TAFSIR AL AHLAM

IBN SIRIN'S

Dictionary of Dreams

ACCORDING TO ISLAMIC INNER TRADITIONS

MUHAMMAD M. AL - AKILI

qadeem
PRESS

Qadeem Press
www.qadeempress.com

Find our titles on your favourite online bookstore using the keyword 'Qadeem Press'

Translation of the Qur'ān

It should be perfectly clear that the Qur'ān is only authentic in its original language, Arabic. Since perfect translation of the Qur'ān is impossible, we have used the translation of the meaning of the Qur'ān throughout the book, as the result is only a crude meaning of the Arabic text.

Qur'ānic verses appear in speech marks proceeded by a reference to the Surah and verse number. Sayings (Hadith) of Prophet Muhammad (saw) appear in inverted commas along with reference to the Hadith Book and its Reporter.

CONTENTS

PREFACE

All praises be to Allāh, Lord and Cherisher of the universes. He created the night for people to rest and the day for them to seek their livelihood. He is the Lord and Sustainer of the Divine Throne. His sovereignty pervades the entire existence. His supremacy governs all actions. He hears and sees everything, including the steps of the smallest black ant crawling over an opaque stone in the middle of a moonless night. There is no god except Him. He chose His messenger, the seal of the prophets and strengthened him with wisdom and protection. He sent him as mercy to humankind, to guide them away from heedlessness, and to lead them out of darkness into light. God's Prophet, upon whom be peace, delivered the message of his Lord, advised the people, brought glad tidings to the believers, and warned them about the consequences of failing to fulfill the commandments of their Lord. May God's eternal blessings shower upon him, his companions, and followers in this world and in the hereafter.

Among the masters and scholars in the field of dream interpretation, Eastern people easily recognize the name of Imām Muhammad Ibn Seerīn (God bless his soul) who is most honored for his outstanding knowledge and piety. He is particularly known for his extensive work *Muntakhab Al-Kalām fi Tafsïr Al-Ahlām* (The Key Declamation on Dream Interpretation) which is considered by dream interpreters in the Muslim world as a major source of knowledge that enriched the spirit of readers as well as dream interpreters for the past one thousand years. However, other Islāmic works on dream interpretation from Arabic sources which must be credited in this dictionary include the book of Shaikh Abdul-Ghani Nabulsi, *Ta'atïr-ul Anām Fi Ta'abïr Al-Manām* (Enchanting the Creations Through Dream Interpretations); the book of Nasr Bin Abi Ya'aqūb Bin Ibrāhim Al-Dinawari on dream interpretation, which he compiled for the Abbassid Caliph Al-Qādir Billāh; the book of Shaikh Ibn Shāhïn Al-Zāhiri, *Al-Ishārah fi 'Ilm-il 'Ibārah* (Hints about Dream Interpretations); the book of Shaikh Imām Ibi Tāhir Burhānud-Deen Al-Maqdisi, *Al-Mu'allam 'Alā Hurüf Al-Mu'jam* (Indexed Paragon of Dreams), which was commented on by Shaikh Imām Muhibbud-Deen Muhammad Al-Maqdisi in his work *Al-Muhkam fi Ikhtiṣāṣ Al-Mu'allim* (Instructive Lexicon on Dream Interpretations); the book of Shaikh Abil-Hassan Al-Khalili which he titled *Al-Muntakhab* (The Select); the book of Shaikh Imām Jalālu Deen Sulaimān Al-Mazni also called *Al-Ishārah fi 'Ilm-il 'Ibāra;* and the book of Shaikh Imām Shahābu-Deen Abi Al-Abbāss Al-Maqdisi, *Al-Badrul-Munïr fi 'Ilmit-Ta'abïr* (The Radiant Moon on Dream Interpretations), among others. Most of these masters, God bless their souls, agree on the basic interpretations, based on their common understanding of the principal references in religious books.

In this book, Ibn Seerīn's Dictionary of Dreams, the reader will find some of the unique treasures of Muslims' inner traditions which have rarely surfaced in the West. The resourcefulness of synonyms and attributes used in this dictionary could only come from rich traditions and elaborate social structures. The opinions stated in this book also represent a wealth of similarities between nations and contain spiritual values that must not be overlooked. This book also reveals cultural elements that were once held as a common human understanding. God willing, it will be a bridge between people, and its wisdom may quench the thirst of students as well as seekers on the path of Islāmic inner traditions.

I have prepared this book in the form of an indexed dictionary of dreams to make it more accessible for readers from all walks of life. It includes the opinions of most masters cited hereinabove. The meaning of synonyms vary, though I have used some contemporary appellations, idiomatic phrases, Arabic terms, specialized definitions, as well as Islāmic terminologies and proper names in certain parts of this dictionary. It is important for the reader to commence by studying the Introduction and the Guide To Using 'Ibn Seerïn's Dictionary of Dreams According to Islāmic Inner Traditions' before sailing in search of the meaning of his or her dream. Except for a student or a professional dream interpreter, one should take what applies to his prevailing circumstances and discount the rest. The reader must use his wisdom and take what benefits him and discard what does not suit him. The more knowledge and background one may have in this field, the easier it is for him to develop a better understanding from this dictionary. However, the less knowledge one has means that his reading from this dictionary will help him discover some helpful hints about his dream on a day-to-day basis. This is particularly true when one lacks the opportunity of knowing a wise shaikh or a respected dream interpreter.

When looking up one's dream in this book, one must realize that the human mind is capable of stretching into endless horizons. Only God knows what the human mind can imagine or what exact interpretation really relates to one's dream. The interpretation of the elements contained in this book remain closely functional and will most surely satisfy the initial quest for interpreting one's dream. Still, the final explanation and joining of the elements should come from a knowledgeable dream interpreter, a scholar, or a true shaikh.

The nouns, adjectives, and sometimes verbs immediately following each entry are put in brackets to indicate related synonyms. At this point, I feel it necessary to say that this book is not a numerical chart, nor is it a how-to-do-it yourself handbook. Each component has to be seen in relationship to one's own state and surrounding conditions. Still, the interpretations provided in this dictionary may represent the common understanding of people to date and, for a learned person, it will prove to be a well established reference for basic interpretations of one's dreams according to Islāmic inner traditions.

A dream interpreter studies the human nature through its own perception and interpretation of the surrounding elements. Attributes used in this dictionary are not intended to portray anyone, though a thorough examination of the character-actor within each element may depict some characteristics or portray a common cultural, social, or spiritual understanding that may affect society's views, knowledge, or judgment. As the reader will recognize in this book, philosophy also dominates the views and values of things. For example, selling in a dream means giving preference and value to something or being in need of a merchandise. In this case, if what is being sold in one's dream is worldly, then the preference is given to one's benefits in the hereafter. Selling in a dream also means exchanging or bartering one condition for another. In Eastern inner traditions, to sell means to part with. In a dream, the buyer represents the seller, and the seller represents the buyer. The principal relating to interpreting each element must be realistic and functional. The common views in interpreting each of the elements in this book seem as if they were taken from the perspective of each element itself. For example, a mosquito sucking someone's blood may feel strong at that moment and perhaps healthy because of the blood flowing through its veins. However, in reality, its scale may not measure up to the creature whose blood it is sucking.

Dreams are connected to one's true spirit and intentions. The value placed on each element highly represents the ideal perception which must be taken from real life. However, one must recognize that whatever a person may do in a dream, the true act is God's act.

The Eastern imagery of these interpretations provide beauty and eloquence. The cultural and spiritual perception of these elements represents the clarity of the seer and the interpreter. It must be noted here that the original names of things came from their function and description. There is also a philosophical attitude in interpreting dreams such as comparing big apples with small apples, a bird with an airplane, a whale with a submarine, and earth with a mother, etcetera. In Islāmic inner traditions, the Qur'ān is seen as a beautiful garden when one looks at it. Its verses are the fruit of knowledge and wisdom the reader can pluck or pearls he can gather. The Arabs call a garden whose owner is not known a *Jannah*, which is also a term used to mean paradise, its comforts and bliss. Jannah in Arabic also carries the connotation of something hidden or invisible to the naked eye. In a dream, dates are like money, for they do not have a long shelve life. The allegorical interpretation of a mosque when understood to denote the ruler of the land means time. Its lights mean the noble retinue and the wise men of his epoque. The ceiling represents the knowledge contained in the books he uses to apply justice. The minaret represents his chief minister or advisor. The pulpit represents his servant. The prayer niche represents his wife, or it may represent his lawful earnings, or it may mean a righteous and chaste woman.

To properly understand one's dream, it is helpful to identify a universal perception of things and to recognize the human qualities in them. However, the shift in cultural understandings throughout the history of mankind could today influence one's perception of things. Moral values also have changed greatly. For example, in contemporary Western traditions, a pigeon represents a fool, a dupe, or a victimized person, while in the original understanding and valuation of a pigeon, it meant a trustworthy messenger, a truthful friend, a comforting beloved, or a chaste wife. What a change and difference in moral standards! Once upon a time piety meant something valuable, though in today's cultures, as the moral standards have degraded and, outside of a religious significance, piety no longer connotes uprightness, devotion, faithfulness, allegiance, or loyalty, etcetera.

Having gone through the experience of preparing this study, I cannot under-estimate the amount of work which is left for the students of this art to complete in order for them to fully document the references cited in this book. I pray that they will use it wisely and in conformity with the dictates of the Holy Qur'ān and the Sunnah traditions of God's Prophet, upon whom be peace. I thank Allāh the Merciful and Compassionate Lord for the opportunity He allowed me to learn from this work and the time needed to complete this part of it.

Philadelphia, Pennsylvania   Muhammad Al-Akili
October 1991

ABOUT
IMĀM MUHAMMAD IBN SEERÏN
(God bless his soul)

He is Muhammad Ibn Seerïn Al-Basri. Born in the city of Basra in Irāq the year 33 A.H. (653 A.D.) Imām Ibn Seerïn was a renowned writer and a respected religious scholar of his time. He lived during the first century of the Islāmic caliphate and studied the Islāmic jurisprudence (*Fiqh*) and the science of prophetic sayings (*Hadith*) at the hand of the early followers of the companions of God's Messenger, upon whom be peace. Among his contemporaries were Imām Anas Bin Mālik, Al-Hassan Bin Abi Al-Hassan Al-Basri, Ibn 'Aown, Al-Fudhayl Bin 'Iyādh, and others.

Mouriq Al-'Ujali once said: "I have not seen a man who is more sagacious in his piety or more pious in his knowledge than Muhammad Ibn Seerïn."

In his biographical dictionary, Khairu-Deen Al-Zerekly describes Imām Muhammad Ibn Seerïn as a pious, God fearing, and a strong believer, who was a generous host and a trustworthy friend.

HIS PIETY & ASCETICISM

Al-Hassan Bin Abi Al-Hassan Al-Basri once said: "There was a time when, if a man sought knowledge, you could see its effects in every aspect of his life, including his piety, conduct, speech, sight, and hearing." Imām Muhammad Ibn Seerïn used to say: "When God Almighty wills to bless His servant, He will direct him to a wise man to admonish him." He also used to say: "If a man wishes to benefit in this world and in the hereafter, he must seek the company of someone who will command him to do what is good and to disuade him from doing evil."

Imām Ibn Seerïn used to fast every other day of his life. The day when he did not fast, he used to have lunch, omit his dinner, and take a bite during the *Suhür* meal, before the dawn prayers. He used to stand up all night in prayers during the entire month of Ramadān, and he used to say: "One must pray during the night and at least for the time it takes to milk a goat." Once Hishām Bin Hassān stayed overnight at Imām Ibn Seerïn's house and commented to a friend, saying: "I used to hear his weeping during the night, though he was a most cheerful host during the day."

Hafsa Bint Seerïn, sister of Imām Ibn Seerïn, once said: "When Muhammad entered before our mother, he used to stand before her with modesty and refrain from speaking to her with his whole tongue." Once, someone visited Imām Ibn Seerïn in the presence of his mother and remarked about his outstanding respect for her. When the man left, he asked: "Is Muḥammad not feeling well?" Someone replied: "He is well, but he reveres his mother so much that he nearly melt away in her presence."

A man asked Imām Ibn Seerïn about his opinion on dream interpretation. Ibn Seerïn replied: "Fear God when you are awake, and do not worry about what you see in a dream." Whenever he is asked to give a religious opinion about two similar interpretations, he took the closest one to God's book. He once said: "In essence, this knowledge is taken from our religion. Thus, consider carefully from whom you learn it!"

Once Mūsa Bin Al-Mughïrah said: "I saw Muhammad Ibn Seerïn entering the marketplace in the middle of the day. He was totally absorbed in his prayers, glorifying and celebrating God's praises. Someone asked him: "O Abu Bakr (that is his patronym), is this the time to engage in such invocations?" Ibn Seerïn's replied: "In a marketplace, one may be distracted by its glitters and become negligent of his devotion."

One time, the call to prayers came during a gathering. When the people stood to perform their prayers, Imām Ibn Seerïn called: "Let only someone who is well versed in Qur'ānic recitation lead us, for there are amongst us people who have memorized it." After the congregational prayers, Ibn 'Aown asked Imām Ibn Seerïn: "Why did you refrain from leading the prayers?" He replied: "I did not want the people to say: 'Ibn Seerïn led us in prayers tonight.'"

Imām Ibn Seerïn used to abstain from even some lawful things in fear of indulgence. He was once invited to a wedding, and before leaving his house, he asked his family: "Give me some sweets to eat!" They replied: "You are going to a wedding, and you will have it there." He answered: "I hate to satisfy my hunger from people's food." He also used to say: "Do not burden your friend with a gift greater than he can bear." Hishām bin Hassān once said: "Whenever Hind Bint Al-Muhallab invited Al-Hassan Al-Basri and Ibn Seerïn to a meal, Al-Hassan obliged, and Ibn Seerïn refrained from going."

Once Imām Ibn Seerïn refused a gift of forty thousand Dirham because of some doubt about the lawfulness of their source. Commenting on that act, Sulaimān Al-Taymï said: "He refused them because no two scholars will disagree about their unlawfulness. When Ibn Seerïn was asked once about two brothers who turned enemies of one another, he replied: "Evil came between them."

Ibn Zuhair once said: "Whenever death is mentioned before Imām Ibn Seerïn, his entire body dies away, limb by limb."

When Imām Ibn Seerïn laid down on his deathbed, he said to his son: "My son! Pay my debts. Pay only what I owe to people." His son replied: "Oh my father, should I free a slave on your behalf?" Ibn Seerïn replied: "God Almighty has the power to reward me and you for whatever good you do on my behalf."

Imām Ibn Seerïn died in the city of Basra the year 110 A. H. (729 A. D.) at the age of seventy-six.

FORWARD

By Dr. Mahmoud Ayoub

Dreams are messenger to us from the unknown. They are voices from our collective sub-conscious, warners of deep inner disturbance in the individual psyche, bearer of glad tidings of good things to come, or echoes of happy or sad and long hidden memories.

As messenger from the unknown, dreams are often prophetic voices of the future. Hence, they have at times directed the course of the history of nations. The dream of the prophet Abraham to sacrifice his son, his obedience to the Divine will and his willingness to submit in absolute faith to God made him the first true *Muslim* and the father of prophets. The true interpretation of the dreams of the king of Egypt by the prophet Joseph saved both the Egyptians and the children of Israel from famine and death. The dreams of the Prophet Muhammad, upon him and all the prophets of God be peace and blessings, marked the beginning of his revelation, the noble Qur'ān which changed the face of human history and civilization.

Although dreams belong to the domain of personal experience, they are a universal phenomenon, and thus have played a crucial role in the formation of human culture. Throughout recorded human history, dreams and the interpretation of dreams have inspired sages and prophets, poets and kings, as well as the most creative psychologist/philosophers of our day. The science of psychoanalysis of Carl Jung and his school rests on the fact that dreams form the inner diary of every human individual, and hence the need to read and interpret them correctly. This fact has for long been recognized by the sages and prophets of traditional cultures and religions.

Not all dreams, however, are either true or authentic. Those of the prophets and friends (*awliya's*) of God are Divine revelations, true and sacred. The dreams of pious men and women are almost always true and meaningful. Some dreams come from Satan, and are thus misleading. Others may be caused by physical or psychological problems such as stomach discomfort or emotional disturbance. It is therefore important to distinguish true dreams from empty fantasies, and inspired dreams from satanic insinuations.

This is a Divine gift to inspired prophets, holy persons and insightful sages.

The author of the original book *Muntakhab Al-Kalām Fī Tafsīr Al-Aḥlām*, of which the present volume is an adaptation, was a well-known and highly revered man of God, religious scholar and mystic. Even though the book looks at dreams and their significance from an Islāmic point of view, the truth on which it is based, and which it uncovers are universal and primordial verities. This book is therefore intended for all those who take dreams seriously as an important aspect of their life, faith and psychological makeup.

The extensive indexes and well organized layout of this valuable book make it a useful manual of types of dreams and their meaning. It is, moreover, the first Islāmic guide in English to authentic dream interpretation. It is hoped that this dictionary of dream interpretation will prove useful to students of culture and spirituality, but above all to seekers after truth.

Professor Mahmoud Ayoub
Professor of Islāmic Studies
Department of Religion
Temple University

In the Name of God,
the Merciful, and Compassionate

INTRODUCTION

All praises be to Allāh, Lord and Cherisher of the universes. May the most sublime of His blessings shower upon His chosen and elect, the light that dawned upon the creation and brought mercy to humanity, God's Prophet Muhammad, upon whom be peace. He is the carrier of the Divine promise of forgiveness for those who repent and walk the avenues of the dwellers of paradise, and he is the loftiest of intercessors on the Day of Judgement, when creation will meet its maker to receive the harvest of its deeds.

Dream interpretation requires vast knowledge, clear perception, and sensitivity. Such knowledge must be based on the fundamentals of one's religion, inner spiritual values, moral and cultural traditions. The beginner in this field must know that there are two types of dreams: one type that comes from God Almighty, and the second type comes from satan. What is good comes from God Almighty, which is a type of revelation that comes to a righteous person and carries either glad tidings, or warnings. Such dreams also cause one's heart to reflect upon his actions and to beware of heedlessness. On the other hand, they could be a reprimand for an ignoble act one is pondering, or an act one may mistakenly thinks that it is the correct thing to do, or a new friendship that could lead him to hell-fire, or a clarification concerning his treatment of his family and friends and about his business dealings, or they may bring spiritual guidance, etcetera. This is the type of dream which is referred to in God's Prophet's sayings: *"A true dream represents one of forty-six branches of a prophecy."* Both religious and irreligious people may see a true dream that could come true. The second type of dream connotes deception, cunningness, contriving, jealousy, or a scare, causes pain, depicts any type of eavesdropping, engaging in mundane conversation, the call of one's mind and desires, or imagination, or occur after eating a heavy late meal or even going to bed hungry, etcetera. This type of dream comes from satan. God's Prophet (uwbp) has said: *"As time draws nearer to the conclusion of this world, dreams will become confused. The most true of dreams are those of a truthful person. Thus, if one sees a dream that he dislikes, he should tell no one about it, and he should immediately leave his bed and perform his prayers."* He also said: *"The best of ropes is steadfastness to one's religious life."*

Some interpreters divide dreams in three categories: 1- a good dream which is a glad tiding from God Almighty; 2- a dream that rises from one's desires and inclinations; and, 3- a distressful dream that is prompted by satan. As a consequence of such dreams, one may wake up either happy or afraid. Some dreams cause elation, while others cause shivers. In fact, the human frailty is subject to such involuntary acts of infringement upon its so-called 'privacy'. Each dream connotes meanings that relate to one's own character, actions, thoughts, intentions, expectations, qualities, associations, dealings, and environment. However, one may wake up in fear from his dream, though it signifies joy and exaltation, or one may wake up happy, though his dream connotes sorrow and distress.

The wife of God's Prophet, Aisha, God be pleased with her, related that God's Prophet (uwbp) has said: "Glad tidings are the only part of prophecies that will remain after me." Someone asked: "What are the glad tidings, Oh Messenger of God?" He replied: "*A true dream that one sees or which someone sees for him.*"

The early revelations that were brought to God's Prophet, upon whom be peace, commenced in the form of true dreams. Then, they continued in the form of revelations (*waḥī*) that were brought by the archangel Gibreel, upon whom be peace. Aisha, God be pleased with her, also said: "The earliest revelations God's Messenger (uwbp) received came in the form of true dreams. Whatever he saw in his dream unfailingly came true." Once God's Prophet (uwbp) related a dream to his blessed companion Abu Bakr, God be pleased with him. He said: "I saw in a dream that we were climbing a ladder. At the end, I reached two steps further than you did." Abu Bakr replied: "O Messenger of God, God Almighty will call your soul back unto His mercy, and I shall live two and one half years after you have departed from this world."

In another dream, he said: "I saw a flock of black sheep tailed by another flock of white sheep following me." Abu Bakr replied: "The Arabs will follow you first, then others will follow them."

In his book '*Ta'tīr-ul Anām fi Tafsīr-ul Manām*', Shaikh Abdul Ghani Nābulsi, God bless his soul, related that dream interpretation is one of the earliest knowledge that was revealed to humankind. All of God's prophets, upon all of them be peace, had to deal with dream interpretation from time to time. God's prophet Joseph (uwbp) was also blessed with such knowledge, as revealed in the Qur'ānic verse: **"Thus will thy Lord choose thee, and teach thee the interpretation of stories."** (*Qur'ān 12:6*), meaning dream interpretation.

The faith of God's prophet Abraham, upon whom be peace, was once tried through a dream where he saw himself sacrificing his own son. **"He said: 'O my son! I saw in a dream that I offered thee in sacrifice.'"** (*Qur'ān 37-102*). As he reached the point of implementing his dream, God Almighty said: **"O Abraham! Thou hast already fulfilled the vision! —"** (*Qur'ān 37:104-105*).

On the eve of the battle of Badr between the believers and the Quraish tribe of Mecca, God's Prophet Muhammad (uwbp) saw a dream as stated in the Holy Qur'ān: **"And remember when God showed them to thee as few in thy dream—"** (*Qur'ān 8:43*). Later on, when God's Prophet (uwbp) led his companions to Hudaibiyyah, he also saw in a dream that he and his companions were entering the Holy city of Mecca. In this dream, he saw them circumambulating the Sacred House with peace and tranquility. God Almighty confirmed his dream in the Holy Qur'ān saying: **"Truly did God fulfil the vision for His Apostle, that ye shall enter the Sacred Mosque, if God wills, with your minds secured, head shaved, hair cut short, and without fear. For He knew what you do not know, and He granted beside this, a speedy victory."** (*Qur'ān 48:27*). Indeed, it was in such a state that God's Messenger and the believers entered the Holy city of Mecca and cleansed God's House from polytheism and idol worship.

In the book of *Tafsīr ul-Aḥlām* by Imām Muhammad Ibn Seerīn, it is reported that Shaikh Abu Saïd Al-Wā'iṭh, God bless his soul, has said: "In essence, dreams are true. They connote wisdom and have emotional and physical traceable effects." Wahab bin Munabbih once said: "The first dream was seen by Adam, upon whom be peace." He added: "God said to Adam: 'Have you seen among my creation anyone that resembles you?' Adam replied: 'My Lord, Thou hast blessed me, and honored me among Thy creation and I have not seen anyone that looks like me. Bless me Lord with a mate, so I may dwell with her in tranquility, and we may both worship Thee and glorify Thee.' God Almighty then caused Adam to repose, and He showed him Eve in a vision. When Adam opened his eyes, he saw Eve sitting near him. God Almighty created Eve from Adam's rib and made her look like him."

Wahab bin Munabbih also related: "Once Joseph son of Jacob, upon both of them be peace, went with his brethren to herd the family's sheep. Each one carried a heavy stick to help direct their sheep and to defend themselves against the beasts of the wilderness. Joseph was a young boy then. During the day, he felt like resting on his brother's lap, where he soon fell asleep. When he woke up, he said to his brothers: 'Should I tell you about a dream I saw?' They replied: 'Indeed!' Joseph then said: 'I saw as though my stick was dug into the ground, then your sticks were brought in and placed in a circle around it. Mine was the shortest. Then my stick kept on growing until it reached the skies. My stick then stood in the ground and took firm roots that grew to push your sticks out of their holes. Then I saw your sticks laying near mine.' Hearing that, one of his brothers replied: 'The son of Rachel is nearly saying that he is our master and that we are his slaves.'" Seven years later, in another dream, Joseph saw the sun, the moon, and the stars prostrating themselves to him. As reported in the Holy Qur'ăn, Joseph went to his father Jacob, upon both of them be peace, and said: "**O my father! I did see eleven stars, and the sun, and the moon prostrating themselves to me!**" (*Qur'ăn 12:4*). Jacob understood the meaning of his son's dream, and said: "The sun and the moon are your father and mother, and the stars are your brethren." Jacob added: "**My dear little son, do not tell your dream to your brothren, lest they concoct a plot against thee, for satan is to man an avowed enemy.**" (*Qur'ăn 12:5*)

Later on, Jacob saw in a dream that he was standing on top of a hill and Joseph was down in the valley. He saw ten wolves surrounding and attacking his little son Joseph. Jacob feared for his son and felt sorrowful for him, though he could do nothing in the dream. Suddenly, the earth split open under Joseph's feet and swallowed him. The wolves then departed. When Joseph's brethren came to their father and said: "**Send him with us tomorrow to enjoy himself and play, and we shall take good care of him.**" Jacob replied: "**It saddens me that you should take him away. I fear lest the wolf should devour him when you are busy and oblivious of him.**" (*Qur'ăn 12:12-13*)

During his imprisonment in Egypt, Joseph taught the truth as he interpreted the dreams of his two fellow prisoners. In the Holy Qur'ăn God Almighty says: "**Two young men entered the prison with him. One of them said: 'I see myself in a dream pressing wine.' The other said: 'I see myself in a dream carrying bread on my head, and birds are eating from it.' They said: 'Tell us the truth and meaning of these dreams, for we see that thou does good to all. He replied: 'Before any food come to feed either of you, I will surely reveal to you the truth and meaning of what will befall you. That is part of the duty which my Lord has taught me. I have abandoned the ways of a people that do not believe in God and that even deny the hereafter.**" (*Qur'ăn 12:36*) Joseph added: "**Oh my two companions of the prison! As for** one of you, he will pour wine for his master to drink. As for the other, he will be crucified, and the birds will eat from off his head. So it is decreed in the matter which you are inquiring about." *(Qur'ān 12:41)*

Joseph (uwbp) also used his knowledge about dream interpretation to clear his name and to explain the king's dream, when the Pharaoh's own council and the palace's dream interpreters failed to explain it, saying: **"A confused medley of dreams, and we are not skilled in the interpretation of dreams."** *(Qur'ān 12:44)*. The cup-bearer went to Joseph and said: **"O Joseph! O man of truth! Expound to us the meaning of seven fat cows whom seven lean ones devour, and a seven green ears of corn and seven others withered."** Joseph's explanation was: **"You shall sow diligently for seven years after your wont; what you harvest leave in the ear, except a little you keep in store. This will be followed by seven hard years, that shall devour what you have kept for them, except the little you have guarded. Then will come a year in which the people will have abundant water and press in season."** *(Qur'ān 12:47-49)*

Ibn Jābir Sulaimān bin Āmir Al-Kalā'i related that Abu Umāma Al-Bāhili had told him: "I heard God's Messenger, upon whom be peace, say: 'Two men came to me in a dream. They took me near a pathless mountain that is difficult to cross and said to me: 'Climb!' I replied: 'It is difficult, and I cannot climb it.' They said: 'We will make it easy for you.' Thus, we commenced out ascent. As we reached the middle of our climb, I heard loud yowling like that of dogs. I asked: 'What is that sound?' They replied: 'This is the cry of the dwellers of hell-fire.' We continued our climb, and I saw people hanging from the tendons of their heels. I asked: 'Who are these people?' They replied: 'These people are the ones who break their fast before the due time.' We then continued our climb, and I saw people whose bodies are swollen, and their stench is similar to that of feces. I asked: 'Who are these people?' They replied: 'These are the adulterers.' As we continued, I saw little children playing between two rivers. I asked: 'Who are these children?' They replied: 'They are the progeny of Muslims.' Then I saw three people from a distance. I asked: 'Who are these people?' They replied: 'These are Abraham, Moses, and Jesus, upon them be peace, and they are awaiting you.'"

True dreams also can be seen by unbelievers. It is related that Pharaoh once saw in a dream a fire that had ignited in Syria. This fire kept on expanding until it reached Egypt, where it burned and destroyed every house and farm of the land. Pharaoh woke-up scared. He called every dream interpreter in the land and asked them to explain the meaning of his dream. One of the interpreters said: "If your dream is true, it means that a descendent from the family of Jacob will be born, who will bring about your destruction and that of Egypt." Immediately, Pharaoh ordered his soldiers to kill every newborn in the land. Despite all of Pharaoh's precautions, Moses was born in God's protection and fulfilled God's Will. God Almighty commanded the mother of Moses by inspiration: **"Behold! We told to thy mother, by inspiration: "'Place the child into the chest, and throw the chest into the river. The river will cast him up to the bank, and he will be taken up by one who is an enemy to Me, and an enemy to him."'"** *(Qur'ān 20:39)*

Some dream interpreters explain that dreams are of three types: 1- glad tidings from God Almighty, and this is what is called a true dream; 2- warnings from the accursed Satan. This type represents false and confused dreams because it is not befitting the accursed one to advise or warn people. Once a man came to God's Prophet (uwbp) and said: "O Messenger of God! I saw my head rolling before me, and I saw myself running after it and seeking it in the dream." God's Prophet (uwbp) replied: "Do not talk about Satan's chicanery." 3- The third category includes dreams that reflect one's personal thoughts. One may see himself sitting with his beloved; or if one is afraid of something, he may see it in a dream; or if he goes to bed hungry, he may see himself eating or vomiting; or if one sleeps under the sun he may see himself burning in hell-fire; or if he has an ailment, he may see himself in a dream suffering or being tortured, etcetera.

There are seven types of false dreams. 1- confused dreams: dreams which are caused by distress, exaggerated hopes, and personal thoughts. 2- The second type represent sexual dreams that require one to take a ritual ablution (*ghusul*) if they end in ejection of semen and they have no interpretation. 3- The third type represent warnings by Satan or scary dreams where they end in a no-win situation. 4- The fourth type represent dreams that are driven by the sorcery of jinn spirits, or their illusions, and they are judged as vain. 5- The fifth type is a dream which is shown by satan, and this type is not considered to be a dream. 6- The sixth type is driven by one's own mind and desire when they are confused or under stress. 7- The seventh type of false dream is one which is caused by pain and suffering from a physical ailment.

As for the true dreams, they are the glad tidings that come from God Almighty. In them, one may see himself in a state of serenity and peace, or wearing a beautiful garment, or eating healthy and appetizing food. Shaikh Abdul Ghani Nābulsi divided the true dreams into five categories. 1- A clear vision of a truthful person that takes place exactly as seen in one's dream. This is the type which is considered to represent one of forty-six branches of a prophecy, including the dream of God's Prophet (uwbp) entering Mecca or the dream of God's prophet Abraham sacrificing his son, etcetera. A dream interpreter once said: "Blessed is he who sees a true dream, for they come directly from God Almighty and without an intermediary." 2- The second category includes a direct warning or a reprimand from God Almighty. God's Prophet (uwbp) once said: "*The best of dreams are the ones where you see your Lord, or your prophet, or your Muslim parents.*" Someone asked: "O Messenger of God, can one see his Lord?" He replied: "*The king represents God, and God is the king in one's dream.*" 3- The third category is a dream that is shown to you by the angel of dreams, and his name is Siddiqūn. This blessed angel may come into one's dream and, by God's leave, reveal some of what God Almighty taught him or made known to him from what is written in the Preserved Tablet. God Almighty also has taught him to give parables and how to tell stories one can understand. 4- The fourth category represent dreams of allegories, apotheosis, or symbols one can decipher. This type comes through good spirits or blessed souls, such as if an angel comes and says: "Your wife wants to poison you at the hand of your friend so-and-so." In this case, the angel or the blessed soul has indirectly indicated that one's friend is having a secret affair with one's wife, for adultery requires a covert scheme, and poison connotes disguise. 5- The fifth category of true dreams is one that includes a true witness. In it, such a witness will manifest a prevailing presence in the dream, such as seeing oneself beating a drum, or playing a string instrument inside a mosque or a place of worship. In this case, it may mean repenting in public from one's sins. The witness element here represents the opposite of what the person sees, such as seeing oneself dancing, or reading the Qur'ān inside a bathhouse. In this case, it means that he will be involved in a scandal, and his reputation will be defiled, for a bathhouse is a public place, where one's privacy may be infringed upon if he is not careful about his conduct therein. Children's dreams are also true, for Joseph was seven years of age when he saw his dream with his brethren. The dream of a woman during her menstrual period also can be true, for some religions do not see it necessary for a woman to take a ritual ablution in order to perform her prayers.

The prophet Daniel, upon whom be peace, explained that the angel of dreams Siddiqūn is a colossal angel. The distance between his shoulders and his earlobe equals seven hundred years of walking. The parable of this angel is like that of the sun. Once it rises, things can be seen with clarity. By God's leave, he teaches the true believers, guides them, and explains some of their hidden destiny, whether it is good or bad, in this world or in the hereafter. When he brings a warning, or disturbing piece of news in a dream, it is intended to help one cross such an adversity with clarity, determination, and without distress when it takes place. Such a true dream usually takes place within a couple of days from seeing it. The best of such dreams are seen before daybreak and during the daylight. Ja'afar Al-Sādiq, God bless his soul once said: "A true dream is one that is seen during a mid-day nap."

Sometimes, one may accomplish something in a dream, when in reality it connotes someone else's accomplishment. This includes his wife, his son, business partner, or someone who has the same name. This was seen in Abu Jahl's dream when he saw himself accepting Islām and pledging allegiance to God's Messenger, upon whom be peace. In truth, Abu Jahl died as an unbeliever, and it was his son that fulfilled the father's dream.

Um-ul Fadhl once came to God's Prophet (uwbp) and said: "O God's Messenger! I saw an awful dream." He replied: "Blessed be it." She continued: "I saw a piece of your flesh put in my lap!" God's Prophet (uwbp) smiled and said: "My daughter Fātimah will beget a son, and you shall take it into your lap." Later on, Fātima, God be pleased with her, conceived a child from her cousin Ali, God bless his countenance, and Um-ul Fadhl placed the newborn in her lap.

According to Imām Jāmi, Zulaikha was a beautiful princess and daughter of a king from a northwestern African country. In her youth, Zulaikha saw a dream of a handsome man who possessed a great beauty, goodness, purity and truth, and she fell in love with him. Zulaikha nursed her love and sorrow in secret. The dream she saw first, occurred thrice and on the third time, she had the courage to ask the man about his name and country. In her dream, the man concealed his name, but he told her that he was the vizier of Egypt. Thus, the man in the dream occupied her entire life. Finally, Zulaikha's father knew her reason for refusing to marry kings and princes from all over the world and arranged for her to marry the vizier of Egypt. When Zulaikha's caravan arrived to Egypt, she peeped from a hole in her curtain to find that the vizier of Egypt was not the man she saw in her dream. Later on, and in another dream, Zulaikha was told that this vizier of Egypt is not her beloved, and that she will be protected by him until she meets her destined love. Armed with a glimpse of her beloved, Zulaikha waited with faith and longing for her beloved. One day, a foreign merchant who had found Joseph inside a well had brought him to sell him in Egypt. During the auction, everyone who was thought to have the means desired to buy Joseph, but destiny made him the prize of Zulaikha, who had a lot to learn about the true price of a divine gift. It was only after her husband died, and she was bereft of her beauty, youth, health and honor, that Joseph became the vizier of Egypt. He knew what is true from what is false and ephemeral. At his prayers, God Almighty restored Zulaikha's health, youth and beauty, and they were married in purity, love, and true worship of God Almighty. (*Also see Joseph*)

The Dream Interpreter

Some dream interpreters agree that dreams are seen by the soul and are understood by one's consciousness. Shaikh Abdul Ghanī Nābulsi explains in his book *Ta'atīr-ul Anām* that "the soul resides within one's heart, and the functions of the heart are dictated by one's brain. When one falls asleep, his soul becomes like an extended ray of light, or like a sun, where he can see what the angel of dreams reveals to him through the effulgent light of his Lord. When one's senses come to wakefulness, it is as though a cloud has come to cover the sunlight. When one wakes up, he may remember through his soul what the angel of dreams has showed him." Someone said: "Spiritual feelings are greater than one's physical awareness. For the soul represents the truth, and the senses can only recognize what is physically perceivable."

For a dream interpreter, it is also necessary to know that the soil is different from one land to another, because each soil is watered by a different quality of water. That is why dream interpretation may vary from one land to another. As we explained earlier, dream interpretation requires a concise knowledge that must be based on the fundamentals of one's religion, inner spiritual values, and moral and cultural traditions. Dreams also are influenced by the atmospheric condition of the land and culture. For example, if one who lives in a hot country sees snow or hail in his dream, it means rising prices or drought. On the other hand, if one lives in a cold country and sees snow, rain, and hail, it means a good harvest and prosperity.

In India, for example, mud means money, while for another country it may mean an adversity. Also in India, breaking wind in a dream means good news, while in another country it may mean hearing bad words. In one out of four countries, fish in a dream means marriage, or money, while in other countries a fish means a bad stench. Quince, which is known in Persian as *Safarjal* in a dream means comfort, beauty, and glory for an Iranian person, while it means travels, or departure for an Arab. Eating a dead animal in a dream means acquiring unlawful money for those who believe in the impermissibility of doing so. As for those who see no harm in eating the flesh of a dead animal, when they see that in a dream, it means benefits, or profits. Timing is also crucial. If one who is stricken with cold symptoms sees himself warming up in the sun, or near a burning bush in the wintertime in a dream, or if he sees himself wearing winter clothing, or using hot water to wash with, etcetera in a dream, it means recovering from his illness, while doing so in the summertime means health complications, or adversities. The meanings of dreams also differ in values. For instance, if a devout worshiper sees himself wearing a soldier's uniform in a dream, it means invalidation of his worship, while if a non-fighting soldier sees that, it means going to war, and victory. As for the rest of people, it means a dispute, an argument, and corruption.

A dream interpreter must also be considerate of other social customs and religious norms. For example, eating raw herbs in a dream means unlawful money and disturbances for Sabians and Judaeo-Christian priests, for it is not permissible in their traditions. The Jews forbid the eating of certain roots, the Greeks forbid chicken, and the Muslims forbid drinking wine. Thus these elements in a dream represent unlawful earnings for such religions. If a Muslim woman sees herself committing adultery inside a mosque in a dream, it means gaining bad reputation, while if a Hindu woman sees that dream, it means rising in station of nearness to her lord, for in Hinduism they consider sexual intercourse an act of worship. The Magians and Zoroastrians worship the fire, so if one of them sees himself kindling a fire or prostrating to the fire in a dream, it has positive connotations and benefits. The same goes for worshipers of the sun or the moon.

The dream interpreter must investigate each dream based on religious opinions, logic, idioms, crucial factors, dictating circumstances, parables, what is deemed correct, and he should not express a firm opinion, as we shall expand on this subject at a later part of this introduction.

A dream interpreter must have knowledge of the Qur'ānic references, Qur'ānic interpretations, sayings of God's Prophet, upon whom be peace, allegorical meanings and parables. He also must know the prophetic traditions, tales of the prophets, the wisdom they imparted to their followers through interpreting their dreams, and the conclusion they themselves have earned from that experience. A refined interpreter in this art also must cultivate the essence of social norms, history, fables, poetry, proverbs, languages, etymology of words, synonyms, homogeneity, contrariety, etcetera. He also must be an honest and respected person, and he must care for the way he earns his living, what he eats, and what he drinks, and he must be a sincere and a God-fearing person.

It is beneficial for a dream interpreter to have knowledge about astrology, numerology, lucky days of the week, lucky hours of the day and the night, natural medicine, and psychology, besides other sciences.

The prophet Daniel, upon whom be peace, has said: "One may forget his dream because of four reasons: 1- his sins; 2- contradiction between his deeds and intentions; 3- lack of sincerity; and 4- changes of his spirit." Imām Ja'afar Al-Sādiq, God bless his soul, once said: "If one forgets a dream he saw at night, he should calculate the numerological value of the letters of his name on the basis of the 'Abjad' system. He then should deduct the number nine from the total. If they result in an even number, then his dream is positive. If the total produces an odd number, then his dream has negative connotations." The dream interpreter also should ask the person who forgot his dream how did he find himself when he woke up. If the person who forgot his dream finds his hand over his fingers, he could have seen little trees. If he finds his hand his hand laid over his ribs, then it could be women that he saw, etcetera. (See Body[1]).

A dream interpreter must listen to the complete story, and its minute details. He also must investigate and find acceptable religious references (Usūl) for each element in the dream. If he does not fully understand the dream, or if he is unable to find such references, then it is better for him to refrain from making up an interpretation. In that case, he will be giving a religious ruling, though dreams relate to psychology. Indeed, it will be a sin to tell a false interpretation, while one will be rewarded if he remains silent when he does not know the answer. Imām Ibn Seerïn was the most renowned master in this science, and he often refrained from interpreting someone's dream. Perhaps, he would interpret only one out of every forty dreams when asked to do so. Of three out of four such dreams, he used to say: "I do not know the meaning of this dream."

The dream interpreter must investigate the dream and establish its acceptable religious references. It is related that Imām Ibn Seerïn used to spend a good part of the day questioning the person about himself, his life, type of work, living condition, and surrounding circumstance, for a dream interpreter is not a prophet and cannot tell about the future.

Beside the religious references, a dream interpreter also must know the basic categories which connect the elements of the dream. Thus he should know that wheat, barley, flour, honey, milk, wool, iron, salt, and earth, etcetera, represent money. He should also know that a weasel, a coyote, a lion, a wolf, a rope, a tree, a bird, or a beast, etcetera, represent men; and that a saddle, a bed, and female birds, etcetera, represent women, and that a pitcher, a pillow, a bowl, a basin, etcetera, represent servants. He should also know that anything that has no end in a dream is not attainable, while leaving a boat in a dream means descending in rank.

In his book *Tabaqāt Al-Mu'abbireen,* (i.e., The Ranks of Dream Interpreters) Al-Hassan Bin Al-Ḥassan Al-Ḵẖallāl, God bless his soul, noted some seven thousand five hundred interpreters. He then divided them in fifteen categories: 1- the prophets; 2- the companions; 3- the followers; 4- the scholars; 5- the ascetics; 6- professional interpreters who wrote books on this subject; 7- philosophers; 8- physicians; 9- Jewish interpreters; 10- Christian interpreters; 11- Magian interpreters; 12- polytheists from the pre-Islāmic period; 13- soothsayers, prognosticators, palm readers, and fortunetellers; 14- Magicians; and 15- physiognomists and allegorists.

♦ The perspective which one assumes in his interpretation of someone's dream is crucial. Once a Caliph saw his teeth falling out in a dream. He called a dream interpreter and asked him about the meaning of his dream. The interpreter replied: "The entire family of my master will perish." The Caliph became upset, and he called for another interpreter and told him the dream. The second dream interpreter replied: "The dream of my master, the prince of the believers, is true, for he shall live the longest amongst his relatives." Immediately, the Caliph embraced the man and rewarded him for his skill and tactfulness. In this case, both interpreters gave the same meaning, though the presentation is different.

♦ Once upon a time, a king hired a private tutor to teach his children the Qur'ān and proper conduct. After the teacher had died, one day the king's children went to visit the grave of their teacher. After paying the customary greetings, they sat beside his grave and engaged in a mundane conversation, ate some fruits, and threw the peels and pits on the side of the grave. That night, the teacher came to the king in a dream and told him: "Instruct your children to refrain from visiting my grave, for they have certainly offended me." When the children learned from their father about what happened, they cried and exclaimed: "God bless his soul, for surely he is still teaching us proper conduct, even after his death."

♦ A man came to Imām Ibn Seerïn and said: "I saw a pot filled with milk, then someone brought a second pot of the same size which was filled with honey. He then poured the honey into the milk, and miraculously, the first pot contained both of them without any spillage. Further on, he poured some foamy substance on the top, and I sat with some friends eating and skimming the foamy substance first. Suddenly, the contents of the pot turned into a head of a camel, and we kept on eating from it." Ibn Seerïn replied: "What a wretched dream you had! The milk represents inherent purity. What is poured into it has nothing to do with inherent purity. Your eating of the scum means waste, and neither you nor your friends will benefit from it, for God Almighty has said: **"For the scum will be thrown off."** (*Qur'ān 17:13*) As for the camel in your dream, it represents an Arab leader, and in this case, he is the Prince of the believers, the Caliph Omar Bin 'Abdul-Azïz, and you are backbiting him and sweetening your calumny with honey."

♦ Once a man came to Shaikh Sa'adu-Deen Al-Dharïr, who was a blind man from Aleppo, Syria, and said: "I saw a dream, whereby I was wearing a shoe of fire that burned up to my ankles." The Shaikh replied: "Come near me, so I may tell you the meaning." Once the Shaikh took hold of the man's arm, he cried out to those who were present to catch the man and to call the police. After an investigation, it appeared that the man used to steal people's shoes at the entrance of the mosque, to which crime the man confessed, and people went to his house to claim their properties.

♦ A woman came to Imām Ibn Seerïn and said: "I saw two pearls in my lap in a dream. One was bigger than the other. Then my sister came and asked me to give her one of them, so I gave her the smaller pearl." Imām Ibn Seerïn replied: "You spoke the truth. You have learned two chapters from the Holy Qur'ān. One of them is longer than the other, and you have taught your sister the shorter one." The woman obliged.

♦ A man said to Imām Ibn Seerïn: "I saw a big bull coming out of a small rock, and I shook hands with him in a dream. The bull then wanted to return inside the rock, but he couldn't." Ibn Seerïn replied: "Indeed; sometimes a man may say a big word, then regrets what he had said, though he cannot change it."

♦ A man said to Imām Ibn Seerïn: "I saw a man swallowing small pearls, then bringing them out of his mouth bigger in size in the dream." Ibn Seerïn replied: "This the type of a person who learns about something once and speaks about it a lot."

♦ A man said to Imām Ibn Seerïn: "I saw a pebble going into my ear in a dream. Then I shook my head and got it out of there." Imām Ibn Seerïn replied: "You mix with people of innovation, and you hear bad words, though God willing, at the end, you will repent."

♦ A man told Imām Ibn Seerïn: "I saw that I was betrothed to a black woman who was short in the dream." Ibn Seerïn replied: "Go and marry her, for her blackness is her richness, and her size represents the span of her life. For you will shortly inherit her wealth."

♦ A man told Imām Ibn Seerïn: "I saw myself drinking from a pitcher with two heads in a dream." Ibn Seerïn replied: "You have a wife, and you are trying to tempt her sister to sin with you, so fear God." The man answered: "You spoke the truth. Bear witness that I repent from my doing."

♦ Once the Caliph Omar Bin Al-Khattāb, God be pleased with him, appointed a judge for Syria. When the man left Mecca, one night he saw in a dream that the sun, the moon, and the stars were fighting against one another. Then, the man himself became a star and participated in the fight in the dream. Halfway through his journey, the man returned to Medina and told the Caliph about his dream. Omar asked: "When you became a star in the dream, did you fight on the side of the sun or that of the moon?" The man replied: "I fought on the side of the moon." Omar replied: "Go away, and do not work for me." Later on, the man joined the army of Yazïd in Syria and died fighting the caliphate during the battle of Siffïn.

♦ Abdullāh the son of Omar, God be pleased with them, reported: "I heard God's Prophet, upon whom be peace, saying: 'I was given a glass of milk in a dream. I drank from it until I could see the quench reaching the tip of my fingers, then I gave what is left to Omar.' Abdullāh asked: 'How did you interpret it, O Messenger of God?' He replied: 'Knowledge.'"

♦ Abdullāh Bin Omar, God be pleased with them both, reported that God's Messenger, upon whom be peace, has said: "Last night, I saw myself at the Ka'aba. There I saw a person with a fair skin and a most beautiful appearance circumambulating the Ka'aba. I asked: 'Who is this man?' A voice replied: 'This is Jesus son of Mary.' Then walked an ugly-looking man, whose skin was wrinkled, and who was blind in his right eye. I asked: 'Who is this man?' A voice replied: 'This is *Al-Masīh al-Dajjāl, the impostor of Christ.*'"

♦ Abu Sa'īd Al-Khidrī, God be pleased with him, reported that God's Prophet, upon whom be peace, has said: "While in my sleep, I saw people presented before me, most of whom wore a garment that covered down to their breast. Then arrived Omar who was dragging his robe behind him." Someone asked: "How did you interpret it, O Messenger of God?" He replied: "Commitment to one's religion."

Relating One's Dream

God's Prophet, upon whom be peace, liked to sleep on his right side. He also taught his companions when they go to bed to pray: **"Lord, I seek refuge in Thee from any disturbing dreams and from Satan's chicanery whether I am awake or in my sleep. Lord, protect me against the sufferings that people will experience on the Day of Gathering."**

After the daybreak, God's Prophet, upon whom be peace, used to ask his companions if they had seen any dreams, and he did interpret their dreams for them. It is reported that he also has said: *"A dream will take effect according to how it is interpreted."* God's Prophet (uwbp) also said: *"A dream sits on the wing of a flying bird and will not take effect unless it is related to someone."* Therefore, one should only tell his dream to a trustworthy person, a pious and a knowledgeable person. He should not tell it to a jealous person, and he should not tell his dream to a child, or a wife. It is related that God's Prophet (uwbp) once said: *"Tell your dreams only to a beloved or a knowledgeable person."* Remember when Jacob (uwbp) told his son Joseph: **"My dear little son, do not tell your dream to your brothren, lest they concoct a plot against thee, for satan is to man an avowed enemy."** (*Qur'ān 12:5*)

In relation to the earlier related saying of God's Messenger (uwbp): "Glad tidings are the only part of prophecies that will remain after me" which is said to mean true dreams someone said: "When a servant of God Almighty falls asleep in the middle of the night during his prostration, God Almighty will say: 'Look at My servant, his soul is standing before Me, and his body is engaged in my service.'" Abi Al-Dardā' once said: "When the servant falls asleep, his soul will be brought before the Divine Throne. If one had gone to sleep abluted, then the soul will be permitted to prostrate before its Lord. Otherwise, the soul will not be permitted to prostrate." Abi Tharr Al-Ghafārī once said: "My beloved advised me never to neglect three things until I reach my death: 1- to fast three days from every month; 2- to perform the pre-dawn (*Fajr*) prayers on time; and 3- never to go to sleep without ablution."

God Almighty has said in the Qur'ān: **"It is He Who takes back the souls at night, then it is He Who gives them back at awakening, except for those for whom death has come. He then takes back the latter and returns the ones that are to remain in this world for a while."** (*Qur'ān 39:42*). God's Messenger, upon whom be peace, has said: **"People are asleep, and when they die, they wake-up."** Describing sleep, he also said: **"Sleeping is the little**

brother of death."

When someone told a dream to God's Prophet (uwbp) he used to say: "God willing, may your dream be blessed. May it be glad tidings you receive and protection against evil. May this be good for us and bad for our enemy. All praises be to God, Lord and Cherisher of all lives. Now, tell your dream." In his tradition, if one says to someone: "I saw a dream." The listener should immediately say: "God willing, may it be glad tidings." (arb. *Khair In-Shā Allāh*).

People mostly went to wise shaikhs in their vicinity. Others travelled to distant places to meet qualified interpreters and to receive the explanations and meaning of their dreams. Even kings and rulers throughout the history of mankind sought someone to interpret their dreams. Such interpretations were used as medicine for one's spiritual, physical (*see Medicine*), or psychological illness, or to amend the course of one's decision. There is a special prayer in Islāmic traditions called *Salātul Istikhārah,* which solicits Divine guidance in one's life or for a specific and immediate need. According to Islāmic traditions, such guidance may come in many forms, including in a dream.

When intending to tell a dream, one should choose the early dawn hours or immediately after sunrise. This will particularly help the interpreter whose mind is mostly clearer at that hour. God's Prophet (uwbp) has said: *"Special blessings are given to my followers in the early hours of the day."* If one is truthful in his life, he will see true dreams. If he lies, or if he likes to lie, his dream will lie to him. However, if he lies but hates to do so, his dream then may be true to him.

One's subconscious understanding in the dream is what counts. The dream interpreter must work with it. Let's suppose that one sees a snake and thinks that it is a frog in the dream! Then the interpretation will be based on the meaning of the frog. Similarly, if one sees a frog, and thinks that it is a snake in his dream, then this is what counts in the interpretation of his dream.

Interpreting dreams is a process of analyzing the nature of things and their opposing possibilities, connecting their roots, and assembling the fragments of one's thoughts to better understand his or her real condition.

In a dream, one may see things that may connote equilibrium or the opposite, while his passive and inert participation urges him to examine the elements and to awaken his consciousness. Sometimes, the elements themselves may be opaque or unclear. In this case, if one recognizes a person in the dream, perhaps the name of that person, or his trade, or his look, or the meaning of the individual letters of his name, or their combined numerological value, etcetera, may provide a clue to the meaning of one's dream.

For example: Selling grains and not seeing the return or money in a dream means ascetic detachment, and gra itude to one's Lord, for the real price of things is gratitude. Castle in a dream mear. sing the vehicle of truth. That is the origin of the proverb: "Truth is a castle." A ording to eastern inner traditions, fever represents atonement for one's sins. Suffering one day from a feverish chill is an atonement for three hundred and sixty-five days of sins. Death is the final phase of practicing one's religion in this world. Shrouding the dead after washing the body means washing it from its impurities. In a dream, one's enemy represents Satan, drugs, alcohol, weaknesses, attachment to the world, sexual indulgences, pride, arrogance, anger, perfidy, jealousy, envy, hatred, impatience, differences, injustice, crimes, hunger, thirst, desires, loves for women, attachment to the world, love for fame, admiring oneself, belittling others, cheating, stealing, bigotry, fanaticism, obstinacy, narrow-mindedness, affectation, idling, cunning, hypocrisy, ostentatiousness, blatancy, blasphemy, excessiveness, haste, dishonesty, immodesty, trials, tribulations, distress, agony, misery, afflictions, wife, son, brother, mistress, worldly ambitions, apostasy, loneliness, anguish, despair, sorrows, pain, carnality, cruelty, antipathy, carelessness, selfishness, forgetting about one's covenant with God Almighty; etcetera, all or which are within oneself. *(See Body¹)*

To reach a close interpretation of one's dream and from studying what each element may connote, one should mostly look at the positive side first and eliminate the negative. One should also refrain from editing his own dream, or using other than the first words that come from his mouth, and he should search accordingly. One also should research the possible different appellation of each word or element. Draw a tree of words, then try to bring together a close understanding of the dream. However, one should definitely find a man of wisdom, or a shaikh, or a known dream interpreter to help him put together any missing elements or even explain hidden meanings in one's dream, when possible.

For example, if a righteous person sees himself standing before God Almighty in a dream, his dream means attainment of divine mercy, and receiving guidance. If an ungodly person sees that, then his dream means a warning of a severe punishment. God Almighty refers to: "**...A day when all mankind will stand before the Lord of the universes.**" *(Qur'ān 83:6)*

One also can find solid references to dream interpretations from the Holy Qur'ān, its firm wisdom, parables, and clear meanings. For example when God Almighty spoke of unity, He said: "**And hold fast to the rope of God.**" *(Qur'ān 3:103)*. When He spoke of women, He said: "**As if they were delicate eggs which are closely guarded.**" *(Qur'ān 37:49)*. When He spoke of the hypocrites, God Almighty said: "**Worthless as hollow propped up pieces of timber.**" *(Qur'ān 63:4)*. About kings, God Almighty says: "**When kings enter a country, they despoil it.**" *(Qur'ān 27:34)*. About backbiting, He says: "**Would any of you like to eat the flesh of his dead brother?**" *(Qur'ān 49:12)*. Other references of wisdom and knowledge also can be found in the saying of God's Prophet, upon whom be peace, when he said about women: "Be careful about the glass pitchers." He also said: "A woman is created from man's rib." Also from the sayings of Jesus son of Mary, upon whom be peace, when he spoke of sleep using a simile saying: "Those who sleep in death will also be raised." *(Corinthians 15.20)*. About parables he said: "I will use parables when I speak of them." *(Mark 4.34)*. About the parable of the hereafter he said: "A man who is looking for fine pearls and when he finds one that is unusually fine, he goes and sells everything he has and buys that pearl." *(Matthew 13.45)*. At another time, he used a metaphor of the doctor and the sick person in comparison with the gnostic and the sinner. He said: "The doctor comes to heal not those who are healthy, but those who are sick." After the passing of God's Prophet, upon whom be peace, Abu Huraira, God be pleased with him, heard someone say: "The Anti-Christ is out!" Abu Huraira replied: "The dyers are lying about the true color of their hides." In other usage of metaphors, similies, and synonyms, dream interpreters used the meaning of disbelief to connote a cover-up and the meaning of forgiveness to denote veiling. When speaking of injustice in a dream, they used the expression: "Putting things in the wrong place", etcetera.

Finally, if one wishes to see a true dream that will reflect his innermost being and true state, he should go to sleep abluted, rest on his right side, then pray: "**Lord, I place my soul in Thy Hand; I turn my face toward Thee; I entrust** my affairs to Thy command; I take refuge in Thee to protect me from all sides. Lord, I turn wholeheartedly toward Thee, desiring Thy blessings and fearing Thy punishment. I have no refuge to seek from Thee except in Thee. I believe in the Book Thou revealed and the Prophet Thou sent. Blessed Thou art in the heavens and on earth. Lord, Thou art the rich, and we are the poor who are in need of Thy help and blessings. Lord, I ask for Thy forgiveness, and I repent unto Thee. My Lord and Cherisher, I ask Thee to let me see a true vision, not a false dream; a blessed and happy vision, not a sorrowful dream and a vision that will benefit my soul and does no harm to it."

In the morning, when one's wish is granted, he should praise God Almighty and thank Him. After performing one's dawn (*Fajr*) prayers, one should seek a Shaikh to interpret and explain the meaning of his dream and, most certainly, he should accept and comply with his views.

The Soul and The Self

Who sees the dream, the soul or the self? People are divided in opinion concerning the subject of the soul (*rūḥ*) and the self (*nafs*). Some say that they are both the same thing (e.g., man and human being), while others hold a different view. The first group argues that the self (*nafs*) means blood. For example, the Arabs say: *"Nafasat-il mar'a,"* when a woman discharges blood during her menstrual period. Also when a woman gives birth they say: *"Nafsā,"* because of the blood discharge that accompanies the delivery of a newborn. They also argue that blood is the only thing that leaves the body of a deceased person. Thus, when referring to death, they used the term: *"Sālat nafsuhu,"* meaning his blood was exuded or that he died. Also in the English language, one can find the term 'bloodless' to mean dead. In this sense, the term *nafs* is used in the Arabic language to mean life or blood.

Others argued that the nature of the (*rūḥ*) soul is cold, and that the nature of the (*nafs*) self is warm. That is why, in their opinion, there was a need to blow the soul into the body to animate it and to give life to it. The Arabs also called the act of blowing, *'Rūḥ.'* They say: *"A'tāhā rūhan,"* meaning blew life into it or gave life to it. In this sense, to blow into the fire means to ignite it, and to blow the soul into the dead bodies means to resurrect them or to make them rise from the dead. Thus, in their opinion, the soul means life. Another group of people considered the soul to be a light spirit, while others may called it an angel or a spirit.

However, despite people's attempts to ascertain such opinions, God Almighty has kept the meaning of the soul in His sole knowledge as He says: **"They ask thee about the soul. Say: 'The soul comes by command of my Lord, and of knowledge, you were given only a little."** (*Qur'ān 17:85*)

The Proper Name

The name of a person or a city one sees in a dream also reflects some of the meanings of one's dream, (e.g., Bait-ul Maqdis [*Jerusalem*], Dar-u Salām [The abode of Peace], Maghrib [Sunset], or among Western cities we find: Salt City, Bellview, New York, New Brunswick, Philadelphia, Bridgewater, Summerside, etcetera.) The industry of a city also has a share in the dream interpretation.

To understand the possible role of a person, a known place or a city in a dream, one should also analyze the meaning of that person's name, or that city's name. Suppose that one sees a man called Robert or Roger in a dream, he then should think of the meaning in relation to bright, praised, boast, or fame. If his name is Charles or Carl, for example, then one should think of something which is fully grown. If his name is Abel or Cane then he should think of the children of Adam and their trials. If his name is Gable, one should think of the head or the upper part of a building. If his name is Mustafa, one should think of the expression chosen or elect. If his name is Baker, one should relate that name to a compassionate leader; an honest livelihood, a just ruler, love, a son, bread, or even the neighborhood bakery. If his name is Harvey, one should think of the subject of fighting, conquering, or a battle taking place somewhere. If one sees a woman by the name of Elizabeth in a dream, he should think of an oath he made to God Almighty, for the name Elizabeth means, "God is my oath." If he sees a girl by the name of Wanda, he should think of base, wind, a rod, authority, a tree, etcetera. If one sees himself in Jerusalem, he should think of the holy city, the furthest Sacred Mosque *Al-Aqsā*, prayers, receiving a great wealth from an inheritance, a pilgrimage to Mecca, or business profits. Other proper names of persons and cities may be found in this dictionary.

♦ God's Prophet, upon whom be peace, once said: "Last night, I saw in a dream that we were visiting the house of 'Uqbah bin Rāfi'; then Ratib Ibn Tāb came and joined us. I interpret it to mean that we will rise in honor in this world and in the hereafter and that our religion will be firmly established." Thus, he took from the name Rāfi' the meaning of honor and exaltation and from the name of Rātib Ibn Tāb the meaning of a blessed religion.

♦ Sharik bin Abi Shamr came to Sa'īd bin Al-Musayyib and said: "I saw all my teeth falling out in a dream." Sa'īd bin Al-Musayyib replied: "What a calamity! If your dream is true, it means that all your relatives will die before you." Thus, Sa'īd interpreted teeth from the root of the word canines (e.g., the family of, or relatives, clans, followers, or age. *arb. Asnān*).

♦ Bishr bin Abi Al-'Āliya said: "I asked Muhammad about someone who saw his jaws fall out in a dream." He replied: 'This is someone who has cut off his ties with his family." Here again, Muhammad went to the origin, and in this case, it is one's teeth. In Islām, breaking relations with one's family is considered a major sin. Jubair Ibn Mut'in reported that God's prophet (uwbp) has said: "One who breaks his family ties will not enter paradise." (*Bukhārī & Muslim*) Abu Huraira, God be pleased with him, reported that God's Messenger, upon whom be peace, has said: "Whoever wishes his fortune to increase and his life to be extended, should preserve his family ties." (*Bukhārī*)

Traditions

Interpreting the dream by subject requires further understanding of one's religious and socio-cultural environment. For example, if one is offered a lemon in a dream, and if it did not connote money or a child, in this case, a lemon in one's dream means fraud, hypocrisy, and falsehood. If one sees his arm longer than usual in a dream, it means that he likes to show off his charities or deeds, or it could mean generosity. This idiom is also used in the saying of God's Prophet, upon whom be peace, when he said to his wives, God be pleased with them: *"Those who have longer arms amongst you will follow me first."* In her case, Zainab Bint Jahsh was the first to die among his wives. Qualifying a sickness in a dream to mean hypocrisy came from the expression, "sick at heart," also meaning poor judgement or emotional disturbance. Sickness and hypocrisy are also noted in the expression, "He is a sick person," meaning a disgusting person. Sometimes people use the expression, "Both his words and actions are sickening," to mean someone whose promise cannot be trusted. In the Holy Qur'ān, God Almighty describes the hypocrites saying: **"There is a disease in their hearts; and God has increased their disease."**(*Qur'ān 2:10*). In some traditions, people use the expression, "The lion sneezed, and a cat came out of his nose." This tradition was transmitted from the folkloric tales about the arc of God's prophet Noah. In this sense, in dream interpretation, snot came to mean an impudent and insolent child or a newborn. In the same sense, ejaculated fluid and snout came to mean a son. (*See Nasal mucus, p. 300.*) Equating slandering with curse, God Almighty says in the Holy Qur'ān: **"Those who slander chaste women—are cursed."** (*Qur'ān 24:23*). The common proverb says, "If you live in a glass house, do not cast stones at others." Here again, the interpreter made an association between one's own faults, weakness, and imperfection, and those of a glass house. Concerning severing relations with one's family, God Almighty says: **"We broke them up into sections on this earth."** (*Qur'ān 7: 168*). Equating washing one's hands with hope, people also say, "I washed my hands from it", meaning I have no further interest in it or any hope in it.

Interpretation by Contraposition

Some dreams are interpreted to mean the opposite when the elements are related. This tradition comes from examples such as crying when one is extremely happy; or when laughing in the face of adversities; or seeing the sun and the moon fighting and interpreting it as a fight between two people; or calling a flood an enemy and an enemy a flood, because both are destructive; or when eating a fig in a dream to mean regret and regret to mean eating a fig, because the fig tree is accursed in some traditions; or when one sees himself dead in a dream, though even if he does not have the look of dead people to mean losses or destruction of part of one's house; or interpreting locusts as warriors and warriors as locusts, because of the destruction they both cause to a land; etcetera.

Interpretation by Correlation, Relativity, and Approximation

In this case, laughing in a dream means sorrow, while smiling in a dream means politeness and correct conduct. Crying in a dream is usually interpreted as happiness, but when accompanied with intonation or wailing, it means a calamity. As for putting grease over one's hair, dream interpreters infer the meaning of adornment, while if it dribbles over one's face, they call it hypocrisy, fawning, or adulation. As for saffron in a dream, they interpret it to mean praises or commendation, while should its color manifest in one's body or clothing, then they call it an illness. As for feathers in a dream, they call them wealth or comfort, but when one sees himself flying with wings, they interpret it to mean travels or rising in station, depending on how high one reaches in his dream. If one's hand is cut off in a dream, and if he sees himself carrying it, it means having a brother or a son, while if he loses it in the dream, it means an adversity or loss of a brother or a son. If a sick person sees himself in a dream walking out of his house in silence, it means his death and funeral, while if he speaks in the dream, it means that he will recover from his illness.

Strength of One's Dreams

The meaning of a dream is stronger when seen at dawn, or during an afternoon nap, or when fruits are ripening on their trees, or at the time of harvest, or when one's star is in the rising position, or at a time when one is intending to sign a business contract, or if one is thinking of getting married, or at the term of a decade, etcetera. Seeing a dream during a daylight nap is also stronger than seeing it at night. On the other hand, the meaning of a dream becomes weaker and less plausible when seen during the wintertime.

The dream of a righteous ruler or governor is considered to be an inspiration from God Almighty. The dreams of community leaders depend on their beliefs. The dreams of servants come true for their employers. Women's dreams may materialize faster than those of men. Sinners' dreams are a proof against them on the day of judgement, unless they repent before their death. The dreams of rich people are stronger than those of poor people. The dreams of rich people materialize faster than those of poor people. The dreams of poor people are slower when they connote benefits and faster when they connote adversities. Because of their innocence, the dreams of little children are truer than those of teenagers. This is because older children may be busy in their mischief and fulfilling their newly discovered desires. The dream of a drunk person has no ground. Shaikh Al-Karamāni explains that "the dream of a scholar is truer than that of an ignorant person, the dream of a chaste person is truer than that of an unchaste person, the dream of a good person is truer than that of a bad person, and that the dream of an elderly person is truer than that of a younger person."

The meaning of a dream also varies depending on how people look in it, their dress, type of work they perform, status, or religion. To someone, the dream may mean glad tiding and mercy, while the same dream could mean the opposite for another person. One may wonder when he receives a gift in a dream, then the same gift reaches him in in wakefulness, or if he suffers an adversity in a dream, then the same adversity takes place in wakefulness. Another person may be promoted in his dream, then the same is conferred on him in wakefulness, or if one sees himself performing his pilgrimage to Mecca in a dream, then he joins the pilgrims' caravan in wakefulness or if one sees someone visiting him in a dream, then the same person arrives in wakefulness, days or hours later.

Finally, in pursuing what we have earlier explained, the elements of a dream are interpreted on the basis of three categories: 1- kind, such as trees, lions, or birds, etcetera, and ; 2- specimen, such as the type and name of that tree (e.g. a conifer, a spruce, or a maple tree, etcetera), or what type of bird (e.g. a magpie, a pewee, or a condor, etcetera); and 3- characteristics, such as the nature, or inherent characteristics of a lion, a cat, a crocodile, or their habitat, etcetera.

Some Rare Dreams

True dreams are rare, and each dream is unique, as we will find in this section of this introduction. As dreams are thus complicated and vary in meanings depending on the source, the contents, interpretations, variations, manifestations, time, season, cultures, acceptable witnesses, elements, conditions, definition, subject, phrasing, perception, purity, wisdom, and one's own understanding of his dream, etcetera, it seems appropriate in this section of the introduction to illustrate some rare dreams and to help the reader better evaluate his dreams.

♦ Abdullāh bin Omar, God be pleased with both of them, related that in his youth, he wished to see a true dream and to hear its interpretation from God's Prophet, upon whom be peace. At that time, God's Messenger (uwbp) used to ask people if they saw any dream and he interpreted them accordingly. Abdullāh once prayed: "Lord, if Thou reserves any good for me, then let me see a dream that will be interpreted by God's Messenger, upon whom be peace." One night, Abdullāh saw a dream where two angels took him, and brought him before a third angel who addressed Abdullāh saying: "You are a righteous man. Do not merely talk!" The angels then took him to visit hell-fire, which was folded up like a well. In it he saw some people he knew, but the angels pulled him away from them to the right. When Abdullāh woke up, he told his dream to his sister Hafṣa, the wife of God's Prophet, upon whom be peace. In turn, Hafṣa, God be pleased with her, related the dream to God's Messenger (uwbp) who commented: "Indeed, Abdullāh is a righteous man. It will be good for him if he increases his prayers at night." Consequently, Abdullāh was more regular about his (Suḥūr) night prayers.

♦ Abdullāh bin Mālik Al-Khuzā'i once related: "I worked as a guard serving at the palace of the Caliph Hāroon Al-Rashīd. In the middle of one night, a messenger came and ordered me to appear before the Caliph at once. He did not even allow me to change my sleeping garment. I was struck with great fear. When we came before the Caliph, I was given permission to enter, and I saw him sitting on his bed and pondering something that appeared weighty. My fear increased. I paid my regards and waited for a long time. I prayed as I was shivering from fear waiting for a longer pause. Suddenly, the Caliph said to me: 'O Abdullāh, do you know why I called for you?' I replied: 'Nay, O Prince of the believers.' He added: 'I saw in a dream as though a fierce looking man came and pointed a spear at my chest and said: 'Either you free Mūsā bin Ja'afar at once, or I will put this spear through your heart.' I replied: 'O Prince of the believers, Let Mūsā bin Ja'afar go.' I repeated this thrice. The Caliph then said to me: 'Go and free him from prison at once, and give him three thousands Dirham as a gift. Furthermore, tell him that should he like to stay in this town, he is welcome, and we shall honor him. Otherwise, should he prefer to go to Medina, he has permission to do so.'"

♦ Abdullāh bin Mālik Al-Khuzā'i went at once, and delivered the Message of the Caliph, and gave the man the three thousands Dirham, then added: "You are a wonder. Tell me what happened!" Mūsā bin Ja'afar replied: "I will tell you. Last night, I was between sleep and wakefulness when God's Messenger, upon whom be peace, came to me and said: O Mūsā, you have been unjustly imprisoned." He added: "Say these prayers, and you will not sleep tonight in jail." I replied: "I beseech thee by my mother and my father, O Messenger of God, what should I pray?" God's Prophet upon whom be peace, replied: "Say: 'O Lord Who hears every single sound, Whose act of mercy precedes every bound, Who clothe the bones with flesh and resurrects the people after death, I ask Thee by the glory and holiness of Thy Beautiful Names. I call upon Thee by Thy most glorious, magnificent, preserved, and all encompassing Name which no one of Thy creation knows. O Lord, Thou art the Most Forbearing and Most Patient, have mercy on one who has no more strength to bear his sufferings. O Lord Whose generosity never ceases and Whose gifts cannot be reckoned, Lord, free me.'" Mūsā added: "This is the result of what you witnessed."

♦ When Um Jareer bin Al-Khaṭfi was pregnant, she saw in a dream that she gave birth to a long braided rope of black hair. A soon as the rope fell from her womb, it began to go from one man to another and strangle them. Um Jareer woke up scared from her dream. The next day, she related the dream to a dream interpreter who told her: "You will give birth to a son who will grow to be a famous poet. His poetry will incur evil, hardships, vigorousness, and disdain." When she gave birth to a boy, she called him Jareer, meaning a pulling rope in Arabic.

♦ The governor of Alexandria was tried once with extreme attachment and love for his five children. All five were steadfast in their religious commitment. One night, the governor saw in a dream as though his five fingers were cut off. He woke up extremely disturbed and told his five children his dream. The children called in a dream interpreter called Shaikh Yusuf Al-Karbouni at once. After hearing the dream, Shaikh Yusuf, God bless his soul, smiled and said: "It is not like you think, but if I tell you the meaning of your dream, you must give me a good reward." The governor thus obliged. Shaikh Yusuf, then said: "Are you negligent of your five times prayers?" The governor replied in the affirmative. Shaikh Yusuf continued: "This the meaning of your dream, so repent to God Almighty, and be steadfast in your religion."

♦ A woman said to Imãm Ibn Seerïn: "I saw myself in a dream sucking on a date and giving my neighbor the rest to eat." Imãm Ibn Seerïn replied: "You will help your neighbor by performing a little deed." On the following day, the woman washed her neighbor's garment.

♦ A woman said to Imãm Ibn Seerïn: "I saw my daughter in a dream after she had died. I asked her: 'Tell me what is the best of deeds?' She replied: 'The walnuts, the walnuts, you must take it out, and distribute it among the poor and the needy, O my mother.' " Imãm Ibn Seerïn replied: "If you have hidden a treasure in your house, then dig it out, and give poor people their share ." The woman said: "You spoke the truth. I hid that money in the past, during a plague."

♦ A man said to Imãm Ibn Seerïn: "I saw my hand cut off in a dream." Imãm Ibn Seerïn replied: "You have the habit of making false oaths." The man obliged and repented from his wrongdoing.

♦ A man said to Imãm Ibn Seerïn: "A man saw himself in a dream piercing eggs from the top, extracting the egg white, and leaving the egg yoke." Imãm Ibn Seerïn replied: "Let him come here and tell me his dream in person." At three different occasions, the man kept on asking about the meaning of that dream, and Imãm Ibn Seerïn insisted on the same reply. Finally, after taking a promise from Ibn Seerïn, the man confessed that he is the person who saw that dream. Imãm Ibn Seerïn asked someone to call the chief of police and to tell him that this man is a body snatcher who digs the graves and steals their contents. The man immediately asked for forgiveness, repented from his doing, and promised never to do it again.

♦ Shaikh Muhammad bin Isã al-Rikhãwï of Aleppo, Syria, once saw in a dream that God's prophet Abraham, upon whom be peace, came and gave him forty camels. Shaikh Muhammad went to Shaikh Ahmad Shahãbu Deen Al-Maghribi and told him his dream. Shaikh Shahãbu Deen replied: "You will live forty years from this day." On the thirty-ninth year, Shaikh Muhammad visited Shaikh Shahãbu Deen who encouraged him to perform his pilgrimage that year. Shaikh Muhammad died three days after his return from Mecca. Shaikh Shahãbu Deen led the funeral prayer and buried him beside his father. Shortly after that, Shaikh Ahmad Shahãbu Deen died and was buried in their vicinity.

♦ A man told Imãm Ibn Seerïn: "I saw myself in a dream digging the bones of God's Messenger, upon whom be peace." Ibn Seerïn replied, "You will establish his traditions in your life."

♦ A man said to the prophet Solomon, son of the prophet David, upon both of them be peace: "I saw a garden filled with fruit trees. In that garden, there were many pigs eating from its fruits, and a large pig who was sitting on a chair said to me: 'O man, this fruit garden belong to these pigs.'" Solomon replied: "The large pig represents an unjust ruler, and the small pigs eating from that garden by his permission are the scholars who receive their reward from him for changing the laws to his liking. These are the people who sell the reward of the hereafter for the price of this world and do not ponder upon God's punishment for their sins."

♦ Once a man saw a big tent and a poor man sitting under it in his dream. The man under the tent was addressing a prince in Turkish and telling him without bending: "One thousand shirts, O Turtur!" When he woke up, the man told his dream to a shaikh, who replied: "The prince in that dream will attain a great kingdom." Sometime later, a man was placed on the throne and was known by Al-Malik Al-Ẓāhir, also known as Abi-Fātih Turtur. Remembering his dream, the man went to Al-Malik Al-Ẓāhir and related his dream to him. Immediately, the king Al-Ẓāhir ordered that one thousand shirts be distributed to the poor people of that town.

♦ A dream interpreter once said: "I saw in a dream a man who was blindfolded with a blue piece of cloth. I asked him: 'Do you know what happened to my father?' The man replied: 'Your father is dead.' Then he took me to may father's grave, where I felt the great loss, and I hugged it, cried, and wailed. When I woke up, I told another dream interpreter, who was a friend of mine, about my dream. He smiled and said: 'Your father's death in the dream means his longevity, and your crying means relief from distress.' I did not accept his interpretation of my dream, for I knew better the meaning of wailing and mourning in a dream. Soon after that, I visited my father, and my friend proudly reminded me of his interpretation. Later on, I travelled away from home. When I returned to my town, I passed by a graveyard. At the gate stood a woman who was guarding that cemetery and whose eye was bandaged with a blue piece of cloth. I knew her, so I stopped and asked her about the news. She said to me: 'May God grant you a long life. Your father has passed away.' Then she took me to his grave, and I fell on it, crying and wailing, exactly as I saw in my dream. Thus, my friend's interpretation did not come true, for he has no hand in it."

♦ During a pilgrimage to Mecca, a shaikh was told in a dream that he would die on such and such date. When he returned home, he held that dream to himself and waited for the time to come. Once he passed that date stated in his dream, he waited a few more days, then told someone about it, saying: "I would have not told you about this dream, had the date not passed." The person replied: "Perhaps you miscalculated the date, or maybe it is a confused dream." After returning to his home, the shaikh died during that same night. This is the meaning of God's Prophet's saying: *"A dream sits on the wing of a bird and will not take effect unless it is related to someone."*

♦ A man said to his close friend: "If you die before me, come and tell me about what you met with." The other man replied: "And you too!" After one of them had died, he came to his friend in a dream and said: "Trust in God Almighty, and depend on Him alone, for I saw no reward better than that of (*Tawakkul*) trust."

♦ Once a man visited a cemetery. Looking at the graves, he said to himself: "I wish that a miracle takes place and that some of these people come out and tell me about what they saw!" He then sat beside one of the graves pondering, when he was seized by slumber. In his sleep, someone appeared to him in a dream and said: "Do not boast about the way you fashion the gravestones and how you maintain the look of the cemetery. For under these gravestones there are people whose cheeks have decayed. Some are blessed and are awaiting God's reward and His paradise, while others are distressed with their past and are suffering the consequences of their deeds. Beware of heedlessness."

♦ A disciple of Husain Al-Hallāj once asked his teacher about the meaning of generosity. Al-Hallāj was killed before telling his disciple the answer. One night, the disciple was depressed. In a dream, it appeared to him as though the Day of Judgment was established, and that people stood before their Lord awaiting their reckoning. Then he saw Husain Al-Hallāj sitting on a seat made from gold and encrusted with jewels and sapphires. He also saw the scholars who signed the decree to kill Al-Hallāj standing before him with humiliation. It seemed to him as though God Almighty asked Al-Hallāj: "What do want Me to do with these people?" Al-Hallāj replied: "Lord, I ask Thee to forgive them all." My Shaikh then turned to his disciple in the dream and said: "My son, this is what true generosity is about."

♦ Imām Al-Junayyid reported that he was once sitting by his doorsteps. A blind man who was asking people to help him passed by him. Al-Junayyid said to himself: "If this man trusted in God Almighty and sat on the corner of a street, or at the entrance of a mosque, God Almighty will surely provide for him without his asking." Al-Junayyid continued: "That night, a copper tray was placed before me in a dream, and that blind man was laid on it. A voice then said to me: 'Eat from the flesh of this man.' I replied: 'God is my witness, I did not backbite him. It was only a thought, and my tongue never uttered a word of that.' The voice then said: 'Remember, O Junayyid, such an excuse cannot be accepted from a person with your level of knowledge.'" Junayyid added: "In the morning, I sat at my doorsteps again, pondering what had happened. Meanwhile, the blind man walked by me and said: 'O Abā Al-Qāsim, was it enough what you saw last night, and did you repent?'"

♦ After Al-Junayyid's death, a disciple saw him in a dream and asked: "What did God Almighty do to you, O Junayyid?" Al-Junayyid replied: "All the knowledge went away, and all the thoughts disappeared. Only a few prayers (Raka'āt) which we used to pray in the middle of the night (Suḥūr) were of any benefit to us.

♦ Once Sufyān Bin 'Ayeenah saw Sufyān Al-Thawri in a dream and asked him: "What is the special virtue that makes God Almighty love you?" Sufyān Al-Thawri, God bless his soul, replied: "Knowing less about people." Ibn 'Ayeenah then said: "Advise me." Sufyān Al-Thawri replied: "Use what I have just told you." Ibn 'Ayeenah added: "God have mercy on you. There are many good brothers here, and each one of them may intercede for his fellow brother on the Day of Judgment." Sufyān Al-Thawri replied: "I wish not to know you from this day on. Have you seen harm coming from other than people you know?" Ibn 'Ayeenah continued: "I suddenly woke up crying from my dream."

♦ Someone used to regularly recite special prayers and offer their blessing to the benefit of the soul of Rābi'a Al-'Adawiyyah, God be pleased with her. One night, he saw her in a dream, and she said to him: "Your gifts are carried to us on trays of light and are covered with light."

♦ Abu Al-Qāsim Al-Maghribi once saw Abdu Raheem Ibn Nabātah Al-Khatīb in a dream and asked him: "What did God Almighty do to you?" He replied: "He passed a small piece of paper, and on it I read two verses of a poem written with red ink. It says:

You used to feel secured and at peace,
and today I will let you into My safety and peace.

Forgiveness is not conferred upon a rightful person,
but upon a sinner, as a kind show of clemency.

♦ Ibrâhîm Al-Khurabi once said: "I saw Bishir Al-Hâfî in a dream. It seemed as though he was leaving the Mosque of Rasâfa. As he walked away from the mosque, the sleeve of his shirt looked weighty, and something kept on moving inside it. I asked him: 'What did God Almighty do to you?' He replied: 'He forgave me, and He was generous to me.' I asked: 'What are you carrying in your sleeve?' He replied: 'The soul of Ahmad Ibn Hanbal visited us yesterday, and it was welcomed with showers of gems and pearls. This is the share I was able to gather from that welcome.' I asked: 'What happened to Yahyâ Ibn Ma'ïn and Ahmad Ibn Hanbal after that?' He replied: 'They were called to visit the Lord of the universes, and they were welcomed with heavenly banquets.' I asked: 'Why did you not eat with them?' He replied: 'My Lord knew how little I care for food, and He allowed me to look at His Divine Countenance.'"

♦ A man said to a dream interpreter: "I saw myself in a dream bartering wheat for barley." The dream interpreter replied: "You have discontinued reading the Qur'ân to become a poet." The man obliged and repented.

♦ A man was asleep when his friend brought an open pitcher of milk and a water melon. The friend then cut a piece of the water melon and placed the milk and the pitcher beside his friend's pillow with the knife on top of the pitcher. He then sat down and waited for him to wake up. When the man woke up, he told his friend an amazing dream. He said: "I saw as though a type of fly came out of my nose, and it stood over a knife before reentering my nose. Then suddenly, I saw myself walking over an iron bridge that stood on top of an ocean." The friend smiled and told him what happened.

♦ It is related that Al-Mustanjid Billâh son of Al-Muqtafi saw during his father's life a dream in which an angel descended and wrote four times the Arabic letter 'H' in the palm of his hand. When Al-Mustanjid woke up, he told the dream to an interpreter who replied: "You will receive the Caliphate from your father in the year five hundred fifty-five, and already five months and five days have passed." Al-Mustanjid became the Caliph as foretold by the dream interpreter.

♦ A man bought a farmland. One night, he saw his nephew in his farm walking over snakes. In the morning, he asked a dream interpreter about it, and the latter replied: "If your dream is true, the land you bought is fertile, and whatever you plant therein will come to life."

♦ One night, a woman who lived in Mecca read the Qur'ân before going to sleep. In a dream, she saw maids of honor circumambulating the Ka'aba and carrying fine sheets covered with safflowers. The woman exclaimed in her dream: "Glory be to God! Who are these women?" A voice said to her: "Do you not know that tonight is the wedding ('Urs) of Abdul-Azïz Abi Dâwüd?" The woman woke up scared from her dream, as she heard a bursting noise coming from the street. She inquired about it to find that Abdul-Azïz Dâwüd has just died.

♦ A man came to Imâm Ibn Seerïn and said: "I saw a big bird that landed upon a jasmine tree in a dream, and he ate all its flowers." Ibn Seerïn's face became alarmed as he replied: "Your dream means the death of scholars."

♦ Once Imām Ibn Seerïn was sitting to eat his lunch when a woman came and said: "I saw a dream." Ibn Seerïn replied: "Would you let me eat first, or would you like me to stop and listen to your dream?" The woman said: "Eat first," and she sat waiting for him. During the course of his meal, Ibn Seerïn said to the woman: "Tell me your dream." The woman said: "I saw the moon merging in Alcyone." (*The brightest star of the constellation Taurus, arb. Thurayyā. See Alcyone.*) The woman continued: "A voice then said to me: 'Go to Ibn Seerïn, and tell him your dream.'" Ibn Seerïn suddenly shook, and said to the woman: "Tell me how did you see it?" The woman repeated her dream, and Ibn Seerïn's face became grim. His sister who was then sitting with him at the table said: "What disturbed you, O my brother?" He replied: "This woman is claiming that I will die in seven days." On the seventh day, Ibn Seerïn was buried.

♦ Imām Ahmad Ibn Hanbal once saw God Almighty in a dream and asked Him: "Lord, how do Thy near ones get to that station?" God Almighty answered: "Through reciting My words." Ahmad Ibn Hanbal then asked: "With understanding, or without understanding?" God Almighty answered: "O Ahmad, both with and without understanding them."

♦ A man saw himself in a dream falling down from a high altitude. When he woke up, he said to himself: "I will avoid going out of my house or seeing people for a while." During the middle of the afternoon of that same day, a close friend came to see him, and called him from downstairs. When the man stood up to look through the window, the shutters broke, and he fell with them.

♦ A man came to Abu Bakr, God be pleased with him, and said: " I was given seventy leaves in my dream last night." Abu Bakr replied: "It means that you will be flogged seventy times." The interpretation came true within a short time when he had to face such a public chastisement for a sin he committed. Within that same year, the man came to Abu Bakr and said: "I saw that same dream again." Abu Bakr replied: "You will receive seventy thousand Dirhams." The man said: "O Imām of the Muslims! Last year when I told you the same dream, you said that I will be flogged, and it took place, and this year you interpreted the dream to mean that I will receive seventy thousand Dirhams!" Abu Bakr replied: "O man, last year when you came to see me, the trees were shedding their leaves, and this year you are telling me the dream at the time when the trees are blooming with new blossoms." Shortly after that, the man received seventy thousand Dirhams from a business deal.

♦ Abdu-Rahmān Al-Salmi related that God's Prophet, upon whom be peace, united between Abu Bakr Al-Siddïq and Salmān Al-Fārisï, God be pleased with them both. One night Salmān saw a dream in which Abu Bakr was involved. Salmān kept his dream to himself and distanced himself from Abu Bakr, because it. One day Abu Bakr saw Salmān and said to him: "My dear brother, why have you abandoned me?" Salmān replied: "I saw your hand tied to your neck in a dream, and I was apprehensive of it." Abu Bakr replied: "God is the greatest. It means that my hand is tied to spare it from wrongdoing." Salmān then related his dream to God's Prophet, upon whom be peace, and added Abu Bakr's interpretation. God's Prophet (uwbp) confirmed the meaning and praised Abu Bakr's good interpretation.

♦ A woman came to God's Prophet, upon whom be peace, and said: "O Messenger of God, I saw in a dream that the central pillar which supports the ceiling of my house broke, and the ceiling caved in." God's Prophet (uwbp) replied: "Your husband will return to his home from a journey." Soon, the husband returned home from a business trip, and the wife was happy. While the husband is in town, the woman saw the same dream again, and she sought to ask God's Prophet (uwbp) about it. When she did not find him, Abu Bakr was present, so she told him the dream, and he replied: "Your husband will soon die."

In the first interpretation of the above dream, the husband was absent, while in the second dream, he was present. The conditions changed, and the meaning also changed.

♦ A man hid his money inside his house and went on a journey. On his way back home, he became sick. The man also owed money to some people, and he thought of telling one of his companions about the place of his money and to ask him to pay his debt, but he aspired for recovery and hoped to return home and pay his debts in person. During his journey, the man died. His son saw him in a dream and asked: "What did God do to you?" The father replied: "My condition is in abeyance, and it depends on some debts that must be paid first. I have some money hidden in such-and-such place. Please go and dig them up, pay people what I owe them, and enjoy the rest." In the morning, the son told a friend about his dream and added: "It is a fairy tale!" A few days later, the father came back to his son in another dream and said: "I have told you about something that will benefit you and that will free me from my limbo, but you failed to do it!" The son woke up in shock and immediately went to the place his father indicated in the dream. When he dug out the money, he paid his father's debts and benefited from his unanticipated inheritance.

♦ A man said to a dream interpreter: "I saw a bird flying off from my chest, then I sought my mother who hid me inside her garment." The interpreter replied: "If your dream is true, then it means your death. The bird represents your soul, and your hiding in your mother's robe means your burial. God Almighty has said: 'From it We created you, and into it We shall return you.'"

♦ A dream interpreter once said: "I saw a ruler sitting in a high place, and people were looking at him. I interpreted my dream to mean the ruler's death and people's deliberation of his work. A few months later, the ruler died, and people engaged in talking about his deeds and judging of his work."

♦ A man said to a dream interpreter: "In a dream, I went to a pond to drink some water. Suddenly, as I reached down to drink from it, a beast appeared from inside the pond and tried to impede my purpose. At a certain point, I turned into another sea creature and jumped into the water, then remained in that pond to help serve the thirst of every person who comes." The dream interpreter replied: "If your dream is true, you will seek an appointment in the government, and someone who is close to the ruler will fight you. Later on, positive circumstances will manifest and allow you to attain your goals and to take the place of that person. People will then come to you for their needs, and you will serve them with honesty, justice, and compassion." The man's dream was true, and as soon as he occupied that chair, he called for the dream interpreter and rewarded him for his knowledge.

♦ A man said to Shaikh Ahmad Al-Far'onï: "I saw Prince so-and-so riding on a high horse in a stately form and people honoring him." The Shaikh replied: "If your dream is true, he will soon be appointed at a high-ranking position." Shortly after that, the prince was appointed to the pilgrims' administration.

♦ Shaikh Salim Bin 'Isā once visited Hamza Bin Al-Habïb Al-Zayyāt, God bless his soul, who had memorized the Holy Qur'ān and read it with great devotion, seeking God's pleasure, and saw him crying and rubbing his cheeks with dust. He exclaimed: "I call upon God's protection for you. O Ḥamza, what is this crying?" Hamza replied: "Last night, I saw in a dream that the Day of Resurrection took place. The readers of the Qur'ān were called in to stand before God Almighty, and I was among them. I then heard an amiable voice saying: 'Only those who lived by the Qur'ān should enter.' I was in shock, so I began to withdraw. A voice called my name: 'Where are you going to, O Hamza Bin Al-Zayyāt?' I cried out: 'At thy command, O caller to my Lord.' An angel then said to me: 'Say: At Thy command O my Lord, At Thy command.' So I repeated what the angel told me to say. I was then led into an abode where I heard the voices of Qur'ān readers. I stood there shaking. I then heard a voice saying to me: 'Be at peace. Rise there and read.' I turned my face to the direction of the voice and saw a pulpit made from white pearls. One step is made from red sapphire, and another is made from green chrysolite. Then I was told: 'Rise and read.' So I did, and I read Al-An'ām chapter, not knowing before whom I am reading. When I reached verse sixty-one, reading: **'And He is the irresistible Lord, Who watches from above over His creation...'** (*Qur'ān 6:61*), the voice then said: 'O Ḥamza, Am I not the irresistible Lord, Who watches from above over His creation?' I said: 'Indeed. Thou speaks the truth.' Then I read Al-A'rāf chapter to its last verse, which says: **'Those who are near to their Lord, do not disdain to worship Him. They celebrate His praises, and bow down in prostration before Him.'** (*Qur'ān 7:206*). As I intended to prostrate before my Lord, my Lord said: 'Sufficient is the reading. Do not prostrate here.' He continued: 'O Hamza, who taught you how to read this?' I replied: 'Sulaimān.' He said: 'True. Who taught Sulaimān?' I replied: 'Yaḥyā.' He said: 'True. Who taught Yaḥyā?' I replied: 'Abi Abdu-Raḥmān.' He said: 'True. Who taught Abi Abdu-Raḥmān?' I replied: 'Ali Bin Abi Talib, the cousin of Thy Prophet.' He said: 'Ali spoke the truth. Who taught Ali?' I replied: 'Thy Prophet, upon whom be peace.' He said: 'My Prophet spoke the truth. Who taught My Prophet?' I replied: 'Gibreel, upon whom be peace.' He continued: 'And Who taught Gibreel?' I remained silent. He said: 'O Ḥamza, say You.' I replied: 'Lord, I cannot say that!' He again said: 'Say You.' I said: 'You.' He said: 'You spoke the truth O Ḥamza. I swear by the Qur'ān, I shall honor its readers and particularly those who lived by it and acted with it. O Hamza, the Qur'ān is My Word, and I love no one better than the people of the Qur'ān. O Ḥamza, come nearer.' So I did, and my Lord anointed me with a musky ambergris. Then He added: O Ḥamza. This is not only for you. I did the same to your companions who are higher than you and to those who are lower than you, as well as to those who read the Qur'ān like you and who seek no reward except Me. What I have reserved for you is still greater than this. So tell your friends about Me and about My love for the people of the Qur'ān, for they are the chosen and elite. O Hamza, I swear by My Glory and Majesty, I shall never punish a tongue that recited the Qur'ān, nor a heart that understood it, nor an ear that heard it, nor an eye that looked at it.' I said: 'Glory be to Thee, O my Lord.' God Almighty added: 'Who are the people of the Qur'ān?' I said: 'Those who memorize it, my Lord?' He said: 'Indeed. Such people. I am on their side until they meet with Me on the Day of Judgement. When they come before Me, I shall raise them a station for each verse they learned.'" Ḥamza, God be pleased with him continued: "Thus, would you blame me if I cry and rub my cheeks with dust?"

Conclusion

In closing, it seems obvious from this reading that the branches, basis, fundamentals, and references of dream interpretation are many, and no single book in this world can encompass them. Should anyone attempt to ascertain the meaning of all the dreams, he will definitely fall short of accomplishing his intent. The examples cited in this introduction may help the dream interpreter as well as the person who is interested in this art. Their purpose is to help one to understand the varying functions of dreams, and an intelligent dream interpreter can understand the reasons behind refraining from further elaboration on this subject.

In this dictionary, the reader could find expressions with which he or she may not be familiar. However, to those who have knowledge, this work is intended to provide explanations by way of short traditions and explaining values that can initiate the groundwork for further study.

It is necessary here to state that if people depend solely on books to explain their dream, they will certainly fail to understand all the meanings. Thus, it is of great importance to seek a knowledgeable dream interpreter, or a wise Shaikh who is familiar with the fundamentals of dream interpretation, their inner and outer meanings. God knows best.

In seeking God's acceptance and invoking His bounteous blessings upon His Prophet Muhammad, upon whom be peace, I hope that this dictionary of dreams will help the reader to further his or her understanding of this art.

By the Grace of God Almighty,
this book was completed this Tuesday
the 1st day of Rabi'u Thānī 1412 A.H.,
October 8th, 1991.
All Praises be to Allāh,
Lord and Cherisher
of the
universes.

GUIDE TO USING
IBN SEERÏN'S
DICTIONARY OF DREAMS

I. THE MAIN ENTRY

This dictionary of dreams contains over 4300 indexed entries. However, the combined multi-usage of nouns, verbs, adjectives, proper names, synonyms, etcetera, provide the reader with a much greater access to vocabulary and interpretation of elements. Interpreting dreams is like reading the meaning of each element and its synonyms in its own mother tongue. Example:

Artichoke, (ärt'i chŏk') *n. arb. Art*, earth -*choke*, thorn.

Omniscient: (äm nish'ent) < *omni*, all + -*sciens*, a prp. of *scire*, to know, discern.

Viscount: (vi'kount') *n. vice*, deputy and -*count*, companion < Earl; Count.

In a couple of instances, I used the meaning of a proper name, followed by the root of the entry word. Example:

Zachariah: (*Zachar*, to remember + *ya*, God; ...)

Dream interpretation also explains how the human mind works. In fact, this art clearly identifies the state of one's innate awareness. Interpreting dreams also portrays the spirit of a culture and may sometimes carry a universal perception of values.

The entries in this book are mostly followed immediately by related synonyms that are placed in brackets. Sometimes the elements inside the brackets represents a cross-reference on such subject. Example:

Medicine: (Drug; Inkwell).

Other entries are followed by a reference in Italics on where to find explanations about the said element. Example:

Immolation: *(See Feast of immolation; Manumission; Offering; Sacrifice; Slave)*

Colors of the face: *(See Colors; Face)*

In this case, for example, one should look under both:

1. **Colors**, and

2. **Face**.

In some cases, the reader is advised to look up the opposite meaning of an interpretation, where he may find further interpretations, with ending instructions in italics. Example:

Incomplete job: (Unfinished business) .... *(Also see Finished business)*

The word *Jāmi* in Arabic means the center of a congregation. In this dictionary of dreams, one can look the word Jami under Masjid (*sajada*, to prostrate oneself, pray. *arb.* place of prostration or place of worship), and under Mosque, (the British version of the Arabic word Masjid, using the Egyptian pronunciation Masgid > *muskey. fr.*

Jāmi: *(See Masjid; Mosque)*

When main entries are spelled alike but each carries a different meaning or usage, as **pit** (snake pit) and **pit** (date pit), they are entered in separate blocks and are followed by subscript numbers immediately following the boldface entry.

Mercury[1]......(planet)

Mercury[2]...... (Quicksilver)

In this dictionary of dreams, foreign words are followed by an abbreviation of their origin, and set in italics (*See List of Abbreviations*). Example:

Hajj: (*arb.* Pilgrimage)

Immediately after the origin of a foreign word, I indicated where to find such entry. Example:

Ṣalāt: (*arb. See Five times prayers.*) Though the word Ṣalāt in Arabic also means: Prayers, Benediction, Blessings, Grace, etcetera.

In some places, I used a phrase to provide an indication of how to build the elements of one's dream. Example:

1- Visiting God's House in Mecca: (*See Pilgrimage; 'Umrah*)

However, the reader can also find other interpretations on visiting God's House, by looking under **Masjid** and **Mosque**. The reader is advised to search for other interpretations and in this case under: (*Also see Imām; Ka'aba; Minaret; Minbar; Muezzin*)

2- Walking on water: ....(*Also see River; Water*)

In some instances, a list of interpretations is provided under one entry. Example:

Sound of birds: ......

Sound of animals: ......

Playing games:......

or one may find his favorite ball game under one entry such as:

Ball: (*Baseball; Basketball; Cricket ball; Football; etcetera. Also see Games*)

Other entries include Arabic words that are sometime used in Eglish such as: **Islām, Muezzin, Saker, Wadi**, etcetera.

II. PRONUNCIATION

In this dictionary of dreams, pronunciation is mostly concerned with foreign words.

When an opening apostrophe (') is placed before a vowel (i.e., 'A; 'E), it means that this letter is a consonant in Arabic and must be pronounced with extra guttural sound of the Arabic letter ع. Example: 'Eid: (*Festival*). When the Arabic letter is not transliterated in the English text, the opening apostrophe then indicates its presence. Example:

Zul-Qi'dah: (*See Arabic months*)

A closing apostrophe is used herein to indicate a glottal stopping or light breathing sound of the hamza letter in Arabic ء. Example: **'Ashüra'**: (10th day of Muḥarram; Anniversary of the martyrdom of Husain at Kerbala).

However, when a closing apostrophe (') is placed before a vowel in the middle of a word such as **Qur'ān**, then the vowel should be pronounced as it is: (e.g. ā; e; o).

ā   This symbol indicates a prolonged aa. Example: **Yaḥyā**: (John).

ï   This symbol indicates a prolonged letter *i*. (k<u>ee</u>n)

ü   This symbol indicates a prolonged letter *u*. (mood)

When (...) are used under an d̲, h̲, s̲, t̲, etcetera, they indicate the Arabic letters ط ، ص ، ح ، ذ , implying a stronger guttural sound.

pronounced by pressing the tongue against the edge of the upper teeth.

Dh	Representing the Arabic letter ض . Example: **Dhuḥā**: (*See Five times prayers*).
Kh	This symbol represents the Arabic letter خ which is a gutteral *ch* as in Scottish "*loch*". Example: **Khimār**: (*Veil*).
Th	This symbol represents the Arabic letter ذ which is pronounced like the article "*the*" in English, and sometime pronounced like "*think*".
Gh	This symbol represents the Arabic letter غ which is pronounced like the French "*r*", *grasséyé*.

For other references on Arabic pronunciation, please refer to any Arabic grammar book or an Arabic-English dictionary.

III. DEFINITIONS

In this dictionary, definitions that follow some entries are arranged in alphabetic order, and they are set inside brackets immediately following the entry.

IV. SCIENTIFIC NAMES

When the name of a plant or an animal is entered in this dictionary, I used an abbreviation symbol of *zool. med.* or *bot.* before sometimes entering the Latin name. Example:

Tragacanth: (*bot. genus Astragalus*).

Elephantiasis: (*med. See Elephant man*).

Mole[3]: (*zool....*).

Proper names of planets are followed by the abbreviation *astr.* ,while others may indicate a group of elements.

1- Capricorn: (*astr. See Moon*).

2- Canis Major: (Constellation. *See Dog*).

V. SYNONYMS

Synonyms are sometimes listed following the entry. In Eastern inner traditions, the synonym may not necessarily agree with today's Western appellation. However, a close examination of the interpretations provided in this dictionary may lead to narrowing the meaning and make it more applicable. The interpretation of the elements themselves provides for a more extensive list of synonyms and may require a specialized dictionary of synonyms for Eastern cultures.

VI. INTERPRETING IDIOMATIC EXPRESSIONS

What is lawful and unlawful in this book does not only represent the legal or illegal, the permissible and the impermissible, but rather treats the same in a religious sense. For example, usury (lending of money for excessive interest) is unlawful. The quality of humankind in a dream maybe represented by the innate character of the like creations. Thus, a beneficial bird may mean a praiseworthy person; a beast represents the like quality in man; an elephant represents arrogance; a harvest projecting a particular person denotes human qualities of a lesser magnitude, etcetera. (*Also see Man*).

In the past, people also used dream interpretation as a tool to understand diseases, to find cures from their interpretations, to discover spiritual guidance, and to provide psychological analysis of their condition. Example: **Medicine**: (Drug; Inkwell.) In a dream, medicine means correcting oneself, or fulfilling one's religious requirements. (*See Grapes; Medicine*). Based on traditional medicine, dream interpretation also emphasizes and educates the public on using certain herbal medicine for their illness by eating seeds and herbs from plants such as pumpkin, cucumber, eggplant, sweet basil, chard, onion, cabbage, Indian corn and melon seeds, etcetera.

As for distilled farm water, or from water lily, or distilled water from similar flowers, they represent medicinal remedies, profits, celebrations and weddings. *(See Distilled water).*

King in the old traditions is substituted here with the noun ruler, governor, mayor, supervisor, or a similar commonly adopted terms in today's usage. Though in Eastern traditions king in a dream is sometimes interpreted by relative nouns such as lion, notable, or luminary, etcetera.

Blessings connote good, goods, money, health, the five senses, wife, husband, children, property, friends, and any worldly benefits the human being enjoys and takes for granted. In a dream, a soldier represents one's deeds while enemy may represent one's poor qualities.

A spool represents the element of religious life. Religion means a way of life. Of course it is connected with faith, though religion is incumbent upon every person while faith is an endowment or a divine gift based on one's performance of his or her religious obligations. In a way, the parable of religion is like that of a laborer who whether he likes it or not, he has to wake up in the morning to reach his work, collect his wages and pay his rent and expenses. Otherwise, his employer will dismiss him, his landlord will evict him, his family will be dispersed and he will lose respect. The same thing goes for being a law abiding citizen. Hence, honor and status in a society depend on hard work, loyalty, devotion and servitude. Thus we can understand how religion is a must and faith is an gift. Religion carries laws which are established by God Almighty and relates to the original covenant between our Lord and his creation. God's attributes and promises are always fulfilled and religious commitment is man's share of duties. Man's increased gratitude and devotion may, God willing, entitle him to further endowments and his sincere love for his Lord may qualify him for a reward.

In many instances, elements in a dream may mean the opposite. Some of the elements must be approximated to construct a closer interpretation of one's dream *(See Introduction).* Business for instance may be connected to one's job, a king or a ruler to one's supervisor or boss, etcetera. On the other hand, the elements themselves define their innate nature. To interpret one's dream from this dictionary one must connect the elements and establish their pertinence. For example, in a dream, ritual impurity (Junub; Janâba) indicates that one is avoiding certain obligations. According to Islamic traditions, one must have ablution when pursuing any interest. Another example, building an edifice from plaster or baked brick encrusted with pictures or forms in a dream means engaging in an unlawful or a deceitful act, for a wall of plaster or a gypsum dry wall carries no strength and has a short life, particularly under the rain. *(See Plaster)* .

Another example, **Kite:** *(Small hawk).* In a dream, it means an insouciant or languorous ruler who is audacious, defiled and stouthearted. This interpretation came from the innate nature of the bird itself which flies low and close to the ground and rarely misses its catch. Understanding the nature of a kite helped the interpreter in this case to discuss such element of a dream. It is said in Eastern traditions that man gets very little from a kite if he uses it for hunting.

Finally, interpreting dreams helps to put things in perspective. It recognizes their nature through scrutinizing and examining their effects in one's heart with analytical wisdom.

VII. MAPPING ONE'S DREAM

Following the explanation given in the *Introduction* about relating one's dream, one should commence by mapping his dream and identifying the elements. For example:

1. If in a segment of one's dream, one sees himself riding a car or running after a car in the middle of the night, then one should look under Car, under night, and even under Running. If one seems impatient or anxious, then he should also look under Patience and Anxiety. If one ends in the city of Jerusalem in the dream, then he should add the element of Jerusalem, etcetera.

In this case, the search consist of looking up the main entries: (Car; Night; Running; Anxiety; Patience; Jerusalem) and their synonyms.

2. If one sees himself flying in the air, feeling comfortable, looking down at the world, then should he see Mount Sinai, or God's prophet Moses, or if he sees Pharaoh, etcetera, then he should look up the main entries: (Mount Sinai; Mountain; Moses; Flying in the air), etcetera, or substitute the proper synonym.

The adjectives, nouns, or verbs explaining each element, and each entry in this dictionary also may need to be researched and explained. For example: Under **Sugar cane**, one finds the elements of charity; women; pious men; knowledge; lineage; ruins; destruction; exhuming the dead; marriage contract; juice; freedom; imprisonment; wailing; grief; sorrow; rabbling; toiling; or clamor; etcetera. Thus, should one need further explanations on the element subject of his dream, then perhaps he should look up these entries under their separate blocks.

Other examples can be found in the dictionary itself.

One also can look through the Index of Entries (pages 489-506) in order to identify his elements and their synonyms.

Please do not forget that you are reading a book about dreams and dream interpretation. The contents herein are not intended to portray any particular person or gender, though sometimes one may discover astonishing similarities between beings, things, or instances. Still, use them as a guide, and definitely seek the counsel of a reputable dream interpreter or a shaikh for further elaborations.

VIII. LIST OF ABBREVIATIONS

A.D.	anno Domino	e.g.	for example
A.H.	after Higra (Islāmic year)	folk.	folklore
approx.	approximately	fr.	French
anat.	anatomy	i.e.,	that is
arb.	Arabic	med.	medicine
astr.	astronomy	spa.	Spanish
bibl.	Biblical	(uwbp)	upon whom be peace
bot.	botany	zool.	zoology

A

Aaron: (The Prophet Aaron, the older brother of God's prophet Moses, upon both of them be peace.) Seeing the prophet Aaron (uwbp) in a dream means exaltedness, leadership, or that one may become an Imām, a vice-regent of a great person, and perhaps suffer from many adversities because of it. Finally, he will triumph and attain his goals, or he may destroy a tyrant and an unjust ruler. If a warrior sees God's prophet Moses or his brother the prophet Aaron, upon both of them be peace and blessings, in a dream, it means that he will be victorious and triumph over his enemy.

Abacus: (Calculator) In a dream, an abacus represents social order, conformity and uprightness. Seeing an abacus in a dream also reflects one's own state and conduct. If the frame and beads are in a good condition, operate smoothly and smell fragrant in the dream, the abacus then denotes one's uprightness and good conduct. If they look dirty, greasy and rough to handle in the dream, then they denote the ill management of one's life or business. If one sees an abacus in such a condition in his dream, it may also represent unsanitary food preparation, a greasy spoon restaurant, or it could mean abating the declared weight or value of a merchandise. An abacus in a dream also may represent a well behaved child, a student, a teacher, or a judge. If one turns into an abacus in a dream, it means an illness or a calamity. An abacus in a dream also means that one's patience, contentment and trust in God Almighty will reserve him a generous reward. *(Also see Record keepers)*

Abandoned infant: *(See Orphan)*

Abattoir: *(See Slaughterhouse)*

Abdomen: (Venter) The surface part of the body between the chest and the pelvis in a dream represents one's strength and health condition, wealth, or it could mean poverty. *(Also see Body¹)*

Abel: Seeing Abel, the second son of Adam in a dream means suffering from people's jealousy, grievance, chicanery, or that one may be killed by his enemy. It also means that an unjust person will envy him. Seeing Abel in a dream also means piety, devotion to God Almighty, feebleness toward a woman or making an offering to please God Almighty and entering the heavenly paradise as a reward. One who sees Abel in a dream should beware of his brethren and close friends, and he should fear for his life.

Abhor: *(See Hate)*

Ablution: Taking an ablution and completing it by giving careful attention to details in a dream means fulfilling one's needs. Taking a second ablution to perform one's prayers without the ritual need to do so in a dream means increase in one's light. Taking ablution with milk or honey in a dream means debts. Ablution is a proper deed in all religions. It is a guard, a clemency, assurance of the divine protection and immunity from punishment. Taking an ablution to perform one's prayers in a dream means entering under God's protection against what one may fear. It is reported in the traditions that God Almighty has said to Moses, upon whom be peace: "When you are seized by fear, take your ablution

1

and direct your family to enter the sacrament of prayers." Washing one's body in a dream is either performed in preparation for prayers or to wash away impurities. Taking ablution inside a tunnel, or taking a complete ritual bath in a dream means recovering a stolen object. Taking one's ablution and engaging in prayers in a dream means relief from distress and offering thanks to God Almighty for His protection and guidance. If a merchant sees himself praying without ablution in a dream, it means that he has entered into a business venture without capital. If a worker sees that dream, it means that he has no home to shelter him. If a ruler sees that dream, it means that he has no soldiers to protect him. If a sick person sees himself taking ablution while in bed in a dream, it means separation from his wife or a close friend. Taking ablution inside one's house in a dream means that one will move to a new house. Taking ablution in the street or the marketplace in public or in a bathhouse in a dream means a scandal, loss and a curse. Taking ablution at the seashore or in a proper ablution area in a dream means dispelling one's fear, sorrow or distress. Taking ablution while standing over a friend's head in a dream means inheriting him. Seeing a friend taking his ablution over one's head in a dream means suffering harm or a scandal that will be caused by such a friend. Taking ablution in a dream also means dispelling fears, recovering from an illness, paying one's debts or repenting from sin. Taking ablution with hot water in a dream means falling sick. Wanting to take ablution and failing to find the proper means to perform it in a dream means failure of a project or facing adversities. (Also see Tayammum; Enacting; Prayers; Ritual bath)

Abode: (See Dwellings; House)

Abominable: (See Shameful act)

Abraham: (God's bosom friend, upon whom be peace. arb. _khalīl_) To see the Prophet Abraham, upon whom be peace, in a dream is a good sign of wealth, blessings, glad tidings, devotion, long life, assiduousness, healing of a sick, noble goals, righteous progeny, commanding good and forbidding evil, discarding bad company, compliance with the divine ruling, knowledge, guidance, success after failure and separation from one's family and kin to seek God's nearness and pleasure. In a dream, Abraham represents the element of compassion toward one's son and family and sometime he represents the element of adversities and finally of reaching safety. (Also see Feast of Immolation; Station of Abraham)

Abscess: (Boil; Tumor; Ulcer. See Pimple)

Absolution: (See Amnesty; Pardon)

Abstention: (See Justice)

Abstinence: (See Ascetic detachment)

Abundance: (See Kawthar)

Abuse: (See Insult)

Acacia tree: (Arabic Gum; Dyes; Mimosa tree; Ornamental flowers; Perfume) Seeing this tree in a dream means stinginess, evil and behaving with the actions of the dwellers of hell-fire.

Accolade: (See Embrace)

Accomplished: (See Finished business)

Accoucheuse: (See Dromedary rider; Midwife)

Accountability: In a dream, accountability has various levels of interpretations. If an employee sees that he has received his account promptly in a dream it means rising in rank and increase of one's income. If one sees himself under a strict supervision or reckoning in a dream, it means humiliation, distress or perhaps loss of his job. If a person is investigated in a court of people he does

not know in a dream, it means that he has strayed into innovation and will remain accountable for his deeds. *(Also see Reckoning)*

Accountant: In a dream, an accountant represents an astringent person who also has the power to carry sentences. If his accounting is strict and detailed in the dream it means that his sentence will be severe and painful. *(Also see Accountability)*

Accumulating debts: *(See Tripping)*

Accursed son: *(See Recalcitrant child)*

Ache: *(See Pain)*

Acknowledging devotion: If one sees himself acknowledging devotion or worship of another human being in a dream, it means enmity with that person. But, if one sees himself confessing his wrongdoing in a dream, it means regaining honor, dignity and true repentance. To confess a murder in a dream means that one will attain peace, leadership or advancement to a supervisory job.

Acknowledgment: *(See Fame)*

Acorn: *(See Gullnuts)*

Acquaintances: *(See Connections)*

Acquittal: *(See Amnesty; Pardon)*

Acrimony: *(See Teeth)*

Acumen: *(See Perspicacity)*

Adam: Father of humanity, upon whom be peace. In a dream, Adam represents the elements of sin and repentance. He also represents one's father or the governor of the land. When seen standing in a noble fashion, Adam also represents attainment and honor. If Adam addresses the person in question in the dream it means that the latter will acquire knowledge. If one becomes Adam or a companion of his and should he qualify for such promotion, it means that he will attain it. Adam also represents the element of temporal existence. Seeing him in a dream also implies understanding, for he was the first to see dreams in this world and to interpret the name of things. Adam also represents reunion with one's family, concerns, forgetfulness and worries.

Adjuration: (Ingratitude. *See Uncertainty*)

Adjuring: (To command solemnly; to swear by God; or to take an oath.) If one sees himself swearing in God's Name before someone in a dream, it means that the other person will deceive him. To swear solemnly by the stars, the celestial signs or by any physical sign in a dream means arrogance, deception, humiliation, hypocrisy or heedlessness. If one is truthful in his oath in a dream it means that he will win his argument, speak the truth or perform an act that pleases God Almighty. To swear by God in a dream when failure to perform requires atonement means following the truth and emulating the leading example of God's Prophet, upon whom be peace.

Adjust: *(See Organize)*

Admonition: (Destruction; Harvest) To impel one's animal to drive faster in a dream means heeding admonition. *(Also see Washing)*

Adobe maker: In a dream, an adobe maker represents someone who earns his money from his own sweat and saves his earnings. Molding these bricks and drying them in the sun in a dream means prosperity. Handling wet adobes or stampeding a wet adobe mix and smoothing it in a dream means distress, toiling, sorrow or corruption. Half-dried molds of adobes placed under the sun in a dream represent workers or servants. *(Also see Adobe; Bricks)*

Adobe: (Money; Sun-dried bricks) Seeing blocks of adobes in a dream signify money. Each adobe represents a denomination of ten, thousand or one hundred thousand units of money, depending on the type of work one does in wakefulness. If adobes are used for construction in a dream, then they mean good work, good deeds or they could represent a religious person. An adobe in a dream also represents a servant. Building a house with adobes in a dream means unity and love between the father and his children. If an adobe falls to the ground in a dream, it means the death of a sick person or disunity in the family or dispersal of one's children. Manufacturing adobes in a dream means increase in the number of one's workers or employees. Each adobe represents a worker. Building a house with adobes in a dream also means leadership. A pile of adobes in a dream means a pile of money. *(Also see Adobe maker; Bricks)*

Adornment: *(See Apparel)*

Adulation: (Flattery; Sociability; Sycophancy) Adulation and sociability in a dream mean showing respect and esteem, lauding someone, being true to oneself or being charitable. *(Also see Flattery)*

Adultery: (Rape) Committing the abominable and forbidden act of adultery in a dream means betrayal. If one sees himself doing so in a dream, it means that he will betray his wife. An unknown woman is better here than a known woman. Adultery in a dream also means theft. If one sees an adulteress soliciting him for fornication in a dream it means that he might be lured to earn unlawful money. If one commits adultery with a young and a beautiful woman in a dream, it means that he will place his earnings in a well-guarded place or a coffer. If a strong person commits adultery in his dream and if he had to face the divine ordinance and chastisement for his sin in the dream, it means that his authority will expand. If the person in the dream qualifies for leadership, then he will be endowed with one. If one sees himself committing adultery with the wife of a close friend in a dream it means that he will take some money from him. If one reads the ruling of the divine ordinance concerning the punishment of adulterers in a dream, it means that he is an adulterer. If one deals with an adulteress or with a woman who has committed adultery in a dream, then such a woman represents the world and its seekers. If a student on the path of God Almighty, who is known to have piety, good conduct and who has the look of a believer sees himself dealing with an adulteress or a woman who has committed adultery in a dream, it means that he will join the company of a gnostic and learn wisdom at his hand. If one sees a man and a woman sitting alone in an intimate setting in his dream, and if he recognizes them, it means that he desires some worldly interests from such a man. If a man sees himself raping a young woman in a dream, it means that he hides his savings in an unknown place. If he is caught after that, and if the divine ordinance is exacted in the dream, his dream means that he will follow the path of knowledge and understanding of religious jurisprudence. If one commits adultery with an adulteress in a dream, it means that he will face severe trials. If one enters a brothel in his dream and finds it impossible to leave that place, it means that he may die shortly. If one sees himself sleeping with someone else's wife, while the husband is not minding in a dream, it means that the husband will entrust him with his home to manage. If one marries an adulteress in a dream, it means that he is an adulterer. *(Also see Sexual intercourse)*

Advantage: *(See Booty)*

Adversary: *(See Cheese; Opponent)*

Adverse: *(See Opponent)*

Advice: If one receives an advice from his enemy in a dream, it means deception, trickery, cheating, duplicity, stratagem, dishonesty and arrogance. *(Also see Soliciting advice)*

Adz: (Adze; Ax) Seeing an adz in a dream signifies continuing progress, permanence, stability, livelihood, profits, money, benefits from one's wife or child. An adz in a dream also could represent the head of a project or the manager to whom one must report about the progress of his work, or it could represent a teacher, a wise man, an educator, one's mouth, one's servant, a greedy person, a sharp tongued woman or it could represent the arrival of a traveller. *(Also see Ax)*

Affectation: Witnessing affectation in a dream is a sign of committing a forbidden act or an evil act in wakefulness. *(Also see Shell)*

Affection: *(See Amity)*

Affiliation: *(See Partnership)*

Affinity: *(See Correspondence)*

Affront: *(See Digging up the past)*

African dances: *(See Tap)*

African rue: *(See Rue)*

Agate: (Quartz. *See Stone²)*

Agent: *(See Bodyguard)*

Aggrandizement: *(See Giant)*

Agitation: Man's agitation or explosion toward inanimate objects in a dream means either business losses, or seizing of one's property by the authority. Agitation in a dream also means a calamity of an unknown disease or a worrisome illness.

Agony of death: If one sees himself struggling with death in a dream, it means arguing about his religion, or doubt about God's revelations. Death rattling in a dream also signifies preparing to take a journey, marriage of an unmarried person, moving from one house to a new one, changing one's trade or repaying one's debt, or divorcing one's wife. If one sees himself in agony in his deathbed, combating the throes and pangs of death in a dream, it means that he is unjust toward himself or others. *(Also see Death)*

Agony: *(See Agony of death; Death; Distress; Gambling; Uptight; Worries)*

Agreement: *(See Conformance)*

Air blower: *(See Bellows; Fan)*

Air: Standing in the air in a dream means being honored or acknowledged by a governor, though it will not last. If one has exaggerated hopes, arrogance, pride, or if he is a self-centered individual, then his floating in the air represents mere disturbed dreams. Walking in the air without ascending or descending in a dream means receiving dignity, honor and earning lawful money. If one does not qualify for it, then walking in the air in his dream means travels. Hanging in the air between the heavens and the earth in a dream represents a concerned heart and uncertainty about what to do! Falling in the air in a dream means despair or loss of status in wakefulness. Falling in a dream also means relief from distress, wantonness, or satisfying one's needs. Clear, fresh and pure air in a dream represents a good time to take a trip for business or pleasure. Air in a dream also represents one's desire and passion. Thus, disobeying one's mind, desire and passion in a dream means entering the heavenly paradise. Following one's desires in a dream means negligence of once religious duties. Standing up in the air and speaking loud in a dream means blessings, favors, money, honor and fame. Sitting in the air in a dream means arrogance and self-deception regarding religious opinions. Building a house up in the air or placing a mat in the air or raising a tent in the air means death of a sick person, and what is built in this case is one's own coffin. If a governor sees that dream, it means his dismissal from his office or his death. Seeing that dream after a wedding or after having marital relations with one's wife means mistrust and loss. It also means involvement in an uncouth action, lacking knowledge of the Holy Book and prophetic traditions, because what one has built lacks a foundation. Flying in the air in a dream may mean travels. Flying with wings in a dream has stronger connotations and is safer. The wings here will represent money or power. Swimming in the air means benefits or business travels. If the air looks opaque in one's eyes, so he cannot see the skies in his dream, it means problems with one's superior. If one does not have a boss, then it means that he may lose his sight. If all the people witnessed the air opaque or red in the dream, then it means a major calamity and a trying adversity. *(Also see Ascending in the Skies; Flying)*

Aircraft: (Airplane; Coffin; Flying ship; Knowledge. *Also see Kite; Ship)*

Airplane: (Aircraft; Coffin; Flying ship; Knowledge. *Also see Kite; Ship)*

'Aisha: (Wife of God's Messenger upon whom be peace, and Mother of the believers, God be pleased with her) Seeing her in a dream means blessings and bounty. If a woman sees 'Aisha in a dream, it means earning a high station, a blessed fame, developing righteousness and earning the love of one's husband and parents.

Al-Azhar mosque: *(See Masjid)*

Alarm clock: (Timepiece) Seeing an alarm clock in a dream means exposing ills, richness of a poor person, or fulfilling a promise. *(Also see Clock)*

Albino: *(See Elf)*

Alcohol: *(See Beer; Intoxicants; Nonalcoholic wine)*

Alcoholic: (Drunkard; Enmity; Evil; Hatred; Inebriate; Temptation; Tippler. *Also see Beer; Intoxicants; Nonalcoholic wine; Wine)*

Alcyone: *(See Constellations)*

Aldebran: *(See Constellations)*

Aldromeda: *(See Constellations)*

Alertness: *(See Wakefulness)*

Alhena: *(See Constellations)*

'Ali: ('Ali bin 'Abi Ṭālib, God bless his countenance, cousin and son in-law of God's Messenger, upon whom be peace.) Seeing him in a dream means victory over one's enemy. Seeing him in a place or a mosque where people are mourning him or performing the funeral prayer on him or carrying his coffin or prostrating to him in a dream means becoming a Shia'it or gathering one's strength for a rebellion or to create divisiveness, or it could mean hypocrisy. If a scholar sees him in a dream, it means that he will earn increased knowledge, asceticism, reverence and strength. Seeing him in a dream also means capture by one's enemy, migrating from one country to another and mostly to die as a martyr. Seeing 'Ali in a dream also means having a blessed progeny, vanquishing one's enemy, presiding over the believers, hardships during travels, booty, manifestation of blessings and miracles, acquiring extraordinary knowledge, following the leading practices of God's Messenger, upon whom be peace, or fulfillment of one's commands. If one sees him as an old man in a dream, it means establishing a connection with the leadership of the land and profiting from it. Seeing him with wounds over his body in a dream means that one will become subject to people's slander and defamation.

Aliment: *(See Product)*

Alimony: *(See Family support)*

Allāh: God Almighty, Lord, Creator and Cherisher of the universes. There is nothing like unto Him and He is the All-Hearing, the Al-Seeing Lord. Seeing Him in a dream can be interpreted according to one's state of being. If one sees Him in His glory and majesty, without descriptive designation, without ascription of human characteristics to Him and without depiction or portrayal in the dream, it is an indication of glad tidings for both this world and the hereafter.

These blessings also may continue to affect the lives of one's progeny. If one sees Him otherwise in a dream, it means confusion, and particularly if the Almighty Lord does not address him. If an ailing person sees Him in a dream, it means that he will soon die and come to meet Him. If a straying soul sees God Almighty in a dream, it will find guidance. If an oppressed person sees Him, it means that justice will prevail and he will triumph over his oppressors. Hearing God's words without designation represents the imagination of the person in the dream. Perhaps hearing His words in a dream appeases one's heart and increases the person's drive for success. Hearing God's words without seeing Him represents the rising of one's station. If one receives revelations from behind a veil in a dream, it means mental confusion and innovation. This is most true if a messenger comes in one's dream and describes the one who spoke as God. In this case, the dream is a nightmare, because God Almighty cannot be depicted according to human descriptions. If one sees a picture of God in his dream, it means that he is a liar who ascribes images to God Almighty that do not befit His Majesty and Glory. If one hears God Almighty talking to him directly and if he can focus at Him in the dream, it means that he will be encompassed with God's mercy and blessings. If one sees God Almighty in a dream, it means that he will look at His Divine countenance in the hereafter. Seeing God Almighty seated on the Divine Throne in a dream means elevation of one's rank, knowledge and increase in his wealth. If one sees himself running away to hide from God Almighty in a dream, it means that he will change the course of his devotion into heedlessness. Seeing a veil separating between the servant and his Lord in a dream means that one will commit major sins and abominable actions. If one sees his Lord frowning at him, whereby he could not bear the effulgence of God's light, or if he is seized by a shock and immediately commences to repent and pray for forgiveness in the dream, it means that such a person is indulging in abominable actions, and that he is a despicable sinner who follows his own mind and desires, and that he is an innovator of religious thoughts who misleads the people. If one hears God Almighty talking to him in a dream, it represents an admonition and a warning to abstain from sin. If one hears God Almighty talking to him in a dream, it also means that one is more assiduous in his recital of the Qur'ān. If one hears God Almighty talking to him with words he cannot understand, then if He anoints him and blesses him in the dream, it means that God Almighty will bring him nigh unto Himself and exalt his station. If one sees God Almighty in a form resembling one's father, a brother or a relative and showing His kindness or blessing him in a dream, it means that he will be afflicted with a calamity and a major illness. If a righteous person sees himself standing before God Almighty in reverence and filled with awe in a dream, it means that mercy will encompass him and help him to further his growth. The same interpretation applies if one sees himself prostrating before Him. If God Almighty speaks to someone from behind a veil in a dream, it can also represent a good worshipper, but if the Divine address takes place without a veil in the dream, it means falling into sin. If God Almighty names someone in his dream with his birth name, then adds another title to it, it means rising in station and rank. If one sees God Almighty angry with him in a dream, it means that his parents are displeased with him. This description includes seeing oneself falling from the skies or from the top of a mountain. If a devoted servant sees God Almighty kissing him in a dream, it applies to his growing devotion and reward. Fearing God Almighty in a dream reflects eminence, peacefulness, quiescence, wealth of being and disregard for material needs. (Also see Carriers of the Divine Throne; Divine Throne; Educator; God's will; King)

Allergic disorder: *(See Hives)*

Alley: (Corridor; Hallway; Lane; Long narrow lane) Entering a lane in a dream means falling under suspicion and particularly if it has curves. A lane in a dream also means breaking one's oath or mixing and confusing values, or it could mean a road, a method of operating a business, or the techniques used by a craftsman in his trade. *(Also see Lane; Road)*

Alliance: *(See Allies; Partnership)*

Allies: In a dream, allies are good news for someone who seeks to find partners. As for a sick person, they mean death.

Alligator: An alligator in a dream represents a knowledgeable person who guides people from darkness unto light. *(Also see Crocodile)*

Allowance: *(See Raise)*

Allurement: *(See Trespassing)*

Almighty God: *(See Allāh)*

Almond: (Cure; Bitter almond; Sweet almond; Truth) In a dream, almond represent a cure for an illness, impeachment of a governor or loss of one's job. In a dream, almond also represent a deceased person in his shroud or in his grave. Yet, seeing fresh green almond in season in a dream means profits and blessings. Sweet almond in a dream represent lawful money or earnings, depending on the quantity one sees in his dream. Eating sweet almond in a dream means profits, though to be earned with a fight. Plucking almond from a tree in a dream means earning money from a niggardly person with a fight. An almond tree in a dream also represents one who is stingy with people, though generous with his wife and children. Eating sweet almond in a dream also means tasting the sweetness of one's faith. Bitter almond in a dream means truth. Eating almond in a dream means money and a good health. An almond tree also represents a stranger. Seeing oneself showered with almond shells in a dream means receiving a new garment. Dry almond in a dream means sorrow, rage and clamor. Eating a leaf from an almond tree in a dream means receiving money from someone in authority and enjoying the gift.

Alms tax: (Tithe) Paying the dues alms tax in a dream means increase in one's income or prosperity. If a rich man sees himself paying the due tithe on his liquid assets in a dream, it means increase in his wealth, a spiritual growth and receiving the blessing of performing one's obligatory prayers on time. Payment of one's due tithe also represents protection from one's enemies. Paying alms tax in a dream also means performing supererogatory prayers during the night, repayment of debts, absolution, or it could mean paying a fine. Alms tax in a dream also means the death of a dear person in the family, or it could mean losing a limb due to an illness or an accident, giving a charity for the benefit of a departed soul, or payment of one's debts. Thus, paying alms tax in a dream may mean increase in one's wealth, recovering from illness or payment of one's debts, all of which earn levels of exaltation and blessings. To pay charity on one's property of silver in a dream means begetting a son, or it could mean getting married. If it is a poor person, then paying alms tax in a dream represents God's acceptance of one's deeds. If he is a sinner, it means that he will repent of sin and earn lawful money, and if he is a disbeliever, it means that he will become a believer. *(Also see Charity; Endowment; Tithe collector)*

Aloe perfume: Seeing or manufacturing aloe perfume in a dream means religious innovation, dirty money, evil reputation, placing things in the wrong place, or it could mean doing good deeds for profit. *(Also see Civet; 'Ud)*

Aloe: *(bot.* Cactus) Eating from an aloe plant or smelling it in a dream means sorrows, sadness, separation between husband and wife or enduring an unhappy life.

Alopecia: *(See Boldness)*

Altar: *(See Temple)*

Alterations: (Couturier; Garment alteration; Hemming; Tailoring) Seeing a tailor doing alterations to a garment in a dream signifies dispelling one's worries, overcoming one's difficulties, eradicating dishonesty, dispelling conceit or perhaps he could denote music, elation, sexual intercourse or someone who exhausts himself and strives in every way to help others. A tailor doing alterations to a garment in a dream also could represent a preacher or a teacher at whose hands many people will repent of their sins and walk on God's path. A tailor doing alterations and handling trims and the ends of things represents a charitable person who makes someone happy by taking something from him and giving it to others. *(Also see Tailor)*

Alum: (Crystalline compound containing aluminum; Fake jewelry) In a dream, owning or having a piece of alum in any form means money. If one melts it in a dream, it means that he argues for the sake of a cheap matter. If one sees a piece of alum or a yellow piece of metal in a dream, it means that he will be addressed with harsh words or become subject to slander and defamation.

Amazaki: (Japanese fermented rice drink; slightly sweetened and a non-alcoholic drink also found in Egypt) Drinking amazaki in a dream means comfort and prosperity. If an unmarried man sees himself drinking this fermented rice drink in a dream, it may mean that he considers it lawful to live unmarried with divorced women.

Amber: (Musk; Spermaceti) To perfume or anoint oneself with amber in a dream means increase in one's earnings through a rich acquaintance or earning money through a notable person or through a man of knowledge. Seeing a person mixing amber in a dream denotes a praiseworthy person, an architect or a builder. Anointing oneself with amber in a dream signifies hearing praises. Amber in a dream also denotes valuable properties, farms, fruit gardens, or a fellowship of knowledge and wisdom. The fragrance of amber in a dream means a storm, wind, a breeze, or it could represent benefits coming from the direction one recognizes in the dream. If one sees himself burning amber in a dream, it means that he is indulging in religious innovations, corruption, losing face, placing something in the wrong place, dealing with tainted money, bribing a government official, lobbying for a selfish cause and supporting a political campaign. *(Also see Incense; Galia moschata; Perfumery)*

Ambergris: *(See Galia moschata)*

Ambiguity: *(See Fog)*

Ambulate: *(See Circumambulation)*

Ambush: An ambush for an assiduous student in a dream, means acquiring knowledge and it could be interpreted as spoiling the performance of one's religion.

Amenities: *(See Dwellings; House; Luxuries shop)*

Amity: (Affection; Benevolence; Love) In a dream, amity between people means a wise judgement, understanding the consequences of things, realizing one's benefits, unity and balance.

Ammonia: Mixing a solution of ammonia in water in a dream means hoarding tainted money and spending it in evil and unlawful ways.

Amnesty: (Absolution; Acquittal; Pardon) To be granted amnesty in a dream means a safe passage in real life. *(Also see Pardon)*

Amulet: (Incantation; Prayer; Talisman; A prayer worn around the neck or cherished to word off evil and attract good fortune.) When a prayer is read in a dream following the prophetic traditions to help a sick person in the dream, it means protection from sufferings, dispelling distress and dissipation of sadness. If the amulet or the talisman carries a personal spell or wish, then it is nothing but lies, falsehood, affectation and hypocrisy. If the person who recites the incantation in the dream is a craftsperson, it means that he defrauds the people and fakes his product. If he is a man of knowledge, it means that he lies or hides his true knowledge, abstains from giving true advice, or perhaps he offers a poor quality of worship. If the one reciting the incantation in the dream is a judge, it means that he will give a wrong judgement. If one is given to drink some water over which specific prayers were recited in a dream, it means longevity. If one sees himself reciting an incantation, or if he hears incantations recited on his behalf in a dream, it will all be false except for a prayer that recites: 'In the Name of God, the Most Merciful, the Most Compassionate' or contains a Qur'ânic revelation.

Amusement: Diversion or amusement in a dream is a sign of glad tidings, recovery for the sick, prosperity for the poor, honor after humiliation, scientific advancement, higher position, or it could mean travel. *(Also see Games)*

Anchorman: *(See Broadcaster)*

Anemones: *(bot. See Red anemones)*

Angel of death: *(See 'Izrā'īl; Robbery; Osprey)*

Angels: (Celestial beings; Heavenly beings) If one sees the heavenly angels *(arb. Malā'ika)* coming before him to congratulate him in a dream, it means that God Almighty has forgiven that person his sins and endowed him with patience, through which he will attain success in this life and in the hereafter. If one sees the heavenly angels greeting him or giving him something in the dream, it means that his insight will grow, or that he maybe martyrized. If one sees angels descending upon a locality that is raging with a war in a dream, it means that the dwellers of that place will win victory. If the people are suffering from adversities, it means that their calamities will be lifted. Flying with angels or visiting the heavens in their company in a dream may mean that one will die in the station of a martyr and receive God's utmost blessings. If one feels scared of the angels in his dream, it means that a fight, an argument or awesome trials will befall that locality. In general, to see the angels descending from the heavens to the earth in a dream means enfeeblement of those who have doubt, and strength for those who have faith and certitude. If one sees the angels prostrating to him in a dream, it means that all his needs will be satisfied and he will be endowed with good conduct, good behavior and a blessed fame. If one sees them looking like women in the dream, it means that he lies before God Almighty. If a pious person sees an angel telling him in a dream: "Read God's Book." It means that one will attain happiness in his life. If an impious person sees an angel in a dream telling him: "Read your own records." It means that he may go astray. If one sees the angels giving him glad tidings and congratulating him in a dream, it means that he will beget a blessed son who will grow to be righteous and an example to be followed. If one sees a gathering of angels in a town in his dream, it means that a pious man, or an ascetic, or a great scholar will die in that locality. If one sees himself looking at the angels in the skies in a dream, it means that he may suffer the loss of a son or his wealth. Seeing the celestial angels *(arb. Rūhāniyyeen)* in a dream means gaining honor, dignity, blessings in one's life, profits and a good fame, developing spiritual inner insight, or becoming a business manager. Near the end of one's life, one who sees such a dream also will suffer from people's slander and backbiting. He will also lose his good reputation to people's envy and evil qualities and he will live in tight financial conditions. If one becomes an angel in a dream, it means tat he will receive honor, power, overcome his adversities, dispel his distress and win his freedom, or it could mean that he will rise in station. If one sees the angels greeting him and shaking hands with him in a dream, it means that God Almighty will endow him with wisdom, clarity and insight. Angels in a dream

10

also represent one's closest witnesses, guardians, police officers or the emissaries of a ruler. Wrestling with an angel in a dream means loss of status. Wrestling with an angel in a dream also means suffering from distress, trouble, humiliation and falling in rank. Seeing angels entering one's house in a dream means that a thief will burglarize such a house. If angels disarm someone in a dream, it means that he will lose his wealth and strength, or that he may divorce his wife. If angels offer the person a tray of fruits in the dream, it means that he will depart from this world as a martyr. If angels curse someone in a dream, it means that he has little care for his religion. If one sees a gathering of heavenly angels together with the angels of hell-fire in a dream, it means enmity and divisiveness. If a sick person sees himself struggling with an angel in a dream, it is a sign of his death. If one sees an angel taking the form of a child in a dream, it represents one's future. If he sees an angel as a youth, the youth then represents the present time and whatever events that will take place during it. If the angel appears in the form of an old man in the dream, he represents the past. If one sees the angels praying and asking for God's forgiveness on his behalf in a dream, it means that one's spiritual and religious life will grow for the better, and that he will become wealthy. If one sees angels descending upon a cemetery in a dream, it signifies the presence of blessed and righteous souls in that place. If one sees angels walking in the markets in a dream, it means that the merchants are trifling with prices and playing with the measures. If the angels who are in charge of punishing the sinner in hell walk before a dying person and he does not fear them in the dream, it means peace and tranquility. If one sees the angels teaching a dying person how to recite his final rites in a dream, it means glad tidings and attainment of what his heart desires, a guarantee of his safety, happiness, joy and of having a blessed and a good heart. If he sees them angry with him or beating him or subduing and taming him in a dream, it means that he may revert to sin, earn the displeasure of his parents, disdain from complying with God's commands, or he could even come to deny the necessity of God's religion. Such angels in a dream also represent the emissaries of a governor or his deputies. If a dying person is told in the dream that no angels have come to see him, then it is a testimony of his good character and piety, or it could mean payment of one's debts or recovering from an illness. Angels in a dream also could represent scholars, gnostics or translators who understand people's languages and speak in many tongues. As for Munkar and Nakïr, the angels who come to one's grave upon his burial to question him, seeing them in a dream means prosperity for a poor person, and finding work for a jobless person. *(Also see Castration)*

Anger: (Fury; Indignation; Rage) Leaving one's home angry in a dream means entering a prison. If one gets angry for material gains in a dream, it means that he has disdain and contempt toward God's religion. However, should he get angry in his dream to defend God's rights, then it means gaining strength and power. Becoming angry for someone else's sake in a dream signifies a corrupt contract, a tainted agreement, a marriage consent with a hidden intent of a divorce to follow, fighting for unlawful earnings, or it could mean accumulating money from usury. In a dream, usury and anger mean falsehood in wakefulness. *(See Foam; Frothing at the mouth; Sneezing; Suppressing one's anger)*

Animal bones: *(See Bones)*

Animals: *(See Sound of animals)*

Animosity: *(See Enemy; Enmity)*

Anklets: In a dream, anklets represent one's son. Wearing golden anklets in a dream means a severe illness, or that one may commit a major sin. However, if a woman sees herself wearing anklets in a dream, it means that she is safe and protected. If she is unwed, it means that she will marry a gracious and a generous person with whom she will live happily and content. If a man sees himself wearing a pair of golden anklets in a dream, it means adversities, distress or imprisonment. It is said that anklets in a dream represent shackles in wakefulness, except for a wedding ring or a necklace. What a woman sees as beauty or imperfect in her anklets in a dream will reflect upon her husband. If she is unmarried, the anklet will then reflect on her adornment or makeup. In a dream, anklets also represent honor, wealth, dignity and beauty.

Annihilation: *(See Evanescence)*

Announcement: *(See Fame)*

Announcer: In a dream, an announcer represents a man of dignity who manages people's business, including the high and the low, who brings unity between people and his services are most beneficial to everyone. *(Also see Broadcaster; Piper)*

Annoyance: *(See Asthma)*

Anoint: Anointing oneself with perfumed oil or with liniments in a dream means acclamation of praiseworthy deeds. Applying a liniment as a treatment to construction laborers, mail carrier or the like people in a dream means renewal of their strength, and increase in their income. *(Also see Amber)*

Antelope: *(See Deer; Gazelle; Oryx)*

Anthill: An anthill in a dream represents a village. *(Also see Village)*

Antichrist: *(arb.* Dajjāl; Imposter) In a dream, the Antichrist represents a contemptuous, deceitful and a tyrant ruler. He does not fulfill his promises and he has a following of wicked people. His appearance in a dream also indicates the supremacy of one's enemy over him or over his land. This will involve massacres, evil, deception, trials and bloodshed. If a traveller sees the Antichrist in his dream, it means that a band of robbers may attack him. His appearance in a dream also denotes the conquest of a land which is saturated with evil. If one becomes the Antichrist or accompanies him in a dream, it means that he will suffer from black magic, sorcery, falsehood, decrepitude or it could denote that a global disease will appear on earth and cause mass physical defects, destruction and death. The landmarks that the Antichrist passes by in a dream represent adversities, trials, injustice, ruins, inundations with floods, destruction of crops and drought. *(Also see One-eyed)*

Antidote: (Cure; Herbs; Ivy; Medicine) In a dream, if one sees himself taking an antidote against a snakebite, it means appeasing of one's fears, or having peace in one's life. *(Also see Ivy)*

Antilla: *(See Constellations)*

Antimony: (Silver-white powdered mixture. *See Kohl)*

Ants: (Army) In a dream, ants represent weak and covetous people, an army, a family, or longevity. Seeing a colony of ants entering a city in a dream means that an army will occupy that city. A colony of ants in a dream also represents a heavy populated area. Seeing ants over one's bed in a dream means having many children. If ants leave one's house in a dream, it means that someone in the family will leave that house. If there is a sick person in a house and one sees ants flying in a dream, it means the death of such a person. Ants leaving their colony in a dream means dying away of the population in that area, or that such a town may become a ghost town. Seeing ants leaving their nest in a dream also means adversities or distress. Though in this case, they represent the small and hard working people. If a sick person sees ants walking over his body in a dream, it means his death. Flying ants in a dream also mean hardships during a journey. Seeing winged ants in a dream means a war and destruction of a large army. Ants in a dream also may signify prosperity. They also represent the person seeing the dream or members of his family or relatives. Understanding

12

the language of ants in a dream means sovereignty, leadership and prosperity. If one sees ants entering his house and carrying food in a dream, it means prosperity in that family. If one sees ants leaving his house and carrying food with them in a dream, it means poverty. Seeing ants coming out of one's nostrils, ears, mouth or any part of his body and rejoicing at that sight in the dream means martyrdom. However, if one seems unhappy to see that in his dream, it means dying in sin. Flying ants in a dream also represent a robbery. Killing ants in a dream means cruelty against weak people.

Anus: (Backside) In a dream, it represents the husband or money. If one sees his anus blocked in a dream, it means that he will die shortly. The anus in a dream also represents a lowly person, a cheap musician, a drummer, someone who holds secrets, a kin or a relative with whom it is not lawful to be married. Seeing the backside of a young person in a dream means separation between the two. If it is an older person in the dream, it means a fight between them. Causing cuts in one's anus means severing family ties. Seeing the anus of one's mother in a dream means nullification of one's devotion, cancellation of one's due interests or the stagnation of one's business. Seeing someone's anus in a dream means meeting with a frowning person. If one's anus bleeds in the dream, it means money. If one sees himself excreting in a dream, it means spending money with a clear intent of benefiting from it. Seeing the anus of an unknown woman in a dream means material losses, or it could mean difficulties in acquiring the necessary money for one's livelihood. Seeing worms coming from one's anus means departing from one's children or loss of one's children. If a cloth comes out of one's anus in a dream, it means severing relations with strangers who took advantage of one's children and abused their rights. Having sexual intercourse with a woman through the anus in a dream means asking for something in the wrong way. If one sees a peacock coming out of his anus in a dream, it means that he will beget a beautiful daughter. If he sees a fish coming out of his anus in a dream, it means that his wife will beget an ugly looking daughter. *(Also see Pederasty; Sexual intercourse; Sodomy)*

Anxiety: *(See Distress; Gambling; Uptight; Worries)*

Anxious: *(See Uptight; Worries)*

Aorta: (Artery) In a dream, the aorta represents man's heart, souls and innermost self because it carries the blood from his heart to all the main arteries. In a dream, the aorta also represents one's happiness, health, sorrows and pain. *(Also see Jugular vein)*

Apartment: (Dwellings; Hardship; House; Journey) Buying or receiving an apartment as a gift in a dream means undertaking a distant and a difficult trip.

Aperture: *(See Attic window; Window)*

Apiculturist: *(See Beekeeper)*

Apiarist: *(See Beekeeper)*

Apparel: (Adornment; Attire; Costume; Garb; Veil) In a dream, one's apparel vary in meaning depending on their contents, colors or type, etcetera. Wearing one's garb in the winter in a dream is better than wearing it in the summer. Wrapping oneself with a cloth in a dream means becoming poor. An attire in a dream represents a man and a leader. An attire for a scholar, or a merchant, or a leader in a dream represents his trade through which one earns his livelihood and which protects him from adversities. If one's apparel is dirty in the dream, then it reflects his life and appearance. If one wears a beautiful garb in the summertime in a dream, it means that he is ostentatious, arrogant and vainglorious. It also could mean that he is under great pressure and suffering from a painful distress, for the heat of a summer in a dream signifies distress. If a woman sees herself wearing a man's apparel in a dream, it means piety and success in her material and spiritual life. If a man sees himself wearing a woman's apparel in a dream, it means that he will be afflicted with fear, depression, subjugation, humiliation, trials, then all of it will be lifted away from him. *(Also see Veil; Yashmak)*

Appeal: *(See Soliciting advice)*

Appearance: (Emergence; Manifestation; Visibility) In a dream, if one sees something that is kept away from him as a secret, it means experiencing comfort after suffering from trials, receiving compensation after suffering from injustice, conceiving a child after having given up hope or the like examples. A revealed secret on time in a dream means fulfillment of a promise, satisfying one's needs, repayment of one's debts, arriving of a long awaited person from a journey, release of a prisoner from his jail, and for a woman, it could mean becoming pregnant. If something emerges at the wrong time in a dream, it means debts.

Appetite: (Sated; Saturation; To eat one's fill) In a dream, to eat one's fill means fidgety or restlessness. If one sees himself satiated with food and could not eat any more in a dream, it means changing of his condition, losing rank, losing business, or his death. This interpretation is applicable unless one finds in his dream extra space to fill with food, then the dream means that his lot in this world will equal the size of that remaining space. Eating to one's fill in a dream also represents working for one's livelihood or recovering extra money. Some interpreters convey that hunger in a dream is better than satiation, while to drink extra water in a dream is better than thirst.

Apple tree: An apple tree in a dream represents a good man who serves his community and cares about it. *(Also see Tree)*

Apple: In a dream, apples represent beautiful children. An apple in a dream also denotes one's determination and good will. To a king, apples in a dream represent his kingdom. To a merchant, they represent his merchandise, and to a farmer they represent his crop. Eating apples in a dream means determination. Eating a sweet apple in a dream means lawful earnings, while eating a sour tasting apple means acquiring unlawful earnings. Sour apples in a dream mean divisiveness and hurt, while its tree represents torpor. If a king throws an apple at one of his subjects in a dream, it means good news or attainment of one's goals. Planting an apple tree in a dream means adopting or caring for an orphan. An apple tree in a dream represents a good man and a believer who serves and benefits his community. Eating an apple in a dream also means earning something people cannot see. Plucking an apple in a dream means money earned through a respectable person. Counting apples in a dream means counting money. Smelling an apple inside a mosque in a dream means getting married. If a woman sees herself smelling an apple during a reception in a dream, it means misconduct and the permeation of sin. If she sees herself eating an apple in a known place in a dream, it means that she will give birth to a handsome son. Biting on an apple in a dream means satisfying one's sexual desires or being sexually obsessed. *(Also see Magician)*

Apricot: (Fruit) In season, seeing an apricot in a dream means money. Seeing apricot out of season in a dream means illness. A fruitbearing apricot tree in a dream represents a rich man. However, it is said that an apricot tree in a dream also represents someone who suffers from a serious illness, and is of little or no use to others. On the other hand, it is said that an apricot tree in a dream represents someone with a cheerful face, who is courageous in defends himself, but who is stingy with his own family. When the apricot is still green and unripened in the dream, it represents little money. When it ripens and becomes yellow in a dream, it denotes greater profits. Eating a ripened apricot in a dream means being generous and charitable, or it could mean recovering from an

14

illness. Breaking a branch from an apricot tree in a dream means a dispute with one's family or with a friend. In general, breaking a branch from a tree in a dream means claiming someone's money or denying him his money, or it could mean failing to perform one's prayers, neglecting one's obligatory fast or misusing and damaging someone else's property. Attending an apricot farm in a dream means trustworthiness and dutifulness. It is also said that an apricot tree in a dream represents a hypocrite, because yellow in a dream means illness, and hypocrisy is an illness. An apricot tree in a dream also represents a wealthy woman. Plucking apricots from a tree in a dream also could mean marrying such a woman. Harvesting any fruitbearing tree in season in a dream means pleasures and work, except for the mulberry tree, for here it means toiling, hardship or waste of time. Plucking apricots from an apple tree in a dream means impressing unjust rules upon others. In general, a yellow colored fruit in a dream signifies illness. A sower tasting fruit in a dream signifies distress and sorrow. Apricot in a dream also signifies fear, bringing things under control, things returning to normal or it could even mean pleasant gains. *(Also see Fruit)*

April: *(See Thunder)*

Apron: *(See Towel)*

Apus: *(See Constellations)*

'Aqīq canyons: (A place near the holy city of Mecca; First segment of God's Messenger's Nocturnal journey.) Seeing oneself performing a ritual ablution, then performing prayers in the Aqīq canyons in a dream signifies confirmation of the testimony of God's Oneness *(see Carnelian-red)*, washing oneself from worldly attachments, witnessing Divine blessings and spiritual favors, rising in station, hearing good words, or it could mean imprisonment, rain, a gift, an offering, or a charity.

'Aqīq: *(arb. See Carnelian-red)*

'Aqīqah rites: (Hair of a newborn; Immolation offered on the seventh day for a newborn; Islāmic tradition of shaving the hair of a newborn on the seventh day after his birth; Sacrament; Weighing the shaved hair of a newborn and distributing an equal measure in gold or silver in charity for his benefit.) The offering of an 'Aqīqah ceremony in a dream represents glad tidings, the arrival of a long awaited person, recovering from an illness, or the release of a prisoner. Participating in the sacrament of the 'Aqīqah rites in a dream also could represent a growing faith and certitude, and emulating the blessed traditions of God's Prophet, upon whom be peace. If the sacrifice presented in one's dream on that day is a permissible one and if one fulfills all the necessary rituals in his dream, then it denotes his praiseworthy character and the success of his endeavors. If one offers a non-permissible sacrifice in his dream and presents it to people to eat from, then his dream represents a recalcitrant child, or a rebellious son. *(Also see 'Aqīq canyons; Carnelian-red)*

Aqṣā mosque: *(See Masjid)*

Aquarium: *(See Fish)*

Aquarius: *(astr. See Moon)*

Aquarius: *(See Constellations)*

Aquila: *(See Constellations)*

Ara: *(See Constellations)*

Arab: (People) Seeing an Arab dressed in his customary garb in a dream means overcoming one's difficulties or easing of one's adversities.

Arabic months: (Lunar months: 1- Muharram; 2- Safar; 3- Rabī-'ul Awal; 4- Rabī'u Thānï; 5- Jamādul Awwal; 6- Jamādu Thānï; 7- Rajab; 8- Sha'bān; 9- Ramadān; 10- Shawwāl; 11- Zul-Qi'dah; 12- Zul-Hijjah) Seeing a dream during the month of **Muḥarram** means that the dream is most true as it is seen. Thus, having a dream during the month of Muḥarram could be even called a vision and it never fails. Such a dream means success, relief from difficulties, release from a prison, or recovering from an illness. If the person had retreated from his town, he will return to it. This interpretation is based on the story of God's prophet Jonah, upon whom be peace, after he emerged from the belly of the whale. Perhaps the person in the dream may face a great spiritual challenge in his life, or it could mean the death of a great man of knowledge or the emergence of such a gnostic or wise man in that city. If the person seeing the dream is a sinner, it means that he will repent of his sins, for God Almighty has accepted the repentance of Adam, upon whom be peace, during that month. If the person in the dream is one who hopes for a station of honor, he will attain it, because God Almighty has raised the prophet Enoch (Idrīs) upon whom be peace, to a high station during that month. If a traveller sees a dream during that month, it means that he will safely return home from a long journey, because it is the month in which the prophet Noah upon whom be peace, was saved with his people, and it is the month in which the arc settle on top of Mount Judiyyi. If the seer desires a son, then he will beget a righteous son, because it is the month in which God's prophets Abraham and Jesus, upon both of them be peace, were born. If the person seeing the dream is suffering from tight financial circumstances and if he desired a way out, it means that he will see the light or escape from the danger of his enemy, because this is the month in which God's prophet Abraham was saved from the fire of Nimrod, or perhaps, if he had followed a path of innovation and falsehood, he will turn back to God Almighty and repent of his sin, because it is also the month in which God Almighty forgave the prophet David, upon whom be peace. If the person in the dream is impeached from his leadership position or stripped from his status, he will return to his office and regain honor, because it is also the month in which God Almighty returned the prophet Solomon to his kingdom. If one is bedridden, it means that he will recover from his illness, because it is the month in which the prophet Job (uwbp) recovered from his illness, or perhaps it could mean that one will be sent as an emissary with a mission, or as an ambassador, because it is during this month that God Almighty spoke to His prophet Moses upon whom be peace. As for the second lunar month, known in Arabic as **Ṣafar**, having a dream during it could be interpreted as follows: If one is pessimistic about what he saw, then it could mean the opposite. If he is sick, it means recovering from his illness. If one is needy, it means that his needs will be satisfied. If one is suffering from stress and worries, it means that they can cause him no harm. If one sees his dream during the third lunar month, known in Arabic as **Rabī-ʻul Awwal**, and if he is a merchant, it means that his business will grow, prosper and that his money will be blessed or perhaps he may conceive a child during that month. If he is under stress and worries, they will be dispelled. If he is persecuted or treated unjustly, he will end in a triumph, or it could mean that he will hear good news, or he may be appointed as a governor, or he may admonish people to do good and discard evil, for it is the month in which God's Prophet Muhammad, upon whom be peace, was born to this world. If one's dream takes place during the fourth lunar month, known in Arabic as **Rabīʻu Thānī**, and if it suggests glad tidings, then one may have to wait and exercise patience, but if it suggests evil, then such happening will come fast. During this month, seeing a dream also means victory over one's enemy, or it could mean conceiving a blessed son who will grow to become a gnostic, or a hero, for it is during this month that the Imām ʻAli, may God bless his countenance and be forever pleased with him was born. As for the fifth lunar month, known in Arabic as **Jamādul Awwal**, seeing a dream during this month means that one should slow down or scrutinize his buying and selling, or it could mean that he may lose his daughter or wife, for it is in this month that the daughter of God's Messenger, upon whom be peace, Faṭima died. May God be forever pleased with her. If the dream happens during the sixth lunar month, known in Arabic as **Jamādu Thānī,** and if the dream carries a good meaning, it will come, but slow and one should not contradict it. If one sees this dream during the seventh lunar month, known in Arabic as **Rajab,** it means that he will gain honor and status, for it is the month of the prophet's Ascension (*Mi'rāj*) and his night journey to the seventh heaven. A dream during the eighth lunar month, known in Arabic as **Sha'bān,** represents honor and ranks, for during this month, every good deed will be honored. As for the ninth lunar month, known in Arabic as **Ramadān,** in it, all difficulties will be suspended, evil will be shun and stinginess will be dispelled. During this month all what is good will manifest and bad dream will dissipate to become null and void. During this month, the dreams of a believer may be differently interpreted than the dream of a disbeliever. If one sees the month of Ramadān in his dream, his dream means blessings, profits, commanding good and forbidding evil. If the person is seeking knowledge, then knowledge will be given to him, for it is during this great month that the Holy Qur'ān was revealed. If the person is inflicted with epilepsy, he will recover from it, for the devils and all evil spirits are shackled and are rendered powerless during this month. As for the tenth lunar month, known in Arabic as **Shawwāl,** if one's dream suggests a war or a conflict, it means that he will come first in it, and that he will triumph. If one sees the month of Shawwāl in his dream, it means that he will come out of difficulties and finds happiness and devotion, for it is the month during which that God's House, known as the Ka'aba was built. As for the eleventh lunar month, known in Arabic as **Zul-Qi'dah,** if one's dream suggests a trip, then the person should refrain from taking that trip or perhaps he should delay it for the better. He also should guard himself where he lives. If the dream denote stress or worries, then he should avoid whatever may cause them. However, if one's dream takes place during the twelfth lunar month, known in Arabic as **Zul-Hijjah** indicates a journey then one may take it, or if it denotes a good business, one should seek it, for it is a most blessed month and it is the month of festivities and sacrifices. If one sees this month in his dream or sees himself offering sacrifices in it, or if he sees himself praying the festival of Sacrifice prayers in it, his dream means paying one's debts or fulfilling one's vows, repentance from sin, guidance or perhaps his dream may indicate the death of great people of knowledge, the impeachment of governors, the changing of governments, or it could mean a sudden war.

Arabic: *(See Language)*

'Arafāt: (Mecca; Mount 'Arafa; Mount of mercy; Plain of 'Arafāt; Reunion of beloveds) If one sees himself standing in prayers in the Plain of 'Arafāt during the pilgrimage season on the 9th day of the Arabic month of Zul-Hijjah, it means the return of a long awaited traveller to his home, a happy reunion, a family reunion, reconciliation between friends or peace between two individuals. Seeing Mount 'Arafa or the Plain of 'Arafāt in a dream also could represent the pilgrimage season, or performing a pilgrimage, visiting Mecca on 'Umrah (*See 'Umrah*), or it could mean the Friday congregational prayers, the sixth day of the week, a marketplace, or engaging in a profitable business. Seeing oneself standing at 'Arafāt in a dream also means rising in station, changing conditions, reversal of one's state from good to bad or from bad to good, or perhaps it could mean death of a beloved such as one's wife, or it could mean relocating to a blessed place or finding a sanctuary. Seeing oneself at 'Arafāt in a dream also could mean losing a battle to one's adversary, though the results or consequences of such a battle will bring him honor and exalted station, or it could mean winning the battle against one's enemy. If a sinner sees himself praying and repenting at Mount 'Arafa or near the Mount of Mercy in the Plain of 'Arafāt in a dream, it means that his repentance will be accepted, or that a secret will be exposed, or it could mean that a reunion of beloveds will take place shortly after one's dream. If one sees himself standing in 'Arafa during the night time in a dream, it means that his goals will be attained and that he will satisfy his quest. If one sees himself standing in 'Arafa after the sunrise, it means that his question will find no answer. *(Also see Circumambulation; Cradle of Ishmail; Ka'aba; Muzdalifa; Pelting stones; Responding; Station of Abraham; 'Umrah)*

Aramaea: (The prophet Aramaea, upon whom be peace.) Seeing him in a dream means that a fire will consume one's city, house or rural district.

Arc: (Noah's arc. *See Coffin; Ship*)

Archangel Gabriel: (Upon him be peace.) Seeing him in a dream and feeling happy for his meeting brings glad tidings. If the archangel Gabriel in one's dream speaks to him, advises him, or admonishes him in the dream, it means receiving a great honor, strength, victory in one's life and glad tidings. If the person is oppressed, it means that he will triumph at the end. If he is sick, it means that he will recover from his illness. If he is in a state of depression or fear, it means that he will overcome it and he shall sail into success. If he had not yet performed his pilgrimage to Mecca, it means that he will fulfill it. Seeing the archangel Gabriel in a dream also means glad tidings of martyrdom, even if the person lives a long life. If one receives some food or fruits from him in the dream, it means that he is one of the dwellers of paradise. However, if a disbeliever sees him in a dream, it means that he will face tribulations and punishments in his life. If he considers the archangel Gabriel and the archangel Michael as equals in a dream, it means that he agrees with the people of Jewish faith. To his own detriment, such a person might steer into an activity that is opposite to God's instructions and consequently earns himself God's wrath. If the archangel Gabriel (uwbp) greets someone in his dream, it means that such a person will become a great man of knowledge and he will be recognized and distinguished in his own field. The archangel Gabriel in a dream also represents the messenger of the king, the confidant, the carrier of glad tidings or the person who announces the birth of a son. Seeing him in a dream also indicates increase in one's devotion, learning and acquiring in-depth knowledge of mystical realities. Seeing him (uwbp) in a dream also signifies the smooth rising of the soul after death for someone who is dying. The archangel Gabriel in a dream also represents a movement, struggle, triumph and understanding the meanings of religious knowledge or learning the secrets of astrology. If one sees the archangel Gabriel distressed in a dream, it means that a calamity will befall the person seeing the dream. If one becomes Gabriel in a dream, it means that he will become generous, magnanimous and blessed in his actions and performances.

Arched bridge: (Bridge; Stone bridge; Viaduct) An arched bridge or a viaduct in a dream represents suspicious matters or mundane questions or worldly vs. ungodly concerns. An arched bridge or a viaduct in a dream also could represents one's wife, or it could mean dispelling of one's worries or trouble. Driving over an arched bridge or through a viaduct in a dream means riding a vehicle. An arched bridge or a stone bridge in a dream also signifies richness, luxury, longevity, a sickness, renouncing one's allegiance, or it could mean breaking a promise. An arched bridge in a dream also could represent a middle man, a wise man, or a ruler, except if the bridge leads to a loathsome place, or to a dead end. Crossing an arched bridge that leads to the palace of a ruler in a dream means receiving money, or it could mean getting married to a noble person. An unknown bridge in a dream represents the world and particularly if it connects the city with the cemetery. It also could represent a ship, or the Bridge of the Day of Judgement, for it is the last hurdle before reaching paradise. If one crosses an arched bridge in his dream, then it means that he will cross the abode of this world into the abode of the hereafter and particularly if one meets departed souls from the world or enters unknown places or sees uncommon structures, or if a bird carries him by air, or if a beast swallows him, or if he falls into a ditch or flies into the heavens in his dream, all of which also means recovering from an illness or undertaking a long journey, or it could mean returning home from a long journey. If on the other side of the bridge one ends in a fertile farm, luscious fields, or meets with an old woman in his dream, it means money, benefits and prosperity. If the other side of the bridge leads to a mosque in the dream, it means that one will achieve his goal, fulfill his intention or perform a pilgrimage to God's House in Mecca. If one becomes a bridge in a dream, it means that he will acquire extensive powers or becomes an inspiration to others, or that people will come to need his authority and help. Crossing a wooden bridge in a dream means meeting with a group of hypocrites. *(Also see Bridge)*

Archer: Seeing an archer in a dream signifies longevity, bravery and victory over one's enemy. In a dream, an archer also represents someone who is reared by a stepfather. *(Also see Arrows)*

Architect: (Engineer) An architect in a dream represents both urban developments and urban destruction. He represents joining what is fragmented and breaking up what is whole. Seeing an architect in a dream also signifies trials, evil, calamities and disunity. If one becomes an architect in a dream, it means longevity because of the architect's aspirations and he will fulfill his intentions, reach a ranking station and a commanding position in his life. If one becomes an architect in a dream, it also means that he may become a judge, or a marriage officiant, or it could represent a poet. Seeing an architect in a dream also signifies richness after poverty and health after sickness. *(Also see Artist; Carpet weaver; Graphic artist; Orthopedist)*

Arctunus: *(See Constellations)*

Argillaceous: *(See Clay)*

Argillite: *(See Clay)*

Argo: *(See Constellations)*

Aries: *(astr. See Moon)*

Arietica: *(See Constellations)*

Arm[1]: (Forearm; Limb; Member; Wing) One's two arms in a dream represent his two brothers, his two close friends, two sons or partners. If one sees a person with short arms in a dream, it means that he is courageous, generous and wondrous. One's arm in a dream represent his brother and supporter or a spiritual example he follows. If one's arm is broken in a dream, it means the death of one's brother or closest friend, or it could mean an accident or a calamity. One's arm in a dream also signifies protection from sin or it cold represent his wife, his mother, his teacher, wealth, craft, source of income, a supporting son or a close brother one can depend on at times of difficulties. If one sees that his arm is missing something in a dream, it could mean that he has little brain, though he is filled with pride and haughtiness. *(Also see Air; Body*[1]*; Forearm)*

Arm[2]: *(See Weapon)*

Armistice: *(See Truce)*

Armlet: Wearing a silver armlet in a dream means giving one's daughter in marriage to one's nephew. Wearing an armlet made from beads in a dream means suffering pressure and distress caused by one's brother or sister. Any jewelry that is worn by a woman in a dream represent her husband. *(Also see Bracelet)*

Armor maker: In a dream, he represents a person who advises people to live in peace and harmony. *(Also see Armor)*

Armor: (Coat of mail; Shield) An armor in a dream means protection and defence. It also means fasting. If weapons are mixed with the armor or shield in one's dream, it means that one's enemies cannot reach him or cause harm to him. If one sees his armor laying down at his reach in his shop or place of business while dealing with his customers in a dream, it means that such a merchant is untruthful and he uses claims of honesty as a shield. *(Also see Coat of mail)*

Armpit: *(See Odor)*

Army general: (Commander; Military) In a dream, an army general or a commander represents someone famous who is self assured and dauntless. If one sees himself as an army general in a dream, and should he qualify for such a position, it means prosperity, honor and blessings. If one does not qualify for such a position, then it may mean his death. If a poor person sees himself as an army general in a dream, it means disturbances and that he will raise his voice. As for a prisoner, it means his release from jail.

Army's flag: (Banner; Flag) In a dream, the flag of an army represents a pious man, a scholar, a religious doctor, a spiritual leader, an ascetic, or a rich and a generous person who is an example to others. A red flag in a dream means war, while a yellow flag means a plague. A green flag in a dream means a blessed journey, while a white flag means rain. A black flag in a dream means drought and doubt, or it could mean a rainstorm. Sighting the flag of an army in a dream means finding one's way or finding guidance. For a woman, seeing a flag in her dream means getting married. *(Also see Banner; Colors; Flag)*

Army: *(See Ants)*

Arrange: *(See Organize)*

Arrival: (Home coming) The arrival home of a traveller in a dream signifies relief after sustaining depression and distress, or it could mean recovering from an illness, or regaining a stronghold. If one finds himself depressed and annoyed with the arrival of the traveller in the dream, then his dream may signify having to ask for something from someone, or needing others, or confronting the unavoidable.

Arrogance: To show arrogance in a dream based on one's success in life and richness means the nearing end of one's life in this world. Arrogance in a dream also means prosperity and a high rank in this world, though evil maybe the end of it. *(Also see Advice; Elephant)*

Arrowhead: In a dream, an arrowhead represents talk, benefits or profits from business travels. An arrowhead which is made of lead in a dream means receiving a letter that explains one's weakness. If the arrowhead is made from copper in the dream, it means material pleasure. If it is made from gold in the dream, it represents a letter one is forced to send. *(Also see Arrows)*

Arrows: In a dream, arrows mean messages, a messenger, writings, victory over one's enemy. If a woman sees her husband's arrows in their quiver in a dream, it means that her husband has turned away from her. Arrows in a dream also are an indicator or a guide. Seeing an arrow outside its quiver, means failure to perform one's duty or inability to deliver one's message. Shooting arrows in a dream means writing letters. If one shoots an arrow but fails to hit his target in the dream, it means that he will send a messenger to do something and his messenger will fail to deliver. If one sees a woman shooting him with an arrow in a dream, it means that she is showing kindness toward him and consequently he may fall in love with her, or he may marry her. If one shoots an arrow and hits his target in a dream, it means that he will reach his goal, or if he wishes to have a child, it means that he will bear a son. An arrow in a dream also represents a messenger, profits, a son, longevity or new clothing. If the arrows are made from reeds in one's dream, they mean falsehood and prattle. If they have arrowheads in the dream, then they represent a talkative person who if he hits his target, it means that he does what he says. If the arrowhead breaks in the dream, it means that he speaks only to protect himself from others' arrows. If the arrow is made from gold in the dream, it means that he is sending a message to a woman because of another woman. The arrowhead in a dream represents strength, power or disturbance. The arrows themselves in a dream also mean the fear of an emissary for his life. Throwing arrows in a dream means backbiting others and slandering them. *(Also see Archer; Shooting arrows)*

Artery: *(See Aorta; Jugular vein; Veins)*

Artificial lake: *(See Water level)*

Artist: (Architect; Painter) Seeing him in a dream means consenting to reason. He also could represent an opinionated person, an expert, a friend, a real estate broker, a scientist, a commander, or an architect. *(Also see Architect; Painter)*

Arts: All types of arts in a dream signify recovering from illness, attaining peace, a picnic, colors, clothing, waters and beautiful people.

Ascending in the skies: (Climbing; Rising) To see oneself ascending in the skies in a dream means falling in rank, or it could mean oppressing oneself. If one sees himself ascending in the skies until he reaches the stars, merges with them and if he becomes a star in the dream, it means that he will receive titles and powers. If one sees himself ascending a mountain it means depression, stress and travels. However, rising in a dream means elevation of status, and descending means a backslide. If one sees himself walking up a steep road in a dream, it means rising in status, but involving toiling and hardships. If one sees himself climbing a mountain, then the mountain in a dream is interpreted as one's goal. Thus, one's dream may mean attaining one's goal as far as he reaches in his climb. In dream interpretation, any ascent of a mountain, a trail, a hill, an elevation or even climbing a roof means attaining one's goal or satisfying one's needs. To see oneself climbing flat on his back in a dream then means uncalled for, or unnecessary hardship. *(Also see Air; Ascent; Climbing a mountain; Flying)*

Ascent: (Incline; Mountain road; Steep incline) If one sees himself climbing a steep incline in a dream, it means toiling to succeed in both his material and spiritual life, or it could mean trying to gather the benefits of both worlds, though with great strain on him . An ascent in a dream also could signify a difficult woman or a stern man who can only be handled with kindness, gentleness and love. An ascent in a dream also represents one's associate, or a business partner who cannot be trusted with one's money or life. An ascent in a dream also represents the road to salvation or the dangers one may have to cross and the deeds that can save him from hell-fire. An ascent in a dream also could represent adversities, difficulties and dangers. Ascending a steep incline in a dream means danger and descending a steep hill means reaching safety. An ascent in a dream also could represent a bridge, an underpass, a wife, a woman, or a scorpion. Walking through a steep incline in a dream also means rising in station because of one's knowledge, politics, good conduct, fulfillment of one's duties, his caring for others or wisdom. Falling through a steep hill in a dream means falling in rank, losing one's prestige, losing one's money, denying the truth, objecting to one's religion or walking into darkness. Climbing in a dream always means attainment of one's goals. Climbing flat on one's back in a dream has negative connotations. Descending from a steep hill, or from a ship, or coming down form a castle or a mountain in a dream also mean that one's goal will not materialize. *(Also see Ascending the skies; Climbing a mountain)*

Ascertain: *(See Sneezing)*

Ascetic Detachment: (Abstinence; Asceticism) To see oneself living an ascetic life in a dream means that one is earnestly seeking to show kindness and love for people and to earn their love. *(Also see Perfume salesman)*

Asceticism: *(See Ascetic detachment)*

Ashes: (Coal; Fire; Fumes; Oven) In a dream, ashes represent unlawful money or they could mean burns. Ashes in a dream are also interpreted to mean money one will receive from someone in authority or directly from the government. Seeing ashes then mean difficulties or toiling for no benefit in the service of a person in authority. Ashes in a dream also mean vain talk, or a knowledge one cannot benefit from. If one sees himself carrying a container filled with ashes in a dream, it means that he is engaged in falsehood, backbiting or in acquiring useless knowledge. If one sees himself blowing air into cold ashes in a dream, it means that he will engage in futile undertaking. Ashes in a dream also denote sadness, sore-eyes or heedlessness. Ashes in a dream also mean quelling the fire of war, suppressing upheaval, or attaining peace. Ashes which are collected from baking in a dream represent charity, or curiosity. *(Also see Coal)*

'Ashürä: (10th day of Muharram; Anniversary of the martyrdom of Husain at Kerbela.) If a descendent of the blessed family of God's Messenger, upon whom be peace, sees himself on the day of 'Ashürä in a dream, it means that he may have to face an adversity. If anyone else sees that in a dream, it means the opposite.

Askance: *(See Eyes)*

Asphyxia: *(See Strangulation; Suffocation)*

'Asr: *(arb. See Five times prayers)*

Ass: *(See Donkey)*

Assassin: *(See Thief)*

Assassination: (Bang; Thunder) Hearing the sound of thunder without seeing lightening in a dream means an assassination or a murder. *(Also see Thunder)*

Assault: (Destroy; Extirpate; An assault which is directed by an enemy or which is aimed at an enemy.) An assault in a dream means a disaster, a calamity, a flood, a fire, locusts or major changes in the world. To devastate someone by looking at him with despise in a dream means that the assailant will suffer from the jealous eye of his victim in wakefulness.

Assert: *(See Naked)*

Assets: If a rich person sees himself in a dream standing within the confines of the Cradle of Ismaïl in the Sacred Mosque in Mecca, it means that he will be debarred from his assets, and his rights to use them will be temporarily suspended.

Assistant judge: *(See Assistant magistrate)*

Assistant magistrate: (Assistant judge) Seeing the assistant magistrate in a dream means either following the traditions of the righteous ones, or the avenues of innovation.

Assistant teacher: (Students' leader; Monitor; Pupil) In a dream, an assistant teacher represents an innovator or someone who advises others the right way, though remains attached to his own innovative ideas.

Assistant: (Beauty; Eye-brow. *Also see Assistant teacher*)

Associate: (Beauty; Eye-brow. *Also see Partnership*)

Asthma: Experiencing breathing difficulties in a dream means boredom, annoyance, weariness or disgust.

Astral: *(See Star)*

Astray: *(See Disbelief; Irreligious; Wandering)*

Astringent: *(See Accountant)*

Astrolabe: (Astrology) In a dream, it represents the assistant or the servant of a governor or ruler. An astrolabe in a dream also represents someone connected with the leadership of a land. Accompanying such a person in a dream then means benefits equal to what one sees in his dream. Seeing an astrolabe in a dream also may connote someone with uncertainty, or an ever changing person who lacks determination, loyalty, or honor. *(Also see Astrologer)*

Astrologer: (Foreseer; Fortuneteller; Predictor; Soothsayer) Seeing an astrologer in a dream means associating oneself with spiritual masters and witnessing some of their miraculous signs. An astrologer in a dream also may mean knowledge of people's secrets, curiosity, inquisitiveness, meddling in people's affairs, divulging people's secrets, soothsaying, fortune-telling, backbiting, predicting the future, hearsay, gossip, distress or trouble. If the one who is seeing the dream suffers from any of the above ills, seeing an astrologer in a dream also means dispelling such misfortunes. Seeing an astrologer in a dream also signifies marriage, divorce, the death of a sick person, travels, delivering a baby, hearing good or bad news. Seeing an astrologer in a dream also may denote knowledge, following the true path and acting upon it, for a God fearing astrologer mostly arbitrates by the prophetic rules. *(Also see Astrolabe; Divination; Fortuneteller)*

Astrology: *(Astrolabe. See Astrologer; Fortuneteller; Moon)*

Astronomer: In a dream, an astronomer represents someone who trades with women, a pimp, or a salesman.

Astronomy: *(See Celestial sphere; New year's day)*

Astute: *(See Perspicacity)*

Atheism: (Ingratitude. *See Darkness)*

Atonement: (Expiation; Penance; Requital) Atonement, distribution of gifts or charities as penance for one's sins in a dream means payment of one's debts, delivering a trust to its rightful owner, paying a fine or reciprocating an invitation. *(Also see Tithe collector)*

Attack: (Charge against; Comeback) Charging against one's enemy in a dream means victory in wakefulness, or it could mean disturbance, anxiety, concern, going through a mental conflict or having doubt, and it may mean regret, repentance and correcting the course of one's actions and thoughts.

Attainment: *(See Fulfillment)*

Attar: *(See Rose)*

Attic window: (Aperture; Peephole; Window) If one's attic window towers over a large and a beautiful property in the dream, it means owning or acquiring a new property, earning respect, honor and fulfilling one's aspirations. If the view from one's attic window is depressing in the dream, then it means relief from difficulties, or if one is sick, then it means recovering from his illness, or if he is unmarried, then it means that he will get married. If a woman looks at an attic window in a dream, it means that she will get married. Discovering an attic window in a house that does not have one in a dream means the spread of one's authority, or the success of one's business. *(Also see Window)*

Attire: *(See Apparel; Veil)*

Attracting attention: *(See Digging up the past)*

Attrition: *(See Worries)*

Auctioneer: In a dream, an auctioneer represents an escort, a station master or a broadcaster. *(Also see Broker)*

Auditorium: *(See Hall)*

Auditory meatus: *(See Earwax)*

Auger: *(See Drill)*

August: *(See Earthquake; Thunder)*

Auriga: *(See Constellations)*

Austerity: *(See Harshness)*

Author: *(See Book; Writer)*

Automobile: *(See Car)*

Avarice: Stinginess, avariciousness, love to hoard things and to never share with others in a dream means finding a cure for one's disease. Avarice in a dream also means hypocrisy associated with acts that lead to hell-fire. Avarice in a dream also means blame and criticism. If one sees himself repugnantly spending his money in a dream, it means his death. Avariciousness in a dream also means falling into sin.

Avenue: *(See Lane; Road)*

Awakening: (Rising-up) To see oneself waking up from sleep in a dream means steadfastness, serious repentance, success in one's business and returning home from a journey.

Ax: (Hatchet) An ax in a dream means receiving help, increase in one's earnings, recovering from a migraine headache, recovering from an illness, or it could mean begetting a son. Holding an ax in one's hand in a dream means becoming a guardian, an executor of a will, a trustee, becoming steadfast in one's religion, or it could mean overcoming one's enemy. It is said that an ax in a dream means harm, disruption and scattering of one's livelihood. An ax in a dream also represents a servant, a housekeeper, strength, victory or perhaps an insolent person or it could denote one's job. *(Also see Adz)*

Azān: (Muezin. *Also see Call to prayers*)

B

Baby crow: *(Fledgling; Nestling)* A fledgling crow in a dream represents poverty, need, separation from one's parents and segregation from one's relatives or clan. If one is experiencing such adverse conditions in wakefulness, then seeing a fledgling crow in a dream means satisfaction of one's needs and reunion with his family. When the egg hatches and the baby crow comes out of it, the parents shy away from their fledgling and remain distant from the nest. Then God Almighty will provide the nestling crow with various types of flies to eat from. Once the baby crow's feathers grow, the parents will return to their nest and care for their baby until it commences to fly.

Back pain: *(See Back; Body¹; Pain)*

Back: (Behind; Posterior; Rear side) In a dream, the back of a human being represents what people hold for him of praises or blame, acceptance or rejection, honor or humiliation, or it could represents one's debts. Seeing the back of a human being in a dream also means following his tracks or practices. If a positive look manifests therein, such as a sweet fragrance or the emergence of a radiant light, or if it turns into iron in the dream, it signifies one's gratitude regarding his own condition. In a dream, the rear side of the human being represents his outward appearance or what renders the human being acceptable, or it could represent his garment, an ostentatious person, a show of grandeur, pride about one's social class, a show of being wealthy, the surroundings of one's house, the outskirts of a town, the outer display of one's religion or his school of thought. A broken back in a dream means fear, distress and sorrow. If one sees his rear side dark in color, black or red in a dream, it means that he may suffer from physical abuse and beating during a fight. Seeing one's own back in a dream also could mean buying new clothing, or it could mean feeling strong because of one's knowledge, his son, power, political connections, wealth or property. Seeing one's back in a dream also could mean to repudiate one's wife. If one's back is seared or cauterized in a dream, it denotes stinginess, or it could mean that he fails to comply with God's rights upon him. If one sees his back bent in a dream, it means a misfortune. If one sees the back of his friend in a dream, it means that his friend will turn his back to him at times when he needs him most. If one sees the back of his enemy in a dream, it means that he will be guarded against his threats. If one sees the back of an old woman in a dream, it means that the world is turning its back to him. If she is in her middle age in the dream, it means that he is seeking something hard to obtain. If she is a young woman in the dream, it means that he is expecting something and must be patient to acquire it. One's back also represents old age. Back pain in a dream means poverty, sickness, debility, imprisonment of one's boss or the death of a brother. One's back in a dream also represents one's dependence on a strong person. If one sees himself carrying a heavy load on his back in a dream, it means debts, or a vicious neighbor. A broken back in a dream means losing one's strength and power, or it could mean one's death. If a sick person sees his back broken in a dream, it means that the person who is taking care of him may die shortly, or it could mean that he will suffer from poverty. Carrying burdens over one's back in a dream means sins. Carrying a coffin or a load of merchandise over one's back in a dream means carrying forgotten debts that will surface at awkward times. Carrying wood over one's back in a dream means backbiting, slandering people and reporting lies. Carrying a heavy load over one's back in a dream also means having many children with little money to sustain them. Seeing a hunchbacked person in a dream means prosperity, longevity or having a large family. (Also see Backbone; Backside; Body')

Backbiting: (Belittlement; Defamation; Harm) Backbiting someone in a dream means driving one's blessings away and nullifying one's good deeds. Backbiting a poor person in a dream means becoming poor. Backbiting someone concerning a scandal in a dream means that one will become subject to defamation and suffers from a scandal. Like that, whatever subject the backbiting is addressing, its harm will come back to the doer. Belittling someone in a dream means that one will suffer the same in wakefulness.

Backbone: (Helper; Loins; Offspring; Spinal column) In a dream, one's backbone represents man's helper or his right hand man. If one has a strong backbone in a dream, it represents his sedate manners, calm and serious composure. Whether one's backbone is weak or strong in the dream, it could also represent his son. If one finds his backbone strong in the dream, it means that he will develop wisdom or beget a son who will grow strong and become a just person. Perhaps one's backbone could be interpreted to mean crucifixion, or it could mean marriage to a virgin. If one sees a tree growing from his backbone in a dream, it means an illness. If a sick person sees his backbone turned into iron in a dream, it means recovering from his illness. (Also see Back)

Backgammon: (Tricktrack) Playing backgammon in a dream means having an imposing character, being highly skilled and efficient, scheming, mental keenness, playing a ruse or eliciting admiration. Playing backgammon in a dream also denotes someone who is highly qualified or it may demonstrate the type of character one assumes in his daily life, or it could mean arguing with others, mockery, deception, gambling, mixing with evil people for business, or it could mean pleasure. It also means indulging in sin, fear of exposure or maneuvering a business scheme. If one sees the game set but no one is playing it in the dream, it means lack of work, dismissal from one's job, walking the wrong tracks. Playing backgammon in a dream also signifies a fight, an argument or a dispute between business partners, each of them seeking his personal interests. (Also see Chess; Games)

Backside: (Backside; Buttocks; Rump) In a dream, the backside represents the wife's property and money, or it could mean one's husband. Dragging oneself over one's buttocks in a dream means becoming poor and needy. Hair growing over one's backside in a dream means money or richness. Otherwise, if one sees no hair on his backside in the dream, then it means insolvency or bankruptcy. Shaving off the hair over one's backside in a dream means fulfilling a promise, repayment of one's debts or giving back a trust to its rightful owner. (Also see Back)

Bactrian camel: (See Milk)

Bad look: To devastate someone by looking at him with despise in a dream means that the assailant will suffer from the jealous eye of his victim in wakefulness.

Bag: (Sack) A travelling bag or a sack in a dream represents a coffer, a keeper of one's secrets, or it could mean a treasure. Seeing a sack or a bag in a dream also means a trip, or a young son one takes pride to carry over his shoulders. (Also see Pouch; Sack, Suitcase; Trunk)

Bagpipe: (Musical instrument) In a dream, a bagpipe represents music, travel, or it could mean profits.

Bairam: *(turk. See Manumission; Festival of Breaking the Fast; Feast of Immolation)*

Baked bricks: *(See Bricks)*

Baker: (Compassionate leader; Honest livelihood; Just ruler; Love; Son) A baker in the dream represents peacefulness and a lucrative life. One who bakes bread on top of limestone in a dream represents a happy and a good person who entices people to work and earn honest income from their own sweat. If he receives money for his bread in the dream, it means that he has made preaching to others his main source of income. Seeing oneself as a baker in a dream means becoming wealthy and prosperous. If one sees himself buying bread from a baker and if the baker does not look at how much money is tendered in the dream, it means that the baker is a noble man, and he is capable of doing good deeds without anticipating a reward. A baker in a dream also represents someone who brings benefits to others, for they all need him. Receiving a loaf of bread from a baker in a dream means earning an honest income. If one who is not a baker sees himself baking bread and selling it to people in a dream, it means that he solicit customers for a prostitute. The profession of a baker in a dream also involves talks, disputes and energy. *(Also see Bread; Sweets)*

Baklava: *(See Pastry)*

Balance: (Scale) A balance and a scale in a dream have similar interpretations. Both represent faith, justice and righteousness in words and actions. In a dream, a balance also may represent a wife, or it could mean payment of one's debts. A steelyard in a dream represents an architect or a builder. A miller's scale in a dream represents a man who considers himself worthy of respect, while his actions, earnings and moves are contemptible. A precision scale in a dream represents a warning against heedlessness and concern for proper accounting for one's actions. The justice scale represents a judge. If it stands balanced in one's dream, then it means that the judge of that locality is a just and a learned person. In a dream, the scales of a balance represents the judge's ears. The money put on a scale for measuring represents the lawsuits, and the weights represent the judgment. If one sees himself standing before God Almighty on Judgment Day and if his good deeds weigh heavier than his sins in the dream, it means that he will reckon himself, reflect about his bad actions and correct the course of his life. Consequently, his reward in the hereafter will be greater. Seeing the Balance of the Day of Judgement in a dream means vulnerability of people's secrets, exposing one's actions in public, recognition of the ultimate truth, joy, happiness, victory and justice. If one's deeds are praiseworthy, then he will be a winner. If one's deeds are blameworthy, then he will be a loser. In general, a balance in a dream represents a guide, an example to follow, a scholar one seeks to learn at his hand, a ruler, a criterion and the Qur'ān. It also may represent one's tongue and correctness, truthfulness, lies, incredulity or trustworthiness. *(Also see Measure²; Measurer; Scale)*

Balancer: *(See Stabilizer)*

Balcony: Sitting in a balcony during the summertime in a dream means comfort, dispelling aggravations, recovering from an illness, or exposing one's secrets. A balcony in a dream also could mean honor, or if seen with the city walls, then it represents the governor of the town, or it could mean the battlement. The parapet on top of the walls represents his armies, his entourage or his ammunition and the stored provisions of the city. If the walls are interpreted to be wealth, then the balconies and the battlement represent its guards and servants. Balconies in a dream also represent the front rows of one's enemy. *(Also see Walls of the city)*

Baldheadedness: *(Also see Baldness)*

Balding: *(See Baldness)*

Baldness: (Alopecia; Baldheadedness; Balding; Hairless) In a dream, baldness means loss of job or falling in rank. If one sees himself bald-headed in a dream, it means that his superior will lose money in business to the authorities or by a fire that will eat up his property. It also can be interpreted as becoming needy, or if he is indebted, it means that he will pay off his loan. If one sees his hair thinned until it reaches baldness in a dream, it means that he may lose his wealth or perhaps it could mean losing face with the people. If one sees himself sitting with a bald-headed woman in a dream, it means that he is engaging in a project that is tainted with suspicion, or it could mean that he will become a victim to temptation. Seeing a baldheaded woman in a dream also signifies drought and scarcity. In a dream, baldheadedness also means money that is received from one's superior at work and requires tremendous efforts to earn. Such earnings will costs more than what they are worth.

Ball of thread: (Hank of yarn; Spool; Thread) For pensioners, seeing a ball of thread in a dream signifies increase in one's benefits or receiving extra income. A ball of thread in a dream also represents an astute worker, an employee, an intelligent and a hard working young man, or it could mean longevity. *(Also see Spool; Thread)*

Ball: (Baseball; Basketball; Cricket ball; Football; Glob; Golf ball; Handball; Ping-Pong ball; Pushball; Snowball; Tennis ball; Volleyball) A ball in a dream signifies a dispute, an argument, a fight to control the world and its resources. Some will desire it and others will reject it. A ball in a dream also could signify travels or moving between places. Usually, a ball in a dream represents a man. If it is made from leather, then it represents a leader, a boss, or a scholar. Playing ball in a dream means a fight. *(Also see Games)*

Ballista: *(See Missile launcher)*

Balloon: Inflating a balloon in a dream means begetting a son. *(Also see Ball)*

Banal: *(See Cat)*

Banana: (Money) In a dream, a banana means money, savings, a fetus, a man in his grave, a prisoner in his jail, a closed book, news from the past, or it could mean inner knowledge. In a dream, a banana also signifies clothing, love, tenderness, a generous man, a monotheist, or it could represent a person of good conduct. If a banana tree grows inside one's house in a dream, it means that he may beget a son. Eating a banana in a dream means profits from a business partnership. For a business man, banana in a dream represents profits and for a renunciate it means devotion and ascetic detachment. If a sick person eats a banana in a dream, it means aggravation of his illness or his death.

Band: (Bond; Tie) To tie or band one's hair in a dream mean amassing huge sums of money and to disband one's hair means to squander one's wealth. *(Also see Bond¹)*

Bangle: *(See Bracelet)*

Banishment: *(See Expulsion)*

Banjo: (String instruments; Guitar; Lute; Mandolin) In a dream, a banjo represents people's common business, double-dealing, scrupulousness, adultery, playing chess, sorcery, a medium, evocation of spirits, calling on jinn spirits, being possessed by jinns or similar effects. A banjo in a dream also represents the leader of such a band of people and it denotes distress and sorrows. Playing a banjo with strings made from animals' intestines in a dream also represents a wise man admonishing or reprimanding people. Playing a banjo in a dream also means sorrow. To tap on a banjo in a dream denotes nostalgia. Listening to the music of a banjo in a dream means turning one's attention to lies. *(Also see Musician; String Instruments)*

Bank draft: *(See Bill of exchange)*

Banknote: (Dollar; Money) A banknote in a dream represents a pure intention, a beautiful son, a treasure, an agreement, a consent, deputyship, devotion, straight path, swearing in, testimony or wisdom. Losing a banknote in a dream means losing one's son or missing one's prayers. If one sees himself moving piles of banknotes to his house in a dream, it means that money will be delivered to his hand. Though banknotes are blessings and they are what people need, nevertheless, they are also Satan's arrows. If one sees himself handling a large quantity of banknotes in a dream, they mean trusts he receives for saving or as a business. If one sees himself holding a banknote in his hand in a dream, it means that he has entrusted something to a friend who will deliver it back to him on demand. A counterfeit banknote means illegal money or income from unknown source. A banknote carrying the denomination five, represents the five time daily prayers in Islām. If one loses one in the dream, it means that he neglects his required prayers. In some interpretations, banknotes represent a book. They also represent benefits to a poor person. Perhaps banknotes in a dream could represent the punishment of a hypocrite, or a person who respects no commitment toward his friends, or perhaps they could represent a beloved, mutual support, helping others, or good news. Common denominations such as one hundred represent working for the government. If one sees himself receiving a coin of money, or a banknote (*e.g.* One dollar), it means that he is suffering from oppression. If one sees himself giving someone a banknote of the denomination one, then if he finds it shred'ded into pieces in the dream, it represents a severe enmity, a grievance, or a fight. If he finds it thrown to the floor in the dream, it signifies heavy fighting between two people. *(Also see Money)*

Bankruptcy: Bankruptcy in a dream signifies both material and spiritual losses. If a sick person sees himself bankrupt in a dream, it means that he is approaching his death, or it could mean loss of his property or changing one's trade into a job of lesser importance. *(Also see Fraudulent bankruptcy; Slave)*

Banner: (Beacon; Distinguished; Excellence; Flag) A banner in a dream represents public knowledge, fame, presidency, laurel of victory, a man of knowledge, an Imām, or an ascetic who is vigilant and courageous, or a rich and a generous man, or a strong and a victorious hero whose example is loved and followed. If the banner is red, then one will reap happiness from the person it represents, or he may engage in a war against him. As for a woman, a banner in a dream represents her husband. If one sees banners flying during a parade, they mean rain. If the banners are black in the dream, they mean that one will meet a man of knowledge. If the banners are white, then they represent a jealous person who will never be married. If they are yellow, they represent an epidemic disease. If they are green, they mean a journey by land. A banner or a flag in a dream also means that one will be wrapped in ambiguity in relation to a particular matter and he will not find a way out. If one sees a flag and a brigade in a dream, it means that he will be able to find his way through the difficulties and overcome his sadness and adversities. His heart will have peace and his path will open before him. If the flag represents a country in the dream, it means that one may visit such a country. If a woman sees herself burying three banners in a dream, it means that she will marry three men who belong to the noble class of the society. Such three people will die one after the other. As for a pregnant woman, a flag in a dream means a son and for an unwed woman, it means a husband. A large banner in a dream means rain and winds. The carrier of the flag is usually interpreted to represent a judge. If one sees himself carrying a banner in his dream, it means that he is seeking the seat of a judge. *(Also see Army's flag: Flag)*

Banquet: (Ceremonial dinner) Attending a banquet or giving a banquet in a dream means dispelling distress and overcoming adversities. A banquet in a dream also means celebrating a new appointment or receiving honorary guests. However, a banquet in a dream also denotes distress, sorrow or grief. *(Also see Colors; Food fare; Food)*

Bar: (Taproom; Tavern)

Barber: (Hairdresser) A barber in a dream represents a person who benefits the meek and the poor, though he harms the rich. A barber, or a sheep shearing person also represents a corrupt police officer, or a street gang leader who taxes local businesses. If shearing the animal is necessary, then the dream will mean comfort and benefits for both the man and the animal. *(Also see Hairdresser)*

Barefoot: In a dream, it means toiling in one's life and exhaustion. This is thus interpreted if one does not actually see himself going through the motion of taking off his shoes and walking barefooted. Otherwise, in that case, it means that he will receive an appointment to a high ranking position. Walking barefooted in a dream is also interpreted as unloading one's burdens and relief from pressure, divorce or death in one's family. If one sees himself traveling barefooted, it represents a debt that he could not repay. If one sees himself walking with one foot bare and the second fitted in the dream, it means breaking up a business partnership. *(Also see Walking)*

Barkeeper: *(See Bartender)*

Barking of a jackal: *(See Sound of animals)*

Barking: *(See Dog)*

Barley: Barley corns in their fields in a dream represent spiritual awakening and a conscious endeavor to do good. Seeing barley in a dream also denotes easy and sweet income. If one barters wheat for barley in a dream, it means that he will forget the Qur'ān and pursue poetry. Buying or carrying a measure of barley in a dream means that one may conceive a son who will grow to be pious and a man of knowledge, though his life will be short. It is also said that barley in a dream represents money spent toward one's health and fitness. Buying barley from its distributor in a dream means receiving a great wealth or an inheritance, though one must pay its due alms tax and charities. If one sees himself planting barley in a dream, it means that he will engage in doing a good deed that will please God Almighty. Walking through barley fields in his dream means that one will be blessed with the opportunity to participate in a holy war. Farming barley fields in a dream represents people's deeds. If one plants barley in a dream, it means that he will prosper from his business or from governing, or that he will receive an endowment from someone in authority. Seeing barley in a dream also implies feelings or perceiving something good that is going to take place. *(Also see Crop)*

Barman: *(See Bartender)*

Barn: In a dream, a barn represents profits, provisions, fodder, food, savings, coffer, bag, one's house, one's shop or one's farm. *(Also see Carriage house; Stableman)*

Bartender: (Barkeeper; Barman; Beverages; Sherbet salesman; Syrup vendor) A bartender in a dream represents a syrup vendor or a sherbet salesman. All of them organize their bar with colorful bottles and different sizes of drinking glasses. Their drinks vary between the sweet and sour, cold and hot or dry. A bartender in a dream also could represent a craftsman in his shop, a business-man in his office, a confidant, or someone who exposes others' secrets and troubles for a price, or one who keeps a secret for a price.

Base: (Column base; Plinth) A column base or a plinth in a dream represents scholars, their circles, or their study room. A column base in a dream also could represent unmarried women, one's wife, knowledge, a trade, or a craft, or religious precepts. Building or owning a column base in a dream also could signify marriage, children, guidance, knowledge, or a chronic illness. The column base of a mosque in a dream represents pious people and the column base of a house represent chaste women.

Baseball: *(See Ball)*

Bashfulness: (Constrains; Modesty; Reserve) In a dream, bashfulness means an excuse. If a bearded person sees himself bashful in a dream, it means that he might suffer imprisonment. Bashfulness in a dream also could represent a myrtle, or any aromatic plant. Bashfulness in a dream also purport a clear excuse, increase in one's income, the arrival of a traveller, or receiving a letter from him. If being bashful beautifies the person in the dream, then it means glad tidings. Otherwise, if one feels ashamed from it, then it means distress and adversities. *(Also see Blushing)*

Basin: (Washbowl) In a dream, a basin represents a servant, a mistress, or a wife who brings her husband a life of cleanliness and purity, or it could mean marriage. A basin in a dream also denotes earnings, a respectful job, or it could mean prosperity. Seeing one's reflection in a basin filled with water, like looking at a mirror in a dream represents one's condition or state. *(Also see Mirror)*

Basket weaver: *(See Caner; Caning)*

Basket: In a dream, a basket represents a woman who guards people's secrets.

Basketball: *(See Ball)*

Basmalah: *(arb.)* Calling the Name of God Almighty in a dream means blessed tidings. Basmalah in a dream also represents attainment, knowledge, guidance and wealth. Reciting the formula: 'Bismillāhi Raḥmāni Raḥeem' (*In the Name of Allāh, the Merciful, the Compassionate*) in a dream also means living to see one's children and grand children. It also means recovering a lost article. Basmala in a dream also means placing the intention to get married, tidings of a good progeny, and receiving guidance after heedlessness. If one writes down such a call: 'In the Name of God' with a beautiful handwriting in his dream, it means that he will receive wealth and recognition in his field of knowledge. If a deceased person writes it in one's dream, it means that such a person dwells encompassed with God's mercy. If the one who wrote it in the dream is alive and if he erases it or if a bird steals it from him in the dream, it means the nearing of his death and exhaustion of his sustenance in this world. If one recites it during his prayers in a dream when it is not his custom to do so, it means borrowing an unnecessary amount of money or giving preference to leaning toward one's mother rather than his father or the opposite.

Bat: *(zool.)* By God's leave, a bat was one of the many signs of God's prophet Jesus son of Marry, upon both of them be peace. In a dream, a bat may represent a monk. It also means glad tidings for a pregnant woman. Seeing a bat in a dream is not considered as a good omen for a traveller. If a bat flies into a house in a dream, it means the demolition of that house or the separation of that family. A bat in one's dream also represents a witch, or an unjust person who may have suffered from deprivation in his childhood. A bat in a dream also signifies blindness, heedlessness, a child of adultery, or a bastard son. In a dream, a bat also means hiding from people because of one's evildoing, such as theft or eavesdropping. Seeing a bat in a dream also means the end of enjoying blessings and not acknowledging their true provider. A bat in one's dream also means having to change one's living standards.

Bath: Taking a bath in a dream means payment of one's debts, dispelling one's fear or stress, release from prison, attending a pilgrimage or recovering from an illness. If in his dream, one shaves his hair when taking a bath, it means loss of his wealth or cheating on his wife. Shaving the pubic region in a dream represents benefits and increases in pubic hair in a dream means increase in money. Bath in itself denotes many things. *(Also see Turkish bath)*

Bathhouse: (Sauna; Steam room; Sweat room; Rest room) Washing one's dirt with hot water in a dream brings benefits. If one builds a bathhouse in his dream, it means committing a sin or searching for a woman to partake in it, then suffering its consequence. If the bathhouse is heated and the water is lukewarm in the dream, it represents his family's compassion toward him, trying to help him out of his breach. If the bathhouse is cold and if its water is cold in the dream, it means that his family has ostracized or banished him. If one witness the hot water pipes breaking, whereby he could not control the flow of water in the dream, it means that someone will betray him with his wife, though he will keep trying to control the situation, but to no avail. A water leak from the boiler that flows through the floors of the bathing quarters in a dream means incurring the anger of one's wife. Entering a bathhouse in a dream means suffering from a fever. Drinking hot water directly from the boiler in a dream means sickness, stress, depression and a scare from evil spirits. If one sees himself drinking cold refreshing water from the regular water tab in a dream, it means comfort and joy. Taking a bath with cold water in a dream means recovering from an illness. A bathhouse in a dream also represents hell-fire, and the attendant represents its keepers. A bathhouse in a dream also represents the judge's court, and its attendant represents the judge himself. A bathhouse in a dream also represents a prison and its guard, the ocean and the ship pilot, the evil bawdy houses and their dwellers, a woman and a pimp, or a cadet posing as her husband. If one goes to a public bath, then after completing his wash wears a white garment, and takes a carriage back home in his dream, it means that he will shortly die and the elements of his dream represent his washing, shrouding, coffin and funeral. The element of a bathhouse in a dream also represent a library, knowledge, guard's post, house of worship, a mosque, a church, idol worship, a prison, or a marketplace. It also represents repentance, guidance, richness, healing, an ocean or marriage. If one sees himself taking a bath with his clothe on in a dream, it means that he will fall prey to an attractive prostitute who will deceive him and lead him to commit his religious life to waste. *(Also see Bath; Bathroom; Hell-fire; Turkish bath)*

Bathroom: (Lavatory; Toilet) In a dream, a bathroom represents the nest of impurities or the seat of sufferings. If one enters it in his dream it means that he will be struck with distress caused by women. For heat and pruriency may develop in one's privacy inside the bathroom. If a person in distress comes out of the bathroom in his dream, it means relief from his depression. *(Also see Bathhouse; Toilet)*

Battering ram: *(See Missile launcher)*

Battlefield: In a dream, a battlefield represents actions, accomplishments, activities, fulfillments, success, victory, warning to children or training them to become professional soldiers.

Battlement: *(See Citadel)*

Bay-color: *(See Maroon)*

Bay: A bay in a dream represents a man and a woman who are entrusted to guard and protect other's personal secrets, belongings or money.

Beacon: *(See Banner; Torch)*

Beads salesman: (Beads; Chaplet; Necklace; Pearls; Prayer beads; Women) In a dream, he is a man who embellishes women's apparels or sells them. When a beads salesman is seen in a dream, he represents a man who interferes with or deals in women's businesses. *(Also see Prayer beads)*

Beads: *(See Counting beads; Prayer beads)*

Beak: (Bill) In a dream, a beak represents wealth, prosperity, honor and power.

Beam: In a dream, the beams of a ship represent religious people, faith, holding fast to one's faith, or it could mean complications. *(See Light; Ship)*

Beans: *(See Lupine)*

Bear trainer: (Circus; Hunter) A bear trainer is the one who hunts it, trains it, teaches it to dance and to obey his orders. A bear trainer in a dream represents a teacher who teaches good conduct to ignorant people, or a coach of a woman singer. He also represents people who illicit unlawful or tainted money from drugs or prostitution.

Bear: (Mammal) In a dream, a bear represents someone with a physical infirmity, who is evil, deceitful, perfidious and betraying. A bear in a dream also represents a dull and a heavy looking woman who takes pleasure in partying, uninhibitedness and enjoying all types of entertainment. Seeing a bear in a dream also means capture or imprisonment, or he could represent a stupid enemy, a thief, an effeminate person, or a trickster. If one sees himself riding over a bear in a dream, should he qualify, it means that he will manage a loathsome business. Otherwise, it means that he will be struck with fear and distress, then he will escape from his trials. A bear in a dream also means travels, returning from a journey or he could represent a prostitute. If one has access to such a woman, he must beware not to commit adultery.

Beard: For a man, a beard in a dream signifies wealth, honor and dignity. If it is moderately long or well trimmed in the dream, it means earning respect, rising in rank, prosperity, beauty and sovereignty. If only the sides of one's beard are long and not the middle section in the dream, it means that one will work to save money for someone else. If one's beard is too long and lacks proper trimming in a dream, it means indebtedness, distress and suffering from depression. If it becomes long to the extent of reaching the floor in the dream, it means death. If one's beard grows long and thick in a dream, it means longevity or increase in one's wealth. If it reaches his belly in the dream, it means that he does not obey God's commands. If it grows longer than one's grip in the dream, it means that one lives from the interest he earns from usury. If the hair of one's beard is black in the dream, it means prosperity and satisfaction in one's life. If its color is greenish-black in the dream, it means extended wealth, power and rulership, unless if one is a tyrant, for the color of Pharaoh's beard was greenish-black. If the color of one's beard yields to yellow in the dream, it means poverty and illness. If its color is blondish in the dream, it means a scare. If one grabs his own beard in the dream and if its hair falls into his hand, and if he keeps holding to the hair, it means incurring financial losses then recovering them, unless one discards the hair in the dream. Pulling someone's from his beard in the dream means inheriting him. If one sees a young boy who has not reached the age of puberty having a beard in a dream, it means the child's death. If the child's beard is just starting to grow in the dream, it means that he will grow to lead and command people. If one's beard is shallow and if it makes him look fatuous in a dream, it means payment of one's debts or easing of his trouble or dispelling of his distress. If one's beard looks childish or completely immature in the dream, it means losing people's respect. If the color of one's beard is gold in the dream, it means that he will lose some respect and perhaps half of his wealth. Seeing one-half of one's beard shaved in a dream means poverty. If an unknown young person shaves one's beard in a dream, it means loss of dignity and injury caused by one's enemy or competitor or someone who carries the same name. If an old man shaves his beard in a dream, it means that he will lose his good reputation at the hand of a profiteer and an overpowering enemy. If one's beard is cut off in a dream, it means financial losses valued at how far it is trimmed. Clipping what is longer than man's grip of one's beard in a dream means paying the due alms tax. Cutting off someone's beard in a dream means swindling his inheritance. A white beard in a dream means honor, dignity and good fame. If one's beard turns gray, leaving few black hairs in the dream, it means earning respect. If all its hair becomes gray in the dream, it means poverty and loss of integrity. Seeing one's wife having a beard in a dream means increase in one's wealth or growth of the son's business, or sickness of one's wife, or it could mean that she will no longer be able to conceive children, though if she had a son, it means that he will control the entire family. If a woman sees herself having a beard in a dream, it means losing her husband and if she is a widow, it means that she will marry a hard-working man who is compatible with her. If a pregnant woman sees that in a dream, it means that she will beget a son, and if she has a quarrel with someone, it means that she will win the battle and stand for herself with dignity and courage. Plucking one's facial hair or beard in a dream means wasting money. If one's beard and head is shaved in a dream, it means recovering from an illness, satisfying one's debts or dispelling sorrow and distress. Having an extraordinarily long beard that one can spin and weave as a cloth, then sells it in his dream means that he will forge a testimony. Clipping one's beard in a dream also means losing money. One's beard in a dream also represents his job, business, clothing, gains and losses. Cutting off the hair of one's beard with one's own teeth in a dream means sufferings, distress and trouble. Swearing by the honor of one's beard in a dream may denote either one's truthfulness or lies, his stinginess or generosity. One's beard in a dream also could represent his wife. If a farmer finds the hair of his beard black in a dream, it means that he should start harvesting his crop. A white beard could denote illness or frailty. If one's beard in wakefulness is gray and he sees its color black in a dream, it means strength, determination, firmness, certainty, having great energy and exuberance. If one's beard in his dream seems longer than the usual, it means being a spendthrift, wasting money, engaging in gambling and sporting games, or suffering from depression, or being troubled by circumstances. If a subversive and a sinful person sees himself having a beard in a dream, it means that he will repent of his sins. If a misguided person sees himself having a beard in his dream, it means that he will receive guidance. If a woman grows a beard in her dream, it means that she is trying to be a man, or it could mean insolence or engaging in wrongdoing. If a child sees himself having a beard in a dream, it means longevity. Loving a beard and kissing it in a dream means lacking determination or will, regardless if it is his own beard or if it is someone else's beard. If a straw or anything sticks to one's beard in a dream, it means hearing bad words. Shaving half of one's beard in a dream means losing one's source of income or loss of one's dignity. Holding the beard of one's uncle in a dream means unjustly inheriting him. If a woman sees herself having a beard like a man in a dream, it means that she will never beget children, unless if she has a reddish beard as the natural color of her hair. However, for a man, to have a reddish beard in a dream means trials and temptation and particularly if some gray hair is also mixed with it. *(Also see Face; Scissors; Shaving; Twisting a rope)*

Beast: (Monster; Wild beast) In a dream, a beast represents mountain people or people living in the wilderness, or an innovator who breaks from the community and introduces his own religious ideas. *(Also see Hunter)*

Beating: (Blow; Hit; Lash; Whip) To hit someone with a staff in a dream means bringing back to life something that died away or investigating the cause of a death or clarifying something. To beat someone with a wooden stick in a dream means failing to fulfill a promise, or it could mean lying to someone. If someone in authority hits his employee in a dream, it means that he will give him a raise. If he hits him on his back in the dream, it means that he will pay his debt. If he hits him on his backside in the dream, it means that he will give him a daughter in marriage. If one hits someone head with a stick in a dream, it means that he desires his position or it may denote his jealousy. If one hits someone between the eyes in a dream, it means that he wants him to get lost. Beating someone in a dream also means to rebuke, revile or insult him, or it could mean to admonish him. Beating someone over his scull in a dream means that the victim in the dream will attain excellence of expression and reach his goals. If he hits him over the earlobe and if it bleeds in the dream, it means that the assailant will rape and deflower the daughter of the victim. Like that, interpreting the subject of beating must be associated with the meaning of the limb affected in the dream. (*See Body¹*). Beatings in a dream also connotes supplications. If one sees himself beating a donkey in a dream, it means that he does not earn his daily bread unless he regularly prays for it. To beat someone in a dream also means cursing him. If he hits him over the head in the dream, it means speaking ill of him and that one cannot retrieve his words or apologize for them. Beating a family member in a dream means that one's wife is committing adultery. Beating someone in a dream also means benefiting him, or it could mean business losses. If one is beaten in a dream, it means profits and benefits, unless if the one beating him is an angel, or a deceased person, or a member of his family. Beating someone with a leather belt or with a cane in a dream means bad consequences in wakefulness. Hitting the floor in a dream means taking a trip. If one receives one hundred lashes on his back in a dream, it means that he has committed adultery, or it could mean that he has the intention to do so. If one receives forty lashes in a dream, it means that he indulges in drinking alcohol or uses intoxicants. If he is lashed eighty times in a dream, it means that he slanders married women. If he is whipped by a deceased person in the dream, it means that he is pursuing wrong ideas and should reverse his course, for a deceased person dwells in the kingdom of truth and follows only what pleased God Almighty. However, if one sees himself in a dream beating a deceased person, this could be interpreted to denote the strength of his faith, certitude, prayers and charitable nature. It also could mean benefits from a business trip or pursuing a lost interest. Beating in a dream when it causes no pain, bleeding or scratches means receiving a new garment, paying debts, or hearing sarcastic comments. Beating an animal in a dream means either training him, or it could mean ignorance and being unfair toward such an animal.

Beautician: *(See Perfume salesman)*

Beautify: (Eye-brow)

Beauty mark: In a dream, a beauty mark means honor and dignity for a woman, and it means wealth for a man. *(Also see Birthmark)*

Beauty: To see one's own appearance in a beautiful state in a dream, including one's look, attitude, clothing or ride reflects the condition of one's enemy.

Beaver: Seeing a beaver in a dream means initiating a project that will not be completed, or it could mean living with false hopes. *(Also see Dog)*

Bed cover: *(See Blanket)*

Bed: (Couch; Mattress; Sleeping pad) A bed without covers in a dream represents travels, a wife, honor or a high rank. Sitting on a bed in a dream means regaining power or authority over something one had lost control. If the bed has it covers on, then it means ruling over a group of hypocrites who live in heedlessness. If it is not covered, then it means a journey. If one sees himself wearing his shoes and sitting on his bed in a dream, it means that he will undertake a trip in the company of an ostentatious person. Sitting on a bed in a pleasant surrounding in a dream means honor and power. The covers of one's bed in a dream represent his wife, his livelihood, or his mistress. Whatever stands on top of a bed represents one's male children and whatever is hidden under it represents one's female children. A bed in a dream also represents happiness, joy and dignity. It may also represent a wife, a ship, or a coffin. If one's bed falls apart or breaks into pieces in a dream, it means loss of authority, dismissal from one's job, divorcing one's wife, or it could mean her death. If one sees himself sitting over an unknown bed in a dream, it means marriage or conceiving a child. Sitting over a bed without a mattress means death, or a business trip. If a woman sees herself bringing a bed into her house in a dream, it means that she will get married. If a sick person sees himself sitting up in his bed in a dream, it means that he will recover from his illness. *(Also see Couch; Mattress)*

Bedchamber: *(See Bedroom)*

Bedmate: (Companion) To share one's bed with a deceased person in a dream means paying a pecuniary penalty which will be exacted by the authorities. Sharing one's bed with someone who is away on a trip in a dream means receiving news from him. Sharing one's bed with evil companions, spirits, satans or jinn in a dream means fighting against a crime ring.

Bedroom: (Bedchamber; Chamber) In a dream, one's bedroom signifies trickery or speaking soft words in fear of retribution, retaliation or rejection. One's bedroom in a dream also represents his inner thoughts. The good and the bad ones. Seeing a new bedroom in one's house, means renewing one's hopes, or affirming a good intention between the one seeing the dream and his Lord. A beautiful looking bedroom in a dream represents one's good qualities, while a bad looking bedroom in a dream represents one's bad character. *(Also see Chamber)*

Beehive: In a dream, a beehive represents one's wife. The bees represent her progeny, and the honeycomb represents her money. A beehive in a dream also means a castle or citadel. The bees represent its dwellers, and its honeycombs represent their property or belongings. A beehive in a dream also could mean distress, sadness, or the outcome of patience, or the consequences of abstaining from offering devotion or any serious input. *(Also see Bees; Beekeeper)*

Beekeeper: (Apiculturist; Apiarist) In a dream, a beekeeper represents a struggle, a caprice, taking the short road, wearing a mask, or it could mean hardships. *(Also see Beehive)*

Beer: A beer drinker in a dream represents a laborer or someone who works hard to earn his livelihood or perhaps it could represent a stingy person, or it could mean reunion of beloveds or expressions of joy. Beer or any yellowish drink in a dream signify illness or earning money by exploiting one's employees or servants. *(Also see Intoxicants)*

Bees: In a dream, bees represent prosperity, or a dangerous adventure. Seeing a beehive and extracting honey from it in a dream means earning lawful money. Taking all the honey from the beehive and leaving nothing for the bees in a dream means being unjust. If bees sit over one's head in a dream, it means winning the presidency over people. If bees sit in someone's hands in a dream, they mean a good crop for a farmer, while for someone else, they means a fight. Bees in a dream also represent an army. Killing bees in a dream means obliterating one's enemy. Bees in a dream also represent scholars, knowledge compilers, striving hard or collecting taxes. Bees in a dream also represent a bread winner who is a hard working person, stern and sometime dangerous, though he does bring some benefits to his companions. A bee sting in a dream means harm driven by a group of adversaries. Bees in a dream also mean taking a beating or falling sick. Bees in a dream also represent the army of believers, while locusts represent the army of disbelievers. A bee in a dream also represents a seer. *(Also see Beehive)*

Beetle: In a dream, a beetle represents a perfidious and a rich enemy, a dull person who travels extensively transporting money between the lands, an odious, dirty and abominable person, or an evil servant. A female beetle in a dream means the death of a woman in childbed, or it could represent a stubborn and a relentless woman. If one sees a beetle turning into a scorpion in a dream, it represents an enemy whose real intention is not known.

Beggar: (Hobo; Mendicant; Poverty; Richness) In a dream, a beggar represents a seeker of knowledge. If he is given what he is begging for in a dream, it means that he will succeed in his pursuit of knowledge. His humbleness and his submission when asking means victory. Beggars in a dream also imply sorrow, worries, distress, or contemplation. If one sees a beggar receiving or taking something from him in a dream, it means being in dire need for something, or he could represent the death of the person intended in the dream. If one sees beggars entering his house or his town in a group in a dream, it means dispersal of his family or household and if they take something from his house, it means a catastrophe. A beggar in a dream also represents a student, and the giver represents the teacher or shaikh. If one sees himself begging, but to no avail in a dream, it means that he will be humiliated. *(Also see Hobo; Poverty)*

Begging: *(See Beggar; Soliciting Advice)*

Behavior: *(See Irrationality)*

Beheading: (Capital punishment; Death; Decapitation) In a dream, beheading means freedom from slavery or dispelling sorrows and dismay, payment of one's debts, or it could mean prospering. If one knows his assailant in the dream, it means receiving wealth at his hand. If one is sick, it means that he will recover from his illness, and if he is not sick, it means that he will attend a pilgrimage. If the assailant is a young boy, then it means comfort, joy and relief from his burdens through his own death. If a healthy person is beheaded in a dream, it means the end of his comfort or loss of his job or authority. If one sees the governor of the town beheading him in a dream, it means that God Almighty will save him from his sorrows and strengthen him in this life. If one sees a ruler beheading his subjects in a dream, it means that he will issue a decree of amnesty for all prisoners. If one is beheaded as a result of a judgment or by robbers in a dream, it means that either one of his parents or a child of his may die shortly. If a condemned person on death row sees himself beheaded in a dream, it means that he will be released from prison and his judgment will be rectified. If an investor or a money exchanger sees that, then it means loss of his capital investment. If a traveler is beheaded in a dream, it represents his safe return home. If rivals see that in a dream, it means loss of their fight. *(Also see Cutting off)*

Behind: *(See Back)*

Belching: (Burping) In a dream, belching means vain talk, or the arrogance of a rich person toward a poor one.

Belittlement: *(See Backbiting)*

Bell: (Cow bell; Sleigh bell) Possessing small bells in a dream means a fight, an argument or vain talk known of the person holding them. Seeing a bell in a dream represents the announcer or the forerunner of a ruler. Generally speaking seeing a bell in a dream means that someone will bring glad tidings. If the bell is roped around the neck of an animal in the dream, it means travel. The bells of a church represent people one can seek their advice and follow their opinion. Bells in a dream also represent calling to prayers or preparing to meet one's enemies, or they could mean the arrival of a caravan or a shipment. Bells in a dream also represent abrogated books of revelations or tampering with God's revelations or they could represent past traditions. *(Also see Hand bell)*

Belligerence: *(See Nakedness)*

Bellows: (Air blower; Blacksmith) If a bellows is made from wood in one's dream, it means loss of dignity, demotion or loss of property. Owning a bellows in a dream means acquiring vast control and sovereignty if one qualifies for that. Otherwise, a bellows in a dream means benefits and blessings. Seeing a bellows blowing fire in a dream means completing a project, satisfying a need, reaching one's goal or earning money. If the bellows are not in use, or if they are not blowing air into the fire, then they signify distress, adversities and trouble. Seeing bellows that are used by a goldsmith or a silversmith in a dream means sincerity in one's faith, certitude and devoting one's life to worshipping God Almighty. Seeing bellows that are used in blowing glass in a dream signify deceit and cunningness. Bellows in a dream also represent a woman who conceive children easily, then quickly has miscarriages. Bellows in a dream also represent a hot tempered man, a prison, a police station, or a torture dungeon. Seeing bellows in use by a blacksmith in a dream means easing of one's trouble. *(Also see Blowing into the fire)*

Belt: (Cincture; Cummerbund; Fastening; Sash; Waist belt) In a dream, a belt depicts the carrier of burdens. It also implies travels, money, savings or stinginess. It also could mean serious endeavors and assiduity in seeking knowledge. A belt or a waistband in a dream could represent one's wife or his property. If a woman sees herself wearing a waistband, then it represents her brother, brother in-law, or father in-law. If she is pregnant, it means that she will beget a daughter. If a man sees himself wearing a waistband in a dream, it represents a woman in his family to whom it is unlawful for him to marry. A broken belt in a dream means a fight with one's wife. If one's waistband becomes a snake in the dream, it means enmity with his brother in-law. If his waistband is drenched in blood in the dream, it means that he may get killed because of his wife, or that he may conspire to kill his wife. Wearing a belt in a dream also represents bundles of money one carries, or an unanticipated misfortune he may attract. Buying a new belt in a dream means protecting one's property, money or knowledge. *(Also see Cincture; Cummerbund; Waistband; Waist belt)*

Bench: (Outdoor bench) If one sees a cement bench in front of his door in a dream, it means that one's wife is having a secret affair. If one sees himself sitting on a bench in a dream, it means that he will gain status, honor, rank, money or should he qualify for it, he could sit on the judges bench.

Bend: *(See Twist)*

Benediction: *(See Blessings)*

Benevolence: *(See Amity)*

Bequeath: *(See Beggar; Soliciting advice)*

Bequest: *(See Will)*

Bereavement of one's child: In real life, it represents the opposite of what is seen in a dream. It means rejoicing, reunions, pleasures and respect. Sometimes it is also interpreted to portray an intention of one's children or wife to separate from the family or to live on their own. *(Also See Child)*

Berries: *(See Plum)*

Besiege: *(See Siege)*

Besmear: (Brand; Stigmatize; Smut) To spread something with an unctuous substance in a dream means being sanctimonious, self-righteous or false.

Bethlehem: *(See City)*

Betrayal: (Deception; Double-cross; Milk; Misleading; Renegade; Trickery; War) In a dream, betrayal of others mean shortcomings or religious disdain and failure in one's life in this world. Betrayal in a dream also means a robbery or being in dire need of the victim.

Betrothal: *(See Book)*

Betting: *(See Casting lots; Gambling)*

Beverages: *(See Bartender)*

Bewitch: *(See Hyena)*

Bias: *(See Bragging)*

Bible: *(See Torah)*

Bicuspids: *(See Tooth)*

Bigfoot: *(See Sasquatch)*

Bill of exchange: (Bank draft; Commercial) If one sees himself paying someone a fee to write him a bill of exchange, or a bank draft in a dream, it means that he will borrow some money to do business and that he will profit from his investment to become known in his field. In a dream, if by mistake, one sends the bank draft to the wrong destination or to another country that produces the same type of products, in this case his dream means that he will lose his investment or recover his capital cost after some hardship.

Bill: *(See Beak)*

Billy goat: In a dream, a billy goat represents a person who has an awesome look, but makes stupid choices. A billy goat also means a great person of an extraordinary destiny. It also could represents one's son. *(Also see Goat)*

Binoculars: (Spy glass; Telescope) In a dream, binoculars represents a notable person or the person who is looking through them. Looking with binoculars from a distance in a dream means victory over one's adversary, attainment of one's goals, rising in rank, spying, or happiness. If a merchant looks through binoculars in a dream, it means sovereignty, prosperity, presiding over his fellow merchants and gaining power.

Bird's nest: *(See Nest)*

Bird: (Fowl; Man; Woman) An unknown bird in a dream represents the angel of death. If one sees a bird diving to the ground to pick a pebble, a paper, or a worm, then if he soars away from a house that hosts a sick person in a dream, it means that the sick person will shortly die from his illness. If one sees a bird diving toward him in a dream, it means a journey. If one sees him standing over his head, or over his shoulders, or sitting in his lap in a dream, it denotes one's work or profession. If the bird is white in the dream, it means that one's work is clean, If his color is tanned in the dream, it means that one's work is tainted. If a male bird sits in the lap of a pregnant woman in a dream, it means that she will beget a boy. If a female bird sits in her lap in a dream, it means that she will beget a girl. Large or predatory birds in a dream represent kings, presidents, leaders, tyrants, men of knowledge or merchants. Water birds, sea gulls, etcetera, represent honorable people who rose in rank in two spheres, the sphere of water and that of the air. They also could mean a journey. If they quack in the dream, they represent lamenting or crying. Singing birds in a dream represent musicians and singers. To see a flock of birds in a dream means money and power and particularly for someone who tends them or cares for them. Seeing birds flying over one's head means gaining authority and power. If one sees birds flying inside his house or shop in a dream, it means angels. If a bird flies into one's hand in a dream, it means glad tidings. A bird in a dream also means work. An unknown bird in a dream means a warning, an advice or an admonition. If one's bird looks beautiful in a dream, it denotes the quality of his work. If one sees himself in a dream carrying an ugly looking bird, it also denotes the quality of his actions or that a messenger may bring him good news. An unknown bird means profits. To see black colored birds in a dream denote bad deeds, while white colored birds represent good deeds. Colored birds in a dream represent mixed actions. Seeing a bird in a dream also could mean honor, power, authority ornament or profits. A bird in a dream also represents a fun and a most entertaining companion. A bird in a dream also represents a boy. If one slaughters a bird in his dream, it means that he will beget a child who will live in sickness during his childhood and that his father will fear for his death. It is said that a bird in a dream also represents a rich and a tricky leader who constantly fights for his earnings and to insure his success or superiority. A bird in a dream also represents a beautiful woman. The singing of birds in a dream means hearing good words or receiving a valuable knowledge. A flock of birds in a dream represents easy earned wealth. A bird in a dream also represents a boy. Capturing a bird in a dream means having control over a powerful person. Killing a bird in a dream means fulfilling one's goal. Plucking the feathers, cleaning and eating a bird in a dream means earnings, prosperity, or a woman. Slaughtering a bird in a dream means raping one's servant. Holding a bird in one's hand or having it inside a cage in a dream means a sickness that will befall one's son. If the bird flies away from one's hand or from its cage in a dream, then it means one's death. A flock of birds in a dream also represents gatherings of love, unity, family reunions and celebrations. However, the gathering of birds in a dream also could mean banding to commit wrong or the dispersal of one's family or friends, or it could mean business losses. *(Also see Blackbird; Bustard; Nest; Osprey; Roller)*

Birds' salesman: In a dream, a birds' salesman represents all types of gatherings, including celebrations or grief.

Birth control: (Condom; Contraceptive device; Diaphragm) To use a contraceptive in a dream means throwing one's money into the drain, wasting one's wealth, depriving one's children from their legitimate inheritance. Using a contraceptive in a dream also signifies impeachment from office or losing the election or divorcing one's wife or changing one's trade.

Birth: If one sees his mother giving birth to him in a dream, and should he be ill, it means the approach of his death. *(Also see Childbirth; Giving birth)*

Birthmark: (Mole; Strawberry mark) If one sees himself having a birthmark in a dream, it means that he will be caught and be accused of a sin, or a crime someone else has committed, or it could mean paying for someone else's fault, or it could mean having a good character or nature.

Bishop: *(See Chess bishop)*

Bitch: *(See Dog)*

Bite off: *(See Pinch)*

Bite: (Champing; Chomp; Love; Rancor) In a dream, a bite signifies perfidy, rancor or extreme love for the one who is bitten in a dream. If one bites himself then spits a piece of his own flesh on the ground in a dream, it means backbiting and belittling others. Biting one's own fingers in a dream means regret or fury, rage and anger. If one's fingers bleed from such bite in a dream, it means tribulations caused by one's own shortcomings. A bite in a dream also signifies extreme anger. If one is bitten by another person in a dream, it means that he will enjoy happiness and success at the beginning of his professional life, then he will suffer from an illness, eye inflammation, ophthalmia, or from heart problems. Biting on an apple in a dream means satisfying one's desires. *(Also see Pinch; Tongue)*

Biting on one's tongue: *(See Tongue)*

Bitter almond: *(See Almond)*

Bitter fruits: (Colocynth; Bitter apples; Bitter cucumber) Its tree represents sadness and stress, a coward, or an uneasy, worried and a restless person.

Blabber: *(See Magpie)*

Black hair: If a woman sees herself having a thick black hair in a dream, it means that she will marry a respected and a handsome looking husband. If she sees herself having a charcoal colored hair in the dream, it means that she will live satisfied with her husband's wealth or inheritance. *(Also see Strand of hair)*

Black magic: *(See Magic arts)*

Black mud: *(See Sludge)*

Black pepper: *(See Pepper)*

Black Stone: (The corner stone of the Ka'aba; God's House in Mecca) Seeing or holding the Black Stone of the Ka'aba in one's dream means paying allegiance to the ruler, or it could mean repentance from sin at the hand of a pious Imām, or it could mean kissing one's son, wife or bosom friend. It also means serving people in the government. If one sees himself touching the Black Stone in his dream, it means that he will follow and learn at the hand of one of the Imāms of the Arabian peninsula. Seeing the sacred Black Stone in a dream is perhaps an indication of going to perform one's pilgrimage. If one sees himself cutting into the Black Stone in a dream, it means that he wants people to follow his personal opinions. If he sees the pilgrims searching for the Black Stone but cannot find it in a dream, it means that he thinks of himself to be right and the rest of the people to be wrong. It also could mean that he possesses a knowledge which he hides from others. If he touches the Black Stone in his dream, it means that he follows the teachings of an Imām from among the Hijazite Arabs. If he sees the Black Stone being a castle for himself in a dream, it means that he follows religious innovations. If he swallows the Black Stone in his dream, it means that he is a affected person who will mislead people. *(Also see Ka'aba; Corner Stone)*

Black: The color black in a dream means prosperity and happiness. In a dream, everything black represents money, dominion and power and particularly for those who are used to wearing black. Otherwise, as for those who are not used to wearing black garments, wearing it in a dream means sorrow.

Blackbird: In a dream, a blackbird represents a diligent and a highly recommended writer. A blackbird also represents a well spoken and a good looking son.

Blackboard: *(See Tablet)*

Blackout: *(See Faint)*

Blacksmith: (Jailer) In a dream, a blacksmith represents a strong personality, a leader, or a powerful and a skillful ruler. A blacksmith in a dream also represents the angel of death. Seeing a blacksmith in a dream or being one, indicates both happiness and adversities. To be brought before a blacksmith in a dream means an accident that will bring one before a person in authority for intercession. Otherwise, it could mean seeking the fellowship of a worthless person. If one sees a sick or a deceased person sitting with a blacksmith in a dream, it means that he is in hell, and particularly when his face is blackened from the smoke, or it could mean that he may be imprisoned. *(Also see Bellows)*

Blade: (Cutting edge) In a dream, a blade is interpreted to be one's tongue, or an energetic and a caring wife, or drawing profits for one's livelihood, or it could represent a pencil sharpener.

Blame: (Censure; Rebuke; Reprimand; Reproof) Blame in a dream signifies pursuing Satan in his evil actions and it means failing one's promise. Blaming oneself in a dream means doubt, disturbance and confusion for which one will be rebuked. He will then be relieved to pursue his enemy, to overcome him and become free from people's reproach. Blaming someone in a dream, means the same in wakefulness, and consequently, one will suffer from people blaming him. If one sees people showering him with money in a dream, it means that they are speaking ill of him or blaming him. If one sees people praising him in a dream, it also means that he is praiseworthy and does good. *(Also see Censure)*

Blanket: (Bed cover; Cover; Lioncloth; Mexican blanket; Overlay; Overspread) In a dream, a blanket represents a woman. If one sees himself wearing a blanket over a wrapper, or a lioncloth in a dream, it means marriage. If he sees a blanket made of pearls in a dream, it means that his wife is a pious woman. Wrapping oneself with a blanket in a dream means marriage, comfort, peace, tranquility and strength. Wrapping oneself with a red blanket in a dream means a fight because of a woman. If a blanket is stolen or burned or taken away from someone in his dream, it means divorce or death of his wife.

Bleacher: *(See Fuller)*

Blear-eyed: *(See Mucous)*

Bleed: *(See Suck)*

Bleeding nose: A bleeding nose in a dream means unlawful money, or it could mean a miscarriage. If one's nose bleeds and if he thinks in the dream that such bleeding will benefit him, then it means that he will receive benefits from his superior at work. Otherwise, if in his dream one thinks that such bleeding will hurt him, then harm will unfailingly come to him from his superior. If he is the boss, then he will benefit or lose accordingly. A bleeding nose in a dream may represent good health. It also could mean correcting one's religious and spiritual attitudes. In fact, it all depends on one's own consciousness in his dream and how he perceives the bleeding of his nose. Thus, feeling bad about it or weak from it means poverty. If the blood stains his clothing in the dream, it means that he will receive unlawful money or commit a sin. If the blood does not stain his clothing, then he might walk free from an ill he had indulged in. If the blood from one's nose drips on the road in the dream, it means that he regularly pays his due alms which he distributes to poor people in the streets. It is also said that seeing one's nose bleeding in a dream means finding a lost treasure. Otherwise, it means distress and depression. *(Also see Bleeding; Cut; Injury; Wound)*

Bleeding: Internal bleeding in a dream means financial losses, or it may imply suffering from the consequences of people's interference in his life. However, one will end by receiving financial compensation for pain and suffering. If one sees himself wounded and that his attacker is smeared with his blood in the dream, it means that he may commit a sin, or acquire unlawful earnings. *(Also see Bleeding nose)*

Blessed Tree: *(See Olive tree)*

Blessings: (Benediction; Grace; Light) In a dream, blessings represent one's life, hearing, sight, good health, wealth, good qualities, contentment, gratitude, faith, guidance, submission to God Almighty, obedience to one's parents, having obedient children, having a husband or a wife, children, lineage, friends, love, compassion, happiness, comfort, endowments, attainments, success, provisions, knowledge, wisdom, balance, intelligence, clarity, truthfulness, work, strength, peace in the land, safety, protection, a just ruler, rain or they could mean a good crop, etcetera. *(Also see Enemy; Introduction page xxvi.)*

Blind in one eye: *(See Antichrist; One-eyed)*

Blindness: (Gold; Heedlessness; Inheritance; Poverty) In a dream, blindness means heedlessness, misguidance or receiving an inheritance. A blind man in a dream represents a poor person and because of his poverty, his actions mostly harm his religious life. Blindness in a dream also means a calamity, an accident, a misfortune, sadness, harm, sorrows and distress. If a blind man sees himself wrapped with new cloth in a dream, it means his death. If one sees himself blind in a dream, it means debts he owes, or a pilgrimage he must attend. If one is blinded in a dream, it means that he will betray his covenant with his Lord. Becoming blind in a dream means suffering from poverty and becoming needy after being rich, or it could mean satisfaction and contentment, or it could mean losing a dear person. If one's sight explodes with a lightning in a dream, it means his death. Blindness also could denote deafness, disregarding the world or renouncing it or hiding one's secrets. As for a foreigner, seeing himself blind in a dream means never returning to his homeland. Blindness in a dream for a prisoner means his release from jail. If a seeker, a student, or a businessman sees himself blind in a dream, it means that he may never reach his goals. *(Also see Body¹; Destruction; Eyes; Fear; One-eyed; World)*

Blintz: *(See Pastry)*

Blister beetle: *(See Spanish fly)*

Blithe: (Cheerfulness; Lightheartedness) In a dream, blithe signifies comfort, a good spirit and particularly for a grateful person. This also applies for seeing a deceased person in a state of cheerfulness. A blithely person in a dream is one who is grateful for the blessings endowed upon him by God Almighty of having a family, love, affection and for the ability to do good deeds. If one is expecting a promise to be fulfilled, then blithe in a dream implies the satisfaction of his aspirations.

Blond: (The color blond) In a dream, the color blond means war, sickness, piety, or a religious person. In a dream, the color blond also could mean contemptible-ness, vileness, meanness or depravity. *(Also see Colors)*

Blood disease: If one is presented in his dream with red unripened dates, then they represent some type of blood disease where the red cells exceed the white cells in number. *(Also see Dates)*

Blood letting: *(See Cupping)*

Blood ties: (Debts; Veins)

Blood: In a dream, blood represents unlawful or illegal money, or an evil act that will emanate from the person seeing the dream. If one sees himself dragging his feet through puddles of blood in a dream, it means that he will finance his business from unlawfully earned money, profit from an illegal business or commit a major sin then be caught. If one sees blood staining his shirt in a dream, it means that someone will lie to him, though he will not recognize it. If his shirt is stained with blood or pus from pimples in a dream, it means that a thief will lie to him. If his shirt is stained with the blood of a lion in a dream, it means that an iniquitous person in authority will lie to him and take advantage of him. If his shirt is stained with the blood of a ram in a dream, it means that a rich, noble and a well respected person will lie to him, and at the end he will consent to accepting corrupt money. Seeing blood flowing from one's body or from wounds is a sign of good health, safety, or it could mean coming home after a long journey. Drinking human blood in a dream means money, profits, escape from danger, safety from trials and adversities, or it could mean committing a sin then repenting from it. Falling into a pool of blood in a dream means that one will be accused of a murder or of stealing money. If one sees a valley filled with blood in a dream, it means that he may be killed in that locality. If one sees blood emanating out of his body without cupping or cuts in a dream, it means giving money to someone. If he is a poor person, then it means receiving money from someone. If one sees himself falling into a cistern which is filled with blood in a dream, it means that someone is seeking revenge from him. Blood in a jar represents a woman in menstruation. Blood in a dream also represents one's life, strength, wealth, business, helpers, clothing, earning praise or blame, weak points, unlawful food, lack of benefits, loss of business or money or esteem, inability to draw benefits from one's usual close ones, such as a father, a son, or a business partner, separation through death from one's beloveds or dear one's, such as wife or a kin. One's blood in a dream also represents his own Satan, or an enemy that dwells inside his house. Drinking one's own blood in a dream means paying one's debts with second loan, or vanquishing one's enemy.

Bleeding naturally in a dream means peace and comfort. Excess bleeding in a dream means the opposite. The bleeding of an unwed woman means finding a husband. Bleeding of a pregnant woman in a dream means a miscarriage and for an elderly woman, bleeding means an illness. If one sees blood coming from his anus in a dream, it means that he is tainted with the consequences of an evil act, or it could mean a bad deal, or that he has earned unlawful money then walked out of such a deal. To bleed in a dream also means being a spendthrift, a money wasting family, or it could mean suffering from a venereal disease. *(Also see Vascular blockage)*

Bloodsucker: *(See Leech)*

Blossoms: In a dream, blossoms represent an inner or an outer light, or guidance one follows for spiritual or material gains. *(Also see Earth; Flowers; Roses)*

Blotch: *(See Freckles; Piebald)*

Blouse: *(See Shirt)*

Blow one's nose: *(See Nasal mucus)*

Blow[1]: *(See Slapping on the cheek)*

Blow[2]: *(See Wind)*

Blow[3]: *(See Shock)*

Blowing into a vagina: *(See Blowing)*

Blowing into the fire: *(Also see Bellows; Blowing)*

Blowing into the ground: *(See Blowing)*

Blowing the trumpet: *(See Blowing)*

Blowing: To blow into fire in a dream means kindling a conflict or exasperating and intensifying it. Blowing into the ground in a dream means unveiling a secret or reprimanding one who does not keep a secret. Blowing into the vagina of a woman in a dream means that she will become pregnant. Blowing the trumpet of resurrection in a dream means salvation of the righteous ones. Hearing the first sound of the trumpet of resurrection in a dream means announcing the truth or hearing shocking and worrisome news. Hearing the second blow of the trumpet of resurrection in a dream means exposure of secrets, recovering of the sick, release of the prisoners, reunion of beloveds, loss of one's capital investment or the flow of wealth. *(Also see Bellows; Trumpet of Resurrection)*

Blue: (Color) In a dream, the color blue represents distress, depression, enmity, or a calamity. *(Also see Colors)*

Blunder: (Foolish talk; Nonsense; or people's foolish talk) Blunder in a dream means disobedience, sin or refusing to accept a good advice. To make a foolish oath in a dream means repentance of a sinner and guidance for a disbeliever. *(Also see Grammarian; Fool; Linguist; Lying)*

Blushing: If one sees his face glowing with red or blushing in a dream, it means dignity, nobility and it could represent a person who is known for his good deeds. If the blushing of one's face is mixed with some white lines in the dream, it means strength and happiness. If one sees his face embellished with red cosmetic makeup in a dream, it means that he will commit adultery, and that he will be exposed thereafter. If one sees his entire body turning red in a dream, it means long sufferings and lack of success in his life. Glowing redness in one's face in a dream also means recovering from an illness, or the home returning of a traveller. *(Also see Bashfulness)*

Boast: (Brag; Feat) Boasting about something in a dream signifies wealth and spending.

Boat: (Ferry; Ferryboat; Fireboat; Fishing boat; Ship; Star) In a dream, a fishing boat represents profits and benefits. To sail on an unknown boat or to pilot a boat or to give orders to sailors who are operating it in a dream means marriage to a woman from a country to which the boat belongs, or it could mean doing business in that land. To ride on a ferryboat in a dream means receiving God's benevolence and kindness in crossing over danger. A boat in a dream also represents one's relatives. Thus, whatever atmospheric conditions the skies exhibits during the crossing or during a journey by boat, they will manifest in one's family. In a dream, a fireboat means dispelling anxieties, overcoming distress and adversities. *(Also see Carpenter; Helm; Ship)*

Body lice: *(See Nit)*

Body snatcher: *(See Grave digger; Exhume; Grave)*

Body[1]: (Abdomen; Anus; Aorta; Back; Bones; Brain; Breasts; Buttocks; Chest; Earlock; Ears; Eyes; Eyebrows; Face; Feet; Fingers; Fingernails; Forehead; Hand; Head; Heart; Heels; Intestines; Jugular vein; Kidney; Knee; Legs; Limb; Lip; Livers; Loins; Lungs; Marrow; Mouth; Nails; Navel; Neck; Nerves; Nose; Rear end; Ribs; Penis; Sexual organs; Shoulders; Skin; Spinal column; Spleen; Stomach; Temple; Testicles; Thighs; Throat; Tongue; Umbilicus; Veins) In a dream, the **head** and the **brain** represent man's controller, strength, benefits, longevity, wisdom or power. One's **ears** in a dream represent his wife, daughter, sister or aunt. The **eyes** represent one's faith, religion or children. The right eye represents his son and the left eye represents his daughter. The **forehead** in a dream represents one's beauty, son, power, honor, wealth, leadership or the point of prostration in one's prayers. A wide forehead in a dream means prosperity, while a narrow forehead means tightness. The **eyebrows** represent one's protection or spiritual guardianship. As for the human **nose** in a dream, it represents honor, longevity and respect. Whatever comes out of one's nose in a dream is good and whatever goes into it in a dream may not be beneficial. A bleeding nose in a dream means receiving or giving money. If one's nose is cut off in a dream, it means circumcision, falling in rank, or it could mean his death. Inhaling water and clearing one's nose in a dream represents someone who deceives his wife. If a bird or an animal comes out of one's nose in a dream, it means that a cattle, a pet, or a domesticated animal will give birth to its babies in such a house. A large nose in a dream represents honor and respect. Smelling a nice fragrance in a dream means begetting a son, or it could mean relief from difficulties. One's **face** in a dream represents his happiness or his sorrow. Seeing the forehead and the face in a dream means money, honor and a beautiful woman. The earlock and the temples represent two noble and blessed daughters. A bright face in a dream means glad tidings, while a yellowish face in a dream means bad news or miseries. **Frowning** in a dream means a misfortune. If a woman sees herself frowning in a dream, it means the death of her husband. The two **lips** in a dream represent one's helpers. The lower lip is stronger in meaning than the upper lip. It is also said that lips in a dream represent one's relatives. The upper lip represents the male relatives and the lower lip represents the female relatives. Sealed lips in a dream mean difficulties or adversities. The **mouth** in a dream represents a key, one's livelihood, the conclusion of one's life, death, illness, strength, a coffer, a marketplace, a door attendant, a chief minister, or a door. If one's mouth is sealed in a dream, it means a scandal. One's **tongue** in a dream represents his or her translator. A long tongued person in a dream may mean winning an argument, or it could mean innocence from allegation. An elongated tongue of a judge in a dream means clarity and justice. A tied-up tongue in a dream means poverty, sickness, depression, a calamity, or it could represent an unworthy person. Having two tongues in a dream means praiseworthiness and acquiring two types of knowledge. Seeing what is inside one's mouth in a dream means exposing one's ills. Biting on one's tongue in a dream means regret. Watching one's tongue in a dream means protecting oneself from pitfalls. Carrying one's tongue by hand in a dream means receiving indemnity for bodily injury or receiving blood money. If one sees his **throat** blocked in such a way that he could not speak in a dream, it denotes his stinginess toward his own family. If one sees one of his **limbs** speaking against him in a dream, it means that someone will report him to the authorities or become a witness against him in court. If one sees himself in a dream riding over the **shoulders** of his enemy, it means that he will commit a wrongdoing or a shameful act. If there is no enmity between them, and if he sees himself riding over the shoulders of a friend in a dream, it means earning something from him. Carrying something over one's shoulders in a dream means debts. If one sees himself carrying a hypocrite over his shoulders in a dream, it means that he may work in a lumberyard or carry wood to earn a living. One's shoulders in a dream also represent his parents, brothers, partners, station, or beauty. Anything that affects them in a dream will manifest in any of the above. In a dream, one's **neck** represents an embrace, a donation with terms, a legal will, or a conditional endowment. The neck and the shoulders in a dream represent one's trust or trustworthiness. A healthy and strong neck in a dream means trustworthiness and ability to meet one's obligations. Wounds, festering or purulence in one's neck in a dream mean betraying God's trust. If one sees a nice bird sitting over his neck in a dream it means benefits or an alibi. If it is not a gentle bird, then it becomes a bad omen, or a rebuke. If one sees a necklace, a rope, a wire, or a thread around his neck in a dream, it means fulfilling one's promise, acquiring knowledge and honor. A long neck in a dream could mean four things, that is: justice, leadership, attainment of one's goals or calling people to prayers. The **left hand** represents one's helper, friend, savings, or a compassionate relative. Long hands in a dream represent a charitable person, or a capable one, and short hands mean the opposite. Long **hands** also could mean longevity, wealth, helpers, borrowing money, governing, fulfilling one's commands, profits from one's business or having business sense. If one's hand is cut off in a dream, it means the death of his brother, his father, his partner, or a close friend or his assistant. If the **right hand** is cut off in a dream, it means a vow one takes to deprive someone from his rights. It also means loss of one's job or cutting off one's blood ties, or it could mean that he has committed a theft. If a righteous person sees his hand cut off in a dream, it means abstaining from wrongdoing or eschewing evil. If one's left hand is cut off in a dream, it means reestablishing his relationship with his family and rediscovering the benefits of good qualities. If one's hand is broken in a dream, it means an adversity, illness, loss of business, or loss of a dear person. The cracking skin of one's hands in a dream means loss of wealth. Stretched hands in a dream means ill caused by a close friend. Stretching one's hands in a dream also could mean generosity. If one's hands are cut off without causing him any pain in a dream, it means that he may fall in love. If one sees his hands joined together in a dream, it means having a family reunion, or a wedding. If one's hands are trembling in a dream, it means weakness, illness, old age or longevity. If one's hands feel dry in a dream, it means that such a person does little good in his life. If one enters his hand under his arm's pit in a dream, then brings it out bright and radiant in a dream, it means that he will acquire knowledge and may develop wisdom. Otherwise, it could mean profits. If he brings forth his hand from under his arm's pit in the dream, and if it reveal a flame in his dream, it represents a manifestation of divine power and a blessed victory. If one pulls his hand from under his arm's pit and it brings forth water in the dream, it means that he will receive great benefits and growth in his life, or perhaps that a long awaited traveller will shortly arrive to his doorsteps. If a right-handed person sees himself being left-handed in a dream, it means hardships. If one sees himself walking with his hands in a dream, it represents his dependence on a relative to provide for his needs. If one's hands say something nice to him in a dream, it means financial comfort. If one's hand is cut-off in a dream as punishment for a sin, it could mean marriage, a bad wife, or lack of trustworthiness. If one washes his hands with soap in a dream, it means that he will abandon something he initiated, or that his intention will not be fulfilled. If a form of life or a good spirit comes out from one's hands in a dream, it indicates benefits. If such a life is a malignant one, then it means the opposite. If one takes someone by the hand in a dream, it means that he will help him and save his life. If something sprouts in one's hands or if one's hands turn into iron, or a vegetable in a dream, it means negative repercussions in wakefulness. Hands in a dream are interpreted in twelve ways: that is a brother, a sister, a partner, a son, a compassionate friend, one's strength, wealth, leadership, money, proof, a craft, or work. The condition in which the **palm** of one's hand looks in a dream indicates the state of one's health and fitness. Clapping one's hands in a dream could either mean joy and happiness, or it could mean nothing. Wearing a glove in one's hand in a dream means ceasing the course of wrongdoing. Slapping one's own face with both hands means sorrow, sadness or calamities. Hitting the back of one's hand into the palm of the other hand in a dream means separation. In a dream, the **fingers** of the right hand represent the daily five time prayers. The thumb represents the pre-dawn prayer, the index represents the midday prayer, the middle finger represents the mid-afternoon prayer, the ring finger represents the sunset prayer, and the little finger represents the evening prayer. As for the fingers of the left hand in a dream, they are interpreted to represent one's nephews. To cross or intertwine one's fingers in a dream means difficulties and poverty. One's **toes** in a dream represent the beauty of his character and denote his straight-forwardness. Any defect or crookedness in them in a dream will mirror in wakefulness. If a toe or a finger is bitten or crushed in a dream, it denotes evil or perhaps an accident. If one sees milk coming forth from his thumb and blood coming forth from his index finger in a dream, it means that he will marry a mother, then will he marry her daughter, or it could mean that he will rape the mother, then her daughter. Cracking one's fingers in a dream means exchanging bad words between relatives or being sarcastic or making fun of other people. If one's fingers are paralyzed in a dream, it means that he has committed an awful sin. If one sees his right hand paralyzed in a dream, it means injustice toward a weak person or inflicting losses upon an innocent person. If one's left hand is paralyzed in a dream, it means the death of his brother or sister. As for the **fingernails** in a dream, they denote beauty, courage, strength, a religious covenant, or money. If one's fingernails are chipped, extracted, or broken in a dream, they means loss of money and strength. If they look nicely clipped in a dream, they mean both spiritual and material benefits. Long nails at the point of a near breaking in a dream mean distress, sorrow, fears and depression. If one's nail becomes a claw in a dream, it means rising against one's enemy and opposition. If one does not have fingernails in a dream, it means bankruptcy. If one's fingernails turn yellow, green or blue or if they are broken in the dream, it means death. Clipping them in a dream means dispelling calamities or distress. If a thorn or a chip of wooden enters under one's fingernails in a dream, it means loss of power or money. If one sees himself in a dream knocking his fingernails against his teeth in a dream, it means committing a despicable and a loathsome act. As for seeing one's **chest** in a dream, if one sees himself having a broad and a nice looking chest (*See Chest*), it means repentance of a sinner, or being eager and willing to follow the truth and to comply with it, or to make easy what was earlier difficult. One's **breasts** in a dream (*See Breast*) represent his daughter. Man's breast in a dream means a woman, and woman's breasts in a dream represents a man. Breasts in a dream mean five things: a little boy, a little girl, a servant, a friend, or a brother. One's **abdomen** in a dream means money, children, relatives or prosperity. If one sees his abdomen being cut open and washed, then stitched back to normal in the dream, it means blessings from God Almighty, forgiveness for one's sins, and it could mean that one will receive spiritual guidance. One's abdomen in a dream also denotes his good conduct, amiable character, blessed enterprises and protection from the evil of the accursed Satan. If one sees a newborn son or daughter coming out of his abdomen in a dream, it means that such a child will be born and will grow to govern that household. As for one's **livers** in a dream, they represent knowledge, money or children. If a man of knowledge sees his livers flying away from his body like birds in a dream, it means that he will forget his knowledge, or if one has children, they may die, or perhaps the government may seize his property even if he has nothing. If one sees himself eating his own livers in a dream, it means earning his livelihood. If they are cooked in the dream, then they represent a lawful income, or they could mean gobbling the property of one's own children. If a liver is removed in a dream, it means the death of a child. Removing a liver in a dream also could mean injustice. One's **kidney** in a dream means having a good business connection, dispelling adversities, distress, trouble, safety from danger, a husband and a wife, one's parents, or it could represent two lovers. One's kidneys in a dream also represent a strong, courageous and a hard working man who serves someone in authority, or he may become a personal guard, or an assistant to the governor. As for one's **lungs** in a dream, they represent joy, happiness, or sorrow. Donating a lung to someone known or unknown in a dream means receiving happiness in return. Eating a broiled lung of a domesticated animal in a dream means profits. Otherwise, it could mean acquiring unlawful money. Seeing one's lung torn in a dream means nearing one's death. One's **spleen** in a dream (*See Spleen*) represents money. As for seeing one's **intestines** in a dream, they represent earnings, leadership, a child, unlawful money, intercession, hatred, livelihood, work or they could mean changing one's mind about doing something which could cause a disaster. One's **stomach** in a dream represents longevity, livelihood or children. A healthy stomach in a dream means enjoying strength and a long life. The same interpretation is given to the intestines or the **umbilicus** or the **navel** and the three of them represent one's relationship with his wife. As for the **ribs** (*See Ribs*) in a dream, they represent women. The **loins** or the **spinal column** in a dream represent one's progeny. One's **back** in a dream (*See Back*) represents his strength, wealth, glory, fame, master, destruction, end, poverty, old age and burdens. If one sees himself carrying a heavy load in a dream, it means that he is carrying his sins. If he carries merchandise in the dream, it means debt. If he carries woods in the dream, it means backbiting others. If one sees himself carrying a dead person on his back in a dream, it means that he takes care of orphans. As for one's **heart** (*See Heart*) in a dream, it means intelligence, vigilance, awareness, guidance, clarity and piety. One's **buttocks** and the **rear end** in a dream represent his earnings, job and profits. If one sees himself licking someone's rear end or buttocks in the dream, it means giving high praises to an unworthy and an impious person or commending him. The male and female **sexual organs** in a dream represent a good father or one's profession. What comes or goes into the male organ or woman's vagina in a dream of good or bad will reflect in their lives. Seeing one's **penis** in a dream means children, money, pride, state, or authority. The **testicles** represent one's livelihood, one's daughters, protection and maintenance. The meaning of the penis and the testicles may be transposed in the dream interpretation. One's **anus** in a dream means a pouch, a store, a resting place, or a coffer. The **knee** represents one's capital or one's attendance to his work and earning his livelihood. As for the **legs**, they too represent one's capital, paying attention to one's work and conduct. Man's leg represents a woman, and a woman's leg represents a man. If one's leg turns into wood or iron in a dream, it means that he will fail to earn his livelihood. One's **feet** represent his parents, his livelihood, a journey or his wealth. (*See Feet; Foot*). If one foot is broken or cut off in a dream, it means either the death of a parent or loss of half of one's capital. If one's feet turn into iron or copper in a dream, it means longevity. If they turn into glass in the dream, they denote his short life. The human **bones** represent his livelihood, religion, glory or money. Collecting bones in a dream means saving money. The **bone marrow** in a dream represents hidden money, good awareness, patience and gratitude. The **veins** and **nerves** in a dream represent one's clan, modesty and progeny. As for seeing the human **skin** in a dream, it means ornaments, presiding over others, a veil, blessings, livelihood, provisions, life and a garment. (*Also see Aorta; Face; Finger; Five fingers; Gall bladder; Heel; Jugular vein; Marrow; Nails; Palm; Pluck; Spleen; Teeth; Tongue; Tooth*)

Body²: (Dwellings; House; State) In a dream, the human body represents his state, and its strength represents his faith in God Almighty. If one sees himself wearing the skin of a snake in a dream, it means that he will avow his enmity toward others. If one sees himself as a ram in a dream, it means that he will beget a son from whose success he will earn his livelihood. If one sees his body turn into iron or clay in a dream, it means his death. If one's body appears bigger in a dream, it means that he will prosper accordingly. Having a fat body in a dream means prosperity and knowledge, and an emaciated body in a dream represents poverty and ignorance. The body in a dream is what envelops and contains the human being. The body is like one's wife, a garment, a house, one's beloved, a child, a guardian, or a master. The health condition and strength of one's body in a dream may denote any of the elements mentioned herein. (*Also see Foot; Leg; Skin; Teeth; Tooth; Thigh*)

Bodyguard: (Agent; Escort; Secret service) A bodyguard in a dream represents someone who deceives people and leads them astray. If one sees his house filled with agents wearing white uniforms, it signifies glad tidings of recovering from an illness, or that he will escape from adversities and dispel his fears. If such agents in the dream are dressed in black uniforms, then they mean a sickness, distress or depression, and what they say during that dream also identifies their purpose. (*Also see Uniform*)

Boil: (Abscess; Tumor; Ulcer. *See Pimple*)

Boiled eggs: (*See Boiled vegetables*)

Boiled vegetables: (Blanched; Boiled eggs; Poached; Stew) In a dream, boiled vegetables, eggs, meat or poached eggs, etcetera, signify fast coming earnings, or a profitable business. Boiled vegetables in a dream also mean paying one's debts, an unanticipated arrival of something expected to happen later, celebrations, a wedding or distress, sorrow or poverty. Cooking mixed vegetables with milk in a dream means mixing lineage, or marriage from a different tribe, or it could mean starting a new and a good tradition. (*Also see Stew*)

Boiler: (Kettle; Roasting) In a dream, a boiler represents the seat of honor. (*Also see Hot water*)

Boiling water: Washing a deceased person with boiling water in a dream means that the latter is already suffering from hell in his own grave. (*Also see Hot water*)

Bolter: (Sieve; Sifter) A bolter in a dream signifies spiritual guidance, repentance from sin, a just judge who examines carefully each case, canvases the truth and discerns between truth and falsehood. A bolter in a dream also represents a man and a woman who do not carry evil in them. It may also signify harm, separation between beloveds or combing one's hair, or a rich man whose wealth is managed by his servant. (*Also see Sieve*)

Bond¹: (Band; Chain; Fetters; Shackle; Strap; Ties) In a dream, a bond signifies assiduity, piety, a pretext, an illness, an ongoing debt, cognizance of the one who puts the chain, or a rope around one's hands. A silver band in a dream means a lasting marriage. If it is a brass band in the dream, then it means decisiveness but with trickery and regarding something loathsome. If the bond is made from lead in the dream, then it means having determination about something weak or unworthy of such attention. A bond made with a rope in the dream signifies piety and religiousness. If it is mad of wood in the dream, then it means persistence in hypocrisy. If it is a bond made of a piece of cloth, or a thread in the dream, then it means attachment to something that will not last. In a dream, a bond also means delays when one is intending to travel, and for a merchant it means salability of his merchandise, and as for someone suffering from depression, it means perseverance of his sorrows. To see oneself tied-up in God's cause in a dream means caring for one's family. Seeing oneself tied-up or fettered in a city or a village in a dream means living there. Being bound inside a house in a dream means living with a difficult wife. Adding extra shackles to an already bound and bed stricken person in a dream means his death and for a prisoner, it means extension of his sentence. Wearing a green garment and seeing one's hands tied-up in a dream means spiritual growth. If one sees himself wearing a white garment, then it means knowledge, understanding, beauty and honor. If one sees himself wearing a red garment, it means that he is a musician, or that he is fascinated by music and a night life of distractions. Wearing a yellow garment in a dream means sickness. If one sees himself tied-up with a golden bond in a dream, it means that he is awaiting to recover money that he lost in an investment. If one sees himself in a dream tied-up inside a palace which is built from glass, it means that he will befriend a noble woman, though their friendship will not last. Seeing oneself being tied-up with another person in the dream means committing a sin and being afraid of its consequences. In general, a bond in a dream signifies distress and poverty. *(Also see Band; Chain; Fetter; Yoke)*

Bond²: *(See Contract; Knot; Friendship; Kinship; Relationships)*

Bondage: *(See Yoke)*

Bondman: *(See Slave)*

Bone breaker: *(See Angel of death; Eagle; Izrāil; Robbery; Osprey)*

Bone marrow: *(See Body¹; Marrow)*

Bones: (Animal bones; Money) Seeing animal bones in a dream means a new garment, one's capital, or a major event. Collected animal bones in a dream signify owning a shop, a house, or a real estate. If a poor person sees bones in his dream, they denote his piety and fulfillment of his religious duties. Bones in a dream also represent one's helpers, family, wife, children, vehicles and properties. Seeing one's bones in a dream means exposing one's secrets. If one sees his bones turned ivory in a dream, it means that his wealth is gathered from unlawful money. Bones also could represent trees and their fruits, while their marrow represents one's good character or knowledge. Bones in a dream also denote one's fitness or sickness. *(Also see Body¹)*

Bonesetter: *(See Orthopedist)*

Book dealer: *(See Bookseller)*

Book: (Decree; Flyer; Letter; Publication; Public announcement; Record; Scroll; Write; Writing) Holding a book or a letter in one's hand in a dream signifies power. A book or a letter in a dream also signifies fame or public knowledge. If one sees himself carrying a sealed letter in a dream, then it means that he will receive confidential news or a report. If a book or a letter is carried by a child in a dream, it means glad tidings. If it is carried by a servant or a housekeeper, then it means glad tidings and good news. If a letter is carried by a woman, then one could expect a quick relief from his trouble. If the letter which the woman is carrying in the dream is an open letter, and if the woman is wearing a veil, it means that the news she is bringing must be treated carefully. If the woman is wearing perfume, then one could expect good news and a commendation for his work. If one sees himself holding a closed book in a dream, it means the end of his life in this world. If one sees a flyer or a public announcement in display by the authorities in a dream, it means that he will gain leadership, happiness and income. If one sends a sealed letter to someone, which is returned to him unopened in the dream, it means losing a war to one's enemy. If he is a merchant, it means that he will suffer losses in his business. If he is seeking marriage, it means the denial of his request. If one sees himself carrying a book, a record, or a letter in his right hand in a dream, and if he had an argument, or a confusing deal, or doubt about something, it means that he will bring clarity to that problem. If he is incarcerated or if he is suffering from persecution, it means that he will bring proof of his innocence and escape from his difficulties. If he is depressed, it means that he will be able to dispel his worries. If he is travelling in a foreign country, it means that he will find a way back to his mother land, where he will find happiness again. Carrying a book or a letter in one's left hand in a dream means that he has done something bad, or something which he will regret. Carrying a book in the right hand denotes a prosperous year. If a stranger takes one's book away from him in the dream, it means that someone will take away from him his most precious and endeared thing. Tearing a book into pieces in a dream means getting rid of one's trouble or becoming free from trials or evil encounters and receiving benefits. Holding to a sealed book, decree, or a letter in a dream also signifies abiding by the rules of one's superior. Holding a sealed book in one's dream also signifies success, leadership and honor. If one is seeking marriage and sees a sealed book in his hand in a dream, it means that his betrothal to someone will end in marriage. Seeing or receiving a blank letter or a book from someone in a dream means absence of his news, or not knowing where he lives. If one sees a book descending to him from the heavens and if he thinks in the dream that he understood the contents, then whatever good or bad news it brings, it will be the same in wakefulness. A book in a dream also represents one's companion, or an intimate friend. Seeing a book in a dream also could signify recovering from an illness. A hardcover book if the content is unknown represents dishonesty, deceit, a cheap product or selling a sealed package with undisclosed contents, or it could represent an old woman. Bringing books into one's home in a dream signify hearing news about an honest and a pious person, learning happy stories from a reporter or becoming acquainted with religious thoughts. (Also see Encyclopedia; Letter; Write; Writer)

Bookbinder: (Bookbinding) A bookbinder in a dream represents an undertaker, or a tailor. In a dream, bookbinding also may mean concealing secrets and guarding one's friendship, or it could mean affection one reserves for a dear person.

Bookbinding: (See Bookbinder)

Bookseller: (Book dealer) In a dream, a bookseller represents someone who has vast knowledge or someone who gathers amazing stories. Seeing a bookseller in a dream also could mean overcoming one's trouble, solving one's problems, marriage, or the repentance of a sinner. (Also see Book; Bookstore)

Bookstore: In a dream, a bookstore represents spiritual guidance, repentance from sin, governments, evil, or arguments. (Also see Bookseller; Marketplace)

Booty: (Advantage; Gains; Profits; Spoils) In a dream, receiving a share in a booty means joy, happiness, profits, benefits, attaining one's goals, blessings in one's earnings, buying power, or it could mean abundance. (Also see Spoils)

Boötis: (See Constellations)

Boredom: *(See Breathing difficulty)*

Borer: *(See Drill)*

Borrowing: (Lending; Loan) If the borrowed object is pleasing in the dream, then it means good that will not last, and if the borrowed subject is despised, then it becomes a bad omen. Borrowing a vehicle, or taking a ride in a dream means unlawfully getting hold of someone else's property. Borrowing a valuable object from someone in a dream means paying indemnity, reparation, or a fine of equal value to the object borrowed in the dream. The borrowed object also could signify prosperity and success in one's life, or it could mean committing a shameful act, suffering from a scandal, or a warning which implies the need to avoid a scandal, deceit or corruption. Borrowing or lending in a dream represents the importance of, or one's need for such an object or his love for it. Thus, the enchantment which is derived from borrowing or lending an object to satisfy such things as love, attachment or need may be temporary. To borrow a bad object or something which is used for evil purpose or something one can do without, or an unnecessary thing means that one will suffer because of it, though one's sufferings will not last. To borrow a vehicle in a dream means to carry the lender's burdens or liability. *(Also see Lending; Loan)*

Bosom friend: (Vinegar)

Bosom: *(See Breast; Chest)*

Bottle: (Glass bottle; Water skin) In a dream, a bottle represents a money pouch, knowledge, a womb, or a despicable person. Seeing or carrying a bottle of honey in a dream means learning a trick from a loathsome person. Seeing or carrying a bottle of fuel in a dream means earning unlawful money through an evil person. Blowing into a bottle in a dream denotes having a son. The same interpretation is given for blowing air or inflating any sack or a balloon. Seeing a bottle of water in a dream may denote a wife, a husband, a host, a merchant, or a pregnant woman. *(Also see Glass bottle)*

Bounce: *(See Jumping)*

Bound: *(See Bond¹)*

Bow: In a dream, a bow means travels, a brother, a wife, a son or closeness to someone. A covered bow in a dream means that one's wife is pregnant. If a pregnant woman hands a man a bow in a dream, it means that she will conceive a girl from him. If a pregnant woman hands her husband a bow in a dream, it means that she will deliver a boy. Stretching the strings of a bow in a dream means longevity. Stretching it without an arrow in a dream means planning to travel. A broken bow in a dream signifies the death of a brother, a business partner, or a son. A bow is broken bow in a dream means that an accident may cause the hand of a brother or a business partner to fracture. Holding a broken bow in a dream means losing one's job or closing one's business. Seeing a young man attaching a string to a bow in a dream represents one's enemy. Attaching a string to a bow in a dream also means marriage, while detaching the string of a bow in a dream means divorce. Seeing oneself standing before a ruler with two bows length between them mean receiving an appointment. The two bows in a dream also represent one's eye-brows. Shooting arrows with a bow in a dream means speaking wrong about something or backbiting someone. Carving a bow in a dream means preparing to get married or begetting a son. Shooting an arrow and hitting one's target in a dream means fulfilling one's needs, or attaining one's goal. Selling one's bow and arrows in a dream means giving priority to one's religious life over that of his mundane one. Shooting hazelnuts in a town in a dream means backbiting people, while shooting hazelnuts in the forest means earning lawful money from hunting. Shooting arrows in front of the city hall in a dream means backbiting or slandering others. Shooting a pigeon in a dream means slandering one's own wife. Bending an arch in a dream means preparing for war. *(Also see Eye-brow)*

Bowels: *(See Intestines)*

Bower: *(See City)*

Bowing in prayers: *(arb. Rukü')* Seeing oneself bowing to God Almighty in prayers in a dream means submission to His will, abstaining from arrogance and establishing God's rules in one's life. Bowing in prayers also means fulfilling one's aspirations in this world and quickly triumphing over one's enemy. If one sees himself standing in prayers, but remains standing without bowing until the prescribed time elapses in a dream, it means that he does not pay his due alms. Bowing in prayers in a dream also means a job for someone who needs it most. Bowing in a dream also means longevity. If a woman sees herself bowing before God Almighty in prayers in a dream, it means repentance and exalting her name by protecting her chastity. *(Also see Prayers)*

Bowl: (Cup; Plate; Tray) In a dream, a bowl represents man's money pouch or what his wife would like to receive from him. If one sees himself receiving a bowl filled with sweets in a dream, it means receiving abundance of love from one's beloved. If the bowl is filled with sour food or some green raw vegetables in the dream, it means that animosity will develop on the part of his beloved, and it will provoke despise and fighting between husband and wife. Seeing a bowl in a dream also means increase in one's earnings. A bowl also represents a servant, a child, a daughter, a nanny, or a handmaiden. Licking a bowl in a dream represents one's earnings, and it could mean that he has consumed his lot in this life, or that he has reached the term of his life in this world. If one sees a large number of people gathering around a bowl to eat from it in a dream, it means a reunion of his clan, or it could represent the place of his dwelling. If they are people of true actions, it means that they will become friendly with him. If one urinates in a bowl or in a jar in a dream, it means that he will sexually abuse members of his own family. A bowl in a dream also represents one's beloveds and its contents represent one's love. Holding a bowl in a dream means a reunion with one's beloved. *(Also see Pot; Wooden bowl)*

Box¹: *(See Punch)*

Box²: (Trunk) In a dream, a box represents a wife, a beautiful woman, one's house, or it could mean one's shop. In a dream, a box also represents marriage for an unwed person and prosperity for a poor person.

Boy: (Young boy) Seeing a young boy in a dream means receiving glad tidings. Begetting a boy in a dream means worries, burdens or sickness, while giving birth to a girl in a dream means relief from distress or easing of one's difficulties. Carrying a young boy in a dream means carrying burdens. Giving birth to a boy in a dream also could mean having a helper. A beautiful looking young boy in a dream also signifies good luck and victory over one's enemy. Seeing a beautiful looking boy in a dream means that beautiful and pleasant things will take place in one's life, or it could mean satisfying one's needs. If one is called a teenager in a dream, it signifies the necessity to take a ritual ablution, or that something good or bad may take place in wakefulness.

Brace: (Corset; Jerkin; Knee brace; Support) In a dream, a brace signifies tight circumstances, difficulties, adversities, pain, sufferings, weakness and need for someone's support. A brace in a dream also may denote resoluteness and determination. If one sees himself using a brace with a support device in a dream, it means fulfilling one's purpose, wantonness, containing one's needs or satisfying them.

Bracelet: (Band; Bangle) In a dream, bracelets represent pride or women's ornaments, and for men they represent the support of one's brother. If the bracelet is made of gold in the dream, then it represents chastisement. If it fits tight in the dream, it means difficulties. If each wrist carries a silver bracelet or a bangle in a dream, it means disappointment or losses caused by one's friends. If a man sees himself wearing a bracelet in a dream, it means tight financial circumstances. Wearing a gold bracelet in a dream could represent a righteous person who strives with all his heart to do good. Should one have enemies, then God Almighty will support and strengthen him against them. Wearing a golden bracelet in a dream could mean either that he will be exploited or restrained, or it could mean that he will be handcuffed. If a ruler or someone in authority sees himself wearing a bracelet in a dream, it means that he will hold that job for sometime to come, that he will be just toward his subjects, and they will live happily and enjoy good earnings during his regency. If one sees his arms fitted with armlets in a dream, it means expansion or spreading of his authority along with fame. A bracelet also represents a son, a servant, or a close employee. If a woman sees herself wearing a bracelet in a dream, it means blessings, favors and joy. A silver bracelet in a dream means increase in one's profits. In general men wearing bracelets in a dream means distress, and for women it means ornaments. If one sees a deceased person wearing a bracelet in a dream, it means that he is in paradise. Wearing a golden bracelet is also interpreted as receiving an inheritance, a marriage, or bearing a child. Silver bracelets in a dream also could be interpreted as piety and observing one's religious duties. Bracelets in a dream also represent the noble people of a town, money, or beauty. If the bracelets are made from bones, ivory or cast iron, then they represent the despicable people of that town. Bracelets in a dream also can be interpreted as sorrows, imitations, the coming events of a town, or events it exports. *(Also see Armlet; Bond¹)*

Bragging: In a dream, bragging represents a tyrant, an unjust person, or an aggressor. If the person seen in a dream is already dead, it is a warning for his family. It also means failure to satisfy one's religious obligations. If the person noted in the dream is sick, then it means that he may be nearing his death. If he is healthy, then bragging while yawning in a dream means affliction with an illness. *(Also see Boast)*

Braiding: (Hair; Intertwine; Plait) Braiding women's hair in a dream is a sign of benefits and the same goes for men who usually braid their hair. As for the rest of people, braiding one's hair in a dream represents complications in one's life, unbearable debts, or confusion. *(Also see Hair)*

Brain: (Cerebrum) In a dream, a brain represents savings. Having an oversized brain in a dream means reason. Having no brain in a dream means ignorance. Eating from one's own brain or the marrows of one's own bones in a dream means suspicious dealing with one's own money. Eating someone else's brain in a dream means that one may die shortly or that he may steal someone's savings. A brain in a dream also may indicate one's beliefs, religious life and the work of one's innermost being. *(Also see Body¹; Marrow)*

Bran: In a dream, bran represents charities, discord, or people's filth.

Brand: *(See Besmear; Cauterize; Seal)*

Brass founder: (Foundry) In a dream, a brass founder represents someone who loves money and the possessions of this world. If one sees brass being shaped over an anvil in a dream, it means a fight. If one who is intending to be married sees brass in his dream, it means that his intended wife will be pertly, though insolent in speech.

Brass: (Money; Yellow) Brass in a dream means enmity. If one sees himself melting brass in a dream, it means that he will engages in a fight about mundane things and consequently becomes himself a subject of people's talk. It is also said that if one sees yellow brass in his dream, it means that he will hear harsh words and false statements. Yellow brass in a dream also represents a person who is proud about his worldly possessions. If one is beaten with a stick of brass in a dream, it means that he is seeking some worldly gains. Brass or similar yellow metals in a dream represent an imposter who swindles money from people, cheats and threatens them. *(Also see Coppersmith)*

Braying: *(See Donkey; Sound of animals)*

Brazier: (Coal stove; Charcoal grill; Grill; Fireplace) In a dream, a brazier or a coal holder represents one's wife, a housekeeper, or a well mannered child. One who befriends them will be honored and well treated.

Breach of a contract: (Betrayal; Death; Emptiness)

Breach: *(See Rupture of relations)*

Bread: (Loaf; Knowledge; Life; Longevity; Money; Mother; Nanny; Needs; Prosperity; Religion; A strong person.) When bread is made from bleached flour in a dream, it means blessed earnings and a comfortable life. When it is made with unbleached flour in a dream, it means disturbances in one's life. It is said that each loaf of bread represents forty years of one's life. Each loaf of bread also may represent money in denominations of tens, hundreds or thousands, all relative to the financial standing of the person in the dream, or the type of work he performs. Whole wheat bread, barley bread or sweet bread made with honey or sugar in a dream means rising prices. Eating bread with its crusts in a dream is like eating honey with its beeswax. Oven fresh bread when eaten in one's dream is best. Bread in a dream represents woman's chastity. Bread made with bleached flour means living a clean life, having pure knowledge, or a beautiful wife. If a student sees himself distributing bread among poor people in a dream, it means that he will attain his goals and succeed in his studies. If he is a preacher, it means that people are accepting his admonitions and advice. Otherwise, if he sees people crowding over him to get their bread in the dream, it means that people will seek what he has to offer. In that case, his position is better than theirs, for the giving hand is better than the receiving one. If one sees a deceased person offering him a piece of bread in a dream, it means that he will receive unexpected money from an unsolicited source. If one sees bread hanging in the skies, over the roofs or hanging down from trees in a dream, it means rising prices and the same interpretation applies for all commodities. If he sees bread scattered on the ground and people walking over it in a dream, it means prosperity in that land which leads to vanity. A good looking loaf of bread represents one's good religious stand, otherwise it means the opposite. Baking bread in a dream means working for one's livelihood. Seeing squandered loaves of bread and not eating from them in the dream means meeting with brothers one has not seen for a long time. Having a loaf of bread baked with coarsely grounded grains in the dream means living a comfortable life, though with insignificant religious attendance. If it is a loaf of barley bread in the dream, it means a strenuous life, though well managed. Corn bread, chick peas bread or millet bread means tight financial conditions and rising prices. If one is given a piece of dried bread in a dream, it indicates the near end of his life. A loaf of bread in a dream means marriage for an unwed person, and for a craftsman, it means progress in his trade. As for a ruler or a judge, a well baked loaf of bread in a dream represents his justice. Small loaves of bread in a dream represent a short life, while large loaves mean longevity. Eating a hot loaf of bread means hypocrisy, because the effect of the oven's heat is still in it. Eating bread without a meal means a sickness or dying alone. Eating from a loaf of bread which is half baked in a dream means that one may suffer from high fever. If a poor person eats sweet bread or a cake in a dream, it means sickness or loss of what he maybe expecting to receive. Eating the thin variety of rock baked bread in a dream means increase in one's earnings. A thin loaf of bread in a dream also could mean a short life. Holding two loaves of bread in a dream means marrying two sisters, one after the other. Eating simultaneously from two loaves of bread, one in each hand in a dream also means a marriage to two sisters. Eating pretzels in a dream means adopting a good health diet. Stale bread in a dream means inexpensive or shoddy prices. Dough in a dream means debts or loans. A flying loaf of bread with two wings means high prices. Eating a flat loaf of bread, or a loaf of pita bread in a dream means easy living or prosperity. Eating a bun in a dream denotes a decent financial stability. In a dream, a loaf of bread also represents little money or little earnings, or a small wage. *(Also see Dough)*

Break: *(See Rupture of relations)*

Breakfast food: (Cereal; Grits; Kasha; Oatmeal; Porridge) Having a tasty breakfast in a dream means honor, promotion or dispelling distress, adversities and illness. *(Also see Porridge)*

Breaking wind: *(See Fart)*

Breast-feeding: (Imprisonment; Suckling; Nursing) In a dream, it means being in need, becoming an orphan, business losses, being emotional or having a temper. If a woman sees herself breast-feeding a man in a dream, it means tightness of worldly means or imprisonment for both of them. Breast-feeding a child after weaning him in a dream means a sickness or imprisonment. Though, if a pregnant woman sees herself breast-feeding a child in a dream, it means that she will have a safe delivery. If one sees himself breast-feeding a hunted animal, or a domesticated one, or if one sees himself suckling their milk in a dream, it means that an affliction, or a calamity will strike at that person, then it will secede. If a man sees himself having milk in his breast in a dream, it means material success and prosperity. Should he breast-feed someone in that dream, it denotes ill consequences for both people. If a woman sees a man suckling milk from her breast in a dream, it means that he uses force with her to give him her money. If a woman sees herself moving between other women and breast-feeding them in a dream, it means that she will never yield milk. If a sick person sees himself suckling milk in a dream, it means that he will recover from his illness. *(Also see Milk)*

Breast: (Woman's milk-producing glands) A woman's breast in a dream represent's one's wife, progeny and a large property. They also represent honor and prosperity. Their beauty is her beauty, and their ailment is her illness. If one sees a woman hanging down from her breast in a dream, it means that she has committed adultery and that she will give birth to a bastard son. If a man sees milk coming from his breast, and if he is poor, it means that his poverty will end, his life will be a long one, and he will even carry the financial responsibility of caring for two of his brothers. If he is unmarried, it means that he argues about his fertility and doubts his own ability to conceive children. If a young woman sees her breasts in a dream, it means that she will bear a child. Otherwise, if a single young girl sees her own breasts in a dream, it means that she will get married. If a female child sees herself having matured breasts in a dream, it means her death. If a man sees himself suckling milk from a woman he does not recognize in a dream, it means a long sickness. Otherwise, if his wife is pregnant, it means kissing his wife's breasts. Suckling milk from a woman's breast also means imprisonment and deprivation, stress and sadness. If an old man sees the breast of a woman in his dream, it means that he will hear bad news. If a teenager sees that, it means that he is in love. If a man sees himself having a female milk suckling breast in a dream, it means friends, children, or a wife who are of no benefit to him. If such breasts look hanging tall in the dream, it means either death of one's child, or it could mean that one will commit a sin. If one's breasts are dripping milk in a dream, they represent a woman who cares about her home duty, or it could mean falling into debts. If one's breasts are transformed into iron or copper in the dream, it means loss of a child. A growth in children's bosom or breasts in a dream means an illness, festering wounds, or it could mean an ulcer. The nipple of the female breast in a dream represents one's personal wardrobe. Woman's breasts in a dream also may be interpreted to mean one's father and mother. *(Also see Body¹)*

Breathing difficulty: (Asthma) Experiencing breathing difficulties in a dream means boredom, annoyance, weariness or disgust.

Brewery: *(See Intoxicants)*

Bribe: (Allowance; Compensation; Reward; Skinning; Wages) A bribe in a dream represents burdens, torments and misfortunes. It also indicates one's jealousy of others and desire to strip them of what they have. *(Also see Compensation; Skinning an animal)*

Brick vendor: If one sees himself as a brick vendor, or if he meets a brick vendor in a dream, it means profits to be made from a business trip.

Brick-kiln: *(See Furnace)*

Bricks: (Adobe; Argillites; Plaster) In a dream, bricks mean lawful money. If they are interpreted to means a child, then they represent a miscarried fetus, or a child who may die in his infancy. If one sees baked bricks in his dream, they represent a son who will grow to be infamous, a backbiter and who will enjoy a long life. *(Also see Adobe)*

Bridal dower: *(See Dower)*

Bride: If one sees a bride on her wedding day, dressed in her beautiful robe, looking beautiful and adorned with flower in a dream, it means wealth in this world. If one sees himself as a bridegroom and could not see his bride or recognize her in the dream, or if she is not named or attributed to him in the dream, it means his death or that he may commit a murder. If one recognizes his bride, looks at her, and if she is named in the dream, it means that he will marry the same woman. If one sees himself getting married in a dream, it means that he will gain power equal to the position of that woman, her role, danger, her family's status, the meaning of her name, and her beauty. *(Also see Star; Wedding)*

Bridegroom: *(See Bride)*

Bridge of the Day of Judgement: *(arb. Ṣirāṯ)* This is the bridge people have to walk on after the Day of Resurrection to meet their Lord on the Day of Judgement. The ease of crossing it depends on the weight of deeds one is carrying. Some cross like lightening, while others have to carry their burdens and move at varying paste. Walking on it in a dream means a journey. If the bridge caves under one's feet in the dream, it means destruction and death. Seeing this bridge in a dream also represents knowledge, truth, believing in God's oneness and following the teachings and example of God's Messenger upon whom be peace. If one's foot slips while crossing in the dream, it means that he will miss the true path. If one sees himself walking the path in a dream, it means that he is on the right track, follows what is commanded and abstains from what is forbidden. It also means that one will undergo awesome changes, undertakes major responsibilities and succeeds to reach safety. If one's foot slips in a dream, it also means that he will fall into sin and deviate from the straight path.

Bridge: (Benefits) A bridge in one's dream represents the pillars of one's faith, the straight path, the Bridge of the Day of Judgement or perhaps it could mean knowledge, guidance, fasting, prayers, or any vehicle which assists one in his escape from the evils of this world or the punishment for one's sins in the hereafter. A bridge in a dream also represents a pious worshiper who patiently bears the harm people may inflict on him. It can also mean the path to fulfill one's needs, having a high ranking connection with the governor, or it could represent one's wife, father or mother. Each bridge in a dream represents its own type. A bridge connecting two streets in a dream may lead to the ruler or to someone in his cabinet, particularly if it is built from stones and covered with baked bricks. If it is a small bridge, then it can represent the secretary, door attendant of a governor, a superior, or it can be interpreted as a pimp. If a bridge which is built from stone is transformed in one's dream to look as if it were made of dirt, it means changing of one's status and vice-versa. If one sees himself transformed into a bridge in a dream, it means that he will be elected for a leadership post, and people will need him, his prestige and what he can offer. *(Also see Arched bridge; Bridge of the Day of Judgement; Contract; Knot; Transformation)*

Bridle: (Harness; Headgear; Reins of power; Restraint; Rope) In a dream, a bridle represents a wife, a battlefield, or a sickness. A bridle in a dream also means obedience, servitude or submission and wealth in the hands of the one who sees himself holding it. If a traveller sees a bridle in a dream, it means slow coming news from home. If a sick person sees the bridle of a horse in his dream, it means shattering of his hopes. If a traveller sees a bridle in his dream, it means being forsaken by others. A bridle in a dream also could mean protection from sin. *(Also see Rein)*

Broadcaster: (Anchorman; Announcer; Newscaster) A broadcaster in a dream represents someone who brings news or conveys both true, as well as false stories. He also represents someone who is punctual or someone who keeps his promises. A broadcaster in a dream also could represent a story teller, an advisor, a preacher, a reader, or an expert in investigating the news.

Brocade: (Silk brocade) Wearing a brocaded garment in a dream means attending a pilgrimage. Owning extensive yardage of silk brocade in a dream means piety, presiding over people, a marriage to a beautiful and a noble woman who is worthy of respect. Buying folded yardage of silk fabric in a dream means getting a housemaid. Wearing a silk brocaded garment in a dream means taking a beautiful and a virgin servant for a wife. If people of knowledge or religious leaders wear brocaded garment in a dream, it represents their love for the world, or misleading the people through innovation.

Broiling meat: *(See Roasting meat)*

Broker: (Auctioneer; Middle man; Stockbroker) A broker in a dream represents someone who brokers for either good or evil, or he could be someone broadcasting his own esteem. Such a person will be well recognized in wakefulness. A broker in a dream also represents a marriage broker, or a pimp. If an unknown broker visits a sick person in a dream, he then represents the angel of death. The visit of the undertaker in a dream means the same. *(Also see Auctioneer; Termite)*

Brooder: *(See Incubator)*

Brook: *(See Pond; Stream)*

Broom: (Boy; Employee) A broom in a dream represents one's family or household. Seeing it in a dream does not indicate a favorable sign. A broom in a dream also represents an employee, a housekeeper, or a servant. Sweeping the floors of one's house with a broom in a dream means becoming poor, or it could mean the death of a sick person in that house, or the distribution of one's property and possessions after his death. Sweeping a floor and collecting the trash in a dustpan in a dream means profiting from a project. A broom in a dream also may mean recovering from depression, overcoming difficulties, or satisfying one's debts.

Brother in-law: Having a brother in-law in a dream and particularly for someone who does not have in-laws means strength, peace and tranquility.

Brother: This category in a dream includes, the grandfather, the maternal and the paternal uncles and whoever has a share in one's inheritance. A brother in a dream means having shareholders in one's business.

Brown skin: (Tan) Brown skin in a dream represents mixed ancestry. *(Also see Colors)*

Bucket: (Well) If one sees himself drawing water from a well with a bucket in a dream, it means that he earns his money through deception, that is to acquire unlawful money. If he finds money inside the bucket instead of water in the dream, it means that he will suffer from a calamity. If he draws water from the well to fill a pitcher in the dream, it means that such money will soon be spent or that its benefits will be mixed with misdeeds. If one sees himself watering a garden from that bucket in a dream, it means that he will get married and benefit from his wife's wealth. If the garden blossoms with flowers in the dream, it means that he will beget a son. If one sees himself drawing water from an old well to give water to his camels or to provide drinks for people in a dream, it means that he performs good deeds and that he is a charitable person. He then becomes like a shepherd. If one draws water from an old well to give drink to animals in his dream, it means that he is a hypocrite and through falsehood, he fabricates as many tricks as the amount of water he draws from that old well. If one sees himself lowering the bucket into the well for himself to drink in the dream, it means that his so-called charitable deeds are solely done for his worldly gains, money, respect or status. If a prisoner sees himself drawing water with a bucket to take a bath in a dream, it means that he will escape from jail or that he will be released shortly. It also means that he will receive money and rejoice after his sorrows. If one's wife is pregnant and if he sees himself lowering a bucket in a well to draw water in a dream, it means that his wife will deliver a son. If he is a merchant, it means that his new merchandise will arrive safely to his shop. If he is sick, it means that he will miraculously wake-up healthy again. Standing by a well in a dream means blessings and benefits. A well in a dream also represents a woman. Otherwise, if one is a student, then the well represents his teacher. What one draws from a well in a dream also represents his luck.

Buckthorn tree: (*Genus Zizyphus; Jujube tree; Lotus tree; Shrubs*) In a dream, this warm climate buckthorn family tree that grows datelike fruit represents a noble and a generous woman, or a noble and a generous man. The greener is its color, the greater is such a person. Seeing the buckthorn tree in a dream means rising in station, developing piety and gaining knowledge. Eating its fruit in a dream means that one may fall victim to a sickness. Climbing a buckthorn tree in a dream means depression and adversities.

Buffalo: (Wild ox) A buffalo in a dream represents a strong, innovative and a forbearing leader, who is courageous and well respected by his followers. If a woman sees herself having buffalo's horns in a dream, it means that she will preside over a group of people or marry a man who is a leader in his community. A buffalo in a dream also represents an intelligent but fraudulent person who travels extensively and who is persistent in his demands. In a dream, a buffalo also means striving, toiling and tight handedness, though others may still benefit from him. If a buffalo is used in plowing in a dream, it connotes an insult, or a misdeed. *(Also see Caw; Counting buffaloes; Steer; Oryx; Ox)*

Bug: (Any small, blood sucking insect.) Seeing a bug in a dream means facing a weak enemy. If a small bug enters one's body in a dream, it means that a poor person will visit him to receive some mental satisfaction or to solicit a small financial support. *(Also see Flea)*

Build: *(See Building; Figure)*

Builder: A builder, or a brick layer in a dream represents a righteous person who brings people's hearts together. If he does not accept wages for his work, then in reality such a person is a man of virtue and moral excellence. A builder in a dream also represents a poet, longevity or he may represent the element of greed and desire to amass the world because of his continuous asking for bricks and cement to fasten them together. A builder, or a brick layer in a dream also means unity, love and support. Demolishing a building in a dream means negating promises and failing to comply with the conditions of an agreement. *(Also see Builder)*

Building: The element of a good building in a dream represents love, affection, unity, progeny, prosperity, a garment of honor, and girls in one's family. A strong edifice means strength and firmness. It also means support, help and a long life. Raising a new edifice in a dream represents either personal or collective material benefits in this world. If one sees himself building an edifice in a dream, it means having intercourse with his spouse. If one builds a church, it defines him as Christian. If he builds a mosque, it defines him as Muslim. If a man of knowledge sees himself building a mosque as an offering to please God Almighty in a dream, it means that he will compile a study from which others will benefit or that people will seek his advice in religious matters or inter-pretations. If a king, or a ruler sees himself building a mosque as an offering for God's pleasure in a dream, it means that he will rule his subjects with justice, command what is lawful and forbid what is unlawful. If he builds a school, it shows him to be a man of knowledge. If he builds a hospice in a dream, it means that he is an ascetic. If a sick person sees himself building a house in a dream, it means that he will recover from his illness and enjoy good health. Seeing buildings in a dream explains one's determination, it also means one's wants for himself when he rejoices at finding something suitable for status. If one sees his house bigger than it is in reality in a dream, it means expansion in one's material resources. If it grows beyond the normal norms in a dream, it means anxiety, or a delegation that hastens to enter that house without permission, announcing a calamity, or it could mean that a wedding will take place in that house. Building a house in a dream also means extending one's connections, strengthening one's relationship with his kin, friends, or if the person in question is a general in the army, or a leader, then it means building a strong army. Building a house in a dream also means regaining power, rejoicing or success in one's business, all of which are relative to the thickness of its walls. On the other hand, demolishing one's house in a dream means disagreement, disintegration or separation of one's family, relatives, friends, associates or dissolution of one's army. If one sees himself working for some people to renovate an old building in a dream, it means correcting the norms of conduct in that community or reviving old traditions. For example if one sees himself reconstructing the house of Pharaoh in a dream, it means that he is reviving or reestablishing Pharaoh's system of government, or adopting its principals. Erecting a foundation for a building, then completing its structure in a dream means seeking knowledge, wisdom or leadership. Building a house in a different county, town or locality in a dream means a marriage with a woman from that neighborhood. Building an edifice from ceramic in a dream means decorating oneself. If the building is from clay in the dream, it means lawful earnings. If one engraves pictures or forms thereon in the dream, it means acquiring knowledge, learning a new craft, a leading position in the government which involves partying, alcohol and mingling with what is unlawful. Building an edifice from plaster or backed bricks encrusted with pictures or forms in a dream means engaging in an unlawful or a deceitful act. Building a house in a dream and strengthening its walls, means to complete the father's traditions, and to continue working in his trade. *(Also see Builder)*

Bull: (Cow; Ox; Steer) A bull in a dream represents the chief of the council or the mayor of the town or village. Seeing a bull in a dream also means winning the mayoral seat for a term or losing it after one year. If one sees himself owning a herd of steers in a dream, it means receiving a governmental office and a vast authority should he qualify for it. His employees' support depends on how manageable is his herd. If a man sees himself riding a steer in a dream, it means dealing with a government employee. It also means that he will acquire what he intends. Seeing a bull in a dream also means fame. If one sees himself eating the head of a steer or a bull in a dream, it also means winning a leadership seat in the government, except if the bull is red. If one is a merchant, then it means profit and prosperity for that year. If a steer is transformed into a wolf in a dream, it means that a government's employee will turn corrupt. A white bull in a dream means glad tidings and profits. If a steer or a cow butts against someone in the dream, it means that God is displeased with him. Eating bull's meat in a dream means financial comfort. If a bull bites someone in a dream, it means suffering from an illness or begetting children who will grow to be honorable and righteous people. If one sees an ox mooing at him in the dream, it means undertaking a distant or a long journey. If a farmer sees an ox plowing his fields in a dream, it means a good harvest for that year.

Bulldozer: In a dream, a bulldozer means leveling things, changing them, changing one's profession, moving from one town to another, or it could mean spreading gossip. A bulldozer in a dream also represents someone who is carrying a difficult responsibility and who depends on a strong and courageous man to help him do it.

Bullet proof jacket: A bullet proof jacket maker in a dream represents someone who makes difficult work easier, one who helps people to attain their goal, a marriage broker, one who teaches people about good conduct, or one who disseminates knowledge or teaches about behavior modification, though he masks hypocrisy.

Bullfight: (Butting; Thrusting) A bullfight or a goat fight with horns in a dream means preparing for war. It also could mean joining a festival, a show of innovation, or participating in heedless activities. Thrusting or bumping someone with the head in a dream means plagues, illness or calamities that will affect both parties. If blood flows from their heads because of such blows in the dream, it means that they will both suffer evil consequences and losses. Thrusting against someone with the head during a fight in a dream also means having pride about one's ancestry.

Bully: *(See Panderer; Pimp)*

Bummer: *(See Hobo)*

Bunch of dates: (Dates) Having a bunch of dates in a dream means savings, family reunion and each bunch of dates represents a member of a clan, or a head of a household.

Bunch of grapes: *(See Grapes)*

Bunch: (Bundle) In a dream, a bunch or a bundle represents atonement for one's sin, or something offered to compensate for failing to fulfill a vow, or it could mean a tainted business or money. *(Also see Bunch of dates)*

Bundle: *(See Bunch)*

Buoyancy: *(See Laughing)*

Burden: (Carrying weight; Forbearance; Porter; Serving others)

Burglary: *(See Robbery)*

Burial ground: *(See Cemetery)*

Burial: If one sees himself being buried after his death in a dream, it means that he will undertake a long journey during which he will be short of money. If one sees himself being buried alive and if he recognizes the one burying him in the dream, it means that the latter will assault him, oppress him, imprison him or cause him injustice. If he dies in his grave after his burial in the dream, it means that he may die from such sufferings. Should he survive such adversities in the dream, it means that he will escape from such fear, prison or injustice. If he sees the other person driving him to the edge of his grave in a dream, it means that he will lead him to his death, though his name will be praised after his death. If the other person places him inside a coffin in a dream, it means that he will move to a new home. If the other person fills the grave with dirt on top of him in the dream, it means that he will be piled with money equal to the amount he is being buried under in the dream. It is said that to be buried alive in a dream means losing one's spirituality or religious commitment, unless one comes out of it alive. If one walks out of his grave covered with dirt, then shakes off the dust in the dream, it means that his state is hopeless or that his repentance has little chance to hold. To be buried alive in a dream means imprisonment or despise by others, or a severe punishment which makes one's chastisement an exemplary lesson to others, If a gnostic or a wise man is seen buried alive inside his own house, or if he is brought out of it alive in a dream, it means that one will inherit him in knowledge, wisdom and status. The same interpretation is given if one sees a prophet or a holy man walking out of his grave alive. To be buried after death, after sunrise, at noon or at the sunset hour in a dream means that one is being warned about doing what is good and abstaining from what is evil. To be buried alive in a dream is wrong and means betrayal. It could also mean marriage, prosperity or peace and tranquility after suffering and hardships. If one sees a deceased person burying him alive in a dream, it means that one's due debts are not payed, or that one will be imprisoned to satisfy his debts, or that his collateral was not accepted. To bury a dead person twice means that one is covering his faults. If one sees a deceased person burying another deceased person in a dream, it means unity, clearing of the hearts, love and friendship between relatives, or perhaps it could mean imprisonment, marriage, a sickness, a trust, or guaranteeing a loan. Seeing oneself being buried after death in a dream means that one needs to repent before death. Should he still walk alive from his burial in the dream, it means that he may repent again. God knows best. *(Also see Cemetery; Grave)*

Buried alive: *(See Burial)*

Burn: *(See Cauterize)*

Burning coal: *(See Coal)*

Burning incense: *(See Aloe perfume; Civet; Incense; 'Ud)*

Burnishing: (Polishing; Shining) A wood finisher burnishing a piece of furniture in a dream represents a minister, or a statesman who deals with the high and the low. It also could mean associating with righteous people who point out one's pitfalls and help him to remove his ills. *(Also see Sanding)*

Burp: Burping in a dream connotes a beneficial discussion.

Burping: *(See Belching)*

Burrow: *(See Tunnel)*

Burrowing: *(See Mole)*

Bushel: *(See Half a bushel)*

Business association: *(See Partnership)*

Business loss: *(See loss)*

Bustard: (Bird; Fowl) A bustard in a dream represents a rich person and a spendthrift with limited benefits to others and a gluttonous personality.

Busy: (Involved; Occupied) Seeing oneself busy in a dream means marriage to a virgin girl, interfering in others' business, or changing one's profession. If the new job is satisfactory in the dream, then it means prosperity, marriage, children, or worship.

Butcher block: In a dream, butcher's chopping block represents a hypocrite who interferes in people's business and takes sides in their arguments.

Butcher's knife: *(See Cleaver)*

Butcher: A butcher in a dream represents the angel of death. Taking a knife from a butcher in a dream means falling sick, then recovering from one's illness to become strong and healthy again. In a dream, a butcher also represents a man who causes destruction or evil, and particularly if he is seen holding his cutting knife, or if he is wearing a white uniform stained with blood. If one sees himself as a butcher wearing clean cloths, it represents longevity. A good looking butcher in a dream represents a prosperous culmination of one's life, or changing one's trade. If someone looks at him with despise or in the wrong way in the dream, it means that something is unlawful in what he sells. If the butcher is a man in the dream, he then represents the angel of death. Whatever place he appears in will bear the consequences. A butcher in a dream also represents an unjust person. In a dream, if one sees a butcher who specializes in selling animal heads, he represents a guardian of people's estates, or a treasurer of a company, he also could represent adversities or death. If the animals' heads cannot be identified in the dream, and if they still have their skin, hair, and are dripping blood in the dream, then it means the disappearance of the people of knowledge and that knowledge will become selectively disseminated by political leaders. Cattles' heads here represent people in danger. Buying an animal's head from a butcher in a dream means asking one's superior for a teacher for a special training, a coach, a continuing education program, or a better job. If a butcher slaughters an animal for fun in a dream, it means suspicion about one's spiritual standing. Walking in a butchers market in a dream means adversities, sufferings, a quick death for sick people, loss of wealth for rich people, or the fear of people who are under oppression, or the scare of a person in debt concerning his family or property, or the fears of a person awaiting a court judgment. It is also said that a butcher in a dream represents tyranny and bloodshed. If a prisoner sees a butcher in his dream, it means that he will soon be released from jail. Seeing a butcher in a dream also signifies safety, dispelling fears, protection, silence, vanquishing one's enemy, or it could mean meeting with a persuasive travel agent. *(Also see Meat)*

Butler: *(See Skewer; Wick)*

Butter: Eating butter in a dream means enjoying one's earnings and using them for worthwhile projects, or it could mean profits from one's business. It is said that eating butter in a dream means visiting the holy land. Eating butter in a dream also represents good harvest, plenitude, prosperity, good deeds, or the ease with which one handles his daily work. *(Also see Cream; Ghee)*

Butterfly: (Moth; Silkworm) In a dream, a butterfly signifies ignorance, lack of experience with people, or inexperience with the proper protocol. A butterfly in a dream also could signify love and sacrificing one's life for others. A butterfly in a dream also represents fire worshipers, fear, or a weak enemy who speaks big words. If a farmer sees butterflies in his dream, it means hardships and lack of work, or consenting to evil by associating with evil companions, or befriending vile women. A silkworm in a dream represents the best of people who spend in charity from their best and who curtail their evil, or it could represent children who live a short life in this world, or people who leave a sizeable estate for their posterity. A silkworm, or a butterfly in a dream also could signify a short life, the near end of one's life, a miller, or it could represent a painter. *(Also see Magician)*

Butterskin: *(See Churn)*

Butting: *(See Bullfight)*

Buttocks: *(See Rump)*

Button: (Buttonhole; Fastener; Man) A button in a dream represents protection, guarding one's honor, a just contract, money, or profits particularly if the button is made of silver or gold. A button and a buttonhole in a dream also represents a man and a woman. If an unwed person sees himself buttoning a shirt in a dream, it means that he will get married, or that he will play an important role in uniting two people, or to bring peace between two partners, or that he will revive an old and a forsaken project. Tying one's buttons in a dream means getting married, or going through difficult financial circumstances. Wearing a buttoned shirt in a dream means experiencing tight circumstances, or reuniting with a traveller returning home, or marriage of an unmarried person. *(Also see Clothing)*

Buttonhole: *(See Button)*

Buyer: A buyer in a dream represents someone under obligation; emergency; or need to acquire something. Buying something, then selling it in a dream means needing people's help. In a dream, a buyer also could represent a demanding situation that may push someone to use tricks and to deceive others. *(Also see Seller)*

Buying: In a dream, buying something means selling it. *(Also see Sale)*

Byre: *(See Carriage house)*

C

Cabbage: A cabbage in a dream represents distress, money or a rough person. In general, a head of cabbage in a dream has negative connotations for everyone and particularly for its farmers.

Cable: (Hawser; Rope) Seeing a cable in a dream means a robbery, profits, longevity or it could mean marriage.

Cactus: (Aloe plant) Eating or smelling a cactus plant in a dream means sorrow, sadness, separation between husband and wife or it could mean enduring an unhappy life.

Cadet: *(See Panderer; Pimp)*

Cadger: *(See Hobo)*

Cage maker: In a dream, a cage maker represents a builder, a tailor, marriage, a teacher, a prison guard or a weaver.

Cage: (Cradle; House; Prison) In a dream, a cage represents a prison, a cradle or a house. Entering one's head into a cage while walking in the markets in a dream means selling one's house. A cage in a dream also signifies complications. Seeing a cage inside a courthouse in a dream means marriage.

Cain: (Murderer) Cain, the oldest son of Adam and Eve, who killed his brother Abel. Seeing him in a dream means concealing a murder. If one who is not a murderer sees Cain in a dream, it means that he will be involved in something which he will regret terribly.

Cairo: *(See Egypt; Masjid)*

Cake: If a poor person sees himself eating modified bread or a cake in a dream, it means sickness or loss of something one is anticipating to receive. *(Also see Bread)*

Calamity: (Catastrophe; Destiny; Fate; Kismet) In a dream, calamity represents the opposite effect in real life, meaning: rejoicing after suffering from great distress.

Calculate: *(See Counting)*

Calculator: *(See Abacus)*

Caldron: (Kettle) In a dream, a caldron represents a practical method through which things can develop properly. It also represents a mediator, a go-between or a friend with important connections.

Calendar year: *(See Year)*

Calf: In a dream, a calf represents a newborn son. A broiled calf meat in a dream means appeasement of one's fears or glad tidings of a firstborn son, or it could mean distress, trouble and disobedience. If a woman sees a calf adorned with golden ornaments and jewelry in her dream, it means happiness, joy and celebrations. On the other hand, an adorned calf in a dream also could mean temptations and corruption. Eating calf meat in a dream means money gained from a man or a woman. If one sees himself carrying a calf into his house in a dream, it means distress, sorrow and dismay.

Calif: (Caliphate; Deputy; King; vice-regent) A calif in a dream represents order, leadership, justice or a deputy who establishes God's Laws on earth. If one sees himself attempting to kill the calif in a dream, it means opportunism or seeking an important advancement that one will attain. *(Also see King)*

Caliphate: *(See Calif; King; Vice-regent)*

Call to prayers: (Azān; Muezzin) Hearing the call to prayers in a dream denotes the pilgrimage season or announces its holy months. It also may indicate backbiting, a theft, announcing a major move or blowing the trumpets of war, or it could denote rank and honor or obeyed commands of the one seeing the dream, or perhaps announcing a wife for an unmarried man, and it could mean telling the truth. Hearing the call to prayers in a language other than the Arabic in which it was revealed in a dream means lies and backbiting. If one sees a woman calling to prayers, standing on the top of a minaret in a dream, it means innovation and trials. If children give the call to prayers in a dream, it means that people filled with ignorance will rule the land. This is particularly true when the call is made outside the proper time. If a suitable person sees himself adequately calling to prayers in a dream, it means that he will be appointed to govern a land which is as vast as his voice can reach in the dream. If one does not fit the conditions of ruling, then it means that his enemies will increase in number. If he is a merchant, it means that his business will grow. Hearing the call to prayers in a dream also may represent invocations, supplications and good prayers. If one sees himself calling to prayers from inside a well in a dream, it means that he will call people from another land to walk the path of God Almighty, to follow the jurisprudence He made obligatory upon humanity, and to adopt the divine laws as their way of life and religion. If calling from inside a well is done from within a Muslim country in the dream, it means that he is a spy or an innovator who is introducing changes to God's laws. If one sees himself calling to prayers from the top of the Scared House of Ka'aba in a dream, it means that he is an innovator. If he calls to prayers while laying down in his bed in a dream, it means that his wife is backbiting and slandering the neighbors. If he makes the call at the door of a king in a dream, it means that he will testify to the truth in a court of justice. If one's call is made while travelling in a caravan or in a marketplace in a dream, it means that he will expose a band of thieves. If he makes the call to prayers from inside a ruin in a dream, it means that such a place will be rebuilt and people will live in it. If one sees himself calling to prayer from inside a bathhouse or while under the shower in a dream, it means that he will suffer from a fever. If he sees himself calling and no one is answering his call in a dream, it means that he belongs to the company of unjust people. If he calls with a beautiful voice and the people hearken to his call in the dream, it means that he is seeking the approval of people in authority. If he sees himself calling to prayer while being naked, it represents his recklessness and contempt about his own religion. Calling to prayer standing on a pile of trash in a dream means calling a stupid person to make peace but to no avail. Hearing the call to prayers given inside a marketplace means the death of one of the merchants.

Call-up: *(See Conscription)*

Call: *(See Shout)*

Caller to prayers: (Muezzin) In a dream, he is the person who calls for what is good and blessed, or he could represent a broker or an officiant who performs wedding ceremonies or the messenger of the king or his door attendant. *(Also see Muezzin)*

Caller: *(See Clouds; Invisible caller; Shouting)*

Calligrapher: (Copyist; Handwriting) A calligrapher in a dream represents knowledge, charting and clarity. Otherwise, a calligrapher may represent distress, trouble, unhappiness, seeing everything dark, or he could represent uptightness. A calligrapher in a dream also represents someone who teaches people tricks, for writing is a trick. *(Also see Writer)*

Calling someone: (Shouting) If one is called by name from a short distance in a dream, it means that he will befriend lowly street people. If one's name is called from the horizon or from the furthest end of a valley in a dream, it means that he will attain an honorable status and rank. If one's name is called from a great distance in a dream, it means that he has disobeyed God's commands and is suffering by being distanced from his Lord.

Calumniation: In a dream, calumniation means fire, harsh words, rebuke or slander.

Camel driver: In a dream, a camel driver represents a manager, a guide, a sailor, the captain of the ship, travels, or death of a sick person.

Camel litter: *(See Palanquin)*

Camel: (Arabian camel; Bactrian camel; Ride) Riding a camel who is obedient to his master in a dream means solving one's problem at the hand of a foreigner. If an Arab helps resolving one's problem in the dream, it means that the person in the dream will perform a pilgrimage to God's House in Mecca. If he dismounts his camel during his journey in a dream, it means that he will be inflicted with a disease that will obstruct his journey. If one sees himself leaping over a camel in a dream, it means distress, a sickness or a growing enmity toward an insolent person. If one finds himself unable to control his camel in a dream, it means being overcome by a strong opponent. If one sees himself holding the reins of a camel and driving it on a paved road in a dream, it means that he will guide a heedless person and lead him on the straight path. If one takes the camel through a side road in a dream, it means that he will lead such a person into wrongdoing. If a she-camel leaves one's house in a dream, it means separation from one's wife through either a divorce or death. A camel in a dream also represents prosperity, trials, a tree or women's holdings. A tamed camel in a dream represents a learned person. Collecting camel's fur in a dream means money. *(Also see Counting camels; Milk)*

Camphor tree: *(See Camphor)*

Camphor: (A gummy compound with a volatile fragrance from the camphor tree. Camphor tree; Evergreen tree) In a dream, camphor represents a commendation, honor or giving charity in secret, conceiving a child, or it could mean good deeds. *(Also see Shrouding; Mummification)*

Canal: (Channel; Water passage; Watercourse) In a dream, a canal represents a woman, money or a scholar. Running a watercourse or a channel in a dream means getting married, building a business, or it could mean finding a job and serving one's family and community. Seeing a canal in a dream also means sufferings caused by a member of one's family. Water channels in a dream represent servants or housekeepers. A canal in a dream also could signify a lavatory, sewage, a marketplace, or it could mean a shop. Thus, digging a canal in a dream also could mean prosperity and spending money to support one's family and dependents. Blocking a canal in a dream means divorce, separation between husband and wife, cutting off one's blood ties, leaving one's homeland, or separation from one's clan. Blocking a canal in a dream also means quitting one's job or cancelling a debt, or it could mean closing a business. Seeing a watercourse running inside one's house in a dream means blessings and prosperity. Urinating in a canal or a watercourse in a dream means committing a sin, engaging in unlawfulness or molesting a servant. A canal in a dream also could represent the housekeeper who cleans people's dirt, a street sweeper, or it could mean a forbidden marriage. A dry canal in a dream signifies cessation of business, unsalable merchandise, a dead market or discord with one's wife, suffering from a urinary bladder, or having kidney problems. If one digs a canal and no water runs through it in a dream, it means deception.

Canary: *(See Roller)*

Cancer: *(astr. See Moon)*

Candleholder: In a dream, a candleholder represents a wife if the person is unwed, and it represents a son for a married man. *(Also see Chandler)*

Candlelight: (Wax) In a dream, a candlelight represents might or a noble son who is generous and giving. Melting wax of a burning candle in a dream represents hard earned, but lawful money. If an unmarried person sees a candlestick in his dream, it means marriage, an important appointment, a righteous man or guidance of a heedless person, or richness of a poor person. *(Also see Chandler)*

Candles store: In a dream, a candles store represents repentance and guidance. *(Also see Chandler)*

Candor: *(See Vulture)*

Candy maker: A candy maker in a dream represents a man of knowledge, or he could mean profits. *(Also see Candy salesman)*

Candy salesman: (Candy shop) In a dream, a candy salesman represents a kind and a gentle person. If he receives money for his candies in the dream, it means that he praises people with kind words and they praise him back with better words. *(Also see Candy maker)*

Candy: (Cash) In a dream, a candy signifies hard earned money, release from prison, recovering from an illness, delivering a child, or it could mean enrolling in a school to acquire knowledge or to learn a trade. Candy in a dream also means cash.

Caner: *(See Caning)*

Canine: *(See Dog)*

Canines: *(See Tooth)*

Caning: (Basket weaver; Caner; Mesh weaver; Reed) In a dream, a caner represents a weaver, a tailor, a builder, an architect or a grave digger.

Canis Major: (Constellation. *See Dog*)

Canis Minor: (Constellation. *See Dog*)

Canopy[1]: (A canopy with drapes covering one's bed; Mosquito net; Transparent hood) In a dream, the canopy that drapes over one's bed represents a good woman or a well mannered man. In a dream, a canopy also may represent one's wife, or it could mean affliction, grief, distress or darkness. *(Also see Bed; Couch; Mattress)*

Canopy[2]: (Pavilion; Tent) Setting up a pavilion in the open air to sit under it in a dream means gaining power and dominion. A canopy in a dream also means visiting the graves of martyrs and praying for them, or to die in their state. Folding a canopy in a dream means losing one's power and dominion, or it could mean nearing the end of one's life. Walking out from under a canopy in a dream means losing some of one's power or business. Walking out from under a canopy in a dream also signifies trueness of one's heart and intention, or earning the station of a martyr through one's true devotion, or it could mean visiting the Sacred House in Jerusalem. *(Also see Pavilion; Tent)*

Canyons: (Mountain pass; Mountain trails) In a dream, deep valleys or canyons represent deception, betrayal, perfidy and trickery. Seeing a mountain pass in a dream also could signify overcoming adversities or relief from difficulties. *(Also see Aqīq canyon)*

Cap: (Overseas cap; Persian toga; Roman toga; Shawl) In a dream, a cap means travels, a wife who is supporting her husband, or a husband who is supporting his wife. A shawl-like attire that is worn over the head and shoulders in a dream represents honor, valor, a new trade, travel, a brother or a father. Taking off a cap in a dream means losing one's authority or loss of his wealth. A torn cap in a dream means the death of one's brother or father. Wearing a cap in a dream also means repayment of one's debts. *(Also see Coat; Overcoat)*

Capote: *(See Coat; Overcoat)*

Capricorn: *(astr. See Moon)*

Captain: Seeing a captain of a sea vessel, or the pilot of an airplane in a dream signifies distant travels, a business, or profits. *(Also see Camel driver)*

Captivated: *(See Fond)*

Car racing: *(See Racing)*

Car: (Automobile; Carriage; Carrier; Coach; Lift; Litter; Transport; Vehicle; Wheels) In a dream, a car represents someone who properly manages his life, for a car is made from many well coordinated parts, and carries many things and transports them from one location to another. If one sees himself riding a litter that is carried by people in a dream, it means that he will preside over people or beget a son who will be elevated in rank. If a traveller sees a car in his dream, it means that his trip will take a slow turn and he will be delayed. A car in a dream also signifies dignity, honor, advancement and attainment. If one sees himself holding to a car or running after it in a dream, it means that he will lobby someone in authority and profit from him as much as his nearness to such a car. If one sees himself riding on a cargo vehicle in a dream, it means suffering from distress and sorrow. *(Also see Carrier; Racing)*

Caraway: (Herb) In a dream, caraway represents a profitable investment.

Carbonize: *(See Coal)*

Carder: (Teasing bow) In a dream, a teasing bow for carding cotton represents a disgraceful and a repulsive woman. The string or spike of a carder represents her groaning husband. Holding a carder in a dream means befriending someone filled with hypocrisy and repugnance. *(Also see Cotton)*

Carding: *(See Cotton)*

Carefulness: (Concern; Conscious; Watchful) Being too careful about something that does not call for extraordinary concern in a dream means hypocrisy, straying from the truth or forgetting the divine admonition of the Holy Qur'ān or any part of it.

Caressing: (Tender touch) In a dream, caressing a bird, a dog, a cat, a horse or a cow, etcetera, means having a soft heart, speaking gentle words, ability to draw people to oneself. Caressing someone during the daylight in a dream means slandering and backbiting him. Caressing a woman in a dream means that one will become a translator, or it could represent a frivolous person or someone who appeals to ludicrous people, or it could mean self-adulation or deficiency in one's craftsmanship.

Cargo: (Load; Shipment) Receiving a shipment in a dream means a burden, impediments, an illness, affliction, uneasiness or anxiety. *(Also see Car)*

Carnal self: (Abode; Bad; Dwellings; Desire; Ego; Good)

Carnation: *(bot. See Gillyflower; Musk)*

Carnelian-red: *(arb. 'Aqīq. A variety of chalcedony; Crystalline mineral; Gem; Jewelry; Precious stone; Stone)* Seeing a Carnelian-red stone in a dream means dispelling poverty. At the beginning of the creation, of all stones, the Carnelian-red was the first stone that testified to God's Oneness. If one sees himself in a dream concluding his ablution or ritual bath with the essence of a Carnelian-red, it means that he owns something blessed. Such blessings will manifest in one's work and success in his material as well as spiritual life. A Carnelian-red stone in a dream also represents one's progeny, good religious conduct, good character, while seeing the white variety of this stone has a stronger meaning and a better attribute than the red. *(Also see Aqïq canyons; Aqïqah rites)*

Carnelian: (Gem; Stone; Semi-precious. *Also see Carnelian-red; Ring*)

Carob tree: *(See Tree)*

Carob: (Carob beans) In a dream, carob beans means debilitation or death of a sick person, whether he eats it in his dream or not. In general, carob in a dream means destruction and perdition. *(Also see Tree)*

Carpal tunnel: *(See Veins)*

Carpenter: A carpenter in a dream represents a teacher or an educator. Seeing a carpenter in a dream also means curbing off the intentions of hypocrites and obliging them to comply with what is correct. Constructing a canoe in a dream means travels. Building a water-wheel in a dream means profits from real estate, building a mill in a dream means disputes. Fixing a door latch in a dream means marriage or children. Building a plow in a dream means farming. *(Also see Construction worker)*

Carpet weaver: (Architect; Engineer; Graphic artist) A carpet weaver in a dream represents a marriage officiant. *(Also see Architect; Artist; Carpet)*

Carpet: (Straw mat) Owning a carpet or a straw mat on which one sits in the wintertime in a dream means comfort, promotion, high ranking status and exaltation. A carpet in a dream also represents the master of the house. All types of carpets or mats are included in this category. If one sees himself sitting on a carpet in a dream, it means that he will purchase a property or a farm. In a time of war, sitting on a carpet in a dream means safety from danger. If one sees himself gazing at a carpet in the dream, and if he sees in it the image reflection of a person he recognizes, it means that the figure drawn on the carpet is a person who has gone astray. It also means that such a person will present him with an amazing report that will be infested with falsehood. A carpet in a dream also means worldly gains for its owner. If it is folded in the dream, it means that his worldly interests are limited. A folded carpet in a dream also means restricted income, difficulties in travels, tightness in one's heart about some concerns or lack of success in establishing a good livelihood. A new and well made carpet in a dream also represents a long life to its owner, prosperity and decisiveness. Seeing a carpet spread for one to sit on it and whose owner is unknown in an unknown place in a dream means that one will emigrate to a foreign land and succeed in establishing a good livelihood for himself. If in such a place the carpet is thin in the dream, it means worldly gains and longevity. Sitting on a carpet in a dream also means associating with leaders and judges. If one's carpet is stolen, burned or thinned in a dream, it means nearing the term of his life in this world, afflictions, illness or emaciation. An old torn carpet in a dream means distress, or a man who boosts about himself, who exalts his status and consequently emerges to be a liar and false.

Carriage house: (Barn; Byre; Coach; Cowshed; Stall) A carriage house in a dream represents the assembly place of politicians, leaders, scholars, merchants, visitors or spectators. The condition in which the carriage house appears in one's dream reflects the state of such groups of people. *(Also see Barn; Stableman)*

Carriage: *(See Car)*

Carrier: (Driver; Mail carrier; Messenger; Renter) In a dream, a carrier means that one will recover from an illness, or fall into one, pay for his sins, carry burdens, endure sufferings, or bring comfort to others. A carrier in a dream also represents a forerunner, a guardian, a mail carrier, or a police officer.

Carriers of The Divine Throne: Seeing the carriers of the Divine Throne of God Almighty in a dream represents glory, integrity, might, unity, affection, concord and the company of the good ones. Seeing them in a dream confirms one's true faith, belief and his nearness from the King's intimate ones.

Carrion crow: (or any common crow and particularly one with a red beak, or a starling.) In a dream, a carrion crow represents a mighty man, or people who like sharing, or it could mean a disturbance without cause or basis. *(Also see Crow)*

Carrot: In a dream, carrots represent reprimand, suppression or an obscene and an odious person. However, if one sees himself holding or eating a carrot in a dream, it means overcoming one's difficulties. It is also said that holding or eating carrots in a dream means grieve and depression. Other dream interpreters hold carrots to represent the opposite and perceived benefits in seeing them in a dream, including the freedom of a prisoner from his jail.

Carrying a torch: *(See Torch)*

Carrying someone: Carrying someone in a dream. If the weight is heavy on the carrier, it means trouble or harm caused by one's neighbor. If a woman sees herself carrying a heavy load, such a load could represent her gluttonous husband. Carrying a load over one's shoulders in a dream also represents one's sins. A pregnancy in a dream means comfort for the baby but discomfort for the mother. Seeing oneself carrying bushes from the woods means backbiting, slandering and reporting lies.

Carrying weight: (Burdens; Forbearance; Porter; Serving others)

Case: (Chest; Coffer) In a dream, a case represents a wife, a beautiful woman, one's house or one's shop. In a dream, a case also represents marriage for an unwed person and prosperity for a poor person. A suitcase in a dream means travels, or it may represent an ambassador.

Cash: *(See Candy)*

Cask: (Barrel; Hiding place) In a dream, a cask means hypocrisy or concealing evil actions.

Casket: *(See Sarcophagus)*

Cast¹: *(See Mold)*

Cast²: (Throw; Toss)

Castanets: *(See Cymbals)*

Castigate: *(See Cauterize)*

Casting lots: (Betting; Gambling) Casting lots in a dream or betting means adversities, rebukes, reprimands or exaggeration. If one wins a bet in a dream, it means that he will overcome his opponent. If one loses the bet to his counterpart in the dream, it means that he may suffer from a life imprisonment. *(Also see Gambling)*

Casting stones: *(See Throwing stones)*

Castle: (Fortress; Stronghold) In a dream, a castle means using the vehicle of truth. That is how the proverb: "Truth is a castle" came about. A castle in a dream also represents its owners, an army's fortification, or it may represent knowledge, the Qur'ān, or it could mean seeking refuge in God's protection from the evils of the accursed Satan and his armies, such as deities, preposterous or exaggerated titles, etcetera. The towers of a castle in a dream represent the leaders. Its battlement represents the solders and spies. Its gates represent the guards. Its fortress represents the minister. Its hospices and barns represent the clan or the coffers. It is also said that a castle in a dream could represent an infallible and a strong person. Seeing it from a distance means rising in rank or guarding one's chastity. *(Also see Citadel; Fortress)*

Castor: *(See Civet)*

Castration: If one intends to bank something with someone as a trust or to confide a secret with someone, then if he witnesses a case of castration in a dream, he should immediately halt that intention, or cancel such arrangement. If one sees himself castrated in his dream, it means that he declines to testifying to the truth. If one finds that he became castrated, or if he does so to himself in a dream, it means that he will be inflicted with humiliation and submission to someone's command. If one meets a castrated person who is unknown to him and who has a dignified look and speaks words of wisdom in the dream, it means that he has met an angle who is conveying glad tidings or bringing a warning from his Lord. If he recognizes the castrated person in his dream, it means that he has met with an acquaintance of his. Seeing oneself castrated in a dream also means increase in one's devotion and guarding of his chastity. Castration in a dream also means negation of favors, loss of one's family or children, or it may imply absence of mannerism, choosing to satisfy one's personal comfort over the interests of others, and it represents evil intent or hypocrisy. *(Also see Impotence)*

Cat: A cat in a dream represents a book of records, one's share from a business, an inheritance, or his work. A cat in a dream also means shunning off one's husband, wife or children, or it could mean a fight, theft, adultery, disloyalty, eavesdropping, backbiting or bearing a child from adultery, a bastard child, or it could represent a gentle speaking person, a toadying person or someone who desires to be accepted by others, and should he find an opportune moment, he will spoil everyone's peace. A cat in a dream also represents a banal woman who likes herself. If a cat steels something from her master, it means that he may pay a fine, have a fight with his relatives or children, and it could mean a robbery. A wildcat in a dream means adversities, toiling and a wretched life. Selling a cat in a dream means spending one's money. The scratch of a cat in a dream means that one will be betrayed by his servant. The bite of a cat in a dream represents a hoaxer or a crooked woman. It is also said that a cat's bite in a dream means an illness that will last one full year. *(Also see Tomcat)*

Catapult: *(See Slingshot)*

Cataract: (Waterfall) To discover oneself having cataract in a dream means suffering from sorrow, sadness and dismay.

Catastrophe: *(See Calamity)*

Caterer: A caterer in a dream represents celebrations or a wedding. A commercial caterer in a dream represents someone who deters benefits. Pastry caterer in a dream represents a man of knowledge, or he could mean profits. A travel caterer in a dream represents migration from one's homeland or changes in one's living conditions. Seeing a caterer in a dream is a good sign for someone who desires to get married. Seeing a hospital's caterer in a dream does not convey the best of meanings. A caterer in a dream also represents someone who encourages people to work and seek an honest livelihood. To see oneself catering a dinner for his own house in a dream represents a wedding.

Caterpillar: (Saturn; Silkworm) In a dream, a caterpillar represents a devious thief who wears the cloak of a pious person, who gently and slowly steals people's money or encourages them to invest in losing business ventures. However, no one will suspect him of wrongdoing because of his good looking appearance. *(Also see Butterfly)*

Cattle dealer: In a dream, a cattle dealer represents someone who prefers dealing with rich people, or he could represent the mayor of a town. A cattle dealer in a dream also represents a hunter or a fisherman.

Cattle-ranching: *(See Stableman)*

Cauliflower: A cauliflower in a dream represents a tidy and a passionate person who usually helps others, benefits them and who possesses an acute or a penetrating personality. Seeing a cauliflower in one's hand in a dream means trying to collect a debt that will not be paid except through imposing one's will and firmness.

Cauterize: (Brand; Burn; Castigate; Punishment; Seal; Sear) Cauterization in a dream denotes a ruler, or it could mean painful words. If one's forehead or sides are seared or cauterized in a dream, it means that he is obviating or hindering the distribution of charities or the due alms tax on one's assets, or it could mean a crack down by the authorities on people who are evading to pay their taxes, or it could mean separation between dear ones. If one is cauterized with gold or silver in the dream, it means stinginess or hindering the payment or distribution of God's rights upon one's earnings to poor and needy people. If one is cauterized with iron in a dream, it means punishment for his sins. Discovering old marks from cauterization in a dream means discovering a treasurer. Cauterizing someone in a dream also means speaking to someone with harsh and painful words. If the mark left by such cauterization looks like a rounded seal in a dream, it means subjugation to a court order or complying with the law. Cauterizing a vein or a knee in a dream means begetting a daughter or getting married, or it could mean slandering a stranger. Discovering a burn caused by cauterization in one's chest in a dream means presiding over people. If one's back is seared or cauterized in a dream, it denotes stinginess, or it could mean that he fails to comply with God's rights upon him. *(Also see Back; Seal)*

Cave-in: (Earthquake) In a dream, it means a threat by the ruler. If one sees the earth caving in under him, he will suffer a severe chastisement. An earthquake usually means a bitter illness or a plague hitting the population of the town or locusts or a severe cold weather, or it could mean a drought. If an evil person sees the earth caving under him in a dream, it means a punishment for his sins or undertaking a long and a distant journey from which he may not return home.

Cave: (Cavern; Woman) Entering a cave in one's dream means reaching safety and trust in God Almighty, or it could mean being saved from one's enemy. A cave in a dream also represents a woman, jealousy, swerving, dodging, or a good luck with one's friends. A cave in a dream also represents one's shelter, guardian, mother, father, teacher, Imãm, wife, business or trade. A cave in a dream also means hiding one's secrets and for a person looking for work, it means finding a job or working for people in authority and ending of one's trouble, or it could mean recovering from an illness, release from jail or longevity.

Cavern: *(See Cave)*

Cease fire: *(See Truce)*

Ceiling: A ceiling in a dream represents a well respected person. If it is made of wood, then it represents a fallacious and a deceptive person. If the ceiling looks as if it were going to cave over one's head in a dream, it means being afraid of someone in authority. If consequently some dirt falls over his shirt from the ceiling in the dream, it means that he will receive money in compensation for his pain and sufferings. If the central pillar that holds the ceiling cracks and falls in the dream, it means the death of the man of that house. If the ceiling collapses in the dream, it means the death of the man of that house. If one hides under a roof in a dream, it means that he will enter his house and rob his family's belongings. If water is leaking from one's ceiling in a dream, it means crying in that house for the sake of a departed soul or crying because of a sick person in that family. If rain dissolves the ceiling in a dream, it means loss of money and falling-out from grace. If one sees himself standing on the ceiling of his house and cannot come down in the dream, it means his imprisonment. In a dream, the central beam that carries the ceiling represents a hypocrite who supports the business of an alliance of profiteers. Should the central beam break down and fall in the dream, it means that such a person will be removed from his office. If the ceiling falls over someone's head in a dream, it means that punishment and sufferings will befall him too. If one sees the stars under the roof of his house in a dream, it means that his ceiling may actually cave-in. *(Also see Cave-in)*

Celebrations: *(See Feast of Breaking the Fast; Feast of Immolation)*

Celerity: *(See Hurry)*

Celery: In a dream, celery represents money earned from someone in authority, receiving a commendation from one's superior, ingratitude to one's Lord, divulging secrets, or it could mean affectation.

Celestial beings: *(See Angels)*

Celestial equator: *(See Constellations)*

Celestial poles: *(See Constellations)*

Celestial spheres: (Constellations; Firmaments; Heavens) Seeing oneself at the first celestial sphere in a dream means associating with a tyrant or a liar or befriending a mail carrier. The second celestial sphere represents the scribes of a king. The third celestial sphere represents a marriage to a woman from a noble lineage. The fourth celestial sphere represents leadership, prosperity and reverence. The fifth celestial sphere represents marriage to a most beautiful woman. Travelling in its orbit together with its stars in that galaxy in a dream means travelling to meet a ruler, a warrior, a pious man, or a perfect man. The sixth celestial sphere represents knowledge, blessings and steadfastness. The seventh celestial sphere represents the inner circles of a ruler. The eight celestial sphere represents the company of a great ruler. The ninth celestial sphere represents the company of a revered man. Seeing the tenth celestial sphere or the all-encompassing sphere in a dream means meeting the greatest ruler. Orbiting a celestial sphere or a galaxy or seeing them in a dream means rising in station and honor, attaining one's goals, or increase in one's power. If one sees the all-encompassing sphere in a dream, it means that he will meet the Almighty Lord, the Master of the universes, God Almighty Himself or become the intimate friend of the greatest ruler in the world. If one sees himself in a dream changing the order of stars, galaxies or constellations, it means being unjust or trying to obscure the truth. If a woman sees herself under the first celestial sphere in a dream, it means that she will marry someone from the ruling class. *(Also see Constellations, Dog; Moon; Skies; Star)*

Cell: *(See Hermitage)*

Cellar: (Mouth)

Cemetery: (Burial ground; Grave; Graveyard) Seeing a cemetery or a graveyard in a dream means appeasement and comfort for a terrified person, and dismay to a comfortable and a relaxed person. A graveyard represents the elements of fear, hope and return to guidance after heedlessness. A cemetery represents the hereafter, because it is its vehicle. A cemetery in a dream also represents the prison of the body, but in a dream, it also means seclusion, devotion, abstinence, asceticism or admonition. A cemetery also can be interpreted as the dead looking drunkard in a bar, a man laying flat in a prostitution house, the home of a heedless person who often sleeps rather than pray or a hypocrite whose deeds are not subject to receiving a heavenly reward, etcetera. If a sick person walks into a funeral procession in a dream, it means that his illness will culminate in his death. If he is not sick and then during that procession he weeps or prays for the deceased person in the dream, it means that he will repent of his sins, join spiritual study circles and serves the people of knowledge. Such a person also may attain a blessed spiritual station and benefit from what he hears and sees. If one sees himself walking in a funeral procession and neglecting respect and contemplation, and instead laughs and jokes, it means that he will befriend evildoers and accept their evil conduct as a standard norm of behavior. If one sees himself visiting a graveyard for seclusion, self-awakening and self-re-straint, then if he reflects about words of truth, wisdom and repentance in his dream, it means that he will be asked to judge between two people, and that he will rule with justice. If one does not contemplate thus in the dream, it means that he will forget about something important or dear to his heart. If one enters the graveyard calling to prayers in a dream, it means that he will admonish people, commands what is good and forbids what is evil. If one sees himself entering a graveyard and walking over the scattered bones of the dead people in a dream, it means that he will die and be buried there. A cemetery in a dream also represents admonition, reading the Qur'ān, crying, reminiscence, piety, surrender to one's destiny and discarding worldly gains. A cemetery in a dream also may represent the scholars, ascetics, governors, leaders, camps or a brothel. The graves of saints or shrines in a dream signify innovation, heedlessness, intoxication, adultery, corruption and fear. A stone tomb or a sarcophagus in a dream signifies profits, war prisoners, a booty or exposing one's personal secrets. *(Also see Burial; Grave; Shrine)*

Censure: (Blame; Calumniation; Rebuke; Reprimand; Reproof) If one sees himself censured by a prophet, a saint, a godly person, or a bosom friend in a dream, it means repentance from sin, refraining from walking the avenues of error and temptation. Censure in a dream also signifies love and compassion. If one rebukes himself in a dream, it means that he had indulged in a wrongdoing which he regrets and that he is blaming himself for it. *(Also see Blame)*

Cent: (Money; Penny) Seeing one cent in a dream means an argument, falsehood, ostentation or pride. Swallowing a quarter and excreting it as a penny in a dream signifies that the person is a zendik or an atheist. Pennies in a dream signify evil, fights and speaking despicable words. If God's name is encrusted on the penny in the dream, it means that such a person who carries it has licensed himself to do evil in the name of God Almighty. Seeing a cent in a dream also could signify cheating, toiling, fights, boredom, atheism, sorrow, sadness, tight circumstances, an argument, meager earnings, dispelling poverty, going to work, wages, insolvency or the spread of mutual defamation among scholars. *(Also see Money; Penny)*

Cepheus: *(See Constellations)*

Cereal: *(See Breakfast food)*

Cerebrum: *(See Body¹; Brain)*

Ceremonial dinner: *(See Banquet)*

Cessation: *(See Truce)*

Chain: (Complications; Longevity; Marriage; Richness; Sin) In a dream, a chain represents an old or a rich woman whose earnings are lawful. A chain in one's hand or around one's neck in a dream may mean threats, menaces, sin or disobedience. Seeing a chain around one's neck in a dream also means marriage to a woman of bad character. A chain in a dream also denotes complications. Seeing oneself chained means sorrow and distress. *(Also see Bond¹)*

Chair: (Seat) In a dream, a chair represents authority, rank or a woman. An iron cast chair in a dream represents power and superiority. If it is a wooden chair, then it means less than that beside added hypocrisy. Sitting on a chair in a dream means becoming a guardian, deputy, attorney or proxy. If one qualifies for governing or for managing a business, then sitting on a chair in a dream means receiving such an appointment. If a traveller sees himself sitting on a chair in a dream, it means that he will return to his homeland to be reunited with his family and to attain his goals. For people in authority, a chair in their dream represents an appointment, a promotion, fame, marriage, children or buying an expensive property, a new vehicle or a new garment. If one finds a chair and sits on it in a dream, it means that he will gain power or be married to a woman whose prestige and sophistication correspond to those of the chair. If one's wife is pregnant, then seeing oneself sitting on a chair in a dream means that she will beget a son. If one sees himself sitting on a chair and wearing a stately garment in a dream, it means that he will occupy the seat of knowledge, honor, reverence and that he will receive immediate benefits. If one's chair breaks in a dream, it may mean his death or that of his wife, or it could mean their separation, or losing one's authority at home or at work. A chair in a dream also signifies happiness and promotion for the one who sits on it, or it could mean spiritual success or winning God's forgiveness in the hereafter and entering the heavenly paradise. If a pregnant woman sees herself sitting on a chair in a dream, the chair then represents her labor and her delivery day. If she is wearing a crown in the dream, then it means that she will beget a son. Seeing the Divine Throne (*Kursï*) of God Almighty in its most perfect condition which is situated in the highest heaven and as it is without attribution of human imagination or depictions of images in a dream means acquiring knowledge, wisdom and rising in station. A chair in a dream also signifies delivering a babe, travels, a vehicle, buying a house or initiating a good practice that people will emulate and follow. As for a sick person, a chair in his dream means being on his deathbed. *(Also see Saddle; Seat; Throne)*

Chalcedony: *(See Carnelian-red)*

Chamber: (Bedchamber; Bedroom; Room; Suite) A chamber in a dream means safety, security, marriage, a newborn, or the lady of the house. Seeing a chamber from a distance means joy, satisfaction and happiness. To be inside a chamber with two or three compartments in a dream also means security. Walking scared into a room whose owner is unknown in a dream means security, safety and appeasement of one's fears. If one is sick, then it means entering paradise or recovering from his illness, rising in rank, enjoying an elevated position in the world, presiding over people through knowledge, experience, leadership or spiritual attainment. If a poor person sees himself inside a new room in a dream, it means satisfaction and wealth. However, if a rich person sees that in a dream, it means loss of money or business. If a destitute sees himself inside an old room in a dream, it means that he will become increasingly poor and penniless, and if he is rich, it means that his wealth will increase. Building a room on the second floor in a dream means marrying a second wife. *(Also see Bedroom)*

Champing: *(See Bite)*

Chancellors: *(See Elders)*

Chandelier: In a dream, a chandelier represents a person of firm and resolute standing. The falling of a chandelier means death or falling prices for that year.

Chandler: (Tallow-chandler; Wax-chandler) In a dream, a chandler represents festivities, joy, happiness, death, illness, guidance, knowledge, wanting something, or crying for it. *(Also see Candlestick)*

Change of life: *(See Old woman)*

Changes: *(See Shade)*

Changing form: *(See Transformation)*

Channel: *(See Canal)*

Chanting: (Swallow; Starling. *See Singing*)

Chaplet: *(See Necklace)*

Character: (Hidden; Manifest; Wild plants; Forest; Woods)

Charcoal grill: *(See Brazier)*

Charcoal: (Den; Lair; Hole. *See Coal*)

Chard: (Swiss chard) In a dream, chard means blessings and profits. If one eats it raw in a dream, it means continuous indebtedness or indulging in loathsome and suspicious acts such as practicing anal intercourse with one's wife or homosexuality or performing the forbidden sexual intercourse with one's wife during her menstrual period. In a dream, chard also means slander.

Charge against: *(See Attack)*

Charity: (Detergent; Discards; Filth; Loan; Tithe) Charity in a dream means repelling calamities, recovering from illness, profits or truthfulness. This is also true when it comes to earning one's money lawfully, but if one gives a dead animal or alcohol or a stolen or mismanaged money in charity, then his charity is not acceptable and it means that he will pursue evil and indulge in sin. If a farmer who is having a bad harvest sees himself giving some of what he plants in charity in a dream, it means that his crop will increase and his produce will be blessed. If one donates his charities to a rich person in a dream, it means that he may suffer from tight financial circumstances, or that he may come to be in need of such a person. If one gives a charitable donation to a prostitute in a dream, it means that she will repent of her sin. If he gives a charity to a thief in a dream, it means that the thief will cease his profession. Charity in a dream also could mean suppressing the envy or spite of one's rivals or subdue the jealousy of one's enemy, averting his dislikes, or suppressing evil in general. If an angry person sees himself secretly distributing charity in a dream, it means that God Almighty has forgiven him his sin of anger. Giving charity in secret in one's dream also could mean seeking the friendship of people in authority, or to join the circles of people of knowledge. If a man of knowledge is asked to give money in charity, and if he complies in his dream, it means that he will expound his knowledge to others. If he is a merchant, it means that he will benefit others with his business or teach them his trade. If he is a craftsman, he will teach people his craft. If one who is under pressures, or if one is scared of something sees himself feeding a beggar who is undergoing his own trials in a dream, it means that one's fears and stress will be dispelled. Charity in a dream also denotes celebrating God's praises, devotion, visiting the graveyards and doing good. To spend money on God's path in a dream means that one will surely receive money in wakefulness. *(Also see Alms tax; Endowment; Good deeds; Loan)*

Charmer: *(See Snake charmer)*

Chasing away: *(See Expulsion)*

Chaste: *(See Virgin)*

Chastity: *(See Climbing a mountain)*

Cheat: *(See Chisel; Crow)*

Checker board: *(See Chessboard)*

Cheeks: In a dream, one's cheeks represent his beauty and a display of his character. In a dream, cheeks are a symbol of love and affection. They denote both good or bad, harm or benefits, health or sickness and increase or decrease. Whatever affects them in a dream will show in one's life. One's cheeks also represent his type of work. If they look rosy in a dream, they denote a good health and a good luck in one's life. Yellow or opaque cheeks in a dream mean fear, sorrow and loss of status. One's cheek in a dream also means humiliation or meekness if seen soiled with dust, soot or dirt in the dream. However, if a religious person sees his cheeks covered with dust in a dream, it means the rise of his spiritual rank, and that he will become exalted in God's sight. *(Also see Face)*

Cheerfulness: *(See Blithe)*

Cheese: In a dream, cheese represents a marriage contract if one is unmarried, a child to a pregnant woman or prosperity and longevity. If an opponent sees cheese in his dream, it means cowardice and disdain to face his adversary. It is also said that cheese suggests a period of humiliation or misery. If a pregnant woman sees any by-product of milk in her dream, it suggests the nearing delivery of her child. Yogurt in a dream represents blessings in one's earnings, though it also indicates that a portion of one's earnings may include forbidden interest made from usury. Cheese in a dream also represents easy profits. However, soft cheese in a dream seems to have a more beneficial interpretation than hardened cheese. Such profits entail current financial success. Hardened cheese in a dream however may mean a journey. Eating bread with cheese in a dream represents miserliness. Mixing bread, cheese and walnuts in a dream means becoming afflicted with a sudden illness. Dry cheese for a traveller means profits while green cheese means profits for a resident.

Cheetah: *(See Lynx)*

Cherries: (Prunes) In a dream, cherries or prunes represent easy money, recovering from illness, happiness, joy and celebrations.

Chervil: (Coriander) In a dream, chervil and coriander represent a good person who helps others in their mundane and religious interests. Both dry and green coriander or chervil in a dream mean money.

Chess bishop: In a dream, the Bishop signifies playfulness, distraction or a chronic illness. *(Also see Chess; Chessboard; Chessmen)*

Chess knight: In a dream, seeing the Knight signifies contracts, deals and money. It also could mean cheating, or the death of a sick person. *(Also see Chess; Chessboard; Chessmen)*

Chess queen: In a dream, the Queen represents a noble rank. *(Also see Chess; Chessboard; Chessmen)*

Chess: (Challenges; Game) Playing chess in a dream means mixing with all kinds of people. Playing chess in a dream also means deception, fights or a ploy. Seeing a chessboard, and if no one is playing it in a dream represents a strike, or people who are dismissed from their job. If one sees people playing it, then such people represent the leaders or the statesmen. The winner in a chess game in a dream is the winner of a political or a military maneuver. Whatever steps one takes in playing chess in a dream will be reflected in the political arena. Playing chess in a dream also could mean intending a fight, but not knowing whether he will win or lose. It also could mean facing dangerous people, so one is warned in the dream to be on guard against their tricks or ploys. Playing chess in a dream also could mean vain talk or a weak fight. If one wins in the dream, it means that he will win in wakefulness. A chess game in a dream also means a war, a fight, booty, discovering secrets, pursuing hints, gradual movement, changing conditions, changing temper, or it could mean travels. *(Also see Backgammon; Chessboard; Chessmen)*

Chessboard: (Checker board) In a dream, a chessboard represents the world in everything it does to its dwellers. It raises someone and abases another or it could represent life and death, the upright, the crooked, sports, wars, jealousy, temptation, envy, perfidy, poverty or richness, etcetera. *(Also see Chess; Chessmen)*

Chessmen: (Castle) Seeing any of the pieces used in the game of chess in a dream denotes rightfulness, balance, privacy, confidentiality, truthfulness, or it could mean a sudden death. If a pregnant woman sees any of these pieces in a dream, it means giving birth to a daughter. *(Also see Chess; Chessboard)*

Chest pain: Having chest pain in a dream denotes a sin one is being punished for, or it could mean being spendthrift, or it could represent one's generosity in other than God's pleasure, and the pain represents the punishment for it. *(Also see Body[1]; Chest[2]; Pain)*

Chest[1]: *(See Case)*

Chest[2]: (Bosom; Heart) If one has a broad and a nice looking chest in a dream, it means repentance of a sinner or being eager and willing to follow the truth and to comply with it, or it could mean making it easy to accept things that were difficult to absorb. If a woman sees her beloved inside her chest in a dream, it means that she is suffering because of him or complaining about him, or if she is ill, it means that she will recover from her illness. To have a broad chest in a dream also means giving preference to others' needs. One's chest in a dream also represents what one may conceal in it of knowledge, guidance, heedlessness or it could represent a coffer where one hides his money. One's chest in a dream also represents a guest, one's wife, a rank, a position, magnanimity or generosity. The narrowness of one's chest in a dream represents heedlessness, or it could mean going astray, loss of money, or one's stinginess. If one sees his chest turned into a stone in a dream, it means that he is a hard hearted person. However, a broad chest in a dream also could signify being unjust. The chest in a dream also represents the house of worries and anxieties. Having chest pain in a dream denotes a sin one is being punished for, or it could mean being a spendthrift or generous in other than God's pleasure, and the pain in the dream represents his punishment for it. If a man sees himself having a woman's breasts in his dream, it means that he will get married, or fall in love with a woman, or have a secret affair that will turn into a scandal. *(Also see Body¹)*

Chewing food: If one sees himself exaggeratedly chewing his food in a dream, it means disdain and indifference about seeking an honest livelihood. Swallowing food one should chew in a dream means debts, or collectors standing at one's door demanding their money. *(Also see Chewing gum; Chewing)*

Chewing gum: (Losing the sense of taste; Masticate) Chewing gum in a dream means committing loathsome sins or indulging in sodomy, for the people of the Prophet Lot (uwbp) used to chew gum. If one sees himself chewing gum in a dream it also could signify talking too much, or constantly complaining about something, or engaging in a major dispute, or sustaining an argument, or it could mean losing one's sense of taste. *(Also see Chewing food; Chewing)*

Chewing: (Greed) To chew food other than for grinding or eating one's meal in a dream means an illness or loss of appetite. Chewing gum in a dream means earning money coupled with ugly words that will grow to become a big fight and that will lead to a court appearance. The source of it all begins with greed. Anything that is chewed in a dream means an exchange of words. The only exception to it is chewing a stick of sugar cane in a dream. In that case, it means lauding someone or hearing pleasing words one desires to hear over and over. *(Also see Chewing food; Chewing gum; Greed)*

Chick-peas: (Garbanzo) Chick-peas in a dream mean hard earned money.

Chicken: (Bird; Fowl) A chicken in a dream represents the woman of the house, while the rooster in a dream represents the man of the house. A chicken in a dream also represents a woman who takes care of orphans and raises charities for their sake, or it could represent a blond woman, or a servant. Owning a chicken in a dream means dispelling difficulties, or it could be a show of happiness. Hunting a chicken in a dream means receiving lawful and easy profits. Slaughtering a chicken in a dream means deflowering a virgin servant. If one sees a chicken or a female peacock hooting inside his house or garden in a dream, it means a calamity which is met with a belligerent character. Seeing one's house filled with a large number of chickens in a dream means wealth or presiding over people, or it could mean dispelling one's fear and establishing one's rank. *(Also see Peacock)*

Chicks: (Baby; Chicken; Fowl) A chick in a dream represents a stolen or a missing child. The sound of chicks in a dream represents the voice of insolent people. Eating chick's meat in a dream means receiving unlawful or stolen money. Chicks in a dream also signify something that will develop fast and produce its results without much effort on the part of the person caring for them.

Child molester: *(See Pederasty)*

Child: (Little boy) In a dream, a child carried in one's arms means responsibility, distress and difficulties. A teenage child represents glad tidings or dispelling one's worries. If one sees a beautiful looking teenage child entering a town or descending from the skies or appearing from beneath the ground in a dream, it means that the glad tidings will take effect shortly. Seeing a mature child in a dream means power and superiority. If one sees himself as a child learning in school in a dream, it means that he will repent of a common sin he is used to commit. If one sees one of the renowned people of knowledge sitting in a kindergarten and learning along with other children in a dream, it means that he will shift to ignorance, lose his rank, or that financial changes will affect his living conditions. If one sees himself receiving instructions like a child in a dream, it means that he will receive an inheritance from his mother. If one sees himself as a newborn child in a dream, it means that he will become wealthy and prosper. If a young boy sees himself in a dream as a child, it has a negative meaning. If a sick person sees himself as a child in a dream, it means his death. If one sees himself as a child being reprimanded in a dream, it means that he will be conquered. In a dream, if one looks in a mirror and sees his face to be that of a child, and if his wife is pregnant, it means that she will beget a son who will look like his father. Carrying a baby child in a dream means distress and burdens. A child in a dream represents a weak enemy who sometime shows friendliness and at other times demonstrates his enmity. If one sees that his wife has just delivered children who are playing around him in a dream, it means distress or misfortune and the consequences could be either good or bad. Carrying a child in a dream means managing an inheritance or a financial investment. If an elderly person sees himself roaming as a little child in a dream, it means that he will commit an act of ignorance or lose his dignity, ideals or sense of honor. On the other hand, if such an elderly person who sees himself in a dream as a little child is suffering from depression or financial difficulties or health problems, then it means relief from distress and good health and that he will become free from his sins, like the day his mother gave birth to him. If one sees that he has a little child who disdains from coming near his father in the dream, it means financial promotion and enjoyment of one's life. If one sees a little child screaming in his lap in a dream, it means that he plays a string instrument. Children in a dream also could mean either sorrow and pain or happiness and joy. If they are one's own children in the dream, then they mean temptation with money. Children in a dream also could mean contentment with little or loss of one's means to earn his livelihood or they could mean money or marriage or a flourishing business. Bereavement of a child in a dream means the opposite in real life. It also means rejoicing, reunions, pleasures and earning respect. Bereavement of a child in a dream is sometimes interpreted to portray an intention of one's children or wife to separate from the family. A little male child in a dream represents worries, responsibilities, hard work, catering to ignorant people or dealing with trivial and time wasting people. If a prisoner sees himself carrying a little girl in his dream, it means that he will be released from his prison. If one who is going through hard times sees himself holding a little girl in a dream, it means that his adversities will be lifted. If he is poor, it means that he will thrive for success and the little girl then represents his glad tidings.

Childbearing: *(See Pregnancy)*

Childbirth: (Giving birth) Seeing one's wife giving birth to a son in a dream when in fact she is not pregnant means wealth. If a pregnant woman sees herself giving birth to a girl in a dream, it means a boy, and if she gives birth to a boy in the dream, it means a girl. Giving birth to a girl means relief from distress, while giving birth to a boy in the dream means distress and worries. If a sick person sees his mother giving birth to him in a dream, it means the approach of his death, for a deceased person is wrapped in a shroud, while a newborn is wrapped with a receiving cloth. If the person in question is poor, it means that his financial conditions will change for the better, but if he is rich, it means restriction of his earnings, for a child is dependent on others while his movements are restricted. If a traveler sees his wife giving birth to a new child in a dream, it means obstruction of his travels and changes in his plans. If a woman gives birth to a child from her mouth in a dream, it means her death. If a man gives birth to a son in a dream it means illness, escape from danger or separation from a bad wife. If a man gives birth to a daughter in a dream, it means relief from distress, happiness or the birth of a child from his posterity who will grow to become a renowned leader. If a woman gives birth to a cat in a dream, it means that her child will grow to be a thief. Childbirth in a dream means relief from hardships, recovering from illness or departure from one's home or neighborhood. Childbirth in a dream also means comfort, relaxation, payment of one's debts and repentance from sin. If a woman gives birth to a son in a dream, it denotes the conclusion of her sufferings, glad tidings, payment of her debts or repentance from sin. If she gives birth to a daughter in the dream, then it means honor, prosperity and ease. If a poor man gives birth to a child in a dream, it means prosperity. If he is rich, then it means distress. If he is unmarried, it means a forthcoming marriage, so that his future wife will give the birth he saw in his dream. In general, if a man sees himself giving birth in a dream, it means his death or the death of a relative, or it could mean experiencing poverty. As for a needy person, it means relief or an escape. As for a merchant, giving birth in a dream means loss of his investment. (*Also see Dragon*)

Children: (*See Dependents*)

Chill: (*See Feverish chill*)

Chin: A chin in a dream represents one's beauty, wealth, a supporting father, a helping son, a servant, an honorable position or a respected status designated uniquely for such a person. Seeing one's chin in a dream also means properly satisfying one's ritual ablution or perhaps it could represent the foundation of one's house. (*Also see Jaws*)

Chirp of a swallow: (*See Sound of animals*)

Chisel: (Cheat; Defraud; Swindle) In a dream, a chisel means using a tool to attain one's goal, or using a helper, or it could represent someone who is forced to travel by unwarranted circumstances or without his consent. A chisel in a dream also represents someone whose wounds do not heal easily because of his greed, inequity and craving for more. A chisel in a dream also represents one's assistant, or one's penis, or his mouth.

Chomp: (*See Bite*)

Chopping off: (*See Cutting off*)

Christian temple: (*See Church; Temple*)

Chronic illness: A chronic illness in a dream means hindrances or suspension of one's travel plans, or difficulties in earning one's livelihood in a work that involves using one's hands and feet, or it could represent impediments to achieving one's goal.

Chrysolite: (Beryl; Gem; Peridot; Stone) In a dream, when these precious stones are placed on one's ring, they mean a ranking authority that combines courage and reverence. Receiving a ring with such a stone from one's son in a dream means that his son possesses an amiable character and good qualities. (*Also see Ring; Topaz*)

Church: For a Christian person, seeing a church in a dream signifies a house of worship, religion, knowledge, devotion, work, ascetic detachment, fear of wrongdoing, penance, lamentation and it could mean crying. A church in a dream also could mean distress, trouble, slander, innovation, injustice, a business club, a meeting house, bingo, wine, alcoholic consumption, communion, weddings or a wife. In a dream, a church also can represent its parish, diocese, ministry, clergyman or a chaplain. If one sees a church turned into a synagogue, or a synagogue turned into a church in a dream, it means mistrust, an argument, or a scheme for tax evasion. Seeing oneself in a synagogue in a dream means that one may become a Jew. If one's house turns into a church in a dream, it means that he will bring its business to his house, or it may mean a fight with one's boss. Seeing a church in a dream also denotes a cemetery, confession, a prostitute, a music house or a place of confinement. If a woman sees herself attending a wedding or a funeral service at a church in a dream, it may mean the same in wakefulness. *(Also see Cincture; Temple)*

Churn: (Butterskin) A churn, a butterskin, or a container in which people make butter in a dream represents a scholar or a renunciate who imparts his knowledge to people but does not act upon it.

Cincture: (Band; Belt; Clerical garment; Rope) The priest's cincture in a dream represents a son. A broken cincture in the dream means the death of one's son. Wearing a cincture in a dream is also a sign of devotion, abstinence, ascetic detachment and a sign of obedience for Christians. As for a Muslim person, wearing a cincture in a dream is a sign of faith, certitude and determination, fulfilling God's commands, goodwill or opposing fallacies. A cincture in a dream also means adultery, fornication or being a middle aged person. Whatever good or bad that may happen to one's cincture in a dream will reflect in his life. If one wears a new cincture over his gown in a dream, it means begetting a son. If one wears his cincture under his gown in the dream, it means fallaciousness, dissent, heinous corruption in one's spiritual life and evil in his worldly aspirations. *(Also see Belt; Waistband; Waist belt)*

Circumambulation: (Ambulate; Ka'aba; Mecca; Walk around) If a sinner sees himself circumambulating God's House in Mecca in a dream, it means that he will be freed from suffering in hell-fire. If one is unmarried, it means that he will get married. If one qualifies for promotion, it means that he will receive it. Seeing oneself performing a pilgrimage in a dream also means circumambulating God's house in Mecca, developing a good character, living a straight and a worthy life, safety from fear, repayment of one's debts, delivering entrusted merchandise to their rightful owners or money to its people on demand, being trustworthy, living an ascetic life, fulfilling a promise, atonement for one's sins, distributing expiatory gifts or interceding on behalf of a trustworthy and a noble Imâm. Seeing oneself circumambulating God's house while riding on a mare in a dream means that one will commit the abominable sin of adultery with a member of his own family or with a consanguineous blood relative with whom it is not permissible to have sexual relationship. *(Also see Ka'aba; Rituals of the pilgrimage; Sa'i)*

Circumcising nurse: In a dream, he or she represents a person who shamelessly exposes his private parts, or one who follows scandalous issues or public profanities, or one who has an inquisitive mind, or it could mean exposing women's secrets, or being sexually obsessed.

Circumcision: Circumcision in a dream means purification, cleanliness, discarding impurity, celebrations or happy reunions. If one sees himself being circumcised in a dream, it means that he did something good which God Almighty has accepted, and by its virtue, God Almighty has forgiven him his sins, or it may mean that he will undergo an operation to open his veins or to bleed them. If a young virgin girl sees herself being circumcised in a dream, it means either marriage, or encountering her first experience with her monthly period. Circumcision in a dream also means undergoing an operation of removing one's testicles, undergoing a prostate operation, or it may mean clearing one's name from slander and accusations, or it may mean separation between husband, wife and children, or children leaving their parent's home, If one discovers that he is circumcised in a dream, it means that he will become an apostate and forsake his religion for monetary gains.

Circus: *(See Bear trainer)*

Cistern: In a dream, a water cistern represents a pouch, a safe, a box, a coffer, a partner, one's wife, a son, or knowing people's personal secrets. If the oil cistern is filled with water in the dream, it means stagnation of any of the above. If one sees a water cistern filled with oil in a dream, then it means prosperity. The cistern of a fellowship house, a khanakah or a mosque in a dream represents its Imām or its supervising spiritual teacher or the caretaker and guard of the property. If one sees the water cistern of the house sitting in an unsuitable place in that house in a dream, it represents the spirit of a jinni who pursues such a person or who may haunt his house. If one sees a well being used as a cistern in his house in a dream, it denotes that the dwellers of that house are of the middle class, or it could mean that the water of that house is salty or non-potable. If one sees the cistern filled with butter or honey or milk in a dream, it means that one's wife is pregnant, or it could mean prosperity for that family. If the family of such a house is thirsty in the dream, and if the cistern is filled with other than water, then it means that they owe alms tax and must pay the necessary charity on their assets, or it could mean that such a family has turned its back to God's path and preferred worldly gains instead, or that they have a knowledge that they do not practice, or it could mean shortage of rain in that locality that necessitates spending money on God's path. A cistern in a dream also could represent a protective shield or a pocket, one's dignity, blessings or attaining a respectable rank or dispelling difficulties. However, this interpretation can only apply for those who use a cistern or a similar water container or a water dispenser and in their case, it also could mean peace and protection from any fears. *(See Urn)*

Citadel: (Castle; Fortress; Stronghold) If a suitable person sees himself inside a beautiful citadel in a dream, it means that he will be appointed as a leader, or that he will he get married, have a child, buy a property, walk the path of the believers, or repent of his sins. If one sees himself inside a citadel or a castle in a dream, it means that he will be endowed with ascetic detachment from this world and with piety, faith and abstinence from sin. His share will depend upon that section of the citadel or castle where he stands in his dream. If one sees himself wandering in a desolate region outside the castle in the dream, it means that he will fall prey to his enemy. If one builds a castle or a citadel in his dream, it means that he will guard himself from his enemy, protects his chastity, property and person from adversities and humiliation. The opposite will take effect if he sees himself demolishing such a castle or citadel. Seeing oneself standing near the battlement in a dream, it means that he will benefit from a brother, a son or a superior who will save his life. *(Also see Castle; Fortress)*

Citron: (Acid; Heartburn; Sorrel) In a dream, a citron means a cure from illness. It also may mean hypocrisy and affectation. *(Also see Citrus medica)*

Citrus Bigaradia: *(See Citrus medica)*

Citrus medica: (Citron; *Citrus Bigaradia; Zollikoferia spinosa*) Seeing any of the citrus medica plants in a dream means combatting illness, distress, trouble or it could represent a beautiful, but a cheap woman.

City: (Knowledge; Town; Village) Entering a city in a dream means appeasement of one's fears. Imām Ibn Seerïn use to prefer entering the city in a dream rather than leaving it. A city in a dream also represents a learned person, a wise man and a scholar. If one enters a city and finds it in ruins in his dream, it means that the learned people of that city no longer live there. It is said that seeing a city in a dream means the death of its ruler or an unjust governor from that place. Seeing a city being built in a dream signifies the growing number of its learned people and represents children who will continue the path of their fathers. Seeing a city with no governor in a dream means rising prices. An unknown city in a dream represents the hereafter, while a known city represents the world. Seeing oneself in an unknown city in a dream is also a sign of righteousness. The best of cities in a dream are the large ones. One's home town in a dream represents his father, while one's homeland in a dream represents his mother. Seeing oneself in a northern city in a dream mean increase of one's cash flow. Seeing oneself in a southern city means increase in one's trickery and deception. Seeing oneself in a low plateau in a dream means difficulties and trouble, while seeing oneself in a high plateau means trustworthiness and truthfulness. Seeing oneself in Egypt in a dream means longevity and a comfortable living. Seeing oneself in a farmland in a dream means pursuing innovation. Seeing oneself in a bower in a dream signifies the coming of a prosperous year. Seeing oneself in Jerusalem or at the feet of Mount Sinai in a dream also means prosperity. Seeing oneself in Bethlehem in a dream means increased religious devotion. Seeing oneself in Damascus in a dream means blessings, prosperity and wealth, or it could mean corruption. A cold city in a dream represents adversities. Seeing oneself in a shore city in a dream means winning people's acceptance. Standing on a sulfuric soil or a salinized soil in a dream means an illness. Seeing oneself in a large and populated city in a dream means prosperity and wealth. Entering a city in a dream also means making peace between people. Driving through an unknown section of a city in a dream means losses. Entering an old city that is rebuilt and restored in a dream means that a great and a pious person will be born in that city and he will grow to guide its people on the path of righteousness. A city in a dream also signifies an oath, meeting with one's beloveds, peace, tranquility and safety. Meeting with God-fearing people in a dream means attaining one's goals and receiving glad tidings. Seeing the cities of Sodom and Gomorrah in a dream means adversities, earthquake, fear and corruption. Seeing a city in a dream also could mean repentance from sin. A province in a dream represents its governor or renowned scholars. Governing a city in a dream means rising to a suitable position, getting married, recovering from an illness, repenting from sin, or receiving guidance at the hand of a learned shaikh. Seeing a deceased person walking alive in a city in a dream perhaps means that he is in paradise enjoying its blessings. Seeing a deceased person in a village in a dream means that he might be in hell laboring with its people. A city in a dream also represents the entertainment it provides for its dwellers. The name of a city one sees in a dream should reflect some of the meanings of one's dream. (*See Introduction*). The industry of a city also has a share in the dream interpretation. Known cities in the world in a dream represent their rulers. Entering a city one already knows in a dream means that one will not die until he enters it again, or it could mean that he will receive news from that city. The walls of a city represent a strong ruler. A demolished wall of a city in a dream signifies the death of its ruler or his removal from office. If one sees a flourishing city with its urban construction, factories and farms, his dream will reflect the spiritual awareness and religious devotion of its people. (*Also see Village*)

Civet cat: (*See Civet*)

Civet: (Castor; Civet cat; A fatty substance with a musklike scent which is secreted by a gland near the genitals of a civet, a deer or a beaver. This substance is also used in making perfumes.) In a dream, a civet represents honorable profits or valuable properties, botanical gardens, a school from which one can acquire knowledge and draw benefits, or a business from which one can make profits, or it could mean a profitable leather trade. If one prepares the civet on fire in the dream, it means that he is preparing amber perfume, musk or aloe perfume that is extracted from an aromatic heartwood of the mezereum tree family.

Clamor: (Noise; Roaring; Hubbub) In a dream, it means witnessing social disorder, a public outcry or participating in a religious festival or an important public event that will attract the interest of people from all walks of life. *(Also see Shout)*

Clapping hands: In a dream, clapping hands represents pagan customs. If one hears hands clapping, or if he claps his hands in a dream, it may indicate an illness or it could represent a vacant house or a ghost town.

Clarity of speech: *(See Eloquence of speech)*

Clarity: *(See Glass)*

Claw hammer: *(See Hammer)*

Claw: (Nail) In a dream, a claw signifies victory over one's enemy, as it provides a weapon, protection and a tool for a bird.

Clay: (Argillite; Argillateous; Mortar; Mud; Plaster) In a dream, clay means sickness, disgrace or ignominy, except for one who works with clay or builds structures with it, then in his case, seeing clay in his dream means benefits, religious awareness and developing faith and certitude. Dry clay in a dream represents a cut in one's earnings or living on a budget. If one sees himself plastering the walls of his house with wet clay in a dream, it means that he is a righteous person. If one sees himself eating clay in a dream, it means that he swindles money. Construction clay in a dream means benefits and money. Seeing clay in a dream also could mean death. If one sees himself waking in mud or wet clay, and if he works with it in a dream, it means falling sick or suffering from disgrace. Dry clay in a dream means money, while wet clay means righteousness. Eating baked clay in a dream means backbiting others, untruth or slander. If a sick person sees clay in his dream, it means his death. *(Also see Bricks)*

Cleaner: In a dream, a floor cleaner represents someone who investigates people's conditions and likes to help them. Cleaning throughout a farmland in a dream means seeking the company of righteous people. Cleaning through a vineyard in a dream means investigating the living condition of a woman. Cleaning a tree in a dream means investigating the living conditions of religious people. Sweeping a street in a dream means travelling an equal distance to such a street. If one sees himself cleaning the road to Mecca in a dream, it means that he will perform a pilgrimage. Cleaning through a grass field without knowing the owner in a dream means becoming a renunciate. Cleaning the floors of someone's house in a dream means finding how he is doing. *(Also see Sweeping the floor; Washer; Washing)*

Cleaning: *(See Sweeping the floor)*

Cleaver: (Butcher's knife) In a dream, a cleaver represents a strong and a courageous man, who distinguishes clearly between right and wrong, easy and difficult and who fosters no enmity, though if someone dares to fight him, he will have the power to disperse him in the land.

Climacteric: *(See Old woman)*

Climax: *(See Pleasure; Sexual intercourse)*

Climb: *(See Ascending in the skies)*

Climbing a mountain: Climbing a mountain, enjoying its vegetations and drinking from its fresh and sweet water in a dream means sheltering one's chastity in the company of one's wife. *(Also see Khimār; Veil)*

Clipping one's beard: *(See Beard; Scissors)*

Cloak: In a dream, a cloak represents marriage or a child bearing wife. If the outside of it is made of cotton, it represents one's good spiritual standing. A cloak in the dream usually represents longevity, prosperity for the one wearing it and protection against a cold winter, that is poverty or the heat of summer, or heaviness in one's life caused by his wife, his spiritual life, his religious attendance, or it could mean a sickness, imprisonment, distress caused by a woman or the stress of war. If a wife sees herself wearing a cloak with the lining made of dark sable fur in a dream, it means that she will have a lover of an iniquitous character. *(Also see Coat)*

Clock: (Timepiece; Watch) A clock in a dream represents money equal to the time setting when seen in one's dream. An alarm clock in a dream means exposing ills, richness of a poor person and fulfilling a promise.

Close: (Shut) If a single man sees himself shutting a door in a dream, it means that he will marry a righteous woman. If a married man sees himself shutting a door in a dream, it means that he may divorce his wife. Locking a door in a dream also means getting married, though unlocking a padlock has negative connotations. If one sees his door locked in a dream, it means that he will choose to pursue his worldly satisfaction instead of fulfilling his religious obligations. If one tries to lock the door of his house and fails to do so in his dream, it means that he will abandon a hard decision he took, or refrain from pursuing the impossible in his case.

Closet: (Safe) In a dream, a closet represents one's wife, a hide-out, protection or a veil. If one sees his closet destroyed in a dream, it may mean the death of his wife. A closet in a dream also represents a made, keeping secrets, confidentiality or intimacy between husband and wife, protecting the reputation of chaste women, beautiful garments or it could represent the day and the night. If one puts something in a closet in a dream, it means that he will find it there when he needs it.

Clot: *(See Vascular blockage)*

Cloth: (Fabric) Weaving a cloth or hanging it in the open air in a dream means undertaking a long journey. *(Also see Wrapping)*

Clothing: (Dwellings; Face; Look; State; Transient) One's garment in a dream represents his innermost thoughts that will eventually show in his attitude in life. If one's thoughts are good, then it will show, and if they are evil, they will also manifest. If one wears a slipper over his head and a turban in his foot in a dream, it means that he is carrying trouble. Depending on its type and name, a garment in a dream could represent a man or a woman. Wearing a new garment in a dream is better than seeing an old one. If a man sees himself wearing a woman's apparel in a dream, it means that he is a bachelor. If a woman sees herself wearing a man's garment in a dream, it means that she is unmarried. Wearing a tightly buttoned shirt in a dream means experiencing tight circumstances or reuniting with a traveller returning home, or it could mean marriage for an unwed person. Wearing a stately apparel in a dream means honor and dignity. Wearing a soldier's uniform in a dream means war. Wearing a scholar's robe or a teacher's vest in a dream means studying to become a learned person. Wearing an ascetic's woolen wrap in a dream means becoming a renunciate. Wearing a salesman's suit in a dream means hard work or looking for work if the suit looks expensive in the dream, for people mostly wear expensive looking suits when they are still searching for work. Wearing a white garment in a dream means pride, honor and dignity. Wearing silk in a dream means strength and occupying a high rank in a business or government. If one sees a deceased person wearing a silken garment in a dream, it means that he is dwelling in the heavenly paradise. Wearing a garment that is adorned with gold in a dream means victory over one's enemy. A black garment means honor, reign and having mastery over people. Wearing a green garment in a dream means martyrdom. Wearing a cotton garment in a dream means following the Prophet's tradition (uwbp). Wearing a woolen garment in a dream means clarity, unless if it is coarse or unfitting and in that case, it means poverty and humiliation. Wearing a linen garment in a dream means enjoying a blessing or a favor. Wearing a brocaded garment in a dream means receiving an important and a revered message, rising in station, enjoying wealth or it could represent the blessing of having a child. Wearing a robe that is trailing behind one's feet in a dream means rebellion and disobedience, while wearing a moderately short coat in a dream means purity, virtues and chastity. Wearing any type of garment in a dream means emulating the character of such people or becoming a prisoner of war. Wearing a kufi or a headdress for prayers in a dream means atonement for one's sins. Wearing a jubbah or a long cloak in a dream means longevity. Wearing an open sports jacket in a dream means ease in one's life or financial success. Wearing a special costume for a festival or a celebration in a dream means prosperity and a wealth that is saved for one's children, or it could mean buying new merchandise for one's shop. Wearing a military uniform in a dream means distress, trouble or a scientific dispute. Wearing one's traditional costumes in a dream, or that of another community means to befriend them and to celebrate their festivities with joy. (Also see Filth; Linen; Used clothing)

Cloud of destruction: (Destruction; Disaster; Tornado) Seeing a tornado or a cloud of destruction in a dream is a sign of punishment for disobeying God's command. Seeing a tornado in a dream also could mean money, a wife, or a servant.

Cloud of smoke: (Adversities; Fight; Pollution) In a dream, seeing a cloud of heavy smoke over a town represents a calamity from God Almighty or a harsh punishment of a ruler. However, if one sees smoke coming out of his house in a dream, it means that he will be defamed, or that he will be struck by a severe illness, an injury or a fever that will result from his work or place of business. He will then recuperate from his illness, regain the upper hand and turn things around. If the smoke is caused by a fire or rises to spread from under a cooking pot in a dream, it means joy after distress and prosperity after poverty. If the smoke has no burning odor in the dream, it means an atrocity or an ugly experience which will be followed by exposure and defamation. If one sees himself shaded under a cloud of smoke in a dream, it means that he will suffer from a high fever. If one suffers from the heat of smoke in a dream, it means difficulties and distress. If one sees clouds of smoke gathering over the hills in a dream, it means that a great scare will befall the people of that locality. If the smoke is not caused by a fire in the dream, it represents the stationing of an army though no war will take place. However, the impact of such fear will have its effects on everyone. If the smoke causes harm to the people and affect their sights or limits their vision in the dream, it means injustice, depression, adversities, pain and suffering from a divine punishment for people's sins. Smoke in a dream also means news from the direction it comes from. (Also see Smoke; Sparks)

Clouds: (Concealment; Gloom; Dream; Life; Rains; Skies; Soldiers; Sufferings; Vapor; Water) In a dream, clouds represent the course of life which provides people with rainwater to drink, water to wash their dirt, water for their crops and sustenance. Clouds in a dream also represent knowledge, understanding, wisdom, clarity as they show the divine kindness. Clouds in a dream also represent an army or friends who carry the water and the water represents life and the original element from which they were created. Clouds in a dream also represent ships, airplanes, or if they are black or carry stones or bring thunder, then they represent the antagonistic character of a leader who deprives his people from their rights or causes them to suffer through restrictive laws or harsh mandates. If one sees a cloud inside his house or descending upon him in his room in a dream, it means that he will join the company of believers or receives an award, or that he is endowed with wisdom, or should he wish for a child, his wife will conceive one. If he is a merchant, it means that his merchandise will arrive to its port of destination. If one sees himself riding over a cloud in a dream, it means exaltation or marriage to a pious woman, or that one will attend a pilgrimage should it be his wish. Otherwise, should he wish for it, he will become renowned for his knowledge and wisdom. Should he qualify, it means that he will lead an army, or that he will rise in rank, or that he will be sent as an emissary of his government or as an ambassador. If people are expecting clouds to water their farms, and should one see masses of clear clouds carrying rains and coming in that direction in the dream, it means a calamity. If the clouds carry poisonous rains or acid rains or polluted rains, or if they are driven by heavy winds, or if they carry fires or dust or ashes or rocks from a volcano, they mean that a calamity will strike that locality, or that they will receive news about travellers the majority of whom will perish during a trip. Clouds also mean innovations and manmade religions that may spread throughout the land. If one sees himself merging with the clouds in a dream, it means that he associates himself with a person in authority or a wise man or a man of knowledge. If one sees himself eating clouds in his dream, it means that he will gain lawfully earned money from such a person, or that perhaps he may gain wisdom. If one sees himself amassing clouds in a dream, it means that he will learn wisdom at the hand of a close associate. If one sees himself mixing with the clouds but does not carry anything out of them in a dream, it means that he will mix with people of knowledge and learn nothing from what they say, or practice nothing of what they teach. If one sees himself riding over the clouds in a dream, it means that he may become famous for his wisdom and knowledge. If one sees his own son turned into a cloud in a dream, it means that he earns his livelihood from teaching wisdom or religious knowledge to others. Black clouds in a dream mean wisdom, forbearance, honesty and joy. If the black clouds also carry a threat or cause fear in the dream, it means that one will be reprimanded by such a wise person. If one sees himself building a house over a cloud in a dream, it means that he lives an honest life, earns lawful money and lives his life with wisdom and integrity. If one builds a palace over a cloud in a dream, it means that through his wisdom, he avoids committing sins. It also means that he prospers from such a wisdom or builds a palace in paradise with his deeds. If one sees a cloud in his hand and rain falling from it in a dream, it denotes the wisdom he speaks. If one turns into a rainy cloud in a dream, it means that he lives wealthy and benefits people from his money. If one turns into a cloud that rains gold in a dream, it means that he will learn wisdom from a great man. Clouds in a dream also represent the people in authority who do others favors and ask for no reward. If one hears a human sound calling him from behind a cloud in a dream, it means that God willing he will attend a pilgrimage. (*See Invisible caller*). A black cloud in a dream also represents a just judge, while a white cloud represents a blessed and a noble justice. Clouds in season in a dream represent benefits, profits and prosperity. A mass of black clouds carrying no rain in a dream mean benefits, extreme cold, sadness or sorrow. Red clouds in a dream mean distress, adversities or a sickness. A cloud covering a town in a dream means blessings. If the person who sees such black clouds in his dream is intending to take a trip, it will take place, though his safety cannot be insured. On the other hand, if he is unhappy about something, then if he sees such a dream, it means that his sorrow will be dispelled. White clouds in a dream are a sign of work, a job or business. Rising fog in a dream means taking a journey, or returning from one. Red clouds in a dream means lack of work. A gloomy cloud in a dream means stress. If one sees clouds welcoming him in a dream, it means glad tidings. If he is an evil person, it means a calamity and a chastisement for his sins. If one sees clouds covering the sun in a dream, it means that the ruler of that land is ill. If one sees himself wearing a shirt of clouds in a dream, it means blessings that God Almighty has favored him with. Clouds in a dream also represent virtues, miracles, favors, rains, love and blessings, because they also appear when a prophet or a saint pray for rain or to shelter a blessed person from the heat of the sun. Clouds in a dream also mean travel by sea or air.

Clove: *(See Musk)*

Cloven foot: *(See Cloven hoof)*

Cloven hoof: (Cloven foot) In a dream, a cloven hoof means toiling, hardships, evil, or sexual intercourse.

Club: (Cudgel) In a dream, a club means scolding and rebuking someone. If used as a baton in a dream, then it means subjugating and humiliating someone, or it could mean having the upper hand or having the wealth and power to do good or evil. *(Also see Knocker)*

Clump: *(See Bunch)*

Cluster: *(See Bunch)*

Coach: *(See Bear trainer; Car; Carriage house)*

Coagulation: *(See Vascular blockage)*

Coal stove: *(See Brazier)*

Coal: (Carbonize; Charcoal; Fuel) Burning coal in a dream means immediate earnings or a ready to fill order for one's merchandise. If one can benefit from it in his dream, it means easy benefits or receiving jewelry as a gift, or having a type of work in which one needs to use coal. Seeing burning coal in a dream also means seeking knowledge and wisdom. Coal in a dream also represents an evil and a dangerous person, or it could mean tainted money, unlawful earnings or receiving a grant from someone in the government. Burning coal in a dream also denotes someone who is unjustly suffering from hardships and trials or someone who's property is unjustly confiscated. Consumed or burned up coal in a dream means the same thing as ashes and signifies falsehood. Having large cuts of coal when one needs small pieces in a dream means worries, distress and concerns, while having fine crushed coal when one needs chunks to light a fire in a dream means diminishing of one's wealth. Seeing coal or charcoal in a dream also could mean increase or rejuvenation of one's sexual desires. Seeing coal in the winter in a dream means money. Fuel for the fire in a dream means corruption. *(Also see Ashes)*

Coarse: (Clothing; Food; Words) If a rich person sees himself either wearing coarse clothing, eating coarse food or speaking harsh words in a dream, it means that he will experience severe changes in his life and that will perhaps affect much of his savings. Should one feel more comfortable about such changes in the dream, or if he prefers them over his usual comforts, it becomes a sign of his humility, contentment, gratitude and the correctness of his way of thinking. Should he feel uncomfortable about such changes in the dream, it means that he will become subject to God's wrath. Exchanging coarse words in a dream means aversion between people who actually love one another.

Coat of mail: (Armor; Kingdom; Money; Peace; Shield) In a dream, a coat of mail represents protection from one's enemy. If one sees himself making a coat of mail in a dream, it means that he will build a castle. To see oneself wearing one means becoming a leader. If a merchant sees himself wearing a coat of mail in a dream, it means that his business keeps growing, being completely sheltered and protected from losses. If the coat of mail is understood to mean a friend in the dream, then it will represent a gracious friend and a good helper when one needs him. A coat of mail also represents one's son who is strong and capable, who suffices himself and helps his father. Wearing a coat of mail in a dream is a blessing and a favor one receives from a third party who will support him and defend him under all circumstances. Wearing one in a dream means protection for one's wife, properties and interests. If a woman sees herself wearing a coat of mail in a dream, it means a husband and protection. It also could mean a supporting brother, a compassionate son, money, clothing or strong supporters. Wearing a suit of mail in a dream also means having a strong son, or it could mean travels.

Coat[1]: (Cloak; Garment; Faith; Overcoat; Religion; Spirituality) Wearing a coat in a dream means honor and respect if new. If it is a shabby or a light coat in the dream, then it means failure in one's proper attendance to his religious duties. A winter coat in a dream represents a poor but vainglorious and boastful person. A coat in a dream is also interpreted as a mean and a profane woman. If a man sees himself wearing a coat, and if it is interpreted to mean a woman in the dream, then it means that one may have committed a sizeable capital to support something that will bring limited benefits. If one loses his coat in a dream, it means that he will be shielded from poverty and boasts about his status in public. A coat in a dream also represents man's trust, because it is placed over his shoulders and around his neck. If a woman sees a coat in her dream, it means suffering from unkindness on the part of her husband. *(Also see Cap; Overcoat)*

Coat[2]: *(See Dip)*

Cocaine: *(See Intoxicants)*

Cock fighting: (Gamecock) Cock fight in a dream means prodding and instigating a dispute between close friends or colleagues, or it could mean provoking enmity between scholars or a dispute between two muezzins who call to prayers in a mosque.

Coconut: Eating a coconut in a dream means that one may have the potential to become a fortuneteller or he may befriend one. Coconut in a dream also indicates the possibility of contracting intestinal inflammations.

Coercion: If one adamantly refuses to obey and resists the coercion of evil people or refuses to be intimidated by evil companions in a dream it represents his faith in God Almighty, fear of wrongdoing and making offerings that are pleasing to God. *(Also see Horn; Recalcitrant child)*

Coffee pot: (Brewing; Utensil) In a dream, a coffee pot represents ascetic detachment, increased devotion, a son, a servant, a small town, a profitable business or travels.

Coffer: (Pomegranate; Treasure box. *See Case*)

Coffin: (Arc) In a dream, a coffin means a great wealth. If one sees himself hiding inside a coffin in a dream, it means fearing one's enemy and that one is incapable of facing him, though this element in a dream also could mean salvation or escape from dangers that will follow. If one sees himself riding on top of a coffin in a dream, it means that either his name is mentioned in a will, or that he will face a dispute regarding an inheritance that will turn to his advantage. If one is given a coffin in a dream, it means that he is given knowledge, peacefulness and dignity. A coffin in a dream also represents stress and worries or a travelling vehicle. A miller's flour mixing container which traditionally used to look like a coffin in a dream represents a just man or a man of knowledge and a true guide. *(Also see Sarcophagus)*

Coitus: *(See Sexual intercourse)*

Colander: *(See Sieve)*

Cold spell: (Congestion; Severe cold) A severe cold in a dream represents an evil person of double-dealing, who is suspicious of others, rough in nature, cool in his speech and who benefits no one.

Cold water: If one sees himself drinking cold refreshing water from the regular water tab in a dream, it means comfort and joy. *(Also see Drink)*

Cold weather: (Swine) Experiencing it in a dream during the summer season means benefits, profits or new and expensive clothing, but experiencing hot weather in one's dream during the winter season means the opposite.

Cold: (Atmospheric) Cold temperature in a dream means poverty. A windy and cold weather in a dream means aggravation of one's poverty. If it is sunny and cold, and if ones sees himself sitting in the sun, then the condition of his poverty will be removed. If one sees himself in a dream under the heat of the sun and seeks refuge away from it in the shade, it means that his stress and sadness will dissipate. If he sees that dream during the summertime, it means prosperity. If one sees himself seeking a fire or a smoke to warm himself with it in a dream means that one is seeking a job that entails danger. If it is burning coal which he seeks for warmth in the dream, then it means that he will swindle money from an orphan. Cold weather in winter is insignificant and in the summer in a dream it means that one's travel plans will not take place. *(Also see Cold weather)*

Colic: (Excruciating abdominal pain. *See Drummer*)

Colitis: (*med.* Gastrointestinal disease; Inflammation) Suffering from colitis in a dream means feeling malaise, languid or indisposed with one's own family, children or relations, or it could mean being niggardly toward one's own family and consequently suffering from a just retribution. As for a woman, suffering from colitis in a dream means getting pregnant or befriending evil people, or it could mean hearing harsh words.

Collapsing walls: If one sees the walls of his house collapsing as a result of a flood in a dream, it means the death of his wife. If one sees his house caving in on him and causing a big cloud of dust in a dream, it means that he maybe afflicted with measles. A collapsed ceiling in a dream means devastation. If one sees a destroyed house standing erect anew in a dream, it means spiritual awakening of its owner. If one is awaiting the return of a member of his family, or if he is awaiting a guest to arrive, and if a part of his house caves in, it means the near arrival of such a traveller. If a daughter or a sister or another woman live in that house, it means that the guest will seek her hand for marriage. If a hurricane destroys his entire house in a dream, it means that death will take locality in that place at the hands of a tyrant. If one sees himself demolishing an old house or edifice in a dream, it means evil. If a woman sees her walls caving in on her in a dream, it means the death of her husband. *(Also see Destruction)*

Collar: *(See Collarband)*

Collarband: (Collar; Neckband; Neckwear) In a dream, a collarband represents the pleasure and pride of a mother or a wife to see her sons or daughter having a jewelry business. If an unmarried woman sees herself in a dream wearing a neckband, a necklace or a collarband made from pearls, peridot or chrysolite, it means that she will marry a noble and a high ranking man, beget children from him and find her ultimate pleasure and love in such a marriage. If the collarband is made from alum, then it means marrying a young eastern man. If the collarband is made from beads in the dream, it means that her husband is a mean and a contemptible person. If a man sees himself wearing a collarband in a dream, it means suffocation, distress or a quarrel. *(Also see Neckband; Necklace)*

Collateral: *(See Hostage; Guarantee; Pawn)*

Collect: *(See Combine; Gather)*

College: *(See Institute; School)*

Collide: *(See Smashing)*

Colocynth: (Bitter fruits)

Colors of the face: *(See Colors; Face)*

Colors: (Black; Blond; Bluish-black; Green; Maroon; Purple; Red; Reddish-brown; White; Yellow) The color black in a dream means prosperity, happiness or sickness. The color blond in a dream means war, sickness, piety, honor or a religious person. In a dream, the color blond also means contemptibleness, vileness, meanness or depravity. Black colored eyes in a dream represent a religious person. A bluish-black colored eyes in a dream connote opposing one's religion. Blue eyes in a dream entail religious innovations. Green eyes in a dream represent a religion that is different from all religions. The color green in a dream also represents a good harvest or prosperity. Green in a dream also means youth or fear of wrongdoing. In a dream, the color blue represents distress, depression, enmity, or it could mean a calamity. The color red in a dream denotes joy, celebration, spirituality or dominion. Red means the world or material gains. In a dream, the color maroon or a reddish-brown color signifies dignity, nobility, power or it could represent a wealthy woman. The color purple in a dream represents a brilliant, skillful and a beautiful woman, or it could mean fragrance, instability, sickness, love and harmony. White in a dream also means beauty or it could represent elderly people. A black flag in a dream means a man of knowledge, a white one represents jealousy, a yellow flag represents an epidemic disease and a green flag means a journey by land. A black cloud in a dream represents a just judge while a white cloud represents a blessed, noble and true justice. A white thread in a dream represents the dawn and a black thread in a dream represents the night. If one sees his cheeks radiant white in a dream, it means honor, bounty, or it could mean achieving a high rank in one's community. Unknown white or green tents in a camp in a dream represent the graves of martyrs. Yellow represents strain, sickness, repentance, a son, or it could mean chivalry. *(Also see Flag; Garment)*

Colossal: *(See Giant)*

Colostrum: (Lactate; Milk) If a pregnant woman witnesses the protein rich fluid that is secreted for few days after giving birth in a dream, it means her deliverance, or a childbirth.

Column base: *(See Base)*

Column: (Pillar; Post) In a dream, a column represents one's religion. If one sees a column descending from the firmament in a dream, it means a divine favor and a blessing to have a just, compassionate and a forbearing ruler in that land. If one is hit with a post, or if he uses it to beat someone in a dream, it means hearing or exchanging harsh words that describe the quality of the one who is struck. If one sees himself leaning against a pillar that he bought or which is given to him in his dream, it means that he will rely upon an old woman for his livelihood, or that he will marry an old woman. A column in a dream also represents a friend one can depend on. A leaning column in a dream represents a worker who cheats his employer, disobeys him and who is a hypocrite. If a worker sees a leaning post in his dream, it means that his employer will lean toward kindness and appreciation of his workers. Columns in a dream also represent important and strong men who are capable of managing their responsibilities. Owning a column or becoming a column in a dream, and if one qualifies, it means that he will become a leader of his community, a pillar in his own field, or a beacon of knowledge and a pillar of wisdom who is sought by knowledge seeking people. If one becomes a pillar in a dream, it also could mean his death, or it could mean crying. A pillar in a dream also represents a father, a son, money, capital, a partner, a vehicle, one's wife or a leader. A marble column in a dream represents a great wealth, a great man, or a great woman. A column made from granite in a dream represents someone who despises himself. If it is from stone, it means fast changing conditions. If it is a wooden column in the dream, then it represents a hypocrite. The pillars of a mosque represent the Imām, the muezzin, the servants and the people who pray in it. *(Also see Base)*

Comb: In a dream, a comb represents a good man who strives to help, serve, comfort and entertain others. A comb in a dream also represents an auspicious time to be involved in a business partnership or accepting an employment in a large corporation, since the teeth of a comb are equal. If the teeth of one's comb are capped with gold or silver caps, then they represent one's workers. The golden caps represent trustworthy workers and the silver caps represent treacherous and disloyal workers. Combing one's hair in a dream signifies paying alms tax, or it could mean distributing charities. A comb in a dream also can be interpreted to denote an honest and a just man, an hour of happiness, or a wise person, a judge, a physician, or a preacher one can benefit from his knowledge. A comb in a dream also represents a hairdresser or one's mother. Combing the hair of an unknown woman in a dream represents a wind that will help pollinate the trees. In a dream, a comb also represents a sifter or a sieve. The teeth of a comb may represent one's own teeth or the teeth of a saw. It is also said that combing hair in a dream means weaving a carpet. Combing one's hair or beard in a dream means dispelling adversities and distress. In a dream, a comb also represents a good man who is just and equitable with all his friends, or it may mean longevity, wealth and victory against one's enemy.

Combat: *(See Duel)*

Combine: Combining or matching coordinates such as pearls with gold, amber with gold, gems and pearls in a dream means benefiting others with one's knowledge, counsel, good conduct or professional opinions.

Comeback: *(See Attack)*

Comedian: (Humorist; Storyteller) In a dream, a comedian represents someone who selects his words, embellishes his presentation, investigates the news or someone who constantly searches for new materials to work with. A comedian in a dream also represents someone who sells immodest clothing. *(Also see Humorist)*

Comfort: In a dream, comfort means dispelling sorrows or paying one's debts. *(Also see Fan)*

Coming down: *(See Descending)*

Coming home: *(See Arrival)*

Commander: *(See Army general)*

Commentator: *(See Critic)*

Committing suicide: *(See Disbelief)*

Commutative contract: (Compensate; Interchange; Substitute) To substitute something for something better in a dream means an adversity and a distressful offense one chooses to bear with patience, contentment and accepts it as his fate until God Almighty removes it and replaces it with a greater reward in this world and in the hereafter. *(Also see Compensation)*

Companion of the road: (Friendship) If a sick person sees himself walking on the road along with a friend or travelling with him in a dream, it means that he will recover from his illness. Accompanying an unknown person on the road in a dream means suffering losses. Walking in the company of a relative in a dream has a negative connotation.

Companion: *(See Book; Dog; Bedmate; Messmate)*

Companions of the Prophet (uwbp): (Followers; Righteous people; Successors) If one sees in a dream that one of the companions of God's Messenger, upon whom be peace, his followers or their successors entering a town or locality that is suffering under natural adversities, oppression or war, it means relief for its people and reversal of their conditions. It could also mean that their leaders will become guided again. To see the gnostics of a land means increase in one's knowledge. To see the wise men of a land, means increase in one's wisdom. To see the preachers of a town in a dream means spiritual growth and increase in one's happiness. To see the righteous dwellers of a land and God's trustees therein in a dream means increase in one's devotion. If one sees past companions alive in a dream, it means prosperity, justice and economic growth for the inhabitants, coming from a God-fearing leadership. If one sees himself resurrecting one of the companions, their followers or successors in a dream, it means that he will revive his practices and traditions. If one sees himself turned into one of the known righteous companion or followers of God's Prophet, upon whom be peace in a dream, it means trials in one's life to equal the exalted station of such blessed beings, though the end is praiseworthy. *(Also see Righteous people; Scholars)*

Comparison: *(See Conscription)*

Compassed: *(See Finished business)*

Compassing the streets: A man compassing the streets in a dream represents a guide or an adviser who admonishes people, strives for conciliation and peace and who endeavors what is good and eschew evil.

Compassion: *(See Mercy)*

Compensate: *(See Commutative contract; Coughing)*

Compensation: If one finds a lost object in his dream, or if he does something that earns him a reward in a dream, this will represent his loyalty, fulfillment of his promises, protecting his friendships and striving for lawful earnings. *(Also see Finding something)*

Competition: *(See Duel; Racing)*

Compilation: *(See Reference book)*

Compiling: (Librarian; Pastry chef)

Complimenting oneself: Complimenting oneself in a dream means committing a sin. If an unknown young person compliments him in a dream, it means that his enemy will yield to him. If a known young person, or if an old man compliments him in a dream, it means attaining success at their hand.

Complications: *(See Solution; Solving a complicated problem)*

Compliments: *(See Felicitations)*

Compromise: *(See Conciliation; Reconciliation)*

Con artist: (Deceiver; Shark) If a con artist sees himself as a king or as a leader in a dream, it means that he will be captured and imprisoned.

Concealing knowledge: *(See Keeping a secret; Secretary)*

Concealment: (Hiding) If one sees himself entering a house to hide in a dream, it means that he will receive condolences, or that he will beget a daughter. Concealment in a dream also means dependence on what one stands behind. If one hides behind a mountain in a dream, it means placing his trust in a revered or a religious person. *(Also see Clouds)*

Concern: *(See Carefulness; Conscious; Watchful)*

Conciliation: (Compromise; Peace; Reconciliation; Settlement) Making peace with one's adversary in a dream means disagreement in wakefulness. However, reconciliation between two adversaries or friends in accordance with the prescribed laws in a dream means unity, repentance from sin, guidance that pleases God Almighty, blessings and profits. It also could mean an argument with the person seen in the dream. If one sees himself making peace with an adversary in a dream, it means that he will call upon a heedless person to walk on God's path. Making a settlement with an adversary over money in a dream means profits for the lender. In a dream, signing a peace agreement between two enemies in the battlefield means safety and prosperity, intending to get married, or building a business partnership. Conciliation between arguing drunkards over what they are drinking means enmity between people. If two groups of opposing trends compromise or consent to respect each others' philosophy in a dream, it denotes the birth of a new ideology, innovations and trials. If someone invites a litigant to making an out of court settlement in a dream, it means that he is admonishing people to follow the divine guidance.

Concord: *(See Correspondence)*

Condiment: *(See Salt)*

Condolences: Expressing one's sympathy or condolences to a well-to-do person in a dream means adversities, while it means a blessing to a person in dire need. Expressing one's sympathy to a person who is experiencing difficulties in a dream means glad tidings.

Condom: *(See Birth Control)*

Confess: *(See Acknowledging devotion)*

Confident: (Companion. *See Book; Secret)*

Confiding: (Secret; Trust) If one sees someone confiding into someone else or telling him a secret in a dream, it means the death of the second person. *(Also see Secret)*

Conflict: *(See Enmity)*

Conformance: (Agreement; Consent) Consenting to obey God's commands in a dream or conformance with the divine laws in a dream means love for one's brethren, associating with the righteous ones and renouncing the fellowship of evil companions.

Confusion: *(See Darkness; Fog)*

Congratulations: *(See Felicitations)*

Congregation: *(See Imām; Five times prayers; Pharaoh; Prayers)*

Conifer tree: (Pitch; Resin) In a dream, a conifer tree means travels. *(Also see Resin)*

Conifers: *(See Resin)*

Conjurer: *(See Juggler)*

Connections: (Social acquaintance) To have important connections in a dream means compelling one's enemy to retreat or to accept one's conditions. To have important relationships in a dream also cools the divine wrath, as when giving charity in secret. This is true unless one's connections or circle holds to a group of evil companions, or if he mingles with a band of conspirators.

Connoisseur: *(See Critic)*

Consanguineous: *(See Sexual intercourse)*

Conscious: *(See Carefulness; Concern; Watchful)*

Conscription: (Call-up; Draft; Enlist; Military service; Mobilization) A military draft in a dream means cognizance of what is good and beneficial for everyone and shows equality between the natives of the land, the poor and the rich, the close relative, the distinguished and the unknown.

Consent to obey God's commands: *(See Conformance)*

Constellations: In a dream, Alcyone means dirt or wealth—Aldebran means retreat or one's sexual organs—Aldromeda means a woman in distress—Alhena means satisfaction or impotence—Antilia means iron—Apus means a heavenly bird—Ara means flying—Arctunus means unlawful earnings or actions—Argo means travelling by sea—Auriga and Corvus mean fortune and blessings—Boötis represents a shepherd or servitude—Castor means advancement—Cepheus represents a ruler—Corona Australis means marriage—Corona Borealis means forgiveness and safety—Cygnus means a swan—Grus means departure—Libra means adultery—The Celestial equator means happiness—The Little Bear, the Great Bear, Aquila, Orion, Spica, Arietica or Aquarius among others, if one sees them or owns them or controls them or recognizes their names in a dream, it means befriending someone or marriage to a woman with that name or zodiac sign or character, or it could mean begetting a son. The celestial pole in a dream represents a devout worshiper or a high ranking commander—Pollux means delays—The Ursa Major and Ursa Minor mean pursuit, following, signs of guidance or tracks of moving around—Triangulum means conditions—Vela means confrontation—Viergo means a contraceptive—and Vulpicula means screaming. *(Also see Celestial spheres; Dog; Star)*

Constipation: In a dream, constipation means miserliness, stinginess and avarice.

Construction worker: (Carpenter; Mason; Woodworker; Workman) Seeing a construction worker in a dream means both poverty or richness, or he could denote travels or uncertainty about what profession one should get into to earn his livelihood, or he could represent someone who patiently carries someone else's burdens, or someone who fabricates a story, or someone who embellishes a story with lies, or someone who mixes the lawful with the unlawful. A construction worker in a dream also represents someone who stirs-up people against one another for a price. If some dust falls over him during his work in the dream, it means that he will benefit accordingly, and if no dust falls over him during his work in the dream, it means that he will get nothing from inciting people against one another. If one sees a construction worker demolishing a wall or a house in a dream, it means that some enmity will grow between friends that could bring about the death of one of them. *(Also see Carpenter; Digging; Labor; Pickax)*

Container: *(See Bag; Pouch; Sack; Suitcase; Trunk)*

Contemptible: *(See Shameful act)*

Contest: *(See Duel; Racing)*

Continuity: Continuity of what is common, such as dwellings, status or being in a dream means a lasting job. It also means increase in one's devotion if one sees himself perpetually glorifying, praising and remembering God Almighty. When one invokes the sovereign attributes of God Almighty at the sight of a cemetery or a ruin, and if he follows that by crying and lamenting in the dream, it means stress caused by affiliation with such monuments.

Contour of a person: *(See Figure)*

Contraceptive device: *(See Birth control)*

Contract: In a dream, a contract represents a necklace of pearls, a marriage contract, a prenuptial agreement or a business agreement. A contract in a dream also could signify a covenant or making a bond with the other signing party. *(Also see Knot; Pledge of allegiance)*

Contrast: *(See Opponent)*

Contribution: *(See Endowment)*

Controversy: *(See Dispute)*

Convent: (Monastery) In a dream, seeing a convent is like seeing a church. Perhaps it means dispelling anxiety or distress and recovering from adversities. If a sick person sees a convent in his dream, it means his approaching death.

Conveying a secret: (Entrust. *Also see Castration; Confiding*)

Conveyor belt: In a dream, it means begetting a son or going on a journey.

Convoy: *(See Escort)*

Cooing of pigeons: In a dream, the cooing of a pigeon represents a person of understanding, a scholar, a well mannered person, a gentle soul who has little money but many friends or the followers of a wise man. The cooing of a pigeon in a dream also represents the voice of a teacher. *(Also see Sound of animals)*

Cook: *(See Caterer; Cooking)*

Cooking pot: *(See Pot)*

Cooking: Cooking on fire in a dream means attaining one's goal or achieving one's purpose. If one sees himself preparing food on fire, and if his food is well cooked in the dream, it means that he will attain success and become famous. Otherwise, if his food is not well cooked in the dream, it means that he will fail to attain his goal. Cooking in a dream also means provoking matters of interest. If the food is well cooked in the dream, then it means money and profits. Cooking raw meat in a dream and finding it hard to cook means getting involved in something that will not mature. Otherwise, if it does cook, and if one can eat from it in the dream, then it means success. Cooking mutton in a dream means living an honorable life, being generous and earning lawful money. If one cooks beef in his dream, it means living a comfortable life using the labor of tradesmen. If one sees himself cooking lion's meat in a dream, it means that he will rise to leadership over unjust people, though one will have to maintain his vigilance and live in constant fear. If one sees himself cooking dog's meat in a dream, it means that he will manage a lowly job. If he cooks the fat with it in a dream, it means that he will earn unlawful money. Otherwise, without the fat, it means that he will perform a lowly job and remains poor and deprived. If one sees himself cooking a bird in a dream, it means governing or managing a business or earning lawful money from associating with rich and noble people. If one cooks his meal with vulture's meat in a dream, it means governing or trading with non-intelligent or heedless people and earning unlawful money. *(Also see Pot; Stew)*

Cookware: *(See Bowl; Pot)*

Cooler: *(See Fan)*

Coordinates: *(See Combine)*

Coppersmith: In a dream, a coppersmith represents evil, adversities, difficulties, headaches, noises, marriage of an unwed person or cherishing the pleasure of having children. *(Also see Brass)*

Copulation: (Breed; Farm; Raise) If one sees himself driving a male animal to copulate with a female animal in a dream, it means a good harvest for that year. *(Also see Driver)*

Copyist: *(See Calligrapher)*

Coral: (Coralline) In a dream, corals mean money, wealth or a beautiful young woman. Wearing a necklace carrying a coral stone in a dream means heedlessness and straying from God's path.

Coralline: *(See Coral)*

Core: *(See Date pit; Pith)*

Coriander: *(See Chervil)*

Corn bread: *(See Bread)*

Corn measurer: *(See Measurer)*

Cornerstone: (Pillar) A cornerstone in a dream represents one's wife or it could mean money. *(Also see Black stone; Ka'aba)*

Corona Australis: *(See Constellations)*

Corona Borealis: *(See Constellations)*

Correspondence: (Affinity; Concord; Likeness) Exchanging correspondence between two friends in a dream means longevity, for it means joining two destinies and it means comfort and happiness each one gets from his friend.

Correspondent: *(See War correspondent)*

Corridor: *(See Alley; Hallway)*

Corrosion: *(See Rust)*

Corset: *(See Brace)*

Corvus: *(See Constellations)*

Cosmetics: (Henna; Makeup) If one sees his face embellish with red cosmetic makeup in a dream, it means that he will commit adultery and be exposed thereafter. Cosmetic makeup in a dream also represents a craftsman's working tools. It also means adornment, money or children.

Costume: *(See Apparel)*

Cottage cheese: Eating cottage cheese in a dream means good and dear money one enjoys beside other pleasures. *(Also see Cheese)*

Cotton ginner: (A professional craftsman who works at separating seeds from cotton.) In a dream, a cotton ginner represents a man of knowledge or a judge who settles disputes. He may also represent the person who mints money or one who separates the good metal from the bad ones, or he may represent a man with many wives and children. *(Also see Carder; Cotton; Cotton ginnery)*

Cotton ginnery: (Gin) In a dream, a cotton gin means commanding someone, satisfying a need, procreation, a righteous progeny, money making capital, marriage, emerging truth and sagacity. A cotton gin in a dream also represents two partners, one of them is a hypocrite and the other is a hard minded person. *(Also see Cotton ginner)*

Cotton plantation: Owning a cotton plantation in a dream signifies having money and trouble. *(Also see Carder; Cotton)*

Cotton: Cotton in a dream means money, but less than that of wool. Carding cotton in a dream means scrutinizing one's sins. Cotton in a dream also represents a year, and the cotton plant in a dream represents a humble man. *(Also see Carder)*

Couch: (Canopy; Furniture; Love seat) A raised couch in a dream represents one's wife, midwife or a high ranking position. If it is made of wood in the dream, it indicates respectability, and if it is not upholstered in the dream, it means lowness or inferiority. A fabric stuffed couch in a dream signifies honor, welfare, promotion, good words, new clothing, love, affection and unity. *(Also see Bed; Mattress)*

Coughing: (Pay; Compensate; Render) In a dream, coughing means complaining about something or reporting someone to the authorities. If one's cough is severe to near suffocation, then it means his death. Coughing in a dream is also interpreted as intending to report or complain about someone, but one may call off his drive.

Councilmen: *(See Elders)*

Counselor: (Politician) A counselor in a dream represents a person who embellishes his words, adorns his actions and who promises everyone he meets to satisfy his needs. Such a person would be truthful as long as he does not ask for a price for his services. However, sometimes he may indulge in an act that will cause his best friends to suffer.

Counting apples: *(See Counting)*

Counting beads: *(See Counting)*

Counting buffalos: *(See Counting)*

Counting camels: *(See Counting)*

Counting cows: *(See Counting)*

Counting gems: *(See Counting)*

Counting money: *(See Counting)*

Counting pearls: *(See Counting)*

Counting sheep: *(See Counting)*

Counting: (Add; Calculate; Enumerate; Number) Counting apples in a dream means counting money. Counting up to the number one hundred, five thousand or twenty thousand in a dream signifies victory against one's enemy. Counting up to the number seven or eight means distress or pressures. Counting up to the number nine in a dream means adversities and joining the company of corrupt and evil people. Counting up to the number ten in a dream means completing a project, or it could mean attending the pilgrimage in Mecca. Counting up to the number forty in a dream means anticipating the fulfillment of a promise. Counting up to the number thirty in a dream means promising someone the impossible or telling a lie. The number one in a dream signifies uniqueness, superiority, having the leading edge in knowledge, money, prosperity, marriage, child, or it could mean languor, solitude or liking to be alone or cessation of activities. The number one in a dream also represents the truth or God Almighty Who has no partner, associate or equal. The number two means help against one's enemy. The number three signifies fulfillment of a promise. The number four means a pilgrimage to Mecca. The number five means doubt and weakness of one's faith. Perhaps the number six also means victory against one's enemy or establishing a proof of guilt against one's adversaries. Counting up to number seven or eight in a dream has negative connotations. Counting up to number ten in a dream could mean atonement for one's sins. If one sees himself in a dream counting money coins that has the name of God inscribed on it in a dream, it means that he celebrates God's praises and glorifies His Name. If one sees himself in a dream counting large denomination of money that has the Name of God Almighty written on it, it means acquiring knowledge. If the money coins or the banknotes are designed with images or portray the picture of known people in the dream, then they mean engaging in innovation, religious innovation, falsehood or polytheism. Counting pearls in a dream means reading the Qur'ān. Counting gems in a dream means learning wisdom or acquiring knowledge at the hand of a gnostic. Counting beads in a dream means getting involved in people's business, using obscene language, or fornication. Counting sheep in a dream means counting money or counting one's children. Counting cows in a dream means longevity or going through a long and difficult times. If a farmer sees himself counting camels in a dream, it means rain and a good harvest. Counting buffaloes in a dream means hardships and toiling in one's life. *(Also see Money)*

Courage: To show courage in a dream means perseverance and having a strong will. It also represents offering supererogatory devotion to reach nearness to God Almighty. It also could mean one's pursuit to be accepted by the people, either by defending them or by daring to face their enemy. The same interpretation is given to daring.

Courier: *(See Dromedary rider; Mailman)*

Course: *(See Food fare; Food)*

Court: If one is investigated or probed in a court by people he does not know in a dream, it means that he has strayed into innovation and will remain accountable for his deeds. *(Also see Digging up the past)*

Courtesy: *(See Kindness)*

Courting: (Flirting; Love poems; Philander) Courting a woman or singing love songs to her or displaying amorous behavior for her in public in a dream represents someone who divulges people's secrets.

Couturier: *(See Tailor)*

Cover: *(See Blanket; Envelope; Irreligious; Shade; Wrapping)*

Covetousness: (Avariciousness; Greed; Niggardliness) In a dream, covetousness means committing a sin. *(Also see Jealousy)*

Cow bell: *(See Bell)*

Cow: A cow in a dream represents longevity. A black or a yellow cow represents happiness, prosperity and a good harvest. A white spot on a cow's face means firmness if seen in a dream at the early part of the year. The piebald cow or a cow blotched with white and black in a dream means the same, though the latter also represents firmness when seen in the middle of the year. A fat cow in a dream represents longevity and prosperity. A fat cow in a dream also may represent a pious woman. An emaciated cow in a dream represents drought. Drinking cow's milk or eating its meat or fat in a dream means prosperity and earning lawful income for that year. If the cow has horns, it represents a rebellious woman. If a dairy cow allows the person to draw her milk in a dream, it means conferring benefits. Otherwise, if it refuses to allow the person to milk her in the dream, it means dissonance and discord. If a servant sees himself milking his master's cow in a dream, it means that he will marry his wife after the master dies, and that he will become extremely rich. If a cow enters one's house and thrusts against him, or butts against him in the dream, it means losses and mistrust in one's own family. If one sees himself hitting a cow with a wooden stick or biting a cow in a dream, the cow then represents his sins. If a cow scratches someone in a dream, it means an illness. If one is attacked by a cow or a steer in a dream, it means that a great punishment will befall him, or it could mean that he may be killed during that same year. If one sees himself riding a black cow, or if a cow enters his house, where he ties her to a pole in his dream, it means money, good business and dispelling of his anxiety, sadness, loneliness or distress. A slaughtered cow in a dream represents a calamity. If a shipment of yellow cows arrives at the port of a city in a dream, it means a plague or the spreading of unknown diseases. If a herd of ugly looking cows enters a city with smoke emanating from their noses, and if the people hate their look in the dream, it means a raid, an enemy, or that unwanted solders will control that town. If one sees himself riding a cow in a dream, it means that he will inherit a woman. If one is offered a cow hide as a gift in a dream, it means that he will receive money from someone in authority. On the other hand, if one is stripped of a cow's hide he owns in a dream, it represents a fine that he will have to pay. To see the calf of the Children of Israel in a dream means dissension, temptation or a murder. It also may mean a miraculous event, or that a heavenly sign will take place in that locality. If the person is disobedient to his mother, he will repent and turn to be good to her. If a cow butts against him in a dream, it means that God is displeased with him. *(Also see Counting cows)*

Cowardice: (Lacking courage) Cowardliness in a dream means training one's horses for a racing business, or it could mean modesty, or defending what is right and opposing what is wrong.

Cowboy: In a dream, a cowboy represents flow of profits from one's business, or it may mean dancing or whirling.

Cowshed: *(See Carriage house)*

Crab apple: *(See Medlar tree)*

Crab lice: *(See Nit)*

Crack in a tree: A crack in a tree in a dream means that one's family members will brace against him.

Cracking of the skin: *(See Face)*

Cracking one's fingers: Cracking one's fingers in a dream means exchanging bad words between relatives, being sarcastic, or making fun of others. *(Also see Body[1])*

Cradle of Ismā́īl: (A section of the Sacred House in Mecca.) Seeing oneself praying or standing at the Cradle of Ismā́īl in a dream means bearing a son who will become the principal provider for the family. If one is rich, then seeing the cradle of Ismāïl in a dream means that he will be debarred from his assets and that his rights to use them will be suspended. *(Also see Circumambulation; Cradle; Ka'aba; Muzdalifa; Pelting stones; Pilgrimage; Responding; Station of Abraham)*

Cradle: Buying a cradle or sitting in a cradle in a dream means blessings, grace, profits and comfort. A cradle in a dream also represents a stepson or the stepchild of a young woman. For men, a cradle in a dream signifies sorrow, distress, imprisonment or a small and restrictive dwellings. As for an unmarried man, seeing a cradle in a dream means that he will get married. As for a woman, seeing a cradle in a dream means that she will bear a child, and it could mean distress, trouble, adversities, uptightness, lamentation and crying. In a dream, a cradle also represents singing, an amusement club, an argument or a dispute. A cradle in a dream also represents a coffin. *(Also see Cage; Cradle of Ismāïl)*

Craftiness: *(See Milk; Milking)*

Craftsman: A craftsman in a dream means profits.

Crafty: *(See Monogram)*

Crane[1]: *(See Wrecking ball)*

Crane[2]: *(zool. Bird)* A crane in a dream represents a poor, meek and a weak person. Catching a crane in a dream means marrying a girl from a family of despicable characters. Cranes in a dream also represent sociable people who like to share. Seeing a crane in a dream also could mean undertaking a distant journey or returning home safely from a distant trip. Seeing cranes flying over a town in a dream denotes a cold winter, rain storms and floods. Eating the flesh of a crane in a dream means receiving money from a thief or a servant. A flock of cranes flying in a dream represents thieves, bandits, highway robbers, pollution or a hurricane. Seeing dispersed cranes flying in a dream means profits and benefits for a traveller, marriage, or a son. Riding on a crane in a dream means becoming poor. Owning a large flock of cranes in a dream means presiding over people and becoming rich. Crane's meat and feathers in a dream means earning money from a poor or a weak person. Raising a flock of cranes in a dream also means presiding over poor people. Fighting with a crane in a dream means fighting with a poor and a weak person. Hearing the cry of a crane in a dream means dispelling distress and worries.

Crash helmet: *(See Helmet)*

Crawling: Crawling on one's knees in a dream represents a chronic illness, or praying in a sitting position while being able to stand up in prayers. It also could mean wavering in one's decision to travel and being reprimanded for it, or it could mean losing interest or lacking vigor. If a poor person sees himself crawling in a dream, it means that his needs will be satisfied. If he is a rich, it means that he will become needy. Crawling in a dream also could mean complaisance and partiality toward people.

Craziness: *(See Insanity; Irrationality; Mental derangement)*

Cream: (Butter; Grease; Milk) In a dream, cream represents a fetus in his mother's womb. *(Also see Butter)*

Crease: Ironing the creases of one's garment before wearing it in a dream represents one's interest in beauty, glitters and ornaments.

Creeping: In a dream, whether it be a human or an animal, creeping means a theft, spying or eavesdropping.

Crescent: (New moon) If the new crescent appears in its correct position in a dream, it means begetting a blessed son or receiving an important appointment or profits from one's business. Seeing the gathering of several crescents in a dream means attending the pilgrimage to Mecca. A red crescent in a dream means a miscarriage. If a crescent falls to the earth in a dream, it means a newborn. Seeing the new crescent when everyone else is looking an failing to see it in a dream represents one's death, or it could mean that one will be aberrant and corrupt during that year of his life. Seeing the new moon at a time other than the time of its birth in a dream means happy news, glad tidings, the home returning of a long awaited traveller or having a newborn. The birth of a new moon in a dream also denotes the truth of one's promise, or it could mean receiving money, for rent is usually due at the beginning of each month. The appearance of the new moon or crescent in the wrong position, such as in the South or the North in a dream means committing or witnessing a despicable action that arouses abhorrence and that may die quickly, depending on how long will that new crescent remain in that position. The new crescent in a dream also represents a leader, an unexpected happy news or it could represent the cry of a newborn or a rebel. If the new crescent stands surrounded with a gloomy darkness, or if water or blood dribbles away from it, even if there is no rain during that night in the dream, it denotes the arrival of a traveler from his journey or the climbing of a muezzin to the minaret to call for prayers or the standing of a preacher on the pulpit to give his sermon, payment of one's debts, performing one's obligatory pilgrimage or the end of one's life. If the new crescent is opaque, or if it is created from yellow copper, or if it has the shape of a serpent or a scorpion in the dream, then it denotes evil. Seeing the new crescent in a dream in the same night it is supposed to be born means that one's wife will conceive a child. In a dream, a new crescent also represents a little child, repentance from sin, dispelling adversities, release from prison or recovering from an illness. Seeing the crescent when it is rising in a dream is better than seeing it when it is declining. If the new crescent suddenly disappears in one's dream, it means that one's project, object or intention will not be fulfilled. *(Also see Moon)*

Crest: (Tuft) In a dream, a crest represents a little boy.

Cricket ball: *(See Ball)*

Crime: Committing a crime in a dream means becoming a reprobate and a heedless person.

Critic: (Commentator; Connoisseur; Reviewer) In a dream, a critic represents guidance and ridding oneself of evil companions. A critic in a dream also represents a connoisseur or one who knows what is best or someone who can discern between true and false. If he is a religious person in the dream, it means that he will chose the best of specialties and the most exalted of knowledge, that is learning and understanding God's religion. If he is a worldly man in the dream, it means that he will chose the most comfortable and pleasureful type of lifestyle. If he is a ruler in the dream, it means that he will chose the highest authority.

Criticize: *(See Digging up the past; Slapping on the cheek)*

Croak: (Frog) Hearing the croaking sound of a frog in a dream means death. *(See Sound of animals)*

Croaking: *(See Sound of animals)*

Crocodile: (Alligator; Thief) A crocodile in a dream represents a policeman. A crocodile in the water in a dream represents a person no one can trust, whether he is a friend or a foe. A crocodile in a dream also represents a thief or an untruthful merchant. If one sees a crocodile pulling him into the water where he kills him in the dream, it means that one will be caught by a policeman who will kill him, then steal his property. If one escapes from the crocodile in the dream, it means that he will escape from such a danger in real life. In general, a crocodile in a dream means insolence, sins, a bandit, unlawful earnings, fear and depression. It may also mean the end of one's life, portrayed by his drowning. Seeing him in water is bad while seeing him on dry land means that he is weak and humiliated. If a crocodile pulls someone into the waters in a dream, it means that someone in authority will force him to do something he despises. If one sees himself eating the meat or flesh of a crocodile, or if one sees himself dragging a crocodile out of the water in a dream, it means that he will triumph against his enemy or opponent. *(Also see Alligator; Policeman; Thief)*

Crop: Planting in a dream means that one's wife will become pregnant. If one sees himself plowing someone else's land in a dream, it means a dispute between the two. A crop that is consumed by fire in a dream means famine and drought. If one sees himself walking through green fields in a dream, it means striving to do good, charitable deeds and leading a devout life not knowing whether his deeds will be accepted by God Almighty or not. As for a married person, planting the fields in a dream means that he will conceive a son, and for an unwed person it means that he will get married, while for a businessman in a dream, it means increase in his profits. Seeing a green crop in a dream means longevity, while a dried crop signifies the near end of one's life. Planting wheat in a dream means charity, and it will multiply one's reward. Spike of grain or ears of grain mean a misfortune or miseries. Seeing barley corns in their fields in a dream means spiritual awakening and a conscious endeavor to do good. If one recognizes his crop in a dream, then they represent his worldly and spiritual deeds. *(Also see Farm; Harvest; Planting)*

Crosier: *(See Scepter)*

Cross: A cross in a dream represents a high ranking person who is worthy of respect or it could represent a religious person. Carrying a cross in a dream could mean marriage, or an unsuitable marriage, or begetting a son. Seeing a cross in a dream also could mean adultery, rape or conceiving a son in sin. Seeing a cross in a dream is also interpreted to mean death, opposites, opposition, war, fight, distress, temptation, lies, false testimony or slander.

Crow: (Carrion crow; Cheat; Hooded crow; Jackdaw; Raven; Swindle) A crow in a dream means adultery, narrow-mindedness or concealing one's evil actions or intentions. In a dream, a crow also represents a stingy, proud, ostentatious and an arguing person. Hunting crows in a dream means earning unlawful money through deceitful actions and corruption. Seeing a crow in a dream also means a bad omen and particularly if seen in the fields. Seeing a crow standing over the roof of one's house in a dream means that one's wife is having a secret affair with one of his friends. If a crow speaks to someone in his dream, it means that he will beget a son who will grow to be a corrupt person. If one sees a crow speaking to him in a dream, it could mean suffering from depression, then feeling better thereafter. A crow in a dream also could signify migration, or separation between beloveds. Eating the flesh of a crow in a dream means receiving money from thieves. Seeing a crow standing before the courthouse in a dream means committing an offense and paying the price for one's crime, or it could mean killing one's brother, then regretting it. If one sees a crow digging the earth in a dream, then it becomes a stronger indication of such a crime. If a crow scratches someone's face in a dream, it means dying from an illness or freezing to death from being lost in a forest during the winter. Receiving a crow as a gift in a dream means happiness. A hooded crow in a dream represents longevity, a wealthy person, elderly people or it could represent wonderment about something when awakened. A crow in a dream is also the messenger of winter, cold weather and adversities. Seeing a crow descending upon a noble house means that a corrupt person will marry a noble woman from that house. Seeing a piebald crow in a dream means an affliction that will befall one's son. Owning such a piebald crow in a dream means having a bad son. Slaughtering such a crow in a dream means receiving news from a distant place. In that sense, if a piebald crow speaks to someone in a dream, it means begetting a son who will grow to be a despicable and a corrupt person. Seeing a flock of crows inside one's house in a dream means gaining wealth and honor up to the end of one's life. It also could represent people who speak ill of others or backbite them. A crow in a dream also represents a vicious fighter who fights just for himself and who is keen at acquiring what he wants, or it could represent a grave digger or bad news, a bad omen, mismanagement of one's life or business, a long journey, trouble, adversities or calling a curse upon someone, adultery or it could represent someone who mixes good with bad qualities. Seeing a jackdaw in a dream means a bad crop. Fighting a crow in a dream means fighting someone of such character. Holding a crow in one's hand in a dream means self-deception and pride. A crow inside one's shop in a dream means a corrupt person in that company. Hunting crows in a dream means gains from unlawful sources. Seeing a crow standing over a grave in a dream means that one will die in that place, or that one will discover something about which he had no knowledge. *(Also see Baby crow; Carrion crow; Raven)*

Crowd: (Throng) Seeing a crowd gathering or standing in line or a large number of people suffering in wretchedness in a dream means increase in one's power, rising in station, gaining fame and recognition. If a merchant or a business man sees a crowd of people in a dream, it means growth in his business and increase in his clientele. If a preacher sees that in his dream, it means that his followers will grow in number.

Crown of a king: Wearing a crown in a dream means increase in money and children. For a woman, wearing a crown means marriage to a foreigner. For a man, wearing a crown in a dream implies overcoming false allegations. If a merchant sees himself wearing a crown in a dream, it means loss of business and influence. If a ruler sees himself wearing a crown in a dream, it means failure in his religious commitment. If a king sees his crown being taken away from him in a dream, it means that he may be killed or lose his kingdom.

Crown of thorn: (Diadem; Garland; Wreath. *See Crown of a king*)

Crown: For a Muslim, a crown in a dream represents the Holy Qur'ān, knowledge, prosperity or marriage to a wealthy woman. Wearing a crown in a dream means begetting a son, moving into a new city or forcing an enemy to retreat. If a woman sees herself wearing a crown in a dream, it means marriage to a noble and a high ranking person. If she is married and pregnant, it means she will beget a son. If a prisoner sees himself wearing a crown in a dream, it means that he will be released from jail and regain his dignity. Wearing a crown studded or inlaid with gems in a dream is better than wearing a plain golden crown. Wearing a golden crown in a dream is also a bad omen. If a widow sees herself wearing a crown studded with gems in a dream, it means marriage to a wealthy person from another country. If the crown is made of gold in the dream, it means that she will marry an old man whom she will shortly inherit. If an unjust ruler sees himself wearing a golden crown in a dream, it means that he will lose his eyesight, while if he sees himself wearing a golden crown inlaid with gems in the dream, it means establishing trading interests with a foreign country. If a woman's crown is stolen in a dream, it means the death of her husband. *(Also see Turban)*

Crucifixion: (Death; Punishment) In a dream, crucifixion means exaltation of the one who is put on the cross, or a high rank he will attain. If one who qualifies for a leadership position sees himself crucified in a dream, it means that he will attain his goals. If he dies of his crucifixion in the dream, it means that he will lose faith or fail to apply the divine laws in his life. If he is crucified in the dream and does not die from it, it means that he will rule with justice. If an average person sees himself crucified in a dream, it means that he will be humiliated and suppressed. If one sees himself raised to be crucified after he had died in a dream, it means that he will attain worldly status, though remains morally defiled and religiously corrupt. If one sees himself crucified and did not know when was he put on the cross in a dream, it means that he will recover lost property or money, or fulfill his goals. If one is crucified after being killed in the dream, it means that someone will lie to him, despite his high rank. If one eats the flesh of a crucified person in a dream, it means that he will backbite him. If blood comes out of the flesh of a crucified person in a dream, it means that he is recruited to cause harm. If one eats the flesh of a crucified person in a dream, it means that he will travel in the mail wagon or on a cargo ship. If one sees himself riding in the mail wagon in a dream, it means that he will shortly die. If one is crucified on the walls of a city and people are watching him in a dream, it means that he will rise in station and rank and that he will command strong men. If he bleeds in the dream, it means that his subjects draw benefits from him. Crucifixion of a poor person in a dream means richness, while for a rich person, it means revelations about his business dealings, exposure of his true character, defamation, or it could mean poverty. As for an unwed person, crucifixion in a dream means getting married.

Crude oil: *(See Petroleum)*

Crumbling: In a dream, seeing a mountain or an edifice or a mausoleum breaking into pieces or being destroyed without an outside interference or blasting, it means fading of one's name or evanescence of one's remembrance after his death or disappearance of one's traces or references. Crumbling in a dream also means fulfilling one's promise.

Crupper: (A leather loop passing under a horse's tail and is buckled to the saddle.) In a dream, a crupper represents a contemptuous and a lowly guardian who profiteers and takes advantage of his position. A crupper in a dream also represents a servant who has a secret affair with his mistress. A crupper in a dream also means money or a money belt.

Crying: Lamenting or crying in a dream means distress, sorrow and stress. If such lamenting or crying is done out of fearing God Almighty, it means that salvation and joy will follow. *(Also see Laughing)*

Crystalline mineral: *(See Carnelian-red)*

Cucumber: (Large cucumber; Snake-cucumber; Squirting cucumber) In a dream, cucumbers represent distress and sadness. If one eats a cucumber in his dream, it means that he will strive for something but with great strain on him and particularly if he sees yellow cucumbers. If one's wife is pregnant and he sees cucumbers in his dream, it means that she will beget a daughter. If one is offered cucumbers as a gift in his dream, it means benefits in the long run. *(Also see Pickles; Snake-cucumber)*

Cuddle: *(See Hug)*

Cudgel: *(See Club)*

Culture: *(See Elegance)*

Cummerbund: (Belt; Cincture; Sash; Waistband) In a dream, the broad band worn around the waist, also known as a sash or a cummerbund represents one's father, mother or paternal uncle. Tying a cummerbund around one's waist in a dream means that one has exhausted half of his life. Owning many cummerbunds in a dream means longevity. A cummerbund in a dream also represents one's son or it could denote a big man. If a ruler offers a cummerbund to someone in a dream, it means that he is appointing him to a high ranking position. Wearing a cummerbund without ornaments in a dream means that one will receive the help of a great and a noble person, including moral and financial support. If one is rich, then it means that he will have a great friend to support him and whose inner thoughts and intentions are better than what one may think. If a poor person ties a cummerbund around his waist in a dream, it means extra earnings or power. If the cummerbund is studded and adorned with jewels in the dream, then such jewels represent one's helpers, supporters or obedient subjects. Such associates will carry on his commands whether they purport good or evil. Somehow, such a leader will also be unjust and hypocritical. If the ornaments are made of iron in the dream, it means that his associates are a group of strong people. If the ornaments are made from copper, then such associates care only for worldly gains. If the ornaments are made from led in the dream, it means that they are weak people. If the ornaments are made from silver in the dream, it means that the master or leader is a wealthy person and he will be followed by a strong son who will carry the work of his father. If one is given a cummerbund, and if he does not wear it in the dream, then it means travels. A broken cummerbund in a dream means loss of power or perhaps one's death. If one sees a snake rather than a cummerbund around his waist in a dream, it represents a money belt. A cummerbund in a dream also means work for a jobless person, a wife for an unmarried person, and should it be carrying many ornaments, then it means the added blessing of having several children. *(Also see Belt; Cincture; Waistband; Waist belt)*

Cunning: *(See Monogram)*

Cup: (Drinking cup; Goblet; Mug) In a dream, a drinking cup represents a woman or a son or a servant. Golden or silver cups in a dream are better than glass cups. A cup in a dream also denotes exposing hidden secrets. A filled cup in a dream represents a pregnant woman, if the water disappears in the dream, it means that she will give birth to a new child. A broken glass in a dream means death. A broken glass in a dream also signifies the death of one's wife. If one sees himself carrying a glass of water, then if the glass falls and breaks, while the water remains in his hand in the dream, it means that his wife may die soon after giving birth to a new son. If the glass does not break and the water is spilled in the dream, it means that she will live and the newborn will die. A cup in a dream also represents a housekeeper, or it could mean money. The substance of a cup in a dream is interpreted the same way as that of a woman. Eating a glass cup in a dream means suffering adversities. *(Also see Drinking; Mug)*

Cupola: *(See Watchtower)*

Cupolead structure: *(See Dome²)*

Cupping: (Sacrification; A medicinal process of blood letting) Cupping in a dream means signing an agreement under pressure, committing oneself beyond one's ability to comply, recovering from an illness, payment of debts, paying alimony to one's wife and children, loss of a business or burying a treasure. If cupping is administered but no blood comes from it in the dream, it represents buried monies that one cannot find. Cupping in a dream also means silence, desistance or abstaining from reply.

Curdled milk: *(See Milk)*

Cure: (Antidote; Herbs; Inkwell; Medicine. *See Almond; Bathhouse)*

Curly hair: If a head shaved person or a bald person sees himself having curly hair in a dream, it means following the leading example of God's Prophet, upon whom be peace. Having curly hair in a dream also means receiving financial compensation from a business, family, wife or husband, or it could mean wearing a new garment. Wrinkling one's hair in a dream is interpreted here as a sign of beauty and liking to wear extra ornaments.

Current: *(See Fan)*

Cursing: (Damn; Profanity) Cursing one's wife in a dream means perjury and yielding to sin, or suspicion about the legality of one's marriage, or having apprehensions about the legitimacy of one's earnings. Cursing in a dream also signifies banishment, dismissal from office, expulsion, exile or pushing someone away or distancing him. Cursing someone in a dream also means losing to him in wakefulness. *(Also see Infringement)*

Curve: *(See Twist)*

Custodian: *(See Legal guardian)*

Cut: (Dismembering) If one sees himself being cut into pieces or dismembered in a dream, it means that the person inflicting such cuts will rule over him. *(Also see Wound; Bleeding; Injury)*

Cutter: *(See Marble cutter)*

Cutting off: (Amputation; Beheading; Cutting; Decapitation; Scission; Chopping off; Severing) Cutting off one's hand in a dream signifies failure to perform one's obligatory prayers or being devoid of any need or an income that eliminates the need to ask others for anything, or it could mean repentance from sin. If one's hand and heels are cut off in a dream, it means corruption in one's religious life or forsaking the spiritual circles, or it could mean being barren or being freed from the duty to raise children. Cutting off one's nose or ear in a dream means a punishment for a crime, or it could mean poverty or missing someone's news. Cutting off one's tongue in a dream means invalidating one's argument or proof, or it could mean preventing him from asking for anything. If one sees himself dismembered in a dream, then it means that he will undertake extensive travels, or that members of his family will disperse into different locations, or it could mean severing one's blood ties or paying a penalty. *(Also see Beheading; Rupture of relations)*

Cutting remark: (Oversight) A slip of one's tongue or to slip in a cutting remark in a dream may mean walking on a slippery surface in wakefulness or vice-versa. *(Also see Slippery surface)*

Cygnus: *(See Constellations)*

Cymbals: (Castanets) In a dream, cymbals represent worldly people, arrogance, conceit, bragging, adversities, bad marriage or loathsome sexual intercourse. If cymbals are played during a festival in front of one's door in a dream, it means doing business in foreign country.

Cynicism: *(See Games)*

Cypress tree: *(See Tree)*

Cypress: *(See Evergreen)*

Cyst: (Sac) If one discovers a cyst in his body in a dream, it means money, determination and courage.

D

Dagger: (Knife) Carrying a dagger in one's hand in a dream means attainment of one's purpose or gaining financial stability. Sheathing a dagger in a dream means committing adultery.

Dairyman: In a dream, a dairyman represents knowledge, lawful earnings, guidance and instinct. *(Also see Milk; Milking)*

Daisy: (Plant; Woman) In a dream, daisies represent a close friend who will bring a gift or contribute something to one's business. A daisy flower in a dream is also interpreted to represent a beautiful woman. Gathering daisies from the foot of a mountain in a dream means that a strong man or someone in authority will introduce one of his daughters or relatives to him for marriage. A daisy flower in a dream is also interpreted to means marrying one's cousin.

Dajjāl: *(arb. See Antichrist)*

Damage: If one suffers a damage in a dream, it means dismay, horror, a scare, a shock or a menace. Complaining about a damage or a loss one suffers in a dream means attaining one's goal in wakefulness.

Damascus: *(See City; Masjid)*

Damn: *(See Curse)*

Dampness: *(See Dew)*

Dancer: (Hoofer; Show; Soft-shoe dancer) A hoofer in a dream represents a man in trouble if he dances for himself. If so, his parable is like that of seeds pupping on top of a fire. If a hoofer dances for someone, then the host will be struck by a calamity that will affect both of them. *(Also see Dancing)*

Dancing: Dancing in a dream means a calamity. If one sees himself dancing for someone else in a dream, it means that he will share his problems with him. Dancing alone in one's house in a dream signifies joy and satisfaction. If a sick person sees himself dancing in a dream, it denotes his anxiety. If one is pulled to a dancing circle in a dream, it means that he will be saved from tribulation or be declared innocent from false allegations. If a child is seen dancing in a dream, then it means that he may lose his speech or become dumb, because when a child dances, he mostly moves his hands to express himself. If a prisoner sees himself dancing in a dream, it means that he will be set free. Dancing on top of a table, a raised stage or on top of a hill in a dream means a scare. Dancing inside one's house, surrounded with one's family members with no outsiders in a dream means joy and celebration. If a sick person sees himself dancing in a dream, it means longevity. Seeing a woman dancing alone in a dream means a scandal. If a traveller sees himself dancing on the road in a dream, it means adversities. If a poor person sees himself dancing in a dream, it means richness. *(Also see Dancer)*

Daniel: (The prophet Daniel, upon whom be peace.) If one sees him in a dream, it means that he will become a great scholar in interpreting the divine revelations. It is also said, that one who sees him (uwbp) in a dream may become a leader, a minister, acquire extensive knowledge, but yet suffers a painful persecution which he will later defeat. If one sees himself carrying the prophet Daniel, upon

108

whom be peace, over his shoulders, sitting him beside a wall or talking to him, or if he sees the prophet Daniel talking to him, delivering glad tidings to him or feeding him honey with his own hand, it means that the person in the dream will become a great scholar or a commentator in religious interpretations.

Daredevil: *(Also see Daring)*

Daring: (Feat) Daring in a dream means perseverance and having a strong will. It also could mean making supererogatory offerings to attain nearness to God Almighty. Daring in a dream also represents one's pursuit to be accepted by the people, either by defending them or by daring to face their enemy. The same interpretation is given to courage in a dream. *(Also see Boast)*

Dark: *(See Evening)*

Darkness: (Atheism; Ignorance; Night; Obscurity) In a dream, darkness means straying from God's path, being lost, committing an error, erring, confusion and perplexity. If one walks out of darkness into light in his dream, it means salvation, safety, guidance, repentance from sin or release from prison. Darkness in a dream also represents an oppressor. Thus, walking into a dark place in a dream means being unjust. Obscurity in a dream means the darkness of one's heart or blindness. It also could mean loneliness, keeping to oneself or hiding from people. *(Also see Injustice; Night)*

Darn: (Invisible stitches; Mend; Patch; Regret) To mend a garment with interlacing stitches in a dream means correcting oneself, piety, godliness, appropriateness, good reputation, being free from illness, arming oneself, or it could mean rain. If one sees his wife's robe ripped and tends to mend it for her in a dream, it means that he will insult his wife, then apologize to her or regret his action. If one sees himself darning his own shirt in a dream, it means that he will have an argument with a relative or befriend a person of evil character. Darning one's clothes in a dream also represents the roar of arguments or disputes. In some circles, it is also interpreted to mean repentance from one's sins, regretting wrongdoing, although one will fail to apologize or adequately compensate the other person for offending him.

Darning old cloth: (Patching) Darning an old garment in a dream represents hypocrisy, fawning, adulation, impertinence, or it could mean to manage by, or to suffer from a lasting poverty.

Date palm: *(See Palm tree)*

Date pit: (Core; Pit) Having a date pit in a dream means winning one's case in a court of justice.

Date spread: (Jam; Paste; Spread) In a dream, date paste represents a lawful and pleasant wealth which is collected from different sources. Eating date paste in a dream means taking a cure for an illness. *(Also see Dates)*

Dates: (Fruit; Palm tree) In a dream, dates mean money or a good message. Eating dates in a dream means earning lawful income. Dates are like money, they do not have a long shelve life. Unripened dates in a dream indicate the availability of water for those who need it. Red unripened dates in a dream may signify some type of blood disease, whereby the red cells grow to exceed in number the white cells. Dates in a dream also mean rain. Eating dates in a dream means reading the Holy Qur'ān and reaping benefits from one's religion. Buried dates in a dream represent one's savings. If one sees himself burying dates in a dream, it also means stealing from the property and money of orphans. Dates placed to dry in the open represent money which does not last. To harvest dates in a dream in season means that one may get married to a noble and a wealthy woman. It also means acquiring knowledge. Harvesting dates out of season in a dream means that one will learn something good but fail to act upon it. If one see that he is fanning himself with a tender and a wet branch of a palm tree in a dream it means learning something beneficial from a hypocrite, or it may mean relief from distress. If a woman sees herself eating ripened dates that are dripping with juices in the dream, it means that she will receive an inheritance from her husband and that her name will be included in his will, even if she is divorced. If one sees himself taking a date, splitting it in half and extracting the date pit from it in a dream, it means that he will beget a son. Eating fresh dates in a dream means hearing good words beside other benefits. *(Also see Bunch of dates; Date spread)*

Daughters: *(See Worms)*

Dauntless: *(See Army general)*

David: (Prophet David, upon whom be peace.) If one sees him in a dream, it means that he will gain power, authority, commit a sin, become an ascetic, be tried and oppressed by an unjust person, then he will be saved by God's leave and regain the upper hand over his enemy. He will also receive an exalted office or rank of honor. It is also said, that if one sees the prophet David (uwbp) in a dream, that his country or town will be governed by a just ruler, an honorable president or a righteous judge. If in fact the ruler or the judge of that town, county or country is an unjust person, then seeing God's prophet David (uwbp) in a dream means that God Almighty will surely replace him with a just and an honorable one. If one becomes God's prophet David (uwbp), or if he wears his robe in the dream it means that he will be appointed as a judge, if he qualifies. If he does not qualify, it means that he will prosper, or that he will grow in piety and become righteous through much devotion, piety, sadness and crying in fear of his Lord and love for Him. Seeing the prophet David (uwbp) in a dream also means deputyship, trials with women, trouble caused by women, or it could mean recitation of the Qur'ān or being in a state of constant remembrance of God Almighty, prayers, supererogatory prayers at night, understanding the meaning of what one reads, repentance from sin, chanting songs of God's love, returning to God's path after heedlessness, manufacturing and processing minerals, or it could represent God's acceptance of one's repentance. Should one be in such a manufacturing or processing business, it means that great wealth will come to him, or that his adversities will be of little importance. Seeing the prophet David (uwbp) in a dream also means reaching a successful conclusion to one's life in this world. If an unjust man of knowledge sees him frowning at him or warning him, then one must be at his guard, fear any wrongdoing and correct himself.

Dawn: The first appearance of daylight in a dream represents the birth of girls or their marriage. Seeing the dawn in a dream also may signify remembrance of God Almighty and reading of the Qur'ān. Seeing the dawn in a dream also means walking into the light of guidance. It also means happiness and continuous joy. If one loses something in the night then finds it at dawn in a dream, it means that his opponent denies something he unjustly took from him, then a witness arrives to testify for one's benefit and to help him recuperate his property.

Day of Gathering: *(See Intercession Resurrection)*

Day of Reckoning: *(See Accountability; Intercession; Reckoning; Resurrection; Rising of the dead)*

Day of Resurrection: *(See Accountability; Intercession; Reckoning; Resurrection; Rising of the dead)*

Day: *(See Daylight)*

Daydreaming: *(See Dream interpreter; Moon. Also see Introduction)*

Daylight: (Day) The dawning of the daylight in a dream means relief from pain, distress and sorrow, or it could mean buying a new garment, marriage, having beautiful children, the emergence of truth, unveiling what is hidden, release from prison or the coming home of a traveller.

Deafness: In a dream, deafness represents religious wickedness or corruption. Deafness in a dream also means heedlessness from the path of truth, a threat, or losing comfort. Deafness in a dream also means blindness of the heart.

Dearth: *(See Famine)*

Death by hanging: In a dream, to see someone or oneself being brought to the gallows to be hung means malice, rejoicing at the misfortune of others, fame or perhaps it could mean rising in station. Consequently, if one's condition in the dream does not change to worst, then his dream could mean slander or backbiting, unless his retribution is held for a crime he committed in the dream, then the dream means satisfying one's debts.

Death of a king: In a dream, it means destruction of a town. *(Also see Death)*

Death sentence: *(See Death; Destruction)*

Death: In a dream, death signifies religious failure, corruption and rising in status in the world. This interpretation applies if one is carried on a bier or on a litter and his funeral is accompanied with crying and lamentation except if he is buried in the dream. If one witnesses his own burial in the dream, then it means that his case is hopeless and that he will be seized by the world. One's followers or assisting entourage will be as many as those who walk in his funeral in the dream. However, he will conquer people and ride over their shoulders. If one dies in his dream but does not have the look of dead people and there is no crying over his death or a funeral in the dream, it means that one of his properties will be torn down, or that a room in his house will collapse, or that a wall will cave in, or it could mean that a pillar will breakdown. Such a dream also may signify weakness in one's religious standing or blindness of his heart. Despite that, he will live a long life. If one dies in a dream and finds himself looking like a dead person, and if his body is washed and wrapped in a shroud, it also means weakness in his religion. All the sorrow and crying one sees in this case, represents his rising in rank and promotion in the world. Death in a dream also signifies travels, or it could mean poverty. One's death and burial in his dream also means that he will die short of repentance. If one comes out of his grave after his burial in the dream, it means that he will repent for his sins before dying. Death in a dream also signifies marriage, for a deceased person is washed and perfumed, and a bridegroom also takes a bath and anoints himself with perfumes on his wedding day. If one dies and is carried over people's shoulders, though they do not bury him in the dream, it means that he will conquer his enemy and should he qualify for leadership, he will attain it. To come back to life after dying in a dream means that one will become rich and dispense with poverty, or it could mean that he will repent for his sins. This dream also means the safe home coming of a traveller. The death of an unknown woman in a dream means absence of rain or dearth, and if she comes back to life in the dream, it means rain. In general, the death of a woman in a dream means the death of a child in wakefulness and vice-versa. If a deceased person tells someone in a dream that he did not die, it means that he is blessed in the hereafter. Carrying a deceased person in a dream means carrying the provisions or .ood supplies of an irreligious and an ungodly person. Carrying a dead person in a different way than one carries a deceased person to bury him in a dream means acquiring unlawful money. Carrying a deceased person to bury him in a dream means working for the governor. If one sees a deceased person sick in a dream, it means that he is being questioned about forsaking his religious attendance during his lifetime. If one sees the dwellers of the graveyards coming out of their grave to eat people's harvest or food supplies in a dream, it means rising of food prices. If he sees them drinking from the wells in a dream, it means that a great plague will befall that town. If one sees a deceased person die, then if he walks in his funeral in the dream, it means that someone among his children or in the family of that person will shortly die. If no crying or sorrow follows his death, then it means that someone in his progeny will get married. What a deceased person says about himself in a dream is true, for he has reached the abode of truth and he can exercise no falsehood in that abode. If a deceased person tells something in a dream, and if it does not take place, then it means that one is experiencing confused dreams. If one sees a deceased person well dressed in a white or a green garment, smiling and happy in a dream, it means that he is in that state one witnessed in his dream. Otherwise, if one sees him disheveled, dirty, frowning or crying in a dream, this also denotes his condition in the hereafter. If one sees a deceased person sick in a dream, it means that his condition is contingent upon the satisfaction of his debts and that he is awaiting the Divine justice to take its course. Performing a funeral prayer for deceased people in a dream means asking for forgiveness on their behalf or visiting their graves, or it could mean admonishing someone with a dead heart, or it could mean bidding farewell to travelling people or taking care of needy people. If one's wife dies and returns back to life in a dream, it means making profits from a plantation or a farm. Discovering a body of a deceased in a dream means finding money. Walking behind a deceased person in a dream means following his footsteps or emulating his trade or traditions, whether they be material or spiritual. If the Imăm of the country dies in a dream, it means destruction of that city by war. On the other hand, if one sees a city in ruins in a dream, it means that the Imăm has died. If one sees that he is immortal in a dream, it means the nearing of his death. Death in a dream also signifies being recalled to account for a major sin or a crime. To die in a dream with no apparent reason or illness and to exhibit no features of a dead person means longevity. To suffer from death-pangs in a dream means being unjust to oneself or to others. To sees oneself dead and naked in a dream means poverty. To see oneself dead and lying on a straw-mat or a carpet in a dream means prosperity and success in the world. If one sees himself dead lying on a litter in a dream, it means rising in rank. If he is lying on a bed in the dream, it means benefits from one's family. If one hears about the death of an unknown person in a dream, it means a warning about his success in the world at the expense of his religious compromises. If one's son dies in a dream, it means that he will escape from an enemy. If one's daughter dies in a dream, it means despair from relief. If one dies and gets buried in a dream, it means his freedom. Otherwise, if he is entrusted with something, it means that he will be required to deliver it back to its rightful owner. If one dies and gets buried in a dream, it means that he will get married. If a sick person gets married in a dream, it means that he will shortly die. If a married person dies and gets buried in a dream, it means that he will divorce his wife or break a business partnership or separates from his brothers, sisters and friends, or it could mean that he may emigrate to another country. Otherwise, if he has already migrated from his homeland, it means that he will return to it. Death in a dream has positive connotation for someone in fear of something or a sad person or a sick person. The death of one's brothers in a dream means the death of one's enemies, or it could mean saving one's capital. Walking amidst dead people in a dream means befriending some hypocrites. Walking in the company of a deceased person in a dream means undertaking a long journey, or it could mean profits from one's travels. Eating the flesh of a dead person in a dream means enjoying a long life. If one discovers that he died suddenly in a dream, it means that he will rejoice. If a deceased person eats something in a dream, it means that such a commodity will become expensive. If one sees himself laying on a washing table in a funeral home in a dream, it means that his sins will be washed away and that his debts will be paid. If a deceased person asks someone to wash his cloth in a dream, it means that he needs the prayers and forgiveness of the person who saw him in his dream, or it could mean that one needs him to pay a debt he left behind or to ask people to forgive him his sins or to fulfill his will. If one washes the deceased person's clothes in the dream, it means that the deceased person will become free from his burdens in the hereafter. Transporting dead people to the cemetery in a dream means that one is doing something right. If he transports them to the marketplace in a dream, it means that he needs something, or that his merchandise will be sold quickly. If one sees that a deceased person has returned to life in a dream, it means that one will recuperate something he considered it dead, or if he happens to be going through difficulties, it means that his adversities will dissipate. If a deceased person comes back to life in a dream, it also means that his progeny will benefit from something he left. If he looks beautiful, happy and well dressed in the dream, it means that such happiness will become the inheritance of his descendants. If one sees a deceased person busy, worried and ill dressed in a dream, it means that he is engaged in a struggle that can only subside by the will of God Almighty. If he is sick in the dream, it means that he is answerable to God Almighty for his religious negligence. If the deceased person's face looks dark or opaque in the dream, it means that he died as an unbeliever. If one sees a deceased person sprightly, pleasant and casual in a dream, it means that one's dream is mere hallucination, or that he is experiencing disturbed dreams, for dead people do not joke and have their own duties to respond to. If one's deceased father or mother come back to life in a dream, it means relief from distress and abolishing of his fears. This is particularly stronger when one's deceased mother is seen in the dream. Resurrecting a deceased person in a dream means giving guidance to an unbeliever or admonishing an innovator. This also could mean admonishing heedless people who will repent for their sins. If one sees a deceased person die again in a dream, it means that someone by the same name will shortly die. If a deceased person complains about a migraine headache in a dream, it means that he is being questioned about his religious negligence or his injustices or his abominable attitude toward his father or mother. If the deceased person complains about his eyes in the dream, it means that he is being questioned about what he owes to his wife or about her dower or about a will or a trust he wasted. If he complains about his left arm, it means that he is being questioned about the rights of his brother, sister, son or business partner or a false oath he made. If the deceased person complains about his side in a dream, it means that he is being questioned about cutting off his relations or clan or failing to fulfil his obligations toward his household. If he complains about his legs in a dream, it means that he is being questioned about wasting his life in corruption and falsehood. If he complains about his feet in the dream, it means that he is being questioned about a wealth he spends in falsehood and on the path of heedlessness he walked. A woman and a man in such dreams are the same. Like that, each limb provides for a specific stand one took during his lifetime in this world. (*See Body¹*). If a living person gives a deceased person something to eat or drink in a dream, it means loss of money. If he gives a deceased person a garment in the dream, it means adversity or an illness. If a deceased person gives the person seeing the dream his own shroud to wear in a dream, it means his death. If a deceased person gives the person seeing the dream a cloak or an adorned shirt in a dream, it means gaining what the deceased person acquired of knowledge, wealth, blessings or status during his lifetime. The shirt means livelihood and the cloak means dignity and honor. If the deceased person gives him some food to eat in the dream, it means receiving lawful earnings from an unexpected source. If the deceased person gives him honey in the dream, it means acquiring a booty. Anything one receives from a deceased person in a dream means good news and a blessed gift in general. If a deceased person takes one by the hand and walks with him in a dream, it means receiving money from an unexpected source. Talking with deceased people in a dream means longevity. Kissing a renowned person who had passed away in a dream means acquiring something from his knowledge, wisdom or inheritance, or it could mean receiving benefits from his descendants. Talking to dead people in a dream means having ingratitude toward one's family or friends. If a sick person sees himself kissing a deceased person in a dream, it means that he will shortly die. If a healthy person sees that same dream, it means that what he says is false. Having sexual intercourse with a deceased person in his grave in a dream means committing adultery or mixing with an evil person or losing money to a deceitful and a hypocritical person. If one sees that a deceased woman has come back to life, and if he engages in sexual intercourse with her, then finds his body spattered with her ova and semen in a dream, it means that he has committed something which he regrets. Consequently he will suffer losses because of it. To have a wedding with a deceased person and to move to his or her house in the dream means one's own death. Walking behind a deceased person and entering an unknown house from which one does not come out again in the dream means death. If one follows the deceased person and does not enter such a house in the dream, it means that he will near his death, then recuperate from his illness. If a deceased person beats the person seeing the dream, it means that one has displeased his Lord and has committed an abominable act from which he should repent, for in the abode of truth, a deceased person accepts only what pleases God Almighty and dislikes what He dislikes. If one sees a living person beating a deceased person who is willingly submitting to his fate in a dream, it represents the spiritual and religious strength and the rank of the living person, his charities, prayers, devotion, piety, or it could mean that he is fulfilling the deceased person's will. If one sees a deceased person asleep in a dream, it means that the hereafter is the abode of rest and comfort for the believers. Sleeping in one bed with a deceased person in a dream means longevity. If dead people come out of their graves to sell merchandise in a dream, it means stagnation of the markets. A dead mouse in one's food in a dream means tampering with that product. If one sees a deceased person doing something good in a dream, it means that he is ordering him to do the same. If it is a bad thing he is doing in the dream, it means that he is ordering him not to do it. If a deceased person comes in one's dream and tells him about the time of his death, then the day may be one month and the month may be one year and the year ten years. If one sees his mother dying in a dream, it means that he will lose his worldly attainments, comfort and that he may become heedless. If he is a seeker on the path, then it means that he will lose the benefits of his work or fail to perform his obligatory prayers. If a sick person sees his brother die in a dream, it means his own death. Otherwise, it could mean someone in his family. If one is poor in the dream, it means that may lose one of his eyes. If one's wife dies in a dream, it means bankruptcy and loss of one's source of livelihood. Performing the funeral prayer in a dream means interceding on his behalf and praying for his salvation. If one answers the call of a deceased person in a dream, it means that he will shortly follow him. If one sees a deceased person drowning in a dream, it means that one is plunged in abominable sins. If one sees dead people coming out of their graves and going to their homes in a dream, it means a mass release of prisoners during a general amnesty. This dream also may mean that God Almighty will give life to a barren land. Death for a believer in a dream means honor, dignity, aloofness and ascetic detachment. The death of a prophet in a dream means weakness in people's religious life, while their coming back to life in a dream means a flourishing spiritual life in that place. The death of a ruler in a dream means the weakness of his army or government. The death of a religious scholar in a dream means the birth of innovation or invalidation of one's proof. The death of a pious worshiper in a dream means failure to attend one's religious obligations. The death of a craftsman mean the end of his craft. The death of one's parents in a dream means tightening of his financial means. The death of one's wife in a dream means the end of a prosperous life. The death of one's son in a dream means the obscurity of one's name after his death. If one sees a deceased person performing the funeral prayer over another deceased person in a dream, it means that one's actions are false, for performing a funeral prayer is a deed and dead people have no more deeds to offer. If a married woman marries a deceased person in a dream, it means her divorce from her husband, while if an unmarried woman marries a deceased person in a dream means that she will get married. In a dream, death also means being inflamed with love or separation from one's beloved, whereby life after death would represent reunion with one's beloved or suffering from separation in a hell-fire. *(Also see Agony of death; Funeral prayers; Giving up the ghost; Izrāil; Relaxation; Robbery)*

Debris: *(See Trash)*

Debt: (Blood ties; Promise; Tripping) Paying one's debt in a dream means returning from a journey. In a dream, debts signify humiliation, abuse and insults. If one sees himself paying his debts in a dream, it means that he will reestablish his connection with his relatives, strengthen his blood ties, feed the poor, solve a difficult problem, acquire a better understanding of religious matters, or return from a trip. If one sees himself paying a debt in his dream but could not recognize it in wakefulness, such debts then represent his sins for which he is responsible and answerable whether he committed them knowingly or unknowingly and their consequences will always hunt him unless he repents. Because of that, the person will suffer in this world in the form of adversities, sickness, fines or other worldly losses. Paying a debt or satisfying a just cause in a dream means feeding a hungry person, reuniting one's family or returning from a journey and returning from a journey in a dream also means satisfying a just cause. *(Also See Promise; Tripping)*

Decapitation: *(See Beheading; Cutting off)*

Deceiver: *(See Con artist; Fraudulent bankruptcy)*

December: *(See Earthquake; Thunder)*

Decency: *(See Justice)*

Deception: (Milk; War. *See Advice; Con artist; Fraudulent bankruptcy)*

Declivity: *(See Descending)*

Decoration: *(See Necklace; Ornaments)*

Decree: *(See Book)*

Deep frying: (Fryer) In a dream, deep frying signifies evil, adversities, arguments, problems, failing to do one's prayers, following one's mind, passion and desires, or backbiting and slandering people. *(Also see Frying)*

Deep waters: Falling into deep waters and not reaching the bottom of it in a dream means prosperity and wealth, for the world is a deep ocean. A sudden fall into water in a dream also means joy and money.

Deer: A deer in a dream represents women and children. Capturing a deer in a dream or receiving one as a gift means prosperity, an inheritance, marriage, having children or overcoming one's adversary. Slaughtering a deer in a dream means deflowering a young girl. Bringing a deer inside one's house means finding a bride for one's son. If one kills and skins a deer in a dream, it means that he will rape a noble woman. A deer jumping at someone in a dream represents a disobedient wife. Owning a deer in a dream means marriage to a noble woman or it could represent wealth which is earned from lawful sources. *(Also see Gazelle)*

Defamation: *(See Backbiting)*

Defeat: If a believer sees himself defeated in a dream, it means that he will wear the helmet of a warrior and win the battle against his enemy. If one sees himself defeated and shows no fear in the dream, it means his death. If one sees soldiers retreating into a city to take shelter therein in a dream, it means that they will ultimately win their war, even if their cause is unjust or if they represented a tyrant, though they will ultimately have to pay for their crimes. If one sees the soldiers of a just ruler entering a city defeated in a dream, it means that they will surely be victorious over their enemy. *(Also see Losing a fight)*

Defecate: *(See Feces)*

Defending someone's honor: In a dream, it means commanding good and forbidding evil, protecting one's family and giving a good advice to the assailant.

Deferment: (Delay; Postponement; Procrastination) Deferment or postponement of fulfilling one's obligations in a dream means separation and annulment of a contract. If a woman defers or postpones her marriage in a dream, it means separation from her husband or losing the opportunity to be married or showing preference to remaining unmarried.

Deflation: *(See Knitting)*

Defraud: *(See Chisel; Mockery)*

Degradation: *(See Descending)*

Dejection: *(See Depression)*

Delay: *(See Deferment)*

Delight: (Happiness; Music; Overjoy) Experiencing delight or overjoy from a musical performance in a dream means being moved by sorrow and grief. To feel overjoyed or raptured in a dream also suggests diligence, a quick mind, intelligence or awareness of someone who is known to be leaden, or it could mean a sudden change in the attitude of a stingy person as he turns to spending his money with generosity. The feeling of rapture or emotional ecstasy in a dream also means indulging in sin, becoming alcoholic, committing adultery, or it could mean love for God Almighty, turning toward Him in truth and with sincerity.

Delirium: (Distraction; Love; Unbalance) In a dream, delirium represents unbalance, bewilderment about the world, utter confusion, giddiness or falling passionately in love, or it could denote a better end for all things. *(Also see Distraction)*

Delivering water: *(See Water Carrier)*

Delouse: *(See Hair)*

Demanding employer: *(See Milking)*

Demanding person: (Ignorant; Obtrusive) It is common among the people of knowledge to describe a demanding person as a stone. *(Also see Darkness)*

Demanding situation: *(See Buyer)*

Demanding: *(See Driving force)*

Demolishing: *(See building; Wrecker)*

Demotion: *(See Descending)*

Den: In a dream, a den represents a bastard son, a child of adultery or the retreat of an ascetic. *(Also see Hole)*

Denial: *(See Repudiation)*

Dependents: (Children; Family; Household) One's dependents in a dream represents richness.

Depilatory agent: *(See Shaving)*

Deposit: (Mortgage; Security; Trust) Depositing something with someone in a dream means trusting him with a secret. Entrusting something to a deceased person in a dream means entrusting someone who can keep a secret, or it could mean that he will entrust someone with an object or money that will be lost, or it could mean confiding to someone who cannot be trusted. Entrusting one's wife with something in a dream means conceiving a child. If she gives him back what he gave her in the dream, it means that her pregnancy will not reach fruition. *(Also see Pawn)*

Depression: (Dejection; Melancholy; Sadness) In a dream, depression signifies the opposite. That is to say joy, happiness and celebrations. However, if one sees his friends depressed in a dream, it means suffering the same in wakefulness. Depression in a dream also denotes an illness or sufferings caused by one's own family, or it could mean imposition, forfeiture of business, cancellation of interest receivable, or perhaps it could mean business stagnation. Should any of that be true in wakefulness, then witnessing such a depression in a dream could mean relief. Depression in a dream could mean either happiness or distress.

Deputy: *(See Vice-regent)*

Derangement: *(See Mental derangement)*

Descending: (Declivity) Descending a mountain, a hill or an elevation in a dream represents losses, migraine headache, humiliation, passing from a higher to a lower condition, separation between husband and wife, losing one's job, demotion, degradation, abandoning one's religion, or it could mean adversities in general. Descending a steep slope in a dream also means safe landing, worldly blessings and nomination for a religious duty. Descending from a mountain in a dream means relief from adversities or change in one's conditions. Coming down from an old ladder in a dream means investing in a business to earn nothing from one's efforts. If the ladder breaks half-way through in the dream, it means losing to one's adversary.

Desert: (Waterless plain) Seeing a desert in a dream means escaping from difficulty to ease, or bidding farewell to adversities to meet with opportunities, or it could mean repenting from sin, reversing the course of one's business from loss to profits, or it could mean recovering from an illness. If one sees himself poor and walking into a desert land or a ruin in a dream, it means his death. Walking through a barren land in a dream means engaging in a futile business or a benign affair. Walking in a plain in a dream means reaching ease in one's life, receiving honor or engaging in good deeds depending on how far one walks in that plain during his dream. A desert in a dream represents joy and happiness, depending on how vast it seems and how green are its plants in one's dream.

Deserted: (Empty; Forlorn; Wretched) A deserted and empty place in a dream signifies poverty or lack of food or sustenance for one's household. An empty place in a dream also could signify distress and trouble.

Desertion: *(See Repudiation)*

Desire: (Dog; Lust; Passion; Wantonness) To feel a yearning or desire to see one's homeland in a dream means a divorce between a husband and wife or separation between friends, or it could mean that one will become rich after being poor, though in general, desire in a dream connotes evil if accompanied with crying or lamentation. Satisfying one's desire with no restraint in a dream mostly denotes the actions of the dwellers of hell-fire. *(Also see Dog; Dryness)*

Desisting from evildoing: Desisting from evildoing in a dream means trusting in God Almighty, turning to Him for one's needs, and victory over one's enemy.

Despair: (Despondency; Disheartened; Discouraged; Resign) To experience desperation or to loose hope in God Almighty in a dream signifies polytheism or attempting to commit suicide or committing a sin, though the consequence of such state in a dream may eventually turn positive in wakefulness. Despair in a dream also means escaping from a great danger, or engaging in the activities of the dwellers of hell-fire. *(Also see Uptight)*

Desperado: *(See Wrecker)*

Despise: *(See Assault; Bad look)*

Despondency: *(See Despair; Uptight)*

Destiny: *(See Calamity; God's will)*

Destitute: (Loafing; Loitering; Tramp; Vagabond) Seeing a destitute or seeing oneself as a destitute in a dream connotes a painful poverty, a self-damaging condition, ingratitude or disbelief.

Destitution: *(See Indigence)*

Destroy: *(See Assault; Wrecker)*

Destroying: *(See Wrecker)*

Destruction: (Admonition; Cave in; Earthquake; Harvest; Violation) In a dream, destruction means dispersion of people, or it could mean death. Destruction in a dream also means the leveling of a town or the death of its ruler or it could represent absence of justice. Experiencing destruction in a dream means suffering from the persecution of people one cannot bear. Seeing a city destroyed by an earthquake in a dream represents the carrying of a death sentence for someone there, or it could mean violation of people's rights or freedom in that town. If one sees an entire town being destroyed with its urban area, factories and fields in a dream, it means that the people of that town have gone astray, or that its leaders are struck with calamities. On the other hand, if one sees it flourishing in a dream, then it reflects the spiritual awareness and religious devotion of its people. *(Also see Collapsing walls; Cloud of destruction)*

Detergent: (Charity)

Devotion: *(See Acknowledging devotion)*

Dew: (Dampness; Moisture) In a dream, the morning dew means glad tidings, liberality, generosity and openhandedness. The same interpretation is given for hail and drizzles.

Dhuhā: *(arb. See Five times prayers)*

Diaper: *(See Swaddle)*

Diaphragm: *(See Birth control)*

Diarrhea: In a dream, diarrhea represents negligence and squandering of property and money, while constipation represents miserliness, stinginess and avarice.

Dig up a grave: *(See Digging a grave; Exhume; Grave)*

Digesting food: In a dream, digesting one's food means steadfastness and assiduousness in one's profession, liveliness and vivacity. Digesting one's food in a dream also signifies safety and protection against fear. *(Also see Food)*

Digging a grave: In a dream, digging a grave means getting married. Digging a grave and talking with the deceased person about one's needs in a dream means solving one's problem. A grave digger in a dream also represents a pander, a procurer, or he could be someone who loves the world, or a treasure hunter. *(Also see Grave)*

Digging up the past: (Affront; Attract attention; Criticize; Excavate; Probe; Sideswipe; Stir up) Digging up the past in a dream means an argument or exposing one's dirty laundry, blocking the road, earning unlawful money, or it could mean excavating hidden valuables, reviving past knowledge or discovering a treasure. Digging up the past and not confronting anyone with it in a dream means relief from distress or receiving glad tidings. *(Also see Court)*

Digging: (Excavate) Digging the earth in a dream means profits equal to the measure of earth one piles-up if the dirt is dry. However, if the ground is wet in the dream, it means deceiving someone else in a business venture, whereby, he gains nothing from it but headache and exhaustion equal to the amount of earth he piles-up. The digger's plot also may backfire. If a sick person or if someone in his household who is sick sees himself digging the earth in a dream, it could mean digging a grave. If a business traveller sees himself digging the earth, it represents his travels and the dirt he gathers represent his profits. Digging a hole, a water well or irrigations and planing to water the plants through them in a dream means looking for a job to earn one's livelihood and to bring its benefits to his family. Eating from the dirt one digs in his dream, means profits earned from deception. Finding oneself inside a hole in a dream means that one may divorce his wife. If one sees himself outside a hole, looking at it in a dream, it means an argument with her which will end in reconciliation. If a sick person sees himself coming out of a hole in a dream, it means recovering from illness or being set free from prison. If one sees himself digging the earth in a dream, it also means muddling in falsehood to earn nothing but wrath. Digging a cavity through a mountain in a dream represents a person who associates himself with a difficult but a beneficial person. Digging a well in a dream also represents a crafty and an artful deceiver. A person digging the ground in a dream also represents a jailer, or veiling abominable actions. *(Also see Pickax; Construction worker)*

Dignity: Being dignified in a dream means humiliation.

Dill: *(bot.)* In a dream, dill represents something that will take place in the future. If one sees himself carrying a bunch of dill in a dream, it means that something unforeseen will happen to him and its effects will show later.

Dining table: *(See Messmate; Table)*

Dinner: *(See Hospitality; Invitation; Table)*

Dip: (Coat; Mix) To dip something into a conflicting element or to mix two incompatible substances or to coat something with the wrong element in a dream means creating suspicion or unlawfully mixing people's monies and properties.

Direction: *(See Road; Wending one's way)*

Dirt: (Earth) Dirt in a dream represents woman's money or property. Walking on dirt means soliciting money. Collecting dirt in a dream means saving money. Sweeping dirt in one's house in a dream means swindling money from one's wife. Sweeping dirt in one's shop in a dream represents lawful earnings. Dusting the ceiling of one's shop and throwing it outside in a dream means business losses. Carrying dirt in a dream means circulating rumors, and it also means dispelling distress, or overcoming depression. *(Also see Earth)*

Dirty clothe: *(See Filth)*

Dirty face: (Filth) A dirty face in a dream represents a rare art, while a filthy body represents a sinful person.

Dirty hair: *(See Filth)*

Disappearing: (Absence; Becoming unknown; Loss of tracks) If one disappears from his house or from the country, and if his tracks could not be located in the dream, it means taking a long journey, turning out to be where he is suspected to be, getting married in that place, falling in love with an unknown person, falling sick in a foreign land, or it could mean death if the person is sick. However the disappearance of God's loving people in a dream perhaps means thinking about one's beloved, or being exposed to uncommon mysteries of the universe. If one disappears within the earth without going through a hole in his dream, and if he remains a long time therein until people think that he will never come out again in the dream, it means self-deception, arrogance and love for the world, and such a person will die in that pursuit as a consequence of adventuring with his own life. *(Also see Evanescence)*

Disaster: (Heavy loss; Serious damage; Sudden great misfortune; Upheaval) In a dream, a disaster means the death of a sick person, poverty, imprisonment or blindness. However, witnessing a disaster in a dream also could mean the opposite, such as hearing good news, or that one's reluctant enemy may secede. *(Also see Cloud of destruction)*

Disband: *(See Band)*

Disbelief: (Astray; Heedlessness; Ingratitude; Irreligious; Profane) In a dream, disbelief represents a rich person or becoming one. Disbelief in God Almighty in a dream also means illness, injustice or causing harm to others. Acting silly or impudent or stupidly, or being censured or discredited in a dream also indicates profanity and disbelief in God Almighty. Going astray in a dream means committing a sin or making a mistake. Making a mistake in a dream also signifies heedlessness in wakefulness. If one's profanity becomes public knowledge in a dream, it means that he will commit a forgery or make false testimony in court. Disbelief in a dream also means ingratitude or it could denote the state of a sick person when he lies in his deathbed and awaits for his soul to be taken back to its Lord. Disbelief in a dream also may signify committing the unforgivable act of suicide. *(Also see Irreligious)*

Disbeliever: *(See Disbelief; Irreligious)*

Discarded: A discarded stone in a dream represents a dead person.

Discerning: *(See Sieve)*

Discharge of the eyes: *(See Mucous)*

Discomfort: *(See Pain)*

Discord: *(See Enmity)*

Discouraged: *(See Despair; Uptight)*

Discovering a treasure: *(See Treasure)*

Discredit: (Defile) To discredit someone's reputation or to defile something in a dream means the same in wakefulness. On the other hand, it may mean defaming and backbiting someone, or it may mean making peace with someone after a long separation.

Discriminating: *(See Perspicacity; Sieve)*

Discrimination: *(See Perspicacity)*

Disdain: (Haughtiness; Superciliousness) If one who desires to earn respect from others shows disdain in a dream, it means grovelling, servility, toadying or losing rank. *(Also see Sneezing)*

Disencumbering: freeing oneself from a burden or obstruction in a dream means giving money in charity and doing good for the benefit of those who appreciate and those who do not appreciate.

Disgraceful: *(See Shameful act)*

Disgust: *(See Breathing difficulty)*

Disheartened: *(See Uptight)*

Disheveled: (Matted hair; Ruffled hair; Unkempt) In a dream, seeing one's hair disheveled means stinginess and love to hoard money, or it could mean doing little for others.

Dishonesty: *(See Advice)*

Dismay: *(See Fear)*

Dismembering: *(See Cut)*

Dismissal: *(See Expulsion)*

Disobedience: (Insubordination) Disobedience to God's commands in a dream means insubordination or indulging in sin. If one denies his act to be a sin in the dream, then such disobedience signifies that he will suffer from a severe punishment for his arrogance. *(Also see Recalcitrant child)*

Disobedient child: *(See Recalcitrant child)*

Dispirited: *(See Uptight)*

Displease: (Displeasing one's parents in a dream. *See Recalcitrant child; Slaughter)*

Disposer of estates: *(See Woodcutter)*

Dispute: (Controversy; Quarrel) If one sees himself quarreling with someone in a dream, it means that he will suffer extreme pressure, stress and sorrow. If one is engaged in a dispute in a dream, it means that he is wrong and must rectify the situation and make peace with the other person. If he does so, it means that he will win what his heart desires.

Disregard: *(See Disdain; Sneezing)*

Disrespectful child: *(See Recalcitrant child)*

Disrobe: If one undresses himself in a dream though not knowing whether he did so for good or for an unlawful purpose, or if he strips himself from his clothing in a public place, feels shy and tries to cover his private parts in the dream, it means that his private life will be exposed and that he will be disgraced. If he takes off his garment in public and does not feel ashamed of his nakedness in a dream, it means that he will be credited for his honesty. If the person is sick in real life, it means that he will recover. If he is indebted, it means that he will repay his debts. If he is seized with fear, it means that he will regain his peace. Nakedness in a dream also means injustice. Stripping a dead person of his shroud means divorce, loss in business, repentance from sins, or it could mean guidance. *(Also see Undress)*

Dissolute: *(See Profligacy)*

Distance: In a dream, distance signifies injustice or being deprived from something. The distance between two people in a dream means a fight, resignation or death. Distance in a dream also means closeness, since it is the opposite. Walking a long distance in a dream means hardships or taking a difficult journey.

Distilled water: In a dream, distilled water represents beautiful children or noble children. Seeing distilled water in a dream also may signify acquiring knowledge from learned people who practice what they teach. It also means learning wisdom from wise people. Smelling rose-water or orange-blossom water or distilled water from jonquil or from any species of the narcissus flower in a dream means joy, happiness, cheers, eulogies and prosperity. In a dream, distilled water also may represent bringing out confiscated or stolen merchandise or discovering hidden goods. As for distilled farm water or from water lily or distilled water from similar flowers in a dream, they represent medicinal remedies, profits, celebrations or weddings. *(Also see Water)*

Distinction: *(See Fame)*

Distinguished: *(See Banner; Fame; Horn)*

Distinguishing quality: *(See Trait)*

Distraction: Distraction in a dream and especially during prayers means envy and desire to rip others of their property and particularly close friends or relatives. If one is distracted during his prayers by a creeping snake or a lion in a dream, it means that he must be on his guard and cautious with his wife or child. Distraction during prayers represents one's passions, desires, or it could mean heedlessness, soliciting temporary gains and declining from the eternal benefits of the hereafter. *(Also see Delirium)*

Distress: (Anxiety; Agony; Grieve; Uptight; Worries) Distress in a dream signifies atonement for one's sins and restitution of his human dignity. To experience distress in a dream also signifies regret for something wrong one has committed. If one's distress dissipates, and if he is relieved from its burden in his dream, it means repentance from his wrongdoing. In a dream, distress and sorrow mean being in love or suffering from one's devotion to his beloved. *(Also see Uptight; Worries)*

Diver: (Go under; Submerse) In a dream, a diver represents a spy, an inspector or a reporter. *(Also see Spy)*

Diversion: *(See Amusement)*

Divination: (Geomancy) Seeing a fortuneteller who practices divination by interpreting random figures that are formed when a handful of earth is thrown on the ground or one who interprets randomly drawn lines on sand represents a fraudulent and a cunning person, a thief, or such a dream could represent profits from importing goods. *(Also see Astrologer; Fortuneteller)*

Divine Throne: (The Glorious Throne of God Almighty.) Seeing the Divine Throne of God Almighty in its perfect form means blessings, glad tidings and correctness of one's faith. If one sees the Divine Throne missing one of its attributes in a dream, it means heedlessness and innovation. Seeing the Glorious Throne of God Almighty in a dream may entail whatever good or evil destiny one may go through. Seeing the Divine Throne in a dream also means receiving a high ranking position or assuming a noble function, if one qualifies, or it could represent one's wife, house, vehicle, victory over his enemy, writing poems, or doing good deeds for the one who sees it in its perfect, radiant and glorious manifestation. If one sees the Divine Throne, and if he sees God Almighty sitting on it in a dream, it denotes his faith, certitude, determination and correct religious adherence. If one sees himself sitting upon the Divine Throne and his Lord sitting under it in a dream, and if one qualifies for governing, then it means that he will oppress the religious scholars, show arrogance and spread evil on earth. If one does not qualify for governing, then it means that he will become a disobedient son to his parents, oppose his teacher, rebel against his superior, issue a verdict without knowledge, commit aggression against others, or if he is a judge, he will be an unjust one. *(Also see Allāh; Carriers of the Divine Throne; Chair)*

Divine will: *(See God's will)*

Diving: (Pearl fishery; Plunge) If one sees himself diving into the ocean for pearls in a dream, it indicates his attachment to worldly treasures. If one sees himself diving into the waters and finds out that he could get nothing out of it except mud in his dream, it means distress caused by someone in authority. If one brings a pearl out of the water in a dream, it means marriage or acquiring knowledge or discovering a treasure. If one dives into a river and finds it difficult to come out of the waters in the dream, it means that he will suffer from burdens he cannot carry, or bear patience with adversities. Diving into the ocean to extract pearls from oysters in a dream also means seeking knowledge or wealth. *(Also see Pearl diver)*

Divorce: (Poverty) If someone divorces his wife in a dream, it means that he will be dismissed from his job. If an unmarried person sees himself divorcing someone in a dream, it means reaching a conclusion to whatever good or bad he is experiencing. As for the divorce of a married person in a dream, it means closing of his business or his death if he is bed stricken. If one sees himself divorcing his wife in a dream, it means that he will become rich, or that his life will run smoother. If one divorces his wife with the intention of returning to her in a dream, it means that he will change his trade for a short time, then engages back in it. If the divorce is irrevocable, then it could mean that he will permanently close his business. Divorcing one's wife in a dream also means disregarding a treasure, renouncing an inheritance, abdicating one's throne, or impeachment from one's office. Divorce in a dream also denotes poverty. Divorcing one's sick wife in a dream means that she may die of her illness.

However, if one divorces his sick wife with the intention of returning to her again in the dream, in that case, it means that she will recover from her illness. *(Also see Pencil sharpener; Repudiation)*

Divulging: *(See Spell out)*

Doctor: *(See Physician)*

Dodging: *(See Cave)*

Dog star: *(astr. See Dog)*

Dog: (Bitch; Canine; Desire; Greyhound; Japanese spaniel; Pekingese; Lust; Puppy; Shepherds' dog; Tyke) In a dream, a dog represents an insolent man who dares to indulge in sinful actions. If he barks in the dream, it means that such a man is impudent and has a repulsive and an abominable character. A dog bite or his scratch in a dream means harm caused by one's enemy and its effects will depend on the amount of pain one suffers in the dream. It could also mean falling sick or suffering from great affliction or harm caused by a close companion or a servant. If a dog tears off one's clothing in a dream, it means that a vile person is slandering and backbiting him. If one does not hear the barking of the dog in the dream, it signifies that one's enemy has left him inflected with a small loss. A dog in a dream also could represent a vile and an insolent woman who belong to a group of evildoing people and who are persistent in their enmity. A puppy in a dream represents a loved child. If it is a white puppy in the dream, it means that such a son will grow to be a believer. If it is a black puppy in the dream, it means that he will grow to govern the household and to presides over its people. A puppy in a dream also represents a child of adultery, a foundling who is left in the street, wrapped in a swaddle and who is brought home by an insolent person to rear him. A shepherd's dog in a dream represents profits and benefits. A pet dog in a dream represents an astringent and a bitter enemy. Seeing a greyhound in a dream means gaining authority, control and wealth. A greyhound in a dream also represents the backbone of an army general or his best helper or it could represent a good strategist, though he lacks principals and moral integrity. A Japanese spaniel or a Pekingese in a dream signifies mixing with, or doing business with a foreign counterpart. Bringing-up a dog for companionship in a dream means befriending a servant for whom one has great love and affection. Hunting with a dog in a dream means satisfying one's lust or desire. Killing a dog in a dream signifies vanquishing one's enemy. Seeing an expedition of hounds leaving a town for a chase or a hunt in a dream means blessings and prosperity for everyone, or it could mean taking action. Seeing the expedition of hounds returning from a hunt or a chase in a dream means dispelling people's fears, or it could mean lack of work. If one sees such expedition entering a town in his dream, it also means a high rate of unemployment. Seeing a sick house dog in a dream means illness and financial losses or loss of appetite or losing the pleasure of living. A barking bitch in a dream signifies harm and deceit which is caused by abominable people. A dog in a dream also means suffering from extremely high fever and in relation to Dog star or the stars Procyon and Sirius of the constellations Canis Minor and Canis Major. In a dream, all breeds of dogs represent lowly, obsequious and despicable people. Seeing dogs that are reared for bantering or dallying with in a dream signify fun and enjoying one's life. In the dream, anything that happens to such a breed of dogs means suffering from distress, sorrow or loss of one's pleasure of living. If one is transformed into a dog in a dream, it means that God Almighty has taught him great knowledge which he abused and discarded, then God Almighty stripped him from such a knowledge. A dog in a dream also represents a police informer or a police dog. A dog in a dream also represents a weak enemy or a niggardly person. If a dog barks at someone in a dream, it means that one will hear something he despises or hates to make public from someone who lacks any sense of honor or virtue.

Eating a dog's meat in a dream means cracking down at one's enemy. A dog in a dream also represents a guard or an innovator. Drinking dog's milk in a dream means a scare. Laying one's head on a dog or relaxing with a dog or using the dog for a pillow in a dream, the dog then represents a friend or a good companion. A dog in a dream also represents a street boy, a beggar or an obsequious, lowly and a despicable person who maintains affection toward his master and jealously guards him, his children and property. A dog in a dream also means greed, love for the worldly pleasures, committing a dogfight to win them and failing to have any reserve or savings. In a dream, all types of dogs also represent people. A hunting dog in a dream represents honor and profits. A shepherd's dog represents a good neighbor who cares more about his neighbors than about his own household. Adopting a dog as a pet in a dream means wavering, or paying financial damages, or it could mean unemployment. Taking a dog for a companion on a journey in a dream means disappearing. A dog in a dream also means disbelief, ingratitude or losing hope, belying, fear, imprisonment, or becoming a fugitive. Seeing a dog in a city in a dream also means renewal of one's business contract.

Dogfight: In a dream, a dogfight means love for the world. *(Also see Dog)*

Dollar: (Dinār; Money. *See Banknote; Counting; Numbers*)

Dolly: *(See Stretcher)*

Dome[1]: (Canopy; Pavilion; Tent) In a dream, a dome represents someone in command. *(Also see Pavilion)*

Dome[2]: (Cupolead structure; Qubba; Shrine) Building a dome in a dream means marriage. Demolishing a dome means death or a divorce. A dome also signifies power and ruling if one owns it, or if he stands under one in his dream. Seeing a dome and birds surrounding it in a dream also means exaltation. Building a dome over clouds in a dream means marriage, power and rank. Seeing green domes standing between the heavens and the earth in a dream means that one's deeds are raised to be worthy of blessing, or that he might die as a martyr. If one sees four men demolishing a dome in a dream, it means that a renowned scholar in that locality will shortly die and his elements of earth, fire, water, air and either will destroy one another. *(Also see Pavilion; Shrine; Tent)*

Donation: (Gift; Grant; Present) The gender of a gift one donates in a dream signifies the gender one may receive in wakefulness. A donation in a dream also represents charity, a present or a gift and they all have the same meaning. *(Also see Endowment; Gift)*

Donkey: (Ass; Obstinate person; Steadfastness) In a dream, a donkey means a boy, a child, a wife, livelihood, a man of knowledge without work, or it could mean travels. Riding a donkey in a dream also may mean easing of one's difficulties. Riding any animal without the required saddling in a dream means imposition upon oneself or others or unnecessary and inadequate going out of one's way. Riding a donkey or a mule in a dream also represents one's ornaments, children, a rich wife, wealth or a profitable business. The braying of a donkey, a mule or a mare in a dream may mean evil, excruciating trouble, an illegitimate child born from adultery or evil spirits. Riding a big donkey in a dream connotes a respectable rank. An upright walking donkey represents worldly benefits. A beautiful looking donkey or a white donkey in a dream means adornment. An emaciated donkey in a dream represents poverty, while a fat donkey means money. A black donkey means happiness, honor and prosperity and a green donkey means fear of wrongdoing. A donkey fit with a saddle in a dream represents a respected son. A donkey with a long tail in a dream represents lasting dynasty. His hoofs represent one's money. The death of a donkey represents the death of its owner, or rupture and breaking of one's relationship with his friends or family, the death of one's supporter, selling a dear property, divorce, travel or death of a husband. A lost donkey with an unknown master in a dream represents an ignorant, obtrusive and a demanding person. To own donkeys in a dream means mixing with a group of ignorant people. If one's donkey becomes obstinate and does not move forward except with beating in a dream, it means that one's sustenance and earnings come only through supererogatory prayers and increased devotion. An obedient donkey in a dream represents the vigilance of its owner. Driving a donkey inside one's house in a dream means bringing new income. Only the braying of a donkey is disliked in a dream, though the rest is generally beneficial. A donkey in a dream represents honesty in seeking one's livelihood and earning clean money. If it indicates the person who is seeing the dream, then it means that he buys and sells impure merchandise, pigs, monkeys, toys or games. *(Also see Zebra)*

Doomsday: *(See Reckoning)*

Door latch: *(See Latch)*

Door lintel: *(See Doorstep; Threshold)*

Door post: (Doorjamb) In a dream, a doorjamb or a door post represent the sire of the house or his bottler. If the door post is removed in a dream, it means dismissal of such a person from his work. If it is taken away from that site, then it means the death of the owner of that house. *(Also see Door)*

Door-to-door salesman: *(See Panderer)*

Door: A door in a dream represents the guardian of the house. An open doors in a dream represents a source of income. The door of a house also represents the wife. If the appearance of one's door looks different from reality in a dream, it means changes in one's life. If it is broken or burned in the dream, it means difficulties for the resident guardian of that house. If one sees a small door within the main entrance door in the dream, it means that he will infringe on the privacy of others bedroom. It also means that one's wife may have a secret affair, or that a betrayal may be uncovered in one's house. If one sees lions jumping at his door in a dream, it means that insolent people will pursue his wife. If one sees himself seeking a door which he couldn't find in a dream, it means indecision. Entering a house from its main door means triumph against one's opposition. If the door of one's house opens to the street in a dream, it means that what one earns will be of benefit to strangers rather than to his own household. The disappearing of a door in a dream means death of the head of that household. Passing through a small door into an open space means relief from difficulties. If one sees himself leaving his house from the main door into a spacious green garden in a dream, it means entering the realms of the hereafter. If one sees two ringlets or door knockers hanging at his door in a dream, it means indebtedness to two people who are demanding to be paid. If one sees fire burning his door in a dream, it means the death of his wife, or it may mean his failure to properly manage that household. The gates of a city represent a righteous governor. In a dream, the door of a house also represents the protection it houses behind it, including one's property, personal secrets and family. If the door is well built in a dream, it means protection of one's private life. Otherwise, whatever may be seen through such a door means exposing one's private life. If one sees a carpenter building him a new door, this means glad tidings of health and wealth. If one sees himself unable to properly secure the closing of his door in a dream, it means difficulties caused by his wife. If one sees himself changing his door in a dream, it means moving into another house. If one sees himself entering his house and locking his door in a dream, it means protection against evil. *(Also see Doorjamb; Door post)*

Doorjamb: (Door post. *See Latch*)

Doorman: In a dream, a doorman represents a royal person or a powerful man. If one sees himself in a dream as a doorman, and if he employs a servant to assist him in the dream, it means that he will climb to a powerful position. To see oneself as the king's doorman in a dream means debts, but if one finds himself working as the prince's doorman or door attendant, it means occupying a seat of authority. *(Also see Keeper of the gate)*

Doorplate: *(See Doorstep; Threshold)*

Doorstep: (Door lintel; Doorplate; Threshold) In a dream, the doorstep of one's house represents one's power, or it could mean marriage. If one sees himself removing the doorstep of his house in a dream, it means losing his power. If he removes the door lintels of his house in a dream, it means divorcing his wife. If the door lintels are taken away and one could no longer see them in the dream, it means his death. If he can still see them in the dream, then it means a sickness from which he will recover. The door lintel in a dream also represents a woman or the house bottler. If a governor sees the doorsteps of his house being removed in a dream, it means that he will be impeached. Whatever happens to the doorsteps in a dream should be interpreted as relating to one's wife or a woman. *(Also see Threshold)*

Double-cross: *(See Betrayal)*

Doubt: Doubting the truth or having doubt about God's revelations in a dream means hypocrisy, having double standards, duplicity, or entrapment of a chaste woman. *(Also see Fog; Uncertainty)*

Dough: (Money) In a dream, dough means debts, money or earnings. Dough in a dream also signifies ease, comfort or awaiting the release of a prisoner, or it could mean awaiting the birth of a new child. Seeing dough in one's house in a dream also means money and business. If the dough becomes sour in the dream, it means business losses. If one sees himself kneading a piece of dough in a dream, it means that he could expect a visitor to arrive suddenly, or it could mean the arrival of an awaited traveller. Kneading in a tight place in a dream means sodomy. Kneading in a spacious surroundings in a dream means getting married. Dough that does not rise in the dream means corruption and financial difficulties. Kneading a piece of dough from barley flour in a dream denotes an effeminate person, or it could mean rising to leadership and winning a race against one's opponents. Seeing someone kneading dough in a dream represents a leader who cares for his subjects, a popular leader, or someone who is sincere in helping others with his words and actions. *(Also see Bread)*

Doughnut: (Sweets) Eating doughnut in a dream means money earned from fun or music and it could represent an escape from a dangerous accident, or a would be fatal accident. Doughnut in a dream also could denote either sorrow and regret, or joy and happiness. Seeing a doughnut baker in a dream is a sign of escaping from danger or it could be a sign of an approaching danger.

Dove: *(See Pigeon; Ringdove; Turtledove)*

Dower: (Bridal dower) If one gives a dower for an undefined purpose in his dream, it means that he will fulfill his obligatory duties or comply with a religious injunction.

Down: (Fuzz; Hirsute) Down in a dream means prosperity, profits, clothing, inheritance or a confiscated property. In a dream, down also represents lawful earnings.

Downgrade: *(See Placing things)*

Doze: (Sleep) To doze or fall forward on one's face in a sleep in a dream means going astray.

Draft: *(See Conscription)*

Dragging: Seeing oneself in a dream dragging something heavy one cannot carry means proper controlling of one's surroundings through diplomacy, kindness, or strength and determination. If one sees himself being dragged, the consequences here may be evil.

Dragon: A dragon in a dream represents a tyrant and an unjust ruler, or it could mean a killing fire. The more heads a dragon has in a dream, the greater is his danger. If a sick person sees a dragon in his dream, it means his death. If a pregnant woman sees herself delivering a dragon in a dream, it means that she will give birth to a child who will be chronically ill. Giving birth to a dragon in a dream also represents a child who will be a great speaker or who will be known by two different names, or that he might become a fortuneteller, a monk, an evil person, a bandit or an insolent person who will be killed later. A dragon in a dream also connotes the stretch of time. If one sees a dragon coming his way without causing fear, and if the dragon talks to him with clear expressions, or if the dragon gives him something, it mean glad tidings or good news. If a giant dragon is transformed into a man or a woman in a dream, it represents an army of male or female jinn (*see alphabetically*), and a marching army of female jinns in a dream means an enemy who conceals his true purpose or identity. Such an enemy has many heads and ways in the arts of ugly actions and evil thinking. Each head from one to seven represents an adversity of a different magnitude or an art of evildoing. If the dragon in one's dream has seven heads, it represents an enemy that cannot be equalled and whose evil designs cannot be paralleled. If one sees himself owning and controlling a dragon in a dream, it means taking advantage of a person who is mentally ill. *(Also see Jinn)*

Drain pipe: *(See Gutter)*

Drain: *(See Suck)*

Drapes: (Cover; Happiness; Fears; Veil) In a dream, drapes means veiling one's private life. Drapes in a dream also represent a confidant or a trustworthy friend or a wife who covers the pitfalls of her husband, protects his business and guards him from looking at other women. If a man of knowledge sees such a dream, then drapes represent his integrity, his honorable wife and children. Unidentified drapes in a dream represent worries or distress. If the drapes are hanging over one's front door in the dream, it means that such difficulties will come from the world. Old drapes in a dream represent adversities which will not last. Torn drapes in a dream mean happiness and joy. If they are torn vertically in the dream, they represent a quick joy. If they are torn horizontally in the dream, they mean slander against one's family. Black drapes in a dream mean worries because of money, a child, or the authorities. White or green drapes mean good results. Drapes hanging over the door of a mosque in a dream represent spiritual problems or religious failure. Seeing drapes out of their place in a dream mean adversities, and seeing them hanging over one's windows has no interpretation. In a dream, seeing drapes hanging over a strange environment means fears which will culminate in satisfaction. Drapes adorned with gold means hallucination or dispelling one's worries. If an unmarried person sees drapes in his dream, it means that he will get married and protect his chastity, or it could mean a business that will shelter him from poverty. If a fugitive or a scared person sees himself covered with drapes in a dream, it means a shelter from what scares him. Falling through a hole while hanging to a drape in a dream means taking a long, frustrating, toiling and a distant journey. The bigger the drapes are in a dream, the more difficult is one's adversity.

Drawers: Looking into the perfumery drawer or the drawer where the precious stone balance is stored in a dream means high winds of profits, satisfying one's needs and reuniting with one's family. A paper storage drawer means longevity. In general, a drawer in a dream represents glad tidings. If one opens a drawer and finds a pearl or a gem inside it in a dream, it means good news or a profit one will receive in few days. *(Also see Table of Contents)*

Dream interpreter: In a dream, a dream interpreter represents happiness for a sad person and sorrow for a happy person. If one who desires to maintain secrecy around his life and goals sees a dream interpreter in his dream, it means that he will find an intimate friend or a confidant to complete his intention. If one is expecting news from an associate or if someone in a different land sees a dream interpreter in his dream, it means that he will receive the desired news. A dream interpreter in a dream also represents knowledge of sings, deciphering messages, analyzing substances, a tracer, a religious scholar, a lawyer, a good advisor, a compassionate friend, a judge or a physician. A dream interpreter in a dream also represents someone who does not keep a secret or someone who brings people both happy or sad news. In a dream, he is also a preacher, an advisor, one who balances things, a money changer, a garment cleaner, an undertaker, a barber, a comedian, a news broadcaster or someone who searches for people's faults. Seeing oneself as a dream interpreter in a dream, and if one qualifies to sit on the bench, it means that he will become a judge. If he is seeking knowledge, he will acquire it. If he is seeking to become a physician, he will become one. Otherwise, he might become a money changer, a banker or any of the earlier mentioned trades. Telling a dream interpreted a dream in one's dream, and if the explanation agrees with the common wisdom and religious norms of the Holy Qur'ān and the traditions of God's Prophet, upon whom be peace, then whatever one is told in his dream is true. If one does not understand the explanation of the dream interpreter in his dream, then he might need to find a qualified interpreter in wakefulness to satisfy his needs. *(Also see Astrologer; Divination; Fortuneteller; Founder; Interpretation; Seer)*

Dresser: *(See Dressing room)*

Dressing room: (Dresser; Fitting room; Wardrobe) A dressing room means what a comb represents in a dream. A dressing room in a dream also represents a husband for a single girl, or a chaste and a hard-working wife for a single man. *(Also see Comb; Wardrobe)*

Dried fruits: Fresh fruits in a dream denote money that does not last, while dried fruits represent money that will last. *(Also see Fruits)*

Drill: (Auger; Borer; Gimlet; Wimble) In a dream, a drill represents a devious and a fierce person. In a dream, a drill also means satisfying one's desire or needs, or it could mean using someone's help to reach one's goal, or perhaps it could mean travelling unwillingly. A drill in a dream also represents drilling a well, or it could represent a prurient, lascivious and a lustful man. In a dream, a drill also represents the male of any large quadruped or a filly. *(Also see Drilling)*

Drilling: Putting holes into pearls to string them in a dream means fulfillment of one's goals, easing of one's passage, or facilitating one's marriage. *(Also see Drill)*

Drink: (Beverage) Drinking an unknown sweet drink or a glass of a cold and fresh water in a dream means guidance, knowledge, having good taste, and the diligence of the people of the path. Drinking a glass of cold sweet water in the early morning in a dream means lawful earnings and profits for everyone, except for someone who is used to drinking hot boiled water which means sickness, stress, depression and a scare from evil spirits. Any yellow colored drink in a dream means sickness. Drinking an infusion of a violet flower in a dream means recovering from an illness, or avoiding certain food in one's diet. If one is unwillingly drinking a bitter medicinal syrup in a dream, it means that he might suffer a light illness. If he drinks apple juice or honey or myrtle drink or any other delicious drink in a dream, it means happiness for a rich person and bad news for a poor person. Drinking a glass of apple juice in a dream means benefits drawn from a servant or an employee, a service offered by a powerful person, or it could mean a stressful life. If one drinks something to cure an illness in a dream, it means recovering from that illness if it exists. Otherwise, it means that he might suffer from such an illness and take such a drink as a cure. Any constipating drink in a dream means stinginess, while taking a laxative in a dream means generosity. A headache reliever or a pain killer means kindness or diplomacy and the same goes for any drink that cleanses the kidney. Beside that, drinks denote architecture, religious studies, addressing matters promptly or hiding secrets. Colorful drinks in a dream represent happiness, joy, festivities, celebrations and correcting one's behavior. Fruit drinks in a dream may denote the fruit itself. Drinking rose water in a dream means lack of trust in someone's promises. Drinking an unknown but fragrant drink in a dream means strengthening one's certitude, loyalty or fulfilling one's vow. Drinking a smelly or a spoiled drink and particularly in a golden cup or a silver cup in a dream means denying the true source of favors or becoming an apostate. If one sees a deceased person handing him a sweet and a fragrant drink in a dream, it means guidance or admonition and it could mean that the deceased person dwells in paradise. Drinking with a regular cup in a dream represents the last drink. Drinking an unknown drink in a dream also represents the drink of the righteous and elect among God's creation. *(Also see Cold water)*

Drinking cup: *(See Cup)*

Drinking: Drinking hot water from the boiler in a dream means sickness, stress, depression and a scare from evil spirits. If one sees himself drinking cold refreshing water from the regular water tab in a dream, it means comfort and joy. *(Also see Cup; Drink; Mug)*

Driver[1]: (Animal driver; Grooming; Tending; Stableman) An animal driver in a dream represents a leader, a president of a group or corporations or a wealthy person. In general, seeing a groomer, an attendant, a driver or a stableman in a dream denotes a bad dream and implies impetuousness, a pimp, a procurer, a pander, an officiant, an adulterer, or one who drives a chained male animal to copulate with a female animal. *(Also see Copulation)*

Driver[2]: (Transportation) In a dream, a driver signifies travels, a marketplace, a carrier, or driving toward good or evil for one who is intending that. *(Also see Car; Carrier)*

Driving away: *(See Expulsion)*

Driving belt: In a dream, a driving belt means begetting a son or going on a journey.

Driving force: (Demanding; Exacting; Pushing someone; Retaliation; Yielding) In a dream, a driving force signifies retaliation by something, or compliance and submission to someone together with vigilance and wonderment about what might happen next. If one is driven by a human being in a dream, it means that he is pushed into committing a murder or that he is hired to attack someone. If one is driven by a beast, a lion or a bird of prey in a dream, it means humiliation by a superior person, or suffering from a disease.

Drizzling: *(See Dew; Rain)*

Dromedary rider: (Courier) In a dream, a dromedary rider represents a midwife, and a midwife represents a dromedary rider.

Dropper: *(See Eyedropper)*

Droppings: (Excrements of a bird.) In a dream, droppings mean a new garment. If the droppings are those of an eagle or a vulture in the dream, they mean dethroning a king or a leader. *(Also see Dung; Manure)*

Dropsy: Dropsy or abnormal accumulation of serous fluid in the body in a dream means humiliation and despise by others.

Drowning: Drowning in a dream means falling into sin and incurring the displeasure of God Almighty. Drowning in a dream also means entering hell-fire. If one dies of drowning in his dream, one should fear going astray or following innovations. Drowning in the sea, then floating in the process of trying to save oneself from death in a dream means indulging in the business of the world and forgetting about one's spiritual commitment. It also means attaining success in one's endeavors and gaining a strong foothold in one's business. If one does come out of the water alive in his dream, it means amending his life for the better and pursuing the correct course of serving one's religious life. If one sees himself after coming out of the water wearing a green garment in a dream, it means that he will pursue the path of knowledge and succeed in acquiring it. If one drowns and plunges to the bottom of the sea in a dream, it means that he will incur the wrath of someone in authority who will persecute him and cause him to perish. Drowning in a dream also means dying from an illness. Drowning in seawater in a dream means revival of one's faith in God Almighty. Drowning in freshwater in a dream means becoming extremely wealthy.

Drug addiction: *(See Intoxicants; Slingshot)*

Drugs: *(See Grammarian; Intoxicants)*

Drugstore: (Pharmacy) If a sick person sees a drugstore in his dream, it means recovering from his illness.

Drum: Seeing a drum in a dream means false news. Dancing on the drumbeat in a dream means that a calamity will befall that house. If one sees himself turned into a drum in a dream, it means that he is experiencing confused dreams. A one sided tambourine represents a woman with many faults. Women's drums in a dream mean a wild business, an esoteric commerce, selling gadgets, hideousness, or a stingy woman with many enemies. Hearing the sound of drums in a parade in a dream means false news. Hearing the drumbeat of an auctioneer's drum, a herald, or a harbinger in dream means death. It is also said that hearing the drumbeat of a procession represents someone who is grateful to his Lord under all circumstances. The sound of pilgrims' drums in a dream represents a wise man and a spiritual guide. *(Also see Drummer; Tambourine)*

Drummer: In a dream, a drummer represents festivities and joy. If a drummer visits a sick person in a dream, it means that the latter will shortly die and that drums will play at his funeral. On the other hand, it could mean that the sick person may recover and people will rejoice for his recovery and play music and drums to express their joy. A drummer in a dream also could represent someone who breaks the news. Seeing a drummer in a dream also may denote a colic illness. A drummer in a dream also represents a strong and an alarming person. A drummer in a dream can also be interpreted as one's abdomen, or someone who brings false news, or a procurer, or someone who calls people to falsehood. *(Also see Drum)*

Drunkard: (Alcoholic; Enmity; Evil; Hatred; Inebriate; Temptation; Tippler. *Also see Wine*)

Drunkenness: (Inebriety) Drunkenness in a dream represents unhappiness, stress, depression, worries, vanity, arrogance, wantonness and abuse of riches. Wine in a dream represents the king of drinks. If one gets drunk from wine, then tears off his shirt in the dream, it means that he has put his life in order and has it harmoniously organized. It also means that he has abused his privileges by indulging in vain pleasures of living to such a degree that he could not bear to live with such comfort or control his passions and wants. If one is seen drinking wine to inebriety in a dream, it means that he earns unlawful money. It also means that such earnings will seem to have power over him in the way of spending them. To become drunk in a dream without drinking alcohol means feeblemindedness or childishness of an old man. Drunkenness in a dream is a bad sign for both men and women for it denotes ignorance and complication in one's life. However, if a scared person sees himself drunk in a dream, it means that he will overcome his fears. Pretending to be drunk in a dream means a false claim. Such a person also may be inflicted with an untrue accusation in wakefulness as a lesson, so perhaps he may refrain from false claims and he will come out of such false adversity as though he is drunk without drinking. If a pious person sees himself drunk in a dream, it could represent his love for God Almighty. *(Also see Intoxicants)*

Dry land: (Terra firma) Seeing a dry land in a dream means reaching safety.

Dry skin: Suffering from dry skin condition in a dream means having spent one's money in ways that do not please God Almighty, borrowing money from people, losing it and failure to repay one's debts. Consequently, one will justly suffer from a forthcoming punishment. *(Also see Skin inflammation)*

Dryness: (Desire; Thirst) Body dryness or lack of humidity whether it affects the human being or even tree leaves in a dream means discomfort, poverty or living a wretched life. In a dream, feeling dry means stagnation of businesses, dullness of the real estate markets and unsalableness of farm products. Dryness in a dream also means poverty, slump, recession or yearning for a beloved, desiring and missing him.

Dubiousness: *(See Fog)*

Duck: In a dream, a duck represent a woman or a maid. If one sees himself eating ducks meat in a dream, it means money earned through the labor of one's workers. It also means that one may marry a rich woman. Ducks live in water and do not get wet. Ducks in a dream also are interpreted as exalted men of piety, purity and virtue who live in this world and are not affect by it. If a duck speaks to someone in a dream, it means that he will be raised in honor by a woman. It also represents comfort and satisfaction in one's life which comes from eating its flesh and the parable of its dependence on water is like that of sailors and fishermen and because of its gentleness. However, if someone hears the quacking of a duck inside his house in a dream, it means difficulties in that place, or an announcement of someone's death. *(Also see Swan's meat)*

Due alms: *(See Cauterize; Property taxes)*

Duel: (Combat; Competition; Contest; Marriage) In a dream, a duel signifies strength or a dispute with someone or disruption, dispersion or a fight. A duel with weapons in a dream means marriage to someone whose character is similar in interpretations to the weapon one is carrying in his dream. Wearing armature during a duel in a dream means marriage to a rich but deceiving person, for part of the human body is covered during the combat. A duel with swords in a dream means honor. Waving a sword during a duel in a dream means becoming known in one's field. *(Also see Marriage; Sword)*

Dull-witted: *(See Tankard)*

Dumbness: (Muteness; Silence) In a dream, dumbness means corruption in one's religious commitment or falsehood. If one sees himself dumb in a dream, it means that he insults the companions of God's Prophet, upon whom be peace, or backbites honorable people, or that he is a reprobate and an insolent person. If one sees himself mute in a dream, it means that he is ignorant. Dumbness in a dream means rescinding a court decision, or to remain silent when one is supposed to speak. Dumbness in a dream also means dethroning or terminating one's employment. If one sees his tongue tied up in a dream, it means that he will gain eloquence, mastery of words, clarity of speech, wisdom in his words and prosperity, and it means that he will win victory over his enemy.

Dummy: *(See Tankard)*

Dump: *(See Garbage dump)*

Dung: Sweeping dung in a dream means collecting money. Horses' droppings or dung in a dream mean money earned from an honorable businessman. Sitting on horse's dung or sheep's dung in a dream means earning money by doing business with members of one's own family. *(Also see Manure)*

Dupe: *(See Mockery)*

Duplicity: *(See Advice)*

Dusk: (Evening; Morning twilight) In a dream, the dusk represents an oath or the political or military moves of a ruler and his deputies.

Dust: In a dream, dust signifies money. Seeing a cloud of dust in a dream means a mysterious happening no one knows how to get out of it. Washing one's hands from dust in a dream means becoming poor. Dust that accumulates after a rainstorm or a thunderstorm and lightning in a dream means drought or adversities. A cloud of dust which is produced from a brisk movement of a car or a horse in a dream means controlling one's affairs, indulging in falsehood or enticing trouble. Dusting one's store and throwing the dirt on the sidewalk in a dream means business losses. If a merchant sees his merchandises covered with dust in a dream, it means depression and unsalability of his merchandise. *(Also see Specs of dust)*

Dwellings: (Cage; Clothing; House; Luck; Robe) In a dream, dwellings are man's abode or his world. One's dwellings in a dream are a reflection of his deeds in wakefulness. If one finds himself in a newly built house which is freshly painted and has all the needed amenities and comforts in a dream, it means prosperity. If he is a poor person, then it means that he will meet his financial obligations with ease. If he is under stress, it means that he will become free from such burdens. If he is a craftsman, it means that he will master his craft or acquire authority equal in dominance to the beauty and perfection, size and details of such a dwelling he saw in the dream. If he is in sin, it means that he will repent. The spaciousness or tightness of one's dwellings in a dream represents his finances, knowledge, sharing, hospitality and generosity. If one's own dwellings looked renovated in a dream, it means regaining or developing one's business for the better. Its fresh paint means fulfilling one's religious commitments. Its tiles or marble floors represent his pleasures or wife. Dwellings of solid iron cast means longevity and authority. If one enters an unknown house and finds departed souls dwelling therein in a dream, it means that he has entered the realms of the hereafter. If such dwellings are built of mud or plaster, this will be a reflection on his adverse conditions. If one enters such dwellings, then walks out of it in a dream, it means that he will become sick and nearly die of his illness before he recovers from it. If one walks out of it angry in a dream, it means that he will be imprisoned. If he sees someone entering his house in a dream, it means that someone will know his intimate life, or that an insolent person will become a close family friend, then betray his trust and have a secret affairs with one's wife. If one sees his dwellings crumbling or caving in on him in a dream, it means that he will receive an inheritance from the belongings of a deceased relative. Building a dwelling for oneself or for others in a dream means the death of a relative or of one's child, or it could mean divorcing one's wife. Dwellings in a dream also represent a transient station. If the dwelling is built from an unsuitable construction material in the dream, it means that one's source of income is unlawful. One's dwellings in a dream also represent his physical form, carnal self and substance. Demolishing a new home in a dream means evil and adversities. *(Also see Cage; Glass house; House)*

Dye: (Color; Expose; Hair; Henna; Hide; Gray hair) Applying henna or a dye to one's hair or hands in a dream represents a pharmacist, celebrations, glad tidings, tenderness, or it could mean compassion. Dyeing one's hair in a dream also means veiling or protecting one's personal life and that of others. To dye the gray hair of one's beard in a dream means ostentatiousness and adorning one's merchandise or deeds to make them look better than reality. Dyeing one's hair in a dream also connotes a display of blessings and favors, or it could mean dictating one's conditions to his enemy, if the person is in such position. However, if not, it means difficulties, aggravation, distress, debts or dropping off one's ties with those who love him. Interpreting woman's dyeing of her hair in a dream is the same as that of a man. To dye one's gray hair in a dream means strength, dignity and valor. Applying henna dye to one's head and not to one's beard in a dream means emulating the traditions of God's Prophet, upon whom be peace. To dye both the head and the beard in a dream means concealing one's poverty, though one will keep asking people to pay him respect or to recognize him in their circles. If one's hair accepts the dye in the dream, it means regaining one's status, though with less emphasis on his pride, or it could mean that he will make contentment his new ornament or trim. If one uses a dye other than what is commonly used, and if it works in the dream, it means that he will be saved from an adverse condition through miraculous events. If the new dye does not work in the dream, it means that his true nature will be exposed and he will have no solutions to protect himself from defamation or public abuse. If he tries to dyes his hair with dry henna clay, and if his hair still accepts it in the dream, it means that he is an ignorant person, though he will ultimately repent for his sins, amend his actions and improve himself. If a woman sees her hands dyed with gold in a dream, it means that she will give all her wealth to her husband and that she will be satisfied to see him happy, though in reality she too will gain power and status in her family. If a man sees his feet dyed and tattooed in a dream, it means that he will be struck with family problems. A dyed hand in a dream means hardship in making ends meet. If one dips his hand into a laying corpse in a dream, it means that he will witness a conspiracy. If one sees his hands dyed in a dream, it also means that he has reached the end of the rope with his money or business. If one sees his dyed hands wrapped or bandaged in a dream, it means that he will lose a trial or a fight with his rivals, or that he will fail to meet such a challenge again. Dyeing only the finger with henna in a dream represents branches of dates or clusters of grapes. In general, dyeing one's hands with henna or one's hair with regular dye as a makeup in a dream represents joy for the husband and wife as long as they do not exceed the norms. Dyeing one's hands and feet in a dream means redecorating one's house. If a poor person sees himself dyeing his hands or hair in a dream, it means that he will cover up the loss of his ablution during prayers or during his reading of the Holy Qur'ān or during other ritual occasions where he is required to have ablution before proceeding. It could also mean that he cares little about attending his prayers. As for women, dyeing means happiness, new clothing, receiving gold, or a wedding celebration. If the dye exceeds the required surface of the hands or the feet in the dream, it means being struck with fear and worries caused by one's business or friends. If a man sees himself in a dream dyeing his hair or beard with other than henna, it means that he will suffer from what he fears most. Dyeing or suppressing one's feelings for a sick person means recovering from his ailment. Dyeing one's hair black in a dream means hiding one's bad conditions, spoiling the benefits of one's deeds, or hiding one's evil intentions. This is taken from the practice of Egypt's Pharaoh who sometimes dyed his hair black, thus trying to hide his appearance and ignorance.

Dyer: In a dream, a leather finisher or a fabric dyer represents a false person, though he also could do good. A dyer in a dream also represents someone of good financial standing or one who is in position to help others, or he could be a man of knowledge, or a person in authority. Seeing a dyer dying a white garment into a green color in a dream means repentance from sins. If he changes the dye of a white garment into black, it means apostasy. If one sees a dyer in his house receiving or taking garments to dye in a dream, he represents an adulterer and means that someone in that house may die in that year.

Dyestuff: *(See Safflower)*

E

Eagle: (Vulture) Eagle is the king of birds. Struggling with an eagle in a dream means distress, fury of one's superior or subjugation to an unjust person. Owning an obedient, well tamed eagle in a dream means prosperity, honor and power. Owning and flying an eagle in a dream means becoming a tyrant. The scratch of an eagle in a dream means a sickness. A killed eagle in a dream means the death of a ruler. If a pregnant woman sees an eagle in her dream, it means seeing a midwife or a nurse. In a dream, an eagle also may be interpreted to represent a great ruler, a prophet or a righteous person. Hearing the cry of an eagle in a dream means a fight. Eating the flesh of an eagle or getting hold of some of its feathers in a dream means receiving money from a ruler. If an eagle catches someone and soars away with him horizontally in a dream, it means travels. If he flies away with him vertically in the dream, it means death. In a dream, an eagle also means longevity, prosperity, innovation or heedlessness. *(Also see Vulture)*

Ear: (Awareness; Deafness; Hearing; Stability) One's ear in a dream represents his hearing, the point of his awareness, his rank, child, property or his status. The ear in a dream also represents knowledge, reason, religion, extent of one's wealth, or pride about one's lineage. If one's hearing becomes clearer or increases in sensibility, or if he sees light beaming from his ears or driving into them in a dream, this dream will represent his guidance, obedience to his Lord and consent to His command. If he sees his ears looking smaller or producing an offensive odor in a dream, it means that he may go astray and indulge in actions that will incur God's displeasure. If one discovers that he has an extra ear in a dream, it means a permission is given to him to fulfill what he intends. The number of ears one sees in a dream also represent the different arts and sciences, but they could also mean that the person in question has no stability. In a dream, one's ear may represent the jewelry a woman attaches to herself as ornaments. To clog one's ears with one's own fingers in a dream means death in a repugnant state of innovation. Plugging one's own ears in a dream also means ignoring a repulsive thought. Plugging one's ears in a dream also could mean becoming an advisor to someone or a caller to prayers in a mosque, i.e., a muezzin. If one's ears are transformed into an animal's ears in a dream, it means losing respect or developing inertness or apathy. As one's awareness, one's ear in a dream represents a pouch, a wallet, a coffer or a safe. Ears in a dream are also interpreted to mean separation from one's wife or daughter. If only half of one's ear is there in the dream, it means the death of his wife. If one finds himself deaf in his dream, it means that he may lose his faith. Having large ears in a dream means shunning or avoiding what is true. If one sees as though his ears have eyes in the dream, it means that he may lose his sight. If one sees himself eating the accumulated wax of his ears in the dream, it means that he is a child molester. If one sees grass growing all over him but does not cover his ears or eyes in the dream, it means prosperity. *(Also see Body¹; Earwax)*

Earlock: *(See Body¹; Temple)*

Early companions: *(See Scholars)*

Early scholars: *(See Scholars)*

Earrings: In a dream, woman's earrings or necklace if they are made of pearls, they represent a gift from her husband. If they are made of silver in the dream, they mean a physical ailment, and if they are made from beads in the dream, they mean being let down by one's friends. Seeing one's wife wearing earrings in a dream means engaging in a profitable business. If a man sees himself wearing a pair of beautiful earrings which are mounted with pearls in a dream, it means that he will enjoy wealth, prosperity and comfort in this life, or it could mean that he will memorize the Holy Qur'ān. If a woman sees herself wearing a pair of silver earrings in a dream, it means that she will conceive a son who will grow to be a pious man. If they are made from pearls, then her future son will sing with music. As for an unmarried woman, wearing a pair of earrings in a dream means marriage. If one sees a child wearing a pair of earrings in a dream, it represents beauty, though it is not praiseworthy if an adult or a man is seen in a dream wearing a pair of earrings or even a single earring. In their case, it means engaging in a loathsome and disgraceful action. Wearing a pair of earrings in a dream also means acquiring a knowledge that exalts the person and raises him in station. It also could mean having musical inclinations, or having a picnic. *(Also see Gold; Ornaments)*

Earth[1]: (Element of earth; Dirt) In a dream, earth represents people, for they are created from the same element. Earth in a dream also means cattle, animals or the world. Dirt in a dream represents money, but it could also mean poverty. Digging the earth in a dream means digging a grave for a sick person. Digging the earth in a dream also means a journey, and its collected dirt means profits from one's journey. If digging the earth is interpreted as seeking marriage, then the earth itself represents one's future wife. Generally speaking, digging the earth in a dream is bad, because it unveils what is hidden. The dirt itself represents woman's property. To shake the dust off one's hands in a dream means business losses, poverty and humiliation. It also means remitting savings to their rightful owners. Walking on dirt means soliciting money. Collecting dirt means saving money. Sweeping dirt in one's house means to swindle money from one's wife. Earth also represents mans longevity. If one sees his wife carrying a bag of dirt in a dream, it means a suspicious pregnancy. Earth in a dream also represents the four elements fire, water, air and either, for it is one of the main elements in nature. Wiping one's face with dirt in a dream means praising others or disappointing oneself. Earth in a dream also means satisfaction of one's needs or fulfillment of a promise, because ink is extracted from its elements. If a merchant sees his merchandise covered with dirt in a dream, it means depression and unsalability of his merchandise.

Earth[2]: (Country; Farm; Floor; Glob; Land; Locality; Place; Property) In a dream, each locality has a particular meaning that relates to its substance and conditions. To see the land of the great gathering on the Day of Resurrection in a dream means the fulfillment of a promise, or that the person seeing the dream is worthy of keeping secrets. Earth in a dream also means becoming rich after poverty, or having peace after experiencing extreme difficulties. It also means a marriage to a beautiful young virgin, or it could mean receiving guidance and attaining a high ranking and an honorable position in the world. To see the glob being carried on the back of a whale or a steer without changing its conditions in a dream means that the king of the country will be dethroned. He will either step down or be replaced by his minister. Sweeping the floor and caring for the floor mat or carpet in a dream means to care for one's community or family. Earth in a dream also represents one's mother, or the governor of the land. Working in a farmland in a dream, seeing its tools, elements, seeds, water, plowing, harvesting, landscaping, blossoming of its flowers, their fragrance, light, whatever positive or negative results one sees therein in a dream represent such success or failure. Seeing an unknown land could denote one's mother, child, husband, wife, partner, guardian, a servant, or it could mean one's heirs. Earth in a dream also may mean arguments, knowledge or clarity of speech. Earth in a dream also represents the element of the world, as the skies represent the element of the hereafter. If both the earth and the skies are seen simultaneously in a dream, it means that they can never be joined together, as the world and the hereafter do not exist in one place. If the top soil of the land is cracked in a dream, it means that the land is rich and arable. Such cracks in a dream also signify the rise of invented religious dogmas and the spread of evil and innovation. Seeing the stretch of the land in a dream means the release of prisoners, or in the case of a pregnant woman, it means the nearing of her delivery. If one sees an earthquake and the destruction of life and property in a dream, this element represents straying from the path, pride and heedlessness. If the earth appears to fold over him in a dream, it means losing one stature in the world, divorce or losing in business. If the earth changes into iron or rocks in one's dream, it means that one's wife will not bear children, or it could mean changing one's trade or profession. If the earth opens and swallows him in a dream, it means that he is ashamed of something he did, or it could mean hurdles in one's business, a journey, or imprisonment. If the earth looks like a desert land in the dream, it may mean that such a person may undertake an urgent trip. Beating the ground with a stick in a dream means taking a business trip. Eating dirt in a dream means earnings an equal amount of money to what one eats in his dream. If the earth cracks and opens, and if a beast comes and speaks to the people in their own tongue in a dream, it means that people will witness a miracle or a happening that will bewilder everyone. This may also mean nearing the end of one's life. Digging the earth in a dream also means plotting and deceiving others. If the earth speaks good words to someone in the dream, it means that he or she will attain whatever they are told. On the other hand, if the earth reprimands someone in the dream, it means that he must amend his actions for the better and ask for God's forgiveness and guidance.

Earthenware pot: In a dream, an earthenware pot means a sharing neighbor. It also means a modestly dressed woman, her estate, family and children. If the pot is made of brass or ceramic in the dream, it may represent a poor woman. An earthenware pot in a dream also means decision making, concealing one's secrets, or it could represent a woman who has frequent miscarriages. (*Also see Earthenware jar; Jar; Pot*)

Earthquake: In a dream, an earthquake represents fear of a higher authority. An earthquake in a dream is also interpreted to indicate major changes in that particular place, or a calamity that will befall a town or a country. If one sees the mountains rumbling, shaking and crumbling, then being restored to their original state in a dream, it means that a great happening will devastate such a place. If one sees the earth shaking or caving in, and if everything sinks into the ground, hitting a segment of the community and sparing another segment of it in the dream, it means that a calamity will befall that place, and it will manifest through social disorder, injustices or a plague. If one sees the earth shaking and the firmament rent asunder in a dream, it means that major adversities will hit their properties, cattle, farms and institutions, etcetera, as a divine chastisement for people's sins. If one sees the earth moving under his feet in a dream, then it represents one's striving and pursuit of his business needs or livelihood. An earthquake in a dream also represents exposing secrets, hearing bad news, a general scare, public disturbances, the surfacing of new diseases. If one sees the walls crumbling and caving in a dream, it means his death. Seeing an earthquake in an arable land in a dream means fertility or a good harvest. An earthquake in a dream also may mean travels, dancing, abstraction of business or having an argument with one's family. If the destruction hits the buildings in urban areas in the dream, it means business growth for construction workers, contractors or related industries. Seeing an earthquake hitting a fruit farm in a dream means a good harvest. If the quake takes place during the month of **May**, it means a fierce battle, fights between people or public disorder. If one's dream takes place during the month of **June**, then it means destruction of evil trades and their people. If the dream takes place during the daylight time, then it means appointment of people of knowledge to leading positions in the government. If one dreams of an earthquake during the month of **July**, it means that a great person will die in that place. If it takes place during the month of **August**, it means that an enemy will attack that country. If it takes place during the month of **September** in the dream, it means that a stranger will enter that town and subsequently, the town will be hit with a severe plague and sufferings. If it takes place during the month of **October** in one's dream, then it represents a common illness, safety of pregnant women and lowering or stabilization of prices. If it takes place during the month of **November** in the dream, it means frequent miscarriages. If it takes place during the month of **December** in a dream, then it represents severe calamities, plagues and death, though no enemy threat is visible. If it takes place during the month **January** in one's dream, then it means the death of young people. If it takes place during the month of **February** in the dream, then it means hunger and miscarriages. If it takes place during the month of **March** in the dream, then it means prosperity and a good harvest. If a pregnant woman sees an earthquake in her dream, it means that she is delivering her baby. *(Also see Cave in; Destruction; Earth; Thunder; Tremor)*

Earthenware jar: *(See Jar)*

Earthworm: Seeing an earthworm in a dream means facing a weak enemy. *(Also see Rainworm)*

Earwax: (Auditory meatus; Cerumen) If one sees himself cleaning the yellowish waxlike secretion found in the canal of his external ear, or if he is cleaning it from someone else's ears in a dream, it means that he will acquire a needed antidote or poison or become free from the plot of envious people. If one cleanse his ears from earwax or from other dirt in a dream, it means that he will hear good and pleasing news. If one sees himself eating the earwax he extracts from his own ears in a dream, it means that he is a child molester. Cleaning the wax of one's ears in a dream also means hearing pleasing news. *(Also see Ear)*

Earwig: (Beetle; Insect; Worm) An insect with pincers that seeks out the human ear to crawl into his body *(folk.)* In a dream, an earwig represents the enemy of the leaders.

Eating to one's fill: *(See Appetite)*

Eating: *(See Food)*

Eavesdropping: In a dream, eavesdropping means backbiting and lies. Perhaps the one who is eavesdropping on others may become despised by the ruler or his superior. On the other hand, if one sees himself in a dream inadvertently listening to a conversation, and if the one seeing the dream is a merchant, it means that he will resign from the leadership of his business, and if he is a ruler, it means that he will be removed from his post. If one sees himself harkening to another person in a dream, it means that he desires to defame him or expose his pitfalls. If one sees himself listening to some talks of which he follows the better avenues in the dream, it means that he will receive glad tidings. If one sees himself listening to admonition but ignoring it in a dream, it means that he lies as a habit.

Ebbing: *(See Ship)*

Ebony: *(bot.)* An ebony tree in a dream represents a rich Indian woman, or a rich strong man.

Eclipse: (Lunar eclipse; Solar eclipse) Seeing a solar eclipse in a dream means that a calamity will befall the leader of a country, while a lunar eclipse represents a calamity that will befall the prime minister. It is also said that a solar eclipse in a dream signifies the death of one's wife or his mother. If a cloud covers the light of the sun in a dream, it means that a sickness will befall the leader of the country or the governor of the land. If one sees the sun moving above the clouds but cannot come from under it in a dream, it means his death. The sun in a dream also may represent a great scholar. A cloud covering the sunlight in a dream means the fall of an unjust ruler. *(Also see Moon; Sun)*

Educator: (Instructor; Master; Mentor; Teacher) In a dream, an educator or a teacher represents himself, or he could represent the principal of a school, or a model, a pillar, a shaikh, a jailer, one's son or one's mother. An educator in a dream also means a coach or an animal trainer. Seeing oneself as an educator in a dream means advancing in one's field. A math teacher in a dream represents intellect and wisdom. Adding, subtracting, multiplying or dividing in a dream represents common benefits and losses one incurs during the course of his life. A Qur'ān teacher in a dream represents singing, honor or favors. An unknown teacher in a dream represents the Almighty God Himself. *(Also see Teacher)*

Edible roots: *(See Taro)*

Edifice: *(See Monument)*

Effeminate: (Lesbian; Sodomy; Transvestite; Vagina) If one sees himself acting effeminately in a dream, it means evil, distress, fear or that a calamity will befall him. If an effeminate person sees himself having a vagina in a dream, it means that he has two faces or that he is satisfied to be knowledgeable as well as a fraud. If an effeminate person or a homosexual looks at his own male organ and finds no female organ beside it in the dream, it means that he will repent and back up from his loathsome conduct and revert to his natural sexual condition. If an effeminate person who is also bisexual sees himself as having a vagina, or if he looks at his penis in a dream, it means separation from his wife or mother or segregation from his friends. *(Also see Sexual intercourse; Vagina)*

Efforts: Making serious efforts to attain something noble in a dream means reaching one's goals. *(Also see Grandfather)*

Eggplant: In season, an eggplant in a dream means earnings with little effort, while seeing an eggplant out of season in a dream denotes negativity and disliked. Eating an eggplant in a dream means falling prices. An eggplant in a dream also represents the element of arrogance, self adulation, perfidy, cheating others, and a man with many faces. As for fishermen, seeing eggplants in a dream means a good catch, joy and success.

Eggs: (Eggs in a basket or a place.) Eggs represent the element of prosperity, or the fear of depleting one's riches. Eggs in a dream also represent marriage for an unmarried person and children for a married one. If one's chicken lay eggs for him in a dream, it means a new born in his family. Eating a boiled egg in a dream means comfort and income while eating a raw egg means unlawful earnings, adultery or distress. If one sees his wife laying an egg in a dream, it means that she will bear a child who will lack faith in God. If the egg breaks in the dream, it means that his newborn will die shortly after birth. If one sees himself raising chicken for eggs, then if the eggs hatch in his dream, it means that some of his affairs that where unsolvable will rejuvenate with success, and it could mean that he will beget a child who will grow to have true faith in God Almighty. He also may beget a child for each egg that hatches in his dream. Eggs in a basket in a dream also represent a family reunion. *(Also see Boiled eggs;*

Omelet)

Egypt: *(See City; Pyramids)*

Eid-ul Adhā: *(arb. See Immolation; Feast of Immolation; Five times prayers)*

Eid-ul Fiṭr: *(See Feast of Breaking the Fast)*

Eid: *(arb. Celebration; Festival. See Five times prayers)*

Elation: *(See Happiness)*

Elderly person: An unknown elderly person in a dream represents one's good luck, happiness and one's assiduity and diligence. If the unknown elderly person looks strong in the dream, he represents one's strength. Otherwise, if he looks feeble, then he represents one's weakness. Whatever physical conditions an elderly person is seen with in the dream, such condition will reflect in one's own state. If an elderly person comes toward the person seeing the dream, it means that someone will help him attain a praiseworthy rank. If one follows an elderly person in a dream, it means that he follows a good path. If one sees an elderly person and displeases him in the dream, it means that he will displease a close friend or reject his advice. If he pleases him in the dream, it means that he will consent with a close good friend and they will walk together on the path to reap material as well as spiritual benefits. If one sees a gathering of friendly people but could not determine whether they are young or elderly in a dream, it means that he will discover new avenues in his life and he will draw material and spiritual benefits from them. If he sees a gathering of young people he does not recognize in the dream, it means that he will associate himself with rich people. If he sees a gathering of elderly people he does not recognize in the dream, it means that he will associate himself with good friends. If a woman sees an elderly person she could not recognize in the dream, he represents the world. If a young man sees himself turned into an elderly person in a dream, it means that he will acquire knowledge and wisdom. Listening to a good looking elderly person in a dream means receiving honor and rank. If an elderly person sees himself turned young in a dream, it represents his strength, wealth, good living and a healthy life, or it could mean material or religious losses, or it could mean his death. If an elderly person sees himself being born again in a dream, it means his death. If he is ill, it could represent his attachment to the world, and if he is poor, it could denote his earning. If an elderly person sees himself as a youth in a dream, it could also mean committing a childish act or an unwise act. A wise elderly person in a dream represents honor, rank, dignity, wealth, blessings and longevity. On the other hand, seeing an elderly person in a dream could represents failure, weaknesses, defeat, disablement or inertness. *(Also see Gray hair)*

Elders: (Chancellors; Councilmen; Leaders; Seniors; Wise men) Seeing the elders of a community, the councilmen of a city, the chiefs of a clan or the shaikhs of a tribe in a dream means victory and glad tidings.

Election: *(See Rising in station)*

Electuary: (Medicinal paste; Ointment; Salve) Licking a paste made from drugs mixed with honey or syrup, or applying a salve in a dream means recovering from an illness or having a sizeable offspring.

Elegance: (Culture; Handsomeness; Refinement; Sophistication) To see oneself handsome, elegant or sophisticated in a dream signifies distress, trouble, false accusations, abstinence, or it could mean freedom.

Elephant man: A chronic disease which is characterized by the enlargement of certain parts of the body, especially the legs and gentiles. In a dream, an elephant man represents love for the world from the wrong angle.

Elephant trainer: An elephant trainer in a dream represents the master teacher of children of noble families, a horse trainer, a sports trainer or a translator.

(Also see Elephant)

Elephant: (Arrogance) In a dream, an elephant represents a respected and feared enemy who is dull-witted, who carries heavy burdens or responsibilities and who is expert in war tactics. An elephant in a dream also signifies arrogance. Riding an elephant or controlling it in a dream means establishing ties with a leader or a politician and profiteering from one's connection. It also means living a long and a prosperous life. Riding an elephant during the nighttime in a dream means rising in rank, and should one be suited for leadership, he will receive it then engage in a war which he will lose. Riding an elephant during the daylight hours in a dream means divorce, perfidy, betrayal or deceit. Milking an elephant or taking something out of its trunk in a dream means either extortion or receiving lawful money from a powerful person. It is also said that an elephant in a dream represents a mighty king who is gracious and generous, patient and tender hearted. If an elephant hits someone with his trunk in a dream, it means receiving benefits from such a person or inheriting something from him, receiving a political appointment, or becoming wealthy through high connections. An elephant in a dream also represents righteous people, scholars and noble ones. An elephant in a dream also denotes hardships, toiling, then relief from adversities. Seeing an elephant in a dream and failing to ride on it means lack of integrity or loss of business. Seeing a dead elephant in a dream means that the ruler or a great person from that land will die, or that a noble person will be killed. Seeing an elephant in a land other than its native land in a dream means adversities. If one faces a threatening elephant in a dream, it means an illness. If one falls under the feet of an elephant in a dream, it means his death. Speaking to an elephant in a dream means receiving a precious gift from someone in authority. Running away in fear of an elephant in a dream means being persecuted by someone in authority. Riding an elephant during a war in a dream means defeat and subsequent destruction. Eating elephant's meat in a dream means money. As for worldly people, seeing an elephant in a dream means benefits, but as for pious and religious people, it denotes adversities. Riding an elephant in a dream also may denote lies or oppression. An elephant entering a land other than its natural habitat signifies an official visit of a king or a president to another country, or it could mean invading it.

Elephantiasis: *(med. See Elephant man)*

Elevation: Elevation in a dream may represent one's wife. *(Also see Hill)*

Elf: (Abnormal; Albino; Elf; Leprosy; Whitish) An elf in a dream represents a person of evil nature who creates disunity and enmity between people through backbiting, insinuations, slanders and who advises them against good deeds. In a dream, an elf also represents poverty, sorrows, humiliation, or adversities caused by people who wander between towns and cities as a habit. If an elf visits a sick person in a dream, it means death.

Elixir: *(See Antidote)*

Eloquence of speech: (Clarity of speech; Fluency) To have fluency and eloquence of speech in a dream means being honored, dignified, becoming a knight or being endowed with immeasurable wealth, or it could mean extension of one's powers and control, prosperity from one's business, fame, or it could mean attaining excellence in one's craft or trade. In general, eloquence of speech in a dream signifies honor and deputyship.

Emaciated: (Poverty; Skin)

Embalming: *(See Mummification)*

Embrace: (Accolade; Hug) Embracing someone in a dream means longevity. Embracing a deceased person also means longevity. If a deceased person embraces the person seeing the dream and does not let go of him in a dream, it means his death. Embracing a known person in a dream means associating with him. Embracing one's enemy in a dream means making peace with him. It is also said that an embrace in a dream signifies exchanging praises. An embrace in a dream also signifies kindness, liking for one another, travels, arriving from a journey and dispelling distress or anxiety. An embrace in a dream is also interpreted to mean having sexual intercourse. Embracing a woman in a dream means love for the world, and despair from receiving any reward in the hereafter. Embracing a man in a dream signifies lending him support and helping him. Embracing the trunk of a tree in a dream means indulging in hypocrisy. Embracing someone and laying one's head in his lap in a dream means entrusting him with one's capital, or working for him. *(Also see Envelope; Hug)*

Embroiderer: An embroiderer in a dream represents a bright and an intelligent person, a trickster or someone who embellishes his words and exaggerates his explanations, or he could represent a writer, a man of letter, a refined person, a poet or a fine singer. *(Also see Monogram)*

Emerald: Seeing an emerald in a dream denotes martyrdom or the blessings that are created for a believer in paradise. If one buys an emerald in a dream, it means that he will win a dear brother, associate himself with a group of righteous brothers on the path, raise well behaving children, acquire a useful knowledge, or earn lawful money.

Emergence: *(See Appearance)*

Employee: *(See Accountability; Office)*

Employment: *(See Accountability; Office)*

Emptiness: In a dream, emptiness represents the dwellings of a foreigner. It may also represent breach of contract, betrayal, death of a sick person, rest after exhaustion or peace after bewilderment. *(Also see Deserted)*

Empty space: *(See Deserted; Emptiness)*

Empty: *(See Deserted; Emptiness)*

Enacting: Enacting ablution rites or performing the acts of ritual ablution without water *(arb. Tayammum)* in a dream means nearing the solution of one's problems. *(Also see Tayammum)*

Enamelist: (Coating; Glazier; Pride) In a dream, an enamelist represents someone who is proud of himself or who is arrogant and deceives himself about his greatness, wealth and attainments, or who mixes with and befriends stupid people and opens his heart to them.

Enamored: (Love; Poverty) To see oneself inflamed with love for someone in a dream represents distress, adversities, blindness, deafness or notoriousness. Such a case may draw people's compassion. If a sick person sees himself in a dream inflamed with love it may mean his death. Fire in a dream also means love. Love in a dream also means heedlessness and failure to fulfill one's religious obligations. It also means financial losses, losing one's child, divorce, despise of one's friends, hunger, travels, sickness or dangers. Being enamored with God in a dream means a strong devotion and certitude. Pretending to be in love in one's dream means straying from God's path. If one finally reaches his beloved to mates with in the dream, it means that adversities may strike at him, or affect his or her beloved. *(Also see Love)*

Enclosure: *(See Hedges)*

Encroachment: *(See Infringement)*

Encyclopedia: *(See Reference book)*

Endowment: (Alms; Charity; Contribution; Donation; Fulfilling needs; Gift; Offering; Profits; Religious endowment) Making a religious endowment in a dream represents good deeds that are done for God's pleasure, seeking to be in

141

His nearness and asking for His blessings. Making a religious endowment in a dream also means rising in station, both in this world and in the hereafter. If what one donates for this purpose is a house or a book or money in the dream, it means repentance from one's sins and guidance on the straight path, or it could mean begetting a son. Offering a swine or wine as an endowment in a dream means rising in rank in the world, injustice, and causing harm to others.

Enemy: (Adversary; Boy; Foe; Hidden treasure; Opponent; Power; Snake; Unjust ruler; Woman) To meet an enemy in a dream signifies honor, signing a treaty, rising above differences, receiving God's help and victory. Facing one's enemy in a dream also means befriending him. If one is threatened by his enemy in a dream, it means that he will win the upper hand. If one is promised good things by his enemy in a dream, it means that he will fall into his trap and lose his fight to him. If one's enemy advises him in a dream, it means that he will betray him. If one sees an enemy invading a land in a dream, it means that a destructive flood will devastate that place. If one's enemy confides to him or pleases him in a dream, it means that he will suffer distress and adversities. If one is captured for a ransom by his enemy in a dream, it means that he indulges in sins and that he is a hostage of his own sins. *(Also see Blessings; Enmity; Introduction p. xxvi)*

Engagement: (Betrothal; Marriage. *See Book*)

Engineer: *(See Architect; Artist)*

English Ivy: *(See Ivy)*

English: *(See Language)*

Engraver: (Goldsmith; Leather craftsman; or any craft using a hammer and a chisel.) An engraver in a dream represents knowledge and pursuit of the prophetic traditions. In a dream, an engraver also means deception, trickery and imposing credulity upon others through dishonesty. A stone carver in a dream represents someone who deals with people of ignorance. A copper engraver represents disputes and illness. Gold and silver engraver in a dream represents clear wisdom and putting things where they belong. An engraver in a dream also represents a worldly person. If he also deals with fabrics in the dream, it means that he is a peacemaker. Seeing him also means spending one's money to serve evil people or investing money in their projects, lies, falsehood and hypocrisy. The customers in the dream represent people who prefer worldly and temporary benefits over the eternal reward and benefits of the hereafter. If the engraver sells the merchandise but does not accept money for them in the dream, it means that he prefers his spiritual life over his temporary material pleasure and that he is grateful to God Almighty. If he asks for a price for his services, then it means the opposite. If the engraver barters what he sells for wheat or flour in the dream, it means that he will become detached from worldly interests, and that he is grateful for his Lord's blessings. An engraver in a dream also represents a person who teaches arts and science.

Enhancement: *(See Eye-brow)*

Enjoyment: *(See Pleasure)*

Enlist: *(See Conscription)*

Enmity: (Conflict; Discord; Rupture; Spitefulness) To show enmity toward someone in a dream means desiring to remain in his company, showing him friendliness, then divulging his secrets or exposing his feelings. To face someone's animosity in a dream, means becoming friendly with him, for enmity means uncovering what is hidden. *(Also see Enemy; Rupture of relations)*

Enoch: *(See Khiḍr; Green)*

Entering a house: If one sees himself entering someone else's house in a dream, it means that he will defeat him, gain the upper hand in business over him or control his interests. To enter the house of the governor and to feel comfortable and at ease therein in a dream means that he is soliciting the governor's assistance in a personal business. The coming of a just person to a house in a dream means blessings. If an unjust person enters a place in a dream, it means that evil and calamities will befall such a house. If it is customary for such a person to enter that place, then no harm will incur from his coming or going. If one sees himself entering a house of unfamiliar substance, ground or structure, and if he meets departed souls whom he recognizes in the dream, it means that he has entered the realms of the dead. If he sees himself going into that sphere, then coming out of it in the dream, it means that he will near his death, then recover from a serious illness. Entering the Sacred House in Mecca in a dream means entering one's house as a newlywed. *(Also see Marketplace)*

Entering hell-fire: In a dream, if one sees himself entering hell-fire, whether he is a believer or a non-believer, it means that he will suffer from fever, become poor, enter a prison, commit a major sin, or mix with disbelievers and reprobates.

Entering Paradise: If one sees himself entering the heavenly paradise in a dream, then his dream represents glad tidings that God willing, he shall enter it. If a pilgrim sees himself entering paradise in a dream, it means that his pilgrimage is accepted or that he will reach God's House in Mecca. If he lacks faith in God Almighty, it means that he will become a believer. If a believer who is bed-stricken sees himself entering paradise in a dream, it means that he will die of his illness. If a non-believer who is bed-stricken sees himself entering paradise in a dream, it means that he will recover from his illness. If he is unwed, it means that he will get married. If he is poor, it means that he will become rich or receive an inheritance. If a sick person sees himself in the abode of the hereafter healthy again in a dream, it means that he will reach it free from the ills of this world, its adversities and temptations. If he is not sick, then entering the realms of the hereafter means glad tidings, business success, a pilgrimage, ascetic detachment from this world, sincere devotion, acquiring knowledge, strengthening of one's kinship or exercising patience toward a calamity which derives from one's own sins. If one sees himself entering the abode of the hereafter to visit and see around, and should he be a person of good deeds and character who is a capable person and who acts upon his knowledge, it means that he will be without work or suffer from business losses. If he is scared of something, or if he is accused of something, or if he is under stress, it means that his fears will dissipate. Mostly, entering the abode of the hereafter in a dream means travels or migration from one's homeland. Thus, if one sees himself returning from a journey to the hereafter in a dream, it means that he will return to his homeland. Entering paradise in a dream means a pilgrimage to God's House in Mecca.

Entertainer: an entertainer in a dream represents a person who claims to be generous, and who commands generosity for others.

Entice: (Incite; Induce; Lure; Research; Urge)

Entwine: *(See Twist)*

Enumerate: *(See Counting)*

Envelope: (Cover; Embrace; Postal package) An envelope in a dream means money, except if it is sealed, then it means travels. In a dream, an envelope also means victory in one's life, attainment of one's goal, learning about a pleasant story, or it could represent a vessel, money, or knowledge.

Epidemic disease: Witnessing an epidemic disease causing a high rate of mortality in a dream represents a tyrant, government, imprisonment or evil happenings.

Error: *(See Darkness; Wandering)*

Escape from danger: Escaping from danger or surviving a would be fatal accident in a dream denotes one's devotion, religious awareness, fasting, charities and good deeds. *(Also see Escape; Running away; Take a flight; Turning)*

Escape: If one sees himself walking across hills in a dream, it means that he is trying to escape from danger. *(Also see Escape from danger; Running away)*

Escort: (Convoy; Guide; Helper) In a dream, an escort means travels, or a barber, a hairdresser, the tithe collector, a collection agent, an emissary or a trader.

Escrow: *(See Guarantee)*

Esoteric: *(See Drums)*

Espalier: *(See Vineyard)*

Establishing the divine laws: If one is required in his dream to circumscribe to the limitations placed by God on man's freedom of action in the world, or if one asks that such judgment be exacted in his case, his dream then represents paying one's debts, or respecting one's limitations, or marriage to protect one's chastity.

Estate: (Farmland) In a dream, a farmland represents wealth and benefits, for cities live from the produce of a farmland. A farmland in a dream also represents stored grains or fruits or vegetables. Anything that affects the farmland, such as drought, inundation, diseases or a fire in a dream will manifest in people's life in the cities. A farmland in a dream also may represents one's livelihood and earnings, a patient and a helping wife, or a hard-working and a patient husband. If one sees a blossoming farmland in his dream, it means blessings, growth and profits from his work. A farmland in a dream also means wasting one's life in useless endeavors, or it could mean heedlessness, lack of comfort, pleasure in one's life or neglecting to seek knowledge while occupying oneself in pursuing mundane objectives. *(Also see Farm)*

Estrangement: *(See Repudiation)*

Eternity: (Heaven)

Etiquette: *(See Perfume salesman)*

Eunuch: *(See Ostrich)*

Euphrates: (River; Sweet water) Drinking from the Euphrates river in a dream means blessings and grace, for the Euphrates is one of the rivers of paradise. Drinking from the Euphrates river in a dream also means being a pious, content and a religious person. If one sees the Euphrates river dry in a dream, it means the death of the governor, or the loss of a country, or perhaps the meaning could apply to the chief minister, or the personal secretary of the ruler. *(Also see River)*

Evanescence: (Annihilation; Disappearing; Non-existence) To vanish or be non-existent in a dream means depression, nullifying all banknotes during a war, cancelling all interests and credits, a bad harvest, a plague, or it could mean a disaster. To be non-existent for the people of the path in a dream signifies an everlasting existence. *(Also see Disappearing)*

Eve: (Mother of humankind, may God's peace be with her.) In a dream, Eve represents prosperity, blessings, a good harvest, a good yield, progeny, profits from a business in textile, farming, smithcraft or similar industries. Seeing Adam and Eve in a dream means being demoted from a station and a place of honor to a lower rank to be raised again after repenting from one's sin. Seeing Eve in a dream also indicates pitfalls, sins, being subject to jealousy and malicious fraud, or trouble with one's neighbors. Seeing Adam and Eve in a dream also means hardships caused by one's wife or children, consent for sexual intercourse, repentance or regret for one's past. If a woman sees Eve in her dream, it means that she will create hardships for her husband because of her association with someone who is unsuitable for her friendship. It also means that a major adversity will befall her, since Eve was the first to experience female menstrual period and the pain of childbirth. It may also mean suffering from the burden of pregnancy, labor and the pangs of giving birth. Seeing Eve in a dream also could mean giving birth to both righteous as well as evil children. If the woman in the dream is separated from her husband, it may mean returning to her conjugal life or earning lawful income for her own needs. It also could mean that someone from her progeny may commit murder or die as a martyr. If a man sees Eve in a dream, it means that he may be deceived by a woman or that he hearkens exclusively to the advice of his wife, or if he follows a woman's advice, it means that he will err and lose his leadership. If one sees Eve with her beautiful countenance in a dream, then she represents his mother, for Eve is the mother of humankind. Should he then be under the pangs of adversities, it means that he will be saved.

Evening: (Dark; Nightfall) In a dream, the evening signifies trickery, lies, corruption and arrogance. The evening in a dream also means celebrating God's praises and remembering Him.

Evenness: *(See Stabilizer)*

Event: *(See Milestone)*

Evergreen oak tree: *(See Oak tree)*

Evergreen tree: *(See Camphor)*

Evergreen: (Cypress; Pine) In a dream, an evergreen tree represents a beautiful woman or a man whose words do not conform to his actions, or it could mean a journey, children, longevity or a generous son. *(Also see Tree)*

Eviction: *(See Expulsion)*

Evil end: *(See Wickedness)*

Evil sound: (Braying of a donkey)

Evil spirits: (Donkey; Braying of a donkey)

Ewe: (Female sheep) In a dream, a ewe represents a woman, a wife or prosperity. Running after a ewe and finding oneself unable to keep-up or to catch it in a dream means chasing a woman and failing to seduce her. Milking a ewe in a dream means good profits for that year. Eating the meat of a ewe in a dream means inheriting a rich woman. If a ewe leaves one's house in a dream, it means divorce or the death of one's wife. If a ewe turns into a ram in a dream, it means infertility. A pregnant ewe in a dream means expecting to receive some money. Fighting with a ewe in a dream means an argument with a woman. Seeing a ewe in a dream also means distress, adversities, loss of one's husband or job. *(Also see Ram; Sheep)*

Exacting: *(See Driving force)*

Exalting God's Oneness: Exalting God's oneness and sovereignty in a dream means receiving financial compensation for pain and suffering. To utter the formula: *'Lā ilāha il Allāh'* (there is no god other than Allāh) in a dream means that one will only die having faith in his Lord. *(Also see Exclamation of God's Sovereignty)*

Examine: (Touch) In a dream, examining means spying, eavesdropping or paying attention to a conversation one should not listen to.

Exasperation: (Infuriation; Irritation; Jealousy) Exasperation without a reason in a dream means a sudden death. Exasperation in a dream also could signify involvement in a scandal or suffering from an illness that will help changing one's attitude about life. If one sees himself infuriated or irritated by someone in a dream, it means that he will suffer the consequences of his qualities or lose his money. Exasperation, infuriation or irritation in a dream all mean poverty and loss of money. *(Also see Infuriating)*

Excavate: *(See Digging up the past; Grave)*

Exchange: *(See Money exchanger)*

Exchanging letters: *(See War correspondent)*

Excitement: *(See Frothing at the mouth; Happiness)*

Exclamation of God's Sovereignty: In a dream, exclamation of God's sovereignty, i.e., uttering the formula *'La Hawla Wa Lā Quwwata Illā Billāh'* (There is no will or power except that of God's Almighty) means constant repentance in wakefulness and hope for salvation. It also means conquering one's enemies. *(Also see Exalting God's oneness)*

Excrements: *(See Dung; Excretion; Manure)*

Excrete: *(See Feces)*

Excretion: (Ritual impurity) If one's bowels discharge excess excrements in a dream, it means hindrance of one's travel plans. If one discharges solid feces in a dream, it means that he does not spend his money on sickness. If it is an abnormal discharge of liquid matters from one's bowels in the dream, it means that he will squander most of his money. If one uses a lavatory near a known ablution area in the dream, it means that his spendings relate to his passion, desires and wantonness. If the location is unknown in the dream, it means that he unknowingly, but willingly spends his wealth in unlawful avenues, whereby he will reap no reward or benefit from it. Discharging feces in the open and covering it with dirt in a dream means burying money in a hole and covering it with dirt. *(Also see Impurity; Feces; Urinating)*

Executioner: (Torturer) An executioner in a dream represents an insolent and an insulting person, or he could denote a sickness, or the law.

Exegesis: *(See Daniel; Piercing a hole)*

Exhaustion from speaking: (Weariness; Tiredness; Fatigue) If one finds himself incapable of carrying a conversation out of exhaustion from speaking, or if he refrains from talking either about good or bad, and if this happens inside a courthouse in a dream, it means that he will give up his alibi and loses his case to his adversary, or it could mean that he will become poor and dependent on people's generosity or that he will become childless.

Exhibition: (Display; Hearing; Honor guards; Inspection of troops; Military review; Portrayal; Presentation; Review officer; Show) If one sees himself standing before a high-ranking officer during a ceremony of reviewing the guards of honor or in a military barrack in a dream, and if the officer is displeased with him in the dream, it means that he will commit a major sin. If one thinks that the officer is pleased with him in the dream, then it implies God's blessings. The high-ranking officer or the review officer in such a dream also represents a compassionate person who cares, and who frequently asks about his friends, helps them solve their problems, and assists them in every possible way. *(Also see Hearing board; Inquisitional court)*

Exhilaration: *(See Knitting)*

Exhume: (Dig up a grave; Unearth) Exhuming the body of a deceased person and finding him alive in his grave in a dream means pursuing his tradition, knowledge, wisdom, trade or practices. It also means acquiring lawful money. If one finds him dead in his grave, then there is no benefit in his striving. A grave robber or a body snatcher in a dream represents a deliberate and a premeditated scheme to unravel a mystery, or forming an expedition to search for a hidden treasure. Digging the grave of a renowned scholar in a dream means studying his school of thought and the restoration of his studies, life, traditions and prominence. *(Also see Grave digger; Grave)*

Exile: *(See Expulsion)*

Expel: *(See Expulsion)*

Expiation: *(See Atonement)*

Explorer: (Traveller; Migrator; Nomad) In a dream, an explorer represents an outgoing woman from a wealthy family. Seeing an explorer in a dream also represents a morganatic marriage or a marriage for pleasure which is governed by duration. An explorer in a dream also represents orphans, or children of sin.

Explosion: *(See Agitation)*

Exposure: Exposing one's hidden knowledge in a dream means exposure to inner knowledge and working a noble trade. If the person in question is already a man of knowledge, then new spiritual revelations or those of material substance will be revealed to him and enrich his life.

Expulsion: (Banishment; Chasing away; Dismissal; Driving away; Eviction; Exile; Expel) Expulsion in a dream means imprisonment. It also means establishing the superiority of the one who gives the order and the proof of the subject's guilt. If one is exiled from his homeland in a dream, it means that he may enter a jail. If one is expelled from paradise in a dream, it means that he may experience poverty. If one evicts a man of knowledge or screams at him, or bewilders him in a dream, it means that he will face an extraordinary misfortune and confront a threatening and a cruel enemy. If a religious and a pious looking person is evicted or driven away from a place in a dream, it means that he is failing to fulfill his religious vow, or it could mean that he is avoiding to remain in the company of true pious people, ascetics, people of knowledge and noble ones. Expulsion in a dream also could denote misbehavior or ill conduct on the part of the evictor.

Extinguishing a fire: Extinguishing a fire in a dream means putting off or quelling a riot, deterring a war or abolishing innovation. If one sees himself in a dream smothering an already dead fire, it means that he is trying to rekindle an old war or to provoke evil between people.

Extirpate: *(See Assault)*

Extracting oils from seeds: (Grinding; Pressing) Grinding or pressing nuts or seeds to extract their oils or butter in a dream means money and prosperity. Pressing ripe olives in a dream represents one's homeland. Pressing olives for their oil in a dream means relief from burdens or overcoming adversities, or it could represent true scholars, satisfying one's carnal desires, engaging in wrongdoing, receiving guidance, seeing the light, walking away from darkness into light, or it could represent one's earnings or benefits. Pressing sesame seeds or walnuts in a dream means prosperity and financial growth. Sesame oil in a dream represents a pious person who admonishes people and entices them to break their attachments to the world or to its temporary pleasures. Pressing sesame seeds in a dream also represents a successful businessman. Extracting hazelnut compound in a dream means money which is earned with hardship or it could mean money that keeps growing. *(Also see Juice; Oil press; Wine press)*

Extravagance: *(See Luxuries shop)*

Eye doctor: *(See Ophthalmologist)*

Eye inflammation: (Disease; Ophthalmia) In a dream, eye inflammation means tightening of one's earnings, or it could mean heedlessness. Seeing one's eyes inflamed in a dream means that one's father or mother may fall sick. Inflammation of the eyes in a dream also denotes near blindness or suffering from a cataract. Any vision loss in a dream represents failing to properly perform one's religion, loss in business or an indication of the state of one's children.

Eye makeup: *(See Kohl)*

Eyebrows: Enhancing and beautifying the eyes. As for a man, his eyebrows represent his good nature and character, being handsome, religious, faithful, trustworthy, his status and esteem. In a dream, eyebrows also mean love and unity. If a woman sees her eyebrows thick or if they are joined together in the dream, it means that she is a person of good character. Eyebrows in a dream also represent one's parents, brothers, partners, associates or assistants. If the eyebrows grow extensively to nearly covering the eyes in the dream, it means changes in any of the above. Eyebrows in a dream also mean longevity. In a dream, eyebrows also indicate the state of one's spiritual standing. When beautiful, one's faith is beautiful, but when wild in a dream, it means that one's faith is deteriorating. Perhaps they could also represent one's guardian, governor or they could represent a bow that launches the arrows of love at one's beloved. *(Also see Body¹)*

Eyedropper: (Dropper) In a dream, a dropper signifies paying one's debts in installments.

Eyelash: If one sees himself pulling someone's eyelashes in a dream, it means that he wants him to follow the avenues of innovation. *(Also see Body¹)*

Eyelid: If one's eyelids are healthy in his dream and particularly for a women, it indicates positive developments in her life. If one's eyelids have little skin, or if they are bleared, or if they develop sores in the dream, they represent difficulties, agony, anger, sickness or distress. Eyelids in a dream also represent one's defenses and protection. They also represent one's teacher, brothers, sisters, family, wife, children, coffer, veil, guards, confidant or trustees. Eyelids in a dream also mean something to be overlooked. Having bleared eyelids in a dream means being in love. If one's eyes are interpreted to represent his wealth, then they mean protection, or paying alms tax. If the outer edge of the eyelid turns white in a dream, it means an illness affecting one's head, eyes or ears. *(Also see Body¹)*

Eyes: Eyes in a dream represent one's religion or wealth. If one sees grass growing all over him but does not cover his ears or eyes in a dream, it means prosperity. One's eyes in a dream also represent his faith and the road to victory in this life and in the next. One's eyes in a dream also could represent his guidance or his heedlessness. Having many eyes throughout one's body in a dream represents one's piety, vigilance and excellence of character. If one sees the eyes of his heart in a dream, it means that he sees with the light of clarity. If one sees a man looking at him with a side glance in a dream, it means that he will suffer from an adversity, mistrust, disapproval, suspicion and disdain at the hand of such a man. If such a man opens his eyes and looks at him straight forward in the dream, it means that he will help him in his business or support his interests. If one's eyes turn into iron in a dream, it means distress, a scandal or serious suffering from one's community. If one sees himself looking at women in his dream, it means that he commits adultery with his eyes by looking and desiring what is unlawful. If one looks at someone's eyes in a dream and likes them, it means that he will suffer from an adversity, religious corruption or jealousy. If one sees himself having an extra eye inside his body in a dream, it means that he is an atheist. If one sees himself having an extra eye over his shoulder in a dream, it means that he will be named to receive money in absentia. If one sees his eyes transfixed in a dream, it means that he looks suspiciously at a relative or someone else's wife. Black eyes in a dream represent a religious person. A bluish-black eyes in a dream denote opposing one's religion. Blue eyes in a dream mean religious innovations. Green eyes in a dream mean a religion which is different from all religions. Sharp sight in a dream means blessings, while weak sight means joblessness and living from the generosity of others. If a father sees weakness in his sight in a dream, it means that a sickness will inflict his children. If one loses his eyes in a dream, it means the death of his children. If a poor person or a prisoner sees that in a dream, it means that he will never become free again, or see any light for the rest of his life. If an oppressed person sees weakness in his eyes in a dream, it means that someone will help him overcome his adversities. If a traveller sees that dream, it means that he will never return to his homeland. If one sees that his eyes belong to an unknown person in a dream, it means that he will become blind. If he recognizes that person in the dream, it means that he will be married to his daughter. If one's eyes fall into his lap in a dream, it means the death of his brother or son. The eyes of a human being in a dream also represent his beloved, his son or his faith. Any defect in them in the dream may reflect in such people. Having one hundred eyes in a dream means money. The eyes of a ruler represent his spies. Eyes in a dream also represent a controller, a man or a spring. Treating one's eyes with medicinal ointment in a dream means correcting one's religious life or begetting a son who will become the jewel light of his father's eyes or if one's brother is exiled or deported from his homeland, it means that he will solicit him and entrust him with duties toward his family. If one sees his sight better than what people think in the dream, it means that his inner character is better than what people think, or if he sees his sight weakened though people do not know about it in the dream, it means that he keeps his faith to himself. If one's eyes become white in a dream, they represent sorrow, or loss of a beloved. If one sees his eyes white, and if the white veil is lifted in the dream, it means that he will be reunited with his beloved and his distress will be dispelled. The right eye in a dream represents one's son and the left eye represents one's daughter. If a father sees one of his eyes being transposed to mix with the other eye in a dream, and if he has a son and a daughter, he should separate their bedrooms. Eating someone's eye in a dream means steeling his money. Seeing one's eyes without eyelashes in a dream means defying God's laws. If one unplugs his eyelashes in a dream, it means that he will expose himself to his enemy. Seeing beautiful eyes in a dream could denote, sorcery, black magic, life or death. Eyes in a dream also represent one's family, relatives, children or workers. Eyes in a dream also signify mourning someone or they could denote a sickness. Smearing one's eyes in a dream means calamities, sufferings and punishment for one's sins. To guard one's eyes from looking at what is unlawful in a dream means heeding God's commands. *(Also see Body¹)*

Eyetooth: *(See Body¹; Tooth)*

Eyewitness: *(See Witness)*

Ezekiel: (God strengthened) Seeing God's prophet Ezekiel, upon whom be peace, in a dream means that one will receive the station of guardianship and trust.

Ezra: (God's prophet 'Uzair, upon whom be peace.) One who sees him (uwbp) in a dream will win leadership by virtue of knowledge, writings and wisdom.

F

Fabulous being: *(See Sasquatch)*

Facade: *(See Cheeks)*

Face mask: *(See Helmet)*

Face: One's face in a dream represents his state. If it appears cheerful and handsome looking in the dream, it represents glad tidings, happiness and a good life, though if it looks opaque in the dream, it means the opposite. In general, a yellow face in a dream means humiliation, loneliness, hypocrisy or illness. If a believer sees his face yellow in a dream, it denotes his devotion and fear of wrongdoing. Yellowness of the face in a dream also could mean being in love. If an African person sees his face white in a dream, it means hypocrisy, impudence and shamelessness. If a Caucasian sees his face black in a dream, it means that his heart and intentions are better than what a stranger may think of him. If one's face appears white and his body black in a dream, it means that he shows decency and disguises inappropriateness. If a whiskerless person sees hair growing over the sides of his upper lip in a dream, it means that he carries burdening debts, or that he has lost dignity. If one's face looks different or missing some of its clarity or beauty in a dream, it denotes someone who jokes excessively, for immoderate jesting, hilarity or mirth decreases people's respect. If there is no skin to cover one's cheeks in a dream, it means that he lives from asking others for his needs. Dust covering one's face in a dream means deficiency in one's religious devotion. If one's face or eyes turn bluish in a dream, it means that he is a criminal in God's sight. An opaque face in a dream represents a liar or an innovator. If the color of one's face is blush or reddish with white spots in the dream, it means joy, happiness and good living. If a righteous person sees his face blush in a dream, it means that he feels ashamed of something he did. If one's face is soaking with sweat in a dream, it represents his modesty and reserve. If one is frowning, and if the color of his face turns red in the dream, it means that he may suffer from distress or losses. Frowning in someone's face in a dream also means suffering at his hand. If a woman sees her face blackened with soot in a dream, it means the death of her husband. If she sees herself putting makeup and anointing herself with perfume in a dream, it means good news for her and for her husband. A smiling and a cheerful face in a dream connotes happiness and righteousness whether the person is alive or dead. The beauty of a woman's face or that of a child in a dream means blessings. Having two faces in a dream mean a grievous and an woeful end, for God Almighty does not look at someone who has two faces. If a scholar sees himself having several faces in a dream, it means that he is utilizing his knowledge in various applications, or giving a subject several possible interpretations. A frowning face, a crying face, a scarred face, or the darkness of one's face in a dream also mean loss of job, fear, or they could represent a liar. If the skin of one's face is cracking in a dream, it denotes lack of modesty or absence of shame. A disgusting look on one's face in a dream means loathsomeness, and loathsomeness in a dream represents a disgusting face. *(Also see Body¹; Jesting)*

Faint: (Blackout; Swoon) To blackout or to faint in a dream means suffering from great sorrow.

Fairness: *(See Justice)*

Fake jewelry: *(See Alum)*

Falcon: A falcon in a dream represents a thief, might, victory over one's enemy, satisfying one's purpose, love to have many children, marriage, slaves, mistresses, precious stones, health, relief, or it could mean love to travel. A falcon in a dream also means cessation of life, capture, hunting, shackles, imprisonment, ties, etcetera. If it appears well trained, obedient and responsive in the dream, it means walking in the company of an important person who is surrounded with an impressive entourage. If one sees a falcon flying and gathering a flock of falcons in a dream, it means building an army. A falcon in a dream also represents an intelligent man who claims importance and dignity, though he is unjust. If one receives or holds a falcon in a dream, it means that he will bear a son who will become a very important person of his time. If one happens to be a politician, it means that he will gain greater advancements in his life. If the falcon flies away in the dream, it means that one will lose his seat but retain his fame. If one catches few feathers of a falcon in a dream, it means that some power will remain in his hand and serve his interests. Slaughtering a falcon in a dream means the death of a king or a ruler. Eating falcon's meat in a dream means a financial endowment given by a ruler. If one kills a falcon inside his house in a dream, it means that he will capture a thief. If a falcon flies away from under one's chair in a dream, it means that he will walk in the company of a person whose earnings are unlawful. *(Also see Indian falcon; Sakr)*

Fall: Falling in a dream means despair or disappointment, or it could mean a mistake that cannot be covered. Falling in a dream also means changing conditions from good to bad, or a marriage failure and changing of spouse. It also means changing profession, country or religion. Falling in a dram also projects the reverse effects and produces positive results if what one falls over is pasture, or if he falls upon a good community or to join a banquet or the like effects, then it may have a positive meaning. On the other hand, falling into the hand of a bad company, or into a beast's den, etcetera, means evil consequences, or it could mean stinginess. If one sees himself falling down from the roof of his house, and if he breaks an arm or a leg in the dream, then it reflects a psychological distress, adverse financial conditions, breaking of a friendship or it may mean suffering from persecution by the local authorities.

Falling in deep waters: *(See Deep waters)*

False testimony: Giving a false testimony in a dream denotes a panderer or a pimp. *(Also see Panderer; Pimp)*

Faltering: (Faith; Penny)

Fame: (Acknowledgment; Announcement; Distinction; Luminary; Recognition; Renowned; Title) Fame in a dream represents a wedding that will be publicly announced, or it could mean rising in rank. If one earns a title of recognition, or if he becomes renowned, or if he is awarded a great prize for his work in a dream, it means that he will learn that his wife has given birth to a beautiful son. Such a son will follow his father's footsteps, learn his trade or work at spreading his knowledge or tradition, or he may govern and lead his people after him.

Family support: (Alimony; Maintenance) To provide support for one's family and relatives in a dream mean prosperity, protection for one's children and concern for one's posterity. Whatever expenses one spends to support his family in a dream will be money he will receive in wakefulness. If one finds himself unwillingly giving family support or alimony to his wife in a dream, it means hypocrisy, or that he is nearing his death.

151

Family: *(See Dependents)*

Famine: (Dearth; Scarcity) If one sees the rulers of his country suffering from a famine in a dream, it represents their greed, terrorization of their subjects and the sufferings of the people. If one sees scholars suffering from a famine in a dream, it signifies their thirst or lust for knowledge. *(Also see Little)*

Fan: (Air blower; Comfort; Cooler; Current; Oscillator; Wind) A fan in a dream means comfort, relief from adversities and prosperity after poverty. In a dream, a fan also represents one's wife, child, money, travels, or a person about whom people generally feel good. In a dream, a fan also represents a mistress, pride, or attachment to something or to someone one thinks that he cannot live without.

Faqīh: *(See Legist)*

Far dh: *(arb. See Five times prayers)*

Farewell: The suggested element contained in bidding farewell in a dream entails ultimate comfort. Wishing someone the best at parting means loss of status or job, divorce, death of a sick person, breaking of a partnership, loss in business, migrating from one country to another, or in general it could mean the reversal of one's conditions. On the other hand, it is said that bidding farewell in a dream also means marriage reconciliation, or the changing of one's conditions for the better.

Farm pond: *(See Water level)*

Farm: (Estate; Farmland; Property) A farm in a dream represents a woman. Its spikes represent her children or property. If a farm in the dream is interpreted to mean a marketplace, then its spikes represent profits, benefits, tools, or financial losses. A farm in a dream also represents a battlefield and its spikes are the soldiers, or it could represent the world and its spikes then represent people, their young and old. A farm in a dream also could represent every deed which is intended for the benefit of the hereafter, meaning that this world is the farmland of the hereafter. *(Also see Crop; Estate)*

Farmer: A farmer in a dream represents a man of good deeds. His planting, plowing, harvesting or any of the phases of his work represents his deeds. When successful in the dream, it means that his business will succeed in real life. When it indicates business in the dream, it means prosperity and when it suggests one's deeds, it means repentance. To see a farmer planting seeds, then when they sprout he recovers them with earth in a dream means that he is ungrateful or irreligious.

Farmland: *(See Estate; Farm)*

Fart: (Breaking wind; Passing gas; Foolishness; Wind) Passing gas in a dream means hearing or speaking vile words, or suffering from adversities, or it could mean dispersing a group of people, telling a shocking news, stupidity, belittling people, lies, using insulting words, or it could represent the sound that could emanate from beating someone. If one breaks wind with a loud sound in a dream, it means that he will address someone with harsh words. If one sees himself sitting with people and unwillingly passes gas or breaks wind in a dream, it means that his difficulties, sorrows or stress will be dispelled, though with horridness and repulsiveness. If one breaks wind intentionally in such a gathering in a dream, then it means committing an evil act and suffering from its consequences. If one passes gas without noise in his dream, it means that he will receive a sarcastic commendation that matches the smell of his fart. If one breaks wind in a dream while sitting with a group of people who are experiencing difficulties, it means that their difficulties will be dispelled, and their suffering will ease. If they are merchants, it means that their merchandise will move faster. If one forces himself to break wind in a dream, it means that he will carry a burden greater than he can bear. If one breaks wind along with passing gas in his dream, it means that he will attain success in his life, and he will receive honor and profits from an important business trip. However, it is possible that his interests will become diverse, or that he could lose his focus, then he will return home free from such burdens. To fart from the mouth in a dream means faltering or a slip of a tongue, an accident, suffering from gum irritation, a stroke that will affect one's speech, or it could mean developing ill habits that will cause him to feel ashamed of himself in public.

Fastening: *(Also see Belt)*

Fasting: (Armor; Protection) Fasting in a dream represents vows and offerings. Interrupting the fast in a dream means an illness, a journey or backbiting someone. If one interrupts his obligatory fast through forgetfulness in a dream, it means that he will receive a pleasing gift or money. Fasting in a dream also means honor, rising in station, or it could mean repentance from sin, repayment of a debt, penitence for a sinner or begetting a son. Observing the obligatory fast of the month of Ramadān in a dream means understanding something about which one has doubt or recognizing the truth without falsification or distortion. If one finds that he is the only person observing the obligatory fast in the dream, and if he is unlettered, it means that he will memorize the Holy Qur'ān, attain a spiritual maturity and receive glad tidings. This dream also indicates that he is a pious and a religious person. If one is sick, it means that he will recover from his illness. If he is lost in heedlessness, it means that God Almighty will grant him guidance. If he is indebted, it means that he will be able to repay his debts. If in his dream, one intentionally breaks his fast during the prescribed fast of the holy month of Ramadān, it means that he could kill someone. Similarly, if one sees himself killing someone in a dream, it means that he has intentionally broke his obligatory fast. Observing the two months of atonement for the sin of breaking the fast during the holy month of Ramadān or for any such fast for the expiation of sins in a dream means that one may fall sick and repent to God Almighty from his sins. Intentionally breaking the obligatory fast of Ramadān in a dream also means neglecting one of the pillars of Islām. If one acknowledges that, then vows to offer the required duties in a dream, it means that he could receive an unexpected gift which will arrive shortly. If one recognizes in his dream the importance of the month of Ramadān, it means that he is on the right path. If he is not fasting, it means that he may go on a journey. Voluntary fasting in a dream means protection against one's enemies. If a sick person sees himself fasting in a dream, it could mean his death, silence, celebrations or recovering from an illness. It could also represent one's faith in God Almighty and sincerity in his words and actions. If one sees masses of people fasting in a dream, it could mean a famine. If one eats during the hours of observing the fast in a dream, it means that he will commit a sin, or it could mean indebtedness or falling sick. Fasting the month of Ramadān in a dream also means safety, protection from evil or repentance from sins. Fasting the extra six days following the festival day which concludes the holy month of Ramadān in a dream means patching one's prayers or paying charity or regretting one's faults. Fasting Monday and Thursday of every week in a dream means strengthening family ties. Fasting the three white days of every month (*i.e., the 13th, 14th, and the 15th days of the lunar month*) in a dream means repayment of one's debts in installments or teaching someone how to properly read the Qur'ān or spreading knowledge. Fasting during the tenth day of the lunar month of Muharram in a dream represents asceticism, piety, renouncing the world or attending the pilgrimage to Mecca. Fasting the day when the pilgrims are standing at mount 'Arafāt in a dream means acceptance of one's charities. Fasting the last ten days of the month of Zul-Hijjah in a dream means attaining a good conclusion to one's life in this world to become a pious person, or it could also mean fulfilling a promise. Fasting the day of 'Ashūrā in a dream means doing good deeds, but it could also mean witnessing adversities and escaping from its dangers, or it could mean living to witness the next religious festival, or if one's wife is pregnant, it could mean that she will beget a blessed son who will grow to be a righteous man. Fasting during the lunar month of Rajab in a dream means working for people in authority, or it could mean that one may be commissioned to work overseas, or it could mean going on a short trip. Fasting an extra day in doubt about one's proper religious performance in a dream means committing a sin or lack of vigilance and certitude about one's devotion. Fasting days of the month of Ramadān one has missed for a permissible reason in a dream means release of a prisoner or repentance of a sinner. Fasting a votive fast or a vowed fast for the purpose of an attainment in a dream means attaining one's goal, joy and happiness. Observing a votive perpetual or an ongoing fast in a dream means undertaking a heavy responsibility or following innovation, or it could mean becoming a loner or abstaining from talking to others, or that one would only talk if the subject is beneficial to others, for fasting in a dream also means silence. Observing a votive perpetual fast in a dream also represents a pious and a religious person. If the person is a sinner, such votive fast in a dream also may mean that he will get nothing out of what he wants. Paying the due charity (_Sadaqat-ul Fiṭr_) after completing one's fast in a dream means recovering from an illness. If one observes a fast for show in his dream, it means that he will receive what he desires. _(Also see Ashūrā; Feast of Breaking the Fast)_

Fat person: (Heavy weight) If one sees himself unusually fat in a dream, it means increase in his wealth and richness. If he is wearing a yellow gown in the dream, then his dream represents a light sickness that will not last. Being fat in a dream represents respect, honor, strong religious convictions, being a special person, or it could mean fame. _(Also see Skin)_

Fat: (Grease; Lubrication; Money; Prosperity; Tallow) If one sees himself having a fat tail like that of a sheep in a dream, it means that his livelihood will depend on the revenues of his offspring. If one eats the fat of a permissible animal (sheep, cattle, etcetera) in a dream, it means profits or owning a sizeable business. If one eats the fat of a non-permissible animal (beats, vultures, etcetera) in a dream, it means earning unlawful money, committing adultery, rejecting one's religion or fostering forbidden acts. Using fat as medicine in a dream means recovering from an illness. Fat in a dream also means joy, happiness or festivities. In general, fat in a dream also could be interpreted to mean clean money, or net profits from which nothing is wasted.

Fate: _(See Calamity)_

Father in-law: Having a father in-law in a dream and particularly for someone who does not have in-laws means strength, peace and tranquility.

Father: (Eyebrow) Seeing one's father in a dream means attaining one's goal. One's dreams are most beneficial when he sees his parents, grand parents or a relative. Seeing one's father in a dream when in wakefulness one needs help means that help will come his way from sources he does not anticipate. If in real life he is awaiting someone's return from a journey, it means that such a person will soon arrive. If one is sick, it means that he will recover from his illness. If he sees that his father is given a dwelling with high fences, it means that he will continue his father's work and manage what he has left for him in this world. _(Also see Governor)_

Fault finding: Finding fault with praiseworthy people in a dream means committing abominable actions or to desist or turn away from one's religion.

Favor: _(Also see Rocks)_

Fear of wrongdoing: *(See Prostration)*

Fear: (Dismay; Fright; Terror) In a dream, fear means the opposite. In fact, fear in a dream represents peacefulness and repentance in wakefulness. If one sees himself scared and running away from fear in a dream, it means that he will win the upper hand. If one sees himself in a dream waiting to battle with fear, it means that he will join a war. If one sees himself afraid, and if a voice says to him: "Do not be afraid, you will not die, nor will you be able to bear this life," it means that he may become blind. If one sees himself as a God-fearing person in a dream, it means that his worldly fears will dissipate and he will develop true devotion and constant remembrance of his Lord. The person or object causing fear in the dream represents harm and aversion. To feel scared in a dream means happiness in wakefulness. Fear in a dream also could mean evil, corruption or suffering from the consequences of wrongdoing one has committed. If one dies of fear in his dream, it means that he does not pay people their rights and particularly if he is afraid of a human being or from his own evildoing. *(Also see Running away; Take a flight)*

Feast of breaking the fast: *(arb.* Eid-ul Fiṭr; Lesser Bairam; Ramadán; 1st of Shawwāl) Witnessing the feast of breaking the fast of Ramadán in a dream means overcoming depression, dispelling stress, regaining joy, ease in one's life, acceptance of one's prayers, repentance from sin, recovering one's losses, relief, finding a lost object, prosperity, comfort, spending money and exchanging gifts. *(Also see Feast of Immolation)*

Feast of Immolation: (Hajj; Eid-ul Adḥā; Feast of sacrifice; 10th of Zul-Hijjah; Greater Bairam; Manumission; Sacrifice; Pilgrimage; Responding) Witnessing the Feast of Immolation *(arb. Eid-ul Adḥā)* in a dream means reminiscing the past, renewal of past celebrations, reviving a state of joy, recapturing moments of one's pleasant past, escape from destruction, salvation, redemption, release from prison or freedom from debts. *(Also see Feast of Breaking the Fast; Ram; Sacrifice)*

Feat: *(See Boast; Bragging; Daring; Exploit)*

Feather: (Clothing; Help; Little; Plumage; Wings) Feathers in a dream may denote evil or they could mean majesty, beauty or strength. Feathers in a dream also represent the house of a pious person.

February: *(See Earthquake; Thunder)*

Feces: (Defecate; Excrete; Human excrements) Feces in a dream represent money. Excreting solid intestinal waste in a dream means that one will spend large amounts of money in caring for his health. Having diarrhea and defecating in public in a dream means that one should be careful about exposing himself or becoming subject to a scandal or saying dirty words. Excreting involuntarily, then cleaning after oneself and carrying one's pickings in a dream means earnings and money. Feces in a dream also mean honey. Defecating in one's bed in a dream means divorcing one's wife. Walking on feces in a dream means distress or depression. Walking away from the bathroom after cleansing one's bowels in a dream means walking away from adversities. Falling into the sewers or a toilet bowl in a dream means entering a prison. Defecating in one's pants in a dream means falling into sin, humiliation, speaking bad words or using despicable expressions. Feces in a dream also represent money, hidden secrets, travels, a fight, recovering from an illness, bad thoughts, whispering of the mind, temptation or trusts. The smell of feces in a dream represents a fine, or overdoing one's duty, or a miscarriage for a pregnant woman. To sally one's clothing with someone's feces in a dream means borrowing money from him or carrying his favor for a longtime to come. Feces in a dream also denote earnings from an unjust and a loathsome person. Excreting in a dream also means dispelling one's worries or getting rid of one's burdens. If one excretes in the ablution room in his dream, it means that his spendings or deeds are recognized to be a fulfillment of his desires, ostentatiousness and love for fame. If one excretes in an unknown place in a dream, it means that his deeds will not be acknowledged, nor will he receive any reward for them. Going to the bathroom in a dream means dispelling one's worries, paying one's debts or paying an unavoidable alimony for his children. Putting a shirt in the wilderness and defecating inside it rather than in the field in a dream means committing a sin and carrying its consequences for sometime to come. Excreting in the wilderness, then covering one's feces with dirt in a dream means hiding money. To defecate in a marketplace in public in a dream means incurring God's displeasure and the curse of His angels. Throwing feces at someone in a dream means starting a fight or opposing him in opinion, being unjust to him, or causing him great losses. The consequences also may backfire at the assailant. If one sees himself standing inside the sewers and searching through the filth with a stick in his dream, it means that he might become a judge and be accused of bribery or misuse of people's money. Seeing human excrements in a dream means abstraction of movement, stalling of businesses, or facing complex and harmful adversities. To soil oneself with people's feces in a dream means sickness or fear, or it could mean good benefits for a person whose acts are filthy and abominable. *(Also see Impurity)*

Feebleness: Feebleness in a dream means strength. However, if one sees himself debilitated or emaciated in the dream, then it means weakness in his faith, failure to properly observe his religious obligations, or it could mean sterility, impotence, or sorrow and distress.

Feeding trough: *(See Manger)*

Feet: *(See Foot)*

Feigned: *(See Fraudulent bankruptcy)*

Felicitations: (Compliments; Congratulations) Felicitations in a dream signify condolences. They also mean relief from difficulties or building financial security against poverty.

Fellowship house: *(See Masjid; Spiritual gathering)*

Fellowship: *(See Friendship; Masjid; Spiritual gathering)*

Felony: To commit a felony or to incriminate an innocent person in a dream means that one will fall into peril. It also can be interpreted as achieving one's goals. If one injures a forbidden animal to kill in a dream, it means that he will be fined with a like value or worth.

Felt: *(See Feltmaker)*

Feltmaker: (Felt) In a dream, a feltmaker represents patience, endurance, or a most needed tradesman. Seeing a feltmaker in a dream represents one's livelihood, earnings and profits.

Female climacteric: *(See Old woman)*

Fencer: (Controversy; Fence; Politicking) Seeing a fence builder in a dream means moving forward, fulfilling one's goals, or he could represent a salesman of specialty outfits.

Fenugreek: (Medicinal solution prepared for women after giving birth; Plant) In a dream, fenugreek represents hard earned money.

Ferro concrete: In a dream, it means an armored, or a reinforced concrete storage space.

Ferry: *(See Boat; Ship)*

Ferryboat: *(See Boat; Ship)*

Festival of sacrifice: *(See Feast of Immolation)*

Festival: *(See 'Ashūrā; Feast of Breaking the fast; Feast of Immolation)*

Fetter: (Bond; Shackle) To see one's feet put in irons or fettered in a dream represents evil people, or it could mean travels or leaving one's homeland. *(Also see Bond¹)*

Fettered: *(See Handcuff)*

Fettering: *(See Patience)*

Fetus: (Cream)

Fever: In a dream, a fever means paying one's debts, for fever in wakefulness is an atonement for sins. Fever in a dream also means a threat and a menace. If one sees someone he knows suffering from fever in a dream, it means that he will get involved in a business that will require him to lose his religious commitment. Fever in a dream also means wearing the garment of a revered person. Fever is the messenger of the angel of death and his warner. It reminds the person to repent before death comes and to corrects his conduct with his Lord before meeting Him. A feverish shiver in a dream means negligence and disdain regarding one's religious duties. If one sees that he died and was washed and shrouded in preparation for burial in a dream, it means that he is persistent in indulging in sins and that he is careless about the consequences. Such a warning is only seen in a dream by an insolent sinner, if he is lucky. Fever in a dream also may connote entering a bathhouse or a sauna and suffering therein from heat, exhaustion and thirst. *(Also see Bathhouse)*

Feverish chill: In a dream, a feverish chill represents a woman with leadership quality who serves people and from whose contributions, or through her, one will earn his money. What may develop because of a feverish chill in the dream will be her share in wakefulness. *(Also see Fever)*

Fictitious creature: *(See Sasquatch)*

Fig tree: *(See Tree)*

Fig: A fig tree represents a good harvest or increase in children for one who eats from it in a dream, or it could represent a wealthy person who benefits his community. Even his enemies will come to benefit from him, because many types of snakes live on a fig tree. No other fruit equals figs in benefits. Figs represent earnings without difficulties and it shows. Fig leaves in a dream represent distress, grief, depression. Eating a fig leaf in a dream means sorrow and afflictions. Seeing black figs in season in a dream means comfort, while seeing white figs in a dream has a better connotation. Eating a fig out of season in a dream means jealousy. On the other hand, figs in a dream also could mean sorrow, representing the latter days of Adam and Eve when they first dwelled in paradise. *(Also see Fig tree)*

Fight: In a dream, a fight means deception, betrayal, misleading or trickery. A fight in a dream also means inflation and rising prices, plague, food lines, adversities or stress. If a soldier sees himself engaged in a battle in a dream, it means that he will receive benefits and a rewarding success. Fighting unjust people in a dream means triumph over injustice, supporting the needs of one's father or mother first, or being protective of one's wife or husband. Fighting against the truth in a dream means aligning oneself with heedless people or going astray. *(Also see Disbelief; Killing; War; Wrestling)*

Figure: (Build; Contour; Frame; Profile) Having a tall figure in a dream signifies pride, arrogance, stinginess, ostentatiousness or pretending to be tall. *(See Tallness)*. If one sees his figure shorter than his normal size in a dream, then it denotes losing respect or nearing the end of one's life. Seeing oneself beyond the common human size in a dream also denotes the near end of one's life, or it could mean falling in rank. If someone in authority sees himself shorter in size in a dream, it means that he will lose his post, or fail to render a just verdict, or it could mean a political fight. Being smaller than usual in a dream means defeat in a war or losing a fight. If a politician sees himself tall in a dream, it means that he will win his political battle. *(Also see Body¹)*

File: (Rasp; Tongue) A file in a dream represents one's tongue. It also means satisfying an innate need or giving a keen edge to an expression. It also represents a helper, a son who provides for the need of his mother or younger brothers and sisters. A file in a dream also represents demands, obligations, or sexual intercourse.

Filly: *(See Drill)*

Filter: In a dream, a filter represents the essence of one's faith and knowledge. A filter in a dream also could mean music, taverns, dancing or insolence. A filter in a dream also represents a man who speaks only the truth and who does not allow for impurities to seep into his life. *(Also see Sieve)*

Filth: (Dirt) Dirty hair, a soiled garment, or a filthy body in a dream mean distress and worries. Dirty clothing in a dream mean sins. If the dirt comprises oil or grease in the dream, it means attachment to mundane and material objects. Washing one's clothe in a dream means repenting from sin and washing them away. Cleaning off the wax in one's ears in a dream means hearing pleasing words. *(Also see Cloth; Dirty face; Garment)*

Filthy body: (Dirt; Filth) A filthy body in a dream represents a sinful person, while a dirty face in a dream means a rare art. *(Also see Filth)*

Finding a lost object: *(See Compensation; Finding something)*

Finding something: (Abandoned; Discarded item; Lost item; Gleanings) Finding something abandoned or discarded or lost in a dream means receiving a precious gift from an employee or a servant one will treasure, or it could mean receiving a cheap item one cares to keep, receiving an inheritance, or it could mean begetting a blessed son.

Finger: (Hand) Fingers help one's worldly needs or craft and serve one's benefits in the hereafter by identifying and pointing at what is true and identifying what is wrong. In general, fingers in a dream represent one's children, wife, father, mother, money, property, wealth or craft. Positive looking fingers or increase in their number in a dream represents growth, while deformed fingers in a dream mean the opposite. One's five fingers in a dream also represent the five daily prayers. Thus, if the fingers are interpreted to mean the five daily obligatory prayers, then the fingernails represent the supererogatory *(arb. Nafl)* prayers. If the fingers are interpreted as money, then the fingernails represent the due alms tax *(arb. Zakāt)*. If they are interpreted to represent an army in the dream, then the fingernails represent their weapons. Fingers in a dream also represent the days, months or years. When fingers are interpreted to mean money, and if someone cuts off his finger in a dream, it means that he will suffer from financial losses. Long fingers in a dream are regarded as greed. *(Also see Body¹; Five fingers; Thimble)*

Finished Business: (Accomplished; Compassed) A finished business in a dream connotes life and continuity. Completing good deeds in a dream means desiring to have children. Completing one's job in a dream is a sign of prosperity for rich people and the strong ones. It also signifies owning properties and having control over a vast land and its people. *(Also see Incomplete job)*

Fire iron: *(See Poker)*

Fire worshiper: *(See Worshipping fire)*

Fire: The element of fire in a dream represents might. Fire in a dream also means love. A product that is touched by fire in the process of its manufacturing or cooking in a dream means arguments and disputes. In a dream, fire also signifies glad tidings, a warning, war, chastisement, power, imprisonment, losses, sins, or blessings. If one sees a blazing fire with sparks shooting in every direction and burning in the forest and raging with tumultuous noise and uproar in a dream, it means insubordination, civic disorder or an adversity through which many people will die. If one sees fire burning inside his own heart in a dream, it means love or depression caused by separation from one's beloved. Seeing two burning bushes trying to consume one another in a dream represents two armies fighting one another. If the two burning bushes remain intact and yield no loss in the dream, then they represent trials and adversities in the place where they are seen. Whichever of the two fires is closer to a water source in the dream means that such an army is more liable to a voluntary retreat or submission. If the water flows and extinguishes that fire in the dream, it also means that the water will be debilitated and consequently consumed. The more black smoke a fire produces in one's dream, the greater is the danger and consequent sufferings. If one kindles a fire in the night for people to see their way through in a dream, it means that he will acquire a knowledge and with it, he will help people through their life, admonish and guide them. If one sees himself kindling a fire on the road during the daylight in a dream, it means that he will embark on the road of innovation and misleading others. If one sees a fire during a daylight time in a dream, it means war and adversities. If it is seen during the night hours, then it means peace and guidance. If one sees himself worshiping the fire in a dream, it means that he loves wars, or follows Satanic allurements. Warming oneself up from a nearby fire during a cold day in a dream means becoming rich. Eating fire in a dream means swindling orphans' property or earning suspicious and unlawful money. If one is condemned to die in the fire in a dream, it means imprisonment. If one enters hell-fire then comes out of it in a dream, it means that he will ultimately enter paradise. If one sells hell and buys paradise in a dream, it means that he will sell a business involving the use of fire such as a bathhouse, a bakery or a forgery and invest his money in a farm or vice-versa. This also may represent his deeds in the world and his reward in the hereafter. Entering hell-fire to pay for one's sins in a dream means financial losses or committing abominable actions that warrant such sufferings. If one sees hell-fire with his own eyes in a dream, it means that he should be weary about his legal standing or that he should be careful regarding the ruler or governor of that town. Entering hell-fire and tasting its punishment in a dream also means suffering from adversities. Seeing a group of people standing around a fire in a dream means blessings. Discovering a burning bush in a wilderness and finding solace in taking refuge near it in a dream means dispelling one's fears and reaching safety. If one is touched by a fire, and if it does him no harm or burn him in the dream, it means that someone will fulfill a promise he made to him. If a fire burns inside a granary in a dream, it means hiking prices. Whatever product a fire burns in a dream means high demand for it and rising prices. If one sees a stove burning with no food in the pot in the dream, it means that the head of the household is engaged in some futile activities and he could suffer because of them. If one sees a governor kindling a fire, and if it keeps smothering, then if it dies off in the dream, it means that he will be dismissed from his office and that his fire will be extinguished. Seeing a burning torch with no smoke hanging in front of one's door in a dream means attending the pilgrimage season during that year, or remodeling one's house, or it could mean getting married. Burning one's fingers in a dream represents an unjust person, or it could mean changing the contents of a book or committing perjury. Seeing fire lit in the palm of one's hand in a dream means cutting ends in one's trade to save money or voluntary violation of the code of a trade. Seeing fire inside one's mouth in a dream means distress. Willingly entering hell-fire in a dream

represents one's love and attachment to the world and its pleasures. A raging fire in one's house or town in a dream means war and destruction. If it is a roaring and a blazing fire in the dream, then it means plagues and mass destruction. If it has no noise in the dream, then it means the spread of a new disease. If one sees a fire falling from the skies in a dream, it means greater calamities. If it causes no harm in the dream, then it means a verbal abuse with no lasting consequences. If one sees a fire rising into the skies in a dream, it means that the people of that locality are challenging God Almighty's decrees with arrogance and indulging themselves in abominable sins and insubordination. Kindling a fire to bring warmth to a group of people in a dream means starting a community project that will benefit several people including oneself. Kindling a fire to broil some meat in a dream means starting a conversation to backbite and slander someone. Eating from such broiled meat in the dream means earnings, distress and feeling heavy hearted. If a fire burns one's garment or causes burns to his skin in a dream, it means a calamity that will befall him or a member of one's family who is represented by that particular limb. To bring live coal into one's house in a dream means stealing money or acquiring unlawful profits. If one is struck by the heat of a blaze and feels its glare over his face in a dream, it means becoming subject to people's slander, jealousy and backbiting. To stand by the light of a fire in a dream means becoming close to someone in authority. If a fire comes out of one's house in a dream, it means a political appointment, a business, strength, or knowledge of one's trade. If one sees a radiant light brightening the skies from the East to the West in a dream, it means fame, recognition and knowledge, or a discovery one will become famous because of it. If one's wife is pregnant, and if he sees a fire coming out of his head to brighten the entire house in a dream, it means that his wife will beget a son who will grow to be a renowned man of knowledge and piety. A fire lighting one's house in a dream also means that one's wife will get pregnant. Kindling a fire on top of a mountain in a dream means seeking nearness to God Almighty by making offerings, giving charities and increasing one's devotion. Consequently all of one's needs will surely be satisfied. If one who sees this dream is on a journey, it represents his safe return to his home. Sitting inside a fire and suffering no harm in a dream means working for, or associating with the ruler of the city or country. It also means becoming the ruler's confidant or intimate friend. Fire in the desert in a dream means war. Setting people on fire in a dream means creating division and enmity between them. To stand in the fire, feeling cool and comfortable in a dream represents one's truthfulness, sincerity, faith and certitude, and it means victory over his enemies. A dying fire in a dream means suppressing a commotion, or containing a troublesome matter that could endanger one's community or life. If a fire that is lighting one's house is extinguished in a dream, it means the death of the father, the husband or a child. An extinguished fire in a dream also signifies the death of the governor, or a great scholar, or a renowned shaikh in that city. Fire in a dream also means a robbery. Fire with no smoke in a dream represents spirits or jinns, for they are created from a smokeless fire. It also represents drought, locusts or a calamity. If a fire is extinguished by rain in a dream, it means poverty or loss of one's job. If one sees a fire talking to him from inside an earthenware jar or from inside a pitcher or any container in a dream, it means that an evil spirit has possessed one's son or daughter. A destructive fire in a dream represents an unjust ruler. If people can benefit from such a fire, it means that he is a just and a righteous ruler or governor. Fire in the wintertime in a dream means fruits. Eating fire in a dream means eating from a golden or a silver plate, or drinking from a golden or a silver cup. It also means poverty and need. *(Also see Body¹; Firewood; Hell-fire)*

Fireboat: *(See Boat; Ship)*

Fireplace: (Hearth; Stove) An iron cast stove or a fireplace in a dream represents a woman who comes from a powerful and a strong family. If the stove or the fireplace is made from yellow copper or brass in the dream, then such a woman may have come from a house of a worldly and rich people. A wooden fireplace in a dream represents hypocrisy in such a family. If the fireplace is made of plaster in the dream, it means that such a family has associated itself with Pharaonic traditions or worship. If the fireplace is made of argillite or form sun-dried bricks in the dream, it means that someone in that family is a godly and a pious person. A fireplace in a dream also represents a state, a government, joblessness or fleeing from one's enemy. If the fireplace or the stove is lit with no food to cook or water to boil over it in the dream, it means that the head of the household, the butler or the house keeper will become angry and infuriated by someone's slander or backbiting. If the cooking pot in the dream is interpreted to represent the wife, then the fireplace would represent her husband who faces the adversities and hardships of life. On the other hand, if the fireplace in the dream is interpreted to represent the wife, then the cooking pot would be her husband who is always sitting on fire. If the fireplace or the stove is not lit in the dream, then it represents distress, worries and trouble, but if it is on, then it means fulfilling one's needs and earning one's livelihood through hard work. A fireplace in a dream also represents one's wife, his tools and instruments, his vehicle, or it could represent a place of gathering, one's rank, a chair, light, a woman in childbed, a father, a mother, a pregnant woman, one's shop or a helper. A fireplace in a dream also could represent the month of January or the cold season. If a bachelor sees a fireplace in a dream, it means that he will get married, and if he is married, it means that his wife will become pregnant. If he is a sinner, it means that he will repent for his sins, for a fireplace is the abode of fire and fire in a dream represents fear, horror and guidance. A fireplace in a dream also represents one's stomach and the firewood in a dream represents a late heavy meal that will cause indigestion or confused dreams. (Also see Brazier; Firewood)

Firewood: Firewood in a dream means slander and backbiting. If one puts two or three logs to burn in the fire in a dream, it means that an argument will take place or that an exchange of rough words will grow beyond one's control. If a religious person sees timber in his dream, it means that he will commits a major sin such as theft, murder, or adultery, he will then be caught and put to justice. If anyone kindles a fire in a dream, it means that he will report someone to the authorities. Carrying firewood in a dream means exchanging harsh words, slander, rebuke or calumniation. Seeing timber in one's house also means profits, fulfilling needs, inheritance or endowments. If the timber needs cutting in the dream, it means earnings that involve great efforts, or earnings that bring about evil. If the timber is already cut for the fireplace in the dream, it represents a person who is favored by someone in authority, or it could mean business success. Firewood in a dream also means adversities or stinginess. Wrapped firewood in a bundle means mixed profits. If an unemployed person sees himself carrying a bundle of firewood in a dream, it means that he will work for a generous person. Gathering firewood in a dream means bringing medicine for a sick person. Attributing the firewood to its mother tree or distinguishing its fruit in the dream means money of a doubtful source. Offering timber to burn in a religious ceremony in a dream means nearness to one's Lord, or it could mean offering a gift to one's teacher, bringing a culpable before a judge, or bringing a sick person to the doctor. In this case, if the timber burns before putting it in the fire, it means that the gift was accepted, or that a guilty person will receive a just verdict. Eating timber in a dream means earning unlawful money. A tree stump or a log in a dream means a chronic illness or paralysis. A prepared log for the fire in a dream means profits for those who use it to earn their livelihood. (Also see Fire; Log)

Firmament: *(See Skies; Star)*

Fish restaurant: *(See Seafood restaurant)*

Fish: (Sea life; Human being) In a dream, if their number is known, fish represent women, but if their number is not known, then they represent money from a doubtful source. If one sees a fish colony gathering at seabed, where he is fishing, bringing them up and eating them raw as he pleases, or if he places them into baskets and divides them into lots in the dream, it means that he will prosper and invest his wealth in different ventures and savings plans. A whale in a dream represents the minister of sea life, while the sea itself represents the king or the country. A whale in a pond with his jaws opened in a dream represents a prison. A large fish colony in a dream represents despised earnings, or earning a large amount money one is accountable for its expenditure. Fishing in a well means homosexuality, or it could represent someone who tries to tempt his servant or his assistant to indulge in a loathsome act. If one sees himself fishing in murky waters in a dream, it conveys evil, sorrows, or distress however it may happen. If one sees himself fishing in clear waters in a dream, it means money or hearing nice words or conceiving a son, while fishing in salty waters in a dream means difficulties. If one sees himself fishing with a fishhook in a dream, it means excitement, pleasure or losing benefits. A soft skin fish in a dream means benefits for someone intending to trick or to swindle people's money. Mostly fishing with a pole and a fishhook in a dream means difficulties or slow coming benefits, or a slow and loose business. Any large cyprinoid freshwater fish or a barbel fish *(cyprinus bynni; barbus)* in a dream denote positive benefits for someone intending marriage or to enter into a business partnership. Seeing a herring or any of its clupeid type fish in a dream represent evil work or toiling for something one will never get. A fish in the pond in a dream is also a sign of benefits, though may be little benefits. Seeing dead fish floating in the water in a dream has an ominous connotation, or they could represent a hopeless case. Taking fish from the water and eating them alive means profits, or an appointment to a high raking position in wakefulness. In a dream, if a sick man or a traveller finds fish in his bed it also connotes bad or a painful sickness or suffering from arthritis, or he may drown because he would be sleeping with them. Seeing sea fish covered with salt in a dream means lasting richness, because fish are preserved in salt, or it could mean burdens. If one's wife is pregnant and he sees a fish coming out of his male organ in a dream, it means that his wife will beget a son. If a fish comes out of his mouth, then it means speaking ill of a woman. A fried fish in a dream means that one's prayers will be answered. A broiled fish in a dream means travels or seeking knowledge. A large fish in a dream means money, while a small fish means difficulties, burdens and stress, because it carries more spikes than meat, beside, small fish are more difficult to eat. Mixed sized of different kinds of fish in a dream represent money, trouble, liking social events or mixing with all types of people, the good and the bad ones. Buying a fish in a dream may mean marriage. Eating a rotten fish in a dream means pursuing adultery and avoiding a lawful marriage. If one sees himself attempting painstakingly to catch a whale in a small pond in a dream, it means money that he will fight for, though he cannot get hold of it without having to cross major obstacles. If one finds a pearl or two in the belly of a fish in a dream, it means that he will marry a rich woman and conceives one or two sons with her. If he finds a ring in the belly of the fish in a dream, it means that he will gain authority and might. Finding fat in the belly of a fish in a dream means acquiring money from a woman. Seeing oneself fishing on a dry land means committing adultery, a sin, or it could mean hearing good news. Catching a fish with excessive bones and scales denotes the necessity to pay one's dues or to distribute alms tax on one's liquid assets, because one cannot enjoy his catch unless he first cleanse it. Seeing sea fish swimming toward sweet waters, or river fish swimming toward the sea in a dream means hypocrisy, falsehood or the rise of an innovator or an impostor. If one sees fish swimming on the water surface in a dream, it means ease in attaining his goals, exposing secrets, unveiling hidden past, reviewing old books or redistributing an old inheritance. If one sees fish that have the look of human beings in a dream, it means business, trading or meeting with an interpreter, or a translator, or associating with people of good character. If such fish with a human face look beautiful, then one's companions are good. Otherwise, if the fish look ugly in the dream, then it means that he has associated himself with evil companions. If one sees an aquarium in his house filled with all types of catfish, or angelfish or similar fish that live in a home aquarium in a dream, it means being charitable or taking care of orphans or adopting children. If one sees himself reaching with his hand to the bottom of the seabed to catch fish in a dream, it means that he will acquire extensive knowledge in his profession and prosper from his trade. Otherwise, it could mean that one will become a spy. If the sea opens and unveils its treasures, and if one catches a goldfish from its belly in the dream, it means that God Almighty will reveal new spiritual knowledge to him in order to help him understand his religion and to receive guidance. If the goldfish leaves his hand and returns to the sea in the dream, it means that he will join the company of righteous people and saints from whom he will learn about the inner spiritual knowledge, or that he will find a good companion for a journey he intends. If one eats a fish without cleaning or cooking it in a dream, it means that he will speak ill of his own friends, slander his associates, commit adultery, acquire money from trickery and falsehood, or become inflicted with a dangerous disease or suffer from a stroke. If one sees fish on the shore rather than in the water in a dream, it means that he may change his profession. The different types of fish in a dream represent human beings and their professions. A fish in a dream also could mean that death will take place where it is found, because of the departure of its soul, its stench, weight and one's responsibility to bury the deceased. Eating a fish in a dream also means receiving easy, lawful and enjoyable earnings. *(Also see Meat)*

Fishbones: (Spikes) In a dream, fishbones represent hypocrisy, backbiting and slander.

Fishery: (Fresh seafood) A fresh fish salesman in a dream represents a jeweler, one who earns lawful money, knowledge, strive, trickery, exposing secrets or defamation. To buy a fresh fish in a dream also may mean getting married. *(Also see Seafood restaurant)*

Fishing boat: *(See Boat; Ship)*

Fishing net: In a dream, a fishing net represents trickery, deception, profits, knowledge, realizing one's hope, and victory over one's enemies if one owns a fishing net. If one sees himself entrapped inside a fishing net, it means that he may be jailed or fall to sickness or marry a rebellious wife, or it could mean money, or a child that will preoccupy him. A fishing net in a dream also represents a harsh employer, hard working laborers. or an adversity they may suffer. As for a clear minded fisherman who earns his livelihood from a fishing net, seeing a fishing net in a dream represents trials, imprisonment, short breath, or it could mean profits or good news. As for a traveller, seeing a fishing net in his dream means his return home. A fishing net in a dream also means increasing difficulties for a worried person. If one who has lost something sees a fishing net in his dream, it means that he will find his lost object.

Fishing pole: A fishing pole in a dream means a ploy and deception. The same interpretation goes for all fishing tools and equipment. It is better to see oneself in a dream holding it, than seeing others fishing with it or carrying it.

Fishing: Fishing in a dream means womanizing. *(Also see Hunter)*

Fist fight: *(See Punch)*

Fitting room: *(See Dressing room)*

Five fingers: (Hand) In a dream, the fingers of the right hand represent the daily five time prayers. The thumb represents the pre-dawn prayer, the index represents the midday prayer, the middle finger represents the mid-afternoon prayer, the ring finger represents the sunset prayer, and the little finger represents the evening prayer. As for the fingers of the left hand in a dream, they are interpreted to represent one's nephews. To cross or intertwine one's fingers in a dream means difficulties and poverty. *(Also see Body¹; Fingers; Thimble)*

Five times prayers: (Communication; Communion; Invocations; Prayers; *arb. Salāt*) To see oneself performing one's obligatory prayers (*arb. Fardh*) in a dream means receiving a high ranking appointment, spiritual advancement, leadership, presiding over people, delivering a message, performing a duty, paying dues, turning over one's trust or satisfying obligatory deeds and enjoying peace. If one sees himself in a dream performing one of the five obligatory prayers on time, having performed the proper ablution and correctly completed its obeisance of the proper standing, bowing and prostrating postures, standing with reverence and piety and facing the Ka'aba, it means that he will perform a religious duty or attend the annual pilgrimage in Mecca. It also means that he will extricate himself from an unjust deed he fell into and repent, or it could mean eschewing evil. Performing the divinely ordained prayers in dream also means loyalty to one's promise, employment for a person who could not find a job, or reconciliation with a long forsaken friend or relative. If one leads the prayers in his dream, it means that he will guarantee something to someone, or it could means that he will borrow money for a term. If one prays behind an Imām in the dream, it means that he will become a burden to others. The midday prayers known in Arabic as Zuhur signify a manifestation, a proclamation or exposing what is hidden. Praying Zuhur in a dream means attaining one's goal, satisfying every need, obtaining everything one has asked for from earthly gains in this world, or it could mean spiritual benefits in the hereafter and particularly if one sees himself completing his prayers in the dream. Completing one's prayers means achieving one's goal. If one is incarcerated because of a debt and sees himself completing his Zuhur prayers in a dream, it means that someone will pay his debt for him and gets him released from prison and he will then prosper. If one sees himself performing his Zuhur prayers in a clear day and feels happy about it in his dream, it means that he will engage in some work that will make him famous and that he will enjoy the fruits of his work as much as he did in that clear and beautiful day in his dream. If one performs his midday Zuhur prayers in a cloudy day in a dream, it means that his work will be distressful. As for the mid-afternoon prayers, known in Arabic as 'Asr, performing it in a dream means taking a vow or making a promise. This prayer in a dream also represents one's liability. If one sees himself performing the 'Asr prayers in a dream, it means that what he is asking for will materialize, though after some hardships and adversities. If one does not complete his 'Asr prayers in a dream, it means that what he is asking for may not take place. If one sees himself performing the sunset prayers, known in Arabic as Maghrib in a dream, it means that what he is seeking has reachd its term. If one completes his Maghrib prayers in the dream, it means that he will get what his heart desires. As for the night prayer, known in Arabic as 'Ishā. If one sees himself performing his 'Ishā prayers in a dream, it means that he will complete his work and get what he wants, or it could mean the end of his life, following which, one usually attends to his resting time, which is similar to death. If one sees himself performing the daybreak prayers before dawn in a dream, it means that the morning has come and it will be soon before he hears either good or bad news. On another level, if one sees himself praying the evening 'Ishā prayers in a dream, it means that he is committed to attend to his family's needs as commanded by God Almighty, such as providing for their food, clothing, shelter and teachings. If one sees himself praying in the middle of the night (arb. Witter) in a dream, it means that he does attend to his family's needs and perhaps they feel comfort in his presence. If one sees himself performing the dawn Fajr prayers in a dream, it means that he will start with the inevitable, such as working to provide for his family. If one sees himself performing the midday Zuhur prayers at the time of the mid-afternoon prayers in a dream, it means that he will repay his debts. If one's midday Zuhur prayers or his mid-afternoon 'Asr prayers are interrupted in the dream, it means that he will pay half of what he owes. If one sees himself performing the mid-afternoon prayers in a dream, it means that his job will shortly be completed and only little work is left for him to finish. Praying the sunset Maghrib prayers in a dream means finishing one's duties and it is time for him to take a rest. The night 'Ishā prayers in a dream means veiling things or entering the privacy of one's home. On a third level, the midday Zuhur prayers mean repentance, dismissal or abrogation of laws. The midday Zuhur prayers also could mean struggling against Satan and one's enemies, which struggle takes place usually at the time of one's midday nap. The mid-afternoon 'Asr prayers in a dream also represents victory in one's life, or it could mean guidance, blessings and observing God's laws. The sunset Maghrib prayers in a dream means losing a parent, the passing away of one's guardian, the death of a close friend or the impeachment of the person the dream indicate. Seeing oneself praying the night 'Ishā prayers in a dream means preparing for a journey, or it could mean marriage, moving from one place into another, or it could mean suffering from cataract, weakness of one's vision, or it could denote the vastness of what is to come, for 'Ishā prayers are distant from the dawn Fajr prayers. Performing the dawn Fajr prayers in a dream indicates a vow one pledges. Praying the mid-afternoon 'Asr prayers in a dream means attaining ease after suffering from hardships. Performing the sunset Maghrib prayers in a dream means having crossed something that will come back later, and performing the night 'Ishā prayers in a dream means deception and a tricks. If one sees himself performing the Friday congregational prayers in a dream, it means that he will attain what he is hoping for. If one sees himself praying inside a garden in a dream, it means that he is beseeching God Almighty for His forgiveness. If one sees himself praying in a farmland in a dream, it means repayment of his debts. If he prays inside a slaughter house in a dream, it means that he will commit the loathsome act of sodomy. If one sees himself praying seated without an excuse in a dream, it means that he will perform a deed which is not acceptable by his Lord. If he prays lying on his side in bed in a dream, it means that he will be bed stricken. If one performs his prayers in a mosque, then leaves it to attend to other duties in a dream, it means that whatever he attends to will be blessed, and he will profit from it. If one sees himself praying while riding in a dream, it means that he is struck with fear, or that he may face a fight. If one sees himself performing the obligatory (arb. Fardh) prayers shortened to two groupings of prostrations (arb. Rak'āt) in a dream, it means travels. If one sees himself praying while eating honey in a dream, it means that he may engage in sexual intercourse with his wife during the fasting hours. If a woman sees herself performing the obligatory (arb. Fardh) prayers shortened to two grouping of prostrations in a dream, it means that she will have her monthly menstrual period on that day. If one discovers that he has missed the time of the prescribed prayer and could not find a place or time to perform it in his dream, it means that he will face difficulties finishing something or paying a debt or satisfy a worldly goal. If one intentionally neglects to do an obligatory prayer, or if he plans to do them later (*arb.* Qaḍā') in the dream, it means that he takes his religious commitment lightly and hopes to correct his attitude at a later time. Performing the Friday congregational prayers in a dream is a sign of happiness, joy, festivities, celebrations, the pilgrimage season, abstaining from borrowing money for one's accessories or luxuries. Performing the festival prayers (*arb.* Eid) at the end of the month of Ramadān in a dream means paying one's debts, recovering from an illness, dispelling difficulties and dissipating one's worries. Performing the prayers of the festival of sacrifice (*arb.* Eid-ul Adḥā. See *Immolation; Manumission*) in a dream means controlling one's business, respecting one's promises or fulfilling one's vows. Performing the mid-morning prayers (*arb.* Dhuhā) in a dream means amnesty, innocence, making a true oath, happiness and being free from polytheism. If one performs the prayer of a sick person in a dream, it means lack of luck and doubt about one's faith. Grouping two prayers at one time or shortening them in a dream, means travels or temptation. Performing one's prayers directly on a filthy, wet and impure ground without a prayer mat means poverty, humiliation and needs. If one sees himself praying without properly covering his or her modesty as required in a dream, it means committing wrong while fasting or giving charity from unlawful earnings, following innovation, falling victim to passions or professing that one is right however he does his prayers. If one performs the prayers of fearing something in a dream, it means creating a business partnership, business activities or suffering the pangs of death. Talking during prayers in a dream means asking to get back a gift one has offered, or failure to focus one's intention, or talking about one's charities in public. In a dream, when performing one's prayers, if one reads loud when he should read inwardly, or if he reads inwardly when he is supposed to invoke outwardly, and if he is called upon to judge between people, it means that his judgment will be wrong or that he may follow his own mind, or it could mean affectation, falsehood, hypocrisy, hiding the truth or unjustly confiscating someone's money. If one changes the order of the ritual prayers in a dream, it means that he disobeys his parents or objects to someone he is supposed to hear and obey, or perhaps he will be afflicted with forgetfulness or staying-up sleepless nights, or it could mean that he lacks intelligence, or that he is unable to memorise or remember things. Performing the late night prayers, (*arb.* Tarāwīḥ) in a dream means toiling, exhaustion, repayment of one's debts and receiving guidance. Performing a special prayer for rain (*arb.* Istisqā) in a dream denotes fears, languid, rising prices, dullness of the market, trouble, unhappiness, attachment and stagnation of the construction business. Performing the solar or the lunar eclipse prayers in a dream means striving to deliver comfort or to appease someone or perhaps it could denote repentance of a sinner, returning to the path of God Almighty, fearing the authorities, difficulties, or manifestation of major signs of the fast approaching Hour of Reckoning. Performing a special prayer of fear (*arb.* Khawf) in a dream represents unity, concord, common consent, peace and tranquility. Performing the funeral prayers (*arb.* Janāza) in a dream means interceding on behalf of the deceased. If the deceased is unknown, then performing the funeral prayers means giving employment to a jobless person, profits from a partnership, or it could denote failure to adequately perform one's regular obligatory prayers, or being forgetful or oft-distracted during prayers. If one sees himself leading the funeral prayers in a dream, and then after completing his prayers intercedes exaggeratedly with special invocations on behalf of the deceased in a dream, it means that he will be appointed by a ruler who is a hypocrite to manage a sector of his business. If one sees himself then invoking blessings upon the deceased in the dream, it means that God Almighty has forgiven him his sins. If one sees himself sitting in a gathering of people praying for departed souls in a dream, it means that he will pray in a funeral. Seeing oneself in a dream performing a funeral prayer, means that one will intercede on behalf of a sinner. If one sees himself performing the Friday congregational prayers (*arb.* Jumu'a) in a dream, it means that relief is coming his way, or it could mean a reunion with a beloved, or satisfying a need one is asking for it to be fulfilled. If one sees himself praying the Friday prayers alone in the dream, it means that such help is exclusive to him. If one loses something and sees himself in a dream celebrating one of the two Islāmic festivals, it means that he will find his lost object. If one sees himself performing the festival prayers (*arb.* 'Eid) of the end of the month of Ramadān in the dream, it means perosperity, and if it is the festival of sacrifice in the dream, it means repayment of his debts, dispelling stress, advancement in one's life or job or release from prison. Performing either the solar or the lunar eclipse prayers (*arb.* Kusüf or <u>Kh</u>usüf) in a dream means that a calamity will befall the leaders of the country or its renowned people, or it could mean the death of a great person of knowledge, whereby everyone will attend his funeral. As for the special prayer for rain (*arb.* Istisqā), performing it in a dream may represent an accident, or it could mean political unrest. If the people offer this prayer from its inception to its completion in the dream, it means that their adversity will be lifted. Praying any supererogatory prayers (*arb.* Nafl) in a dream represents piety and devotion to the leading example (*arb.* Sunnah) practiced by God's Messenger, upon whom be peace. If a woman sees herself leading men in prayers in the dream, it means that she will shortly die. Performing supplementary prayers (*arb.* Sunnah) following the leading example of God's messenger, upon whom be peace, in a dream means serving one's community wit sincerity, purity and good qualities. If one sees himself performing extra supererogatory prayers in a dream, it means that he cares about the success of his life in the hereafter, and that he shall enjoy the fruit of his devotion both in this world and in the hereafter. Performing one's obligatory prayers (*arb.* Far<u>dh</u>) in a dream means providing the necessary care for one's family, while performing the supplementary prayers (*arb.* Sunnah) means working to provide extra comforts for one's family. The same interpretation is provided for performing the congregational night prayers of the month of Ramadān known in Arabic as Tarāwī<u>h</u>. Seeing that in a dream means taking care of the family needs and bringing comfort to their hearts. During a congregational prayer, if the rows are straight in the dream, it means that such people are in a constant state of celebrating God's praises. Supererogatory prayers in a dream also mean striving for unity with one's community, love for one's brethren and constantly trying to serve and please them with deeds, money, moral and financial support. If the person seeing the dream is unmarried, it means that he will get married. If he is married, it means that he will beget two children. If a poor person sees himself performing voluntary prayers in a dream, it means that he will earn enough to satisfy his needs. If one performs the middle of the night prayers known in Arabic as Tahajjud in a dream, it means that he will rise in station. Performing special prayers for the fulfillment of certain wishes in a dream means attending official ceremonies, or being punctual at one's appointments. To perform one's prayers after the due time (*arb.* Qadā') in a dream means paying one's debts, repentance from sins or fulfilling one's vows. Performing one's prayers sitting in a dream means an illness, failures, contentment, or a warning about an affliction that will befall one's father, teacher, or a beloved. Performing a special prayer for forgiveness (*arb.* Istighfār) in a dream means forgiveness for one's sins and acceptance of his repentance. If this prayer is performed in congregation in one's dream, it means rain, prosperity, begetting children for a barren person, a good harvest, or the purchase of a new property. Performing the special prayers of celebrating God's praises, known in Arabic as Tasābī<u>h</u> in a dream means a receiving a gift, an endowment of divine grace, blessings and prosperity. Performing a special prayer of soliciting guidance for a specifi<u>c</u> <u>need</u> or circumstance in a dream (*arb. Istikhārah*) means dispelling doubt or confusion, receiving guidance for one's problem, or it could denote the success of a project. If the one performing such a special prayer is known to follow the guidance of a spiritual teacher or shaikh, then his dream means lowering of his spiritual status, for a true seeker has no questions. Performing a special prayer for the safe return of a traveller in a dream (*arb.* Ghā'ib) means asking for suitable weather conditions for one's own needs or for people's needs. Performing a special prayer over the grave of a deceased in a dream means offering special gifts that warrant no reward, or it could mean distributing charity to needy people. Performing a special prayer of greeting the mosque in a dream means spending one's money to help his relatives and the needy people among his friends. Performing a sudden and an unexpected prayer in a dream means giving charities in secret, or asking for employment from unjust people. Performing any supererogatory prayer, whether during the day or the night in a dream means performing a good deed that brings someone closer to his Lord, or reconciling adversaries, or fostering love between people. If one sees himself laughing during his prayers in a dream, it means that he oft-forgets his prayers and that he is delinquent about performing them properly and on time. If one sees himself praying while drunk in a dream, it means that he will give a false testimony in court. If one sees himself praying without the required ablution in a dream, it means that his religious performance is worthless and that his adherence is despicable. If one sees himself standing in prayers toward the wrong direction in a dream, it means that he does the opposite of what he is required to do, or that he acts the opposite of what God Almighty has ordained. If one sees himself turning his back toward God's House in a dream, it means that he is an apostate who rejects God's religion or that he does not care about it. If one sees the people in the mosque facing another direction in his dream, it means that their leader or judge will be dismissed from his office, or that he neglects to follow the prescribed rules of his religion, or that he follows his own mind and desire in making religious interpretations. However, performing one's prayers and turning with helplessness toward any direction and crying for help in a dream means seeking God's nearness, or asking to be accepted by other believers for an unacceptable indulgence or a non-permissible opinion, or it could mean travelling in the direction he faced in his dream. If one sees himself praying eastward or westward and beyond the point of God's House in Mecca in a dream, it means that he is a despicable person who is full of arrogance, who backbites and slanders others and who is daring to indulge in sin and disobedience to his Lord. If one could not find the direction of the Ka'aba in his dream, it means that he has doubt about his faith. However, if one sees himself facing the holy Ka'aba in the dream, it means that he is walking on the straight path. If one sees himself wearing a white garb and reading the Qur'ān in the dream, it means that he will join the caravan of pilgrims to Mecca. God knows best. *(Also see Death; Imām; Pharaoh)*

Flag: (Banner; Woman) In general, flags in a dream represent leaders, governors, judges and scholars. Carrying a flag in a dream means signing a marriage contract. A flag in a dream also means avoiding a dispute. Carrying a flag and a spear in a dream represents one's death or the sudden death of his son. A hoisted banner inside one's house in a dream means a funeral. Carrying a flag in a dream also connotes a woman. Carrying a red flag in a dream also could represent an evil woman. If it is a white flag, then it represents a pious and a chaste woman. Carrying a flag of many colors in a dream represents a corrupt woman. If one is given a flag to carry, and if he leads a parade of colorful flags in his dream, it means that he will rise in station and receive honor. To take a flag away from someone in a dream means removing him from office. If one sees a black flag in a dream, it could represent an ominous woman. A black flag in a dream also represents a man of knowledge. A white flag in a dream represents jealousy. A yellow flag represents an epidemic disease and a green flag means a journey by land. *(Also see Banner; Colors; Honor; Laurel)*

Flagship: *(See Flag)*

Flattery: (Excessive admiration or adulation of someone in a dream.) Ingratiating oneself to someone for worldly profits, or to gain access to knowledge, or to find a job to help him better apply his religious obligations in a dream means honor, correcting one's religious practices or attaining one's spiritual goals. It also means evil consequences if one does not usually strive after such needs, or if he presents his needs too favorably, or if he does so in a dream soliciting favors from a woman he knows. It also means escaping from the dangers of his enemy. However, flaterry and ingratiating oneself to others in a dream also could mean giving preference to others' needs over one's own, trueness and being charitable. *(Also see Adulation)*

Flea: Any leaping bloodsucking insect when seen in a dream represents a weak person who uselessly occupies himself at defaming others. Fleas in a dream also represent God's soldiers. If one sees an army of fleas stinging him in a dream, it means threats and distress caused by a rubbish type of people. A flea bite in a dream also means earnings. A wounded flea in a dream represents a weak enemy and its blood represents receiving money from a lowly person.

Fledgling: *(See Baby crow)*

Flesh: (Meat) Human flesh in a dream represents one's health, strength, earnings, sickness or one's shop, piety, religious attendance, fear of wrongdoing, scrutinizing the difference between the lawful and the unlawful, patience, forbearance, anger, distress, sexual desires, suffering from adversities and punishment for sins. If one's flesh grows bigger than what one actually has in a dream, it means prosperity, and if one is sick, it means recovering from his illness. If one sees himself having less flesh than what he actually has in a dream, it means stagnation of his business or loss of his money and property. If a devoted worshiper sees growth in his physical fitness in a dream, it means slackening in his devotion and occupying himself more in material gains and worldly pleasures. If one sees himself emaciated in a dream, then it means the opposite. Buying a piece of human flesh in a dream means having a stagnant merchandise. If a judge or a ruler finds that his flesh has grown in a dream, it means that he will become famous for his verdicts, rulings or that he will become rich, or perhaps he might grow in fury or develop anger. Growth in one's fitness in a dream also denotes happiness, joy and celebrations, while emaciation in a dream represents distress and adversities. If one sees his flesh black or blue, or if his skin is cracking in a dream, it denotes suffering from adversities, an illness or a punishment for his sins. Eating the growth of one's own flesh in a dream means usury, or living on income from usury and saving one's capital. Eating from one's own flesh in a dream also means using one's own capital, or doing something that will be followed by regret and sorrow. *(Also see Meat)*

Flies: (Insect) In a dream, a fly represents a weak, lowly and a slanderous person. If he ever benefits anyone, it will be someone of his own kind. Eating flies in a dream means earning loathsome money. Seeing flies ruminating inside one's stomach in a dream means earning money from a loathsome and a despicable man. Seeing flies inside one's body in a dream means mixing with loathsome people. Whatever profits one may gain through them will not last. A large size fly in a dream represents a great enemy who will bring harm to the people and to the economy of the land. Flies flying over one's head in a dream represent a weak enemy who is desiring to triumph over him. It could also mean that someone in a high ranking position is influencing their moves or forcing them to do what he wants. If someone who intends a journey sees flies sitting on him in a dream, perhaps he should delay his travel plans for while. If one sees flies inside his mouth in a dream, it means that some thieves will take refuge or hide in his house. If a fly or a mosquito enters one's ear in a dream, it denotes blessing, status, authority or profits. Killing a fly in a dream means preserving one's health and fitness. If one sees a swarm of flies inside his house in a dream, it means that his enemies will cause him losses. Flies are a weak but a tough enemy. In a dream, a gathering of flies somewhere means profits, medicine, cure, abominable actions or committing an act that will bring rebuke.

Flint stone: (Fire stone; Hard; Siliceous rock; Steel) In a dream, a flint stone means searching for something that could bring profits or hoping for something to happen, and both will take place. If one sees himself striking a flint stone with a piece of steel to produce fire for cooking or for light, and if he sees the sparks coming from them in a dream, it means that he will take advantage of his friendship with someone in authority who is rock hearted to help him overcome his poverty and to make his life more manageable. The flint stone in a dream also represents the rock hearted man, and the steel represents his might. On the other hand, if one strikes a flint stone with a piece of steel and produces sparks from them in his dream, it means that he will witness an awesome fight between two rock hearted and cruel people. Striking a flint stone in a dream also means marriage of an unwed person. If a woman sees herself striking a flint stone with a piece of steel, and if she can produce sparks in the dream, it means that she will beget a son. If a spark starts a fire in the dream, it means that one's wife will become pregnant or perhaps it could represent a fight between the husband and the wife, or a fight between two partners. If the sparks burn one's gown in the dream, it means that harm will affect that house and such harm will bring about losses in money, family honor or bodily injury. If the sparks burn a notebook in the dream, it means deviation from God's path.

Flirting: *(See Courting)*

Floating in the air: *(See Air)*

Flood: (Inundation; Torrent) Flood in a dream represents enemy attack, harm, destruction, sickness, a toiling journey or the inundation of a town. If the water flows toward a river in a dream, it means that he will escape from a dangerous enemy. Fighting a flood or trying to prevent it from entering one's house in a dream means fighting with one's enemy to protect one's family and property. However, if people still benefit from its waters for their wells or farms in the dream, then it represents a prosperous year and a good harvest, or it could represent good irrigations and strong dams. In a dream, a flood also represents lies, hypocrisy, wasting one's speech, or it could mean falsehood. If one sees his town flooded with blood in a dream, then it represents God's wrath and punishment for people's sins. Inundations in a dream also could represent a rainfall, one's tongue or a sharp spoken woman. If one's house is flooded in a dream, it represent past deeds that will bring later benefits. Flood in a dream also represents liquid nourishment such as honey, milk, or oil. If one sees himself collecting the waters of a flood in jars and people seem happy about it in the dream, it means the availability of food products in abundance and falling or stabilization of prices. A flood in a dream also means blocking the roads to extremism or isolating a danger. When one sees a flood in his dream but outside of its season, it means that he is following some psychic influences or pursuing religious innovations. It also means wrath, destruction, impeachment, penalties or a plague, unless if it is falling from the skies, then it means rains and blessings. If one sees himself coming out of his home to swim into an inundated town in the dream, it means that he will escape from a ruthless tyrant. Should one fail to cross, and if he is rather forced to return to his house in the dream, it means that he should be careful about staying in that town or about disobeying his boss. Stopping the flood from reaching or entering one's home in a dream also means reconciliation with one's enemy.

Floor: *(Also see Earth)*

Flossing: *(See Tooth)*

Flour: (Wheat; Rice flour; Semolina) In a dream, flour means money or blessings. Semolina in a dream represent a husband who is compatible with his wife. Flour in a dream also means acquiring exalted knowledge, travels, money, shop, tools, castle, defense, religious nature, guidance, or recovering from an illness. However, eating it in a dream means poverty. A bowl of wheat flour in a dream represents one's savings, or it could represent one's family and children. Mixing wheat flour to make bread in a dream means that a friend will travel to meet one's family. Mixing and kneading whole-wheat flour in a dream means faith, deputyship and victory over one's enemy. Flour in a dream means immediate profits, the surfacing of the truth and enjoying comfort after toiling.

Flower garden: *(See Garden)*

Flower shop owner: In a dream, he represents someone who has gratitude and contentment, or someone who faces his adversities with patience.

Flowers: Flowers in a dream are a sign of joy and benefits. If one sees himself crowned with a garland of flowers in the dream, it means that he will get married, enjoy his marital life excessively and take pleasure in experiencing his success in this world. Seeing flowers out of season in a dream means depression. If an impostor sees himself carrying a bouquet of flowers in a dream, it means constipation, while if a sick person sees that in a dream, it means his death. A bouquet of many varieties of flowers and colors in a dream represent the world, its constantly renewed youthfulness and its material pleasures. As for a woman, seeing flowers in a dream means getting pregnant or overcoming her difficulties. *(Also see Blossoms; Earth; Iris)*

Fluency: *(See Eloquence of speech)*

Flute: (Fold; Instrument) In a dream, a flute represents good news. To hear the sound of a flute in a dream means announcing someone's death. Playing the flute in a dream means developing a good understanding of things. If one is given a flute in a dream, it means an appointment to a high ranking job, protection from trials, becoming pious and living an ascetic life. *(Also see Oboe)*

Flyer: *(See Book)*

Flying ants: *(See Ants)*

Flying: Flying in a dream means travels. If one sees himself flying lying on his back, then it means comfort. Flying for other than a traveller means joblessness. Flying from one roof into another in a dream means changing from a man of dignity into a man who has no moral standards. In a dream, a roof also represents a woman or a wife. In this sense, flying between two roofs could mean having a mistress beside one's wife. If a woman sees herself flying from her house into the house of a man she knows in the dream, it means that she will marry him. Flying from a known abode into a distant and unknown abode in a dream means death. If a prisoner sees himself flying in a dream, it means that he will be released from jail. Flying with wings in a dream also means travels, and flying without wings means changes in one's status or conditions. If a foreigner sees himself flying in a dream, it means that he will return to his homeland, or it could mean that he travels excessively. If one who has pride and exaggerated hopes sees himself flying in a dream, then his dream represents mere hallucination. If one sees himself in a dream flying in a race with someone else, and if he wins the race, it means that he will conquer his opponent and rise above him in station. Flying over a mountain in a dream means power and sovereignty. If one who qualifies for leadership sees himself flying in a dream, it means that he will attain a leadership position. If he falls over something in the dream, it means that he will own or control whatever he falls into. If one does not qualify for leadership and sees himself flying in a dream, it represents pitfalls in his religious performances, or it could mean falling sick. If one does attain his intended destination in the dream, then his dream connotes a successful journey. If one flies in his dream and disappears beyond sight, it means his death. If one flies from his own house into an unknown house in the dream, the latter house represents his grave. Flying in a dream also represent a sickness that could lead a person near his death before he could recover from it. If one flies from a low elevation into a higher one and without wings in his dream, it means fulfillment of his aspirations. If one soars in the air like a pigeon in a dream and sees people below him, whereby he can benefit or harm whomever he wants, it means that he will preside over people and reach a rank of honor and dignity. If one becomes tired during his flight between tow cities or places and finds himself incapable of benefiting or harming anyone, and if he seeks nothing from his flight but is still happy about flying in the dream, it means that he is trying to find money for his personal needs or business. If one sees himself flying from one land into another in a dream, it means that he will attain honor, power, comfort and satisfaction. If one sees himself flying horizontally in the dream, it means that his wife will straighten her act and without much effort on his part. If one sees himself flying vertically with his head up and his feet pointing to the ground in the dream, it means that he will receive benefits. The more he rises, the greater are his benefits. If rich people or craftsmen see that dream, it represents a leadership position they could occupy. If a foreigner sees that in a dream, it means that he will return to his mother land, or it could mean that he will never return to his homeland again. Flying with wings in a dream means benefits in general. Soaring high in the air and without wings in a dream means fears and hardships. Flying over people's homes and over the streets in a dream means difficulties and disturbances. Flying near a flock of birds in a dream means associating, living or working with unknown people. If an evil person sees that, it means a bad omen, and for a fisherman it means sufferings or death. Flying in the air at a low altitude in a dream means taking a short trip. If one sees himself flying at will and ceasing to fly at will in a dream, it means easing of his burdens and expectation of great benefits to come his way. Seeing oneself in a dream flying upside-down means evil happening. If a sick person sees himself flying in the air in a dream, it means that he will die from his illness. If one sees himself laying over his bed and flying with it in a dream, it means a severe illness or an ailment that will strike at his legs. Enjoying flying between the sky and the earth in a dream means having exaggerated hopes. Flying in a dream also means seeking a destructive knowledge, or pursuing an evil idea, or associating with villainous and notorious people, or it could mean being in a hurry, or that one takes lightly a serious project, then fails to accomplish it because of his angry character. Flying in a dream also denotes extreme happiness, or it could mean superstition. If one flies from a bad place into a good place such as a farm or a mosque in his dream, it means benefits and growth. *(Also see Air; Wadi)*

Foam: (Anger; Froth; Suds; Water scum) In a dream, foam or water scum represents something worthless. However, water scum may create initial wonderment in the mind or perhaps be of value. If one accumulates or collects some foamy substance in his dream, it means that he has gathered something worthless, the efforts needed to collect and preserve it could be lost time.

Fodder: *(See Stableman)*

Fog: Fog in a dream means going on a journey or returning from one. Fog in a dream also means confusion or obscurity about a material or a spiritual matter. If one sees himself walking through fog in a dream, it means that he is intending something despised by God Almighty and he should desist from it. Fog in a dream also means ambiguity, dubiousness, tangle or doubt. Fog in a dream also means trials or a fight between people. *(Also see Clouds)*

Fold: *(See Pleat)*

Followers: *(See Companions of the Prophet)*

Fomenter: *(See Poker)*

Fond: Feeling captivated by something in a dream represents one's love for money and wanting to amass the wealth of the entire world if he could. If one is fond of his own hair or ties, or if he sees himself as a collector of fine ties in the dream, it means that he is a professional business person who amasses large sums of money. *(Also see Band; Tie)*

Food basket: (Picnic basket; Traveller's pouch) A food basket in a dream represents an important journey, financial comfort, or interchanging conditions between poverty and distress. If a traveller sees himself carrying a food basket in a dream, it means that he will take a positive look at things, or that he will walk a step forward that will bring benefits to him and to his family.

Food fare: (Banquet; Course; Meal) If one organizes and invites people to a food fare or a banquet in a dream, it means that he will spend money to establish a business, or that he will seek the help of someone against a rival. *(Also see Food)*

Food: (Man's food; Dinner; Digesting food; Invitation; Lunch) Food which is placed on a ceramic plate or on a clay plate in a dream represents lawful earnings. If food is served on a forbidden golden or silver platter in the dream, it represents unlawful money, extensive debts, eating and chewing one's food with desire and gluttony. Swallowing what one is chewing means debts or collectors demanding their money. Eating with the right hand in a dream means success. Eating with the left hand in a dream means falling in the trap of one's enemy and displeasing one's friends. Eating from someone else's hand in a dream means good abstinence and trusting in God Almighty as one's sole sustainer. Eating from someone else's hand in a dream also can be interpreted as a sickness or inability to eat with one's own hand. Eating sweets in a dream means solving a problem through kindness. If the food is greasy in the dream, it means that one's problem is a lasting one. Sour food in a dream means steadfastness. Sour food in one's mouth in a dream also means pain and sufferings. Yellow food in a dream means sickness, except for fowl's meat. Drinking food the way one drinks liquids in a dream means increase in one's earnings. Eating at a wedding in a dream means glad tidings. Eating at a reception after a funeral in a dream means distress and sorrow. Any food that has a long shelf life in a dream means profits and continuous benefits. Meat, eggplant, squash or the like food in a dream represent temporary benefit or seasonal earnings. Eating at the tables of royalties or rich people in a dream means rising in rank, or renewing the mandate of one's office. Eating squash in a dream also means guidance, following the true religious precepts, or it could mean vigilance. Eating food from the table of people of knowledge in a dream means acquiring knowledge, guidance, wisdom and blessings. Eating food from the plate of a policeman or a soldier in a dream means committing adultery or receiving money from an unlawful source. Eating the food of poor people or pious ones in a dream means repentance from sin or receiving guidance. Eating the food of nomads or bedouins in a dream means travels, rising in station or changes in one's conditions. Eating a meal that is cooked with meat in a dream means richness for a poor person. Eating a meal that is cooked without meat in a dream also may mean poverty, or it could mean devotion. If one's meal turns into something better in the dream, it means

173

advancement in one's spiritual life. If one's food turns bitter or sour in the dream, it means changing a spouse or a job. If one cookes a tasty meal in a dream, it means attaining a high ranking job, or it could mean prospering after suffering from a painful poverty. If someone else cooks one's meal in the dream, it means dealing with a treachrous person and in this case, it means that one should fear for his life or about doing business with him, or it could mean that he may receive a helping hand in doing his job. If one eats an unbearably hot food in a dream, it means adversities. If one finds his mouth filled with food, and if there is still a cavity for more food in the dream, it means confusion, or it could represent the balance of his life in this world. If one manages to grind and swallow the food in his mouth in a dream, it means that he will overcome his difficulties. Receiving a sour or a bitter tasting food from someone in a dream means hearing harsh words, and the same interpretation is given if one offers someone sour or bitter food in a dream. If he eats it, then it means sorrow, sadness and distress. If one finds himself eating it patiently and thanks God Almighty for it in the dream, it means that he will escape from such dangers. *(Also see Chewing food; Guest; Hospitality; Swallowing; Table)*

Fool: (Impudence; Shamelessness; Silliness; Stupidity) To make fool of oneself in a dream means ignorance. To play silly before people in a dream means spiritual losses or foolishness. However, silliness in a dream is also interpreted to mean victory over one's enemy, rising in station or expansion of one's authority, if he is pretending.

Foolish talk: *(See Blunder; Fool)*

Foot pain: *(See Body¹; Pain)*

Foot: In a dream, feet represent man's uprightness, for with them one stands erect. If anything happens to one's feet in a dream, it will reflect on his financial standing, work, toiling, his boss or his delegations. If one sees his feet pointing toward the heavens in a dream, it could denote the death of his child. If one's feet turn green, it means that he will suffer business losses. If one sees himself committing loathsome sexual acts with his feet in a dream, it means that he will pursue an unlawful sexual intercourse. Walking bear footed in a dream means toiling in life, difficulties and fatigue. If one sees himself eating the foot of another human being in a dream, it means that he will become a close friend with him, acquire his intercession, reap success from his connection, fulfill his needs, receive benefits in his travels, or if he qualifies, he may preside over a group of poor people or guide seamen to their catch. If he is a poor person, it means that his benefits to others are greater than if he were a rich person. If a rich man sees himself eating the foot of another person in a dream, it means illness, weakness or blindness. As for evildoers, eating someone's foot in a dream means imprisonment, sorrow and blame. If one sees one of his feet turning into a stone, it means that he will be deprived of its use. If one steps over a king or a ruler in a dream, it means that he will step over a coin of money that carries the figure of such a ruler. If one's foot is amputated in a dream, it means that he will loose half of his wealth. If both his feet are amputated in the dream, it means that he will lose all of his wealth, or that he may die shortly. One's feet in a dream also represent his parents or the leaders of the land. If one's foot is fractured in a dream, it means that he should not near the people of authorities for some days or he better leave town for sometime and pray for his safety. If a sick person sees his foot broken in a dream, it may mean his death. If one sees one of his feet longer than the other in a dream, it means that he will travel and profit from his journey, or receive the needed help during his journey. If he is rich, it means that he will become sick. If a poor person sees himself having four legs in a dream, it means that he will travel and receive help to accomplish his goals. A rich person in that case may get sick, or it could mean longevity.

Walking on three feet in a dream means either that one will grow to be old, or that through an ailment, he will not die until he uses a cane to help him walk. If a ruler or a judge sees himself having many legs in a dream, it means that he has many helpers. If one's feet turn into iron in a dream, it means longevity and prosperity. If they turn into glass in a dream, it means that he will live a short life and suffer a debilitating illness. If they turn gold in the dream, it means that he will use them to seek a lost property or a desired wealth. If they turn silver in the dream, it means that he is a philanderer and he will live in poverty, for lust for women and wealth cannot exist together. If one's feet turn into led in the dream, it means that he may suffer from paralysis, unless if the dream contains other elements that denote actions which are pleasing to God Almighty. If one sees his foot without a covering skin in the dream, it means longevity. In a dream, one's toes represent good deeds. Experiencing foot pain in a dream means sins and punishment or repentance and endurance. *(Also see Measure; Body¹; Leg; Thigh; Travels)*

Football: *(See Ball)*

Forage: *(See Stableman)*

Forbearance: (Burdens; Carrying weight; Porter; Serving others) If a worthy person displays forbearance in a dream, it means that he will rise in station, but if an unfit person displays forbearance in a dream, it could mean burdens, responsibilities, sins or a sickness. *(Also see Patience)*

Forbidden tree: *(See Tree)*

Forearm: (Fortify; Help) Using one's forearm in a dream means lack of helpers. A hairy forearm in a dream means debts. Seeing the forearms of a woman uncovered in a dream means desiring worldly status. Feeling pain in one's forearm in a dream means sorrow. *(Also see Arm)*

Forehead: The forehead in a dream represents the honor, standing and dignity of the person. If it is seen blemished or fractured in the dream, it means humiliation or loss of authority. If one sees a growth in his forehead in a dream, it means bearing a son who will attain leadership and glory in his life. If one sees his forehead made of stone, iron or copper in the dream, it denotes positive effects and particularly for a policeman. Otherwise, for the majority of people, seeing one's forehead made of any solid element causes them to be despised by others. A normal broad forehead in a dream represents a good character, while a tight forehead in a dream means the opposite. If one sees his forehead broader in a dream, it means that he will develop stupidity after being intelligent, or become ignorant after being knowledgeable, or become stingy after being generous. If one sees his forehead turning black in the dream, it means disdaining from paying one's due alms tax. However, its brightness represents one's concern and caring for others. The forehead in a dream also represents one of the seven points in one's prostration and in that sense, its growth or transformation may affect one's devotion and assiduity in his prayers. *(Also see Body¹)*

Foreseer: *(See Astrologer)*

Forest: (Jungle; Wild plants; Woods) A forest in a dream represents loneliness and fear and it could represent a brothel, immorality and corruption.

Forgetting: (Inadvertence; Distraction) Forgetting something in a dream means worries, trouble, misplacing things or heedlessness.

Forging money: In a dream, forging money means using vile words, or words without action. *(Also see Minting)*

Forgiveness: Asking for forgiveness in a dream means expansion in one's wealth, victory in one's life, repelling calamities, long life and bearing children. If asking for forgiveness is done after completing one's prayers in the dream, it means that one's prayers will be answered. If one confronts the necessity of asking for forgiveness, then if he disdains from doing so in the dream, it means that he is a hypocrite. If a person is asked to repent and to ask for forgiveness in a dream, it means that he or she will commit adultery.

Forgiving one's sins: If one's sins are forgiven in a dream, it means receiving guidance, abstinence from sin, protecting one's chastity, hoping for God's forgiveness, engaging in charitable actions and offering atonements.

Forlorn: *(See Deserted)*

Form: *(See Mold)*

Fornication: *(See Adultery; Sexual intercourse)*

Fortress: (Castle; Citadel; Stronghold) A fortress in a dream means obliterating something from its roots or eliminating one's trouble. A fortress in a dream also represents a positive power that eliminates negative forces, or it could represent good verses evil. Entering a fortress in a dream also could mean growing in piety or developing ascetic detachment. Seeing a distant fortress in a dream means travelling from one place to another and gaining fame. Taking refuge in a fortress in a dream means victory. A fortress in a dream also means repenting from one's sins, or it could represent a great person. To conquer and capture a fortress in a dream means deflowering a virgin girl. *(Also see Castle; Citadel)*

Fortuneteller: (Magic practice; Medium; Prophecies) If a fortuneteller sees himself gathering white sand in his dream, it means profiting from his trade. A fortuneteller in a dream represents someone who can explain the meaning of things, a man of knowledge, an emissary, a dream interpreter, a treasurer or a supply controller. Seeing a fortuneteller in a dream also signifies stagnation of businesses, a recession and a slump. Coming before a fortuneteller to ask about some understanding in a dream denotes distress, burdens or dismay. If the fortuneteller replies with a truthful answer in the dream, one should accept his answer. If the fortuneteller maintains silence and declines to answer in the dream, it means abolition of one's intent or dismissal of any benefits. *(Also see Astrologer; Divination; Dream interpreter; Seer)*

Forwardness: (Daring; Courage) In a dream, forwardness means a battle between good and evil and it could be interpreted according to one's standing in that case. Forwardness in a dream also means lack of determination and disdaining to serve one's true needs.

Founder: (Casting metals; Glass; Gold; Mixing ores) In a dream, a founder represents a spendthrift, someone who cannot keep a secret, one who does not keep a promise, a minter, one who separates good from evil, a just judge who distinguishes between good and evil, an assiduous craftsman or a dream interpreter who distinguishes between true dreams and confused ones, a seer, a launderer or a garment bleacher. A founder in a dream also represents a person about whom people speak negatively, or a person who is appointed to lead a high ranking function.

Foundling: *(See Orphan)*

Fountain: In a dream, a fountain placed in a suitable place or as a decorative item in the middle of a yard or a park represents honor, dignity, dispelling worries or adversities, hearing good news or listening to good music, squandering money, dispersal of one's interests, breaking a gathering, or adding and subtracting if seen near an accountant. A fountain in a dream also means avoiding evil actions. If one is told that such a fountain is a blessed one in the dream, it means the opposite, and should one wash himself with its water or drink from it in a dream, it means depression and trouble. A fountain in a dream also could represent a beautiful, rich and a noble woman. If no water is coming from the fountainhead in the dream, then it represents a poor woman or a barren woman. *(Also see Fountainhead; Spring)*

Fountainhead: A fountainhead in a dream represents blessings, grace, bounty and attaining one's goal. If one sees many springs gushing forth inside his own house in a dream, and if he is not a discrete person, it represents a calamity that will bring him and his family to their knees with sorrow and tears. If one sees himself taking a ritual ablution for prayers from a fountainhead in a dream, it means that he will receive lawful money. Discovering a fountainhead in a dream means prosperity. If the spring gushes forth inside one's house or from the walls of one's house in the dream, then it means a calamity or a misfortune that will be caused by a woman, a brother or a brother in-law. If the water flows into the street in a dream, it means that such a calamity or adversity will leave that house and peace will finally prevail. If the water is pure and clean in the dream, it means depression along with a strong and a healthy body. What is disliked in such dreams is the murky water. If one owns a stream in a dream, it represents one's livelihood, his shop, business, work, or one's good deeds that remain beneficial even after his death and until the Day of Judgment such as a blessed progeny, a school or a mosque he builds, a road he opens, a book of knowledge he leaves behind, or a charitable endowment. Seeing waters overflowing from a fountainhead and flooding one's property means sadness, crying and sorrow and the same applies if one drinks from that water in his dream. If one sees several springs gushing forth in a dream, it means prospering through dirty actions and corruption. Seeing a spring in the valley in a dream means blessings for most people and particularly for the sick and the needy. A dried well in a dream means the opposite. If one who is suffering from depression sees a spring in his dream, it means relief from his difficulties, repayment of his debts, recovering from his illness, or repentance from his sins. A spring of sweet water in a dream also means collecting one's profits or rents. If one sees a rivulet carrying pure and sweet water to his house in a dream, it means profits, easy life and blessings that will be driven to him. (Also see Rivulet; Spring)

Fowl: (See Chicken)

Fox's fur: (See Fur)

Fox: A fox in a dream represents a lethal enemy, a perfidious person, a liar, a poet, someone who defraud people, a schemer and a trickster. Somehow, a fox in a dream is also interpreted generally as a fortuneteller, a dangerous state inspector, a physician or a good business manager. Killing a fox in a dream means taking advantage of a noble woman. A fox in a dream also means ingratiating oneself before a noble man or a noble woman. If one sees a fox toadying him and seeking his protection in a dream, it represents his fear of spirits, jinns or human beings. If one sees himself battling a fox in a dream, it means that his wife has committed adultery. Capturing a piece of fox skin or his hair in a dream means victory and strength, or it may be interpreted as receiving an inheritance. A fox in one's dream also represents profits, new clothing, one's wife or marriage. (Also see Fur)

Frailty: (See Feebleness)

Frame of a person: (See Figure)

Frankincense: (Incense) In a dream, frankincense represents the occasion for which it is burned. (Also see Incense)

Fraud: (See Fraudulent bankruptcy)

Fraudulent bankruptcy: (Bankruptcy; Deceptive; Feigned; Misleading) Fraudulent bankruptcy in a dream represents income or suffering from an actual bankruptcy. If one is called fraudulent in a dream and there is a legitimate witness to such allegation, it means increase in his earnings. If the circumstances in the dream denote evil, it means that he will go into bankruptcy or become ill mannered, or that he will use vile language, or become filthy, or lose his integrity. *(Also see Bankruptcy)*

Freckles: (Blotches; Speckles) Freckles in a dream represent crimes or sins one has committed just for the sake of making money.

Freedom: *(See Manumission)*

French: *(See Language)*

Fresh produce: (Damp; Food; Humid; Produce; Ripe; Tender) Fresh vegetables or fruits in a dream and in their season represent a political appointment in a populated village or a small town. Eating fresh produce out of season in a dream means an illness. As for a merchant, eating fresh produce in a dream means profits and plenitude. Fresh or ripened fruits in a dream represent glad tidings, spiritual awareness, victory over one's enemy, chastity, lawful earnings or absence of trouble. Eating a ripened fruit out of season in a dream also may mean a miraculous recovery from illness and a blessing.

Friday eve: *(See Night of Power)*

Friday: (*arb.* Jumu'a, the sixth day of the week.) Recognizing Friday, the sixth day of the week in which the believers gather for their congregational prayers in a dream means receiving God's blessings, recuperating a lost property, receiving compensation for one's losses, and changes in his financial conditions from tightness to ease. If one sees people gathered to pray the congregational Friday prayers at the grand mosque while he is still in his house or shop, and if he hears the call and segments of their prayers, or if he suspects people to be leaving the mosque to return to their homes in the dream, it means loss of his status in that town. If one joins the congregational prayers in the dream, it means that he will receive protection and honor in that town. If one thinks it is Friday in his dream, then the meaning will be more pejorative than laudatory. Joining the congregational Friday prayers in a dream also may connote a pleasant journey with anticipation of a financial reward one may receive. Joining the Friday congregational prayers in a dream is a sign of joy and living to join one of the two festive congregational prayers of the end of Ramadān or that of the pilgrimage season. The Friday congregational prayers in a dream also represents the pilgrimage of the poor people, or satisfying one's debts. It also means anticipating a relaxed financial conditions, or meeting with an old friend or a beloved after a long separation. *(Also see Pilgrimage; Preachr)*

Friendship on the road: *(See Companion on the road; Friendship)*

Friendship: Fostering a friendship or seeking the fellowship of the righteous ones or the men of knowledge in a dream represents one's sincerity and love for others, devotion to family ties and serving their interests. It also indicates one's true sincerity in his or her religious duties. *(Also see Bond; Companionship; Fellowship; Kinship; Spiritual gathering)*

Fright: (Alarm; Shy) A fright in a dream means sickness or stress. If a sick person or one who is suffering from stress is seized by fear in a dream, it means that he will recover from his illness or dispel his stress. *(Also see Fear; Horse fright)*

Fringes: (Saddle fringes; Hanging ornaments) Fringes in a dream represent a fight, an argument or vain talk. *(Also see Tassels)*

Frivolity: *(See Laughing)*

Frog: A frog in a dream represents a pious and a religious person. Sitting with frogs in a dream means having a good relationship with one's family and being friendly with one's neighbors. Eating a frog in a dream means receiving benefits through a relative or a neighbor. Eating a frog in a dream also means gaining authority or accumulating extensive wealth. Frogs in a dream also represent people who practice magic arts and sorcery. If one earns his livelihood from dealing with sea life, or if he sells spring water for living, then seeing frogs in his dream means profits. If one sees frogs leaving a town in a dream, it means that a calamity is lifted through prayers and atonement. Hunting frogs in a dream means winning over one's rivals or competitors. Frogs in a dream also represent lobbyists, readers, dervishes, ascetics or they could represent noisy people or someone who is on a constant move from one place to another. Frogs entering a town in a dream represent a calamity that will befall the dwellers of that town. In a dream, frogs also represent a chaste, pure and a religious woman who never cause harm to anyone.

Froth: *(See Foam)*

Frothing at the mouth: Frothing at the mouth in a dream means excitement, madness or infuriation in wakefulness. *(Also see Foam)*

Frowning: (Knitting one's brows; Scowling) Frowning in a dream connotes a misfortune.

Frozen assets: If a rich person sees himself in a dream standing within the confines of the Cradle of Ismāïl in Mecca in a dream, it means that he will be debarred from his assets and his rights to use them will be suspended.

Frugal: *(See Middle course)*

Frugality: (Humiliation. *See Middle course*)

Fruit pickle: (Relish) Pickled fruits in a dream means apostasy, corruption, emulating evil people, wasting one's money foolishly or breaking one's promise. Pickling fruits in mustard in a dream means speaking the truth at an inappropriate time, or speaking the truth then meeting with rejection. *(Also see Pickles; Preserves)*

Fruit: (Dried fruits; Fresh fruits) In a dream, a sweet tasting fruit represents blessings, knowledge or money. Even a sour tasting fruit means the same when it suits the taste of the person eating it in his dream. When a sour tasting fruit does not agree with the person's taste in the dream, then it means unlawful earnings or aggravation of his illness. Eating or drinking any by-product that is made of fruit in a dream means debts or facing challenges in a foreign land. Seeing one's most preferred fruit in a dream represent profits earned from one's own sweat and such profits will equal the amount of efforts exerted to earn them. A large size fruit in a dream represents earnings that are not yet free from due alms. A fruit without seeds or hull in a dream represents success and lawful earnings. Eating fruits out of season in a dream means prosperity and comfort. A fruit that grows or which is plucked in cluster or as bunch in a dream means love and unity. Imported fruits in a dream represent their country of origin. Fruits in a dream also represent one's wife, children, business agreements, exchanging knowledge, good deeds, family reunion, weddings, recovering from sickness or recovering lost money. Grapes in a dream represent wine, and water melon represents the alcoholic beverage which is fermented from its juices. To pick up a fruit that fell from a tree in a dream means leading a fight against a righteous person. If one sees a tree that bears fruit in warm weather bearing fruit in the winter in a dream, it means that he will associate with someone expecting to make a business deal, though their friendship will end in wasting time and money. To pluck a fruit from a tree other than its own in a dream represents a good brother in-law, an honest partner, or a profitable partnership. Wild berries in the mountains or prairies in a dream represent innate arts, abilities and knowledge given directly from God Almighty and no other teacher has a claim in it. Figs in a dream represent the best of fruits in a dream. Fresh fruits in a dream signify money that does not last, while dried fruits represent savings. Fruits for a poor person in a dream signify prosperity and for a rich person they signify increase in his wealth. If one is showered with fruits in a dream, it means that he will become known for his good deeds. *(Also see Apricot; Dried fruit; Fruit salesman)*

Fruits salesman: (Fruit) In a dream, a fruit salesman represents a trustworthy person who is entrusted with people's money and confidentiality. In dream interpretation, a fruit salesman also represents a good person unless he takes money for his fruits. Seeing a fruit salesman in a dream is also interpreted as listening to a worthwhile lecture or listening to a touching sermon or hearing an official report from the government delivered by a special announcer, or it could mean marriage, children, fast coming money and worthwhile efforts. *(Also see Fruit)*

Fryer: *(See Deep frying)*

Frying: Frying meat or eggs or fish, etcetera in a dream means separation or turning away from someone or something. It also means satisfying one's needs, attaining one's goal or identifying it. Frying in a dream represents the skill of cultivating one's personal entitlements, or it could mean the home returning of a long awaited traveller or the release of a prisoner. Frying something with sugar in a dream represents a profitable business partnership. *(Also see Deep frying)*

Fuel: *(See Coal)*

Fulfilling needs: *(See Endowment)*

Fulfilling one's goal: Fulfilling one's goal in a dream means increase in knowledge, guidance on the path of God Almighty, earning lawful money, marriage or becoming wealthy.

Fulfilling one's needs: (Endowments; Inheritance; Profits. *See Endowment; Fulfilling one's goal)*

Full moon: (Qur'ān)

Fuller: (Bleacher; Tinner; Whitewasher) A fuller in a dream represent a wool bleacher. A whitewasher in a dream implies covering people's faults or giving someone a new dress or he could represent a tailor. A fuller or a whitewasher in a dream both signify dignity, honor, richness, praises and correcting the course of one's life or managing one's life in a useful way. A tinner in a dream represents a righteous man who endeavors to do good privately as well as in public.

Fun: *(See Jesting)*

Funeral prayers: Performing the funeral prayers *(arb. Janāza)* in a dream means interceding on behalf of the deceased. If the deceased is unknown, then performing the funeral prayers in a dream means employment for a jobless person, profits from a partnership, or it could denote failure to adequately performing one's regular obligatory prayers, or being oft-forgetful, and distracted during one's prayers. Leading the funeral prayers in a dream and interceding with exaggerated invocations on behalf of the deceased in a dream means receiving a political appointment by a ruler who is a hypocrite to manage a sector of his business. Invoking blessings upon the deceased in a dream means that God Almighty has forgiven him. Sitting in a gathering where people are praying for those who passed away in a dream means attending a funeral. Performing the funeral prayers in a dream also means interceding on behalf of a sinner. *(Also see Death; Five times prayers; Funeral)*

Funeral: Joining the funeral prayers in a dream means fostering brotherhood with people on God's path. Walking by a funeral procession in a dream is interpreted to represents a hypocrite who destroys or kills an evil person. If one sees himself laid in a coffin though no one carries it in a dream, it means that he will be imprisoned. If one's coffin is carried by a group of people, it means that he will support and serve a man of authority, then collect a financial reward for his support. Involuntarily following a funeral procession in a dream means serving a non-religious person in authority. Sitting on top of a coffin in a dream means increase in one's wealth. If one sees himself lifted and placed in a coffin in a dream, it means that people will appoint him to a leadership position. If one sees a group of people performing a funeral prayers and crying over the loss of the deceased in a dream, it means that the conclusion of his life will be commendable. Otherwise, if they express no sorrow for his loss or cry over him, but instead criticize him in the dream, it means that the conclusion of his life will be contemptible. If a merchant, a governor or a leader sees himself sitting over a coffin that is moving freely by itself in the dream, it means taking a trip by sea. If one sees the coffin flying in a dream, it means that a great man of knowledge will die in that town and people will not know of it, or that a known person will die in a foreign land or on the way to or back from a pilgrimage. If a funeral reachs the cemetery in a dream, it means that people will surly regain their rights. If one sees a large number of coffins scattered in a specific locality in a dream, it means that the people of that community will break into violence, adultery and evildoing. Carrying a coffin in a dream means earning unlawful income. If a woman sees her own funeral in a dream it means that she will get married. If she is married, it means payment of her debts. A funeral crossing a marketplace in a dream means liquidation of merchandise. Paying tribute to a funeral in a dream means bidding farewell or paying respect to a travelling friend. Paying tribute to a passing funeral procession in a dream represents one's concern for his own comfort. If the deceased in the coffin points at the person seeing the dream, it means that the latter will conduct his funeral, and he will receive a reward for his service. If he serves that funeral till the burial and the closing of the grave in a dream, it means that he will receive double that reward, the value of which reward is known only to God Almighty. *(Also see Cemetery; Death; Funeral prayers)*

Fungus: *(See Herpes)*

Fur coat: A sable fur coat in a dream means a war, a fight or deception. It also denotes vulgarity, meanness, or it could represent a powerful man, his wealth and children. *(Also see Fur; Sable)*

Fur: Wearing a fur coat in the winter in a dream means benefits and profits, for cold in a dream signifies poverty. If it is in the summer, then it means benefits accompanied with a sickness, distress and trouble. Sable, squirrel or tiger's fur in a dream represents an iniquitous and an unfair person. Sable's fur in a dream also means dominion, ungodliness and wickedness. It is also said that squirrel's fur in a dream signifies pride, ostentation, a high rank or beauty, though without any religious or moral concerns. Wearing a fur coat inside-out in a dream means showing one's wealth and being excessively ostentatious. Mending or repairing a piece of fur in a dream means suffering from an unexpected illness. Fox fur in a dream represents an insidious, crafty and a deceitful person. Sheep's skin in a dream represents a noble, strong and an unassailable person. *(Also see Furrier)*

Furnace: (Kiln; Oven) In a dream, a furnace means distress, burdens, trouble and suspicion. Seeing a limekiln in a dream means backbiting people of knowledge or religious scholars. As for a brick-kiln in a dream, it means oppression, injustice or polytheism. A furnace or a kiln in a dream also represents hell-fire and its people.

Furrier: Seeing a furrier in the summer in a dream signifies trouble, distress and sickness. Seeing a furrier in a dream in the winter means health, energy and dispelling difficulties. *(Also see Fur)*

Fury: *(See Anger)*

Fuzz: *(See Down)*

G

Gabriel: *(See Archangel Gabriel)*

Gadget: *(See Drum)*

Gains: *(See Booty)*

Galaxy: *(See Celestial spheres)*

Galia moschata: (Oils; Perfume made of a mixture of musk and ambergris) Anointing oneself with galia moschata in a dream means happiness, joy, peace, praises, commendations and celebrations. Anointing oneself with this perfume in a dream also could mean performing a pilgrimage to Mecca or begetting a son. Wearing galia moschata in a dream also could denote distress from an allegation that will be handed down by someone in authority.

Gall bladder: Cutting someone's gall bladder with one's teeth in a dream means perfidy and jealousy. If he drinks any blood that comes out of such cut in the dream, it means that he will confiscate or appropriate someone's money having no right to do so. A gall bladder in a dream also means anger, sexual excitement, sexual climax, laughter or one's personal secrets. *(Also see Body¹)*

Gambling: (Betting; Casting lots; Games; Risk) Gambling in a dream denotes something groundless, distress, falsehood or an unattainable goal. If one bets money or something with an adversary and wins his bet in a dream, it means that he will overcome him. Generally speaking, betting or gambling in a dream means quarrels, disputes, uptightness or agony in wakefulness. *(Also see Casting lots; Distress; Games; Uptight; Worries)*

Gamecock: *(See Cock fighting)*

Games: (Amusement; Cynicism; Playing games; Playing) To play games or to act sprightly in a dream means pride, arrogance, being cynical, profanity or defiling what is sacred in one's religion and lacking reverence for it. Playing backgammon in a dream means exaltation, gaining power, honor and rank, or it could denote one's pride, arrogance and cynicism. Playing with a wedding ring in a dream means concealing secrets, except if someone else appears in one's dream, then it could mean looking for a missing person. Sitting and playing with one's heels in a dream means governing. Playing football in a dream means reconciliation or making peace with one's enemy. If a sick person sees himself playing a game in a dream, it means recovering from his illness and returning to a normal healthy life. Playing cricket ball in a dream means a fight followed by reconciliation and peace. *(Also see Backgammon; Cock fighting; Gambling; Ball; Bullfight)*

Garb: *(See Apparel)*

Garbage dump: (Dump; Garbage) In a dream, a garbage dump represents the world and its refuse represents money. If one's house becomes a garbage dump, or if one buys or inherits a dump, or if he manages one in a dream, it means dispelling fear, recovering from illness or pursuing the road to prosperity and success in this world. It also means dispelling poverty, receiving an inheritance or getting married. Otherwise, the dump represents one's business, office or store. As for a governor, a garbage dump in a dream represents his treasury. If one takes off his clothing and stands naked on top of a pile of trash in a dream, it means that he will lose his office, and if he is sick, it means his death, and if he is wealthy, it means renouncing his wealth and status, or pursuing an ascetic life.

Garbage: (Money; Refuse; Trash) Seeing garbage in a dream is good news for poor people, though it represents bad news for rich people. Garbage also could mean money or receiving a variety of merchandises. *(Also see Sanitation; Sweeping the floor; Trash collector)*

Garden greens: *(See Garden herbs; Lentil; Sprout)*

Garden heliotrope: *(See Gillyflower)*

Garden herbs: (Garden greens; Herbs; Legume; Sprouts) A bouquet of fresh garden herbs in a dream represent a man in sorrow and distress. Gathering a bunch of mixed herbs from one's garden in a dream signifies trouble caused by a female members of one's family. If it is a bunch of fresh sprouts, then one should be careful about an evil mishap. Dry sprouts in a dream signify money that will salvage a bad investment. *(Also see Sprouts)*

Garden: (Flower garden) A garden in a dream means repentance, and repentance from sin in a dream means a garden. Watering one's garden in a dream means having marital relations. If one sees his garden dry in a dream, it means that his wife has commenced her menstrual period during which he is not permitted to have sexual intercourse with her. If he sees someone else watering his garden in a dream, it means that such a person will betray him with his wife. If one sees himself entering an unknown garden with its trees unattended and its pasture unkempt in a dream, it means distress and worries. A garden in a dream also represents a woman. They both need water and they both bear fruits or children. In this case, if the garden is interpreted to represent a woman, then its trees and fruits represent her tribe, family and children. An unknown garden in a dream also represents the Holy Qur'ãn. A garden in a dream also represents a marketplace, a new bride's house, a property, an animal domesticated for service, a shop, a business, a tavern, a bathhouse, generosity, an army made of slaves, cattle or personal assets. If one sees himself inside a garden in a dream, it means comfort and growth in his life. If the house to which this garden belongs is God's house, then the man seeing it is in paradise. If he is sick, it means that he will die from his illness and enter that paradise. If the garden is unknown in the dream, it means martyrdom and particularly if he finds inside the garden a woman calling him to herself, or to drink milk or honey from the garden's rivers and the same is true if the garden does not look like the ones he is accustomed to see in the world. Otherwise, If one sees himself looking at a garden, and if he is unmarried, it means that he will meet a suitable woman and get married. If he is married, it means that he will receive joy from his wife equal to that which he received from the garden in his dream. If one finds within such a garden a group of associates or colleagues, the garden then represents a marketplace. If one sees a servant or a worker of his urinating inside a well or a stream inside such a garden in the dream, it means that a relative will betray the interests of the family. A garden whose owner is known in a dream represents a mosque, a park, people of knowledge, ignorant people, the generous ones or the stingy ones. It also represents a meeting place where the rich and the poor, the righteous and the insolent gather. A garden in a dream also may indicate a religious center, a school, a center for scientific research and studies, a place of worship, etcetera. If one enters a garden at the season of plucking its fruits in a dream, it means glad tidings, money and increase in one's good deeds, marriage or children. On the other hand, if he enters a garden in the fall in a dream, it means defamation, indebtedness, divorce, or it could mean loss of a child. Seeing a deceased person in a garden means that he is in paradise. A garden in a dream also represents a source of nourishment. Its fruits are colorful and their taste ranges from sweet to salty and from sour to bitter. *(Also see House garden; Qur'ān)*

Gardener: In a dream, a gardener represents a feminist, but he also may represent joy, happiness, benefits, sustenance, a school guardian, a mosque attendant or a parishioner.

Garlic: Garlic in a dream means agony and distress. Eating raw garlic in a dream means receiving unlawful money, speaking bad words, making sarcastic praises or bartering good for evil. However, eating cooked garlic in a dream means repentance. Only a sick person can benefit from eating fresh garlic in a dream. Gathering garlic in the fields in a dream means suffering from harm caused by one's own family.

Garment alteration: *(See Alterations)*

Garment: Wearing a good quality garment in a dream means prosperity in this world and in the hereafter. Wearing a woolen garment in a dream means renouncing the world and calling on people to do the same and to desire the benefits of the hereafter. Wearing a green robe in a dream brings benefits and no harm. If a living person sees himself or someone else wearing green in a dream, it denotes his religious devotion. As for a deceased person, it means a good state and acceptance before God Almighty. It is also said that wearing a green garment in a dream means receiving an inheritance. Wearing a white garment also means glad tidings. If a fabric merchant or a tailor sees himself wearing a white garment in a dream, it means lack of work. Wearing a black garment in a dream means a bad omen, but if one is used to wearing black clothing, then it means honor, wealth and receiving a high ranking position. Wearing a red garment in a dream means excess earnings that are not yet free from due alms. Such a person then must immediately pay the proper share of his earnings. A red garment in a dream means death, sickness and to a poor person, it means increase in his difficulties. Wearing a red garment in a dream can mean good only if the person wearing it is an unmarried woman. Otherwise, wearing red during festivals or social gatherings in a dream has no meaning. Wearing a yellow garment in a dream or any of its derivative colors in general means ulcer or other internal festering illness. Wearing a silken garment in a dream means loss and negligence of one's religious life. Wearing a blue garment in a dream means distress and difficulties. Wearing a patterned garment of mixed colors in a dream means being reprimanded by one's superior. It also could represent a flower merchant. Wearing a double sided coat means duplicity and affectation. A washed garment in a dream means poverty and indebtedness. Wearing a brocaded garment in a dream means attending a pilgrimage. Otherwise, if the person qualifies, it means controlling interests in a farmland, or it may represent a good harvest for that year. Wearing a garment which is brilliant in colors for a man in a dream represents his pride and arrogance. If one sees himself wearing a silken raiment and portraying a religious jurist in a dream, it means that he is a seeker of worldly titles who may invent something new. Announcing lost and found garments in a dream means attending a pilgrimage to Mecca or a journey to an Arab country. A woman wearing a thin garment in a dream represents her integrity, while if she is wearing a thick garment, it represents her labor and hardships. If one sees himself putting on a new garment after taking a ritual bath in a dream, it means prosperity or repayment of his debts. If one's new garment is torn and cannot be repaired in the dream, it means inability to bear children. If the garment can be repaired in the dream, it means that there is an evil spell over the person wearing it. Wearing two torn garments in a dream means death. A torn garment in a dream also means a shattered religious or spiritual life, or it could mean that one is pursued by an evil person, or it could mean poverty or striving to satisfy one's basic material needs. If one is stripped of his clothing in a dream, it means loss of his status. Destroying or wasting garments in a dream brings glad tidings, unless if the person seeing the dream is incarcerated, or if he is a poor person, or if he is in debt. If a man sees himself wearing a woman's outfit in the dream, and if in his consciousness he intended to act effeminately, it means that he will face a calamity and carry a great burden. If he thinks in his dream that he is a woman, then his humiliation will be greater. Receiving used garments but in a good condition as a gift in a dream means money, though if they are in bad condition, they mean trouble. A dog wearing a woolen cloak in a dream represents a just ruler. If one sees a lion wearing a cotton or a linen cloak in a dream, it represents a ruler who confiscates people's properties and money. Wearing linen cloak in a dream also means living a dignified life. Eating a clean garment in a dream means receiving lawful earnings, and eating a dirty garment in a dream means living from unlawful money. Burning one's garment in a dream means the end of his difficulties. Ironing off the creases of one's garment before wearing it in a dream means interest in beauty, glitters and ornaments. *(Also see Closet; Colors; Filth; Trader)*

Gastrointestinal disease: *(See Colitis)*

Gate: (City gate; City. *See Lane)*

Gathering: Seeing a group of people gathering in a dream may represent business losses or a trial that will end in mercy and success. If one sees a group of people surrounding the corps of a dead, or visiting a sick person, or standing around his bed in a dream, it means relief and success. Sitting in the company of a beloved means unity, marriage happiness, prosperity or reunion. *(Also see Spiritual gathering)*

Gazelle: (Antelope; Deer; Woman) In a dream, a female gazelle represents a beautiful woman. Capturing a female gazelle in a dream means taking advantage of a woman, or it could mean marriage. Throwing a stone at a gazelle in a dream means raping a woman, or committing a sin, or divorcing one's wife or being violent with her. Hunting a gazelle in a dream means profits. Shooting a gazelle with arrows in a dream means slandering a woman. Slaughtering a gazelle in a dream means deflowering a female servant. If one sees himself turned into a deer in a dream, it means that he lives solely to satisfy his pleasures, lust and sensual desires in this world. If one receives the gift of a gazelle in a dream, it means that he will receive an inheritance and become wealthy. A gazelle in a dream also represents a child. If a gazelle enters someone's house in a dream, it means that he will marry off his son. If a gazelle jumps at someone in his dream, it means that his wife will rebel against him. Running to catch a gazelle in a dream means gaining strength. Owning a gazelle in a dream also means earning lawful money or a marriage to a noble woman. If one kills a gazelle in a dream or if a gazelle dies in his arm in a dream, it means distress, sorrow and difficulties. *(Also see Deer)*

Gecko: *(See Wall gecko)*

Geese: In a dream, geese represent beautiful women, handsome men or money. Honking gees in a dream represent death, drowning, crying or women in mourning. Herding geese in a dream means becoming a leader or presiding over people, earning their respect and becoming wealthy through them. A goose in a dream represents a man under stress. Geese in a dream also represents survivability and control of life in water and on land. Wild geese in a dream represents travels, business, property, moving into a new neighborhood. Geese eggs in a dream represent wealth.

Gem polishing: (Polishing) In a dream, a gem polisher represents the polisher of the hearts, a wise man, a teacher, a shaikh, a sage, a refiner of characters or a gnostic. On the other hand, a gem polisher in a dream may also represent evil, belligerence, hesitation, or travels. A stone polisher in a dream represents someone who offends or injures people's feelings with his words.

Gemini: *(astr. See Moon)*

Gems of the eyes: (Children)

Gems: (Jewel; Son. *See Counting gems; Carnelian-red; Sapphire; Zircon)*

Gemstone: Owning a gemstone in a dream could mean buying one in real life. *(Also see Carnelian-red; Ring)*

Genealogist: *(See Linguist)*

Generosity: (Horse; Kindness) Generosity or openhandedness in a dream means acknowledgment of God's favors and expressing one's gratitude for them. Generosity in a dream also could represent the return to noble thinking, proper moral conduct, good character and finding guidance after heedlessness.

Geomancy: *(See Divination)*

Getting lost: *(See Lost; Wandering)*

Getting married: *(See Grave)*

Ghaib: *(arb. Unseen. See Five times prayers)*

Ghee: (Butter; Purified butter) In a dream, ghee represents knowledge, spiritual excellence or purity of faith that is free from doubt. Ghee in a dream also could represent a woman who can win people's hearts, though she exaggerates a little in her expressions of friendliness. If a woman sees herself unusually fat in a dream, it means that a swagger will take advantage of her. When ghee is seen in a bowl in a dream, it means knowledge, spiritual awakening for the right people, medicine for a sick person, or it could mean his recovery. Extracting ghee from butter in a dream means lawful and blessed earnings, prosperity, comfort, and healthy living.

Gherkins: (Cucumber; Small pickle) Gherkins in a dream represent a son who looks like his father and mother and acts like them. *(Also see Pickles; Preserves)*

Ghost: (Phantom; Spook) A ghost in a dream represents money earned from a friendly person. If a pregnant woman sees a ghost in her dream, it means that she will give birth to a son. *(Also see Mirage)*

Ghusul: *(See Ritual bath)*

Giant: (Aggrandizement; Colossal; Death; Hulk; Magnification) If one sees his body grown to be gigantic and beyond the normal size in a dream, it means his death.

Gibbon: (Monkey; Primate) A gibbon in a dream represents someone of little intelligence who leads himself to a serious nerve breakdown. Such a person disrupts his life through his own actions and sins and is despised in people's eyes. A gibbon in a dream also represents a toadying person, though proud. He also represents astonishment and forgetfulness. *(Also see Monkey)*

Gift: Receiving a gift in a dream is a sign of happiness, joy, love and friendship. A gift in a dream also means reconciliation between adversaries, promoting unity, or it could mean betrothal of one's daughter to a good man. *(Also see Donation; Endowment)*

Gigantic: *(See Giant)*

Gilder: (Gold leaf) In a dream, a gilder represents a decorator, someone who makes things attractive and pleasant or someone who coats things with sugar. In general, a gilder in a dream represents someone who is truthful in his words and actions. If a gilder overlays gold leaf over the cover of a book in a dream, it means that he is lying, falsifying things, innovating and that he is a heedless person who loses his money in loathsome entertainments, corruption, or it could mean that he works for a religious institution.

Gillyflower: (*bot.* Carnation; Garden heliotrope; Wallflower) In a dream, gilly-flowers signify the death of a newborn, a celebration that will not culminate in peace, a short lived happiness, a new job that will be quickly terminated, or they could mean wearing stylish clothing, or treasuring the art effects of another culture.

Gimlet: *(See Drill)*

Gin: *(Cotton ginnery)*

Ginner: (Machine. *See Cotton ginner)*

Ginseng: (Medicine. *See Ivy)*

Giraffe: (Hoof) Seeing a giraffe without a necessary reason in a dream has a negative connotation. In fact, it may mean an illness or business losses. On the other hand, a giraffe in a dream could represent a beautiful woman, or learning astonishing news coming from a foreign land, or hearing comforting news coming from a close friend, a wife or a child. A giraffe in a dream also represents a wife who is keen to protect her married life or who stands behind her husband under all circumstances.

Girl: *(See Boy; Virgin)*

Giving birth: *(See Childbirth)*

Giving up the ghost: (Death) In a dream, the return of one's soul back to its Lord means remitting of a trust back to its rightful owner, the recovery of a sick person from his illness, the release of a prisoner from jail, or perhaps it could represent a reunion of people who love one another. *(Also see Death)*

Giving: (Allot; Distribute; Gift; Offer) Giving something in a dream indicates the value or worth of the giver. If one gives his workers or a needy person little money when they merit more, it denotes his disobedience to the commands of God Almighty, or straying away from the prophetic traditions. If one is denied what he is asking for in a dream, it means failure in his religious practices, suffering from the consequences of challenging others and arguing about religious laws, or it could represent one's perilous pursuit of heedless thoughts. If a sick person sees himself paying his debts in a dream, it means his death or the spoiling of his wealth. If he is healthy, then it denotes a case of mental derangement, anger, lack of self-control or raising one's voice unnecessarily. If a poor person sees himself paying someone's debt in a dream, it means that he will receive benefits. Receiving monetary compensation by a court order in a dream denotes lawful earnings.

Glass blower: A glass blower in a dream represents happiness in one's life, clarity of one's thoughts, understanding others' pitfalls, handling ignorant people with wisdom, exposing secrets, or seeing him could mean paying for one's crime.

Glass bottle: A glass bottle in a dream represents a servant, a housekeeper, a son or a woman. A glass bottle in a dream also represents a woman who does not keep a secret, a slanderous companion, sickness, an adulteress or a prostitute. A glass bottle filled with oil in a dream represents a woman and her makeup. If one grooms his hair with oil from such a bottle in a dream, it means adorning himself or being proud about his love for such a woman. If the oil spills over one's face during the process of applying it in the dream, it means that he will suffer from distress. The broken chips of a glass bottle in a dream represent money. A urine testing tube in a dream represents a prostitute. Thus, if one sees himself urinating inside such a tube in his dream, he should beware not to commit adultery. A bottle of wine in a dream represents a housekeeper who is hesitant about carrying money on her. A bottle of wine in a dream represents a pregnant woman who could suffer from hemorrhaging though she will deliver her child safely. Glass bottles of different colors and sizes in a dream represent people of different nationalities. A glass bottle in a dream also could mean exposing people's secret life or slandering disloyal people. If a glass bottle falls and breaks inside one's house in a dream, it means avoiding corruption or escaping from temptation that could take place inside such a house. *(Also see Bottle)*

Glass house: (Dwellings; House) Sitting on the rooftop of a glass house in a dream means marriage to a beautiful woman from a noble family and who may die soon after her wedding. *(Also see Dwellings)*

Glass pitcher: For an unwed person, seeing a glass pitcher in a dream means marriage to a rich and a beautiful woman. *(Also see Bottle)*

Glass slippers: *(See Slippers)*

Glass: (Clarity; Perception; Wisdom; Woman) In a dream, glass represents an early stage of a temporary anxiety, depression or stress. Such condition is less serious when glass is seen collected as broken chips in a container in a dream. Seeing through glass in a dream means uncovering something that is hidden. In a dream, all glassware, stained glass, engraved glass, or decorative glass of green, red or yellowish color represent a suspicious person, money earned from a suspicious source or suspicion about one's wife, or even suspicion about one's true children, or it could mean eavesdropping, affectation or hypocrisy. In a dream, any glass by-products represent people of knowledge, scholars, gnostics, sages or people of wisdom. Buying a glittering glass ornament, or a house made of mother of pearl in a dream means choosing the pleasures of this world over the everlasting joy of the hereafter, or it could mean disdaining to obey God's commands, or it could mean becoming an apostate. A drinking glass cup in a dream represents a woman. Receiving a glass of water in a dream means that one's wife is pregnant. An unknown kind of glass cup or a roughly cut drinking glass of water in a dream means that there is a fetus in the mother's womb. If the glass of water breaks and the water remains in the dream, it means that the mother may die after giving birth and the infant will survive. If the water spills and the glass remains intact in the dream, it means that the fetus may die and the mother will survive. The breaking of a glass in a dream also denotes the death of the one who is serving it. If a sick person is given a glass of wine, or water, or a bitter apple drink, or a laxative in a dream such a drink represents his last cup. *(Also see Glass blower; Glass bottle)*

Glazier: *(See Enamelist)*

Gleam: *(Also see Light)*

Glitters: (Money; Sequins; World)

Glob: *(See Ball)*

Glorifying: Glorifying God's sovereignty in a dream is a confirmation of one's true faith. If in real life the person is ill, imprisoned or in fear, glorifying God Almighty in a dream means his cure, freedom and peace. If one sees himself performing his prescribed prayers, then following that with invocations of God's glory in a dream, it means that one will receive a verdict of innocence, fulfil a vow, comply with the divine command, or that God Almighty will provide him with resources to pay his debts from sources he does not anticipate.

Glorious Throne: *(See Divine Throne)*

Glue: (Gum; Past; Tree) In a dream, glue represents blessings, nobility, or one who shares some of the good qualities and attributes pertaining to such a tree.

Gluttony: (Bustard, *zool.*)

Gnat: *(See Mosquito)*

Goat: A goat in a dream means prosperity, richness, a servant, associating with a cheap woman or a prostitute. A fat goat in a dream represents entertaining girls, or it could mean orphans. If one brings a goat into his house in a dream, it means that he is inviting poverty into his life. *(Also see Billy goat; Bullfight)*

Goblet: *(See Cup; Mug)*

Gocart: *(See Palanquin)*

God's House: *(See Entering Paradise; Ka'aba; Masjid; Mosque)*

God's will: (Destiny; Divine will) Acknowledging God's will in a dream signifies receiving great benefits, prosperity or reaping the fruits of success in whatever good project one undertakes. *(Also see Allāh)*

God: *(See Allāh)*

Gold: In a dream, gold is a disliked element which cause damages, anxiety and losses. Wearing a golden bracelet in a dream means receiving an inheritance. Wearing a golden ornament in a dream means marriage to an incompatible person. Any wedding gift one receives from such a person means trouble. Receiving a golden bar in a dream means losing money or business. If one sees himself melting a bar of gold in a dream, it means that he will be persecuted for committing a loathsome act and he will become the talk of the town. Seeing broken chips of gold or a whole coin of gold in a dream means meeting with the ruler of the country or with the governor of town. Minting gold in a dream represents evil, death or destruction. Seeing one's house turning gold in a dream means that a fire will consume his house. If one's hand turns gold in a dream, it means that it may be paralyzed. Seeing one's eyes turning gold in a dream means that he may become blind. Wearing a golden necklace, or a silver necklace, or a necklace studded with gems in a dream means that one will become a leader, or that he could receive something in trust. Gold in a dream also represents the elements of festivities, joy, profits, good deeds, dispelling stress, marriage, children, knowledge, spiritual guidance, or literally the business of goldsmithing. If one sees gold turning into silver in a dream, it means decrease in value, or changing conditions in relation to women, children or properties. The opposite is also true. If one sees silver turning into gold in a dream, it means increase in value, the rising moon of one's wife, children, business or clan. Any gold embroidered garment or fabric in a dream means religious offerings. Any gold plated ornaments in a dream means emulating mundane people, or outwardly imitating spiritual people, or ostentatiously acting like them. Pure gold or silver in a dream means purity and sincerity of one's intentions, making a true covenant or signing a peace treaty. Gold plated or silver plated ornaments or gold leaf objects in a dream represent a short life, changing circumstances, spending long and sleepless nights, or it could mean forgetfulness. Wearing any manufactured or handmade piece of jewelry in a dream means perpetual earnings. The same interpretation is given to gold foils. *(Also see Goldsmith)*

Golden cage: *(See Marriage)*

Golden calf: Seeing a golden calf in a dream means pursuing the path of greed, or disobedience or celebrating falsehood.

Golden oriole: *(See Oriole)*

Goldsmith: (Jeweler) In a dream, a goldsmith represents celebrations, joy, happiness or perhaps mixing truth with falsehood. A goldsmith in a dream also could represent falsehood, lies, cheating, forging, defrauding, or he could represent a poet, knowledge, guidance or children. A goldsmith in a dream also represents an evil person, for he molds words from fire and in smoke. If one is seen heating gold or silver in a dream, it means lies and deception. If one is seen placing gems on a ring in a dream, it means that he will bring unity between people and deal with a subject matter that begins with evil and ends in goodness. *(Also see Gold; Jeweler)*

Golf bag: In a dream, a golf bag represents the keeper of one's secrets, or it could represent one's mistress. If any of its contents are exposed, or if they peak from its opening end in the dream, it means divulging one's secrets. A gulf bag in a dream also represents the carrier who turns against his employer or betrays him.

Golf ball: *(See Ball)*

Goliath's head: (Arrogance; Deception; Defeat; Death; Giant; Mocking; Slingshot) Goliath's head in a dream represents a perfidious man who entices people to engage in treachery, deception and falsehood. If one sees himself nicknamed as Goliath's head in a dream, it means that he will be accused of treachery, deceiving others or defaming them, though he maybe innocent of such allegations.

Gomorrah: *(See Lot¹)*

Good deed: Doing a good deed in a dream means repentance, reestablishing the connection with one's blood relations, uniting one's family with love or being charitable in helping a poor person. If one sees himself calling people to God Almighty in a dream, it means that he will be saved from hell-fire. Doing good deeds in a dream such as charity, prayers, invoking God's blessings, helping others, protecting the rights of others, commanding what is lawful and shunning what is forbidden incurs the divine pleasure and bounty, and brings profits to one's business, pays his debts, dispels his fears and leads him to receive a leading position in his community. Thanking God Almighty for His favors in a dream means receiving an inheritance. Doing a good deed in a dream also signifies receiving encouragement or having encouraging ambitions. To spend money on God's path in a dream means receiving money in wakefulness.

Good luck: *(See Hunchback)*

Good manners: *(See Perfume salesman)*

Goodwill: (Alms; Generosity; Secondhand; Thrift shop; Torn garments. *See Used clothing*)

Gospel: (Injeel) If a person sees himself carrying the gospel in a dream, it means that he devotes his life to worship, asceticism and gives preference to solitary life. If a ruler sees that in his dream, it means that he will conquer his enemy. Carrying the Gospel in a dream also could represent a false witness, or slandering a chaste woman. If a sick person sees himself carrying the gospel in a dream, it means that he will recover from his illness. In general, seeing the gospel in a dream may represent science, geometry, copying knowledge from its people or it may indicate images and music.

Gourd: *(See Pumpkin)*

Government: (Ocean. *See Swimmer*)

Governors: If one sees them in a good state in a dream, it means that he will attain his goals, be it profits, knowledge, guidance or uprightness. A governor in a dream also represents an orthopedist, an engineer, gentleness or conformity. If a governor sees himself hearing a petition from a deranged person, a stupid person, a street sweeper, a baker, a trash collector, a servant, a dancer or a musician in a dream, it means that the governor will consent to the opinions or advice of others in his ruling, or perhaps he will lean toward the interests of some opportunists. A governor in a dream also represents a father or a mother who teach their children justice and righteousness and in turn, the child will benefit from them and particularly if he follows their advice. *(Also see Earth)*

Gown: *(See Cloak)*

Grabbing: Grabbing to a wall, a tree or a branch in a dream means the nearing end of one's life, depending on how firmly one is grabbing to it. Firmly grabbing to something in a dream is also means holding dearly to a strong man. *(Also see Gripping; Hug)*

Grace: *(See Blessings)*

Grain merchant: In a dream, a grain merchant represents a man of dignity whose earnings are blessed if he does not need to sell his merchandise in the dream, but if he is eager to dispose of his merchandise, then it will bring him humiliation. If one sees the governor of his town selling grains in a dream, it means that he will lose his post. A grain merchant in a dream also represents the head of merchants, a union boss, the chief craftsperson, or a popular and a magnanimous ruler. Selling grains and not seeing the return or money in a dream represents one's ascetic detachment and gratitude to his Lord, for the real price of things is gratitude. *(Also see Wheat)*

Grains: *(See Wheat)*

Grammar teacher: *(See Teacher; Writer)*

Grammarian: (Linguist; Philologist) A grammarian in a dream represents preventive medicine, drug prescriptions, avoiding evil pranks, or it could mean a cover for one's head. A grammarian in a dream also means embellishment of one's words, making a flowery speech, falsification or exaggeration. Seeing a grammarian in a dream also means balance, unbalance, gossipry, pretension and ostentatiousness. If a falsifier becomes a grammarian in a dream, it means that he will turn truthful and become known for it. If he is a heedless person, it means that he will receive guidance. If he is a sinner, it means that he will repent for his sins. If he stammers, it means that he will prosper after having suffered from poverty. The same interpretation is given for one who suffers from dumbness. If he is sick, it means that he will recover from his illness. *(Also see Linguist)*

Granary: *(See Underground granary)*

Grandfather: To become a grandfather in a dream means longevity or earning respect. Seeing one's grandfather in a dream also means enjoying a happy life. A grandfather in one's house in a dream represents one's own father. Therefore, any interpretation relative to one's father should apply here. If one's grandfather dies in a dream, it means loss of one's determination and will. *(Also see Father)*

Granite: *(See Column)*

Grant: *(See Donation)*

Grape juice: *(See Juice)*

Grape wine: *(See Juice)*

Grapes: (Bunch of grapes) In a dream, a sweet tasting bunch of grapes means receiving benefits through a relative or a close friend. If the grapes taste sour in the dream, then they mean regret. Grapes in a dream also represent money, profits, earnings, a growing capital, savings or a needed capital to support a business venture. Seeing grapes in season in a dream means material gains, and out of season, they mean quick profits or unlawful earnings. Picking a bunch of grapes in a dream means receiving money from a woman. Black grapes in a dream represent the night and white grapes represent the daylight. Black grapes in a dream has little benefit in wakefulness and may represent money that does not last. White grapes in a dream represent recovering from an illness, for the prophet Noah (uwbp) was once inflicted with tuberculosis and God Almighty inspired him in a dream to eat white grapes and by God's leave they brought about his recovery. Grapes hanging on a grapevine in a dream denote fear. Extracting the seeds and throwing away the pulp in a dream means an argument with one's wife that will end in regret. Seeing grapes in season in a dream could mean distress and out of season they mean a sickness. Seeing grapes in season in a dream also could mean success associated with women, love, tenderness and compassion. Eating grapes in a dream also means drinking wine. *(Also see Tuberculosis; Wine)*

Grapevine: (Vineyard) A grapevine in a dream represents a wife, wealth or a servant. *(Also see Vineyard)*

Graphic artist: *(See Architect; Artist; Carpet weaver; Painter; Weaver)*

Grass pea: A grass pea in a dream represents profits and resting after a long journey.

Grass: (Lawn) In a dream, grass represents religious awareness and blessings. If one sees grass growing in the palm of his hand in a dream, it means that he will discover his wife having a secret affair, and he will find her in the company of someone else. If one sees grass growing over his hand in a dream, it means that he will die shortly and grass will grow over his grave. If he sees grass growing in a place where it is not supposed to grow, such as inside one's house or inside a mosque in a dream, it means a wedding. If one sees grass growing all over him but does not cover his ears or eyes in a dream, it means prosperity. If he sees grass growing on people's hands or floating on water in a dream, it means a good harvest and prosperity for everyone. If weeds grow at the same time in the dream, they connote negative effects. If a sick person sees such a dream, it means that he is nearing his death. Grass growing over one's stomach in a dream means his death or his burial after death. If grass grows all over one's body but does not cover his head in the dream, it means prosperity and wealth. If the grass covers one's eyes and ears in the dream, it means that he will become heedless and loses the advantages of his religious life. The same interpretation is given if one sees feathers growing over his body. If poisonous weeds grow over one's body in a dream, they represent an illness or death. As grass is cattle's food and cattle represents people's wealth, then gathering and eating grass in a dream means prosperity. If an ascetic sees himself eating grass in a dream, it means that he will revert to desiring the world and its pleasures, and consequently, he will be deceived by it. Wild grass in a dream represent bad earnings and a miserable life. Cutting and selling grass in a dream means dispelling stress and difficulties, or it could represent a police officer or a tithe collector. *(Also see Meadows; Weeds)*

Gratitude: To be grateful to God Almighty in a dream means dispelling stress, gaining strength, wealth, blessings, prosperity or a good harvest. If someone in authority sees himself thanking God Almighty for His blessings in a dream, it means expansion of his authority. Gratitude to God Almighty for His blessings in a dream represents a monotheist, or one who submits to God's Will. If he is a hypocrite, it means that he will turn sincere, and if he is a true being to his Lord, it means that he will join the company of a noble, powerful, wise and a renowned person. *(Also see Prostration)*

Grave digger: In a dream, a grave digger represents a person toiling in difficulties. One cannot be at peace with him until he dies. If one sees a grave digger asking about him in a dream, it means calamities for the person in question, and peace for those who will help bury him. *(Also see Body snatcher)*

Grave: (Burial; Tomb; Sepulcher) A grave in a dream represents a prison and a prison in a dream represents a grave. If one sees himself living in a grave in a dream, it means that he will be incarcerated in a prison. Building a grave in a dream means building a house. If one enters a grave but does not witness a funeral in his dream, it means that he will buy a house. Digging a grave in a dream means getting married, though through tricking the woman to get her consent. Standing over a grave in a dream means committing a sin. If one sees himself digging a grave and upon completing his work, if he discovers that what he has dug is standing on the surface of the earth and has no walls in the dream, such ground represents the abode of the hereafter. If he then enters it in his dream, it signifies that his life term in this world has come to its conclusion. If he does not enter it in the dream, then there are no consequences to his dream. Seeing a known grave in a dream is a proof of what is true and a sign of what will unfailingly come. An unknown grave in a dream represents a hypocrite. Building a tomb on the roof of one's house means longevity. Visiting the graveyard in a dream means visiting people in prison. Raining over the graves in a dream means blessings from God Almighty upon the people of the graves. Graves in a dream also represent distant travels, bewilderment, a wife, or they could mean a prison. Filling a grave with dirt in a dream means longevity and living a healthy life. Seeing oneself buried alive in a dream means a calamity, tightening of one's means or imprisonment. Seeing oneself buried alive and wearing one's shroud in a dream also could mean marriage. To unearth someone's grave in a dream means seeking to pursue his trade. If it is the grave of a scholar, then it means wanting to acquire his knowledge. If it is the grave of a rich person in the dream, then it means becoming rich or receiving an inheritance. If one sees the deceased person alive in his grave in a dream, it means that such money will constitute unlawful earnings, while in the first instance, the knowledge or wisdom one is seeking will be true, except if the person in the grave is dead in the dream. A stone tomb or a sarcophagus in a dream means profits, a war prisoner, a booty or exposing one's personal secrets. *(Also see Burial; Cemetery; Exhume; Sarcophagus; Shrine; Tower)*

Gravel: (Pebbles) Gravel or pebbles covering the riverbed or stream bed in a dream mean hard work. *(Also see Pebbles)*

Graveyard: *(See Cemetery; Grave)*

Gray hair: For young people, gray hair in a dream means dignity and it could mean longevity, weakness or poverty. If gray hair grows in one's beard and head in the dream, it means poverty. Seeing half gray hair mixed with one's beard in a dream means strength, dignity and honor. If one's wife is pregnant, and if he sees his hair turned gray in the dream, it means that she will beget a son. If one sees himself plucking out gray hair from his beard in a dream, it means that he respects the elderly people and honor religious scholars. If a woman sees her hair turned gray in a dream, it means the arrival of guests, or it could mean that her husband is having a mistress. If a rich person sees his body covered with gray hair in a dream, it means major business losses, while for a poor person it means debts that he cannot repay. The gray hair of an unknown woman represents a drying crop. If a soldier sees his hair gray in a dream, it means his weakness or defeat in the battlefield. If a sick person sees his hair gray in a dream, it means his death and shrouding. If a person is afraid of something then sees his hair gray in a dream, it means appeasement of his fears, or amnesty given by a ruler or a judge deciding in his favor. It is also said that woman's gray hair in a dream means that she will be insulted by her in-laws, or it could mean divorce. If one's gray hair increase, but still include some black hair in the dream, it means dignity and reverence. If no black hair remains, then it means a rebuke or a reprimand one will hear from his superior. If one's black beard turns gray in a dream, it means that he may fail in his religious life, or lose his wealth. If one discovers two or three gray hairs in his black beard in a dream, it means that he will beget a son or that someone he loves will return from a long journey. If the hair of one's chest turns gray in a dream, it means that his food will become spoiled. Seeing one's beard brilliantly gray and beautiful in a dream means honor and fame throughout the lands. To pluck a gray hair in a dream also means disrespect for the elderly. Gray hair in a dream also means poverty, debts, pain, distance from others, being harsh with others, or imprisonment. *(Also see Dye; Elderly person)*

Gray: (Color) In a dream, the color gray means a high rank or authority.

Grease[1]: (Lubrication; Oil) In a dream, grease is a sign of distress or depression. If one sees himself smearing his hair with excess grease, and if grease starts to run over his face in a dream, it means adversities, burdens and a painful depression. If it is a normal quantity, then it means beautifying oneself. If the grease smells bad in the dream, it means sarcastic praises equivalent to the degree of its stench, or it could represent a prostitute, or an insolent man.

Rubbing oneself with mercury or a fragrant cream mixed with musk in a dream means hearing favorable praises and earning a good reputation. Lubricating someone else's head in a dream means evil and the subject should take precautions toward the one greasing his head. Having a jar of grease or cream to rub one's body with it or to apply it to others in a dream means fawning, adulation, flattery, hypocrisy, falsehood or backbiting, etcetera. If one sees his own face rubbed with grease in a dream, it means a lifetime of abstinence and religious fasting. Rubbing oneself with a cream as a treatment or as a medicine to lessen one's pain in a dream means that one will correct himself, or save money as a bridal dower or as a down payment toward a purchase. *(Also see Lubrication; Stuffed turkey)*

Grease[2]: (Fat. *See Stuffed turkey*)

Great Bear: *(See Constellations)*

Greater Bairam: *(See Feast of Immolation)*

Greed: (Avariciousness; Covetousness; Niggardliness) Greed in a dream means committing a sin.

Green fields: *(See Crop)*

Green: (Fertile; Good harvest; Longevity; Paradise; Youth) Wearing a green garment in a dream is a sign of piety, religious attendance, assiduity and devotion. Green silky garments are the robes of the dwellers of paradise. Seeing a departed person wearing a green raiment in a dream means that he or she are living in a good state and reaping the benefits of their deeds in the world. It could also mean inheriting the deceased person. As for the deceased person himself, it could also mean that he has left this world in a state of martyrdom. All green garments in a dream represent benefits. Green in a dream is also interpreted to mean submission to God's will. *(Also see Garment)*

Greenhouse: *(See Nursery)*

Greetings: Greeting someone in a dream means receiving benefits from him. If one greets an opponent in a dream, then it represents evil or war between them. If one sees an unknown old man greeting him in a dream, it means safety from the divine chastisement for one's sins. If the old man is known to him, then it means prosperity. If one is a farmer, it means that he will buy seedlings of fruit trees for his farm. If the greetings are given by an unknown young person in the dream, it means that one will escape from the blow of his enemy. If one is seeking marriage, then the greetings mean a positive reply. Otherwise, if one greets someone he does not know in a dream, and if the other person does not reply, it means that his request for marriage will be denied. If two merchants greet one another in a dream, it means that their business will succeed, and if the second merchant does not reply to the greetings in the dream, it means that their partnership will dissolve. If one's enemy greets him and brings a gift to him in a dream, it means that he is seeking reconciliation and is willing to pay damages for a settlement. If one is greeted with an unknown expression and to which he replies with a common greeting in the dream, it means that he will be saved from a fatal accident, though he will be rewarded for his reply. However, if he does not accept it, or reply to it in the dream, it means the opposite. If one sees himself shaking hands with someone, then embracing him in a dream, it means that he will receive glad tidings, good news, hear good words to which his reply will be the same, or it could mean a knowledge he will teach to others. If one sees himself shaking hands and embracing his enemy in a dream, it means that their disagreement will cease. If one sees the angels greeting him in a dream, it means that his insight will grow. Greetings in a dream represent submissiveness, surrender, or the need for a reply concerning an interest one has with the other party. If one commences talking to someone before greeting him in a dream, it means innovation, and the same interpretation is given if he does not reply to a greeting, or if he replies with a gesture. Paying the regards of peace at the end of one's prayers in a dream means pursuing one's path, following the proper traditions, completing one's job, resignation from one's job, appointment, dismissal, travels and profits. If one ends his prayers beginning his greetings from the left, then proceeding to the right in a dream, it means that he pursues the road of evildoing and innovation. If one ends his prayers without the traditional greetings in a dream, it means that he is more interested in collecting his profit, than in protecting his capital investment. *(Also see Prayers²)*

Greyhound: *(See Dog)*

Griffin: (Legendary bird; Mythical monster) In a dream, a griffin represents a haughty person, an innovator or a powerful person who disdains to follow the advice of the people of the faith. If a griffin talks to someone in his dream, it means that he will receive money from someone in authority, or that he could become an assistant to a strong man. If a griffin drops something to someone in a dream, it represents a divine blessing that will come at the hand of a ruler. If one sees himself riding a griffin in a dream, it means that he will rise in station and rank. If one hunts or kills a griffin in a dream, it means that he will deceive someone. If he sells a griffin in his dream, it means that he will oppress someone. If he captures it without a trick in his dream, it means that he is a courageous young man. Hugging a griffin in a dream means marrying a beautiful woman. A griffin in a dream also represents a beautiful woman, news from a distant land, distant travels, or idle talk about what is true and what is false.

Grill: *(See Brazier; Oven)*

Grimness: *(See Harshness)*

Grinder: *(See Mill)*

Grinding: *(See Extracting oils from seeds; Hand mill; Mill; Miller)*

Grindstone: *(See Hone)*

Gripping: (Holding; Seizing) Gripping to something by the hand in a dream means buying a new property, renewal of one's control over something, getting married or begetting a son. *(Also see Grabbing; Hug)*

Grits: *(See Breakfast food)*

Groaning: (Moaning) If a pregnant woman sees herself groaning in a dream, it means that she is in labor.

Grocer: (Butter; Cheese shop; Ghee; Milk products) A grocer selling any milk products represents a gnostic, a man of great knowledge, a well known man of piety and good deeds who shares his knowledge, wisdom and wealth with others. Seeing a grocer in a dream also could mean marriage for an unwed person with a wealthy and beautiful woman. A grocer also represents a rich person who sustains those who live near him or follow him.

Grocery bag: In a dream, a grocery bag means good news. Though, mostly its interpretation relates to what it contains. For example, if it carries grapes or eggs, then it means money and profits. A grocery bag in a dream also means glad tidings or warnings.

Grudge: (Rancor; Hatred) In a dream, to see oneself having a grudge, of suffering from one means earning a high rank or becoming a governor.

Gruel: *(See Porridge)*

Grumble: *(See Murmur)*

Grus: *(See Constellations)*

Guarantee: (Bail; Collateral; Escrow; Security; Surety) In a dream, a guarantee means commitment or a promise to take responsibility for something. If the content of the guarantee is of good nature, such as charity, or a guarantee of safe conduct, or a promise to satisfy a need, or a promise to save someone in need, then the dream represents the good character and nature of the person seeing it. If the guarantee is promising alcohol, wine, unlawful money or contempt, then the dream means confinement, need, poverty, parsimony, or tightfistness, because the guarantor in the dream is the debtor and the guarantee in a dream represents a fine. If one sees himself guaranteeing someone for something in a dream, it means that he will learn something good from the one he is guaranteeing, or that he will he regret something he already guaranteed. *(Also see Sponsorship)*

Guard: If one sees himself guarded in a dream, it means complications in his life, business, security or health. If one is experiencing difficulties at that time, then his dream means relief and reversal of his condition for the better. Being guarded in a dream also may mean status, rank or peace for the guarded and difficulties for his guard. *(Also see Night guard)*

Guardian: (Herder. *See Woodcutter*)

Guarding post: (Dwellings; Niche) In a dream, a guarding post represents a spiritual retreat, a votive seclusion, prayers, hunger, fast, depression, humbling oneself, controlling one's passions and desires.

Guest: If one's wife is pregnant, receiving a guest in a dream means glad tiding of a son. Otherwise, a guest in a dream means honor and fast coming money. *(Also see Food; Invitation; Hospitality; Table)*

Guidance: (Wall) Guidance in a dream means oppression. To receive guidance in one's dream through seeing a light, or hearing the admonition of the holy Qur'ān means walking one the straight path and abstaining from falsehood, or it could mean mixing with its people.

Guide: *(See Escort)*

Guitar: *(See String instruments)*

Gulf: A gulf represents one's partisans or his immediate entourage, or it could represent a gate if the seawater thus indicates in the dream. If the water level of such gulf rises at a time when the tides are low in the sea in a dream, it means a rebellion in the land. The same conclusion is made when the opposite is true. In a dream, a gulf also represents a shelter and safety from havoc. Gulf in a dream also indicates the middle road, a middle man, an average person the level of whose righteousness or spirituality is summed from the degree of his ease, or it could represent serious devotion.

Gull: *(See Gullnuts)*

Gullet: (Life; chastity)

Gullnuts: (Acorn; Gull; Oak apples) In a dream, gullnuts represent an endowment or a growing capital investment.

Gum¹: *(See Chewing gum)*

Gum²: *(See Glue)*

Gun salesman: (Arms) In a dream, a gun salesman is like a police officer and represents an oppressor in general. *(Also see Gunsmith)*

Gunsmith: (Arm) In a dream, a gunsmith represents war, arguments, or victory. *(Also see Gun salesman)*

Gurgle of a camel: *(See Sound of Animals)*

Gutter of Mercy: (Mīzaab) If one sees the Gutter of Mercy in a dream, which is located on the roof of the Holy Ka'aba in Mecca inside a mosque or a house in a dream, it carries the same interpretation as that of seeing the Well of Zamzam in a dream. Standing under the Gutter of Mercy at the Holy Ka'aba in a dream means that one's wishes will come true, and particularly if pure fresh water pours through it. However, if murky water comes through it, then it means the opposite. *(Also see Gutter; Ka'aba; Zamzam)*

Gutter: (Drain pipe; Gutter of Mercy; Roof gutter) In a dream, a gutter represents someone who is gracious from time to time. Seeing water flowing through gutters without a rainfall in a dream means corruption, or people who are spreading evil in that locality. Each gutter in such a dream also represents the loss of one life. Gutters in a dream also represent servants and housekeepers who faithfully manage their duties, or they could mean relief from distress or pressures. A gutter in a dream also may represent a trustworthy emissary or a reliable letter carrier. If blood flows through a gutter in a dream, then it represents a tyrant and bloodshed that will take place in that locality. If fresh water flows through it, and if people seem to benefit from it in the dream, then it represents economic growth, peace, safety and tranquility. If murky water or odorous and filthy water flows through it in a dream, it means plagues that include ulcers, tumors and smallpox. *(Also see Gutter of Mercy; Roof)*

H

Haft: (Handle of a dagger, or handle of a knife. *See Knife handle; Turquoise*)

Hag: *(See Old woman)*

Hail: (Icy rain) In a dream, hail means calamity, sufferings, hunger, loss of property, poverty, mass persecution, or torture. In nature, this element cools the earth and eliminates many harmful insects, worms or scorpions and limits the danger of snakes. Thus, seeing hail in its proper season in a dream means eliminating the source of one's stress and overcoming one's difficulties, enemies, or jealous competitors. Seeing hail in the summertime in a dream means business losses, but if it falls in the winter in a dream, it means success and prosperity. Heavy falling hail in a dream means destruction of businesses, interruption of communication and damage to roads and highways. In that sense, hail in a dream means obstruction of public interests. In a dream, hail also represents a strange type of business that will come from the direction of the wind carrying such a storm. If no harm occurs in one's dream, then hail represents glad tidings and especially if people start collecting it in bowls. If hail falls over a farmland without damaging it in a dream, it means a good harvest. If one gathers hail in his garment, or inside a cloth in a dream, it means that he will lose his riches, or it could mean the loss of an awaited shipment. *(Also see Dew; Ice)*

Hair: In a dream, hair represents money and longevity. If a rich person ties a strand of hair to a bun of his own in a dream, it means increase of his wealth and growth of his business based on a business loan or a mortgage. If a poor person sees that in a dream, it means that he will borrow money to pay for his debts and still borrow more money to pay for his daily expenses. If one sees his straight hair frizzed or curled in a dream, it means that he will be honored, and if he sees his frizzed hair straight in a dream, it means that he will suffer from humiliation or lose his rank. If one with a straight and lanky hair sees it longer than usual in a dream, it means that money belonging to someone for whom he works will be distributed, wasted, or lost. If one's hair is soft and lanky but still looks longer than usual in a dream, it means that his manager's authority will expand, and his interests will diversify. If a strong man or a warrior sees himself having a bun of hair in a dream, it means protection and respect inspired by a strong personality. Otherwise, if he is rich in the dream, a bun here means more wealth, and if he is a poor, it represents his debts. If one's hair looks curly in a dream, it means that power, honor and praises will be the lot of his superior. If a woman sees her hair straight in a dream, it denotes benefits and particularly if she uses a hair pieces or a wig as part of her makeup. Women receive benefits from braiding their hair in a dream and it means saving money or investing it. Otherwise, if a poor person, or a blind person braids his or her hair in a dream, then it means complications and difficulties, and particularly when they are accustomed to doing so. If a sick woman sees herself braiding her hair in a dream, it means that she will die from her illness. If one sees his hair long to the extent that he could braid it together with his beard in a dream, it means debts. Shaving one's moustache, or under one's armpit in a dream means paying one's debts, dispelling distress, or following good hygienes. Braiding one's hair in a dream also means mastering one's craft. Shaving one's head during the pilgrimage season in a dream means safety and protection. Shortening one's hair, or removing unwanted hair during makeup in a dream means dispelling stress, or being coerced to pay one's debts. If a thief or a fugitive sees himself grabbing to his own long and lanky horse like hair in a dream, it means that he will be captured. If one sees himself having hair like that of a hog in a dream, it connotes major calamities. If an unhappy person sees himself hairy in a dream, it means aggravation of his depression and unhappiness, while if a happy person sees himself hairy in a dream, it means increase of his happiness. The black hair of a woman in a dream represents her husband's love for her. If a woman sees herself wearing a veil, or putting on a head piece in a dream, it means a journey that will take her husband away from her from sometime, or a journey from which he may never return. If she sees people looking at her hair in a dream, it means that she will suffer slander and defamation. If a man sees himself with horns formed from his own hair in a dream, it means might and adroitness. If one sees the hair in the back of his head disheveled or rumpled in a dream, it means that he will suffer humiliation. If he sees his hair on the right side of his head tousled in a dream, it means that he will molest male children from among his relatives. If he sees his hair on the left side of his head tousled, or disheveled in a dream, it means that he will molest female children from among his relatives. If one does not have relatives, it means that he will suffer harm from his evil actions. If one sees long hair under his armpit in a dream, it means he will attain his goal, or it could denote his generous character. If he sees it thick in a dream, it denotes his thirst for knowledge, search for a business, or profiting through patience and endurance. If one sees his hair infested with lice in a dream, it means that he has a large family. If one sees his hair longer or thicker, and if he wishes in the dream to have that in wakefulness, it means that he will attain his goals, pay his debts, or prosper. If the length or thickness of one's hair is uncommon, and if one feels no offense to walk with it in the streets in his dream, it means debts, distress and inability to take care of one's family. Long hair in a dream also means naughtiness and adversities. Thick and long hair in a dream also can be interpreted as having many children, or it could represent fear of wrongdoing, or thinking about an important person, or it could represent common daily concerns. Having less hair in a dream means diminishing difficulties. If one sees someone pulling out his hair in a dream, it means that he may have to face a financial disaster. If a woman sees a strand of her hair being cut in a dream, it means a fight between her and her husband, or it could mean that someone is encouraging her husband to seek another woman. If one sees himself grooming his hair with oily dressing in a dream, it means adorning oneself for the world. If the oil runs over one's face in the dream, it means trouble. Discovering a bad odor emanating from one's hair in the dream means hearing praises. Delousing one's hair in a dream means discovering some of one's own faults. If some lice fall during the combing of one's hair in a dream, it means that he will spend a portion of his inheritance in charity, or that he will clean his act, or correct his attitude. If one sees his hair growing anew in a dream, it means that he may lose most of his wealth. If one sees hair growing on his face where hair does not usually grow in a dream, it means debts. If one sees hair growing in the palm of his hand in a dream, it means benefits from a business. A hairy chest, or hair growing over one's tongue in a dream means wisdom, clarity, or diligence, except if it grows beyond control, then it becomes adversities, stress, sorrows, debts and so forth. If one sees the hair on his forearm scattering, or falling in a dream, it means that he may lose all his savings. Braiding the hair of one's legs in a dream means earning money through improper methods, or engaging in something which contradicts the divine laws. Woman's hair in a dream represents her protection, husband or family. Hair in a dream also denotes farming, money, a wife, a husband or marriage. If one's hair looks ugly and smelly in a dream, it represents the living condition or the state of the husband and wife. Nicely combing one's hair in a dream means loyalty and fulfilling a promise. As for a person who lacks loyalty, shaving his hair or cutting it short in a dream means squandering money, though in general shortening one's hair means knowledge and guidance. Combing the hair of one's wife in a dream means divorce. Good looking hair in a dream represents a person of good character. Hair in a dream also means feeling apprehensive about something. If one's hair turns into an animal's hair in a dream, it means toiling and difficulties. If a poor person sees that dream, it means that his basic needs will be adequately satisfied. The eyebrows, eyelashes, hairy arms, hairy legs and a hairy chest in a dream also represent man's virility, beauty, protection, or lasting wealth. Hair in one's ears in a dream means knowledge, or admonition. Seeing hair in one's noses in a dream represents a beneficial thing one breezes, though it may involve some hidden trouble, or it could mean money. Hair covering woman's body in a dream means remaining celibate and for a married woman it means taking care of her parents and children. A hairy child in a dream means longevity. If a beardless man sees himself hairy in a dream, it means that his wife will soon be pregnant. If one's hair turns white in a dream, it means loss of money for a rich person, or paying the debts of a poor person. *(See Black hair; Dye; Shaving; Strand of hair)*

Haircut: A short haircut in a dream means failure to properly fulfill one's duties. *(Also see Hair; Shaving)*

Hairdresser: (Barber) In a dream, a hairdresser represents a person who justly manages people's assets, or directs them through the right channels.

Hajj: *(arb. See Feast of Immolation; Pilgrimage; Responding; 'Umrah)*

Half a bushel: *(arb. Mudd.* Unit of dry measure equal to 2 pecks, or 16 quarts.) A container measuring half a bushel in a dream means sanctity, chastity, cleanliness and purity. This interpretation comes from understanding the practice of God's Prophet (uwbp) of regularly taking his ritual ablution from such a measuring container. *(Also see Unit of measure)*

Hall: (Auditorium; Large hall) A large hall in a dream means comfort, overcoming financial difficulties, a helping wife, a good mistress of the house, a high ranking position that involves little danger, a highway sign, a praiseworthy son, a hard working employee, or a good investment. If the hall is dark, dirty and filled with insects and spider webs in the dream, then it means the opposite.

Hallway: (Corridor; Doorman) In a dream, a hallway represents a servant who controls and manages the business and life of his employer. It also represents a doorman, or one's actions that guides him to his purpose, or one's deeds that could lead him either to paradise or to hell-fire. A hallway in a dream also represents one's grave, since the grave is a hallway to either heaven or hell, or it may represent the steps of a sick person or a handicapped person. Its lights, size and the ease of crossing it in the dream reflect the outcome.

Hammer: (Claw hammer; Mallet; Sledge; Stone hammer) A hammer in a dream represents the one who has the upper hand, advantage, or influence. Holding a hammer in a dream means receiving honor and great benefits. A hammer in a dream also represents one's helper and it could mean money for one who uses it to earn a living. A hammer in a dream also connotes evildoing, or expressing oneself loud with clamor.

Hand bell: A hand bell in a dream represents a jobber, a broker, a wife and her children, or the muezzin of a mosque. A hand bell in a dream also means a scandal. Ringing a hand held bell in a dream means propagating falsehood. Holding a hand bell in a dream also means associating with a useless person, or it could represent a liar. Ringing a hand bell in a marketplace in a dream means making a false oath.

Hand grinder: *(See Hand mill)*

Hand mill: (Laboring; Livelihood; Millstone; Travel) A hand mill in a dream means overcoming distress, pain, or satisfying one's needs. It could also mean richness after poverty, marriage, a servant, or moving into a new house. If someone sees a hand mill in a house that is not accustomed to grinding its own grain or spices in a dream, it means adversities, defeat, or arguments. If one then grinds bread, or meat or honey with in the dream, it denotes a despicable character of the people of that house, their falsehood, affectation, lesbian or pervert nature. If one sees a hand mill grinding stones in a dream, it means that he will be seized by terror. If one grinds barley or grains for food in a dream, it means solving the family's problems, prosperity, recovering from illness, or refurbishing one's business. If one sees a huge hand mill in the center of a town in a dream, it means war and destruction and especially if he sees it grinding rocks or emitting fire or sparks. Otherwise, it means a plague if the hand mill is grinding spoiled and moldy grains, mud, or spoiled meat. If one sees the millstone tilted in a dream, it means rising prices. If the hand mill is turning with nothing to grind in the dream, it means toiling aimlessly. If the hand mill turns using a wheel in the dream, it means prosperity. If one sees the hand mill turning and not grinding in a dream, it means travels. If it turns for no useful purpose in a dream, it denotes the nearing of one's death. A pair of small hand grinders in a dream represent two loathsome partners that no one can correct or guide. If one sees himself operating a millstone by hand in a dream, it means that he earns his livelihood following the required religious conduct, and earns his money from his own sweat. A millstone in a dream also may denote loathsome actions. If a prisoner sees a broken millstone in a dream, it means that he will be soon released, and if he is under a death sentence, it means that the judgment will be rescinded, or that he may die before the judgment is carried out. As far as the question of livelihood, the better looking and effective is the hand mill, the better are one's earnings and vice-versa. If one buys a hand mill in a dream, it means that he will get married, or that he will marry off his daughter, or that he will travel on business. If the millstone is interpreted to mean a husband or a wife, then it represents respectful people. A hand mill in a dream also means comfort, relief, evil, fight, dispute, wife, servant, livelihood, travels, gourmandism, or a woman who gives herself priority in everything. *(Also see Water mill; Windmill)*

Hand: *(See Body¹; Fingers; Five fingers)*

Handball: *(See Ball)*

Handbarrow: *(See Palanquin)*

Handcuff: (Fettered; Marriage; Shackled; Tied-up) If one sees his hand tied to his neck in a dream, it means that he does not pay God's rights upon what he earns. If one's hand is tied around his neck in a dream, it also could mean that he will desist from wrongdoing. If both hands are tied-up in the dream, it denotes his stinginess. If one is captured and handcuffed by the authorities in a dream, it means that he will be thrown into jail or fall into difficulties. Seeing oneself handcuffed in a dream also means marriage, wrongdoing, or hypocrisy. *(Also see Bond¹; Rancor)*

Handkerchief: (Head kerchief; Kerchief) In a dream, a handkerchief represents money, benefits, honor, a wife, a son, or authority. Seeing an embroidered head kerchief in a dream means learning a pleasant poetry, or it could mean favors, sponsorship, or protection. A head kerchief in a dream also represents a prayer mat, leadership, or a servant. Tying a knot on a handkerchief in a dream means that one may marry a prostitute, or it could mean helping her out of sin. A handkerchief in a dream also denotes either stinginess or generosity. Carrying a handkerchief in a dream also means getting married to a beautiful woman.

Hands clapping: *(See Clapping hands)*

Handsaw: *(See Saw)*

Handshake: Shaking hands with someone in a dream means signing an agreement, receiving benefits, a pledge of allegiance, honoring one's promise, making a commitment, good intention, signing a contract, or cherishing a friendship. Shaking hands with someone then embracing him in a dream means glad tidings, good news, good words to which one's reply will be the same, or it could represent a knowledge he teaches to others. *(Also see Greetings)*

Handsomeness: *(See Elegance)*

Handwriting: *(See Calligrapher)*

Hanging clothes: (Spread; Unfold) To hang a garment in the sun to dry in a dream may indicate that someone will shortly arrive from a long journey.

Hanging loosely: If one sees himself hanging down loosely from a high place in a dream, it means that he will turn pious and for the sake of his faith, he will give preference to his life in the hereafter over that of this world. One's fall in the dream connotes despair or disappointment. Hanging loosely to reach a lion, a serpent, a scorpion, or the like creatures in a dream means hanging around with evil companions, soliciting marriage from a corrupt family, or seeking the friendship of the wrong people. Hanging loosely to reach some cattle or a herd of sheep in a dream means delivering charities or spending money in a good way.

Hanging: *(See Death by hanging)*

Hank of yarn: *(See Ball of thread)*

Happiness: (Elation; Excitement; Joy) In general, happiness in a dream means sorrow. To be happy about something which the heart does not feel comfortable with, or which the heart does not qualify as correct conduct or behavior in a dream means sadness and sorrow in wakefulness. Happiness in a dream also means being indifferent about following God's commands. If one's happiness in his dream is derived from the release of a prisoner or the recovery of a sick person, then it means positive changes in one's life. If one is told something that is supposed to make him happy, when in fact it made him sad in the dream, such as being told in a dream that so and so has just arrived from a long journey, when in fact such person has just died, it means that his sadness will be dispelled and his sorrows removed. Feeling happy in a dream means sadness, sorrow, or crying. If one sees his friends happy in a dream, then it means happiness for him too.

Harbinger: *(See Herald)*

Hard hat: *(See Helmet)*

Hard work: *(See Labor)*

Hardness: *(See Harshness)*

Harm: (Damage; Loss) Suffering from harm in a dream means dismay, horror, a scare, a shock, or a menace. Complaining about a harm one is suffering or a loss in a dream means attaining one's goal in wakefulness.

Harness: *(See Bridle; Yoke)*

Harrow: *(See Shovel)*

Harshness: (Austerity; Grimness; Hardness; Rigor; Severity) To be unpleasant, sharp, lacking restraint and wittingly incisive in a dream, or to display a harsh character, or to have one's heart blocked to receiving admonition, or to be defiant when God's words are spoken in a dream means pride, arrogance and indulgence in sinful actions.

Harvest: Harvesting one's farm in a dream means ease after difficulty, or seeing a fast return on one's investment. It also could represent destruction, or it could mean receiving admonition. The portion harvested in a dream will equal the size of destruction that will befall the area. If one sees people harvesting a field in the middle of the marketplace or a road in a dream, it means that a calamity will befall them because of their sins. On the other hand, it also means profiting from one's business. If worshippers are seen harvesting inside a mosque with no outside help in a dream, it means reaping the reward of their devotion and sincerity. Throwing the harvest back into the fields means that one's deeds are worthless. To see oneself harvesting outside the season in a dream means devastation, war, or death. Harvesting a green crop in the dream connotes the death of a young person. If the color of the harvest is white in the dream, it means death of an elderly person. If one sees the crop being harvested before its time, or much later than its due time in the dream, it means death or a war. *(Also see Crop; Earth; Grammarian; Planting)*

Hash: *(See Mincemeat)*

Hashish: *(See Intoxicants)*

Haste: *(See Hurry)*

Hastiness: (Regret) In a dream, hastiness represents regret and regret represents hastiness. If a sick person sees himself running hastily in a dream it means the nearing of his death. The only positive connotation of hastiness in a dream is to hasten to do good when the results in one's dream are good. Otherwise, it means evil. *(Also see Hurry)*

Hat: *(See Helmet)*

Hatchery: *(See Incubator)*

Hatchet: *(See Ax)*

Hate: Hate and abhorrence are the cause of divisiveness and enmity between people, and people need one another in order for them to reach their common goal. If one sees himself suffering from despise, or if he hates someone in a dream, it means a bad omen for everyone involved. To hate someone who loves you in a dream means having perfidy, jealousy and rancor. Hatred in a dream also may connote wanting to do what is right and abstaining from what is wrong. *(Also see Grudge)*

Hatred: *(See Grudge)*

Haughtiness: (Disdain; Superciliousness) If one desires to earn respect from others, then haughtiness in a dream means grovelling, servility, toadying, or losing rank.

Haunted by evil spirits: (Possessed) If one sees himself haunted or possessed by evil spirits in a dream, it means that he engages in usury, performs secrets arts, or that he may lose his wealth to become unhappy, or to suffer from stress or depression.

Hawk: *(Also see Hunter; Kite'; Sparrow)*

Hawser: (Cable; Rope) A hawser in a dream represents a robbery, profits, longevity, or marriage.

Hazelnut tree: A hazelnut tree in a dream represents a mature and a strong person, while its fruit represents money. However, throwing hazelnut at someone in a dream means stoning him to death. *(See Hazelnut; Stoning)*

Hazelnut: In a dream, hazelnut represents a stranger who is rich, generous but dull, unpleasant though he has the ability to bring people together. It is also interpreted as hard earned money. In general, nuts in a dream represent roar, or even melancholy. A hazelnut in a dream also means news that one's homeland is ravaged by war and its children are taken prisoners. In a dream, a hazelnut also represents the marriage of the first born girl to an unknown person. *(Also_* *see Hazelnut tree)*

Head cover: (Headdress; Scarf) If a religious Muslim woman sees herself without a head cover in a dream, it means that her husband has left her with the intention not to return to her again. If she is not married, it means that she may never marry.

Headdress: *(See Head cover; Head)*

Head kerchief: *(See Handkerchief)*

Head lice: *(See Hair; Nit)*

Head: (Balance; Beauty; Capital; Craft; Death; Father; Knowledge; Life; Measuring cup; Oven; Parents; Teacher; Tent) In a dream, the head represents leadership, presidency, or one's capital. If one's head looks bigger than usual in the dream, then it represents his father, or it could mean rising in rank and receiving honor. If one's head looks smaller in the dream, it means loss of respect, rank and honor. If an intelligent person sees his head smaller in a dream, it means that he will turn to ignorance, or perhaps lose his job. Seeing oneself in a dream having two or three heads means victory over one's enemy, wealth for a poor person, blessed children for a rich person, marriage for an unwed person, or attainment of one's goal. Seeing oneself in a dream without a head cover means disobedience to one's superior. If one sees his head down, or hanging loose in a dream, it means confessing to one's wrongdoing, or experiencing a long life of humiliation and striving to please someone. If one's head is fixed backward in a dream, it means delays in attaining his goals, hindrance of one's travel plans, or it could represent someone's return from a business trip slowly and without greed. If one sees his head severed without beheading in a dream, it means that he will shortly die, or it could mean his freedom. Seeing one's head turning into a lion's head in a dream, it means that he will rule and prosper. If it turns into a sheep's head in the dream, it means that he will be just and equitable. If it turns into a donkey's head in a dream, it means that he will revert to ignorance. If it turns into a dog's head, a donkey's head, or a horse's head, or any of the domesticated animals in a dream, it means toiling and hardships. If it turns into a bird's head in a dream, it means that he travels a lot. If it turns into an elephant's head, or a wolf's head, or a tiger's head in a dream, it means that he is looking to do things beyond his means, though he will still benefit from his ambition. If one's head is hit with a stone in a dream, it means that he neglects to perform his night prayers before sleeping. If one contracts any pain in his head or neck in a dream, it means an illness. If one sees his head anointed with fragrances or oils in a dream, it represents his good endeavors and piety. Eating someone's head raw in a dream means backbiting him. Eating it cooked in a dream means steeling money from him if he recognizes him. Otherwise, it means steeling from one's own property or share. Holding one's head between one's hands in a dream means reorganization of one's debts. Seeing someone's head on a tray drenched with blood in a dream represents the head of a leader who lies, or wh is lied to. Blood in a dream means lies or falsehood. A turban in a dream represents a crown or a flying ship. One's head in a dream also represents knowledge, wisdom, respect, children, followers, or money. Losing one's head in a dream means carelessness, heedlessness, or inability to properly manage one's interests. Cutting off one's own head in a dream means committing suicide, severing one's connection with one's family, or betraying one's father or teacher. Looking at one's own head in a dream means examining one's investment or capital worth. Seeing cattle heads gathered somewhere in a dream means profits. If one sees a king beheading him in a dream, it means that God Almighty will cleanse him from his sins and dispel his agonies and distress. If a money changer loses his head in a dream, it means that he may go bankrupt. *(Also see Body¹)*

Headache: Headache in a dream represents one's sins. Suffering from a migraine headache in a dream means that one should repent of his sins, curtail his plans, distribute money in charity, observe voluntary religious fast, seek a spiritual retreat, or have a change of heart toward doing good deeds. Headache in a dream also means suffering from unhappiness and misery in one's life. Headache in a dream also could represent one's employer or supervisor.

Headgear: (Tiara; Turban) A headgear in a dream means a presidency, travels, or marriage. If one receives a headgear, or a tiara in a dream, it means that he may undertake a distant trip. If one wears a headgear in his dream, it means that he may hold a seat in the government. If one is accustomed to wearing a headgear then wearing it in a dream represents his superior, the governor, his brother, his father, his uncle, his teacher, or a scholar, for they all have equal right upon him. Wearing a dirty and a worn out headgear in a dream means sorrow, difficulties and distress. If one's headgear is stripped off his head, or if it falls to the ground in a dream, it means the death of his superior, or any of the abovementioned people. If a king offer someone a headgear or a tiara in a dream, it means that he will have the power to appoint people in different administrations. If a mishap befall one's headgear or the turban of an Imām in a dream, it will reflect upon his faith and the state of his congregation. Wearing a black turban in a dream means authority, or it could mean sitting in the judges' bench. Wearing a headgear which is topped with a white feather in a dream means becoming a leader. Wearing a headgear that is made from animal fur or hide in a dream means becoming unjust and blinded to one's own injustice, or it could portray the wicked personality of one's superior at work. A headgear, a turban, or a tiara in a dream also could represent an ascetic. *(Also see Overseas cap; Turban)*

Healing: *(See Medicine)*

Health: To take care of one's health in a dream means trying to amend one's life for the better. The same meaning is applied if one sees himself applying an ointment to his eyes. *(Also see Medicine; Physical fitness)*

Hearing a voice: *(See Invisible caller)*

Hearing board: (Cabinet; Council; Court; Inquisitional court) If one's name is presented before a hearing board for review, and if he is nominated to fill a seat in any governmental department in a dream, it means that he may satisfy the requirements of such a position. If he loses the nomination in the dream, it means his death, or that he may never return to that building again. *(Also see Exhibition; Inquisitional court)*

Hearing: *(See Speaking)*

Heart pain: *(Also see Body¹; Pain)*

Heart palpitation: *(See Palpitation)*

Heart: (Daughter; Pulsate; Servant) In a dream, the human heart represents his awareness, diligence, intelligence, master, king of the human body and its governor. Seeing a heart in a dream also represents good conduct, good spiritual awareness, religious assiduity and clarity of speech. If one's heart is stolen from him in a dream, it means fear, yearnings, bad religious practices, an accident, or a calamity. Seeing one's heart blackened, or covered with an opaque seal in a dream, it means heedlessness, sinfulness and blindness of the heart. *(Also see Body¹; Chest)*

Heartburn: (Sorrel) In a dream, heartburn means recovering from an illness, or it could mean hypocrisy and affectation.

Hearth: *(See Fireplace)*

Heat: (Weather) Experiencing hot weather in the winter in a dream means benefits, profits, or new and expensive clothing, but experiencing it during the summer season in a dream means the opposite.

Heater: *(See Furnace; Oven)*

Heavenly beings: *(See Angels)*

Heavens: (The eight heavens; Firmament; Planets; Skies) If one sees himself dwelling in the lower heaven, and if he qualifies, it means that he will be appointed at a ministerial office, or work for a minister in the government. This is because the lower heaven is the sphere of the **Moon** and the moon is interpreted as a chief minister or as a secretary. The second heaven is the sphere of the planet **Mercury**. If one sees himself in the second heaven in a dream, it means that he will acquire knowledge, diligence and writing style. In turn, people will seek him to learn from him. The third heaven is the sphere of the planet **Venus**. If one sees himself in the third heaven in a dream, it means that he will prosper, or employ a female servants, or it could mean possessing jewelry and living in happiness and comforts. The fourth heaven is the sphere of the **Sun**. If one sees himself in the fourth heaven in a dream, it means that he will reach leadership, gain authority and win respect, or that he will serve such people. The fifth heaven is the sphere of the planet **Mars**. If one sees himself in the fifth heaven in a dream, it means that he will preside or leads a police squadron, a mountain patrol, a small army, a band of thieves, or manage a brothel. The sixth heaven is the sphere of the planet **Jupiter**. If one sees himself in the sixth heaven in a dream, it means that he will acquire deep spiritual understanding, religious assiduousness, or become a judge, if he qualifies. He also could become an ascetic, or a true worshiper and he will have strong faith, good managerial ability, or he could become a treasurer. The seventh heaven is the sphere of the planet **Saturn**. If one sees himself in the seventh heaven in a dream, it means that he may buy a house, a property, a farmland, or it could mean longevity. If one does not qualify to receive any of the above, then such award will reach his superiors, or someone in his progeny, or a close friend. If one sees himself standing beyond the seventh heaven in a dream, it means exaltation, though his new station will be the direct cause of his death. *(Also see Mars; Jupiter; Skies)*

Heavy weight: *(See Fat person)*

Hebrew: *(See Language)*

Hedgehog: *(See Porcupine)*

Hedges: (Enclosure; Fence; Surrounding) If the green hedges of a fruit garden climb toward the outside of the fence and the trees remain inside the garden in a dream, it means improper attitude toward one's religion, or loss of worldly status, business losses, failure to repent, or giving preference to the company of ignorant and boastful people over the company of righteous people, or it could mean lack of adequate religious devotion, rejecting one's religion, or raising the esteem of commoners above the elect. If one sees that the green hedges are replaced with a wall, a fence, or a ditch in the dream, it represents the rising star of the owner of such a garden. Hedges in a dream also represent one's religion and the trees represent one's religious duties. Hedges in a dream also represent one's family, relatives, or his trade. If hedges are interpreted to mean the world, then they could also represent one's family, relatives, progeny, one's religious life and the deeds that could save one from suffering in hell-fire.

Heedful angels: *(See Record keepers)*

Heeding: To impel one's animal to drive faster in a dream means heeding admonition.

Heedlessness: *(See Disbelief; Ingratitude; Irreligious)*

Heel: In a dream, heels represent one's children or heirs. If one discovers that he has no heels in a dream, it means that he has no heirs in his family. If one's heel is broken or cut off in a dream, it could mean the death of his child. A broken heel in a dream also means an adventure that one will regret. A broken heel in a dream also could mean depression, calamity, sorrow, a trial, or one's death. The right heel in a dream represents the son and the left heel represents the daughter. One's heels in a dream also imply the conclusion of his life in this world and his judgment in the hereafter. One's heels in a dream also represent his estate. Strong heels in a dream represent good deeds. Dark heels in a dream represent heedlessness and disobedience to the divine commands of God Almighty. Heels in a dream also signify punishment for one's sins. One's heels in a dream also may represent a son who is a gambler. A low heel and tendon in a dream represent a daring, courageous and a forward person. As for a bachelor, seeing his heels in a dream means marriage. Heels in a dream also mean vain talk. Playing with one's heels in a dream means enjoying one's success over his opponent. A broken heel in a dream means an illness. One's heels also represent his property and money. Having no heels in a dream means losing one's wealth. A nice looking heel in a dream means glad tidings and blessings. *(Also see Body¹)*

Height: *(See Tallness)*

Hell-fire: Entering hell-fire in a dream means committing major sins such as murder or adultery. If one comes out of it unharmed in the dream, then it represents worldly adversities. If one sees the fire of hell coming near him in a dream, it means difficulties, debts, losses, fines and adversities from which one will not be able to escape. If one sees himself entering hell-fire and holding his sword unsheathed in a dream, it means that he speaks evil of others and commits abominable actions against his own soul. The same interpretation applies if one enters it smiling in his dream. Finding oneself prisoner in hell not knowing when was he incarcerated in the dream means constraint, poverty, deprivation, failure to pray, fast or to remember his Lord. Walking across burning coal in a dream means exceeding one's bound regarding people's rights. Eating food from hell means becoming a tyrant and a blood thirsty person. If one sees himself inside hell-fire, where his eyes turn dark-blue and his face charcoal black in the dream, it means that he befriends God's enemy and consents to their deception and chicanery. Consequently, he will surely be humiliated and despised by people, and in the hereafter, he will suffer the consequences of his sins. Seeing hell in a dream means that one should avoid incurring the wrath of a ruler. Entering hell in a dream also means notoriety, or becoming known as an evil person. It also means heedlessness and pursuing one's indulgence in abominable actions. Whatever knowledge such a person acquires will bear evil consequences. Hell in a dream also represents loss of one's prestige, status and it means poverty after wealth, despair after comfort, unlawful earnings, insolence, and if it leads to an illness, it will end in a shocking death as a punishment. If it leads to employment, it will be a job serving a tyrant. If it leads to acquiring knowledge, it means inventing vain religious practices. If it leads to bearing a son, he will be the child of adultery. In general hell in a dream means excessive sexual desires, a slaughter house, a public bath, an oven, inventing a new religion, innovation, absence of truth, indulgence in what is forbidden, stinginess, denying the Day of Judgment, a blazing fire for the devils, joining with a group of evildoers in committing atrocities, denying the sovereignty of God Almighty and ascribing human characteristics to Him. Seeing Mālik, the guardian angel of hell-fire in a dream means receiving guidance after heedlessness. If one sees Mālik coming toward him in the dream, it means his salvation and the restoration of his faith. However, if one sees Mālik turning his back to him or going away from him in the dream, it means that he will commit an act that will deliver him to the blazing fire of hell. The angels in charge of punishing the sinners in hell in a dream represent the authority, soldiers, or tax collectors. If one enters hell-fire then comes out of it in his dream, it means that, God willing, his life will culminate in paradise. If he sees his limbs reprimanding him in the dream, it means that one's own body is telling him something, or admonishing and trying to awaken his conscious to the realities of the hereafter and the Day of Reckoninh. *(Also see Bathhouse; Fire; Mālik; Mental hospital)*

Hell: *(arb.; Jahannam. See Hell-fire; Mālik; Mental hospital)*

Helm: (Tiller; Wheel) In a dream, the helm or the tiller of a boat represent true knowledge, the seat of authority, solid credentials and a reliable reference. *(Also see Boat; Ship)*

Helmet: (Crash helmet; Face mask; Hard hat; Warrior's helmet) In a dream, a helmet means safety, money, a wife, employment, travel, or one's head. A white helmet in a dream means relaxing, or peace in one's life, or it could mean recovering from a migraine headache. Wearing a warrior's helmet in a dream also means safety of one's property and protection from an accident. Wearing a rounded expensive helmet in a dream means betrothing a beautiful and a rich woman. A helmet made of iron in a dream represents a leader who defends people, or it could mean trust, status, rank, a wife, or might. Wearing a white helmet in a dream means honor and protection of one's property.

Help: (Honor) To help or honor poor people in a dream, or to give their needs preference over one's own means rising in station or rank, though working under higher authorities.

Helper: *(See Backbone; Escort)*

Hemming: *(See Alterations)*

Hemorrhaging: *(See Glass bottle)*

Hemp: *(See Intoxicants; Marijuana)*

Henna: (Dye; A reddish-orange cosmetic dye produced from the stalks and leaves of henna plant) Henna for a man represents his working tools. It also means adornment, money, prosperity, or children. If a man sees his hands dyed with henna in a dream, it means that he keeps praising his Lord. If only the right hand is dyed with henna but looks ugly in the dream, it means that he may commit a murder. Dying one's hands with henna in a dream also means carelessness about exposing one's good and bad qualities in public, or it could mean that he delivers his merchandise or work in any condition without acknowledging blame, fault, or recognizing his improper behavior with his customers. If one's hands are tattooed with henna in a dream, it means that he cheats to acquire his earnings. Eventually, he will be exposed and his opponents will rejoice at his misfortune. If a woman sees her entire body dyed with henna in a dream, it means having a good relationship with her husband. If after applying the henna to her hands, the dye does not work in a dream, it means that her husband does not show his love for her. If only the fingers are dyed with henna in a dream, they then represent branches of dates, or clusters of grapes. In general, dyeing one's hands and hair with henna as a makeup in a dream represents joy for the husband and wife as long as they do not exceed the common norms. *(Also see Dye; Tattoo)*

Herald: (Harbinger; Messenger) In a dream, a herald represents an escort, a station master, or a broadcaster.

Herbal medicine: *(See Ivy; Solomon)*

Herbs: *(See Antidote; Caraway; Garden herbs; Onion. Also see other herbs)*

Herder: In a dream, a herder represents a guardian.

Hereafter: *(See Entering Paradise)*

Hermaphrodite: *(See Hyena)*

Hermitage: (Retreat; Sanctuary) A hermitage in a dream represents a spiritual retreat, abstinence, good character, seclusion, ascetic detachment, controlling one's desires and wants, divorcing one's wife, abandoning one's friends, or it could mean an illness. If a sick person sees himself in a hermitage in a dream, it may mean his death, or it could mean suppressing one's sexual desires. Occupying a hermitage or building one in a dream means rising in station. A beautiful and a newly built hermitage in the dream represents a wife. A hermitage in a dream also could mean migration, bewilderment, severing a friendship, hiding, power, or it could represent one's son. Whatever may affect a hermitage in the dream also could manifest in the life of one's son. *(Also see Retreat; Temple)*

Herpes: (Fungus; Ringworm; Tetter) Suffering from herpes, or ringworm, or tetter in a dream means stinginess, or having resources to repay one's debts and concealing such knowledge from the lenders and being afraid of their asking for their money.

Hiccup: (Spasmodic inhalation) Hiccups in a dream mean anger, interference in people's business, or falling sick. As for a sick person, a hiccup in a dream means death, while for anyone else, it represents money.

Hickory: *(See Tree; Walnut)*

Hidden goodness: (Herbal medicine; Medicinal plant; Wild plants)

Hidden road: *(See Road)*

Hidden treasure: (Boy; Enemy; Power; Snake; Troves; Unjust ruler; Woman) If the treasure one discovers in his dream is hidden by a previous generation, it means receiving an inheritance, lawful earnings, a booty, a son from adultery, or it could represent an orphan because it comes from someone else's earnings.

Hide: *(See Concealment; Dye; Irreligious)*

High prices: (Cost of living) Seeing a winged loaf of bread flying in a dream means high prices. *(Also see Bread)*

High tides: (Ocean) In a dream, swimming in troubled waters or high tides means adversities, or having to face a strong opponent.

Highway: *(See Wandering)*

Hiking: *(See Naturalist)*

Hilarity: *(See Laughter; Menstrual period; Mirth)*

Hill: (Elevation) In a dream, a hill represents a powerful and a dangerous person. Any construction surrounding such a hill represents one's wealth. If one sees a flat land adjacent to a discarded high ground or a hill in a dream, such a hill represents a rich man whose wealth compares to the size of the surrounding property. A valley of green pasture surrounding a hill in the dream represents his strength, justice in method of dealing with others, or it could mean religious devotion. Following that line of thoughts, it also means rising in rank at the hand of a powerful person. Crossing hills in a dream means escaping from danger. Standing on top of a hill in a dream means presiding over a religious person. Descending a hill or an elevation in a dream represents losses, migraine headache, or humiliation. Imprisonment on the top of a hill in a dream means a high ranking job. If the elevation is made of trash in a dream, it means worldly and material status. An elevation in a dream also represents one's wife.

Hind: *(See Deer; Gazelle)*

Hindering: Hindering someone's work in a dream means ingratitude or disbelief.

Hindu: *(See Language)*

Hirsute: *(See Down)*

Hissing: *(See Sound of animals)*

Hitching: *(See Limping)*

Hitting: *(See Beating)*

Hives: (Allergic disorder; Rash; Urticaria) A blood disease that manifests through breaking out of the skin with red spots. If seen in a dream, it means fast richness, money spent in celebrating a wedding, the outrage of injustice, or expediting a punishment.

Hobo: (Bummer; Cadger; Homeless; Tramp; Wastrel) A hobo wandering in the streets, collecting refuse and litters from garbage cans and rubbish in a dream represents someone who accumulates both lawful and unlawful earnings, or someone who divulges or exposes people's secrets, or launders their private lives, or someone who does not mind his own business and asks questions that are of no concern to him. *(Also see Beggar; Poverty)*

Hodgepodge: *(See Magpie)*

Hodman: *(See Mortar carrier)*

Hog-like wolf: *(See Hyena)*

Hold: *(See Gripping; Hug)*

Hole: (Deception; Plot; Profits; Fall) Digging a hole, a water well, or an irrigation and planning to water the plants with them in a dream means attending one's needs and serving the interests of his family. Eating from the dirt one piles from digging in his dream represents a swagger, or someone who acquires money through deception. Seeing oneself inside a hole in a dream also means divorce. To see oneself outside of such a hole looking at it in a dream means having an argument with one's spouse that will end in reconciliation. If a sick person or a prisoner sees himself coming out of a hole in a dream, it means that he will become free from his trials. Falling into a hole and crying for help to no avail in a dream means taking a short trip. A hole in a dream also represents a poor woman who strives to cover others pitfalls, though she cannot veil her own. Hiding inside a hole in a dream also means appeasement of one's fears, or ending of one's adversities. If while hiding, one finds food, or fresh water, or a cloth to cover himself in the dream, it means profiting from sources one does not anticipate, or making peace with an opponent. To put a hole in one's shoe in a dream means facing trouble and adversities. *(Also see Den; Mouse hole; Tunnel)*

Holy Book: (Qur'ān; The Last Revelation) In a dream, the Holy Book, or the Qur'ān represents a king or a judge who deals with Islāmic jurisprudence. If a king, a ruler, or a judge sees that the Holy Book does no longer exist, or if he sees it burning, or if its contents are washed away in a dream, it means his death. If one sees a ruler or a governor handwriting a copy of the Holy Book in a dream, it means that he is a just person who uses the divine laws in making his decision. If a judge sees himself handwriting a copy of the Holy Book in a dream, it means that he does not share his knowledge, and that he is audacious about his rank and status. If a religious scholar or a theologian sees himself writing a copy of Holy Book in a dream, it means that he will profit from a business deal. If one sees a king, or a ruler swallowing the Holy Book in a dream, it means that he may die soon. If a judge swallows the Holy Book in a dream, it means that he accepts bribes. If a ruler sees himself erasing what is written in the Holy Book in a dream, it means that he will be exiled. If a judge erases what is written in the Holy Book in a dream, it also means his death. If he erases it by licking it with his own tongue in a dream, it means that he will commit an awful sin. If a witness erases it in a dream, it means that he will deny his own testimony. Carrying the Holy Book, or buying a copy of the Qur'ān in a dream means living by its criterion. Reading from the Holy Book before God's Prophet, upon whom be peace, in a dream means that one will commit himself to memorizing it. Eating the pages of the Holy Book in a dream means accepting bribes. If a layman eats the pages of the Holy Book, or few lines from some pages in a dream, it means that he earns his livelihood from reciting the Holy Qur'ān or teaching it. Eating the pages of the Holy Book in a dream also means earning one's livelihood from copying and selling it. Seeing the Holy Book in a dream also mans growing in wisdom. Handwriting copies of the Holy Book in a dream denotes one's piety, or it could represent a religious scholar who lives by the book, act by its commands and shares his knowledge with others. Tearing off the pages of the Holy Book in a dream means ingratitude toward God's revelations, or denying God's favors, or questioning some of them. If one does something to the Holy Book in his dream that he would abhor to do in wakefulness, it means that he has lost his religious devotion and faith. Carrying a copy of the Holy Book in a dream means attaining power and acquiring knowledge. The Holy Book in a dream also represents a husband, a wife, a son, or wealth. If a sick person sees it in his dream, it means that he will recover from his illness. If the one who sees it in his dream is facing an enemy, it means that he will triumph over him. If he is a sinner, it means that he will repent of his sins and turn to his Lord, or it could mean that he may receive an inheritance. If one sees himself following innovations and he recognizes that in his sleep, his dream denotes a warning from God Almighty. Seeing the Holy Book in a dream also could mean seeing wonders, witnessing a miracle, hearing news, receiving happy news, or it could mean longevity for one who browse through it from cover to cover in his dream. The Holy Book in a dream also represents gardens, heavens, places of worship, or a person one is commanded to obey, such as a ruler, or a father, a mother, one's teacher, or shaikh, or it could mean making a true oath, receiving glad tidings, admonition or a warning. Seeing the Holy Book or any of the early divine revelations in a dream means that one may preside over people. If one sees himself carrying the Holy Book, or even any book of revelations, and if when he opens it finds the pages blank with no writing inside it in the dream, it means that he portrays himself to be what he is not, or that he impersonates a scholar, or pretends to be religious. Kissing the Holy Book in a dream means revering what it contains and adhering to what it commands. If one looks into the pages of the Holy Book and finds its lines crooked in a dream, it means that he lives satisfied with what he has, and fulfills his required duties accordingly. Stealing a copy of the Holy Book and hiding it in a dream means that one cheats in performing his own prayers, or fails to do them properly. If one sees himself looking in the Holy Book, then writing from what he is reading on his own garment in the dream, it means that he interprets the Qur'ânic revelation according to his own liking. If one sees a Holy Book sitting in his lap, then if a chick comes and picks all the words written therein in a dream, it means that one will beget a child who will memorize and read the Holy Qur'ân as an inheritance, and benefit from the piety of his father, and as a trust, a lawful earning and a source of strength in his life. Buying a copy of the Holy Book in dream means benefits, prosperity and becoming a renowned and a distinguished religious scholar. If the Holy Book is snatched away from someone's hands in a dream, it means that he will lose his knowledge, or perhaps lose his employment. If one sees himself spreading the pages of the Holy Book on a flat surface in a dream, it means that he is seeking wisdom which he will get, or that he may receive an inheritance. If one sees himself putting the Holy Book over his shoulders in a dream, it means that he will receive an appointment, or be entrusted with a duty to guard, or that he will memorize the Holy Qur'ân. If one finds himself trying to eat the pages of the Holy Book in a dream, it means that he is a regular reader of the Qur'ân. If one sees himself trying to eat the pages of the holy Book but is unable to do so in a dream, it means that he tries to memorize the Holy Qur'ân from time to time but keeps forgetting what he learns. *(Also see Qur'ân)*

Holy Ka'aba: *(See Ka'aba; Mecca)*

Holy Mecca: *(See Ka'aba; Mecca)*

Homage: *(See Pledge of allegiance)*

Home coming: *(See Arrival)*

Homeland: To feel a yearning or desire to see one's homeland in a dream means divorce between a husband and a wife, or separation between friends, or experiencing richness after poverty. Such a yearning in a dream also connotes evil if accompanied with crying or lamenting.

Homeless: *(See Hobo; Poverty; Stableman)*

Homosexuality: *(See Pederasty; Sexual intercourse; Sodomy)*

Hone: (Grindstone; Razor strop) In a dream, a hone, or a razor strop represents guidance, forthrightness and knowledge. A hone in a dream also means incitement or promoting an activity, or encouragement to continue one's course of actions. A hone in a dream is also interpreted to represent a woman, or someone who causes division between a husband and a wife, or between friends and beloveds. A hone in a dream also signifies tribadism, or lesbianism when in use in one's dream. In a dream, a hone also signifies movement, activities, sharpness and good nature.

Honesty: *(See Justice)*

Honey: (Love) In a dream, honey represents lawful money, love, prosperity, or wealth which is accumulated from a business partnership, or from a successful business. As for a pious person, honey in a dream represents the delight of his religious life and good deeds, while for profane and worldly people, it means little earnings which are acquired through toiling and hardships. If one sees the skies raining honey in a dream, it means confirmation of the social order, fostering proper moral standards, easiness, religious assiduity, blessings and plenitude. Honey in a dream also could represent a husband and a wife, or their private moment, taking a rest, or engaging in a marital relationship. However, honey in a dream also means distress, trouble, bad-temper, jealousy, or worrying about people's perfidy, for honey also attracts flies and wasps. Purified honey in a dream means relief after suffering from a depression, or recovering from a nervous breakdown, or giving birth to a child after completing a full pregnancy, or it could mean marrying a woman after she had observed her Iddah of either the passing of her husband or divorce *(See Iddah)*, or it could represent clean money, or earnings which are purified through paying the due alms and charities, or it could mean knowledge that is free from innovation, doubt or suspicion, or a final guidance after which there is no heedlessness. Purified honey in a dream also means hard earned money, a medicine, or the embrace and kisses of lovers. Licking honey in a dream means getting married. Eating bread and butter with honey in a dream means living a rich life. *(Also see Lick; Love)*

Honeycomb: In a dream, a honeycomb represents an inheritance of a lawfully earned money, or money from a business partnership, or profits in general as long as the fire does not touch it. If a honeycomb is placed before someone in a dream, it means that he has knowledge which he wants people to hear about or to learn. If the honeycomb is placed as if on a table in the dream, it means a booty, or blessed earnings. If it is placed in a bowl in the dream, it means lawful profits. If one sees himself feeding it to the people in the dream, it means that he will chant the Qur'ān with embellishment and awaits people's praises and request to encore his recital. Eating from a honeycomb with honey still in it in a dream means having sexual intercourse with one's own mother. Eating a honeycomb in a dream also could mean martyrdom, or mixing between diversified interests. Purified honey in a dream means good deeds, lawful earnings, displeasing one's parents, recovering from an illness, or testifying in a court of justice. *(Also see Honey)*

Honor: (Laurel) To honor someone in a dream means rising in rank. *(Also see Help; Laurel)*

Hooded crow: *(See Crow)*

Hoof[1]: (Slippers) In a dream, an animal's hoof, or an ostrich's hoof means strength or travels. It also means to wend one's way and prepare for the better. *(Also see Slippers)*

Hoof[2]: (Cattle; Horse) In a dream, a hoof represents knowledge and pursuing its references or tracks. It also represents wealth when the hoofs are those of the kings' horse or of his messenger's horse. Hoofs in a dream also imply making a compulsory move from one location to another. Hoofs in a dream also mean guidance for a lost soul. Hearing the sound of hoofs running through the streets in his dream means rain or floods.

Hoofer: *(See Dancer)*

Hoopoe: (*zool.*) In a dream, a hoopoe represents a truthful messenger, an intimate person, a spy, an arguing scholar, escape from adversities and sufferings, or leveling a building. A hoopoe in a dream also represents one who knows God Almighty and understands the value of the Divine Laws. If a thirsty person sees a hoopoe in his dream, it means that he will find water. A hoopoe in a dream also represents a great scholar who is constantly barraged with accusations and blame because of the bird's offensive smell. Seeing a hoopoe in a dream also means profits, honor and wealth. Eating a hoopoe in a dream means receiving news from the governor, or hosting a traveller. A hoopoe in a dream also represents the king's advisor, the court's seer, an astrologer, a writer, a scribe, or a critic. Holding a hoopoe in one's hand in a dream means glad tidings, or profits from a business in another market or town. Owning a hoopoe in a dream means having influence over someone in authority, or it could represent a writer, or a perspicacious person but who has no religious commitment. Slaughtering a hoopoe in a dream means getting hold of such person. Owning a female hoopoe in a dream means getting married. Slaughtering a female hoopoe in a dream means deflowering a young girl.

Hop: *(See Jumping)*

Horizontal wound: In a dream, a horizontal wound means enmity, backbiting and slander.

Horn: (Distinguished) In a dream, a horn means strength and invincibility. Having a horn in a dream means conquering one's enemy. If one sees a ruler having two horns in a dream, it means that such a ruler will control interests throughout the East and the West. A horn in a dream also represents a relative from whom one can draw benefits. If one grows two animal horns in a dream, it means that he will die from grief and coercion. A horn in a dream also represents a century, years, weapons, money, children, or the reason behind one's pride or his distinguished look. *(Also see Trumpet)*

Hornet: A hornet in a dream represents a fighting enemy, a builder, an architect, a thief, a highway robber, a despicable person whose earnings are unlawful, a singer who sings in the wrong key, eating poisonous food, or disclosing something. A hornet in a dream also represents a slanderer, a troublemaker, a strong fighter, a strong enemy that will argue against the truth, or merciless people, a vile person, a blood thirsty person, a stinging personality, or a harmful connection. Fighting attacking hornets in a dream means a war with evil people.

Horoscope: (Stars. *See Moon*)

Horse fright: Shying, as in a horse fright, in a dream means hastening to undertake a journey, moving quickly from one place to another, or substituting one school of thought for another, adopting a new ideology, or changing one's religion. *(Also see Horse)*

Horse litter: *(See Palanquin)*

Horse race: *(See Racing)*

Horse: (Castle; Chivalry; Generosity; Goodness; Merchant; Nobility; Partner; Son; Travels; Wife) Owning horses in a dream means prosperity, or victory over one's enemy. Riding a horse in a dream means dignity, honor and wealth. Perhaps it could mean that one will befriend a noble person, or meet a good companion on the road. Owning a mare in a dream means begetting a beautiful son. If it is a nag or a workhorse in the dream, it means that he will live satisfied, or that he may marry a rich and a noble woman who will bear his children. Seeing a horse in a dream also may connote owning a good house. If it is a blond horse in the dream, it means knowledge, devotion, piety and fear of wrongdoing. A nag in a dream represents a wife or a husband. A saddled horse in a dream means a woman in her menstrual period, during which time it is not permissible for the husband to engage in marital intercourse with her. A gathering of horses in a dream represents a gathering of women for a funeral or a wedding. Owning a herd of horses, or taking care of their feed in a dream means presiding over people, or it could mean managing a business. If a horse dies in one's presence in a dream, it means loss of his house or business. The fit of a horse in the dream represent man's own state. Descending from a horse in a dream means committing a sin that will force one to resign from his position, or be dismissed from his work. A hairy horse in a dream represents a large family. If the tail of one's horse is cut off at its end in a dream, it means that one may come to see the death of his children and clan before his own eyes. If the tail of one's horse is simply clipped in the dream, it connotes his own death and that his name will be quickly forgotten. If one is attacked by a horse in a dream, it means that a noble person, or a young boy will stand to him and require a just retribution from him. A flying horse with two wings in a dream means that one may be tried with affections toward a perverted boy or a woman who will tempt him then follow him. If a descendent of the family of God's Prophet, upon whom be peace, sees himself flying on a winged horse in a dream, it means that he will rise in station and preside over people. If one sees horsemen coming through the skies in a dream, it means that a war may take place in that land. Riding a horse and holding a spear in one's hand in a dream means forcing people to do something, or forcing them to pay what they owe. If one sees his horse drowning in a dream, it means that he may die from an illness. Buying a horse and tending the money to the seller in the dream means profits in one's business, or earning money from teaching. Selling one's horse in a dream means doing good and being grateful for it. If one's horse bites him in a dream, it means that he will lead an army in a war. If one kills a horse in his dream, it means that he will be awarded status, rank and money. Slaughtering a horse for other than food in a dream means spoiling one's livelihood. If one sees a horse whose owner is not known entering a town in a dream, it means that a noble person will enter that town and people of his trade will fear his competition or his becoming a danger to their business. If such a horse reverts his course and leaves that town in the dream, it means that a great, though unknown person from that locality will die shortly. Horses running across the streets in a dream represent a destructive rain or devastating floods. A feeble horse in a dream represents the weakness of his owner. *(Also see Dung; Horse fright; Nag)*

Horseman: To see a horseman leading a procession, a caravan, or a group of travellers in a dream means going on a distant journey, recovering from an illness, or it could mean business activity. *(Also see Ride)*

Hose: *(See Watering hose)*

Hospitality: (Dinner; Food) In a dream, hospitality means getting together for a charitable cause or to perform good deeds. If one invites people for a dinner and they eat to full satisfaction in the dream, it means that he will preside over them. Preparing a guest room in one's house in a dream means the arrival of a long awaited traveller. *(Also see Food; Guest; Invitation; Table)*

Hostage: (Pawn; Deposit) If one sees himself as a hostage in a dream, it means that he has earned himself an accumulation of sins that made him a pawn for repayment of his debts. If one sees himself holding someone as a guarantee for a promise, or keeping him as a pawn until his demands are met in a dream, it means that he is veering toward injustice. A hostage in a dream also represents mistakes, errors, exposing people's private life, divulging people's secrets, slander, or a debt that keeps the person subject to constant harassment. Being a hostage in a dream also means adversities, trials, or falling in love with someone, whereby, one's heart becomes a hostage of his beloved. *(Also see Enemy; Enmity)*

Hostel: (Inn; Hotel; Lodge; Pub) In a dream, a hostel represents fornication, adultery, temporary marriage for pleasure, renting a space, renting tools or machinery, leasing an area for storage, or renting a garment. If a sick person rents a room in a hostel or an inn on the highway in a dream, it means his death, or it could mean that he will recover from an illness, or dispel anxiety, or take residence in a new country, or it could mean marriage after being single for a long time, or buying a vehicle, finding a money pouch, or something one can sell to help him during his financial crises. A married person resting in a hostel in a dream means that he will beget a son who when he grows will help his father in his trade and bring him happiness and comfort. If one's child is disobedient, or recalcitrant, it means that he will repent and come back to live under his father or mother. If a heedless person sees a hostel in a dream, it means that he will find guidance and return to walk on God's path. *(Also see Hotel)*

Hot water: Washing one's dirt with hot water in a dream means benefits. Drinking hot water from the boiler in a dream means sickness, stress, depression, or a scare by evil spirits. *(Also see Bathhouse; Drink; Hot)*

Hot: (Bathhouse; Boiling water; Hot pepper; Pungent) Eating hot food, or drinking a hot drink in a dream may represent arduous earnings, or abundance that becomes a burden. It may also represent unlawful earnings, illegal profits, losses, or losing any blessing which maybe contained in one's deeds. Washing a deceased person with boiling water in a dream means that he is destined for hell-fire.

Hotbed: *(See House garden; Nursery)*

Hotel: (Hostel; Inn; Travelling to a foreign country) A hotel in a dream represents one's house, body, name, property, glory, bathhouse, oven, or a court of justice. Whatever may happen to him in that dream could take place in conjunction to any of the above elements and in relationship to his condition. Staying overnight in an unknown hotel in a dream means travel, or it may indicate the abode of this world from which one travels to reach the abode of the hereafter. *(Also see Hostel; Travel)*

Hourglass: (Sandglass) In a dream, the two bulbs of a sandglass represent two sons, or two brothers, or two partners. Whatever happens to them in the dream will reflect in such people. An hourglass in a dream also means makeup, beauty, or marriage. The sand trickling from the upper bulb into the lower bulb in a dream represents man's semen.

House garden: In a dream, a house garden means protection of women's chastity, the honor of men's abstinence, denial of suspicion regarding the lawfulness of one's earnings, or protection of children's innocence. A private garden in a dream may mean stinginess, or refusing to satisfy the needs of someone who asks for help, whether his needs are financial or relating to acquiring knowledge. A house garden in a dream also represents one's private devotion, fasting, asceticism, piety, fear of wrongdoing, celebrating God's praises and exalting His holiness. A house garden in a dream also could mean a marriage within the family, insanity on the part of that house dwellers, paying a financial penalty, or it could mean an imposition. *(Also see Garden; Nursery)*

House: (Cage; Dwellings) In a dream, one's house holds different meanings. One of them is the wife. If one sees himself entering his house in a dream, it means that he will get married, or have sexual intercourse with his wife. Building one's own house in a dream means that a sick person will recover from his illness. If such construction is hard and if it is customary in that family to bury its dead within the compound of the same property, then it means the death of a sick person in the family. If no one is sick in that house and the construction is accompanied with music and celebrations in the dream, then it means adversities, trials and hardships. If under such circumstance the person in the dream is unmarried, it means marriage, and if he is married, it means that he will marry off one of his daughters. If one sees himself tied up and imprisoned inside a house in a dream, it means that he will receive glad tidings, or it could mean good health and prosperity. If one sees himself carrying a house over his shoulders in a dream, it means that he takes care of a needy woman or a wife. If one sees his house made of gold in a dream, it means that a fire will burn it down. If the house has no roof, whereby one can see the skies, sun or moon in a dream, it represents the marriage of a woman from that household. If one sees a big house within his own house in a dream, it means that a righteous woman will live their or move into that family to become a blessing for such a house. If there is a tunnel under such a house in the dream, it denotes deception or that a perfidious person is having access to that household. A house without lights in a dream represents a woman of evil character, and if a woman sees that house in her dream, then it represents a man of evil character. Demolishing one's house in a dream means a fight within that family. If one sees grass growing inside his house in a dream, it means a wedding. *(Also see Cage; Dwellings; Glass house)*

Household: *(See Dependents)*

Housekeeper: *(See Lantern; Wick)*

Hubbub: In a dream, hubbub means witnessing social disorder, a public outcry, participating in a religious festival, or joining an important event that involves the interest of all people. *(Also see Shout)*

Hüd: (God's prophet Hüd, upon whom be peace, who was sent to the people of the king 'Ãd.) If one sees God's prophet Hüd in a dream, it means that he will suffer harm from ignoble and ignorant people, then he will escape from a great distress, and be saved from their evil. Seeing God's prophet Hüd (uwbp) in a dream also means that one will receive guidance, blessings and be able to save others from plagues and destruction.

Hug: (Cuddle; Embrace; Hold) To embrace a living person in a dream means to associate with him and to love him. To give a deceased person a short hug in a dream means longevity. To give a deceased person a long and a continuous embrace in a dream means one's own death. To embrace a woman in a dream means embracing the pleasures and attractions of this world and to despair of any reward in the hereafter. To hold tight to a piece of fruit, or to endear certain food one loves in a dream means easy profits or lawful earnings. If an unmarried person holds tight or embraces a garment in a dream, it means that he will get married. If one hugs a pair of shoes in a dream, it means that he will hold a new position or a job that will make him extremely happy. *(Also see Embrace; Grabbing; Gripping; Sexual intercourse)*

Hulk: *(See Giant)*

Human being: To see one of the children of Adam (uwbp) one does not recognize in the dream perhaps may represents oneself. If he does good, then it represents one's own deeds, and if does evil, the seer may pursue the same. If one recognizes such a being in the dream, it means that he will receive something from him. If one likes what he receives from him in the dream, it means that he will attain his personal goals. If he receives a shirt in the dream, it means an appointment to a high ranking position. If he receives a rope in the dream, it means an agreement, a commitment or a covenant. If he takes money from him in the dream, it represents something he will lose and forgo in despair, or perhaps that a fight will take place between them. Each human being in a dream represents himself, his kind, look alike, someone by the same name, his town, or his craft. If the person whom he recognizes in the dream holds an elevated rank, it means that he will lose it, and if he holds a lower rank, it means that he will be promoted. *(Also see Man; Mankind)*

Human body: *(See Body¹)*

Human brain: *(See Body¹; Brain)*

Human call: *(See Shout; Voice)*

Human cry: *(See Shout; Voice)*

Human flesh: *(See Flesh)*

Human rights: *(See Destruction)*

Human voice: (Human sound. *See Voice*)

Humiliation: To see oneself humiliated in a dream means that one will triumph and rise in station. However, humiliation in a dream also may mean poverty, frugality, lack of spiritual depth or religious attendance. Suffering from humiliation in a dream also means earning a rank of honor. *(Also see Meekness)*

Humorist: (Comedian; Storyteller) In a dream, a humorist represents frivolity, prankishness, satire, falsehood, deceit, or sarcasm. *(Also see Comedian)*

Hump: A hump in a dream represents a condition that will make one a celebrity, or it could represent a debt one is unable to pay. This is because one's back is the point that carries his burdens. A hump in a dream also may be interpreted as a burden, longevity, or bearing children. *(Also see Hunchback)*

Hunchback: (Friend; Good luck; Money; Prosperity) A hunchbacked in a dream means prosperity, longevity, or having a large family. Seeing oneself in a dream as a hunchback means acquiring wealth and a large property through an influential person in one's family or a son. One who sees that in a dream will also be gifted with vigilance and astuteness. *(Also see Back; Body¹; Hump)*

Hunger: In a dream, hunger means wearing the garments of mourning, being seized by fear, or tightening one's fist. Hunger in a dream also represents financial losses, eagerness to maintain a certain level of standards, persistence in seeking one's livelihood or pursuing one's trade, or love for the world. Some dream interpreters prefer hunger over satiation and thist over thirst-quenching in a dream. If one sees himself hungry during the winter season in a dream, it means that he will be tried with gluttony. If one's hunger lasts long in the dream, it means that he will receive benefits after a long wait. Hunger in a dream is also considered to mean money, bad company, jesting, asceticism, fasting, inflation, deprivation, poverty and perhaps sometimes it may mean piety and fear of wrongdoing, or remembering and thanking God Almighty.

Hunt: (Food) In a dream, a hunt represents a booty or profits. If one hunts a deer or a rabbit in his dream, it means money and profits. If one hunts for sport in the dream, it means backbiting or slandering a woman. If one sees himself hunting with hunting dogs in a dream, it means that he will fulfill a long desired wish. If one sees dogs going to hunt in a dream, it means good news for everyone, or it could mean engaging in an act, or establishing a business. If he sees the dogs returning from the hunt in a dream, it means dispelling fears, or shortage of work. If one sees himself fishing with a fishing instrument in a dream, it means making an honest living, or seeking lawful earnings. Hunting in a dream represents one's diligence and determination to succeed in his life, and to earn his livelihood with his own sweat. If one happens to be unmarried, then hunting in a dream means that he will get married. If one is married, it means that he will beget a son. If a woman sees herself hunting in a dream, it means that she has control over her husband's money, her father's assets, or it could mean that she will receive an inheritance or control vast interests in a business. Hunting small preys in a dream represents knowledge, a trade, or an inheritance. *(Also see Dog; Hunter)*

Hunter's snare: *(See Trap)*

Hunter: In a dream, a hunter represents a philanderer, a womanizer who rounds women, or a pimp. If one sees himself befriending a hunter, or if he helps him, and if the hunter is pursuing what is lawful to kill for food, one's dream then connotes personal advantages. If the hunt is after an animal which is unlawful for food, then the dream means sufferings. Hunting a lion in a dream means acquiring great power through deception. Hunting sparrows, hawks, or falcons in a dream also means gaining power. Hunting birds or pigeons in a dream represents a tricky merchant. Hunting beasts in a dream means cheating travellers. Fishing means womanizing. A beast hunter in a dream represents someone who takes advantage of foreigners. A bird hunter in a dream also represents a school teacher, a music teacher, or a preacher. *(Also see Beast; Dog; Hunt)*

Hunting dog: (Lust; Desire; Want. *See Dog)*

Hunting: *(See Dog; Hunter; Shooting)*

Hurl: *(See Thrust)*

Hurricane: *(See Collapsing walls; Destruction; Wind)*

Hurry: (Celerity; Haste; Hastiness; Quick pace) Walking with dispatch, or with a quick pace in Mecca or in any town in a dream means victory over one's enemy. Celerity in a dream also represents haste, or the dispatch through which one leaves this world. Moving with a quick pace in a dream also means loss of one's position, or it could mean attending the pilgrimage season in Mecca. *(Also see Hastiness)*

Hurt: *(See Pain)*

Husk: *(See Shell)*

Hyacinth: (Bulbs; Gem; Sapphire) These bulbous and bell-shaped flowers in a dream differ in meaning depending on their type, shape and fragrance. If one smells a hyacinth flower in a dream, it means relief from sorrow, end of adversities, good deeds, or making a true promise. If one sees a deceased person carrying such a flower, or offering him a hyacinth flower to smell in a dream, it means that the deceased person is dwelling in paradise. If an unwed person sees a hyacinth flower in his dream, it means that he will get married. If a married person sees a hyacinth flower in his dream, it means that he will beget a son, or he may acquire knowledge, or specialize in a scientific project that will add to his pride. Perhaps, a fragrant hyacinth in a dream could mean distur-bances, distress, or a sickness. It is said that any flower from the lily family may represent death when presented to a sick person in a dream. A healthy hyacinth plant in the ground means a beautiful son, or good words. A garland of hyacinth flowers in a dream means honor. A hyacinth flower salesman in a dream represents a worrisome person, for such flowers do not remain long in his possession. If any of the flowers of the lily family are cut, or made into a bouquet in the dream, then they mean sorrow, and if they are seen on their mother plant, they mean happiness, a husband or a son. If one sees a hyacinth flower being raised to the heavens in a dream, it means the death of a gnostic or that of a renowned scholar. A hyacinth in a dream also represents a son when standing erect in the fields, and it represents a woman when gathered as a bouquet of flowers, while it means a calamity if seen cut and placed inside a flower pot, a vase, or in an inappropriate place. A hyacinth flower in a dream also represents a beautiful woman or blessings, its fragrance represents one's love for his wife, and its tenderness represents one's concern and support for his family. Seeing branches of hyacinth spread inside a house in a dream means lauding or commending someone. If one is offered a hyacinth flower but find that it carries no fragrance in the dream, it means an adversity. If one throws a hyacinth flower to another person in a dream, it means that the receiver will experience sorrow at his hand and that their friendship will be hampered. If one sees another person sitting inside a mosque and surrounded with hyacinth in a dream, it means that the other person is backbiting him though what he is saying is not true. *(Also see Lily of the valley; Water lily; Stone²)*

Hyena: (Hog-like wolf) A hyena in a dream represents a fierce, an unjust and a perfidious enemy whose actions stem from the directives of an evil and an ugly old witch. If one sees himself eating the meat of a hyena in a dream, it means that he is bewitched and does not know it, though subconsciously, he will desire and seek to be free from such an evil spell. Riding a hyena in a dream means marriage. A lame hyena in a dream represents a witch, or the wife of an unknown person, a jobless person, a loafer, or a cheater. Riding a hyena in a dream also means gaining authority. A hyena in a dream also may denote exposing one's secrets, interfering in people's business, effeminacy, a hermaphroditic person, a wretched wife, or an ugly, treacherous and a disloyal woman. Thus, when interpreted to means a woman, it means that one may marry such a woman. Shooting a hyena with an arrow in a dream means corresponding with such a woman. Throwing a stone or a walnut at a hyena in a dream means slandering a woman. Hitting a hyena with a sword in a dream means lashing at such a woman with bad words. Drinking hyena's milk in a dream means suffering losses at the hand of such a woman through betrayal. Stabbing a hyena in a dream means doing business with such a woman, or managing her business, or getting married to someone in her family. Getting hold of the skin, bones, or hair of a hyena in a dream means taking advantage of such a woman and using her for her money. If it is a male hyena in the dream, then it represents a criminal and a despised person.

Hymn: *(See Zikr)*

Hypocrisy: (Lumber; Wood)

I

Ibex: *(See Mountain goat)*

Ice cream salesman: (Cooling) An ice cream salesman in a dream represents a hard working person who labors to provide comfort to others, whose efforts are praiseworthy, and whose earnings are blessed.

Ice: Buying a container of ice during a hot weather in a dream means profits that will bring financial stability to one's family, or hearing good news that will comfort and cool one's heart. Winter's ice in a dream means washing away one's difficulties and trouble. It also means forcing one's conditions upon his opponents. A snowstorm that culminates in icy roads, freezing and impeding the traffic in a dream means economic depression and slowing of the travel industry. Ice in a dream also represents men's endurance. Filling a pot of water to make ice in a dream means saving money, or locking a coffer.

Icy rain: *(See Hail)*

'Iddah: *(arb.* Mourning period. A prescribed waiting period of three month during which a divorced or a widowed woman may not remarry. *Islāmic Law)* If a woman sees herself in a dream observing the 'Iddah period, it signifies distress, adversities, trouble, concern, sickness, or divorce. If she is observing the 'Iddah period because of her husband's death in the dream, it means her divorce, or the death of her husband, mother, father, or anyone for whose sake one will renounce comfort, beautiful clothing, tasty food, the pleasures of this world and the company of others.

Idiot: *(See Tankard)*

Idle talk: *(See Moon)*

Idol: *(See Statue)*

Ignominy: *(See Clay)*

Ignorance: (Demanding person; Obtrusive person) It is common among the people of knowledge to describe an ignorant person as a stone. *(Also see Darkness)*

Illness: Having an illness in a dream represents a sickening character, or a hypocrite. Finding oneself ill in a dream means enjoying a good health for that year, or it could mean loss of devotion and lack of piety. If a warrior finds himself sick in a dream, it means that he will be wounded. If one sees his wife sick in a dream, it means that she is negligent of her religious obligations. If a sick person sees himself riding an ox, or a swine in a dream, it means his death. A feverish illness in a dream means pressure caused by a ruler. Feeling sick, or feeling down with an undiagnosed illness in a dream means spending money, or wasting it in ways other than on God's path. In a dream, illness mostly denotes religious disobedience and religious disdain. If one's sick child recovers from an illness in a dream, it means his death. If one sees the entire city suffering from an illness in a dream, it means a war, or a siege. If one sees himself ill in a dream, it also means victory over his enemy and enjoying a happy life. Otherwise, seeing anyone suffering from an illness in a dream means lack of work, and for a rich person it means becoming needy. If a business traveller sees himself ill and desiring something in his dream, it means that his business deal will not fall through, for physicians mostly do not grant their patients their wishes. If a bedridden person sees himself freeing a slave from bondage in a dream, it means his death, for a dead person has no property. Seeing a friend sick in a dream means that one will suffer from the same illness. Illness in a dream also signifies spending money, repentance, prayers, supplications, imploring, while falling in love in a dream means a sickness. Seeing two of one's children sick in a dream means that one may suffer from trachoma or ophthalmia, for one's eyes in a dream represent his children. Illness in a dream means that one has lost something to his adversary. Seeing one's father ill in a dream means having a migraine headache, for one's father in a dreams also represents his head. An illness in a dream also signifies falsehood and corruption. If one sees himself suffering from a terminal illness in a dream, it means that his sins will be forgiven, and he will die with God Almighty pleased with him. An illness in a dream also signifies a calamity, distress, fear of something, desiring something, or trouble. The illness of a woman in a dream represents her step daughters from her husband. Man's sickness in a dream also could signify abstaining from sexual course with his wife during her menstrual period. The illness of scholars means weakness in their religious adherence. The sickness of a ruler means religious failure, or that he may die in that same year. The illness of a teacher in a dream means separation from his students. The illness of a child in a dream means distress and worries for his parents. The death of a suffering old person, or someone with a terminal illness in a dream means relief. The death of an animal in a dream means lack of benefits. A plague in a dream means drought, or prosperity for physicians as well as for undertakers. Complaining about some pain in a dream means distress, unless if the one complaining in the dream is an opponent, then it means victory and joy for the person seeing the dream. *(Also see Thief)*

Illusion: *(See Magician; Magic arts; Rainbow)*

Illusionist: *(See Juggler)*

Illustrator: *(See Painter)*

Imām: *(arb.* The person who leads prayers in a mosque; Guide; Leader; Ruler) If one sees himself building a prison in a dream, it means that he will meet a righteous man or an Imâm who will guide him on the straight path. An Imâm in a dream also represents the spiritual leader of all Muslims. *(Also see Five times prayers; Pharaoh)*

Imitating: If a woman sees herself wearing men's clothing and imitating them in their look and actions in a dream, it means progress in her life if she is dressed handsomely, and it means digress and fear if not befitting. To dress oneself in a traditional costume of another religious group means to celebrate, befriend and to participate in their religious festivities.

Immolation: *(See Feast of Immolation; Manumission; Offering; Sacrifice; Slave)*

Immoral: *(See Profligacy)*

Impacting: *(See Smashing)*

Impartiality: *(See Justice)*

Impel: To impel one's animal to drive faster in a dream means heeding admonition.

Impetuousness: *(See Driver)*

Imposing structure: *(See Monument)*

Imposition: (Saddling)

Impotence: (Infertile; Sterile) Impotence in a dream means protection from sin, asceticism, abstinence and renouncing the pleasures of this world. If one sees himself castrated in a dream, it means that he will gain power and fame. If one marries a woman and finds himself incapable of performing sexual intercourse with her in a dream, it means that he will engage in a commerce without a capital.

Imprecation: *(See Spit out)*

Impurity: (*arb.* Junub. A state of ritual impurity that inhibits performance of one's prayers. Feces; Semen; Urine) In a dream, to be in a state of ritual impurity means that one is avoiding to comply with fundamental religious obligations. According to Islamic traditions, one must have ablution even if when pursuing any of his daily interests. If one sees himself performing his prayers without the required ritual ablution in a dream, it means corruption in his religious practices, though it also could be interpreted as committing oneself to serve God's religion. Being in a state of ritual impurity in a dream also could mean confusion. If one sees himself in such a state and finds no water to perform his ablution in the dream, it means adversities and inability to sustain one's needs in this world, or to satisfy one's aspirations in the hereafter. Washing oneself or washing one's clothes of impurity in a dream means paying someone his due rights.

In-laws: (Adversities; Benefits; Brother in-law; Distress; Father-in-law; Mother-in-law; Profits; Son in-law; Stress) Having in-laws in a dream for someone who does not have in-laws means strength, peace and tranquility.

Inactive: *(See Log)*

Inattentiveness: (Absent-mindedness; Distraction) Inattentiveness in a dream represents worries and trouble, misplacing things, or it could mean heedlessness.

Incantation: *(See Amulet)*

Incense burning: *(See Aloe perfume; Civet; Incense; Frankincense; 'Ud)*

Incense: Perfuming oneself with sweet incense in a dream means having a good friendship. An incense burner or holder in a dream represents a certitude that is praiseworthy. Perfume in a dream basically means good, though to a bedridden person it means death. This category includes: amber, henna plant (*Lawsonia inermis, bot.*), or fumigating oneself with sweet incense, though there is a danger that could arise from the smoke in the dream. Perfuming oneself with amber in a dream means increase in earnings that will come through the labor of a rich person who is associated with the one seeing the dream. The seeds of any dark colored perfume such as carnation, clove, or their powder, etcetera, means receiving praises. The elements encompassed herein include: richness after poverty, knowledge after ignorance, peace with one's adversaries, bribery, divulging one's secrets, ingratiating oneself to a superior for personal gains, or adulation. Incense in a dream also represents the heat of one's love or passion. In a dream, perfuming oneself with incense also means using an amulet or a charm to repel jealousy, or to break through the stratagem of sorcery. Incense in a dream also means using charm to bring peace, tranquility and profits if one intends so in his dream. *(Also see Aloe perfume; Civet; Frankincense; 'Ud)*

Inch: *(See Measure)*

Incisors: *(See Tooth)*

Incite: (Entice; Induce; Lure; Urge) Inciting someone to work for his livelihood, or to impel one's animal to drive faster in a dream means heeding admonition. *(Also see Prompting)*

Incline: *(See Ascent)*

Incomplete Job: (Unfinished business) An incomplete job in a dream signifies joblessness, inactivity, indolence, or it could mean an unattainable desire for leadership. An incomplete job in a dream also means despair. *(Also see Finished business)*

Incubator: (Brooder; Hatchery) In a dream, seeing an incubator or a hatchery means marriage, progeny, suspicion, a bastard son, a kindergarten, a theater, spectators, a park, a promenade, release from prison, an effeminate male, homosexuality, or cowardice.

Indemnification: (War tax) Paying war tax in a dream means either humiliation, or regaining one's integrity.

Indian falcon: (*zool.* Shāhïn) In a dream, an Indian falcon or a Shāhïn represents an unjust ruler who keeps no promises. If one sees himself turned into a Shāhïn in a dream, it means that he will be appointed at a high ranking seat of authority, then be quickly dismissed or impeached from office.

Indian meal: *(See Boiled vegetables; Stew)*

Indian stew: *(See Boiled vegetables; Stew)*

Indigence: (Destitution; Poverty) To express one's need to God Almighty and to receive an answer for one's prayers in a dream means satisfying one's needs.

Indignation: *(See Anger)*

Indigo plant: *(See Tree)*

Indolence: (Laziness. *See Incomplete job)*

Induce: *(See Prompting)*

Inebriety: *(See Drunkenness; Intoxicants)*

Inequitable: *(See Judge)*

Infertile: *(See Impotence)*

Infidel: *(See Irreligious)*

Inflammation: *(See Colitis; Pleurisy)*

Inflation: Inflation in a dream means bread, rising prices, greed, taking advantage of the meek, and manipulating people's interests.

Inflorescence: *(See Pollen)*

Infringement: (Encroachment; Transgression) To infringe upon someone's rights, or to slander him, or to insult him in a dream means losing to him, unless if there is a legitimate reason, or a legal point for trespassing. If someone infringes upon your rights in any way in a dream, it means that your ultimate victory over him is sure. Infringement in a dream also means prosperity and success in this world, though the end results may not be as positive as the beginning. *(Also see Cursing; Injustice; Insulting)*

Infuriating: (Anger; Fury; Rage) Infuriating someone without reason in a dream means distress, trouble, sorrows or sickness. *(Also see Exasperation; Frothing at the mouth)*

Infusion: (Soaking; Steeping) Drinking an infusion of dried fruits as a medicine in a dream means taking a medicine, using a charm, or pursuing the path of knowledge, reading the Qur'ān, or walking on the straight path.

Ingratiating: *(See Flattery)*

Ingratitude: (Denial; Adjuration; Uncertainty) If one sees himself denying what is true in a dream, it means that he will become an atheist. If he denies what is false in the dream, it means that he will defend what is true and attack what is false. To deny others' favors in a dream is an indication of injustice, and to deny the Godliness of our Creator, Sustainer and Cherisher in a dream means ingratitude and atheism. *(Also see Disbelief; Irreligious; Uncertainty)*

Inhaling spasmodically: *(See Hiccup)*

Inheritance: (Endowments; Fulfilling needs; Profits)

Injection: *(See Intoxicants)*

Injury: *(See Wound)*

Injustice: (Infringement; Oppression; Transgression) If strong men, or if the people in authority are unjust in a dream, it denotes a time of wars and destruction. If injustice is practiced by people of knowledge, or religious scholars in a dream then it denotes God's forgiveness for one's sins. Seeing an unjust person in a dream means poverty. If one sees himself confessing to being unjust in a dream, it means that he will repent for his sin. If one sees an oppressed person invoking a curse upon him in a dream, it means that he should await a painful punishment from God Almighty. The oppressed in a dream will always triumph over the oppressor. If one sees his oppressor cursing him in a dream, it means glad tidings, for the oppressor is always a loser. *(Also see Darkness)*

Ink: (Knowledge) In a dream, ink signifies honor, dignity and the rising of one's star. If one's shirt or garment are stained with ink in a dream, it means disgrace, though one will eventually overcome his adversities and regain his former status. Seeing a spotted garment with ink in a dream could mean leprosy, or perhaps that ink will soil one's shirt as seen in one's dream. Ink in a dream also signifies power and dominion. Writing with ink in a dream means strength and authority. Using ink or seeing someone using it in a dream means honor, rank, assisting others, and it may represent a learned person, or a religious scholar.

Inkwell: In a dream, an inkwell represents honor, governing power, exaltation, wife, or money. An inkwell in a dream also represents marriage, business, or a servant. If one is presented with an inkwell in a dream, it represents a fight with a relatives or with a woman. If a respected witness is present when the inkwell is handed to the person seeing the dream, then it means a marriage to a relative. Licking an inkwell in a dream means engaging in sodomy or homosexuality. An inkwell in a dream also could mean that one may seduce his servant for an unlawful sexual intercourse and that she will no longer serve that house. To buy an inkwell in a dream means that one's marriage will see no happiness since one's writing pen comes out of it with ink only. An inkwell in a dream also means ulcer. The pen represents iron *(See Iron)*, and the ink means time. If one sees a section of his body transformed into an inkwell, whereby he can draw ink from it and write in a notebook in the dream, it means that he will receive an inheritance. An inkwell in a dream also means medicine. If one is sick, then seeing an inkwell in a dream also means finding the right medicine and, God willing, one will be cured from his illness. *(Also see Pederasty; Sodomy)*

Inn: (Hostel; Pub. *See Hotel; Travels*)

Inner struggle: (*arb.* Jihād; Inner struggle; Outer struggle; Struggle) In a dream, one's inner struggle means hastening to serve the needs of his family, an act for which the person receives blessings, praises and gratitude. Inner struggle or Jihād in a dream means prosperity, paying one's debts, challenging arrogant people or oppressors, and walking on the straight path.

Inner: (Hidden)

Innovation: (Investigation) If one sees himself being investigated in a court of justice by people he does not know in a dream, it means that he has strayed into innovation, though he remains accountable for his actions.

Inquisitional court: In a dream, the inquisitional court represents the heart of all problems, or the nerve center of worldly adversities. *(Also see Hearing board)*

Insane asylum: *(See Mental hospital)*

Insanity: (Craziness; Excitement; Madman; Mental derangement) In a dream, insanity or any of the above conditions represent prosperity, merit and prestige. Insanity in a dream also indicates desiring the world, festivities, or social fun for one who seeks such connections. If one acts irrationally as a consequence of something that affected his life in a dream, it denotes profits he earns from usury. Seeing oneself extremely happy and excited in a dream means entering paradise. In general, insanity represents profits equal to the degree of one's irrational behavior in his dream. How mad is he in his dream may indicate how rich he will become. However, such profits will be spent in sinful ways and in the company of an evil companion. Insanity in a dream also can be interpreted as receiving an inheritance. The madness of one's son in a dream represents the father's benefits. The madness of a woman in a dream represents a good harvest for that year. Insanity in a dream is also interpreted as being madly in love. It also could signify suffering from harsh beating, or perhaps it could mean offering good deeds without anticipating any reward. *(Also see Irrationality; Mental derangement; Mental hospital)*

Insidious man: *(See Fox's fur)*

Insomnia: *(See Sleeplessness)*

Inspection of troops: *(See Exhibition)*

Inspector: *(See Examine)*

Installments: *(See Eyedropper)*

Instinct: *(See Sexual intercourse)*

Institute: (College; School) In a dream, one's college or school represents his commitment, an agreement, a covenant, an oath, reminiscence or memories. To visit one's institute in a dream means remembering a place which is fraught with memories, plans, emotions, anxieties, hopes, or it could denote one's old home. Visiting one's college, institute, or school in a dream also may mean that one will revisit them again. *(Also see School)*

Instructor: *(See Educator)*

Insufficient: *(See Little)*

Insult: (Abuse; Cursing; Swearing; Vilify) Insulting someone in a dream could represent the dignity of the one impugning upon the other person, and the unworthiness of the person who is insulted. There is an exception to that interpretation when the person insulting the other in the dream has suspicious motives, and the one who is abused in the dream is supposed to command respect. It is also said that the one who is insulted or abused in the dream may owe something to his assailant and must repay him. If the one insulting is of a higher social rank, then the victim in the dream is better than his attacker. However, in general, an abused person in the dream is ultimately the victorious one in wakefulness. *(Also see Insulting)*

Insulting: (Affront; Dishonor) Insulting someone in a dream means a murder. To insult ignorant people in a dream also means commanding them to follow the path of righteousness. To insult one's parents in a dream means disobedience to God's command. *(Also see Insult)*

Intercession: (Mediation) Interceding on behalf of someone in a dream represents honor, a seat of authority, or influence. Intercession in a dream also means cheating, or earning a wage for one's work without humiliation. If one sees the Day of Reckoning in a dream and people searching for an intercessor among the prophets, upon all of them be peace, it means social unrest and privation of the poor and needy from one's assistance. If one's neighbor intercedes for him on such a day in a dream, it means that one will benefit from his neighbor, or receive his help, or find a helper in a friend in times of difficulty. If one sees his own son interceding on his behalf in a dream, it means that he will benefit from him or through his business connections, and the same is true if one intercedes on behalf of someone else in a dream. *(Also see Day of Reckoning)*

Interchange: *(See Commutative contract)*

Interlacing: *(See Contract)*

Interlocking one's hands: (Intertwine) In a dream, interlocking one's hands means a partnership, a contract, marriage, stagnation, stillness of business, delinquency in one's prayers, negligence of one's duties, difficulties with one's family, or a meeting that purports evil.

Interpretation: Personal interpretation of matters in a dream means false reports. However, if a known knowledgeable and a truthful person interprets something in a dream, his recommendations and explanations should be heeded. *(Also see Dream interpreter)*

Intertwine: *(See Braiding; Interlocking one's hands)*

Intestinal worms: *(See snakes)*

Intestines: (Bowels) In a dream, intestines represent one's personal property, or they could mean a pouch. If the intestines are seen outside the stomach in a dream, they represent one's step daughters, or an illness in that house. If the tissue of the intestines has a cut, or if it breaks in the dream, then it means death. Intestines in a dream also mean money. Exposed intestines in a dream mean the surfacing of hidden money. Eating someone's intestines in a dream means denying him his money, or discovering a hidden treasure. If one's intestines and bowels are taken out from his body for washing, then placed in a container in a dream, it means his death and the washer represents the undertaker. Noting here that embalming is not permissible in Islām. *Islāmic Laws. (Also see Body')*

Intimate friend: *(See Book)*

Intimidation: *(See Coercion)*

Intoxicants: (Alcohol; Beer; Brewery; Cocaine; Drugs; Hashish; Injection; Inebriant; Marijuana; Opium; Sedatives; Spirits; Wine) In a dream, all intoxicants signify suspicions, apprehension and doubt about one's resources, or the lawfulness of his earnings, the legitimacy of his children, or the religious legality of his marriage. Drinking alcohol in a dream means losing a fight. Using drugs or intoxicants in a contemptible way in a dream signifies apostasy, loss of honor, negation of the truth, corruption of one's wife, or it could mean profanity. This is because the raw material and herbs used in the preparation of such drugs and herbs are sacred in their intrinsic state. Once mixed and taken to induce inebriety in a dream, they will produce the reverse effects. *(Also see Drunkenness; Marijuana)*

Intruder: In a dream, an intruder represents a stranger, a low spirited person who is much humiliated by others because of his cast or origin. In a dream, an intruder also may represent a messenger, a lively person, or a restless one.

Inundation: (Torrent. *See Flood*)

Invasion: In a dream, invasion means poverty, failure, facing danger and destruction, or seeking to do business overseas. *(Also see Elephant)*

Inverted: *(See Pimp)*

Investigation: *(See Innovation)*

Invisible caller: (Voice) Hearing the voice of an invisible caller admonishing, commanding, forbidding, blessing, or reprimanding the person seeing the dream means exactly what one has heard and has no further interpretations. This includes all voices. *(Also see Voice)*

Invisible stitches: *(See Darn)*

Invitation: An invitation to lunch or dinner in a dream means taking a long journey. If in the mid-afternoon, it signifies a rest or taking a break from a troubling job. If it is an invitation to dinner in the dream, it means betraying someone under the cover of darkness. If one sees himself planning to invite people to a lunch or to dinner in a dream, it means that he wants to do business with them, or perhaps enter their circles. Consequently, he will be blamed for interfering or entering such a venture. If one sees himself hosting a dinner at his house, and the guests have finished eating in the dream, it means that he will preside over them. If a sick person sees such an invitation at his house in a dream, it means that he will recover from his illness. Serving food to guests in a dream means the returning home of a dear person from a long journey. If one sees himself sitting at a table covered with all types of food and fruits in a dream, it means that he will be called upon to serve his Lord and to win paradise. *(Also see Food; Guest; Hospitality; Table)*

Invocation: *(See Prayers)*

Involved: (Occupied) Seeing oneself involved or busy in a dream means a marriage to a virgin girl, or interfering in others' business, or it could mean changing one's profession. If the new job is satisfactory in the dream, then it means prosperity, marriage, children, or worship.

Iris: (*bot.* Perennial plant; Flower) Seeing an Iris flower in a dream signifies recurring festivities, continuing success, happy news, a rainbow of colors, or a foreigner.

Iron: In a dream, iron represents longevity. If one sees himself holding a piece of iron in his dream, it means wealth and strength after poverty and weakness. If one sees himself eating a piece of iron in a dream, it means victory in his life. If he eats it with bread in the dream, it means bearing difficulties in his livelihood. Discovering iron as a mineral in a dream means prosperity and strength in one's livelihood. Forging iron in a dream means becoming competent and qualified in one's craft. To own iron in a dream means wealth which is accumulated with great pain. *(Also see Bond[1]; Fetter)*

Irrational behavior: *(See Insanity; Mental derangement)*

Irrationality: If one acts irrationally in a dream, it means that he will act with disgrace, stupidity or shamelessness in real life. Being irrational in a dream and intentionally using violent or insulting words, and acting deliberately in an evil way means despair of God's mercy. It also means refuting or opposing something. It is also interpreted to mean attending to one's prayers without the ritual ablution. Irrationality in a dream also may mean insolent behavior, or ill speaking of peoples' honor or chastity. *(Also see Insanity; Mental derangement)*

Irreligious: (Cover; Hide; Farmer; Infidel; Ingratitude; Profane; Unbeliever; Ungodly) In a dream, seeing an irreligious person means meeting an enemy. Seeing an elderly person who is irreligious in a dream means meeting an old enemy whose hatred is clearly shown on his face. Seeing an irreligious housekeeper, or an old employee in a dream means suffering from the hidden evils of an avowed enemy. Becoming irreligious in a dream means embracing innovation, or whatever practices one considers and uses as his religion. Seeing an irreligious person sitting on a table with a plate of honey before him and refusing to eat from it in the dream means that he is ungrateful to his Lord, and that he does not confess to the innumerable favors which God Almighty has given him during this life. A gathering of irreligious people in a dream represents one's children in their infancy. An irreligious person in a dream also represents a farmer who plants a seed, then when it becomes a seedling, he covers it with earth again. *(Also see Disbelief)*

Irritation: *(See Exasperation)*

'Ishā prayers: (arb.; See Five times prayers; Night prayers; Smashing)

Ishāq: (Also known as John in Western traditions. God's prophet Ishāq, son of the prophet Jacob, upon both of them be peace.) In a dream, seeing him indicates adversities and hardships. If one has a son who ran away in disobedience to his father, and if he sees God's prophet Ishāq in a dream, it means that he will return to his home and be obedient again. This dream also indicates a surge of glad tidings, peace and tranquility. Seeing Ishāq (uwbp) in a dream also means suffering from persecution by the senators of one's town, or from some of his relatives, and finally God Almighty will come to his help, and grant him back his integrity and honor. If one sees him in his best form and radiant beauty, it becomes a sign of glad tidings, whereby one's progeny will engender leaders, governors and righteous people. Seeing him in a dream also may mean coming out of tight circumstances into a more relaxed ones, changing from heedlessness into guidance, poverty into richness, and from disobedience to one's parents to obeying them again. If one sees himself transformed into Isḥāq (uwbp) or to wear his robe in a dream means that he may near his death then be saved from it.

Islām: (Religion of Islām; Surrender to God's will; Submission) To see oneself as a Muslim, praising God Almighty, thanking Him, facing the Ka'aba in one's prayers, or to see oneself embracing Islām in a dream means straightening one's life, or repentance from one's sins. If one sees himself renewing his Islām in a dream, it means safety from plagues, sickness, or adversities. To proclaim the two testimonies: "There is no god other than Allāh, Muhammad is the Messenger of Allāh," in one's dream means relief from distress, or guidance after heedlessness. Saying these testimonies in a dream also may mean returning to one's parents after having abandoned them. It also means returning to a place one has earlier deserted, or to using earlier criterions in one's life. If a Muslim recites these proclamations in a dream, it means that he will testify to the truth in a court of justice, or become known for his truthfulness. *(Also see Exalting God's one-ness; Exclamation of God's sovereignty; Imām; Meadow; mosque; Qur'ān; Pil-grimage)*

Islāmic festivals: *(See Feast of Breaking the Fast; Feast of Immolation)*

Ismāīl: (The prophet Ismaïl, son of the prophet Abraham, upon both of them be peace.) If one sees him in a dream, it means that he will gain clarity of speech and preside over his colleagues. He also may build a mosque, or participate in such a project. It also means that someone will make a promise and be truthful about fulfilling it. If one sees Ismaïl in a dream, it means that he may suffer at the hands of his father, then God Almighty will relief him from such sufferings or pain.

Isrāfīl: The archangel Isrāfīl upon whom be peace. Seeing him in a dream means resurrection, reanimation of the dead by God's leave, compelling one's enemies to accept his conditions, and refuting the claims of disbelievers and atheists about the resurrection.

Istanbul: *(See Masjid)*

Istikhārah: *(arb. See Five times prayers)*

Istisqā: *(arb. See Five times prayers)*

Italian: *(See Language)*

Itch: *(See Itching; Plague; Scratching)*

Itching: In a dream, itching means poverty and suffering from the pressures of a demanding wife and children. If one's itching results in bleeding or puss in the dream, it means that they will get what they want. Otherwise, one's toiling for his livelihood will prolong. If one sees himself itching in a dream, it also means that he will investigate the conditions of his relatives and suffer from their state. If one's itching seems to last with no solution in sight in the dream, it means that he will suffer from a condition he cannot bear in wakefulness. If one sees people on the road afflicted with itching in a dream, it means that he will earn money but with a headache. A state he will become known by it. *(Also see Mangy; Plague; Scratching)*

I'tikāf: *(arb. Retreat; Seclusion)* In a dream, it represents a spiritual retreat, prayers, hunger, fast, depression, humbling oneself, controlling one's passions and desires. *(Also see Retreat)*

Ivy: (English ivy; Ginseng; Herbal medicine) Ivy in a dream represents a physician. Seeing it in a dream means that one will use homemade medicine to cure his illness. Ivy in a dream also signifies a bad character, or it could represent an ill will.

'Izrāïl: (The angle of death; Bone-breaker; Death; Longevity) The archangel of death. Seeing him in a dream means martyrdom if one is inspired by it. If one sees the archangel 'Izrāïl angry with him in a dream, it means that one will die unrepented. If one sees 'Izrāïl standing above him, or battling him in a dream, it means that he will recover from a severe illness. Seeing the archangel 'Izrāïl in a dream also means longevity, or going through unavoidable circumstances, or experiencing extreme fear. If one sees himself being 'Izrāïl in a dream, it means rising in status to govern and to oppress others, or he might become an executioner, or perhaps that some major events may take place at his hand. Kissing 'Izrāïl in a dream means receiving an inheritance. Seeing 'Izrāïl in a dream also means separations, death of sick people, losses, destruction, fire, bad news, forfeiture of properties, stagnation of the economy, losing one's source of livelihood, imprisonment, breach of promise, forgetting one's knowledge, neglecting one's prayers, obstruction of charities, hindrance of alms distribution, negating the rights of others, retreating to one's privacy, rising prices, bad crop, a tyrant ruler, glass blowing, or bankruptcy. As for one who loves to meet his Lord, seeing the archangel 'Izrāïl in a dream means attainment of one's goal, fulfillment of a promise, freedom from prison, good news and glad tidings. If an unknown or a common person approaches someone in the street and whispers something in his ear in confidence, the commoner here represents the angel of death. It is said that each human being will see the archangel 'Izrāïl three times during his lifetime, and it is the third time that 'Izrāïl, upon whom be peace, will

J

Jackal: In a dream, a jackal represents a man who deprives people from their rights, or one who causes evil. A jackal in a dream also could mean friendliness, or a light and fun companionship.

Jackdaw: *(See Crow)*

Jacob: (The prophet Jacob, upon whom be peace.) Seeing God's prophet Jacob (uwbp) in a dream means strength, living in God's blessings and having many children. Some of the children will cause their father grief, though his distress will later dissipate. Seeing God's prophet Jacob (uwbp) in a dream also means dispersal of one's family that will be followed by a joyful reunion. Seeing God's prophet Jacob (uwbp) in a dream also means earning God's nearness through devotion, prayers, charity and good deeds. It also could mean temporary loss of one's sight, finding a missing child, or suffering a trial because of one's attachment to his blood ties, though God willing, the results will be positive. Seeing him in a dream also means a calamity, or loss of family and wealth. The person in the dream also will be endowed with great patience and will come out of it victorious. If a sick person sees him (uwbp) in his dream, it means that he will recover from his illness. If he has a prayer or a need, they will be fulfilled. If one sees himself wearing Jacob's robe in a dream, it means that he will be afflicted with calamities, distress, separation from his family and beloveds, or it could mean an illness. At the end, his sufferings will vanish to be replaced with happiness. Seeing God's prophet Jacob (uwbp) in a dream also means business, travels, rising prices, stashing merchandise then revealing it. If a woman sees Jacob's wife in a dream, it means that she will be stripped of her wealth and become subject of defamation, though again, the conclusion of her case will turn positive. It also could mean the imprisonment of one of her children. If a sick person sees her in a dream, it means that he will recover by God's mercy and grace, since her name was '*Raḥma*' (Mercy). *(Also see Joseph, upon whom be peace.)*

Jahannam: *(See hell-fire)*

Jailer: (Blacksmith; Digging) A jailer in a dream represents a grave digger.

Jamarāt: *(See Pelting stones)*

Jamādu T̲h̲ānī: *(See Arabic months)*

Jamādul Awwal: *(See Arabic months)*

Jami: *(See Masjid; Mosque)*

Janāza: *(arb. See Five times prayers)*

January: *(See Earthquake; Thunder)*

Japanese spaniel: *(See Dog)*

Jar: (Any broad-mouthed earthenware container.) In a dream, an earthenware jar represents a deceiving employee who is entrusted with the accounting department of one's business. Drinking fresh water from an earthenware jar in a dream means earning lawful money and comfort in one's life. Drinking half of the water contained in a jar in a dream means having consumed half one's life span. Drinking from a tight mouthed earthenware container in a dream also means tempting a female worker. If one's wife is pregnant and he sees himself carrying an earthenware jar that falls and breaks, it means that his wife may die from complications during her delivery or after giving birth to the newborn. In a dream, an earthenware jar also can be interpreted as a hard-working woman, or a servant, though a copper jar represents a noble woman. A jar of wine in a dream represents woman's menstrual period. If one drinks from a jar of wine, it means that he will have sexual intercourse with his wife during that period, which act is forbidden in Islām. If the jar is filled with eating oil, honey, or milk, it represents a hidden treasure. The same interpretation applies for a small clay jug, a mug, a cooking earthenware, or a tin pot. *(Also see Pot)*

Jasmine: In a dream, jasmine denotes happiness, blessings and benefits. It also represents religious scholars and spiritual teachers. If one sees heavenly angels descending from the heavens to pick jasmine flowers in a dream, it means the death of scholars. Jasmine in a dream also means despair, or making a false oath. It also could mean dispelling anxieties, distress and adversities. As for a bachelor, jasmine in a dream means getting married. Seeing a jasmine flower in one's hand in a dream also means recovering from a chest cold or a fever.

Jaundice: (Jealousy; Prejudice) In a dream, jaundice means experiencing a bitter state of mind caused by jealousy and envy, or it may represents a new garment, or an unsuitable, or a non-compatible wife. *(Also see Jealousy)*

Javelin: (Lance; Spear) Seeing it in a dream represents a fight, evil, or disunity, and if it denotes the emblem of a religious man or a scholar, then it means innovation. Holding a javelin in a dream also means strength, power, a strong son, or a profitable business. If a poor person sees himself carrying a javelin in a dream, it means earnings. If a rich man sees himself carrying a javelin in a dream, it means increase in his wealth and power, or expansion of his control. *(Also see Lance; Lancet)*

Jaws: (Chin; Indignant talk) The lower jaw represents the chief of a group of people who has a large offspring. If one sees his chin elongated in his dream, it means that he will become reproving of others, and he will gossip in vain. It also means weakness after strength. *(Also see Body¹; Chin)*

Jealousy: Jealousy means losses for the one experiencing it in the dream. A jealous person has an evil quality, and jealousy is evil. If one who suffers from people's jealousy sees his condition improving in a dream, it means poverty, rancor, spite, black magic, or malice for the jealous person and benefits for the victim of jealousy. In a dream, jealousy also represents covetousness, grudges, avarice and love for the world. To devastate someone by looking at him with despise in a dream means that the assailant will suffer from the jealous eye of his victim. *(Also see Jaundice)*

Jerboa: (Rodent) A jerboa in a dream represents a liar who often swears in God's Name that he is speaking the truth. Fighting with a jerboa in a dream means having an argument with a person of such qualities. A jerboa in a dream also represents a body snatcher or a researcher.

Jerkin: *(See Brace)*

Jerking: *(See Limping)*

Jerusalem: Seeing oneself performing prayers at the sacred mosque in Jerusalem in a dream means receiving a great wealth from an inheritance. Facing Jerusalem during one's prayers instead of the Ka'aba in a dream means a pilgrimage to Mecca. If one performs a ritual ablution in Jerusalem in his dream, it represents profits from his business. *(Also see Canopy; City; Masjid)*

Jester: *(See Piper)*

Jesting: (Fun; Joking) Jesting in a dream represents a state of poverty, adverse conditions, apathy, a low spirit, uncertainty, torpor, or low self-esteem. Jesting in a dream also represents an ailment, hunger, love, or sorrow.

Jesus: (God's prophet Jesus son of Mary, upon both of them be peace.) One who sees God's prophet Jesus upon whom be peace, in a dream is a blessed man, a generous one, an ascetic who pleases his Lord, who is filled with contentment, who travels excessively and may acquire knowledge about medicine and herbs. It is said that whoever sees Jesus in a dream will be protected against calamities for that year. If he asks or wishes for something, he will receive it, and if he learns a trade, he will become successful at it. One who sees Jesus upon whom be peace, in a dream will become an ascetic, travels throughout the land, escape from his enemy and may become a renowned physician. If one sees Jesus son of Mary in a town looking into people's conditions, it means that calamities will be lifted away from that place, and people will live in peace and tranquility for a while. If one sees him together with his mother, upon both of them be peace, it means that a great miracle, or a sign of divine magnitude will manifest in that location. If one sees himself in a dream as Jesus (uwbp), or if he wears one of his garments, or performs a duty suitable for God's prophet, it means that he will rise in rank. If he is a scholar, it means that his knowledge will be widely spread and his virtues and servitude will benefit others, or if one is a physician, it means that he will become renowned and most successful. If one who sees him is struck by fear and reverence in his dream, it means honor, power and blessing wherever he may go. If a sick person sees him in a dream, it means that he will recover from his illness. If one sees Jesus sick, it means one's own death. In general, to see Jesus in a dream means miraculous events, social justice and economic growth. If a pregnant woman sees Jesus upon whom be peace, in her dream, it means that she will beget a child who will grow to become a physician. Seeing Jesus upon whom be peace in a dream also could denote doubt about one's religion, philosophical disputes or a discord. Seeing him in a dream also signify the rise of some of his followers. If one sees Jesus in a dream, he could be accused of something of which he is innocent, or that someone may lie to him or slander his mother. Seeing Jesus and his mother, upon both of them be peace in a dream also could mean distress, sorrow, defamation, moving from one country into another, or it could mean miracles. Seeing Jesus upon whom be peace in a dream also means glad tidings, for he was the last of God's prophets who gave the glad tidings and spoke of God's Messenger Muhammad, upon whom be peace, as the praiseworthy comforter. (*Poclete; Proclytos*. See John 14-15/18, 25/26, 29/30) Seeing Jesus upon whom be peace in a dream also means answering one's prayers, or wrath against people from the upper social class, or against those who challenged him to bring down a table of food from the heavens then had doubt about God's power again. Seeing him in a dream also represents bounty, good luck, or having good friends. If a child sees Jesus in a dream, it could mean that he will grow up as an orphan, or be reared by his mother and live as a scholar and a righteous person, or he may travel frequently between Syria and Egypt. If one who is impotent, or sterile sees him in a dream, it means that he will regain his fertility and fruition. If one sees Jesus upon whom be peace descending upon a town, it means that justice and righteousness will prevail and permeate that place, as it will be when he shall, by God's leave, descends upon the earth to kill the impostor (Antichrist) and destroy his followers, obliterate infidelity, and he shall fill the earth with justice, blessings and lend victory to the believers.

Jet: (Lignite; Velvet-black coal used for jewelry.) In a dream, jet denotes festivities, celebrations, happiness, honor, or marriage. In a dream, jet also represents suspicious money, tainted profits, or a friend for interest, and if one's wife is pregnant, it means that she will deliver a son.

Jewel light of the father's eyes: In a dream, it means one's sons or daughters.

Jewel: (Gem; Son. *See Carnelian-red*)

Jeweler: A jeweler in a dream represents a pious person, an ascetic and an assiduous worshiper. He also could represent a gnostic, or a magnanimous leader and a good example who is a man of knowledge and piety, and whose words are well respected. A jeweler in a dream also represents a man with a large family, or a rich person. *(Also see Goldsmith; Jewelry shop)*

Jewelry shop: A jeweler's shop in a dream means happiness, celebrations, a wedding, ornaments, Adam's apple, or a Qur'ān study circle. *(Also see Jeweler)*

Jihād: (Inner and outer struggle) Joining the warriors in the battlefield in a dream means that one is a true worshiper who attends to his regular prayers and pays his charities and due alms. If one sees the people charging toward the battlefield, it means that they will receive an endowment of divine forgiveness, victory, might and unity between the believers. To die as a martyr on God's path in a dream means joy, happiness and prosperity. Joining a jihād battle in the sea in a dream means poverty, failure and walking toward destruction. Winning a sea battle in Jihād against a tyrant in a dream means restoring one's religious commitment, and it could represent a protective jealousy for one's wife, or winning a struggle in favor of one's parents. Victory in the battlefield during Jihād means profits in one's business. Returning from a holy war against an oppressor in a dream means that one may lose his religious commitment or disobey his parents, which is a major sin in Islām. *(Also see Inner struggle)*

Jinn: *(Sing.* Jinni) A creation from a smokeless fire. Among the Jinn, some are believers while others are satans. This is in contrast to human beings who are created from earth and among them some are believers and others are human satans. Jinn in a dream represent fraud, deceit, cunning, perfidy, treachery, theft, alcoholism, invented religious practices, travels, music, bars, tricks, sleight of hand, illusion, sorcery and magic. If one is transformed into a Jinni in a dream, it means that he will acquire such qualities. If one meets a Jinni who displays truthfulness, knowledge and wisdom which is recognizable by the person in the dream it means that he will receive good news. Seeing Jinn standing by one's door in a dream means losses, a vow that must be fulfilled, or experiencing bad luck. Seeing Jinn entering one's house and doing work there in a dream means that thieves may enter that house and cause major losses. If one sees himself teaching the Qur'ān to a gathering of Jinn in a dream, it means that he will be appointed to a leadership position. Accompanying Jinn in a dream means familiarity with, and keeping the company of men of knowledge, or people of inner knowledge. If one marries a female from amongst the Jinn in a dream, it means that he will marry an insolent wife, or that he may suffer a great calamity. If a righteous person sees himself chaining Jinn in a dream, it means that he holds fast to his prayers, fasting, controls his carnal self and base desires. Engaging in a battle with Jinn in a dream means that one will be safe from their evil. To befriend a known leader from amongst the Jinn in a dream means becoming a police officer and make it one's profession to pursue criminals and bandits. It also could mean that one might become a guided man of knowledge or a teacher. Seeing Jinn gathering in a known locality in a dream also may indicate the presence of snakes, scorpions, or what human beings may fear in the wilderness. *(Also see Dragon; Pumpkin)*

Jogging: (Hustle) Jogging in a dream means working to provide for one's family. *(Also see Walking)*

John the baptist: *(See Yaḥyā)*

John: *(See Isḥāq)*

Joking: *(See Jesting)*

Jonah: (God's prophet Yūnus, upon whom be peace.) Seeing God's prophet Jonah (uwbp) in a dream means making a hasty decision that will lead one to prison and tight circumstances. He will then be released to enjoy his life for a while along with a group of bewildered people. He also will be emotional, impulsive, easy to get angry and easy to please.

Jonquil: *(bot. See Distilled water)*

Joseph: (God's prophet Joseph, upon whom be peace; *arb. Yūsuf*) Seeing God's prophet Joseph (uwbp) in a dream means attaining high rank or a vice-regency. Seeing him (uwbp) in a dream also could denote a time of rising prices, drought, loss of one's family, or suffering from people's stratagem, entering a prison, then be released by God's grace. It also denotes one's luck with women and adversities related to one's beauty and good character. Seeing God's prophet Joseph in a dream also means acquiring knowledge about dream interpretation, or catching one's enemy, then forgiving him, or digging a river, a water irrigation, or transporting dead people from one country to another. It also could represent a great advent or a miracle by the fact that he (uwbp) had performed a miracle by God's leave and returned his father's sight. Joseph's shirt in a dream means dispelling distress, sorrows and recovering from illness. If the shirt is spotted with blood in the dream, then it means separation and imprisonment. If his shirt is torn from the back in the dream, it means a false accusation. If a woman sees Joseph (uwbp) in a dream, it means that she will lose her comfort and sight. She will also live unhappy because of her separation from her beloved, and she will fall in love with a great man. If the woman who is actually suffering from such adversity sees such a dream, it means that God Almighty will turn to her with mercy and guide her to repentance. If she is unmarried, it means that she will get married. If she is poor, it means that she will become rich, and her life in this world as well as in the hereafter will turn to her advantage. Seeing Joseph (uwbp) as a young boy in a dream means having little or no luck with one's brethren. He will be lied to, suffer from imprisonment and other trials before he recuperates, to rise and triumph over them. They will all then become his subject. One who sees God's prophet Joseph (uwbp) in a dream will also be a pious, generous, charitable, and shares his good advice with those who need it, or ask for it. If Joseph (uwbp) talks to someone, or gives him something in a dream, it means that one will understand dream interpretations and learn about Chronicles, or the two biblical books of History. Seeing him (uwbp) in a dream also means marriage to a beautiful woman who will truly love her husband. *(Also see Jacob; Sale; Introduction p.p. xvi, xvii, xviii)*

Jot down: *(See Write)*

Journal: *(See Reference book)*

Journey: *(See Return)*

Joy: *(See Happiness)*

Judge: (Man; Person) Seeing a judge or a governor in a dream means involvement in the judicial business. If one is appointed to be a judge in a dream, it means that he will be just and righteous. If one sees himself sitting on the bench, but finds himself unable to handle people's cases with justice, it means that he is an unjust person. If one presides over people in a dream, it means that he may be dismissed from his job. If a traveller becomes a judge in a dream, it means that he will be held up by robbers, or it could mean that God's blessings upon him will turn into a curse. If one sees a known judge being unjust in a dream, it means that the people of that locality are inequitable and that they cheat in their weights and measures. If one sees himself standing before a judge, and if the judge treats him fairly in the dream, it means that he will find justice concerning a personal case involving himself and an adversary, or it could mean relief from depression and stress. If the judge is inequitable in the dream, it means that one will lose to his adversary. If someone sees a judge holding the scale of justice and that the scale tilts to one's favor in the dream, it represents glad tidings of a great reward from God Almighty for one's deeds. However, if the scale of justice tilts to the opposite direction, then it represents a warning from God Almighty for one to repent of his sins, or abandon his involvement in a sinful ventures. If one sees the judge weighing pennies or bad monies in the scale of justice, it means that one will give a false testimony which will be accepted. If one sees himself as a judge, a wise man, a scholar, or a righteous man in a dream, it means that he will attain fame, good reputation, ascetic detachment and spiritual knowledge if he qualifies for that. If one is not suitable for such blessings, then it means that he will be falsely accused of a crime, or that he may be robbed during a trip. If a judge looks cheerful in a dream, it means glad tidings. Seeing the bench of a judge in a dream means a scare or a fight. Seeing the seat of rulers, judges, speakers, scholars, or teachers in a dream means disturbance, sorrow, money, business losses, sickness, depression, or the surfacing of hidden secrets. If a sick person sees himself standing before a judge in a dream, it means his death. However, if the case is decided to his favor in the dream, it means that he will recover from his illness. If one who is facing adversities sees himself sitting in the judges bench in a dream, it means that he will triumph. An unknown judge in a dream represents God Almighty. A known judge in a dream represents a physician.

Jugular vein: If one's jugular vein splits open and blood gushes forth from it in a dream, it means one's death. A jugular vein in a dream also represents a strong covenant, or tying a kerchief over one's head during a hot and a hard-working day. *(Also see Aorta; Veins)*

Jug: *(See Water jug)*

Juggler: (Conjurer; Illusionist; Prestidigitator; Trickster) In a dream, a juggler represents amusement, distraction, a sleight of hand, sarcasm, mockery and lies. A juggler in a dream also represents a prostitute, an adulteress, a procuress, or a servant. *(Also see Juggling)*

Juggling: (Conjuring; Magic arts; Sleight of hand; Tricks) In a dream, jugglery means deceit, pride, artificiality and a temptation. *(Also see Magician)*

Juice: (Grapes; Sugar cane; Wine) Pressing grapes to make wine in a dream means prosperity and a good harvest. The same interpretation is given for pressing sugar cane or other fruits. If a poor person sees himself pressing grapes to make wine in a dream, it means that he will prosper. If one sees everyone pressing grapes to make wine, or pressing olives for their eating oil in a dream when the economic conditions are down in one's homeland, it means economic recovery. If a scholar or a student on the path, or a prisoner sees that, it means that they will escape from a potential danger. If a lender sees that, it means that he will recover his money from people. If a student on the path sees that, it means that he will succeed in his quest for knowledge. If a bachelor sees that, it means that he will get married and have many children. Making wine in a dream means good luck with one's acquaintances, or earning unlawful and tainted money. *(Also see Extracting oils from seeds)*

Jujube tree: In a dream, a jujube tree represents a handsome looking wise man. *(See Buckthorn; Jujube; Lot tree; Tree)*

Jujube: (Fruit) In a dream, a jujube fruit represents a noble, strong and a cheerful person who benefits people at large, and who is firm and patient in the face of adversities. Sucking the juice of a jujube fruit in a dream means gaining power. In a dream, a jujube fruit also represents the fingers of a woman who had applied henna to her hands for a wedding or for a religious ceremony. *(Also see Henna; Jujube tree)*

July: *(See Earthquake; Thunder)*

Jump: To jump from one place into another out of fear or with haste in a <u>dream</u>

represents accusations, blasphemy, or disturbing news surrounding one's name. To jump down from a high altitude in a dream means separation, or changing of one's conditions from convenience to discomfort. An ascending rapid jump in a dream means rising in station and a plummeting jump in a dream means deterioration of one's status. *(Also see Jumping)*

Jumping: (Bounce; Hop; Leap) To see oneself hopping on one leg in a dream means moving from an old place into a new one. If one takes a broad leap with one jump in his dream it means travels. Hopping on one leg because of an illness or an impairment in a dream means loss of half of one's money or property and finding it difficult to sustain one's needs with the balance. Playing football or hopping with a ball, or jumping while performing acrobatic exercises, or gymnastic feats in a dream means profits or benefits for someone who is used to play such games, or participates in such training. Otherwise, it could mean facing dangerous or severe adversity. In a dream, jumping from place to place also means false news, fabricated accusations, changing moods with one's friends, or finding oneself bored with them. If one jumps over a wall in a dream, it means that he will change from a believer into a disbeliever or follow the advice of a disbeliever. *(Also see Jump)*

Jumu'a: *(arb. See Five times prayers)*

June: *(See Earthquake; Thunder)*

Jungle: (Forest) In a dream, a jungle means people one cannot benefit from their company. Among them there is an intruder, for jungles grow on plants intruding upon one another, behind which hunters hide to jump at their prey. If the jungle belongs to someone, then it represents enemies one will have to fight. *(Also see Forest)*

Junk dealer: (Ragman) In a dream, a junk dealer represents a hoax, a liar, a fortuneteller, or a superstition and fable teller. A junk dealer in a dream also represents one who sells fake jewelry.

Junub: *(arb.; See Impurity)*

Jupiter: (Planet) The planet Jupiter in a dream represents a treasurer. Seeing it along with the Moon in a dream means business trading, prosperity, or rising in station. If one sees it descending, or star-crossed, or burning in a dream, then it represents literary gatherings, poetic recitals, dream interpretation, poetry, singing, prayers, fasting, making a pilgrimage to God's House in Mecca and offering religious devotion. *(Also see Heavens)*

Justice scale: *(See Balance; Judge)*

Justice: (Abstention; Decency; Fairness; Honesty; Impartiality; Resignation) Witnessing injustice practiced by the authority in a dream represents the opposite. In fact, seeing an unjust ruler in a dream could signify comfort, peace, tranquility, protection of the society, or it could mean urban developments. Being just in a dream may imply the necessity to do justice regarding members of one's family. If a heedless person, or a sinner, or a tyrant, or an oppressor sees himself being just in a dream, it means that he will repent to God Almighty from his sins. *(Also see Injustice; Judge; Unjust ruler)*

Juvenile Correctional House: *(See Oven)*

K

Ka'aba: (God's house in Mecca.) In a dream, the holy Ka'aba represents the calif of all Muslims, his chief minister, a leader of a country, or it may represent a wedding. Seeing the holy Ka'aba in a dream also means that one may enter it, or it could mean receiving glad tidings and dispelling evil. Praying inside the holy Ka'aba in a dream means enjoying the guardianship and protection of someone in authority, and safety from one's enemy. Entering inside the holy Ka'aba in a dream means entering before a ruler. Taking something from inside the holy Ka'aba in a dream means receiving something from the ruler. If one of the walls of the holy Ka'aba crumbles in a dream, it means the death of the Calif or the local governor. Entering the holy Ka'aba and failing to perform any of the prescribed rites in a dream means standing before God Almighty on the Day of Judgment having performed one's obligations, or it could mean repenting from one's sins. To look at the holy Ka'aba in a dream means safety and protection against fear. If one is given a job in Mecca in a dream, it means that he may become an Imâm. Stealing anything from the holy Ka'aba in a dream means committing a sin. Walking toward the holy Ka'aba, or seeking it in a dream means correcting one's religious standing. Seeing oneself in Mecca mixing with departed souls who are inquiring from him about the world in a dream means to die testifying to the Oneness of God Almighty and to the prophethood of His Messenger, upon whom be peace. Seeing the Ka'aba inside one's own house in a dream means that one is still in power and living with grace. If the holy Ka'aba does not look right in one's eyes in the dream, then it means adversities. If one sees the holy Ka'aba as his own house in a dream, the holy Ka'aba then represents the Imâm of all Muslims who is the representative and vice-regent of God's Messenger (uwbp), and it means that one truly follows the Imâm. Praying on top of the holy Ka'aba in a dream means becoming an apostate. Entering the holy Mosque in Mecca and praying on the roof of the holy Ka'aba in a dream represents peace, tranquility, presiding over others, it also means that one will become victorious wherever one goes, though with a questionable conduct, he also may follow innovation and depart from the traditions and teachings of God's Messenger, upon whom be peace. Walking by the holy Ka'aba, or leaving it behind in a dream means going against the traditions of God's Prophet, upon whom be peace, following the path of innovation, or interpreting things according to one's own mind and liking. If one sees angels descending from the heavens to lift away the pillar of God's House from Mecca and place it in a different town in the dream, it means that people have gone astray and the time of destruction has come. It also means that the pillar of the faith, the righteous guide of the believers and God's vice-regent on earth Al-Mahdi will soon emerge to dwell in that town. If one sees the holy Ka'aba burning in a dream, it means that one has neglected or abandoned his prescribed prayers. Any changes, decrease or increase in the shape of the holy Ka'aba, moving of it away from its place, or changing its look in a dream will reflect upon the Imâm, or the guide of all Muslims. Circumambulating the holy Ka'aba or performing any of the prescribed rites in a dream means walking the path of righteousness, or correcting one's religious life as much as one does in his dream. Failure to perform some of the prescribed rites that are associated with being at the holy Ka'aba in a dream indicates one's deviation from God's path, and such innovation is equal to changing the direction (*arb. Qiblah*) of one's prayers. The holy Ka'aba in a dream also represents one's prayers, for it is the focal point of all praying Muslims. The holy Ka'aba in a dream also represents God's House, a mosque, a community center of all Muslims, and it represents a teacher, a guide, Islām, the holy Qur'ān, the prophetic traditions, one's son, a religious scholar, a shaikh, a master, a husband, one's mother, and the heavenly paradise. The holy Ka'aba is God's House, and thereat people will be gathered and led into paradise. The holy Ka'aba in a dream also represents the annual pilgrimage to Mecca, the gathering of believers, the local markets and the vicinity of the holy Mosque. If one sees that his own house has become the Ka'aba and people are seeking it and crowds are gathering at his door in a dream, it means that he will be endowed with wisdom, gain knowledge and act upon it, and that people will learn at his hand and follow his example. Performing some of the required rites at the holy Ka'aba in a dream also means that one may work for someone in authority, or serve a man of knowledge, a shaikh, a renunciate, one's father, one's mother, or it could mean that one has a master who demands clarity, true following and hard-work from his students and disciples. (*Also see Circumambulation; Entering Paradise; Gutter of Mercy*)

Kajawah: (*See Palanquin*)

Kasha: (*See Breakfast food*)

Kawthar: (Plenitude; Abundance; A river in paradise.) To drink from the Kawthar river of paradise in a dream means acquiring knowledge, developing correct deeds, having perfect certitude and truly emulating the leading practices and character of God's Messenger, upon whom be peace. Drinking from the Kawthar river in a dream also means repentance from sin, abandoning innovations, marriage to a chaste and a pious woman, replacing unlawful earnings with lawful ones, endowment of leadership and victory. (*Also see River*)

Keenness of mind: (*See Wakefulness*)

Keeper of the gate: (Personal guard; Prison guard) If a notable or a public figure sees his keepers of the gates, or his personal guards standing-up in a dream, it means that they are performing their duty correctly. If they are sitting in the dream, it means that they are failing their duties. The governor's keeper of the gate in a dream represents glad tidings. Usually he represents a notable person, or a great person who is sought for advice, whereby both great and little people depend on him for access. The keeper of the gate in a dream also represents abeyance, or blocking one's access. (*Also see Doorman*)

Keeper: (*See Rural warden*)

Keeping a secret: (Secretary) In a dream, hiding a secret means concealing knowledge from those who need it, or it could mean having good nature, or having good qualities. (*Also see Secretary*)

Kerbela: (*See 'Ashūrā*)

Kerchief: (*See Handkerchief*)

Kernel: (*See Pith*)

Kettle: (Boiler) Seeing a kettle in a dream means sitting in the seat of honor, or it could represent a public roast.

Key: A key in a dream represents money, a helping hand, entering the path of knowledge, or it could mean receiving divine guidance. Carrying a bunch of keys in a dream means prosperity, knowledge and security against one's enemy. Keys in a dream also represent one's children, emissaries, spies, servant, wife or wealth. Keys in a dream also mean attaining one's goal, or fulfillment of one's prayers. A key in a dream also may mean victory over one's enemy. Holding a wooden key in a dream indicates the character of one who refuses to help others, or if he holds their money in trust, it means that he does not repay them, for wood in a dream means hypocrisy. Holding to a key that has no teeth in a dream means cheating an orphan of his inheritance, or becoming a guardian of an estate and deceiving its rightful heirs. Holding to the key of Paradise in a dream means acquiring knowledge, lawful wealth, or receiving an inheritance. Keys in a dream also represent the coffers they open. Seeing a key in a dream also means performing a pilgrimage to Mecca. A key made of iron in a dream represent a strong and a dangerous man. It also means openness in one's life. Turning a key to open a door or a padlock in a dream means attaining victory over one's enemies. Opening a door or a lock without a key in a dream means attaining the same through prayers. Finding a key in a dream means finding a treasure, or profits from a farmland. If a wealthy person finds a key in his dream, it means that he owes alms tax and he should immediately distribute what he owes, pay charities and repent for his sins. Holding to the key of the holy Ka'aba in a dream means working for a ruler or an Imām. If a woman receives keys in a dream, it means her betrothal. Having difficulty to open a door, even with a key in a dream means hindrances in one's business, or failure to attain one's goal. A key in a dream also represents new knowledge for a scholar or a learned person. Putting a key inside a door in a dream means placing a deceased person inside his coffin or grave, or it could mean having sexual intercourse with one's wife.

Khadija: (Mother of the believers, wife of God's prophet Muhammad upon whom be peace.) Seeing her in a dream means happiness in one's life and a blessed progeny.

Khaṭïb: *(arb. See Preacher; Sermon)*

Khawf: *(arb. Fear. See Five times prayers)*

Khānqāh: (Cave; Den; Harbor; lodge; Refuge; Retreat; Sanctuary) Visiting a khānqān in a dream means travels, asceticism, piety, fear of wrongdoing, reading the Qur'ān, ceasing to seek worldly gains, observing sexual abstinence, or it could mean suffering from asphyxia.

Khidr: *(arb.* God's prophet Enoch (uwbp); Companion of Moses upon both of them be peace.) Seeing God's prophet Enoch (uwbp) in a dream means prosperity after depression, being at peace with what one carries, inexpensiveness after a juncture of soaring prices. Khidr in one's dream also represents longevity, or attending the pilgrimage in Mecca.

Khimār: (A piece of fabric worn by some women as part of their headdress; To conceal one's face; Attire; Cap; Garb; Mantle; Mantilla; Veil) In a dream, a khimār represents a husband, protection or an ornament. The extent of its size shows the man's prosperity. Its finesse connotes clarity and the color white represents honor and dignity. If a woman sees herself wearing a mantilla in a dream, it means maliciousness, a bad omen, or rancor and falsehood of female companions that might cause difficulties, or separate between a husband and a wife. If the khimār is made of black torn fabric in the dream, it means poverty of one's husband, or his being natural, or unsophisticated. Damage to one's veil in a dream means difficulties affecting one's marriage, loss of business or a calamity caused by a guardian, a father or a brother. If a man sees himself wearing a mask in a dream, it means that he will commit adultery with his servant. If a woman sees herself removing her veil in public in a dream, it means that she will be tried with a calamity that will take away her sense of shame. If she loses her khimār in the dream, it means that she may lose her husband. If she finds it again in the dream, it means that her husband will return to her. In a dream, a khimār also represents one's religion. *(Also see Veil; Yashmak)*

Khusūf: (arb. Lunar eclipse. *See Five times prayers*)

Kicking: Kicking something in a dream means ingratitude. If one is kicked in a dream, it means that someone will demean him in public, or cast down his achievements, or despise him for his poverty, or show haughtiness in dealing with him.

Kidneys: (Daughter; Son; Servant. *See Body¹*)

Killing: (Murder; Suicide) Killing in a dream represents a major sin. If one kills himself, or commits suicide in fear of the consequences of his sins in a dream, it means that he is offering true repentance from his sins, though committing suicide is a major sin that will lead its author to eternal sufferings in hell-fire. Killing a human being in a dream means committing an evil and an atrocious sin. On the other hand, committing an outrageous sin, or a conspicuously objectionable act in a dream may mean killing someone. If one is killed in a dream, it means longevity and that he will acquire a great wealth from the one who kills him in the dream. If one kills someone without slaughtering him in a dream, it means that the victim will benefit greatly from his assailant. Slaughtering in a dream means injustice. Killing someone in a dream also means relief from depression, grief, affliction and sorrow. Killing oneself in a dream also means recognition of the value of lost benefits. If one is murdered in a dream and did not know who killed him, it indicates his failure to fulfill his religious duties. If one recognizes his murderer in the dream, then it means triumph over one's enemy. If one sees a victim swimming in a pool of blood that is pouring from his jugular veins in the dream, it means that the victim will suffer greatly from the defamation and slander of his assailant. If one intentionally commits suicide in a dream, it means that he is a subversive rebel and a disobedient servant of God almighty. Confessing to a murder in a dream means gaining the upper hand. Killing in a dream also could mean that one is missing his prayers, or neglecting them. Killing one's own son in a dream means receiving money. If one dies as a martyr in a dream, it also means profits, fulfillment of a promise, business success, or perhaps that he maybe assassinated, or drown, or die under a collapsed structure. If the victim in the dream is a witness in court, it means that his testimony will be accepted, or perhaps it could mean that he will enjoy abundance of blessings in his life. *(Also see Fight)*

Kiln: *(See Furnace; Oven)*

Kindness: (Courtesy) If a respected person sees himself showing friendliness and kindness toward lowly people in a dream, it means self-degradation, loss of status, dismissal from one's position, poverty and need for other's assistance.

King: (God Almighty; Governor; Mayor; President; Royalty; Sultān) The true King is God Almighty. If the king is pleased with someone in a dream, it means that God Almighty is pleased with him, and if the king is angry with him in the dream, it means that God Almighty is displeased with him. If one sees the king frowning in a dream, it means that he fails to properly perform his prayers or show true religious devotion. If one sees him smiling in a dream, it means profits in one's material as well as spiritual life. If one sees that God Almighty has appointed him as a king over a land, it means that he will receive such a regency, should he qualify. Later on, unrest will bring tyrants, or dictators to justice, while people of knowledge and piety will survive and regain their authority. If one sees himself as a calif or as an Imām in a dream and should he qualify, it means that he will receive such an honor, rank, trust and fame in the land, though his vice-regency will not become hereditary. However, it is a bad omen if he becomes a calif in the dream and does not qualify for such an appointment. In such a case, and by contrast, he will be humiliated and dispersed, and his own helpers will become his superiors, while his enemies will rejoice at his misfortune. If one sees himself as a king in a dream, though in reality he does not qualify, it means that he may die quickly, and the same is true if a sick person sees himself turned into a king. If he is healthy, it means that someone in his family may die shortly. Seeing a king in a dream also denotes exposing hidden secrets. If a philosopher or a fortuneteller sees himself transformed into a king in a dream, then it denotes glad tidings should he not complain about it in his dream. If a slave sees himself becoming a king in a dream, it means that he will be set free. If one sees himself becoming one of the great kings of this world in a dream, it means that he will attain worldly success in his life, though it will be accompanied with religious failure. If the person is a natural con artist, it means that he will be captured and imprisoned. If a man sees himself awarded a knighthood that is suitable only for woman, then it means his death. If one sees the king reprimanding him in a dream, it means peace between them. If one sees himself arguing a case with knowledge and wisdom before a king in a dream, it means that he will win his case and receive what he came for. If one sees himself complaisant with the king about his case in the dream, it means that he will lose his case and the judgment will go the king's way. If one sees himself walking with a king and rubbing shoulders with him in the dream, it means that he will oppose the king or disobey him. If he sees himself following the king in a dream, it means that he will pursue the king's traditions during his lifetime or after his death. If one enters the king's palace prostrating in a dream, it means that he will be appointed in a leadership position and receive the king's pardon. If one sees himself mixing with the king's harem, or sleeping with them and should there be signs of comfort, trueness, or wisdom in his act in the dream, it means that he will enter the king's inner circles. Otherwise, should he in the dream fear the consequences of what is happening, or if he lacks trueness, or if he slanders them, or indulges in what is unlawful for him to do, then should he reach the king's door, it means that he will triumph against his enemies inside that palace, and they can cause no harm to him. If in his dream, the king gives him a gift, it means that he will win victory and honor in his life to equal the value of that gift. If the king gives him a brocaded silk garment in the dream, it means that he will give him a wife from the royal family. If the king speaks to someone in a dream, it means honor, fame, wealth after poverty, release from jail, expansion of one's business, or victory over one's enemy. If an appointed governor sees himself looking into a mirror in a dream, it means that he will be dismissed from his post. If an appointed king sees someone who looks like him sitting in his throne in a dream, it means that he will beget a son. If he divorces his wife in a dream, it means that he will abdicate his throne. To see oneself sleeping with the king in the same bed and without a curtain between them, and if the king leaves the bed while one remains resting therein in the dream, it means that his mixing with the king will incur jealousy, or that he will inherit him. If one leaves the bed before the king, it means that he will escape from a great danger. If one sees himself sleeping alone in the king's bed in a dream, it means that he will marry a woman from the governing family, or that he may spend from his own money for the sake of a woman in that palace. If the bed is in the palace though unknown in the dream, it means that he will become a member of that government. If a king hears his subjects praising him in a dream, it means that he will show good qualities. If his subjects shower him with money in a dream, it means that they speak ill of him or cast blame at him. If they shower him with sugar in the dream, it means they speak nicely of him, and if they shower him with stones in the dream, it means that they will speak harshly of him. If one sees the people paying obeisance and bowing to him in a dream, it means that they will stand humbly before him. If they prostrate themselves before him in a dream, it means that they truly praise him. If a king sees himself following the opinion of a woman in a dream, it means that he will lose his kingdom or fall victim to depression, or that he will be thrown into jail. If he opposes her in the dream, it means that he will escape from a great danger. If a king sees himself walking in a dream when a common subject comes near him and whispers something in his ear, the commoner here represents the angel of death 'Izrāïl, and it means that the king may die a sudden death. Eating from the hand of one's servant in a dream represents the growing of one's authority, increase of his business, knowledge, or wisdom. If a king sees himself preparing a banquet for guests in a dream, it means that his opponents will come to argue their case, though he will win over them. If he sees himself placing food on the table in a dream, it means that a messenger will come to see him concerning a dispute. If the food is sweet, then the problem will end nicely. If the food is greasy, then the problem will be a lasting one. Sour food then means steadfastness. Eating on the table of a just and a righteous king in a dream means blessings and honor. If the king is seen walking alone in the markets in a dream, it means that he is a humble, just, and a strong ruler. A sick king in a dream represents weakness in his faith and injustice toward his subjects. If the king is carried over people's shoulders in a dream, it means lack of faith and lack of attendance to one's religious obligations, or weakness in his ruling. If the king dies and does not get buried in a dream, it means that the king and his subjects are deviates. If he is buried and the people walk away from his grave in the dream, it means that one will pursue something of no benefit, unless God Almighty decrees otherwise. If one sees the king's head transformed into a ram's head in a dream, it means that the king is a just and a kind ruler. If his head is transformed into a dog's head in the dream, then it represents his vile nature. If his chest turns into a stone in the dream, it means that his heart will become like a rock. If one sees his own hand turn into the king's hand in a dream, it means that he will receive a leading job. If one sees the king flying with wings in a dream, it means that his authority will spread. If his fingers increase in shape or number in the dream, it means that his greed and injustice will manifest. Any dream about a deceased king will manifest in his successors or in his progeny.

Kismet: *(See Calamity)*

Kiss: (Love; Passion; Rose; Tenderness) A kiss in a dream means satisfying one's need, want or desire, or it could mean subordinating one's enemy. Kissing a man or embracing him lustfully in a dream means getting hold of what one intends to acquire from him. If it is a lustful kiss, then it means accomplishing one's pursuit of benefits, knowledge, or guidance. If it is an amicable kiss, it means that the one who received the kiss will receive benefits from the one who kissed him, or learn something from him, or reap a new understanding of things through him. Kissing a child in a dream means love, care and tenderness toward that child. Kissing a servant in a dream means soliciting the friendship of her master or employer. Kissing a married woman in a dream means seeking friendship with her husband. Kissing someone in authority in a dream means replacing him in his function. Kissing a judge in a dream means that one's testimony will be accepted by the court. If a judge kisses someone in a dream, it means that the latter will win a court case, or benefit from such a judge, and the same interpretation applies if a leader or a boss kisses someone in a dream. Kissing one's father in a dream also means benefiting from one another. Kissing one's son with passion in a dream means saving money for him, or building a business for him. Giving one's son a tender kiss in a dream means receiving joy or money from him or from his mother. Kissing someone between the eyes in a dream means marriage. Kissing someone's eyes in a dream means pursuing both heterosexual and homosexual life and such a dream carries a warning to cease such loathsome and unlawful practices before contracting unknwon illness. Kissing one's beloved from the mouth in a dream means money. Kissing a woman in a dream means desiring her, or receiving news from one's beloved. Kissing an old woman in a dream indicates an excuse or regret for a slip of the mouth. Kissing a young girl in a dream means drinking a glass of wine. If a scholar kisses a beautiful woman in a dream, it could mean reciting the Qur'ān, or speaking words of wisdom. If such a scholar is known to love the world and its pleasures, then what he has kissed in his dream is the world itself. Kissing God's right Hand in a dream means attending a pilgrimage to Mecca and kissing the black stone. Kissing God Almighty in a dream means kissing the holy Qur'ān, or kissing God's holy Name. If one sees God Almighty kissing him in a dream, it means that his deeds are accepted. Kissing an adorned woman or sleeping with her in a dream means marrying a wealthy widow. Kissing a known deceased person in a dream means benefiting from his knowledge or inheriting his money. Kissing an unknown dead person in a dream means that one will receive money from an unexpected source, or perhaps do business with his heirs. If a deceased person kisses someone in a dream, it means that the latter will receive unanticipated benefits. Lustfully kissing a deceased person in a dream means satisfying one's needs, lust, or completing a project. If a sick person sees himself kissing a deceased person in a dream, it means his own death. Finally, if a healthy person kisses a deceased person in a dream, it means that his words are not true. *(Also see Rose)*

Kissing a snake: *(See Weasel)*

Kitchen: A kitchen in a dream means preparing food, or it could represent a servant, menial work, a cook, a greasy spoon restaurant, ruins, loss of status, spoils taken from others by force, or it could mean a craft, heat, lust, tampering with the elements, or meddling with people's business. *(Also see Ladle)*

Kite[1]: (Small hawk) In a dream, a kite means an insouciant or a languorous ruler who is audacious, defiled and stouthearted. If one catches and trains a wild kite to hunt for him and he finds that it is not obeying him or holding fast to his wrist in a dream, it means that he will bear a son who will become a ruler. Otherwise, if the kite flies away from his wrist in the dream, it means that the fetus may die before birth. Its chicks represent boys and girls banding at wrongdoing. A kite in a dream also represents an adulterous wife and a secret affair. *(See Introduction)*

Kite[2]: (Aircraft; Soar) In a dram, a kite represents exaltedness, rising in station, determination, or gaining respect. A kite in a dream also means being dismissed, or banished, or it could mean sorcery and magic. If one sees himself playing with a kite in a dream, it means that he might suffer from a spell of black arts. If a kite falls over one's house in a dream, it means that he will be evicted from it.

Kneading: *(See Dough; Flour)*

Knee brace: *(See Brace)*

Knee: (Brotherhood; Health; Kneeling in prayers; Movement; Partnership; Prayers; Servants) One's knee in a dream represents his efforts, toiling, purpose and share in earning his livelihood. If the skin covering the kneecap appears healthy and flawless in the dream, it means that one's livelihood will become easier to manage, and his financial standing will become stronger. However, if the skin of one's kneecap is detached or hangs loosely in the dream, it denotes coming hardships. If the skin looks rough and swelling in a dream, it means that his hard earned money will be lost in a bad investment, and subsequently his earnings will be scarce and hard to get. Knees in a dream also represent the condition of one's health, movements, freedom and level of professionalism. Healthy knees in a dream also represent travels or business activities. If a sick person experiences knees pain in a dream, it may mean that he is nearing his death. As for a traveller knees in a dream represent his travelling vehicle. They also connote giving and receiving, quietness, one's residence, savings, expenditures, or immobility. A broken kneecap in a dream means separation between friends, or damage to one's vehicle.

Knife handle: (Haft; Saber guard; Sword hilt) Seeing a knife handle or a sword haft in a dream means that one still has a property or a minimum amount of property, including but not limited to livestock, gold, silver, or cash savings that is subject to the obligatory (*Zakāt*) alms tax.

Knife sharpener: A knife sharpener in a dream represents someone who teaches people skills, sagacity and adroitness. A knife sharpener in a dream also represents sobriety, a dignified bearing of adversities, or he could represent a vile person, a trouble maker, or a decisive person.

Knife: (Dagger; Kitchen knife) In a dream, a knife represents the servant of the house or its sire who strives to serve and benefit his family and friends. Its sharpness represents the effectiveness of his commands, the force by which they are carried, or one's magnanimity and distinct personality. If a woman sees herself carrying a knife, or if she gives someone a knife in a dream, it represents her love for a famous person. A pencil sharpening knife in a dream represents an author or a writer. A slaughtering knife in a dream represents a butcher, while a soldier's knife means strength and service. If a kindergarten teacher is seen stealing a knife in a dream, it means that he is tempted by one of his children, and that he may abuse him. A table knife in a dream represents a lazy person who does not like to work and who cheats when he does go to work. Using a table knife in a dream means voidance of a project one supports. A knife in a dream also implies a proof. A knife in a dream also means acquiring strength and prosperity at the hands of a servant or an employee. Swallowing a knife in a dream means depriving one's son from his inheritance, or stealing his money or property. If one's wife is pregnant, then seeing a knife in a dream means that she will beget a son. If one who is going to appear in court sees himself carrying a knife in a dream, it means that he will win his case. If one is given a knife as a gift in a dream, it means that he will beget a son, or have a new brother. If one is not expecting a son or a brother, then it means that he will receive money or an inheritance. Cutting one's hand with a knife in a dream means that one will see wonders. Sheathing a knife in a dream means getting married. If one is married, and if his wife is pregnant, then it means that she will beget a boy, unless if what she carries with her in the dream is more suited for a girl, then it means that she will give birth to a baby girl. If one needs a witness for a trial, and if he sees himself carrying a knife in a dream, it means that he will find such a witness. If the knife is sharpened in the dream, it means that one will find a true witness. If the knife is dull in the dream, it means that his witness is shabby, or that his witness may be hurt before the trial. If the knife is sheathed in the dream, it means that the witness will cowered and the court will be satisfied with one's own testimony instead. On the other hand, a knife in a dream could mean profits, benefits from a brother, a close friend, or a servant.

Knight: *(See Chess Knight)*

Knighthood: *(See Raiment)*

Knitting one's brows: *(See Frowning)*

Knitting: (Interlacing yarn or thread; Weaving) In a dream, knitting represents a problem solver, garments, travels, or hesitation. Knitting in a dream also means the passing of one's life and the nearing of its end. Knitting in a dream also means living under acceptable conditions, or experiencing the gifts of life between exhilaration and deflation. Knitting a garment in a dream means travels. If one sees himself wrapping the knit in a dream, it means that his mind is set on travelling. If one unravels his knit after completing it in a dream, it means that his goal was reached then obstructed. In such a dream, if one is incarcerated, it means that he will be released. If he is disputing something, it means that his disagreements will be solved. Knitting in a dream also could denote sodomy.

Knock: (Door) Knocking on one's door in a dream means a fight waged by an intruder. *(Also see Close; Door)*

Knocker: A door knocker in a dream represents the door attendant, the announcer, a messenger, a warning guard, a security system or a guard dog. If the knocker is made of gold or silver in the dream, it represents honor and prosperity of the people of such a house. If one sees two door knockers at his door in a dream, it means a debt he owes to two people. If one pulls out the door knocker, and if it brakes in his hand in the dream, it means that he follows a path of innovation. *(Also see Club)*

Knocking: *(See Smashing)*

Knot: (Bond; Bridge; Contract; Liaison; Tie) To make a knot in one's shirt in a dream means engaging in business. Tying a knot with a rope in a dream represents one's religious commitment. Tying a knot with a handkerchief in a dream means giving fringe benefits to a servant or to an employee. Tying a belt over a pair of pants in a dream means marriage. Tying a knot with a thread in a dream means asserting one's intention, or stipulating one's plan, or it could mean sorcery and an evil spell. If one sees himself tying a rope or a thread around a pouch or a bag and could not open it again, and if an unknown person comes-by and unties the knot in the dream, it means distress, stress, uptightness, or suffering from political persecution, or financial adversities that will be lifted unexpectedly by God's leave. *(Also see Contract; Thread; Tie; Untying something)*

Knowledge: (Bread; Learning; Wall) To see oneself acquiring knowledge in a dream means marriage and rising in status. Such a wedding will be announced publicly. If one earns a title of recognition, or if he becomes renowned, or if he is awarded a great prize for his work in a dream, it means glad tidings of a beautiful son he will beget and who will follow his father's footsteps, learn his trade, or work at spreading his father's knowledge or traditions, or he may govern or lead after him. To learn about God Almighty, or about the prophetic traditions of His Messenger, upon whom be peace, in a dream means being encompassed with God's mercy and subtle kindness. To learn about sorcery, black magic or similar arts in a dream mean following innovation and walking the path of heedlessness. *(Also see Learning)*

Kohl jar: In a dream, a kohl jar represents a woman who serves others, advises them in managing their finances and teaches women about their religious and spiritual role. One's eyes in a dream represent his religious standing while the kohl is used to beautify them or as a cure. Putting the kohl brush or stick inside a kohl jar to extract kohl powder and apply it to his eyelid in a dream means marriage for a single person, profits for a poor person, or knowledge for an ignorant person. If the kohl jar contains ashes, or butter, or a foamy substance, or feces in the dream, it means that one is seeking earnings from falsehood and innovation. A kohl jar in a dream also may represent a coffer, lost money, a box to keep one's personal papers or documents. *(Also see Kohl)*

Kohl: (Eye makeup; Makeup) Kohl in a dream represents money and clarity. If one is given some powdered kohl in a dream, it means money. If a righteous and God-fearing person places kohl on someone's eyes in a dream, it means blessings and guidance. Finding a container of kohl in a dream means receiving money. Smearing one's eyes with kohl in a dream means becoming more religious. If a blind person smears his eyes with kohl in a dream, it means that he will miraculously recover his sight. If one smears his eyes with a silver-white powdered mixture or antimony in a dream, it means that he will have two wives.

If one coats his eyelids with butter or lather in a dream, it means that he is pursuing an unlawful heterosexual, or a loathsome homosexual relationship. Beautifying childrens' eyes with other than kohl or antimony in a dream means molesting them. If one uses kohl as medicine for his eyes in a dream, it means that he will correct his religious performance and commit his life to a godly cause. If his intention is made to beautify himself with kohl in the dream, it means that he is seeking material success, or worldly promotion. If someone smears one's eyes with kohl to the degree of blinding him in the dream, it means that he will defraud him of some money. If a virgin girl or a widow places kohl over her eyelids in a dream, it means her marriage. Coating or encrusting one's eyes with blood or ashes in a dream means corruption and a non-acceptable marriage, or an illegal marriage. *(Also see Makeup)*

Kursï: *(arb. See Chair; Divine Throne)*

Kusüf: *(arb. <Solar eclipse> See Eclipse; Five times prayers)*

L

Labor pangs: *(See Tremor)*

Labor throes: *(See Tremor)*

Labor: (Hard work; Toil) Hard labor in a dream means comfort in wakefulness. If a businessman or a rich person sees himself working as a laborer in a dream it represents conceit and a sham, or that he is deceiving people to control their money, or defrauding them of their assets. If one sees himself laboring in a dream, it means thriftiness, discretion, or virtuous along with satisfaction and ease in one's life. Laboring in a dream also means a misfortune or one's peril. *(Also see Laborer)*

Laborer: A laborer in a dream represents an honorable worker who possesses dignity, integrity, and whose earnings are blessed. *(Also see Construction worker)*

Lactate: *(See Colostrum; Milk)*

Ladder: A wooden ladder in a dream means distress and toiling one may endure during a journey. A ladder in a dream also represents peace and safety. Climbing a ladder in a dream means receiving a warning or an admonition to do good and eschew evil for someone who does not oblige. If one's ladder turns into concrete stairs in a dream, it means assiduity and veiling or protecting of one's privacy. A ladder laid on the floor in a dream means authority, while a raised ladder means recovering from an illness. A ladder also represents travels, comfort to a person who is struck by sorrows, or it could represent a great person. Climbing a new ladder in a dream means reaching new spiritual attainments, or it could represent his business success. Even climbing an old ladder in a dream means success in one's bushiness, exaltation and profits. Falling from a ladder in a dream means adversities, spiritual fall and temptation. Climbing down a ladder in a dream means business losses. If the ladder breaks in the middle of one's assent or descent in the dream, it means losing to one's competition. If one fixes a ladder to descend upon something he knows in a dream, it means safety from danger, arrogance, fears, or escape from an accident that might cost him his life. Climbing a ladder in a dream also means seeking the help of people who are filled with hypocrisy. If one climbs a ladder to hear something in a dream, it means that he will achieve success and attain power. A ladder in a dream also means authority, eavesdropping, or spying for evil people.

Ladle: (Kitchen; Stew) A ladle in a dream represents a household manger, or the lady of the house who properly manages its finances. Eating meat cooked with vinegar from a ladle in a dream means living happily with dignity from money one has earned from his own labor, or it could mean serving the domestic needs of others, working for rich people and making good money, making healthy profits from one's trade, or winning an important political appointment. *(Also see Kitchen)*

Lair: *(See Hole)*

Lake: A lake in dream represents judges and governors who serve others without conspiracy. A lake in a dream also represents difficulties in completing one's journey. A small lake in a dream represents a rich woman, or a woman with a military spirit, or a woman who likes to be approached.

Lamb: In a dream, a lamb represents one's son. If one sees himself slaughtering a lamb in a dream, it means that either his son or the son of one of his relatives may shortly die from an illness or an accident. If one is offered a lamb as a gift in a dream, it means that he will beget a noble and a blessed son. If one sees himself eating lamb in a dream, it means that he will earn his money through such a son. If one sees himself herding sheep in a dream, it means that he will profit from a blessed money and acquire honor and fame thereafter. *(Also see Sacrifice)*

Lameness: To walk lamely in a dream means concealing God's favors and blessings for selfish reasons, or pretending to be poor when in fact one is rich, or claiming to be in need when his claims are false, or it could mean cunningness, deceit and fraud. *(Also see Limping)*

Lamenting: (Mourning; Wailing; Yowling) Lamenting and desiring something in a dream connotes evil. Lamentation in a dream also represents a preacher or it could represent a putrid odor that comes from opening the door of a filthy lavatory. Lamentation in a dream also represents dogs' yowling, drum beating, the ringing sound of cymbals, or it could mean a wedding. Sitting in a place where people are lamenting and mourning their dead in a dream means that an ominous evil may take place in that locality, or perhaps it could mean separation between families and friends. If one sees himself mourning a deceased person in a dream, it means that harm will come to him from the descendents or family of the departed person. Lamenting with great pain and sorrow and mourning over a deceased person in a dream also means waking up to a great joy and happiness. Lamenting in a dream also means adversities which are driven by the person who is lamenting. It also means going astray, or it could denote a flute, as the flute denotes lamenting in a dream. Lamenting in a dream also represents the work of ignorance.

Lamp stand: In a dream, a lamp stand represent humankind and their characteristics. The lamp itself represents one's soul, the oil represents one's blood, and the wick represents his temperature. Once the wick is used up, and the oil is burned in the dream, it means one's death. If one sees the wick in good condition, and the oil clean and radiant in the dream, it means that he will enjoy a life of purity and happiness. If the wick is black and the oil is murky in the dream, it means experiencing a wretched life. If the stand itself has some deficiencies in the dream, it means an illness in one's body. If the stand is strong and clean, it means that one's body and blood are free from illness. A broken lamp stand in a dream represents a terminal illness. *(Also see Lamp¹; Wick)*

Lamp¹: (Candle; Flame; Light; Torch) If a pregnant woman sees herself carrying a lamp in a dream, it means that she will beget a son. As for a sick person, a lamp represents his life. If the lamp is dimmed in the dream, it means his death. If one sees himself repairing a lamp in a dream, it means that he will recover from an illness. A lamp with a weak battery, or low electrical current represents health problems for a pregnant woman. A strong lamp that lights one's entire house denotes righteousness in that house. If one turns off the light in his house in a dream, it denotes the suspicious character of the owner, his financial troubles, his death, the death of a father, a mother, a wife, a child or a sick person. If one sees a sick person rising to the sky and carrying a lamp in a dream, it means the return of his soul to its Lord. If one draws light from someone else's lamp in a dream, it means that he will acquire knowledge. Extinguishing the light of an oil lamp in a dream means attempting to conceal the truth by opposing a truthful witness, yet he will fail to win his case. Carrying a lighted lamp in the daylight in a dream represents a religious and a righteous person. Walking with a lamp during the night in a dream means observing a night vigil and prayers. If such a person is religious by nature, then it represents benefits. Otherwise, it means that he will see wonders. Carrying a lamp at night in a dream also means repentance from one's sins. Carrying an unlit lamp, candle, or torch in a dream means business losses, or problems at the workplace. If one sees a lamp filled with oil that does not burn in a dream, it means sorrow and distress. *(Also see Lamp stand; Wick)*

Lamp²: (Housekeeper; Lamp¹; Steward; Wick) In a dream, a lamp represents a steward, a housekeeper or a butler. If the oil burns up in one's dream, it means the death of any of the above. If a spark falls on a piece of cotton fabric and burns it in the dream, it means that he or she will face a mishap. If the lamp is put off in the dream, it means that a sick person in that family will soon die from his illness, or that the family will receive news of the death of a relative.

Lance: In a dream, a lance represents a branch of wood, stability based on one's strength, or stepping away from the wrong path. A lance in a dream also represents a woman, a child, testifying to the truth, or going on a journey. A lance in one's hand in a dream represents a grand son or a blessed son who will grow to preside over people and defend them with his own life. A broken lance in a dream represents an incurable deficiency or a disease that will inflict one's child. Carrying a lance while riding a horse in a dream means authority with honor. If someone denies his ownership of a lance in a dream, it means an accident or a betrayal. If the lance belongs to a brother, then it means a calamity. If one does repair a broken lance in a dream, it means recovering from an illness. A lance without a spearhead in a dream means the death of one's brother or child. A lance in a dream also represents a brother or a friend who will part with his brother or friend, or it could mean loss of one's job. Walking with a lance in one's hand in the middle of a marketplace in a dream means walking or strolling with one's son. As for a pregnant woman, a metal lance means that she will deliver a girl, and that she will receive a gift of money or a present after her birth from other daughters. Carrying a lance with a flag raised on top of it in a dream means attaining a position that will earn fame. If one is challenged by someone holding a lance against him in a dream, it means that someone will hurt him with his words, or slander his family. Owning an extra lance in a dream means having a brother or a friend who will stand for one's defence when needed. A long spear means injustice, or it could mean good health. If one bleeds from a wound caused by a lance in a dream, it means that he will be compensated for pain and suffering, or that he will return home from a long journey. Multiple wounds from a lance in a dream mean financial compensation, though the source of money is loathsome. Fighting one's enemies with a lance means earning dirty money. A person holding a lance in a dream also represents a teacher, an educator, or someone who helps his brothers and friends. *(Also see Javelin)*

Lancet: In a dream, a lancet represents a slanderer. To cause a horizontal cut to someone with a lancet in a dream means backbiting him, slandering him and causing enmity between people. If the wound is vertical in the dream, then it means speaking well of someone and bringing people's hearts together. *(Also see Javelin; Lance)*

Land: *(See Earth)*

Landmark: *(See Milestone)*

Landscaping: *(See Earth)*

Lane: (Avenue; City gates; Path; Road; Trail) Seeing a lane in a dream is like seeing the city's gates. If it is closed during the daylight time in the dream, it means that an accident will take place inside the city or at the end of the lane, and that such an accident will necessitate the closing of its gates, or the blocking of the lane. A lane in a dream also represents a servant or cohabitation.

Whatever shape the lane takes in one's dream, one will see the same in wakefulness. Following that trail of thinking, walking a lane in a dream means suffering the wrong treatment of a merchant, a person in authority or a craftsperson. An open road in a dream means that one may work for someone in the government. *(Also see Alley; Road)*

Language teacher: *(See Engraver; Language; Teacher; Writer)*

Language: (Tongue; Speaking; Speech) Speaking the language of another people in a dream may represent their country or culture. Speaking Arabic in a dream means honor and dignity. Speaking Persian in a dream means associating with a higher class of people and benefiting from them in business. Speaking Hebrew in a dream means receiving an inheritance. Speaking Turkish in a dream means hearing pleasing words. Speaking Italian in a dram means eagerness to amass money. Speaking French in a dream means drawing benefits from one's profession. Speaking English in a dream means love for the world. If one can speak in all tongues in a dream, it means that he will acquire wealth, strength and fame. *(Also see Reading; Speaking)*

Languid: *(See Log)*

Languor: *(See Lassitude)*

Lantern: (Housekeeper; Light) The lantern of a house in a dream represents the housekeeper or a woman. *(Also see Lamp; Minaret)*

Lapidate: (Stoning to death. *See Stoning*)

Large hall: *(See Hall)*

Lark: *(zool.)* A lark in a dream represents a little boy.

Lashing: (Beat; Hit; Whip) Lashing someone with a whip in a dream means speaking ill of him, or slandering him. If he bleeds in the dream, then it means business losses. *(Also see Beating)*

Lassitude: To see oneself in a state of listlessness or stillness in a dream is a sign of deviating from one's intention and goal. It also means depleting one's resources, or the conclusion of his life.

Last Day: *(Also see Day of Resurrection; Reckoning; Trumpet of Resurrection)*

Lasting Dynasty: *(See Donkey)*

Latch: (Doorjamb; Door latch) A door latch or a doorjamb in a dream represents a door attendant, a guard dog or a servant.

Latent: *(See Log)*

Laughing: Laughing in a dream means happiness and joy in wakefulness, except if one bursts with a horselaugh or falls over his back from laughing in his dream. If so, then it means crying. If one's laughter in his dream is caused by a joke, then it denotes his dishonesty. The same goes for laughing by imitation in a dream which means falling into sin. Laughing in a dream also could mean sorrow in wakefulness. Laughing in a dream also means that one will receive news about a newborn son. If one's laughter in a dream is as gentle and soft as a smile, then it denotes his good character and means happiness, or it could denote exactly what he shall see in wakefulness. If one sees the earth laughing in a dream, it means a good harvest in that land. If one sees a deceased person laughing in a dream, it means that he is in paradise, and enjoying the blessings of the hereafter. Laughing in a dream also represents lightheadedness, frivolity and buoyancy. This is particularly true when it denotes capable people, or people in authority, where laughing in a dream could mean their dismissal from office. *(Also see Crying; Laughter)*

Laughter: (Menstruating) Uncontrollable mirth in a dream means a misdeed that one desires to eliminate but to no avail. If one does control his hilarity, or even if he repents, he will fall again into the same misdeed. *(Also see Menstrual period)*

Laurel: (Honor) If one who qualifies to be honored for his achievements is crowned and honored with the laurel of fame or a crown of victory in a dream, it means blessings in one's life. If one does not qualify for that, then it denotes his mere passion, want, or desire. *(Also see Flag; Honor)*

Lavatory: *(See Toilet)*

Lawful: (Lawful earnings; Permissible; Legal) Earning a lawful income in a dream means the repentance of a sinner, and the guidance of a heedless person. The opposite represents the unlawful.

Laxative: *(See Medicine)*

Lay: (Lie; Repose) In a dream, if a man sees himself lying on his back over the floor, it means having good strength, or gaining one. It also means winning worldly profits, or expansion of one's control. If one sees himself lying on his back on the floor with his mouth open and bread loaves coming out of his mouth, it means that he will lose control over his business, meanwhile, he may win something totally different.

Laziness: *(See Incomplete job; Lassitude)*

Lead: (Chemical; Hunt; Pipe) Discovering lead as a mineral in one's dream means prosperity and strength in one's livelihood. Forging lead in a dream means becoming competently qualified in one's craft. Lead in a dream also represents earnings from a despicable source based on passion and wantonness. Lead in a dream also means becoming courageous, or unfailingly speak what's on one's mind. Carrying a container of liquid lead in a dream means that one should be careful about his expenses. Melting a bar of lead means a dispute or a prattle.

Leaders: *(See Elders; Star)*

Leaf: *(See Tree leaves)*

Leaking water: *(See Seeping)*

Leap: *(See Jumping)*

Learning: Learning the Qur'ān, the prophetic traditions, or a craft in a dream means richness after poverty, guidance after heedlessness, or marriage after celibacy. It also means begetting a son, or walking in the company of a spiritual guide. If one sees himself learning an evil act in a dream, it means that his is going astray, or that he is experiencing poverty after richness. *(Also see Knowledge; School; Uncertainty)*

Leather shield: (Suit of mail) In a dream, a leather shield means the same as a coat of mail, though providing more protection. Buying a leather shield in a dream also means getting married. *(Also see Armor; Coat of mail)*

Leaving one's body: Leaving one's body in a dream means that changes will take place in one's status, marriage, or property.

Leech: (Bloodsucker; Sponger) In a dream, a leech represents the grave's worms that eat one's flesh, or it could denote one's own children. If a leech falls from one's nose in a dream, it means that his wife will have a miscarriage. Leech in a dream also represent a base and a despicable enemy.

Leek: (Herb; Regret) In a dream, leek represents a deaf person. Eating it raw in a dream means earning unlawful money, though feeling good about it. Eating it cooked in a dream means refraining from pursuing such avenues. Taking a bunch of leek in a dream means saying something one will regret.

Left hand: *(See Body¹; Food)*

Leg: (Thigh; Limb) In a dream, one's legs represent longevity, old age, or his source of income. If one sees his legs turned into iron in a dream, it means that he will live a long life. If they turn into glass in the dream, it means that he will die shortly. If he sees his legs crossed in a dream, it means that he has neared the term of his live, or that he is going to face a major challenge in his life, or that he is a liar. If one sees the thighs of a woman he recognizes in the dream, it means that he will marry that woman or a friend of hers. Hairy legs in a dream mean debts, or that one may die in a prison. If one sees his leg twisted in a dream, it means that he will commit adultery. Legs in a dream also represent man's wealth or his livelihood. In that sense, if one's legs turn into iron in a dream, it represents a lasting prosperity. If his legs turn into wood in a dream, it means that he will grow weaker and unable to earn for himself. If one's legs become glass or pottery in a dream, it means that he may die shortly, and that his property and wealth will be distributed to his heirs. If one finds his leg shorter than usual in a dream, it means that he will lose some of his money. If one walks on one foot in a dream, it means that he will lose half of his wealth. If both legs are amputated in a dream, it means that he will lose everything he has. If one's leg seems fat in the dream, it denotes a good financial standing, or it could mean buying a good car, or receiving a pleasing gift. If a woman sees herself having hairy legs in a dream, it means humiliation or a trick that she will play before her husband, or that her private life will become public knowledge, or that she will receive spiritual guidance after that she lived in heedlessness. A leg in a dream also denotes hardships. If one sees his legs banded or tide together in a dream, it means fear, poverty and adversities. Exposing one's legs in a dream means abandoning prayers, and it could mean humiliation. Legs in a dream also signify writing, admonition, advice, reading a book, wisdom, one's rank, pleasure, pitfalls, fault in advising, or wrong interpretation of religious matters. *(Also see Foot; Thigh)*

Legal guardianship: (Custodian; Trustee) If one receives instructions from a testator in a dream, it has six interpretations: either that what he is told is true, or that he may be put in charge of an important project, thus, it represents rising in rank, increase in knowledge, celebrating forty years of age, a blessing of a spiritual attainment, or protection from sin. *(Also see Sponsorship)*

Legendary bird: *(See Griffin)*

Legist: *(arb. Faqïh; Religious scholar; Scholar; Theologian)* A legist in a dream represents intelligence, awareness, knowledge and seeking to study different branches of religious knowledge. Seeing a legist in a dream also represents a physician, repentance from one's sins, or receiving guidance on the straight path. *(Also see Masjid; Mosque; Scholars)*

Legume: *(See Garden herbs; Lentil; Sprouts)*

Leguminosae: *(See Garden herbs; Lentil; Sprouts)*

Lemon tree: A lemon tree in a dream represents a man who serves and benefits others, or a auspicious and a pleasant woman who also has an eccentric opinion about herself. *(Also see Lemon; Lime; Tree)*

Lemon: Eating a lemon in a dream means blame or falling sick. However, if one sees a lemon and does not eat it in the dream, then it means money. Giving someone a lemon in a dream means criticizing him, or it could mean a bust, total loss, or a bad deal. *(Also see Lemon tree; Lemon; Tree)*

Lending money: Lending an object or lending money to someone in a dream means profits of equal value. *(Also see Borrowing; Loan)*

Lent: *(See Fasting; Ramadān)*

Lentil: (Sprout) In a dream, lentils represent lawful money if sprouted, or they could mean depression, or earning loathsome money.

Leo: *(astr. See Moon)*

Leopard: *(See Tiger)*

Leprosy: (A blood disease; An infectious skin and nerve affecting disease; Albino) To see oneself as a leper in a dream means that one may receive an inheritance, money, or a garment without ornaments. Leprosy in a dream also means working in vain, or losing the benefits of one's deeds because of one's arrogance toward his Lord, and consequently, he will earn God's displeasure. It also means being innocent from false allegations, or being subject to people's slanders. If one's leprous condition spreads throughout his entire body in the dream, it means a lasting prosperity. If one sees himself praying under leprous condition in a dream, it means possessing unlawful and forbidden earnings, or forgetting whatever one has memorized from the Qur'ân. *(Also see Albino)*

Lesbian: (Sopphism; Tribadism. *See Hone; Meat; Sexual intercourse*)

Lesser Bairam: *(See Feast of breaking the fast)*

Letter carrier: *(See Mailman; Minaret; Ostrich)*

Letter: (Message) Sending or receiving a letter in a dream represents a respectable person, a rank, or a word of authority when personally delivered. If one sends a letter addressed to someone known, exhorting him to do good and eschew evil in a dream, it means satisfying one's needs and fulfilling one's purpose. If one receives a letter containing glad tidings in a dream, it means appeasing his condition, and calming his fears, whether it is bearing a son, or getting married. If one repulses the messenger or letter carrier in a dream, it means renouncing one's religion, or dropping one's profession, or it could mean innovation, or that he maybe murdered. *(Also see Book; Papers)*

Levying taxes: (Well; Circumcision)

Liaison: *(See Connections; Contract; Knot)*

Libra: *(See Constellations; Moon)*

Librarian: (Compiling literary works; Pastry chef; Sweets)

Lice nest: *(See Nit)*

Lice: Lice in a dream mean worldly success and prosperity. If one finds lice in his shirt in a dream, they mean receiving an endowment, or renewal of a leadership position. In a dream, lice in one's shirt also may represent something one does not care for it to last. If one's shirt is made of a rag, or if it is tattered in the dream, it means indebtedness. Lice on the floor in a dream represent weak people. If they surround the person in his dream, it mean that he mixes with such people. If he hates them in the dream, then they represent his enemies, though they cannot cause him any harm. If they bite him in the dream, then they represent people who slander him. If a louse flies away from one's chest in a dream, it means that one's son or an employee has run away from his house or place of business. If a large louse comes out of one's skin in a dream, it means losing one's life. A louse in a dream also represents a woman, a housekeeper, a son, an illness, an invading army, soldiers, depression, or distress. For a ruler or a policeman, lice represent his helpers. As for a teacher, lice in a dream represent his students, and for merchants, they represent his envious competition, while for a craftsperson or tradesmen they mean taxes. As for sick people, lice in a dream represent what seems to be a lasting illness. Cutting a louse in half in a dream means being good toward one's children. Eating a louse in a dream means backbiting someone. A colony of lice in a dream represent punishment. Lice in a dream also represent one's dependents or relatives who backbite, slander and divide the family. An invasion of lice in a dream means blessings, wealth, relief from difficulties, dispelling all worries and sorrows. Killing a louse in a dream means the same in wakefulness. If one wakes up from a dream in which lice were attacking him, it means that he will not escape from depression, difficulties or adversities. Picking up a louse from one's shirt or garment in a dream means hearing lies. If one becomes allergic to lice and starts itching in a dream, it means debts. Plant lice in a dream represent wrath, a calamity or a punishment. *(Also see Nit)*

Lick: Licking milk, water, honey or a dash of anything in a dream denotes frugality, tight handedness, or meager earning. To dip one's finger in a plate of tasty food and lick it in a dream may denote a precious metal, a jewel, or a pendant. To lick up one's fingers or any element in a dream means money, or benefits from the substance one is licking in his dream. *(Also see Electuary)*

Licking a bowl: *(See Lick; Wooden bowl)*

Licking an inkwell: (Homosexuality; Inkwell; Lesbian; Sodomy)

Licking honey: (Love. *See Electuary; Honey; Lick)*

Lies: *(See Lying)*

Lieutenant: (Military) In a dream, to see oneself as a lieutenant in the police or in the army means strength, respect, fame, commendation, or perhaps such a person may become a muezzin in a mosque. *(Also see Policeman)*

Life: (Bread; Clouds; Concealment; Rain; Soldiers; Vapor; Water)

Lift: *(See Car)*

Light: (Beam; Gleam; Radiance; Shine) Light in a dream means guidance. Walking from a dark place into the light in a dream means receiving guidance, divine acceptance and protection in this world and in the hereafter, and it represents richness after poverty, honor after humiliation, repentance following sin, sight after blindness and the opposite is also true should one see himself walking from light into darkness in a dream. Light in a dream also means Islām, or submission to God Almighty. Seeing light in a dream denotes good deeds, knowledge, the Holy Qur'ān, or a righteous son. In a dream, light also may mean trials and tribulations. Wearing a raiment of light in a dream means receiving knowledge, or it could represent one's growing devotion. If one sees light beaming from his body in a dream, it means that he will be gifted with a son who will grow to be a man of great knowledge, spiritual rank, and whose prayers are accepted. Thus, whatever he ask, God Almighty will grant. Light in a dream also represents a messenger, knowledge, or it could mean accomplishing one's needs in the light. Light in a dream also represents the sun, the moon, the daylight, sunshine, moonlight, the crescent moon, or the Arabic proper name Shams. *(Also see Earth; Lantern)*

Lightheartedness: *(See Blithe)*

Lighthouse: *(See Minaret)*

Likeness: *(See Correspondence)*

Lily of the valley: (Flower) In a dream, a lily of the valley denotes harm or a despised act. Receiving a lily flower in a dream means displaying bad conduct, or showing a bad example. *(Also see Hyacinth; Water lily)*

Lily: *(See Lily of the valley; Water lily)*

Limbs: (Arm; Member) Limbs in a dream represent one's family. Seeing oneself dismembered in a dream means the dispersal of his family, or that he will cut off his blood ties, or it could mean undertaking a long journey and separating from one's family for a long time. *(Also see Body¹; Tooth)*

Lime: In a dream, a lime represents money and profits. *(Also see Lemon)*

Limekiln: *(See Furnace)*

Limping: (Hitching; Jerking; Lameness) Limping in a dream means becoming incapacitated, or being unable to conclude a project one is pursuing. Limping in a dream also means acquiring knowledge, understanding one's religion, or growing in wisdom. Limping in a dream also means travels. If the limping is caused by one's right leg in the dream, it could mean that an illness will inflict one's son, If the limping has affected the left leg in the dream, it could mean that one's daughter will be engaged. If one has no children, or if he has no plans to travel, then limping in a dream means a warning to set back, slow down and to be careful about his next move. If one's leg is dislocated in a dream, it means that his wife may get sick. Limping in a dream also means longevity, knowledge and religious understanding. Seeing a woman limping in a dream means receiving something deficient. The same goes if a woman sees someone limping or hopping on one foot in her dream. Limping in a dream also represents trickery, perfidy, or treason. *(Also see Lameness)*

Linen merchant: (Linen shop) A linen merchant in a dream represents trials with women, depression, distress, toiling, adversities and humiliation.

Linen: (Clothing) Wearing a linen shirt in a dream means living an honorable life, earning lawful money and savings. *(Also see Clothing)*

Linguist: (Blunder; Genealogist; Grammarian) In a dream, a linguist represents blunder and foolish talk, or he could represent a translator, a guide, a road expert, a genealogist, emulating a good example, or he could represent a talkative person who does nothing about his habit, or one who does nothing in relation to what he says. *(Also see Blunder; Grammarian)*

Link: (Ring; Bond; Door knocker) In a dream, a link represents the religion of Islām. Holding to the like of a chain in a dream means steadfastness in one's religion. In general, a door knocker in a dream represents the door attendant, an announcer, a messenger, a warning post, or a guard dog. If the knocker is made of gold or silver in the dream, it means honor and prosperity of the people of the house. If one pulls off the door knocker, and if it brakes in the dream, it means that he follows a path of innovation.

Lintel: *(See Doorstep)*

Lion: (A tyrant; An unjust ruler; Death; Healing from a sickness; Receiving an inheritance) A lioness in a dream represents ignorance, pride, affectation and perfidy. Seeing a lion without being seen, means escape from harm one may fear, attaining knowledge and growing in wisdom. A struggle with a lion that does not lead to one's death in a dream means observing a long lasting diet caused by an illness. If one fights with a lion and eats or snatches off a piece of his flesh, bones or hair in a dream, it means that he will attain success, leadership, wealth or conquer his enemy. Sleeping beside a lion in a dream means safety from illness, or protection from one's enemy. If one sees a lion inside his own house in a dream, it means that he will gain the upper hand, or it could represent longevity and a high position in the world. A lion entering a town in a dream means a plague that will strike such a town. *(Also see Lioness)*

Lioncloth: *(See Blanket; Lion)*

Lioness: In a dream, a lioness represents an evil woman, or a despot who is also affectionate toward her cubs, or she could represent the daughter of a king or a ruler. Sleeping with a lioness in a dream means conquering one's enemy. Eating the flesh of a lioness in a dream means that one may become wealthy. *(Also see Lion)*

Lips: In a dream, lips represent man's pride, strength, virility, his helper, clarity of expression, eloquence, or special love for one's friend. The lower lip has more advantages than the upper lip in a dream. The upper lip represents a close friend, or someone one depends on in everything. Anything that affects one's lips in a dream, will manifest in any of the above. Lips in a dream also represent one's wife, child, or relatives. If one suffers pain from his lips in a dream, it means that such pain will come from one's friends. If one's lips are chopped off in the dream, it means that he engages in backbiting others. If only the lower lip is chopped off in the dream, it means that one may lose a helper or a provider. If the upper lip is missing in a dream, it means that one's life is void of blessings. If the lower lip is missing in the dream, then it represents a dying wife. If the upper lip is split in one's dream, it denotes double the effects concerning the person who is understood to be meant in the dream. If the lower lip is split or chapped in the dream, it means conducting a secret relationship with two women. If it is the upper lip, it means having two friends. If his chapped lips heal in the dream, then it means reconciliation between two friends, or winning their consent regarding one's opinion or decision. If one's upper lip is cut off in a dream, it means severing relationship with a close friend. Lips in a dream also denote relatives or kinship. Lips in a dream also mean recovering from an illness, or forcing a jealous friend to follow one's directives, or hearing good news that will heal one's heart. Lips in a dream also represent a door attendant, boys, guards, locks, knowledge, guidance, food, drinks, marriage, happiness, sadness, or keeping secrets. Having no lips in a dream means loosing any of the above, or one's dream could mean a broken door, or loosing one's keys, or perhaps it could mean the death of one's parents, husband or wife. Lips in a dream also represent the livelihood of singers or musicians who play wind instruments for a living, or the livelihood of a glass blower. If one's lips look thin and rosy in a dream, they denote clarity of speech, guidance, good food, good drink and happiness. Thick lips with black or blue color in a dream represent laziness, languor, failure to present a verifiable proof or to bring a strong witness, or they could mean discomfort, or difficulty in earning one's livelihood. If a sick person sees his lips black or blue in a dream, it could mean his death. Closed lips in a dream represent one's eyelids, a vagina, the anus, the banks of a river or a well. *(Also see Body[1])*

Listening: In a dream, listening to the Qur'ān, or to the teachings of God's Prophet, upon whom be peace, or to words of wisdom, or to an admonition, or a discourse of knowledge in a dream means receiving guidance, and it means turning repentantly to God Almighty. Otherwise, if one sees himself listening to backbiting, slandering, defamation, or eavesdropping in a dream, then it means that some harm will befall him. Listening to good advice and following its best guidance in a dream means receiving good news. Eavesdropping in a dream means that one intends to defame the other person. Listening, though pretending not to hear what is being said in a dream means that one makes it a habit to lie. The sound of a crowd in a dream means money beside other benefits. The bleating of sheep in a dream means distress and fear. The neighing of horses in a dream means might and honor. The barking of a dog in a dream means vein talk and meddling in people's business. The sound of a lynx in a dream means pampering oneself, or wantonness. The cooing of pigeons in a dream means crying, sorrows or marriage. The chirp of swallows in a dream means beneficial words. The croaking of frogs in a dream means beatings. The sound of bells and the hissing of snakes in a dream means a fight, an argument, a warning, or a war. The braying of donkeys in a dream means cursing in the darkness. The braying of mules in a dream means vein talk, or indulging in suspicious acts. The mooing of a cow in a dream means temptation. The gurgling of camels in a dream means travels and difficulties. The roaring of a lion in a dream means threats. The yowling of a tomcat in a dream means uproar, backbiting, defamation and insinuation. The yapping of foxes in a dream means a warning to escape, or to move from one field into another. The howling of a wolf in a dream means a robbery. The squeak of a mouse in a dream means profits, reunion, love and peace. The crying of a female gazelle in a dream means longing for one's homeland. The barking of a jackal in a dream means a mission of good intent, or a forthcoming evil. *(Also see Eavesdropping; Sound of animals; Speaking)*

Litter: *(arb. Maḥmal. See Car; Palanquin; Stretcher)*

Little Bear: *(See Constellations)*

Little boy: *(See Child)*

Little girl: A little girl in a dream represents prosperity, wealth after poverty, and ease after a passing adversity. Seeing a baby girl of milk suckling age is even better in a dream. It means a new and a praiseworthy development in one's life, or it could mean receiving benefits one is hoping for, or living a new world. A little girl in a dream also represents something exclusive for the one who saw her in his dream. Carrying a little girl in a dream means release of a prisoner, or if one is suffering from difficulties, or if he is at fault in an argument, or if he is indebted or poor, it means that all of his worries will be dispelled by the glad tidings of this little girl. If none of these conditions apply, then it means distress or misfortune. If a mother delivers a sick baby girl in a dream, it means relief from her difficulties. If she gives birth to such a child from her mouth, then it means death. A little girl in a dream also means a new world, while a young girl in a dream implies getting a new job. If a woman sees a little girl in a dream, it means that she cannot conceive children. If one hires a little girl to work for him in a dream, it means that he will receive glad tidings. If he hires a little boy, then it means bad news. Carrying a little girl in a dream is better than carrying a little boy. If one carries a baby boy wrapped in a swaddle in a dream, it means imprisonment or a sickness. If one is poor, then it means that he will live to an old age in misery. If he is rich and diligent in the dream, it means that he will lose his money and reason. *(Also see Child; Young woman)*

Little: (Insufficient; Scarce) Having little of something after having abundance of it in a dream represents unlawful earnings, or money earned from usury, or it could denote heavy financial obligations, or liabilities. However, having little of something in a dream also could signify having plenty of it. *(Also see Famine)*

Liver pain: *(Also see Body¹; Pain)*

Liver: *(See Body)*

Lizard: (Bewitch; Free; Gecko; Independent; Wall gecko; Witch) Seeing a lizard in a dream means greed, gluttony, or difference in opinion and taste. A lizard in a dream also represents a person who swindles people's money. It also means a sickness, or it could represent a wicked, damned and abhorred person, or a lonesome person. Perhaps seeing a lizard in a dream may mean suspicious or tainted money, someone of an unknown lineage, a reincarnated or transformed person in the form of a lizard. Noting here that transformation of the human being into another creature in reality represents a divine punishment, though it may not last for more than three days. God knows best. *(Also see Wall gecko; Monitor; Transformation)*

Load: *(See Cargo)*

Loaf of bread: (Money) In a dream, a loaf of bread represents little money, little earnings, or a small wage. *(Also see Bread)*

Loafer: *(See Destitute)*

Loan: (Borrowing; Charity; Lending money) Loaning someone something in a dream represents a charity to be paid to the borrower, or that in fact the lender will need something from the borrower. A loan in a dream also represents repentance of a sinner, or guidance for a heedless person. Loaning someone money in a dream also means generosity and giving due preference to others' needs. Lending people money with generosity to please God Almighty in a dream means spending money on God's path. As for a sick person, being under the constraint of debts in a dream signifies further health complications. If a sick person sees himself in a dream borrowing to pay his loans, it means his death. If a borrower finds that his lender has died in a dream, it means relief from his stress. Signing a loan in a dream means being put under court restraint. *(Also see Borrowing; Charity; Lending money)*

Loathsome: *(See Shameful act)*

Lobster: In a dream, a lobster represents a strong and a perfidious person who is untouchable, difficult to deal with and who is difficult to associate with, or who requires delicate handling. Eating lobster meat in a dream represents earnings from a distant land. Eating his meat also may mean earning unlawful money.

Locality: *(Also see earth)*

Lock: (Padlock) In a dream, a lock represents a trustworthy person or a virgin girl. Opening a padlock in a dream means escaping from jail, or release from prison. If one who is suffering from depression sees himself unlocking a padlock in a dream, it means that his sorrows or sadness will be dispelled. A lock in a dream also represents a proof, a strong point or a tool. Unlocking a padlock in a dream also means divorce. Locking a door in a dream means seeking a cosigner for a loan or a guarantor. If one who is seeking to get married sees a lock in his dream, it means that he will meet with a trustworthy and a caring woman. A padlock for a traveller in a dream means safety. A metal lock in a dream means dignity, safety, piety, deciphering a language, symbols, or acquiring knowledge. Wooden locks in a dream represent a husband, children, knowledge, wisdom, ease in one's life, or guarding one's promise. Locks in a dream also mean heedlessness. A wooden lock means hypocrisy, or hesitation in one's words and actions, or it could mean accepting a bribe. *(Also see Close; Padlock)*

Locksmith: A locksmith in a dream represents a broker. If he locks the door of his own house in the dream, it means that he arranges marriages, or works as a wedding consultant. If he locks the door of his shop in a dream, it means that he brokers merchandises and businesses. Seeing a locksmith in a dream also means concealing a secrets, or it could mean marriage.

Locusts: In a dream, locusts represent an adversity, a trial, a calamity or a punishment. They also represent a destructive rain, or an occupation by a vehement army. Eating locusts in a dream means that one will receive money. If one fills a cup or a pitcher with locust in a dream it also means earnings. Any place locusts fly into without causing harm in a dream means overcoming from adversities. If a rich person who has lost his wealth sees a swarm of locust falling all over him in a dream, it means that he will recuperate his wealth.

Lodge: (Cave; Den; Harbor; lodge; Refuge; Retreat; Sanctuary. *See Inn; Hostel; Pub)*

Log: (Inactive; Latent; Languid) In a dream, a log represents a chronic illness, or paralysis. As for a butcher or a shoemaker, a log in a dream represents money and profits. *(Also see Firewood)*

Loins: *(See Backbone; Body¹)*

Loitering: *(See Destitute)*

Loneliness: (Aloneness; Isolation; Solitude) Loneliness in a dream means fame, artistry or attaining excellence in one's craft. If a ruler or a governor sees himself alone in a dream, it represents his impeachment from office. Finding oneself alone in a dream also means poverty, or separation from one's beloved. Loneliness in a dream also means humiliation, infamy, or segregation.

Longevity: *(See Teeth)*

Looking at a sexual organ: (Sexual organs; Vagina) Lustfully looking at the vagina of one's wife or that of another woman, or touching it in a dream means engaging in a rotten business. Seeing a naked woman without her knowledge in a dream represents common pitfalls and mistakes one makes in his life.

Looking stern: *(See Scowling)*

Loom: In a dream, a standing loom represents travels or business activities. A loom laying flat in a dream means inhibition, restraint, or seclusion. In a dream, a loom also means support or a gift for a needy person. It also means a high ranking position or becoming a respected chairperson. If a woman sees another woman pushing her away from her loom to sit in her place in a dream, it means death.

Losing a fight: (Defeat; Depression) Losing a fight in a dream means joy. Losing a fight in a dream also could mean vanquishing one's enemy if they are compatible. Otherwise, the winner of a fight is a dream denotes the loser in wakefulness. *(Also see Defeat)*

Losing sight: (Blindness) If one sees in his dream as though the world is totally destroyed and that he remained alone therein, it means that he may lose his sight.

Loss of tracks: *(See Disappearing)*

Loss: (Business) If one's losses relate to his earnings, then his losses in the dream mean decadence of one's principals, religious downswing, or they could mean heedlessness after guidance, disbelief after following one's religion, or losses in general. This sin is man's own. If one suffers a loss in a dream, it means dismay, horror, a scare, a shock or a menace. Complaining about a harm one suffers, a damage or a loss in a dream means attaining one's goal. *(Also see Penny)*

Lost object: *(See Compensation; Finding something)*

Lost: (Getting lost) If a man of knowledge sees himself lost in a dream, it means that he will benefit people with his knowledge, that his teachings will spread widely and that he will be remembered for a long time after he dies. Getting lost in a dream also means bad luck. If one loses a garment or a house in a dream, it means extra expenses, repairs, or taxes he will pay for his property. If one is stripped of his entire wardrobe in a dream, it means that he will avoid an evil and a costly incident. *(Also see Wandering)*

Lot tree: (Heavens; Highest goal; Ultimate results) Seeing the heavenly Lot tree in a dream means attaining one's highest goal and reaching the ultimate promise. *(Also see Buckthorn; Lotus tree)*

Lot[1]: (God's prophet Lüt; Nephew of God's prophet and bosom friend Abraham, upon both of them be peace) Seeing the prophet Lot in a dream means distress and trouble caused by one's own people and wife, or perhaps it could mean victory over one's enemy and witnessing God's wrath toward them. Seeing the prophet Lot in a dream also denotes obliteration of a nation, effacement, earthquake and destruction if the people who displease their Lord and follow the conduct of the dwellers of the two cities of Sodom and Gomorrah. Seeing the prophet Lot's wife in a dream means that one's wife will rebel against him and strive to destroy his life and perhaps she will also be destroyed during that process. If everyone sees Lot's wife in a dream, it means that evil will spread among the women of that land. Seeing the prophet Lot, upon whom be peace, in a dream also denotes a warning against sodomy, and it means that one's wife is a corrupt woman.

Lot[2]: (Batch; Clump; Cluster) In a dream, a lot or a cluster represents atonement for one's sin, or something offered to compensate for failing to fulfill a vow, or it could mean earning tainted money.

Lotus tree: (Lotus; Jujube tree) In a dream, a lotus tree means money and profits. Eating from its fruit in a dream means having a good spirit and a praiseworthy religious standing, or if one qualifies for leadership, it means that he will attain it. In a dream, a lotus tree is also a noble tree. As for religious people, seeing a lotus tree in a dream means spiritual growth, and for a ruler, it means gaining power. *(Also see Jujube tree)*

Loud steps: *(See Tap)*

Loud: *(See Spell out)*

Louse: *(See Nit)*

Love for the world: *(See Elephant man; Love)*

Love poems: *(See Courting; Poet)*

Love seat: *(See Couch)*

Love: (Beloved; Enamored; Honey; Hostage; Lover; Platonic love) Love in a dream means trials and temptations. If one does something he loves in a dream, it means that he will engage in an act that has no limitations. If a man says to woman: "I love you," in a dream, it means that he truly hates her. If one sees himself indulging and satisfying every desire he has and without feeling any restrictions in the dream, it means that he will stray from God's path and lives a corrupt life. Love in a dream also means distress, worries and sorrow. Love in a dream also represents one's ability to express something. Otherwise, it could mean that he keeps to himself. Love in a dream also means trials and fame that incurs people's compassion for the person in love. Love in a dream also means poverty, sickness and death. In fact, death in a dream also could mean love, or living distant from one's beloved or life after death. To burn in the fire in a dream also means love. To enter paradise in a dream also means love and to enter hell-fire in a dream means separation from one's beloved. Yearning for one's beloved in a dream means heedlessness, and love in a dream also indicates corruption in one's religious life, or loss of money. To love someone in God in a dream, means mercy between people. Otherwise, to love one another for personal interests in a dream means a partnership that will end in betrayal or it could mean a marriage without family consent. Pretending to be in love in one's dream means straying from God's path. If a knowledgeable person or a scholar pretends to be enamored in a dream, it means that he will deceive people with his ornate presentations and contradict their standards. *(Also see Enamored; Honey; Lick; Pretending)*

Lover of boys: *(See Pederasty)*

Lowland: (Basin; Cavity; Depression) Walking through a lowland in a dream means suffering from adverse conditions, or it could mean depression and hoping to reach a time of recovery.

Lubrication: (Fat; Oil) A motor lubricator in a dream represents knowledge, guidance, serving the people of knowledge, or being close to people in authority. *(Also see Grease)*

Luck: (Dwellings)

Lumber merchant: (Wood) In a dream, a lumber merchant represents the chief of hypocrites. One's dream also could mean building homes and roads.

Lumber: (Hypocrisy) In a dream, lumber represents a person who mixes with hypocrites, or one who mixes goodness and hypocrisy in his life, or one who appears better than he is in reality. Damp lumber represents boys. If a traveller on a boat sees lumber in his dream, it represents the boat he is travelling on.

Lumberman's saw: *(See Saw)*

Luminary: *(See Fame)*

Lunar eclipse: *(See Eclipse)*

Lunar months: *(See Arabic months)*

Lunatics: *(See Mental hospital)*

Lunch: Having lunch in a dream means taking a brake out of exhaustion from one's work. *(Also see Invitation)*

Lung pain: *(See Body¹; Lungs; Pain)*

Lungs: (Anger; Pulmonary; Soul; Woman) In a dream, lungs represent the abode of the soul. Damaged or decaying lungs in a dream represent the nearing of one's death. If one sees his lungs turned black in a dream, it means cessation of his business or source of his livelihood. Healthy lungs in a dream represent longevity. Lungs in a dream also represent one's wife, anger, or one's composure. *(Also see Body¹)*

Lupine: (*bot.*) A green lupine plant in a dream represents poverty and struggle to earn one's livelihood, or it could mean knowledge without actions. Boiled lupine beans in a dream represent medicine, or fast earnings.

Lure: (Entice; Incite; Induce; Lure; Urge)

Lust: *(See Dog)*

Lute: *(See Musician; Singing; String instruments)*

Luxuries shop: (Amenity; Extravagance) Luxuries salesman in a dream means enriching oneself at people's expense. Luxuries shop owner in a dream means enslaving others, or he could represent a cattle merchant, or celebrating happy or sad anniversaries.

Lying: (Blunder; Lies; Tell a lie) Lying in a dream means giving false testimony in court, fabricating a lie, slandering someone, or it could mean constant failure in one's life. Lying in a dream also means talking nonsense, or letting one's imagination do the talking, or spreading a sharp idea. If someone hears that in a dream, and if he spreads the word, then the negative effects of his doing will bring more harm than good. If one sees himself lying to God Almighty in a dream, it means that he has no brain. *(Also see Blunder)*

Lynx: (Cheetah; Panther) Lynx, a cheetah, or a panther in a dream represent might, exaltation, cuddling and coquetry, along with anger, rage and enmity. A lynx in a dream also represents an enemy who does not show either his enmity nor friendliness. Fighting with a lynx in a dream means fighting with someone with such qualities and character. Using a lynx to hunt with in a dream means prosperity and might.

M

Mace: *(See Scepter)*

Madman: *(See Insanity; Mental derangement)*

Madness: *(See Mental derangement)*

Maghrib: *(arb. See Five times prayers)*

Magi: *(See Worshipping fire)*

Magic arts: (Conjuring; Jugglery; Tricks) In a dream, magic arts mean deceit, pride, artificiality and temptations. To learn about sorcery, or black magic, or about similar arts in a dream means innovation and heedlessness. *(Also Magician; Sorcery; Spit out)*

Magic practice: *(See Fortuneteller; Magic arts; Sorcery; Spit out)*

Magician: (Illusion) In a dream, a magician represents a seducer. If he uses an apple in his illusion in the dream, it means that he will seduce his own son. If he uses a butterfly in his performance in the dream, it means that he will rape his own wife. *(Also see Magic arts; Sorcery; Spit out)*

Magnification: *(See Giant)*

Magpie: (Blabber; Hodgepodge) In a dream, a magpie represents a man who keeps no promise, who has neither honor nor does he feel comfortable with anyone. Such a man is rich, accursed and opportunistic. If a magpie speaks to someone in a dream, it means that he will receive news concerning a distant person. Catching a magpie in a dream means overcoming a corrupt and a perfidious person. Fighting with a magpie in a dream means engaging in a futile adventure and gaining nothing from it.

Magus: *(See Worshipping fire)*

Mahaleb: (Fragrance; Seeds used in perfumes and in making sweets; Prunus Mahaleb, *bot.*) In a dream, a mahaleb tree represents blessed and sweet earnings. Seeing a mahaleb tree or a branch of it in a dream also may mean begetting a son.

Mahmal: *(arb. See Palanquin)*

Mail carrier: *(See Carrier)*

Mail: Mail in a dream means activities or travels. Mail in a dream also means being led by one's evil actions and sins into the road of destruction or consequent death. *(Also see Mailman; Ostrich)*

Mailman: In a dream, a mailman represents the caller to God, a preacher, a news carrier, an emissary, a letter carrier or a courier. *(Also see Dromedary rider; Mail; Ostrich)*

Maintenance: *(See Family support)*

Majesty: Majesty and reverence in a dream represents glad tidings, or rising into a high raking position and earning an exalted station in God's sight whether the person seen in such a state is alive or dead. To recognize a state of reverence and majesty in a dream also means receiving guidance on the straight path, or repenting from one's sins.

Makeup: (Cosmetics; Henna; Kohl; Medicine) Cosmetic makeup in a dream represents a craftsman's working tools. Makeup in a dream also means adornment, money, or children. *(Also see Blushing; Kohl)*

Malā'ika: *(arb. See Angels)*

Male organ: (Penis) To look at one's sexual organs in a dream means profits, children, fame, carnal desires, want, family, strength, virility, conduct, or longevity. If a man sees himself without a male organ in a dream, it means that he will lose a son who will either die or travel away from his father, and who will leave no tracks of his whereabouts. It also could mean that he will have no more children. If a sick person sees himself without a male organ in a dream, it means that he will die from his illness. If he is a king or a governor, it means that he will be deposed. Having two male organs in a dream means that one will beget two sons. Castration in a dream means that one will bear no more daughters. If a pregnant woman sees herself having a male organ in a dream, it means that she will beget a son. If she never had children before, it means that she is barren. If one is circumcised in a dream, it means that he will fulfil his religious covenant, or pay a debt. A pubic area which is excessively hairy in a dream represents an insolent person. Feeding one's sexual organ in a dream means dying an ugly death. If one's male organ turns into a female organ in a dream, it means that he has lost his virility, or that he will become submissive. If one sees himself touching his wife's sexual organ which then turns into a male organ in a dream, it means that she may undergo an operation in relation to abnormal sexual trend. A male organ in a dream also represents a craftsman's tools. Playing with one's male organ in a dream means that one does not shy from God's presence and that of His angels, or that he has forgotten about proper conduct or common moral standards, or if he is a learned person, it means that he will forget what he has learned.

Male: (Gender; Fertilizing; Masculine virility) A human being of the male gender in a dream represents a positive element, a decisive force, or someone who is extremely lucky. *(Also see Man)*

Mālik: (The archangel Mālik; The guardian of hell-fire) Seeing the archangel Mālik in a dream means standing before a policeman or a police commissioner for questioning. If he smiles in the dream, it means that one will be saved from imprisonment. If a sick person sees such a dream, it means that he may die shortly. If one becomes the archangel Mālik, or eats something sweet from his hand in a dream, it denotes that one is a true follower on the path of God Almighty and His Prophet, upon whom be peace. It also means that one loves his brethren on the path. It also means that one will be honored, gain power, abstain from sin or from any act of disobeying God's commands, and he will become free from hypocrisy and heedlessness. It also could mean that one is guided and that he loves God's religion. Eating something that is given by Mālik in a dream also means abstinence and repentance from sin, or it could mean submitting to guidance after having gone astray. If one sees the archangel Mālik walking toward him in a dream, it means peace and safety from hell-fire. It also means salvation and restoration of one's faith. However, if he sees the archangel Mālik walking away from him and showing displeasure in the dream, it means that one will commit an act that will deliver him into the blaze of hell-fire. *(Also see Hell-fire)*

Mallet: *(See Hammer)*

Man of the year: *(See Boiler; Kettle; Roasting)*

Man: (Person) When a man is recognized in a dream, he is the same person in wakefulness, or it could be his brother, or a person with the same resemblance or name. If he takes something valuable or cherished from the person having the dream, it means the opposite, and one will receive from such a man what he wishes for in wakefulness. If he takes a shirt or a rope in the dream, it means

263

that he will accept a promise from the person seeing the dream. If he takes a child away from him, it means enmity between the two. As explained under 'Human being' p. 217, seeing the children of Adam in a dream is an exalted thing in general. Each category of people conveys a different interpretation. The category of rulers and judges in a dream means courts. The category of government authorities represents fear. Soldiers mean travels. Craftsmen in a dream mean profits, or they could represent their respective trades. Women in a dream signify temptation, while pious people represent devotion. *(Also see Human being; Mankind)*

Mandolin: *(See String instruments)*

Manger: (Feeding trough) Seeing a manger or a feeding trough in a dream means having power, receiving a gift, or it could represent one's intelligence, diversification and qualifications. A manger in a dream also represents a woman. Seeing two animals feeding from a trough in a dream means that one's wife is hiding a secret affair.

Mangonel: *(See Missile launcher)*

Mangy: (Skin disease of domestic animals; A bacterial disease) In a dream, mangy represents pestilence or a plague. If one sees himself struck by such a disease causing him to itch though no puss or malignant festering runs from his sores in the dream, it means that his troubles and adversities are caused by his own progeny or relatives. If one's body is afflicted with mangy in a dream, it means that his troubles will come from his friends or from his working environment. If it strikes at his right hand or his cheek in a dream, then his adversities will come from his clan. If it strikes at his left hand, then his troubles will come from his business partner or brother. If his illness forms puss in the dream, it means hard earned money that will also cause headache. Such a disease means money for a poor person and it could mean leadership for a rich person. Following this trail of thinking, mangy or any skin disease in a dream signify less harm compared to other diseases. If an employees experiences such skin disorder in a dream, it means that he does not qualify to work in that company. If it is one's son in the dream, it means that he will disobey his father concerning an undesired friendship. If it is one's wife in the dream, it means that she is engaged in something awful that will bring shame to the entire family.

Manifest character: (Character; Hidden; Forest; Wild plants; Woods)

Manifestation: *(See Appearance)*

Mankind: (Conduct; Quality; Magnitude) The quality of humankind in a dream may represent the quality of the like creations. Thus, a beneficial bird may mean a praiseworthy person, a beast may represent the like quality in man, a harvest projecting a particular person denotes human qualities of a lesser magnitude, etcetera. *(Also see Human being; Man)*

Manna: (Food; Valuable gift; Unexpected favor) A gummy saccharine secretion found on a species of a Tamarisk tree. A manna tree is also found in the Egyptian Sinai. Eating manna in a dream means receiving lawful money without any labor or hardships, or it could mean a favor and a bestowal by the grace of God Almighty. Seeing manna in a dream also means spending money on God's path, or escaping from a fatal accident or danger. Exchanging manna for green sprouts and garlic in a dream means humiliation and poverty. Eating manna in a dream means earnings lawful money.

Mantilla: *(spa. See Khimār)*

Mantle: (Attire; Cap; Garb; Mantilla; Khimār; Veil)

Manual: *(See Reference book)*

Manumission: (Abraham; Ismāïl; Immolation; Liberation) Manumission of a slave in a dream represents a ritual sacrifice, or the offering of an animal during the Feats of Immolation, on the 10th day of the Arabic month of Zul-Hijjah, and following the annual pilgrimage to Mecca. If one gives permission to his wife to leave him in a dream, it means that they will be divorced. If a bondman sees himself liberated in a dream, it means that he or his master may die shortly. If a bondman dies in a dream, it means that he will be liberated. Manumission means departure from bondage. If a sick person sees himself liberated from bondage in a dream, it means his death. If he is a sinner, it means that he will repent for his sin. If he is an atheist, it means that he will become a believer and God Almighty will forbid his flesh to hell-fire. If a free man sees himself liberated from slavery in a dream, it means that he will repay his debts, or repent for his sins. *(Also see Feast of Immolation; Slave)*

Manure: (Dung; Excrement) Manure represents money for one who eats it, or for one who collects it in his house or in a barn in his dream. Any animal excrements that are used to fertilize the soil, or if they are used as fuel represent profits when seen in a dream and particularly dried dung. Pigeons' droppings, or the refuse of any type of fowl in a dream represent unlawful money. Cow dung in a dream is a sign of prosperity and a good harvest for farmers only. *(Also see Droppings; Dung)*

Map: In a dream, a map means money. A map in a dream also represents a trainer, a craftsman, one's helpers, or a friend one takes pride in associating with them.

Maple syrup: *(See Sugar)*

Maple tree: *(See Mulberry tree)*

Maqām Ibrāhïm: *(arb. See Abraham; Pilgrimage; Station of Abraham)*

Marble cutter: In a dream, a marble cutter represents wealth, a palace, high class, beauty, unity and love. Laying marble in a dream means preparing oneself for the next move, or completing a pathway. *(Also see Marble)*

Marble saw: *(See Saw)*

Marble: (Beauty; Eulogy; Hardness; Wealth) In a dream, marble represents prosperity, a beautiful wife, respectable people, class, servants, or properties. If a poor person sees the floor of his house covered with marble in a dream, it means prosperity, marriage, purchasing a business, acquiring knowledge, learning a poem, bearing righteous children, or if he qualifies, it could mean that he will receive a high ranking appointment, or that he may actually work with marble, or in sculpturing marble or in manufacturing fountains from marble, or work in masonry, or as a stone cutter, or he may change his attitude toward things, signaling the end of depression and the start of a joyful time in his life, living in high rises, or spending money for leisure and vacations. If one sees gravestones made of marble, or if one sees marble pillars in a dream, it means a good reward for one's deeds, or it could mean eulogy, or lauding. An architecturally sound edifice made from marble in a dream represents good writing, skillfulness, dowry or a generous prenuptial agreement. If the marble is used excessively in the dream, it means suspicion and doubt about one's resources or source of income. The marble bases of a pillar in a dream represents social benefits. As for marble tiles in a dream, they represent beautiful and noble women, or dignitaries. As for marble jars, tiles, or basins in a dream, they represent the positive and negative effects one overlooks during the course of this life. *(Also see Column; Marble cutter)*

March of an army: In a dream, it means sorrow, or earnestly seeking knowledge, desiring to become wealthy, preparing to perform a pilgrimage, or celebrating a religious festival. If one sees himself marching alone in a campaign in a dream, it means that he might endanger his own life, lose his wealth, or that he may face an awesome trial that will bear heavily on him.

March: *(See Earthquake; Thunder)*

Mare: A mare in a dream represents a noble woman. If one sees himself riding a mare in a dream, it means that he may rape a chaste and a noble woman. In general, a mare in a dream represents people who are known for their honesty and good conduct. Buying a mare in a dream also means getting married. If one is already married, then it means that he will own a property or a farm. A mare in a dream also represents a rich person, a beautiful woman or a handsome looking man, a religious person, a comforting wife, a forbearing husband, or a sick person. If one loses his mare, or if it dies in the dream, it means that he will lose his source of income. Dismounting a mare in a dream may mean loss of one's business, a divorce, or loss of one's house. Hearing the squealing of a mare in a dream means increase in one's income, or it could mean one's promotion at work. Drinking the milk of a mare in a dream means developing a beneficial relationship with a politician. *(Also see Donkey; Horse)*

Marijuana: Intoxicating drug and a wild grass obtained from the hemp plant. In a dream, marijuana means contemptible earnings, a sickness, and a miserable life. *(Also see Intoxicants)*

Marjoram: *(bot.* Mint; Sweet marjoram; Wild marjoram) Smelling a marjoram plant in a dream means recovering from an illness and enjoying a good health for that year. Planting a marjoram in a dream means begetting a healthy and a beautiful child who will grow to possess a good character. Marjoram in a dream also could mean marriage, or something that will not last. *(Also see Mint)*

Marketplace: Going to the marketplace in a dream means seeking knowledge, or looking for work. A marketplace in a dream also represents a mosque, or winning a war. In fact, the merchants and the customers bargain with one another, some win and some lose. If a knowledge seeking student sees himself in a marketplace that he does not recognize, then if he walks away from it in the dream, it means that he will cease schooling or interrupt his studies and fail to acquire his degree, or it could mean that he has missed his Friday congregational prayers. It also could mean that the knowledge he is seeking is not intended to please God Almighty. If one sees himself shoplifting in a dream, it means that he steals, or holds contempt and conceit in his heart, or if he is a man of knowledge, it means that he will foster falsehood or become affected. If one sees a common marketplace on fire, or filled with people, or with a stream of fresh water running in the middle of it, or if it is fragrant with perfumes in the dream, then it represents good business for everyone and increase in their profits, though hypocrisy will later on spread among the people. Otherwise, if one finds the shops closed, the merchants drowsing and spiders webs spreading in every corner and covering the merchandise in the dream, it means stagnation of business or suffering major losses. Seeing the marketplace in a dream is also interpreted to represent the world. Whatever affects it will show in people's lives, in their mosques, churches, or temples including their profits, losses, clothing, recovering from illness, lies, stress, sorrows or adversities. If the market is quiet in the dream, then it represents the laziness of its salespeople. *(Also see Entering a house)*

Maroon: (Color; Bay-colored; Reddish-brown) In a dream, the color maroon means dignity, nobility, power, or it could represent a wealthy woman. *(Also see Colors)*

Marriage bond: To rescind one's bond of marriage in a dream means either death or dismissal from work. To revoke the bond of marriage in a dream also may mean selling a product for a term, requiring its return, or it may mean apostasy. *(Also see Marriage; Yoke)*

Marriage for pleasure: (Morganatic marriage. *See Explorer)*

Marriage: (Cage; Digging a grave; Duel; Golden cage; Pearl; Sanctuary; Silver cage) Marriage in a dream represents the providence of God Almighty and care for His servants. Marriage in a dream also means imprisonment, indebtedness, sorrow, distress, depression, carrying a liability, or endeavoring to achieve a high ranking position. If one marries a known woman in his dream, it means that he will endeavor to satisfy the normal responsibilities of a husband. If one marries an unknown woman, and if he could not see her in his dream, it denotes the nearing of his death, or it could mean moving from an old house into a new one. If a sick woman sees herself getting married to a man she does not recognize or know his name in a dream, it means that she may die from her illness. If the man who sees himself getting married in the dream qualifies, it means that he will attain a high ranking job or a suitable position. If one's wedding ceremony is made with witnesses only in the dream, it means that he has made a covenant with God Almighty. If he performs a traditional wedding ceremony with its celebrations and festivities in the dream, it means a new job, or it could mean acquiring fame, or becoming renowned for one's good reputation or character. Marriage in a dream is also interpreted in association with a trade. If one marries a woman who dies shortly after her wedding in the dream, it means that he will perform a job that earns him nothing but hard labor, toiling and stress. If one marries an adulteress in a dream, it means that he is an adulterer. If one marries a vicious, aggressive or a dominating wife in a dream, it means that his movements will be hampered with various restrictions. If one marries a deceased woman in a dream, it means that he will revive a profitable project he had earlier abandoned. If a man offers his mother in marriage to one of his friends in a dream, it means that he will sell his house. If a pregnant woman sees herself getting married in a dream, it means that she will give birth to a girl. If she sees herself in her wedding night in a dream, it means that she will beget a son. If a mother who has a son sees herself getting married in a dream, it means that she will marry off her son. In general, the marriage of a married woman, or of an unwed woman in a dream means benefits. If a woman marries a deceased man in a dream, it means that she will become lost and impoverished. If a married man sees himself getting married to a second woman in a dream, it means profits. To marry the daughter of a known man of knowledge in a dream means prosperity. If a sick woman marries a man of knowledge in her dream, it means recovering from her illness. If a man sees himself marrying a living relative who is in a degree of consanguinity that precludes such a marriage in a dream, it means that he will sever his ties with such a relative, or with her family. Otherwise, if that relative is already dead, it means that he will contact her immediate relatives and establish a friendly relationship with them. *(Also see Cage; Duel; Sanctuary; Wife; Yoke)*

Marrow: In a dream, bon marrows represent hidden treasures, a library, ammunition or an inheritance. Bone marrows in a dream also mean hoarding money. If a sick person sees his bone marrow in a dream, it means that he will find a cure and recover from his illness. *(Also see Body¹; Bones; Brain)*

Mars: (Planet) The planet Mars in a dream represents evil, calamities, trouble, fear, or blood shedding. Seeing the planet Mars descending or burning in a dream means calamities, injustice, burglaries, divorce, or demolishing one's habitat. The planet Mars in a dream also represents a warrior, an army, or the police force. *(Also see Heavens)*

Marsh mallow tree: *(See Mill)*

Marsh: *(See Meadow)*

Marten: *(See Weasel)*

Martingale: (Pith) In a dream, a martingale represents braces for a broken rib, bone setting, ointment for chest pain, the support by which one finds courage, feeling good about oneself, or the core that evokes pride about one's achievement. A martingale in a dream also could mean self-restraint, or self control.

Martyr: Seeing a known martyr alive in a dream means following his good traditions and aspiring for his character and conduct. Seeing a known martyr in a dream also means striving to attain God's pleasure and to reach His nearness.

Marwa: (*arb.* Hill of Marwa; Mecca. *See Rituals of the pilgrimage; Sa'ī*)

Masjid: (*arb.* God's House; Mosque; Place of worship) In Arabic, the word masjid means a place of prostration, while the word Jāmi means a place of gathering. A masjid or a mosque in a dream represents a scholar and its gates represent men of knowledge and the guardians, or the attendants of God's House. Building a masjid in a dream means emulating the traditions of God's Prophet, upon whom be peace, fostering the unity of one's family, or becoming a judge, should one qualify for such an office. A masjid filled with people in a dream represents a gnostic, a man of knowledge and wisdom, or a preacher who invites people to his house, advises them, brings their hearts together, teaches them the precepts of their religion and explains the wisdom behind the divine revelations. Seeing a masjid being demolished in a dream means that such a gnostic, or religious scholar and devout believer will die in that locality. In a dream, if the roof of a masjid caves in, it means that one will indulge in an abominable action. If one sees a stranger performing his prayers in a masjid in a dream, it means that the Imām of that masjid will dies from a terminal illness. If one enters a masjid in the company of a group of people, and if they dig a small hole for him inside the masjid in the dream, it means that he will get married. If one's house becomes a masjid in a dream, it means that he will attain piety, purity of heart, escetic detachment and an honor he will receive from his brethren. He will also call upon them to follow what is true and to abstain from what is false. If a masjid is transformed into a bathhouse in a dream, it means that a chaste person will turn corrupt or become heedless. A masjid in a dream also represents a marketplace or a business. If one has to climb up a staircase to reach the masjid in a dream, then the masjid represents a thrifty person who does not like to share what he has. If one has to climb down a staircase to reach the masjid in a dream, it means that his needs will be satisfied. If a masjid in the city is moved to a remote village in a dream, it means stagnation of one's business, being ostracized from one's community, or it could mean legal complications related to one's inheritance. If a ruler builds a house for God Almighty or a masjid in a dream, it means that he will be a just ruler and he will govern his subject by the divine laws. If a religious scholar builds a masjid in a dream, it means that he will author a book that will benefit others, or delivers a commentary on a complex religious issue, or if he is wealthy, it means that he will pay the alms tax due on his assets. Building a masjid in a dream also means getting married, or conceiving a child who will grow to become a righteous and a knowledgeable scholar, or if one is poor, it means that he will become rich. Otherwise, it means that one will serve God's House and fill it with invocations, supplications, serving the interest of the community, leading the people to unity and love, and teaching them to value obedience to God's commands. Building a masjid in a dream also could mean becoming a real estate agent, or repenting from one's sins, or receiving guidance on God's path, or to die as a martyr, hence, what one builds for God Almighty in a dream, represents his house in paradise. Such interpretation applies if one builds a masjid following the proper procedures and with lawfully earned money, and using proper materials. Otherwise, building it with what is unlawful of money or materials in the dream, or changing the direction of the prayer niche, etcetera, then one's dream will carry the opposite meaning. If one builds a masjid or a fellowship house in a dream, it means that he will seek the path of knowledge and wisdom, or that he will attend a pilgrimage during that same year, or establish a permanent business, such as a hotel, a bathhouse or a shop, etcetera. Building the roof of a masjid in a dream means taking care of orphans, or sponsoring homeless children. Expanding a masjid in a dream means increase in one's good deeds, repentance from a sin, adopting good conduct, or being just. Seeing oneself inside a new masjid one does not recognize in a dream means attending the pilgrimage to God's House in Mecca during that same year, or joining religious circles to learn about one's religion. If one's shop becomes a masjid, or if the masjid becomes a shop in the dream, it denotes lawful earnings, or it could mean mixing lawful and unlawful earnings. A forsaken masjid or mosque in a dream means intentionally ignoring the value of gnostics and religious scholars, or denying the necessity to command what is good and to eschew what is evil. A forsaken masjid in a dream also denotes the presence of ascetics who have renounced the world and its people and care less about their material possessions. A known mosque in a dream represents the city where it is erected. For instance, the Aqsā mosque in a dream represents Jerusalem, the Sacred mosque represents Mecca, the Prophet's Mosque (uwbp) represents Medina, the Omayyād mosque represents Damascus, Al-Azhar mosque represents Cairo and the Blue mosque represents Istanbul, etcetera. A known mosque in a dream also could represent the renowned scholars who live in that place, or the ruler of that country, or any of his ministers. If one enters a mosque and immediately after crossing the entrance gate, he prostrates himself to God Almighty in the dream, it means that he will be given the opportunity to repent for his sins. If one comes to a masjid and finds its doors locked, then if someone opens the door to him in a dream, it means that he will help someone in paying his debt, then extol his good virtues in public. If one enters a mosque riding on an animal in a dream, it means that he will cut off his connection with his relatives, leave them behind and forbid them to follow him. If one dies in a masjid in a dream, it means that he will die as a true penitent. If the carpet or the straw mat of a mosque becomes a shredded rag in the dream, it means that the community of that masjid is divided and corrupt. Building a masjid in a dream also means overcoming one's enemy. Entering the Sacred Mosque in Mecca in a dream means arriving with one's bride to their new home and it could mean fulfillment of a promise, being truthful, dispelling one's fear and reaching the shore of safety. (*Also see Minaret; Minbar; Mosque*)

Mask: (Veil) If a man sees himself wearing a mask in a dream, it means that he may commit adultery with his servant or his housekeeper. Wearing a mask in a dream also means developing gratitude and contentment. (*Also see Helmet*)

Mason: (*See Construction worker*)

Master: (*See Educator*)

Masticate: (*See Chewing gum*)

Mat: (Plaited fabric; Seat; Woven straws) In a dream, a mat represents a servant, or the court of justice. Sitting on a mat in a dream means that one will commit an act which he will regret. (*Also see Straw mat*)

Math teacher: (*See Educator*)

Matrimony: (*See Yoke of matrimony*)

Mattock: (*See Shovel*)

Mattress: (Bed; Sleeping pad) In a dream, a mattress represents comfort or a woman. Selling one's mattress in a dream means divorcing one's wife. If one's wife is sick, then selling one's mattress means that she may die from her illness. If one sees a dog or a pig sleeping on his mattress in a dream, it means that an insolent person is having a secret affair with one's wife. If the mattress is stuffed with wool, cotton, or down in the dream, it represents a wealthy woman. If the mattress is made of brocade or silk in the dream, it represents a Hindu woman.

If the color of the mattress is white in the dream, it represents a religious and a pious wife. A green mattress in a dream represents a pious and a religious wife. A black mattress in the dream represents a woman who is engaged in doing something for other than God's pleasure. Buying a new and a beautiful-looking mattress in a dream means marriage to a chaste and a beautiful woman. If the new mattress is torn or damaged in the dream, it means living with an impious woman. Changing the place of one's bed in a dream means divorce. If one finds himself unable to sleep on his bed in a dream, it means that he cannot have marital relationship with his wife, or perhaps he could be suffering from impotence. If one tears his mattress in pieces in a dream, it means that he will commit adultery. If he sees his mattress placed in front of the city hall in a dream, it means that he may assume an important political appointment. An unknown mattress in an unknown place in a dream means buying, receiving, or inheriting a farmland. A mattress in a dream also means bearing a son. Changing one's mattress in a dream means leaving one's wife for the sake of another woman. If one does not like to sleep on his mattress in a dream and prefers to find another place to rest, it means that he will renounce his conjugal life. Folding one's mattress and placing it aside in a dream means leaving one's home for a long journey, divorcing one's wife, or avoiding to sleep with her for one reason or another, or it could mean the death of either the husband or the wife. Sitting over one's bed in a dream means gaining authority, or managing someone's business. Sleeping in a dream means heedlessness, or it could mean peace and tranquility. (Also see Bed)

May: (See Thunder)

Mayor: (See Bull; Cattle dealer; King)

Mazdaism: (See Worshipping fire)

Meadow: (Beauty; Grass; Green; Knowledge; Paradise; Wisdom) In a dream, a meadow represents an easy and a trouble free money, or it could represent a wife who has little reservation and tactfulness. Seeing a meadow in a dream also means receiving inner knowledge that is imparted directly by God Almighty through mystical inspirations, or it could mean establishing a charitable endowment. A meadow with its pasture, streams, perennials and spireas in a dream represents the world, its ornaments, attractions and wealth. A meadow in a dream also may mean a place of business or a work place. To see and cherish a green meadow without being able to unfold its reach in a dream represents the vastness and essence of Islām. If a poor person sees himself walking through the meadows, gathering grass, leaves, herbs, flowers and eating them in his dream, it means prosperity. If a rich person sees that in his dream, it means that his wealth will increase. If someone who has renounced the pleasures of this world or an ascetic sees such a dream, it means that he will return to desiring it, or that he will be seduced by the world again. Walking between meadows in a dream means going on a business trip or changing one's profession. The same interpretation is given if one sees himself walking between two different markets. If one sees a deceased person sitting in the meadows in a dream, it means that he is in paradise. Meadows in a dream also represent the world and its pleasures, or they could represent a rich wife. Seeing an unusual meadow which is admired only when beheld, and enjoyed especially when visited in a dream represents a revered place, a house of God, a mosque, the grave of a prophet, or the graves of the righteous ones. A meadow in a dream also may represent the Book of revelations, the Qur'ān, knowledge, wisdom, or paradise. If one sees himself walking from the midst of meadows into a salt swampland or a marsh in a dream, it means that he follows innovations, or that he indulges in sinful actions. Hearing the call to prayers from inside a meadow in a dream means a good deed, guidance after heedlessness, repentance, attending the congregational prayers, or following a funeral procession.

Meal: *(See Food fare; Food)*

Measles: (Collapsing walls) In a dream, measles mean money which is earned from an official person, though one could lose it. If a farmer is afflicted with measles during the harvest season in a dream, it means a devastating damage to his crop.

Measure[1]: (Foot; Inch; Span; Spread; Width) In a dream, a measure or any of its related elements means travels. Measuring a wall with the span of one's hand in a dream means that he may travel to a nearby town. If he measures the same distance on the ground in a dream, it means that he may travel to a distant place. If one measures the ground up to two arms length in a dream, it means that he will attend the pilgrimage in Mecca. If one measures a house or a shop with his thumb in a dream, it means that he may buy that place.

Measure[2]: (Percentage; Proportion; Ratio) A measure in a dream represents a magician, a thief, trickery, or wasting money. *(Also see Scale; Scale beam; Unit of weight; Weight)*

Measure[3]: (Weight) In a dream, a measured weight represents guidance, knowledge, wisdom, a wife, profits, distress, trouble, or poverty. *(Also see Weight)*

Measurer: (Balance; Corn measurer; Measuring controller; Quantity surveyor; Scale) In a dream, one who metes out or dispenses measures and weights represents a ruler, a leader or a judge. If his measurement is exact, it means that he is a just person. Otherwise, it represents a tyrant. If one is given a scale for measuring, or if he becomes a measurer or a measuring controller, or a surveyor in a dream, and if he qualifies, it means that he will be appointed as a judge, or as a leader. If he does not qualify, it means that he will grow in wisdom, righteousness, justice and balance which he can use to help himself and others. *(Also see Measure*[2]*; Scale)*

Measuring controller: *(See Measurer)*

Meat: (Flesh; Knowledge; Money; Substance; Wealth) Cooked meat in a dream means money. Eating raw meat in a dream means illness and pain. Eating raw meat in a dream also may mean benefits. Seeing raw meat and not eating from it in a dream could have adverse meaning. Eating cooked meat in a dream means increase in one's wealth. Eating a meat dish with an old man in a dream means becoming renowned, or entering the inner circle of a governor. Buying meat from the butcher in a dream means adversities. Tender meat in a dream mean death or backbiting. Eating the flesh of a human being in a dream means backbiting him. Eating one's own flesh in a dream means earning money from one's own sweat. If a woman eats the flesh of another woman in a dream, it means that they are lesbians. If a woman eats her own flesh in a dream, it means that she will commit adultery. The meat of a yellow cow in a dream means illness. The cooked meat of a snake in a dream means receiving money from one's enemy. The uncooked flesh of a snake in a dream means slandering one's enemy. The meat of a lion in a dream means receiving money from a ruler and the same goes for the flesh of all predatory animals or birds. Hog or swine's meat in a dream means unlawful money. Eating sausages or dried meat in a dream means speaking ill of deceased people. Camel's meat in a dream means earning money from a rich and a powerful enemy unless if the one seeing it does not touch it in his dream. However, touching camel's meat in a dream means suffering from such a strong person. Eating it cooked in a dream means defrauding someone, then falling sick and recovering from one's illness. It is also said that eating camel's meat in a dream means earning money from a ruler. Beef in a dream means hardships, toiling and lack of work. Holding a mutton inside one's house

271

in a dream means meeting with a new person, accepting an invitation, or inviting a person one has never met or known to share a meal. Seeing a whole skinned but uncut mutton inside one's house in a dream means a sudden adversity, loss, calamity, or death. If the mutton is fat, it means that one may receive an inheritance from a will which is left by a deceased relative. If it is skinny, it means that one will inherit nothing from him. Eating broiled beef in a dream means standing before a judge or a ruler. Eating a chicken in a dream means receiving benefits from a woman. Meat in a dream also means forbearance and patience for someone who is hot tempered, or who gets angry easily. Eating meat in a dream also could mean recovering from an illness, an end to one's distress, trouble and adversities. Eating the meat of an unlawful animal in a dream means receiving unlawful money. Eating a suspicious meat in a dream means earning suspicious money, or having an illegitimate marriage. Eating fowls' meat in a dream means profits for a traveller. Eating a fish in a dream means easy, lawful and enjoyable earnings. Cooked or broiled fowl meat in a dream means profits and money earned from a woman through deception and dishonesty. If it is uncooked in the dream, then it means backbiting or slandering a woman. Eating the meat of an unlawful bird in a dream means deceiving, defrauding, or stealing money from unjust people. Eating swan's meat in a dream means benefits drawn from pious and religious people. Eating fired or broiled chicks in a dream means hard earned money. Unknown meat in a dream represents the hidden treasures of past nations, or buried treasures. *(Also see Butcher; Flesh; Mutton; Pot)*

Mecca: (Holy Mecca; Imām) In a dream, the Holy Mecca represents the Imām of all the Muslims. Whatever happens to it in a dream will manifest in his life. The city of Mecca in a dream also could represent the spiritual and religious standing of the person seeing such a dream. If one sees himself living or owning a house in Mecca in a dream, it means honor and knowledge. If one sees himself living in Mecca in a dream, it also may mean that he will give his daughter in marriage to a noble person. Walking away from Mecca in a dream means separation from one's superior. If one sees that Mecca is demolished in a dream, it means that he does not perform his prayers. Entering Mecca in a dream also could mean getting married to a girl everyone is hoping to marry. If a sinner sees himself entering the city of Mecca in a dream, it means that he will repent for his sins. If one has a dispute and sees himself entering Mecca in a dream, it means that he will lose his argument. Entering Mecca in a dream also means reaching safety and peace in one's life. Leaving one's homeland and travelling to Mecca in a dream means that God willing, he will shortly join the pilgrimage caravan and perform his Hajj. If a sick person sees such a dream, it means that his illness will be long and that he may die from it, or he may join the company of the dwellers of the heavenly paradise. Seeing oneself in Mecca and residing in the lodge one usually uses in a dream means extension of one's contract, or reappointment at a previously held position. If Mecca becomes one's home in a dream, it means that he may move to live there. Seeing oneself in Mecca mixing with departed souls in a dream means that one will die as a martyr. Visiting the holy Ka'aba in Mecca during a business trip in a dream means concern and attachment to material gains and worldly profits. Walking on the road to Mecca in a dream means going on a pilgrimage. If one sees Mecca fertile in a dream, it means benefits, and if he sees it barren in a dream, it means the opposite. *(Also see Circumambulation; Masjid; Visiting holy sites)*

Medal: *(See Necklace)*

Mediation: *(See Intercession)*

Medicinal paste: *(See Electuary)*

Medicine: (Drug; Inkwell) Taking medicine in a dream means correcting oneself, or it could mean fulfilling one's religious obligations. If one takes a medicine for his illness in a dream, it means that he will correct his conduct. If it denotes knowledge in the dream, it means that he will benefit from what he learns and accepts the good advice. If one refuses to take his medicine in the dream, it means that he will deviate from the path of his Lord and shift his interests to his allotment or luck in this world. Medicine in a dream also denotes an inkwell. Licking medicine with one's index finger in a dream means proclaiming the truth, or it could mean profits from the direction the index finger is pointing at in the dream. Swallowing medicinal powder means greed, self-absorption, reclusion and withdrawal. Taking liquid medicine orally means profits. Swallowing pills in a dream means obliging a sinner to correct himself, to repent, or to go on the straight path. It also could mean caring to teach an ignorant person. If a woman applies a medicinal make-up in a dream, it represents her menstruation. As for an unwed girl, it means marriage, and for a barren woman, it means a child. Inserting a suppository into the rectum in a dream means spying or eavesdropping. To take a laxative in a dream means attempting to correct one's religious devotion, or it could mean washing one's body from impurities. The success of one's attempt depends on the potency of his medicine. Seeking good health in a dream means trying to amend one's life for the better. The same meaning applies if one sees himself using an ointment for his eyes. A yellow colored medicine in a dream means illness. A laxative in a dream means a cure for a sick person and a warning for a healthy person to correct himself. A bad tasting medicine in a dream means a fever followed by a chill. Good tasting medicine in a dream is beneficial for rich people, though bad for poor people. Interpreting a cure with a medicine in a dream is not like interpreting recovering without a medicine. *(Also see Grapes)*

Medina: Visiting the Holy city of Medina, the city of God's Prophet, upon whom be peace, in a dream means profits and blessings in this world. Standing at the door of the Sacred Mosque in Medina, or in front of the Blessed Chamber of God's Prophet, upon whom be peace, in a dream means repenting from a sin and acceptance of one's repentance. Seeing the Holy city of Medina in a dream can be interpreted in six ways to reflect peace, mercy, forgiveness, salvation, relief from distress and enjoying a happy life. *(Also see Masjid; Visiting holy sites)*

Medium: *(See Fortuneteller)*

Medlar tree: (Crab apple; *Crataegus azarolus; Mespilus germanica*) Eating a bitter tasting applelike fruit of the medlar tree or any of such varieties that are also used in making preserves, or eaten yellow, spoiled, or unripened in a dream means a sickness. The more yellowish is its color in the dream, the more pain and suffering such an sickness will bring. Eating a green medlar fruit in a dream represents no such danger. Eating any yellowish fruit in a dream represents a sickness, except for citron, apples, or the lotus fruit, for their yellow color in the dream does not cause any harm, since their substance is a viable medicinal cure.

Medlar: *(See Medlar tree)*

Meekness: (Humiliation; Submissiveness) If learned people, scholars, or leaders show meekness, or if they are humiliated in a dream, it represents weakness in their faith, and submissiveness to the demands of their enemy. *(Also see Humiliation)*

Melon: A water melon in a dream represents a sick person with many problems including suppression of urine. A melon in a dream also means that one will be struck with an adversity for which he will find no solution, and he will not understand its consequences for sometime to come. Eating a water melon in a dream also means release from prison. If one sees himself extending his hands to the heavens from where he receives a water melon in the dream, it means that he is seeking a job in the government or a wealth which he shall shortly receive. A ripened water melon in a dream means a sickness, while a green and unripened melon means youth and a good health. Honeydew in a dream represent a group of men and women who possess good character and manners. In a dream, a melon also represents a beautiful woman though with bad qualities.

Member: *(See Arm)*

Men of knowledge: *(See Scholars)*

Mend: *(See Darn)*

Mender: (Patching) A mender in a dream represents happiness and prosperity. *(Also see Darn)*

Mendicant: *(See Beggar; Poverty)*

Menopause: *(See Old woman)*

Menstrual period: (Discharge; Menstruation; The Curse of Eve) Experiencing one's menstrual period in a dream means that one has committed a wrongdoing, or it could mean confusion. If a woman sees herself taking a ritual ablution thereafter in the dream, it means that she will repent for his sin and her adversities will be dispelled. If an aged woman sees herself experiencing that in the dream, it means that she will bear a son. If a widow or an unmarried woman experiences her menstrual period in a dream, it means that she will get married. If a man sees himself experiencing women's menstrual period in a dream, it means that he will commit an unlawful act, or that he lies. If he sees his wife in her period in the dream, it means that she will close herself to him, or that he will lose money in his business. *(Also see Garden; Hilarity; Mirth)*

Mental derangement: (Madness) Mental derangement in a dream means cognizance of evil people, or it could mean forgiveness of one's sins.

Mental disorder: *(See Delirium; Distraction)*

Mental hospital: (Insane asylum; Hell-fire; Lunatics; Prison) In a dream, a mental hospital or an insane asylum represents a bathhouse, or a sauna which is the dwelling of evil spirits, the place of uncovering one's private parts, or showing unpleasant conduct in public. A mental hospital in a dream also represents a training school, caring for children's education, teaching children to behave themselves, a place of learning, a school, a playground, a place of clamor and noise, using vile words, stealing money, or separation from one's family and children. If a deceased person is seen in a mental hospital in a dream, it means that he is dwelling in hell-fire, for a mental hospital sometime uses force with its patients and ties them up, or imprisons them. If one sees himself in a mental hospital in a dream, it means that he might go to jail for a crime he committed. Mixing with lunatics and insane people in a dream also means imprisonment and mixing with criminals, or it could mean falling sick, or dying from a terminal illness. If a poor person sees himself inside a mental hospital in a dream, it means financial success, receiving outside help, comfort and joy in his life. *(Also see Insanity)*

Mental keenness: *(See Perspicacity)*

Mentor: *(See Educator)*

Mercenaries: In a dream, mercenaries represent soldiers of punishment. *(Also see Soldiers)*

Merchandise: *(See Returning the merchandise)*

Merchant: If one sees himself as a store owner, sitting in his shop, surrounded with his merchandise, giving orders, buying and selling in a dream, it means a commanding post in his own field. If the person is not a businessman, but still sees himself in a dream carrying some trade tools such as a scale, a scoop, etcetera, it means financial balance in his life. Merchants in a dream also

274

represent travel, news, profits or a high position. A merchant in a dream also may represent a spendthrift, or negligence of several religious obligations set by God Almighty. A woman merchant in a dream represents an enemy. *(Also see Grain merchant)*

Mercury[1]: (Planet; Policeman) The planet Mercury in a dream represents people of authority, writers, commanders, secretary of state, minister, traveling from one country to another, distress, adversities, or fights. If in wakefulness the Moon and Mercury are appearing simultaneously in the skies, then all dreams will be false and one may have to face lies, poverty, scary news, murders, or robberies. The planet Mercury in a dream also represents a policeman. *(Also see Heavens)*

Mercury[2]: (Quicksilver) In a dream, mercury means a project, or an intention that will not be brought to completion. If one sees himself giving mercury to someone, or if he holds it in his hand in a dream, it means that he fails his promises. It also means that he disinclines in his religious practices, follows his own mind and desire, or it could mean that he is a hoax, a betraying person, or a treacherous person. If he eats it in a dream, it means that one of his children will grow to be one who fails his promises.

Mercy: (Compassion) Seeing a merciful person showing compassion toward a weak person in a dream means clarity about one's spiritual commitment, and that one's religious devotion will grow stronger. If one sees himself being treated with mercy in a dream, it means that he will receive forgiveness. If one is granted divine mercy in a dream, it means that he is endowed with favors and blessings. If one sees himself being merciful and happy in a dream, it means that he will memorize the holy Qur'ān by heart.

Message: *(See Letter)*

Messenger: *(See Herald; Prophet)*

Messmate: (Sharing a table; Table companion) To share a table with a deceased person in a dream means that one will be paying a pecuniary penalty that will be exacted by the authorities. Sharing a table with someone who is away on a trip in a dream means receiving news from him. Sharing a table with evil companions, evil spirits, satans, or jinn in a dream means fighting against a crime ring.

Meteor: *(See Star)*

Mice: *(See Mouse)*

Michael: *(See Mikā'īl)*

Middle course: (Frugal; Taking the middle course) Taking the middle course in a dream, or following one's own interest, or being frugal, or adopting restraint in one's dream means finding an appropriate woman to marry, choosing a suitable partner, or pursuing a spiritual path to learn about good conduct. If one finds himself limiting his outdoor walks, or intentionally staying away from crowds in a dream, it denotes his humility and good character.

Middle man: *(See Auctioneer; Broker)*

Midges: (Fly) In a dream, a midge represents a boy, a woman, a servant, or money.

Midwife: (Accoucheuse) In a dream, a midwife means revealing hidden secrets that when unveiled, they will cause injuries or death. Seeing a midwife in a dream also denotes good advice. Seeing her in a dream also indicates walking through adversities, reaching peace, initiating fascination, or she could represent trials, evil, crying, or paying a fine. *(Also see Dromedary rider)*

Migraine headache: In a dream, headache represents sins. If one suffers from a headache in a dream, he should repent for his sins, refrain from what he is doing, distribute money in charity, observe voluntary religious fast, seek a spiritual retreat, or strive to do good deeds. Headache in a dream means suffering from unhappiness or misery in one's life. Headache also represents one's employer or supervisor. If one who is suffering from a migraine headache in wakefulness sees his temples transformed into iron in a dream, it means that his illness will be cured.

Migrator: *(See Explorer)*

Miḥrāb: *(arb.* Alcove; Niche; Prayer niche) In a dream, a prayer niche or a miḥrāb represents a leader, a guide, or the Imām of a mosque. Praying at the miḥrāb in a dream means glad tidings. If a woman sees herself praying at the miḥrāb of a mosque in a dream, it means that she will beget a son or a daughter. In a dream, the alcoves or shelters that poor people use for their retreats in a mosque represent sincerity, love, devotion, remembrance of God Almighty, standing in night prayers, and aloofness. Building a miḥrāb inside one's house in a dream means bearing male children. Otherwise, it means that such a property will be donated by its owner for religious use. Seeing an incorrectly positioned prayer niche in a mosque in a dream means deviation for God's path and erring in one's words and actions. In a dream, a miḥrāb also represents lawful sustenance or a pious wife. If one sees the prayer niche of a mosque misdirected, or if it emits a vile odor, or if one sees the corpse of a dead animal lying inside it in a dream, it indicates that the one who is seeing the dream is an unbeliever, an innovator and a hypocrite.

Mikā'īl: (The archangel Michael, upon whom be peace.) Seeing the archangel Mikā'īl (uwbp) in a dream means prosperity, wealth, blessings in one's life, good harvest and rain. If a pious person sees him (uwbp) in a dream, it means success, attaining one's goals and fulfilling his intentions in this world and in the hereafter. If an ungodly person sees him in a dream, it represents a warning that could precede the destruction of a town or a village, or a calamity during which the person seeing the dream also could suffer. If one sees him (uwbp) in a town in a dream, it means a rainfall, good harvest and low prices for that year. If he speaks to the person seeing the dream, or gives him something in the dream, it means joy, blessings and glad tidings of entering the heavenly paradise, for he is the angel of mercy. If one sees him (uwbp) during a rainy season, it means prosperity, or listening to the singing of birds, or such a dream could imply the building of an army and raising the banners of war. Seeing him (uwbp) during a dry season in a dream could then represent a trustworthy treasurer, a good accountant or a successful business manager. The archangel Michael (uwbp) in a dream also represents a compassionate ruler who is to his subjects like a father to his children. Seeing him (uwbp) in a dream also may mean drought, or perhaps the dream could mean that a barren woman will conceive a child, or that a difficult and a controversial issue will be resolved. If a traveller sees him (uwbp) in a dream, it may mean adversities on the road, or a rain storm that could delay his journey. Seeing him (uwbp) near someone to whose trade a rainy weather means business losses in a dream means distress and adversities. If seen near a farmer in a dream, it means a good harvest and profits from one's business. If one becomes the archangel Mikā'īl (uwbp) in a dream, it means wealth, prosperity and earning a good reputation.

Milepost: *(See Milestone)*

Milestone: (Event; Landmark; Milepost) In a dream, a milestone represents a son, an emissary, a messenger, travels, or a pious person who serves people's needs.

Military review: *(See Exhibition)*

Military service: *(See Conscription)*

Military: *(See Army general)*

Milk: (Instinct; Nature; Profits) In a dream, milk represents nature, instinct, or easy and lawful money. However, curdled milk in a dream represents unlawful money. If a man or a woman discover that they are carrying milk in their breast in a dream, it means building of one's savings. If a man sees milk flowing from his breast in a dream, it means wealth, prosperity and that new opportunities will rise from every direction. Woman's milk in a dream means recovering from an illness. If a woman sees herself carrying milk in her breast in a dream, when in reality she does not have it, it means that she will breast feed a new born. If a woman sees herself breast-feeding a baby, a man, or another woman in her dream, it means that the source of earnings will be hampered or restricted to both the suckling person and to the one who is breast-feeding him. Hiring a wet-nurse to breast-feed one's child in a dream means raising a child to be like his father, or to have the character of one's father. Sucking milk from a woman's breast in a dream also means prosperity and profits. Drinking the milk of a horse in a dream means receiving love and affection from someone in authority and earning benefits from such a relationship. Drinking the milk of a mare in a dream means a meeting with a ruler. In general, cow's milk, goat's milk, or sheep's milk in a dream represent lawful earnings. Milking in a dream means craftiness and cunning, or it could mean prosperity. Milking an Arabian she-camel in a dream means working in an Arab country. Milking an Asian Bactrian camel in a dream means working in another country. If blood comes out of the glands of a she-camel instead of milk in a dream, it means deviation from God's path, or it could represent a tyranny. If a venom flows from one's glands instead of milk in the dream, it means earning unlawful money. If a merchant, or a business man milks any milk producing animal in a dream, it means profits. Sucking the gland of a pregnant she-camel, one, two, or three times in a dream means steadfastness in one's religion, performing one's obligatory prayers, distributing charity, acquiring knowledge and wisdom. Milking a camel and drinking its milk in a dream also means marriage to a pious and a chaste woman. If one is already married, then it means that his wife will beget a blessed son. If a poor person sees himself milking a cow and drinking its milk in a dream, it means that he will earn enough money to satisfy his basic needs. Drinking sheep's milk, or goat's milk in a dream means profits, happiness, comfort and joy. Lioness milk in a dream also means money or conquering one's enemy, or justly opposing the ruler of the country. The milk of an eagle in a dream means power and victory. Tiger's milk in a dream means avowing one's enmity toward someone. Drinking the milk of a jackal or a wolf in a dream means paying a fine, extreme fear, suffering losses, or lack of determination, or it could mean presiding over people and skillfully defrauding them of their wealth. Drinking swine's milk in a dream means changes in one's state, altering one's mind and focus. However, drinking a little of it in a dream may mean acquiring lawful earnings, though drinking a lot of it in the dream could mean receiving unlawful money. Drinking bitch's milk in a dream means feebleness of mind, or senility, or it could represent money earned from an unjust person, or it could mean presiding over one's local community, or becoming the governor of the town. Drinking the milk of any beasts in a dream represents doubt about one's religion. Drinking zebra's milk in a dream also means an illness. Drinking the milk of a deer or a gazelle in a dream represents small earnings. The milk of non-milk producing animals or birds in a dream means that one's wish will come true. The milk of predatory animals and stingers in a dream means making peace with one's enemy. Drinking snake's milk in a dream means performing a deed that is pleasing to God Almighty, rejoicing, or escaping from a calamity. The milk of a fox in a dream denotes a passing illness which will be followed by borrowing a small amount of money, or it could mean recovering from an illness. Drinking donkey's milk in a dream also represents an illness, while drinking the milk of a she-ass in a dream means profits. Cat's milk in a dream represents an illness, experiencing life's adversities, or it could denote generosity. Seeing milk spilled on the ground in a dream means corruption, tyranny and blood-shed on earth that will equal the amount of the spilled milk. Sheep's milk in a dream means honest earnings. Cow's milk also means wealth. A mule's milk in a dream means financial straits, adversities and horror. The milk of a sable in a dream means an illness or fear. Pouring milk into the drain or wasting it in a dream means losing money, or it could mean longevity, pregnancy, knowledge, or a scandal that will expose one's private life. Curdled milk in a dream means distress. Rabbit's milk and horse's milk in a dream means having a righteous name, or giving a righteous name to one's newborn. Human milk in a dream represents a trust one should not waste or give to other than its rightful owner. The milk of an unknown animal in a dream means energy and strength for a sick person, release from prison, illegal seizure of property, or extortion and blackmailing. *(Also see Breast-feeding; Colostrum; Dairyman; Milking)*

Milking a camel: *(See Milk; Milking)*

Milking a cow: *(See Milk; Milking)*

Milking a deer: *(See Milk; Milking)*

Milking a donkey: *(See Milk; Milking)*

Milking a fox: *(See Milk; Milking)*

Milking a gazelle: *(See Milk; Milking)*

Milking a horse: *(See Milk; Milking)*

Milking a jackal: *(See Milk; Milking)*

Milking a lioness: *(See Milk; Milking)*

Milking a she-camel: *(See Milk; Milking)*

Milking a swine: *(See Milk; Milking)*

Milking a zebra: *(See Milk; Milking)*

Milking: Milking a cow in a dream represents a demanding employer. Milking a goat may mean good neighborly relations, toadying, diplomacy, or seeking to earn one's livelihood. If an employee sees himself milking a cow or a goat in a dream, it means that he will marry his employer's wife. If a poor person sees himself milking a goat or a cow and drinking her milk in a dream, it means financial stability. If he is rich, it means that he will rise in station. Milking a camel in a dream means receiving a significant gift from a person in authority. If the milk turns into blood in the dream, it means that he will acquire illegal funds. Milking any domesticated animal in a dream also means marriage to a righteous person, or bearing a blessed child. The element of milk in a dream also can be interpreted as deception. *(Also see Dairyman; Milk; Trader)*

Milkmaid: Seeing a milkmaid in a dream depicts benefits, a person with good character, or to seek and hear gentle words. A milkmaid in a dream also could represent an employer demanding refunds from his workers. A milkmaid or a milkman in a dream also represents a righteous person. *(Also see Dairyman)*

Milkman: *(See Milkmaid)*

Mill: (Grinder; Press) In a dream, a mill represents a school, a courthouse, a balance, justice, righteousness, benefits, blessings, money, food, charity, or marriage. The millstone in a dream represents a wife and a husband. The flour that issues from between the two grinding stones represents sperms or children. A mill in a dream also means distress and adversities, uptightness, headache, a rivulet, or a windmill. If one sees a mill grinding human beings in a dream, it means loss of lives and adversities. If one sees a mill grinding something that is not edible in a dream, it means drought and rising prices. If the amount of flour coming from the mill is plentiful in the dream, it means lowering of prices, or recovering from an illness. Grinding lupine seeds, henna seeds, potash, saltwort, salsola kali, jojobe seeds or any seeds from the marsh mallow tree in a dream means washing oneself from sin, overcoming difficulties, paying one's debts and recovering from an illness. *(Also see Oil press; Press; Sugar mill)*

Miller's scale: *(See Balance)*

Miller: (Flour; Moving around in a circle) In a dream, a miller represents a selfish person who is particularly interested in acquiring worldly gains and at whatever price it may cost. If one sees an old man being a miller in a dream, the old man here represents his grandfather, or one's bosom friend and consequently one will prosper and become extremely wealthy from his business. If the miller is a young and a strong man in the dream, then he represents a strong helper. A bakery miller in a dream means that one will attain his own goals through hard work. If one sees himself grinding a sufficient quantity of wheat for two, three, or four people in a dream, it means that he labors for his own need and can barely provide for his family. If the miller is a young man who has gray hair in the dream, then he represents both prosperity and strength. Seeing a miller in a dream also means adversities, fights, a spendthrift, usury, or a hard working guardian. Grinding other grains in a dream means dispelling distress and bitterness from one's heart. *(Also see Saffron)*

Millstone: In a dream, a millstone represents a husband and a wife. *(Also see Hand mill)*

Mimosa tree: A Mimosa tree in a dream connotes stinginess, evil and behaving with the actions of the dwellers of hell-fire. *(Also see Tree)*

Mina: (Pilgrims' camp; Pilgrimage) Seeing oneself in Mina in a dream means fulfilling one's wishes in this world and in the next, and it could mean dispelling all fears. *(Also see Arafāt; Circumambulation; Cradle of Ismāïl; Ka'aba; Muzdalifa; Pelting stones; Pilgrimage; Responding; Station of Abraham; 'Umrah)*

Minaret: (Spiritual guide; Letter carrier; Lighthouse; Minaret of a mosque) In a dream, the minaret of a mosque represents a righteous man who fosters unity and love between people, who calls them to live by their religious covenant and guides them on the path of God Almighty. If a minaret is demolished in a dream, it represents the death of such a spiritual guide, fading of his name, dispersal of his community, and perhaps it could lead to the reversal of their conditions. The minaret of the city's central mosque in a dream represents a letter carrier, or a guide calling people to God's path. Falling down from the top of a minaret into a well in a dream means marrying a strong minded woman who uses vicious expressions, when one already has a pious wife with whom he enjoys peace and tranquility. It also means losing one's authority or control. Climbing a wooden minaret and calling people to prayers in a dream means attaining authority and rising in station through hypocrisy. Sitting alone on the top of a minaret, praising God's glory and glorifying His oneness in a dream means becoming famous, while the loud glorifications mean that one's distress and sorrow will be lifted by God's leave. The minaret of a mosque in a dream also represents the chief minister of the ruler, or it could represent the muezzin. *(Also see Lantern; Mailman; Masjid; Mosque; Muezzin; Watchtower)*

Minbar: *(arb.* Pulpit; Sermon) A pulpit in a dream represents the Imām, the spiritual guide and commander of all the Muslims who also represents God's Messenger (uwbp) on earth. A minbar in a dream also represents a blessed abode in the hereafter, and an exalted station through which God's Name is glorified. Standing one a pulpit and delivering a poised sermon in a dream means attaining an honorable station. If one does not qualify for such a position, then it means that he will acquire good fame. If a ruler or a governor is forced to come down from the pulpit in a dream, it means loss of his status, or it could mean his death. If one is seen standing on a pulpit and if he does not speak or deliver a sermon, or if what he says denotes evil in the dream, it means that he will be unjustly executed, or it could mean that God Almighty will protect him against such injustice. The pulpit in a dream also means rulership and subduing one's enemy. Rising on a pulpit in a dream also could mean a betrothal or proposing a marriage. Otherwise, it could mean a scandal. If a ruler stands on a pulpit in a dream, it represents the continuity of his reign. Standing on a pulpit with one's hands tied in a dream means carrying out an execution which is brought about by one's own crimes.

Mincemeat: (Hash) Mincemeat in a dream represents what follows in the food preparation process. First it is minced, then mixed with other ingredients, where its identity changes, then it becomes a dish with a different taste. For an unmarried person, minced meat in a dream means marriage and children, and for a pregnant woman, it means a boy. Minced meat in a dream also means merging of capitals, establishing a business partnership and the advantages that come from a stronger corporation.

Minor ḥajj: (See 'Umrah)

Mint: (Bot.) In a dream, mint means an announcement of someone's death. (Also see Marjoram)

Minter: (Money) A minter in a dream represents a well spoken person who tricks others with his fancy words. If he does not receive a wage for his work, a minter in a dream represents a reliable and an honorable person of a pleasant character and company. However, if he asks for wage in the dream, then he represents a hypocrite, a slanderer, one who follows hearsay, or he could be a poet. Minting in a dream connotes an appointment at a high ranking position for a qualified person. A minter in a dream also represents the ruler, his chief minister, a religious leader, a spiritual person, an artist, a scribe, a tax collector or an employee of a collection agency. A minter in a dream also represents religious jurisprudence, or one who observes his religious rites. A minter in a dream also represents a srotyteller, a religious doctor, or a dream interpreter. Forging money in a dream means speaking bad words, or speaking words without acting upon them.

Mire: (Mud) To sink, stick, or walk in mire in a dream means fear, distress, difficulties and adversities. The same interpretation is given for muddling in the rainwaters, or walking in the rain. If a sick person sees mire in his dream, it means suffering from a prolonged illness. Walking out of mire in a dream means recovering from an illness. Walking in mire in a dream also means imprisonment, poverty, or sufferings caused by one's sinfulness and lack of attending to his religious duties. If a woman sees mire in her dream, it may mean that she may shortly conceive a child. In a dream, mire also means stagnation, disrupting communications, the past, pride about one's wealth, or it could mean apostasy. If the color of mud turns from black into red in a dream, it means moving from one's country to another, or from one wife to another. During a drought, if one sees mire or mud in his dream, it means rain. Mire inside a well in a dream means an inheritance, or the surfacing of blessings, or any related interpretations to what a well represents in a dream.

Mirage: (Phantom; Spook) In a dream, a mirage represents falsehood, or something that will not take effect. If one desires something, then sees a mirage in his dream, it means that his desire is impossible to attain, or that he will be deprived from attaining it. A mirage in a dream also represents hypocrisy and ingratitude, disbelief in God's oneness and love to amass the world and to indulge in its pleasures. A mirage in a dream also may denote false hopes, or unattainable goals. If one is summoned by the court to testify in a case, and if he sees a mirage in his dream, it also means that he will give a false statement. A mirage in a dream also represents a story that has no basis, or deception and lies that are reported as if they were true. *(Also see Ghost)*

Mirror: A mirror in a dream means illusion, arrogance, pride, or a woman. If one looks into a mirror and sees his beard black in a dream, it means honor, respect and dignity. If one looks into a mirror and sees the reflections of someone who looks like him in a dream, it means that he will beget a son who will look like his father and carry his trade. Looking into a mirror in a dream also means loss of one's position, or getting married. If one is already married, then it means the return of his wife from a journey. Looking at the back of a mirror in a dream means loss of one's crop, or entering one's wife from the anus during sexual intercourse. It is said that a mirror in a dream also represents manhood, virtues and station, all of which are subject to the size of the mirror one sees in his dream. Looking into a silver mirror in a dream means loss of one's status, it also means suffering from adversities, distress and fear. Looking into a golden mirror in a dream represents the strength of one's faith, religious commitment, prosperity after poverty, redemption and regaining one's position and status. A broken mirror in a dream means the death of one's wife, for a husband and a wife are mirrors to one another. Looking into a mirror and seeing the reflection of a youth means facing an adversary or a competitor. If one sees an old person, then he has seen a good friend. Looking into a clean and a shiny mirror in a dream means dispelling one's distress. A corroded mirror in a dream connotes a bad state or a trying situation. If the mirror is spurious, or not genuine in one's dream, then it represents a great distress or a calamity. Gazing at a mirror and looking at oneself extensively in a dream means that God Almighty is not pleased with him and that he is disobeying God's commands both in public and in private. Consequently, one will suffer from financial losses or feel down. If a sick person looks into a mirror in his dream, it means his death. A mirror in a dream also means travels or a pregnancy. If a woman looks into a mirror in a dream, it means that she will beget a girl, and if a man looks into a mirror in a dream, it means that he will beget a boy. Looking into a mirror and seeing the reflection of someone else in a dream means hallucination, craziness, or loss of money. If a man looks into a mirror and sees the reflection of a woman in a dream, it means either begetting a daughter, or getting married. If a prisoner looks into a mirror in his dream, it means that he will be released from jail. If one becomes a mirror in a dream, it means that he will meet with people's wrath and despise. *(Also see Basin)*

Mirth: (Laughter; Menstrual period) Uncontrollable mirth in a dream means a misdeed one desires to eliminate but to no avail. If one does control his hilarity and excuses himself in the dream, it means that he will fall back into the same misdeed. *(Also see Laughter)*

Misery: Miseries and adversities in a dream mean poverty, illness, divisiveness, or enmity.

Misfortune: *(See Bribe)*

Mish'ar Al-Ḥarām: *(See Muzdalifa)*

Misleading: (Betrayal; Deception; Milk; Swindle; Trickery; War) If one sees that someone is misleading him or tricking him in a dream, it means that God Almighty will grant him victory over his enemy. The deceiver in the dream will be the loser, and the misled person in the dream represents the real winner. *(Also see Fraudulent bankruptcy)*

Missile launcher: (Ballista; Battering ram; Mangonel) Seeing a mangonel or a missile launcher for hurling heavy stones in a dream means calumny, slander and a false accusation of fornication, untruth, or deceit. A missile launcher in a dream also means victory for the oppressed and destruction for the unjust ones. If the commander who is operating the missile launcher in the dream is a ruler, then it means that he will write a letter with strong words to the other party. The stone or the missile itself represents the messenger, or the carrier of such a letter. If a superior launches a stone against a subject or an employee in a dream, it means that he will send an investigator, a controller or a supervisor of a stern nature. Watching the launch of a mangonel in a dream implies treachery, betrayal and a cause of losses and sufferings. It also means defamation of the learned ones, or forcing them to downplay the ruler's injustice, or to give utilitarian and opportune opinions about sacred religious values. Seeing a missile launcher in a dream also may signify corruption, adversities and trials that will befall the target of such missiles.

Missile: *(See Missile launcher)*

Mist: *(See Fog)*

Mix: *(See Dip)*

Mixed vegetables: *(See Boiled vegetables; Stew)*

Mīzaab: *(arb. See Gutter of Mercy)*

Moaning: (Groaning) If a pregnant woman sees herself moaning in a dream, it means that she is in labor.

Mobilization: *(See Conscription)*

Mockado carpet: *(See Rug)*

Mockery: In a dream, mockery means to dupe or to defraud someone.

Moisture: *(See Dew)*

Molar Tooth: Teeth in a dream represent the elderly members in one's family, or their most distinctive ones. If a molar tooth falls in a dream, it means loss of money or life. Molar teeth in a dream represent one's relatives, or his friendliest relatives, or his own young children. Teeth of the upper jaw represent a male person and those of the lower jaw represent a female person. Whatever may affect them in a dream, will show in wakefulness. For example, if one's molar tooth falls in a dream, it means that the particular person it represents may die shortly, or it could mean being absolved of one's debts, or perhaps repayment of one's debts. If one suffers from a tooth ache in a dream, it represents ill words which are spoken against him by such family member, or that he feels hurt from the treatment he receives from such a family member. *(Also see Teeth; Tooth)*

Molars: *(See Teeth; Tooth)*

Mold: (Cast; Form) In a dream, a mold represents what it is made for. A silver casting mold in a dream means profits. Pastry molds in a dream also denote profits. A shoe mold in a dream represents the property one walks on, and a mold for a hat represents the leading person, or the head of a business, or the head of a household. *(Also see Molder)*

Molder: A mold maker in a dream represents a gnostic, or a genius who teaches each and everyone of his students what they particularly need. Since molds are containers, then he represents a man of knowledge who understands and protects people's secrets. A mold maker practicing his trade, buying and selling what he casts in a dream represents someone who is well acquainted with his profession, and who knows how to promote his services. A molder in a dream is also interpreted as a person who encourages people to travel even as far as China to acquire knowledge. *(Also see Mold)*

Mole[1]: (Burrowing; Body snatching) In a dream, a mole represents an evil and an accursed man.

Mole[2]: (A permanent skin mark) In a dream, moles mean a lasting attainment.

Mole[3]: (*zool.*) A mole in a dream means blindness, uncertainty, unavoidable circumstances, disappearing from social circles, or it could mean incompetence in one's field. A mole in a dream also could mean having sharp hearing, or correcting one's vision if one happens to have hearing disability or sight problems. If a mole is seen beside a deceased person in a dream, it represents hell-fire. Seeing a mole in a dream also may indicate finding support in mundane endeavors. It also means trickery, insolence, or finding a permanent residence.

Molesting a child: *(See Pederasty; Sodomize; Sodomy)*

Monastery: *(See Convent)*

Money bag: *(See Wallet)*

Money belt: *(See Wallet)*

Money exchanger: In a dream, a money exchanger represents knowledge, poetry, speaking the right words, richness after poverty, a school, the fellowship of a wise man, or a scale. In a dream, a money exchanger also could represent someone who has knowledge, though no one benefit from what he knows except in mundane matters. His work relates to scientific writings, scientific arguments, dispute of authority, or questions and answers. Perhaps his only balance or criterion is his own judgment. His balance represents his tongue and ears. His weights are his only instrument for justice and judgment. His measuring pennies are his fights with people. A money exchanger in a dream also represents a religious doctor or a scholar who takes religious questions and interprets their definitions. He also could be a dream interpreter who measures everything he takes in and gives an appropriate answer. He takes a pearl necklace for a price and gives words in return, or he takes scattered words and gives a beautiful pearl necklace in exchange. If one who is experiencing difficulties in wakefulness changes some money in a dream, it means that his difficulties will diminish. If one buys gold coins and gives silver money in exchange in a dream, it means reparation, financial obligations or liability. Seeing a money exchanger in a dream also represents wealth, or quick richness from suspicious sources, or he could represent an accountant, a bookkeeper, or a ledger keeper.

Money pouch: *(See Wallet)*

Money: (Bones; Banana; Brass; Bread; Coin; Dirt; Dough; Pennies; Pie; Poison) A plated coin in a dream means lies, falsehood, or triviality. To shower someone with money in a dream means listening to a filthy conversation, or impersonating someone. Money in a dream also means vain talk, or missing one's prayers. If one sees himself swallowing a coin of money in a dream, it means that he will betray his trust. Money in a dream is also interpreted as knowledge, faith, guidance, or becoming a government employee. Giving money away in a dream means dispelling agony, difficulties or burdens. If one receives money in his dream, it means that he is entrusted with something. Handling one to four coins in a dream is a lucky number. Money in a dream is also interpreted as women's talk. Having a lot of money in a dream means disputes. Receiving money from a known source in a dream means stress. If the source is unknown in the dream, it means a calamity. If one receives an engraved coin in a dream, it means that he may be hurt by his own family, or for the sake of a protégé of his. If one sees a deceased person giving him a coin of money in a dream, it means that he will be spared from an unjust trial. If he refuses to take the money from the deceased person in the dream, it means that he should beware not to be unjust toward others or fall prey to their injustice. If one who has ten coins finds that he only has five coins in the dream, it means that he will lose accordingly. If he has five coins then sees them doubled in the dream, it means that he will double his money. *(Also see Banana; Banknote; Bones; Counting money; Pastry; Voice)*

Mongoose: *(See Weasel)*

Monitor lizard: *(See Monitor²)*

Monitor¹: *(See Assistant teacher)*

Monitor²: *(zool.* Lizard; Monitor lizard; Varanidae; *Varanus Niloticus)* A monitor lizard in a dream represents a vile, mean and a contemptible enemy who has little determination, though he is feared, and who is short of proof.

Monk's cell: *(See Hermitage)*

Monk: (Abstinence; Asceticism; Bat; Celibacy; Extremism; Fear; School of thought) Living a monastic life in a dream means walking away from common traditions. Becoming a monk in a dream means receiving praises, respect, or commendation, though one will become uptight because of it, or have limited resources, little money, lives meekly, have constant fears, or it could mean hiding away from people.

Monkey: A monkey in a dream represents someone with every type of faults. Fighting with a monkey and beating him in a dream means falling sick then recovering from one's illness. If the monkey wins the fight, then it means falling to an illness that has no cure. A monkey in a dream also represents a sinner and a criminal. Monkey's bite in a dream represents a fight or having an argument with someone. A monkey in a dream also represents a deceitful person, a sorcerer, or an illness. If one becomes a monkey in a dream, it means profiting from sorcery, or engaging in adultery. A monkey in a dream also represents a defeated enemy. Riding on the back of a monkey in a dream means winning a war against one's enemy. Eating monkey's flesh in a dream means suffering from depression, becoming poor, alcoholic, deprived, or suffering from an illness that could lead one near his death. If one is offered a monkey as a gift in a dream, it means that he will defeat and capture an enemy, or it could mean that he will betray a trust. Carrying a monkey over one's shoulders in a dream means stealing something from one's house, or something that belongs to his family. A monkey in a dream also represents a filthy and a loathsome person. Owning a monkey in a dream means suffering major losses in one's life. A monkey in a dream also means committing a sin, disobedience to God's commands, or becoming despised. *(Also see Gibbon)*

Monogram: (Crafty; Cunning; Embroidering) A craftsman who applies a monogram or embroiders a garment in a dream represents a cunning and a crafty man of knowledge. *(Also see Embroiderer)*

Monster: *(See Beast)*

Month: *(See Arabic months)*

Monument: (Edifice; Imposing structure) In a dream, a monument means lies, falsehood, arrogance, or destruction. An imposing monument in a dream also may mean spiritual guidance.

Mooing of a cow: *(See Sound of animals)*

Moon: (Reverie; Satellite) The moon in a dream represents a just ruler, his chief minister, a great scholar, a handsome looking boy, a tyrant, or a liar. Seeing the moon as it is in the skies in a dream represents the chief minister of the land. Seeing the moon sitting in one's lap in a dream means getting married. Sitting in the moonlight and talking to one's friend in a dream means reverie and idle talk. If a woman sees that the moon has fallen inside her house, then if she takes it and wraps it in a swaddle in a dream, it means that she will beget a son who will shortly die after his birth and she will suffer great sorrow from his loss. Seeing the moon turned to the dark side in a dream means dismissal of the chief minister from his post. Seeing the moon advancing before the sun in a dream means that the chief minister will rise against his master. If the moon disappears in the skies in a dream, it means that one's business has come to a halt, or that something he has asked for will not materialize, whether it be good or evil. If the moon reappears in the dream, it means that one will receive what he is seeking, and again, whether it is good or bad for him. Seeing a bright and a radiant moon in the skies in a dream means justice and prosperity. Seeing the moon inside one's house in a dream means that a guest or a traveller will soon arrive. Seeing the moon laying on the ground in a dream means the death of one's mother. Walking on the moon in a dream means endearment and love for one's mother. The sun and the moon in a dream represent one's father and mother. Seeing the reflection of one's face in the moon in a dream means one's death. If one's wife is pregnant, and if he sees his resemblance reflected in the moon in a dream, it means glad tidings of a son. If one is looking into the skies and he suddenly sees the moon in his dream, it means that his enemies will be subjugated to him. Holding the moon in a dream means receiving a gift from a ruler or a rich person. If a ruler sees the moon dimmed in a dream, it means that his subjects will rise against him. If the moon turns into a sun in a dream, it means receiving honor and wealth from either one's father or wife. The moon in a dream also represents one's wife, sons, daughters, sister, properties, business, craft, a vessel, a ship, or it could mean travels. As for a sick person or a traveller, seeing the moon in a dream means one's destruction or death. If the moon is veiled by clouds in the dream, it means a short sickness. Seeing the moon through the clouds in a dream means losing one's job. If a rich person sees clouds covering the moon in a dream, it means losing his wealth. If the moon speaks to someone in his dream, it means that he will receive a high ranking appointment. If a pregnant woman sees herself trying to reach the moon with her hand but to no avail in a dream, it means that she is wishing to have a son. Prostrating oneself to the sun or the moon in a dream means committing an awesome sin. If one sees the sun and the moon prostrating themselves before him in a dream, it means that his father and mother are pleased with him. If the moon splits in two halves in a dream, it means that harm will befall a great person, or that a major sign will manifest to show the divine power in that locality. If one sees a lunar eclipse, or if the moon becomes opaque, or turns reddish in a dream, it means that major changes will take place in one's life. The moon in a dream also represents one's bosom friend, an unjust governor, his chief minister, his assistant, a gambler, an oath, recovering from an illness or suffering from eye irritation. Seeing a full moon during the early days of the lunar month, when it is supposed to be only a crescent in a dream means benefits while the opposite means harm. The moon in a dream also represents a scholar, an astrologer, an astronomer or a guide. Seeing the moon at its highest point in a dream means honor and blessings while seeing it at its lowest point in a dream means the opposite. Seeing the moon in the position of **Aries** in a dream means benefits for someone who desires to meet with high ranking people, though it could also have a negative connotation for someone who works in construction. Seeing the moon in the position of **Taurus** in a dream means losses for a business traveler. As for seeing it in the position of **Gemini** in a dream, then it means profits from a ranch and raising livestock. Seeing the moon in the position of **Cancer** in a dream means good time to get married and conceive children. Seeing it in the position of **Leo** in a dream means bad business for partnerships, securities, or mixing capitals. Seeing it in the position of **Virgo** in a dream is good for health and fitness oriented people. Seeing the moon in the position of **Libra** in a dream means water loss for a pregnant woman. Seeing the moon in the position of **Scorpio** in a dream means benefits for health oriented people, or for buying new clothing, though it also could connote negative results for travellers. Seeing the moon in the position of **Sagittarius** in a dream means bad time for planting or seedling. Seeing it coupled with **Capricorn** in a dream is a bad sign for construction or laying a foundation to a structure, or for starting a business. Seeing the moon in the position of

Aquarius in a dream means bad time for sending messages or engaging in any enterprise. Seeing the moon in the position of **Pisces** in a dream is good for contracts and receiving a leadership position. If one sees the sun, the moon and all the planets assembled before him, and together they all produced a radiant and a magnificent light in a dream, it means that one's words are respected by people in authority. If the stars and the planets have no light in the dream, then they mean a calamity. In a dream, seeing a sun and a moon on one's right side and the same on his left side, above him, in front of him and behind him means a calamity and a defeat that will force one to retreat or to escape but to no avail. *(Also see Astrologer; Crescent; Eclipse; Night)*

Moonless night: *(See Night)*

Moonlight: *(See Light)*

Morganatic marriage: (Marriage for pleasure. *See Explorer*)

Moringa tree: *(See Tree)*

Moringa: *(bot.* Willow) In a dream, a moringa plant represents a serious and a hard working man who cannot sit idle, though he is not steadfast when confronted with adversities. It also represents a rough and a stern person who brings no significant benefits to his immediate circle.

Morning star: *(See Wedding; Star)*

Morning: In a dream, the morning represents the fulfillment of a promise, or it could mean an unavoidable happening. If one sees himself unhappy and miserable in the morning hours in a dream, it will denote a low spiritual state, lack of religious coherence, or it could mean sinfulness. If an honest person sees the morning in his dream, it could mean either glad tidings of a new born if he is generous, or loss of his wealth if he is stingy. If a farmer sees the morning in a dream, it means a penalty, a punishment, or financial losses for that year. If one loses something then finds it in the morning in his dream, it means that he will provide a proof that will inculpate his enemy. If a sick person sees the morning in his dream, it means either recovering from his illness, or it could mean his death. If one leads others in prayers in such a dream, it means travels, or making a pilgrimage to Mecca. If the dream is interpreted to be his death, then it means a good end to his life in this world, light in one's grave, or that God willing, he will enter paradise. If one sees the morning and solicits water to drink, or purchases food, or barters for some barley in his dream, it means that he will overcome his difficulties and dispel his adversities. If a prisoner sees the morning in his dream, it means that he will be released shortly. If one's travels are impeded by whatever cause, then seeing the morning in his dream means solving such problems and proceeding on with one's plans. If one is having difficulties with his wife, then seeing the morning in a dream means divorce or separation. If a sinner sees the morning in his dream, it means repentance from his sin and egress from heedlessness. If a merchant or a businessman who is having trouble in his trade sees the morning in his dream, it means good news and business growth. In general, seeing the morning in a dream means relief from difficulties, escape from danger, a good harvest, or winning one's freedom.

Mortar & Pestle: In a dream, a mortar and a pestle represent a husband and a wife. None of the two works without the other. They perform hard work that no one else will do for them. The mortar represents the man and the pestle represents his wife.

Mortar carrier: (Clay; Hod) In a dream, a mortar carrier represents a person who veils people's ills and hides scandals. To see oneself as a mason in a dream means getting involved in a good project and seeking to do a good deed. Seeing a mason using mortar or hod in a dream means becoming strict, giving oneself hard time, or toiling hard to serve others. Seeing a mortar carrier in a dream also means distress, misfortune, or hardships.

Mortar: *(See Steamroller)*

Mortician: If a sick person sees a mortician in a dream, it means his death or relief from adversities. A mortician in a dream also means payment of one's debts, or repentance of a sinner. *(Same as Undertaker. Also see Intestines)*

Moses: (God's prophet Moses, upon whom be peace.) If one sees God's prophet Moses, upon whom be peace, in a dream, it means that God Almighty will destroy a tyrant at his hands. Following that, the person seeing the dream will rise in station, continue to attain one victory after another, and he will never be humiliated or defeated. Seeing Moses (uwbp) in a dream also denotes the strength of righteous people, and the inevitable defeat of iniquitous people. If at the time of seeing a dream with God's prophet Moses (uwbp) there exist a tyrant or an ungodly leader, it means that God Almighty will destroy him, and one will be saved from his evil. If someone in authority becomes Moses (uwbp) in a dream, or if he wears one of his cloaks, it means that he will vanquish his enemy and fulfill what his heart desires. If one sees him (uwbp) in a prison or persecuted, or if one fears a major event that could put and end to his life, or an accident that could kill him, or a dangerous sea trip that could drown him, it means that God willing, he will escape and survive such adversity. Seeing Moses (uwbp) in a dream also means the end of tyranny, or victory in a war. If one is oppressed, worried and distressed by his own family, and if he sees Moses (uwbp) in a similar situation in a dream, it means that God Almighty will guide him to a way to overcome them, or if a traveller sees such a dream, it means that he will return safely to his home. Seeing Moses (uwbp) in a dream also indicates trials during one's childhood, separation from one's family, witnessing uncommon miracles, or that one may suffer from his own family because of an admonition, or it could represent a will he will leave to them, or it could mean commanding good and eschewing evil. Seeing Moses (uwbp) in a dream also means love for travel, praiseworthy intercession, sea travels, a safe return, profits, suffering from slander and false accusations, or perhaps it could mean that one may have weakness in his speech, or tottering, or that he may suffer from a head ill or injury. If someone who has renounced worldly pleasures, an ascetic, or a pious person sees Moses (uwbp) in a dream, it means increase in his wisdom, light in his heart and elevation of his station. If a woman sees Moses (uwbp) in a dream, she must fear loss of her child, or her dream could represent an adversity that should have a happy ending. If a child sees Moses (uwbp) in a dream, the same interpretation applies. If one sees himself carrying the staff of Moses (uwbp) in a dream, it means that he will reach a high rank and win victory over his enemy. If he is suffering from an evil spell or a sorcery, it means that it will be nullified. *(Also see Orphan)*

Mosque: (Jami; Masjid) The main city mosque or the central mosque in a dream represents the king, the governor, or the ruler of a Muslim country, since he takes care of establishing the divine laws as well as he is the symbol of Islām and the decisive judge between the lawful and the unlawful. Smelling an apple inside a mosque means getting married. A mosque in a dream is like the central market that people intend daily and endeavor to make profit therein. It is a place where people will profit according to their deeds and efforts. A mosque in a dream also represents one who is to be obeyed, respected and revered such as a father, a teacher, a shaikh or a man of knowledge. It also asserts justice if one who enters a mosque in his dream is unjustly treated. The main city mosque in a dream represents the Qur'ānic revelation, the ocean of knowledge, a place of purification and washing one's sins, the graveyard where submissiveness and contemplation are evoked, the washing and shrouding of the dead, medicine, silence, focusing one's intention and facing the qiblah at the Ka'aba in Mecca. Seeing the main city mosque in a dream also means to recognize something good and to act upon it. It also could be interpreted as the shelter from one's enemy, and a sanctuary and a shelter of the believer from fear, and a house of peace. The ceiling of the mosque represents the intimate and vigilant entourage of a king. Its outstretch represents the dignitaries. Its chandeliers represent its wealth and ornaments. Its prayer mats represent the king's justice and his knowledgeable advisors. Its doors represent the guards. Its minaret represents the king's vice-regent, the official speaker of the palace or it announcer. If the main mosque in the dream is interpreted to represent the ruler of the land, then its pillars represent the element of time. Its lights represent the noble retinue and the wise men of his epoch. The ceiling represents the knowledge contained in the books that protect his justice and his references. The minaret will then represent his chief minister or advisor. The pulpit represents his servant. The prayer niche represents his wife, or it may represent his lawful earnings, or a righteous and a chaste wife. If one sees a mosque burning in a dream, it means death, losses and political changes in the country. The main mosque of the town also represents the pious people dwelling therein, the men of knowledge, the wise men, devotion, or a hermitage. Its niche represents the leader of the people (Imām). The caller to prayers (Muezzin) represents the judge or a gnostic from that town or country who calls people to the right path and whose call is harkened to by the believer. The doors of a mosque in a dream represent the trustees and guards who shelter people from outside attacks. If one sees any of that in a dream, or whatever condition these elements are in, they represent the current condition of the people, and this is what the central mosque represents in one's dream. If one sees grass growing inside a mosque in a dream, then it means a wedding. *(Also see Imām; Ka'aba; Masjid; Minaret; Minbar; Muezzin)*

Mosquito net: *(See Canopy)*

Mosquito: (Gnat) In a dream, a mosquito represents an enemy who will cause bloodshed and mutilation. A mosquitoes in a dream also represents a confidant, an associate or a strong person. A mosquito's bite in a dream means receiving money in compensation, or as blood reparation.

Mote: (Particle; Speck) In a dream, it means extensive wealth, an enemy who has no honor, a weak opponent, a selfish person, or someone not worth mentioning.

Moth: *(See Butterfly)*

Mother of pearl: Buying a glittering glass ornament, or a house made of mother of pearls in a dream means choosing the pleasures of this world over the everlasting bliss of the hereafter, disdaining from obeying God's commands, or it could mean becoming an apostate. *(Also see Pearl)*

Mother: (Educator; Eye-brow; Governess) Seeing one's mother in a dream has a deeper and a stronger meaning than seeing one's father. All the same in one's dream, seeing her means attaining one's goal. Man's dreams are most pleasing when he sees his parents, grand parents or a relative. If one is going through difficulties and sees his mother in a dream, it means that help will come his way from sources he does not anticipate. If in real life he is awaiting someone's return from a journey, that person could arrive shortly. If one is sick, it means that he will be cured from his illness. If one sees his mother giving birth to him, should he be ill in real life, then it means the approach of his death, for a deceased is wrapped in a shroud, while a new born is wrapped with a receiving cloth. If the person in question is poor, then seeing his mother in a dream means that his financial conditions will change for the better. If he is rich, it means restrictions of his earnings, for a child is dependent on others, and his movements are restricted. *(Also see Earth)*

Mount 'Arafa: *(See 'Arafāt)*

Mount of mercy: *(See 'Arafāt)*

Mount Sinai: *(See City)*

Mountain goat: (Ibex; Oryx; Sasin; Wild goat) In a dream, a mountain goat represents a foreigner who will be passing by one's town. Catching a mountain goat in a dream means receiving money from a king or from a wealthy and a powerful person, for the mountain in a dream represents such a person and the goat represents the prize. Looking at a mountain goat in a dream means slandering a person who holds an important position in the government and who is well connected with the ruler. Catching a mountain goat in a dream means harm and sufferings, though eating its meat in a dream means that one will receive money from such a person. *(Also see Oryx)*

Mountain pass: *(See Canyon)*

Mountain road: *(See Ascent)*

Mountain trails: (Canyons) In a dream, deep valleys, or mountain trails represent deception, betrayal, perfidy and trickery. *(Also see Aqïq canyons)*

Mountain: A mountain in a dream represents a great and a noble man who possesses a strong and a commanding voice, who commands good administration of his affairs and an excellent leadership. It also can be interpreted as a son, a difficult and austere woman, or a businessman. If the mountain is rounded or flat in the dream, it means difficulties or distress. A mountain in a dream also could mean achieving one's goal, a journey, or fulfilling a promise. If the mountain is standing distinct from other mountains in the dream, the above meanings become stronger. If the mountain has pasture and stores a source of water, and if it is used as a permanent guarding post, then it represents a pious ruler. However, if it stores no water, and if no pasture grows therein in the dream, it represents a tyrant and a ruler who is an atheist, for in that case, it is dead and does not glorify God Almighty, nor can people benefit from it. In a dream, a mountain that stands high is alive, but a crumbling mountain which has turned into a pile of rocks is dead. If a person sees himself climbing an erect mountain, eating from its plants and drinking from its water, and if he qualifies to govern, it means that he will be appointed to a governing post under the auspices of a stringent ruler, though his subjects do receive benefits from his government. The size of benefits the governor will acquire is equal to the quantity of food and the measure of water he drinks from it in his dream. If the person is a merchant or a business man, a mountain in his dream represents profits and earning a good reputation. If climbing the mountain is easy, then there are no benefits in that climbing in the dream, for there are no benefits without hardships. If at the end of his climbing one thanks God Almighty for what he has reached in the dream, it means that he will become a just ruler. If he calls to prayers on the top of a mountain or performs his prayers thereat in the dream, it means that he will be appointed to govern. If one sees himself descending a mountain in a dream, it means loss of rank, business losses, or regret. If one is accompanied with his king and soldiers in a dream, it means that he is in the company of God Almighty and that of His angels, therefore, he shall be victorious, whereby, he can win a war, conquer an enemy, or renounces his attachment to the world. If climbing a mountain with difficulty means distress, then descending it in a dream means relief. If climbing means gaining a higher station, then descending in a dream means losing rank. If one sees himself climbing a mountain, though at a certain height he finds himself no longer able to climb or to descend in the dream, it means that he will die young. If one sees himself falling from a mountain in a dream, it means that he will fall into sin. If he falls and breaks a leg in the dream, it means that he will become despised by his superiors. A mountain on fire in a dream represents the death of a dangerous person. Leaning against a mountain in a dream represents friendship with someone in authority. Living in the shadow of a mountain in a dream means earning one's livelihood from such a person and living happily there. Carrying a mountain in a dream means carrying the responsibility of managing the business of a notable merchant, and such responsibilities will bear heavy on him. If the mountain is radiant with lights, it means that one's responsibilities will be light too. If he sees a mountain descending from the heavens in a dream, it represents a visit of the local governor to that locality. If one sees the mountain rising into the skies in a dream, it means that the governor of that town will be dismissed. Throwing stones from the top of a mountain in a dream means insulting others. If the mountain is beautifully dressed in the dream, it means that one will command a greater authority. Seeing a mountain at a distance in a dream means a journey. If one sees an earthquake hitting a mountain in a dream, it means that calamities will befall that land or country. If an evildoer sees a mountain in his dream, it means that he will surely suffer for his sins. Swallowing a mountain in a dream means commanding and controlling ruthless and strong men. Climbing a mountain until one reaches a flat surface in a dream means serving orphans, or nursing sick people. Entering a cave inside a mountain in a dream means reaching safety. The good or evil emanating from seeing a mountain in one's dream depend on its fertility or bareness. Climbing a mountain and enjoying its vegetations and its sweet fresh waters in a dream means sheltering one's chastity in the company of one's wife, or learning a knowledge or a trade that will satisfy one's needs. Climbing a mountain through a straight path in a dream means facing things the way they are. If one sees mountains moving forward with him, it means a war or a major conflict between people of knowledge. Falling down from the top of a mountain into the middle of beasts, crows, vultures, snakes, mammals, mire, filth, or rats and their different kinds in a dream means abstaining from sins, or refraining from innovation if escaping from them leads one into a mosque where he can enter to pray, or a garden where he can rest in peace. If the mountain crumbles, and if it is transformed into ashes or dirt in the dream, it means that whoever is meant in that dream shall lose his devotion and waste his life. *(Also see Ascending in the skies)*

Mourning period: *(See Iddah)*

Mourning the dead: *(See Lamenting)*

Mouse hole: (Den; Lair; Hole; Burrow) In a dream, any hole or den of such mammals means pursuing innovations in one's religious practices, or being attached to following leaders of such ideas and who will lead people astray. A den in a dream also represents the element of charcoal. If one sees an animal coming out of a hole or a den in a dream, it means that he will utter words that befit the character of such an animal.

Mouse: (Rodent; Thief; Woman) A mouse in a dream represents a dissolute and a sinful woman, a thief, or someone who feels flattered at exposing people's private life. To see a large family of mice in one's house in a dream means money and prosperity. If one sees a mouse playing inside his house where there is plenty of food in a dream, it means relief and money. If a mouse leaves one's house in a dream, it means that blessings will depart from that house and its earnings will diminish. Owning a pet mouse in a dream means having a servant or a housekeeper. A black mouse and a white mouse in a dream represent the night and the day. Seeing a mouse of either black or white color going about its own business in the daylight in a dream means longevity. If one sees a mouse nibbling into one's garment in a dream, it means that one will announce his intentions or goals. A mouse digging a hole in a dream represents a thief. A mouse in a dream also could represents a girlfriend, an opportunistic woman, or a lady friend who is hiding her true intentions. Catching a mouse in a dream also means befriending a woman, or marriage. Mice in a dream also mean elation, or ecstasy unless they are of mixed colors. Mice in a dream also represent the members of one's household. Killing or catching a mouse in a dream means taking advantage of a woman. Throwing a stone or shooting an arrow at a mouse in a dream means backbiting or slandering a contemptible woman, or corresponding with her eliciting the unlawful. Seeing a family of mice inside a well or near a slanting land in a dream means nearing the end of one's life. Seeing a large family of mice inside one's house in a dream also could represent a gathering of women, or holding a party in one's house. A mouse inside one's shirt in a dream represents a woman friend out of whom no good can come. The skin of a mouse in a dream means little money which is taken from a vile woman.

Moustache: Shaving, clipping or adjusting one's moustache in a dream means lessening one's burdens. A moustache in a dream also means money. A bad cut in one's moustache in a dream means a mishap or losing money. Having an unusually long moustache in a dream means going against the currents, or it could mean an illness that will deprive one from eating solid food, or it could mean religious innovation. A long and an ugly looking moustache in a dream means difficulties, sorrows, distress, becoming an alcoholic, refusing to surrender to others what belongs to them, or refusing to pay charity, or pretending to ignore the necessity to pay the obligatory alms tax. Shaving one's moustache in a dream for someone who follows that trend means comfort and dispelling sorrows. If one dislikes to shave his moustache and sees himself shaving it in a dream, it means that he will lose his rank, earn a bad reputation, or it could mean poverty or business losses. Having a small moustache or a short one in a dream means languor or laziness.

Mouth: (Cellar) In a dream, one's mouth represents his life from inception to completion. One's mouth in a dream also represents the course of one's livelihood and the source of his strength. Putting medicine in one's mouth in a dream means correcting one's life for the better. If one puts food in his mouth in a dream, it means worldly gains and profits, unless one puts something that tastes bad, or which is spoiled, then it means losses, distress and depression. Putting good and tasty food or sweets in one's mouth in a dream means living a happy and a rich life. If one's mouth is buckled in a dream, it means death, sickness, dumbness, silence, helplessness, or defeat. If one's mouth looks larger than usual in the dream, it denotes growth and greater benefits, but if one's mouth looks smaller in the dream, then it means the opposite. If one's mouth smells good in the dream, it means speaking good words. Infection of one's mouth in a dream means a disaster or business losses. If something nice comes out of one's mouth in a dream, it means kindness toward others. If one sees his mouth sealed in a dream and did not know who did it, it means a scandal or defamation. In a dream, one's mouth is interpreted in seven ways: It could mean knowledge, a coffer, a cellar, a bookcase, a market, a doorman, a minister, or a door. If a pious person sees a harness around his mouth in a dream, it means fasting from food. If an impious person sees that, it means rebuke and reprimand. (Also see Body¹)

Mowing: (See Scythe)

Mucous: (Blear-eyed; Discharge of the eyes; Rheum) To see one's eyes dimmed with foul discharges, or to see oneself blear-eyed in a dream means gazing at what is unlawful, becoming apathetic toward evil people, or suffering from financial difficulties, and for a woman it means inability to conceive children.

Mucus: (See Nasal mucus; Phlegm)

Mud: (See Mire; Tattoo)

Mudd: (arb.; See Half a bushel)

Muezzin: (Caller to prayers; Muslim caller on the hour of prayers) In a dream, a muezzin represents someone who calls for what is good and blessed, a broker, an officiant who performs the wedding ceremony, the messenger of the king, or his door attendant. If a muezzin recites the entire call to prayers in a dream, it may denote the pilgrimage season. The call to prayers in a dream also may represent a siren announcing a burglary or a fire. If a woman calls to prayers on top of a minaret in a dream, it means innovation and that a major trial will emerge in that locality. If a child calls to prayers from the top of a minaret and at a time other than the hour of prayers in a dream, it means that ignorant people will rise to govern and lead his community. The call to prayers in a dream also represents an official announcement. An unknown muezzin in a dream represents the governor, or the ruler of that land. *(Also see Cock fighting; Minaret; Masjid; Mosque; Ram)*

Mug: (A small drinking cup; Tankard) A mug in a dream represents one's progeny, love to raise children, knowledge and understanding. *(Also see Jar; Tankard)*

Muhammad: (God's Prophet Muhammad, blessings and peace be upon him; The Seal of the prophets; The last Messenger) It is related that God's Messenger, upon whom be peace, has said: *"One who sees me in a dream will see me in his wakefulness, for Satan cannot impersonate me."* He also has said: *"One who sees me in a dream, it is as if he has truly seen me, for Satan cannot impersonate me."* He also has said: *"One who sees me in a dream will not enter the fire of hell."* Muslim theologians and scholars differ in opinion about the meaning of seeing God's Prophet (uwbp) in a dream. Imām Ibn Seerīn used to ask someone who tells of such a dream to describe the Prophet, upon whom be peace. If any of the details did not fit his description, Ibn Seerīn's reply was: "You have not seen him." Āsim Bin Kulayb once said: "I related to Ibn Abbās, God bless his soul and that of his father, that I saw God's Prophet (uwbp) in a dream. Ibn Abbās replied: "Describe him to me." Āsim Bin Kulayb added: "I described him as resembling Al-Hassan son of 'Ali, upon both of them be peace." Ibn Abbās replied: "Indeed you have seen him." Ibn 'Arabi once explained that the essence of seeing God's Prophet (uwbp) is cognizance of his presence and understanding the reality of his character and example. Thus, recognizing the presence of the blessed being is as affirmation of the truth, while seeing the physical form represents his example and attributes, for being earthly does not change the essence of prophethood. When God's Prophet (uwbp) said: *"He will see me in wakefulness,"* it means: 'Expounding upon what he saw,' for what one sees in such a dream is the truth which resides in the realms of the unseen. In the second saying, when God's Prophet, upon whom be peace, said: *"It is as if he has truly seen me,"* it means that if one had seen him during the time of delivering God's massage, the example will be the same. Thus, the first saying signifies what is real and true while the second saying implies the physical reality and its example. If one sees God's Prophet, upon whom be peace, coming toward him in a dream, it means blessings and benefits, and if one sees God's prophet (uwbp) turning away from him in a dream, it means the opposite. Al-Qādī 'Iyād, God bless his soul, interpreted the words of God's Prophet (uwbp) in his saying: *"Has truly seen me,"* to mean: "has truly seen my physical form," that the blessed companions knew, while seeing him in another form in a dream means that one's dream connotes personal interpretations. Following the explanation of Al-Qādī 'Iyād, Imām Al-Nawawi commented by saying: "This is a weak explanation. A stronger interpretation is to say that one who sees God's Prophet (uwbp) in a dream has seen him in reality however his resemblance may appear. Whether the resemblance in the dream is known or not." In a separate commentary, Shaikh Al-Baqlānī added: "What Al-Qādī 'Iyād has said does not contradict what Imām Al-Nawawi has said." This is because the first dream does not require interpretation, according to Al-Qāḍī 'Iyāḍ. In the second type of dream, that is discussed in Imām Al-Nawawi's comments, one's dream does require interpretation or analysis. This is to mean that since no Satan can impersonate God's Prophet (uwbp), then whatever appearance he displays in one's dream is true. The meaning of God's prophet's saying: *"For Satan cannot impersonate me,"* implies that since God's guardianship ('Isma) is inviolable, and since God's Prophet, upon whom be peace, is sacrosanct, then as he was protected during the time of delivering God's message to humanity, he is still protected by the same guardianship after God Almighty took him back to Himself. Thus, whoever sees God's Prophet (uwbp) in any appearance in a dream, it is as if has seen him in reality, regardless whether one sees him as a young man, or at the time of delivering his message, or as an old person. If one sees him looking old in a dream, it means peace. If one sees him looking young in a dream, it means war. If one sees him smiling in a dream, it means that one is truly emulating his traditions. Seeing God's Prophet (uwbp) in his known and recognized appearance in a dream means that the one seeing the dream is a pious person, that his integrity is inviolable, and that his success is unquestionable. Seeing him (uwbp) in a dream frowning represents the ill state of the one seeing the dream. Ibn Abi Jumrah once said: "Seeing Him (uwbp) in a beautiful appearance denotes the good religious standing of the person seeing the dream. Seeing him with some disfeatures in a dream, a deficiency or distortion in one's application of his religious duties, for God's Prophet (uwbp) is like a mirror that portrays the one standing before it." In this sense, the person seeing the dream can recognize his own state. This interpretation is also given by Ibn Hajar Al-Hutaymi, God bless his soul. Like that, in the book of 'Sharh al-Shamā-il' of Imām Al-Tirmiṯhï, it is also stated that Satan cannot impersonate God Almighty, His signs, prophets or angels. If someone suffering from distress sees God's Prophet (uwbp) in a dream, it means that his difficulties will be removed. If a prisoner sees him in a dream, it means that he will be released form prison. If one is living at a time of economic chaos, and if high prices are exploiting the people of the land, or if injustice is tyrannizing everyone, then seeing God's Prophet, upon whom be peace, in a dream represents an end to such adversities. Seeing him in his beautiful, radiant and impeccable appearance as best described by his companions in a dream means glad tidings of attaining a successful conclusion to one's life in this world and in the hereafter. The state and clarity of one's heart and how well polished is his own mirror determines in what appearance he may see him, upon whom be peace. If God's Prophet (uwbp) comes toward someone in a dream, or leads him in prayers, or if one sees himself accompanying him on the road, or if one eats something sweet from his blessed hand, or receives a cloak, or a suitable shirt, or if God's Prophet promises him something, or prays for him, then if the one seeing the dream qualifies for leadership, and if he is a righteous and a just man who commands what is good and forbids what is evil, and if he is learned and practices what he knows, and if he is a pious worshipper and a devout Muslim, he will then attain the station and company of the blessed ones. If the one who sees the dream is a disobedient servant of God Almighty, it means that he will repent for his sins and return to his Lord. If he is living in heedlessness, it means that he will be guided. Perhaps, he might attain his goals in acquiring knowledge, or learn how to reconstruct his innermost being to befit a human being who is grateful to his Lord. If one is fearing oppression, persecution, or loss of his property and wealth sees him (uwbp) in a dream, it means putting an end to such fears, for he is the best of intercessors to restore anyone before God Almighty. If one who follows innovations sees God's Prophet (uwbp) in a dream, it means that he should fear God Almighty, heed to His warnings and correct himself and particularly if he sees Him (uwbp) walking away from him, or turning his back to him. Seeing God's Prophet (uwbp) in a dream also means receiving glad tidings and happy news, or it could signify justice, establishing the truth, fulfillment of a promise, reaching a high rank among the members of one's family, or perhaps it could mean that one may suffer from their envy and jealousy, or leave his homeland and migrate to another country, or it could mean that he may lose his parents and become an orphan. Seeing him (uwbp) in a dream also could mean seeing miraculous events (*Karāmāt*), for his companions witnessed and testified to a deer greeting him, a camel who kissed his foot, the broiled leg of mutton talking to him, trees moving to give him cover, pebbles glorifying God's praises in his hand, among countless miracles, including his Nocturnal Journey and ascension (*Mi'rāj*) to the heavens to meet his Lord. If an ophthalmologist sees him in a dream, it means that he will acquire great expertise in his field and become renowned in the land, for God's prophet upon whom be peace, did return the eye of his companion Qutādah to its place and made his sight sharper than it was by God's leave, after Qutādah had lost his eye during one of the battles with the unbelievers. If a traveller in the desert sees God's Prophet (uwbp) in a dream, or if there is drought somewhere, it means that rain will fall and springs will gush forth, as water gushed from between his blessed fingers when he placed his blessed hand over a half filled cup to quench the thirst of an entire army. If calamities, starvation and drought has befallen a land and someone sees Him (uwbp) in a dream, it means that such calamities will be lifted and life will return to normal in that place. If a woman sees him in a dream, it means that she will reach a high spiritual station, honor, righteousness, chastity, trustworthiness and perhaps be given a blessed progeny, or if she is wealthy, it means that she will spend her wealth on God's path. Seeing him (uwbp) in a dream also means facing adversities, bearing patience and suffering from one's enemy. If an orphan sees him (uwbp) in a dream, it means that he will reach an exalted station and the same goes if a foreigner sees him in his dream. If a physician sees him (uwbp) in a dream, it means that people will benefit from his medicine. Seeing him (uwbp) in a dream also means victory over one's enemy, or consolidating and paying one's debts, or recovering from an illness, or attending a pilgrimage to God's House in Mecca, or triumphing over one's trials, or cessation of one's adversities, or fertility of a barren land, or the pregnancy of a barren woman. If a visitor to his mosque sees himself in a dream coming before God's Prophet (uwbp) and finds him standing up, it denotes one's correct religious standing, and it means that he will have commanding authority over the Imām of his time. If one finds him (uwbp) deceased in the dream, it means that a noble person from the family of the person seeing the dream will shortly die. If one sees the funeral of God's Prophet (uwbp) in a dream, it means that a calamity will befall that country. Following his funeral procession up to his grave (uwbp) in a dream means that the person seeing the dream will yield to innovations. Visiting his grave (uwbp) in a dream means receiving a great treasure. If one sees himself as the son of God's Prophet (uwbp) in a dream, and even if one is not one of his descendents, it denotes one's sincerity, true faith and certitude. Seeing God's Prophet (uwbp) by one person does not exclude the remainder of the believers, but the blessings encompass all of them. Receiving something from him (uwbp) such as food or a drink in a dream means benefits and profits. If one receives food which substance connotes negative circumstances, such as a melon or the like elements in a dream, it means that one will escape from a great danger, though he will toil and suffer from hardships during his trials. If one sees that one of the limbs that belong to God's Prophet (uwbp) has become his own in a dream, it means that he is following innovation and making changes in the laws God's Prophet (uwbp) brought to humankind. If one sees himself in a dream embodying the form of God's Prophet, upon whom be peace, or wearing one of his garments, or receives his ring, or sword, then if the person is seeking to govern, he will attain that and the people will accept his leadership. If one is suffering from persecution, or humiliation in the land, then seeing God's Prophet (uwbp) standing in a dream means that God Almighty will grant him victory and make him rise above his enemies. If one is poor, his needs will be satisfied, or if he is unmarried, he will get married. If one sees him (uwbp) in a ruined place in a dream, it means that such a place will be rebuilt. If one enters a room and finds him (uwbp) sitting there in a dream, it means that a miraculous sign, or a major event will take place in such a locality. If one sees him (uwbp) making the call to prayers in a dream, it means that prosperity will spread in that place. If one sees him establishing the prayers (Iqāmah) in a dream, it means that the Muslims will reunite and dispel their differences. If one sees him (uwbp) placing kohl over his eyelids in a dream, it means that he will find safety and correct his religious stand, or it could mean that one will study and become a scholar in the field of the prophetic sayings (Aḥādīth). If a pregnant woman sees him (uwbp) in a dream, it means that she will beget a son. If one sees him (uwbp) having a black beard with no gray hair in it in a dream, it will bring happiness, joy and prosperity to one's life. If God's Prophet (uwbp) is seen as an old man in a dream, it means strength in one's life and victory over one's enemy. Seeing him (uwbp) in his most exalted state in a dream means that the Imām, or the ruler of the country will rise in station and that his authority will expand. If one sees his blessed neck wide, it means that the Imām is holding firmly to his trust. If one sees him (uwbp) having a large chest in a dream, it means that the Imām or the ruler of the country is generous toward his subjects. If one sees his blessed stomach (uwbp) empty in a dream, it means that the treasury of the country is empty. If one sees his right hand closed in a dream, it means that the Imām or the ruler of the country does not pay his employees, or distribute the collected alms tax. If one sees his blessed right hand (uwbp) open in a dream, it denotes the generosity of the ruler and his compliance with the distribution of charities and alms tax as prescribed in God's book. If his hands are locked together in a dream, it means complications in the life of the Imām, or the ruler of the country. The same will affect the life of the person seeing the dream, including suffering from distress and adversities. If one sees his blessed leg beautiful and hairy in a dream, it means that one's clan will become stronger, and his tribe will grow. If one sees the blessed thighs of God's Prophet tall in a dream, it denotes longevity of the Imām or the ruler of the country. If one sees him (uwbp) standing in the midst of soldiers and everyone is laughing and joking in a dream, it means that the Muslim army will be defeated and humiliated in a war. If he is seen with a small army that is ill equipped and everyone is looking down in the dream, it means that the Muslim army will triumph in that year. If one sees him (uwbp) combing his blessed hair and beard in a dream, It means that one's distress and adversities will be dispelled. Seeing him (uwbp) in his own mosque, or in any mosque, or in his usual place in a dream it means gaining power and honor. If one sees him standing in the midst of his companions delivering a revelation in a dream, it means that one will acquire a greater knowledge, wisdom and spiritual understanding. Seeing the grave of God's Prophet (uwbp) in a dream means prosperity and profits for a merchant, or the release of a prisoner from his jail. Seeing oneself in a dream as the father of God's Prophet (uwbp) means that one's faith will diminish and his certitude will weaken. If a woman sees herself in a dream as one of the wives of God's Prophet (uwbp), it represents her growing faith. If one sees him (uwbp) looking into one's affairs in a dream, it means that God's Prophet (uwbp) is admonishing the one seeing the dream and commanding him to render his wife her due rights. To walk behind him (uwbp) in a dream means following his (Sunnah) traditions in wakefulness. To eat with him (uwbp) in a dream means that one is commanded to pay the annual alms tax (*Islāmic law*) due over one's money making assets, or liquid assets, gold, silver, jewelry, savings, etcetera, excepting one's home or vehicle. If one sees God's Prophet (uwbp) eating alone in a dream, it means that the one seeing the dream refuses to give charities and disdains to help those who ask for his help. In this sense, it is as if God's Prophet, upon whom be peace, is commanding the person to give charities and to help the needy. If one sees him (uwbp) bare footed in a dream, it means that one has neglected to do his regular prayers. To see him (uwbp) and to shake hands with him in a dream means that one is truly his follower. If one sees his blood mixed with that of God's Prophet (uwbp) in a dream, it means that one will marry a woman from among his descendents, or that one will marry the daughter of a great religious scholar. If God's Prophet (uwbp) gives someone some type of greens or herbs in a dream, it means that one will escape from a great danger. If he (uwbp) gives him something fresh or honey in the dream, it means that one will learn the Holy Qur'ān and acquire a great knowledge and wisdom according to the amount he receives in his dream. If one returns the gift to God's Prophet (uwbp) it means that he will follow innovation. To see him (uwbp) delivering a sermon in a dream means that he is commanding people to do good and to eschew evil. If one sees the color of his skin (uwbp) tan in a dream, it means that one will think about repenting from his sins and abstain from young people's ignorance. If the color of his skin is white in the dream, it means that one will repent for his sins and turn to God Almighty for acceptance. If he (uwbp) reprimands someone in a dream, it means that one must refrain from innovation and follow the prophetic traditions. If one finds that God's Prophet (uwbp) has died in a specific location in a dream, it means that the person seeing the dream will die in that same place and God knows best. (*Also see Visiting holy sites*)

Muḥarram: (*See Arabic months*)

Mulberry Tree: (Sycamore, *bibl.*) In a dream, a mulberry tree represents a person in a high position who has many children, who is big in size but ill mannered, who benefits no one, though he remains well respected. If one gets some of its fruits in his dream, it means that he will receive something from such a person. If he is hurt by its thorns in the dream, the same will take place in wakefulness. When maple trees, tamarisk trees and shrubs are mixed together in a dream, they mean victory and glad tidings for one who is contemplating a war or gearing for a fight. However, for the rest of people, these trees in a dream mean poverty and meekness.

Mulberry: Eating mulberries or strawberries in a dream mean increase in one's earnings, praiseworthy religious assiduity, good faith, certitude and leading a healthy life. Blackberries in a dream represent gold. The mulberry tree in a dream represents a wealthy person with many children. Mulberry in a dream also could mean borrowing money. A mulberry tree in a dream also represents a wealthy and a generous man with a large family. Eating black mulberry in a dream also means prosperity.

Mule driver: (Muleteer) A muleteer in a dream represents a policeman, a sheriff, a businessman, or business success. (*Also see Carrier*)

Mule: In a dream, a mule represents an obstinate and a stupid person, an imbecile or a bastard. A mule in a dream represents an illegitimate child who is born from a foreign father in adultery. Riding a mule in a dream means longevity or marrying a barren woman. If one sees himself mounting a saddled mule which is travelling toward Mecca in a dream, it means that he will soon perform a pilgrimage. Wandering on a mule in a dream means benefits. An obstinate mule in a dream represents a cunning person. Riding a mule in a dream also means having a dispute with someone. A weak mule who cannot be controlled in a dream represents a niggardly and a wicked person. Riding on top of loads a mule is carrying, and if the mule is consenting in a dream means controlling one's environment.

Muleteer: *(See Mule driver)*

Multiple spouses: *(See Polygamy)*

Mummification: Embalming the body of a deceased person in a dream is a cause of happiness for a sad person and repentance of a sinner. *(Also see Shroud)*

Mummy case: *(See Sarcophagus)*

Murder: *(See Killing)*

Murmur: (Grumble; Rumble) Murmuring or grumbling in a dream denotes the impeachment of the governor, recovering from an illness, a journey for someone who loves to travel, losses for arguing people, or perhaps it could mean marriage and celebrations. To murmur in a dream also means to follow innovations and to lock one's destiny on the path of error.

Mushrooms: Eating mushrooms in a dream means longevity, recovering of a sick person from his illness, marriage of an unwed person, acquiring knowledge, guidance, money or a job. *(Also see Food)*

Musical instruments: *(See Flute; Oboe; Tambourine; String instruments)*

Musical performance: *(See Delight)*

Musician: Seeing a musician in a dream could mean relaxation, comfort, forgetting one's problems, weddings, parties, fun, a repetition, mourning, or complaining. *(Also see Singing; String instruments)*

Musk: In a dream, musk represents a private charity, pregnancy, a profitable business, a valuable property, a farm, fruit trees, olive trees, or advanced knowledge. When associated with a deceased person, musk in a dream may mean that he is in paradise. If musk is burned as incense in a dream, it means innovation, loss of money and respect, putting things in the wrong place, or serving a strong person for a fee. In a dream, musk also represents one's beloved, his servant, his son or a beautiful woman. If a thief sees himself carrying musk in a dream, it means that he will cease robbing people, for a sweet fragrance points to its carrier and exposes what he hides. Musk in a dream also means money, gold, comfort, glad tidings, good news, or innocence. The same interpretation is given to carnation, clove, nutmeg and other dark seeds, all of which mean triumph and happiness. Grinding them in a dream means receiving praises. Offering them whole in a dream means doing good to an ungrateful person. *(Also see Amber; Anoint; Galia moschata)*

Muslims' festivals: *(See Feast of Breaking the Fast; Feast of Immolation)*

Mustard seeds: (Mustard; Money; Poison) In a dream, mustard means poison. If one eats mustard in his dream, it means that someone may poison him, or that he may fall into a vicious circle, or acquire an evil reputation. It also means that he may receive clean money, though through awesome hardships. Mustard seeds in a dream only denote good if seen by a physician. Otherwise, for the majority of people, seeing mustard or sesame seeds in a dream means a sickness, a fever, or poison.

Mute: (Dumbness)

Mutton: (Meat; Sheep) To see a slaughtered and skinned sheep hanging in one's house in a dream means death in such a house. Herding sheep in a dream means presiding over people. Owning a herd of sheep or managing them in a dream means wealth and profits. Eating mutton meat in a dream means prosperity. *(Also see Meat)*

Muzdalifa: *(arb.* Mish'ar Al-Harām; Rituals of the Pilgrimage) Seeing oneself at Muzdalifa in a dream means receiving a commendation because of one's endeavor to fulfill his prescribed duties, or it could mean payment of debts, or fulfillment of a promise. To see the sacred station at Muzdalifa *(arb. Mish'ar Al-*

Harâm) in a dream means observing God's commandments and fulfilling the divine injunctions. If one finds himself standing before the sacred station of Muzdalifa, seeking refuge in its sanctuary in a dream, it means that he will receive guidance and dispel his fears. *(Also see 'Arafât; Circumambulation; Cradle of Ismâïl; Ka'aba; Mina; Pelting stones; Pilgrimage; Responding; Sa'ï; Station of Abraham; 'Umrah)*

Myrtle: *(bot.* A shinny evergreen shrub.) When seen in a dream, a myrtle means health, money, covering one's face with long hair, bashfulness, or it could mean a new garment. Cutting or gathering myrtle leaves in a dream means consolidating one's interests and attaining one's goals. It is also interpreted as a reliable and a just person. Seeing oneself crowned with a branch of myrtle leaves in a dream represent a life lasting marriage. Seeing it in one's house means lasting blessings.

Mythical monster: *(See Griffin)*

N

Nafl: *(arb. See Five times prayers)*

Nag: *(See Workhorse)*

Nail: (Fastener) In a dream, a nail represents a commander or a governor. A nail in a dream also represents attainment of one's goal. Fastening a nail to a piece of wood in a dream means getting married. Nails in a dream also could represent an army, and they could signify strength and benefits. Swallowing nails in a dream means swallowing one's anger. Nails in a dream also represent someone who associates with evil people.

Nails: (Capture; Fingernails; Strength; Victory) Fingernails in a dream represent victory over one's enemy. Having long fingernails for someone who needs them for his or her work in a dream means prosperity. Long fingernails in a dream also mean a trend that opposes what is common and practical. Long fingernails in a dream also mean strength, power and protection from one's enemy. Long fingernails in a dream also denote shame. Losing one's fingernails to a sickness in a dream means losing one's wealth, or reaching a dead end. Clipping one's fingernails in a dream means following the common norms, lending money, or collecting gold jewelry. White fingernails in a dream mean understanding, vigilance, or memorizing things. Fighting someone with nails in a dream represents a cunning person. Long and beautiful fingernails in a dream mean money, or business. If the length of one's fingernails reaches near breaking in a dream, it means losing to others what otherwise could remain under one's own control, or it could denote the need to pay alms tax or to distribute charity. Seeing one's fingernails broken or chipped in a dream means loss of money, status or health. If one's fingernails become claws in a dream, it means that he will triumph over his enemy. *(Also see Body¹; Claw)*

Naked: (Assertion; Nude; Stripped; Unclothed; Undressed) Nakedness in a dream represents inward purity and clarity, or it could mean committing an act that will culminate in regret. Undressing oneself in a dream means facing a reticent, hidden, unexpected and notorious enemy who will publicly assert his enmity. If one sees himself alone and naked in a dream, it means that one of his enemies, knowing his weaknesses, is demanding capitulation from him, or threatening him, or blackmailing him. If one sees himself naked during an assembly or a party in a dream, it means that he will be exposed or defamed. If one sees himself naked in the midst of people, though he does not feel shy and is not aware of it in the dream, it means that he engages in a project then exaggerates the degree of his involvement, suffer hardships and gains nothing out of his adventure. If one sees himself naked in front of people, and if he finds himself embarrassed, or tries desperately to find a cover but to no avail, it signifies loss of property and wealth. If he stands out naked and people keep looking at his private parts in the dream, it means a scandal or suffering from defamation. Nakedness in a dream also could mean divorce, or death of one's wife. Taking off one's clothing in a dream means loss of position and prestige, loss of work, demotion, or recovering from an illness. If a sick person sees himself changing his soiled garment in a dream, it means that he will recover from his illness, or escape from an adversity or an accident, or that he will be declared innocent from a false accusation. Nakedness in a dream also means death. As for religious and pious people, nakedness in a dream means renouncing the world, or increase in their devotion. If a farmer sees an unknown woman naked in a dream, it means that the time has come to turn the earth over and to prepare it for a new crop. If their is a true witness or an acceptable reference, then one's nakedness in the dream means attending the pilgrimage in Mecca. Nakedness in a dream also means putting on a new garment. The nakedness of a woman in a dream means separation from her husband, or it could mean her her divorce. *(Also see Nakedness)*

Nakedness: In a dream, it means belligerence and injustice. *(Also see Naked)*

Nanny: *(See Bread)*

Narcissus: *(bot.)* In a dream, a narcissus flower represents a woman. A garland of narcissus in a dream represents a short lived marriage. If an unmarried woman sees herself carrying a coronet of narcissus in a dream, it means a short lived marriage that will end either in divorce or in the death of her husband. Blooming narcissus in a dream represents a son. A bouquet of narcissus in a dream means the death of a son. Seeing the narcissus flower in a dream also means happiness, money, gold, or silver. The narcissus flower in a dream also signifies longevity or gray hair. *(Also see Distilled water)*

Nasal mucus: (Blowing one's nose; Snot) In a dream, nasal mucus means a son or a daughter. To blow one's nose in someone's house in a dream means marrying someone from that family, or betraying the house master by having a secret affair with his wife. If a mother blows her nose in a dream, it means that she will wean her child. If the wife of such a friend wipes the nasal mucus of her husband's guest in a dream, it means that she will betray her husband and carry the child of his friend. If one blows his nose in a dream, it also means paying a debt, or it could mean rewarding someone for a favor. Blowing one's nose and using someone's bed sheet in a dream means betraying him with his wife. Blowing one's nose in someone's handkerchief in a dream means betraying him with his house servant. Clearing one's nose from a nasal congestion in a dream means dispelling distress. Wiping and washing someone else's nose in a dream means concealing his secret life in front of his wife. Eating one's nasal mucus in a dream means cheating one's son in his money. A congested nose in a dream represents a pregnant wife. If a beast or a bird comes out of one's nose when he sneezes or blows his nose in a dream, it means that he will beget a son from a secret affair with a servant or an employee. If a sable comes out of one's nose in a dream, it means that he will beget a son who will grow to become a thief. If a pigeon comes out of his nose in the dream, it means that he will beget a girl that will grow to be insane. Blowing one's nose and using one's own shirt in a dream means committing adultery with a sacrosanct member of his own family or a blood relation. If one sees his nose gloppy with mucus in a dream, it means that his fecundity and sexual appetite will bring him many children. Nasal mucus in a dream also means an illness, a cold, charity or a will. *(Also see Phlegm)*

Nasal speech: *(See Twanging)*

Naturalist: (Hiker; Mountain person) A naturalist in a dream represents travels, a graveyard, or he could represent a wedding.

Navel pain: *(See Body[1]; Pain)*

Navel: (Umbilicus) In a dream, one's navel represents his mother, his father, or it could mean his earnings, wife, servant or a coffer. If one's navel looks abnormal in a dream, it means that something bad may happen to his family. This also may affect any of the above members of his family or property. If a sick person sees his navel swollen in a dream, it means his death. To open one's navel by hand in a dream means opening one's coffer to get some spending money. One's navel in a dream also means happiness, and could represent the wife's lover, a beloved, or one's will. Thus, if one's navel looks beautiful in the dream, its beauty will show in his life; but if it looks ugly, it means that he may live a wretched life. A navel in a dream also represents one's homeland. Any pain one suffers from his navel in a dream represents the adverse conditions of his family or country. If an immigrant suffers from any affliction to his navel in a dream, it means that he will return to his homeland. (Also see Body[1])

Neck pain: (See Pain)

Neck: In a dream, a neck represents an embrace, a donation with terms, a legal will or a conditional endowment. The neck and the shoulders in a dream represent one's trust or trustworthiness. A healthy strong neck in a dream means trustworthiness and ability to repay one's debts. Wounds, festering, or purulence in one's neck in a dream mean betraying God's trust. If one sees a nice bird sitting over his neck in a dream, it means benefits or an alibi. If it is not a gentle bird, then it becomes a bad omen or a rebuke. If one sees a necklace, a rope, a wire or a thread wrapped around his neck in a dream, it means fulfilling a promise, acquiring knowledge, status and honored. (Also see Body[1])

Neckband: (Collar; Necklace) In a dream, a neckband represents stinginess. A neckband in a dream also could represent woman's kindness, gentleness, softness, protection and respect for her husband. Thus, for a woman, a neckband in her dream represents her husband. If her neckband is made of silver, and if it is wide, comfortable and well strapped to her neck in a dream, it denotes her husband's generosity, richness and forbearance. If the neckband is thin, then it implies difficulties. If it is made of iron in the dream, it represents a strong person. If it is made from wood in the dream, it represents a hypocrite. If a man wears a neckband over a white or a green collar in a dream, it represents victory in his life and comfort he will receive from an unexpected source. If he is a merchant, it means profits, fame, honor and dignity. If he is a common person, then the neckband means earning respect and fame. If a tight neckband is strapped around one's neck in a dream, it represents a stingy person no one can benefit from. If he is a learned person, it means that no one benefits from his knowledge. If he commands authority, it means that he disdains from giving true judgment. To hire a servant who wears a silver neckband in a dream means establishing a profitable business. A neckband in a dream also means impiety, or it could be a sign of trustworthiness. If a man sees himself wearing a neckband that is made of gold, silver, iron, copper or lead in a dream, it means that he has abandoned his religious trust, forsaken his covenant and has become a profligate. (Also see Necklace)

Necklace: (Decoration; Medal; Pendant) In a dream, woman's necklace or earrings if they are made of pearls represent a gift from her husband. If they are made of silver in the dream, they mean a physical ailment, and if they are made from beads in the dream, they mean being let down by one's friends. A necklace in a dream also represents women's adornment. If a man wears a necklace that is incrusted with gold, precious gems or sapphire in a dream, it represents a high ranking appointment, carrying a great responsibility, or fulfilling an important duty. If one's decoration also carries some silver coins in the dream, it means marriage to a beautiful woman. Wearing a decoration necklace that is made from silver and adorned with precious gems in a dream represents a political appointment which will be coupled with honor and wealth. If the necklace is made from iron, it represents a political appointment that will expand one's power. If an ornate necklace is made of copper, then it represents mundane profits. Wearing a necklace that is made from beads in the dream represents an appointment with no authority. Woman's necklace in a dream represents money entrusted to her by her husband. As for a pregnant woman, wearing a necklace in a dream means giving birth to a son. A broken necklace in a dream means the impeachment of the governor of one's town. As for a woman, a red necklace in a dream represents a mask. A necklace for an unmarried woman in a dream represents a husband. Wearing a heavy necklace in a dream means carrying heavy burdens, or it could mean failure to perform one's duties at work. Any defects or perfection a necklace shows when worn by a woman in a dream represent the condition or the state of her husband or guardian, or it could mean a trust she carries. *(Also see Gold; Neckband; Ornaments; Pearl necklace)*

Neckwear: *(See Collarband; Neckband; Necklace)*

Needle: A needle in a dream represents a wife for a bachelor, though for a poor person it means satisfaction. To hold a needle in a dream means to correct oneself. If the needle is threaded in the dream, it means finding a way to improve one's life. A broken needle in a dream means difficulties and trials. If one's needle is stolen in a dream, it means that one's unfavorable conditions may last. *(Also see Sacking needle)*

Negligence: Negligence or lack of concern in a dream is a bad omen for a regular person, and it means injustice for a person in authority. If one sees an unknown old man treating him without the proper attention or with neglect in the dream, it means poverty, and the old man in the dream could represent his grandfather.

Nenuphar: *(See Water lily)*

Nerve center: *(See Inquisitional court)*

Nerves: One's nerves in a dream represent his comportment, bearing and presence. Irritation of one's nerves in a dream means distress and sorrow. If a nerve is cut off in a dream, it represents a broken life, and for a sick person it represents his death. In a dream, a nerve also represents a master, or a sire, piety, a signing witness, agreements, provisions, property, or family ties. Whatever affects one's nerves in a dream will reflect upon any of the above. *(Also see Body¹)*

Nest: (Abode; Dwelling) In a dream, a nest represents the type of bird that dwells in it. A nest in a dream also represents one's wife, house, or the boundaries one must not cross. As for a pregnant woman, a nest in a dream means giving birth.

Nestling: *(See Baby crow)*

Net: (Hunting) In a dream, a hunting net means deception, duplicity and fraud. If one falls into a hunting net in a dream, it means that he will be victimized. If one spreads a hunting net and catches an animal or a bird with it in a dream, it means that he earns money through deception and fraud.

New moon: *(See Crescent)*

New year's Day: Celebrating the new year's day in a dream means a short lived happiness, reminiscing the past, the passing of sorrow and adversities, or recovering lost money. In the dream, if the new year's day coincide to be on a Friday, it means the spread of evil, corruption, or political turmoils for that year. If it is a Saturday, it means drought, hardships during a difficult year, plagues and illness. If it is a Sunday, it means a cold winter and a blessed crop for that year. If it is a Monday, it means floods, winter illness and perhaps a partial loss of the crop. If it is a Tuesday, it means shortage of rain and a cold winter. If it is a Wednesday, it means scarcity and deficiency of water, and a cold weather by the end of summer and beginning of autumn. If it is a Thursday, it means a prosperous year, except for the livestock. This interpretation was given by Ptolemy, the Alexandrian astronomer 367-283 B.C. during his residence in Egypt.

Newborn: *(See Aqīqah rites)*

Newlywed: Entering the Sacred House in Mecca in a dream means entering one's house as a newlywed.

Newscaster: *(See Broadcaster)*

Niche: *(See Miḥrāb)*

Niggardly: (Avariciousness; Covetousness; Greed; Niggardliness) In a dream, niggardliness means committing a sin.

Night guard: Standing as a night guard in a dream means obeying God's commands and following the avenues of righteousness. If a sick person sees himself returning from his night guard shift in a dream, it means that he will recover from his illness.

Night of power: (The night in which the Holy Qur'ān was revealed.) Seeing and experiencing the night of power in a dream means that one's wish will come true, even if one desired a kingdom or a great treasure. The same interpretation applies for seeing a celebration of the night of the Nocturnal Journey during which the Prophet Muhammad, upon whom be peace, ascended to the heavens to meet his Lord. The same interpretation is given to seeing the Friday eve in one's dream.

Night: (Darkness; Heedlessness; Ignorance) In a dream, a moonless night represents lack of work, stagnation, or losing one's job. If one sees the whole world in the dark and the moon is still radiant in the skies in a dream, it means that the governor will temporarily relinquish his entire duties to his chief minister or secretary, and that thieves and robbers will cluster around them for business. If one then sees the daylight in his dream, it means that such an adversity will pass. If people are under siege in the dream and the daylight dawns after a long dark night in a dream, it means that their siege will be lifted. If people are suffering from high prices and someone sees that dream, it means that prices will go back to normal. If they are suffering from tyranny, it too will pass. The night in a dream also means marital relations, while the day means separation between them. In a dream, the darkness of night also represents heedlessness and particularly if one witnesses thunder and lightning in his dream. Seeing a complete darkness inside one's house in a dream means taking a long journey. The night and the day in a dream represent two adverse rulers, or two competitors or adversaries. The night in a dream also represents an atheist, while the day in a dream represents a believer. The night in a dream also signifies comfort and rest, while the day means toiling and hardships. In a dream, the night also means sexual pleasures, while the day means divorce or separation. The night in a dream signifies economic stagnation, while the day means business, travels and hypocrisy. If the night in a dream is interpreted to represent the ocean, then the day means land. The night in a dream also means death, while the day represents life and resurrection. The night and the day together may represent the two guardian angels who record each person's deeds and who are God's witnesses. If a sick person sees the dawn in a dream, it means that he will recover from his illness, or die from it. If he is imprisoned, it means that he will be released. If he is a sinner, it means that he will repent for his sins. If he is a merchant and his business is not moving, it means that his merchandise will be finally sold. The nightfall at the end of the day in a dream also could mean the opposite. Seeing the night in a dream also denotes constant changes in one's life, poverty, hunger, starvation, or death. The night and the day in a dream also represent wisdom and protocols, or indulging in something one will regret. The nightfall in a dream also may denote changing times, or changing trends. The night in a dream also could represent an African woman, while the day may represent a Caucasian woman, or a pregnant woman. The night in a dream also represents the evening gown, while the day represents work. The night in a dream also means veiling one's difficulties and taking refuge in a safe place, except if the one seeing the dream is a traveller, then the night in his dream means injustice and ignorance. The night in a dream also denotes devotion, holding a night vigil, attaining one's goal, or meeting with one's beloveds. *(Also see Darkness; Evening; Moon; Night of power)*

Nightfall: *(See Darkness; Evening; Night)*

Nightingale: In a dream, a nightingale represents a wealthy man or a wealthy woman. It is also interpreted as having a son in his early childhood who recites the holy Qur'ân beautifully. If one sees himself as a nightingale in a dream, it means that he depends on his assistant to provide professional advice, wisdom and good management of his business.

Nip: *(See Pinch)*

Nipple: The nipple of the female breast in a dream represents one's personal wardrobe, or it could mean marriage. If water or milk comes out of it in a dream, it means finding a compatible husband. Otherwise, it may mean loss of a child or a sister.

Niqāb: *(See Khimār; Yashmak)*

Nit: (Egg; Louse; Vermin) In a dream, lice eggs represent contemptible people. If one sees them and could not remove them in the dream, it means that contemptible people will pursue his wife, and he will fail to persecute them or even avoid them. *(Also see Lice)*

Noah's Arc: Noah's arc in a dream represents happiness, joy, festivities, salvation, relief from distress and worries, protection against drowning, a wedding, a leading position, or winning victory over one's enemy. *(Also see Noah; Ship)*

Noah: (God's prophet Noah, upon whom be peace.) In a dream, God's prophet Noah (uwbp) represents longevity, adversities, sufferings, triumph, children from a disgraceful wife, though one will remain content and grateful to God Almighty for His gift. It is said that one who sees the prophet Noah (uwbp) in a dream will become a scholar, an assiduous worshipper and an obedient servant who exercises patience and forbearance. He will also triumph over his enemies and receive a magnificent endowment from his Lord. His companions will disobey him and by God's leave, he will win over them too. Seeing God's prophet Noah (uwbp) in a dream also means rain and floods. Seeing him (uwbp) in a dream also means suffering from many enemies, and from the jealousy and envy of one's neighbors. At the end, they will all suffer from God's punishment, and he will be saved from their evil. Seeing God's prophet Noah (uwbp) in a dream also signifies the destruction of the unbelievers and the victory of the believers. If one sees him in a ship in a dream, it means that such a ship will escape from destruction, or that all its people will be saved from drowning. Seeing God's prophet Noah (uwbp) in a dream also means facing a strong army of unbelievers, their blatant attitudes, their verbal and physical abuse of the believers, and their unrestrained persecution of the physically weak among them. It also denotes the weakness of people's faith and their lack of trust in God Almighty. Seeing him (uwbp) in a dream also means spending a lifetime in devotion and servitude to one's Lord, commanding good and forbidding evil. If a ruler sees God's prophet Noah (uwbp) in a dream, it means that his subject will disobey him. Seeing him (uwbp) in a dream also means crying and lamentation, disputes with one's family, rising prices, relief from distress, adversities and having recalcitrant children. Seeing him in a dream also represents a flourishing business, farming, a ship building industry, travelling with several types of food, or mixing different species of animals. God's prophet Noah (uwbp) in a dream also may represent a genealogist, a zoologist, a botanist, a phytologist, a horticulturalist, an ecologist, or a mammalogist. Seeing God's prophet Noah (uwbp) in a dream also may mean regretting something, distress, penitence for an attitude toward one's own family, or perhaps that one's son will stray away from God's path, or it could mean the death of a son because of his disobedience

304

to his father. If a woman sees God's prophet Noah (uwbp), or God's prophet Lot (uwbp) in a dream, it means that she is disobedient to her husband, and rather she obeys her own family and clan. On the other hand, if a woman sees **Egypt's Pharaoh** in a dream, it means that she is a true worshiper and an obedient believer in God Almighty.

Noble intention: *(See Efforts)*

Nocturnal Journey: *(See 'Aqïq canyons; Night of Power)*

Noise: In a dream, noise means witnessing a social disorder, public outcry, participating in a religious festival or in an important public event that will involve the interest of all people. *(Also see Shout)*

Nomad: *(See Explorer)*

Non-existence: *(See Evanescence)*

Nonalcoholic wine: Drinking nonalcoholic wine in a dream means distress, sorrow, a wretched life, poverty, or unexpected expense. In a dream, drinking nonalcoholic wine also represents lawful money that is earned from one's toiling and sweat. However, drinking alcoholic beverage in a dream means money that is acquired through rough words and arguments, and for a governor in his dream, it means loss of his job. Alcoholic beverages in a dream mean money of suspicious source, or they could mean distress or depression. *(Also see Wine)*

Nonsense: *(See Blunder; Fool; Lying)*

Noria: (Water wheel) In a dream, a noria represents a trustworthy servant. The water wheel itself represents business fluctuations, or changes in people's life. *(Also see Water wheel)*

Nose bleeding: *(See Bleeding)*

Nose ring: In a dream, a nose ring represents an unjust person and a tyrant. Piercing the nose of an animal to insert a nose ring in a dream means money, or it could mean vanquishing or defeating one's enemy.

Nose: In a dream, nose relates to the sense of smelling. It represents the element of comfort by taking in needed oxygen for the body to satisfy its needs. The immediate sense of physical tranquility produced by inhaling through one's nose in one's dream represents liveliness and comfort. If breathing in also includes smelling a sweet fragrance in the dream, then it reflects the immediate results of one's satisfaction. Nose in a dream also represents an aspect of one's beauty, or what one adorns himself with, such as wealth, or pride he takes in his father, a son, a brother, a wife, a just partner or an employee. A beautiful nose in a dream represents the good conditions of one's life. A large nose in a dream means oppression or compulsion. Smelling a good fragrance in a dream means rising in station. If one sees himself in a dream having many noses, each of them represents the renewal of his comfort. If one's nose is transformed into iron or gold in a dream, it means an illness, an adversity, or a crime that one may commit. A nose in a dream also represents news, spying, buttocks, or the uterus. If one's nose shrinks in a dream, it means that he is arrogant. If it becomes crooked in the dream, it also means stupidity and humiliation. If it expands in the dream, it means stupidity. One's nose in a dream also represents his parents. If what is breathed through the nose is good, the consequences will be good. Otherwise, smelling a bad odor in a dream brings about negative results. *(Also see Body¹)*

Notary: In a dream, a notary represents violence, aggression, and a swagger.

Notebook: (Records) In a dream, a notebook means managing one's expenses, or remembering the past. A notebooks in a dream also represents an estate, a treasure chest, benefits, profits, distress, burdens, or bad comments. If an unemployed person sees a notebook in his dream, it means that he will find work. *(Also see Paper)*

Notorious: *(See Naked)*

November: *(See Earthquake; Thunder)*

Nubile: *(See Water lily)*

Nude: *(See Naked)*

Numb: (Lack of feeling; Sleepiness) Numbness of the hand or of any limb in a dream indicates the same in wakefulness. It is as though such a limb will not perform, or that it will wane away when one needs it most.

Numbers: *(See Counting)*

Nurse: A nurse treating one's wounds in a dream represents healing of one's sickness or sufferings. If a nurse visits a healthy person in a dream, it means that he may be wounded, and in that case he will need such assistance.

Nursery: (Greenhouse; Hotbed) In a dream, a nursery represents profits, annual return or a fertile woman. Owning or attending a nursery in a dream means victory, prosperity, marriage, acquiring knowledge, training in arts, or repenting from sin and harvesting the fruits of one's repentance. If the fruits of one's plants turn into gold or silver in one's dream, it means either benefits, profits, or that a disease will impair the growth of one's plants, or it could mean unsalability of one's crop.

Nursing: (Suckling. *See Breast-feeding*)

Nutmeg: *(See Musk)*

Nymph: *(See Water lily)*

O

Oak tree: (Evergreen) An oak tree in a dream represents profits, prosperity, honor, or associating with heedless people who live in the mountains, or perhaps it could mean visiting righteous people, ascetics and renunciates who live in the wilderness or in uninhabited ruins. An oak tree in a dream also may mean homosexuality or sodomy. An evergreen tree in a dream represents the element of longevity and strength, but it could also imply slavery because of its needles. *(Also see Oak; Tree)*

Oak: Oak in a dream represents a difficult person who loves to hoard money, or it could represent a great shaikh, or a rich person. *(Also see Oak tree; Tree)*

Oars: (Paddles) Oars in a dream represent the movement of a ship, or they could mean having a secret affair. Oars in a dream also mean reaching safety, or finding a helping friend. *(Also see Boat; Ship)*

Oatmeal: *(See Breakfast food)*

Obituarist: *(See Piper)*

Oboe: (Flute; Musical instruments; Wind instruments) In a dream, an oboe means amusement, distractions, entertainment, pleasures, celebrations, weddings, enticing rebellion, or corruption. If one receives an oboe as a gift from a governor in a dream, it means that he will preside over an administration. Placing one's fingers over the holes of an oboe in a dream means learning, memorizing and understanding the Qur'ānic revelations. Playing the oboe in a dream also means having a beautiful voice and good diction. Carrying a golden oboe in a dream represents a wise man. If a sick person sees or holds an oboe in his dream, it means his death. If a backbiter holds an oboe in his dream, it means slander, and if one who desires to have a son sees himself carrying an oboe in a dream, it means that he will beget a son. *(Also see Flute)*

Obscurity: *(See Darkness; Fog)*

Obsequious: *(See Dog)*

Observatory: *(See Watchtower)*

Obstinacy: (Obtrusive; Stubbornness) Obstinacy in a dream means witnessing or committing evil in wakefulness. To be obstinate, demanding and persistent in a dream also means running away from something, or turning one's back to a fight, a dispute, an argument or a business. Obstinacy in a dream also may denote a presumptuous and an arrogant person who is disliked by people. Being obtrusive and obstinate in a dream also may mean being exasperated or annoyed about something, or that people dislike to be in his company and have serious reservations about him. *(Also see Obtrusive person)*

Obstinate person: *(See Donkey; Darkness; Obtrusive person)*

Obtrude: *(See Darkness; Obtrusive person)*

Obtrusive person: (Demanding person; Ignorant person; Obstinate) It is common among the people of knowledge to describe an obtrusive person as a stone. *(Also see Darkness; Obstinacy)*

Obviating: *(See Cauterize)*

Occupied: *(See Busy)*

Ocean: (Government) The element of ocean in a dream represents a prison where sea lives are incarcerated, and it means losses, fear, despair, limitless knowledge, a city without walls, or the world, its trials and wonders. An ocean or a sea in a dream also represents a strong ruler who is just, compassionate toward his subjects and whom people revere, have access to, and seek for their daily needs. If a businessman sees an ocean in a dream, it represents his merchandise. As for a worker or an apprentice, the ocean in a dream represents his veteran teacher or master. If one sees the ocean in a dream, it means that he will succeed in his goals. If one sees himself entering into the ocean or sea in a dream, it means that he will enter before a ruler, or stand before someone in authority. If one sees himself sitting or lounging at the sea shore in a dream, it means that he will work for such a person or a ruler, though he will be observing caution and diplomacy with him. If one sees himself drinking the entire water of the sea though no one sees him except the king in a dream, it means that he will reign and live a long life. Drinking any portion thereof also means equal earnings to what he takes in. If one sees himself drinking from it to quench his thirst in the dream, it means riches, strength and longevity. If one sees himself asking for some of its water to drink in a dream, it means that he is seeking to work for such a strong person or ruler. If he pours its water in a pitcher in the dream, it means prosperity, or that he will receive a bounteous gift from God Almighty to encompass a high rank as well as riches. However, his status will last longer than his money. To drink water from the sea in a dream means acquiring knowledge and adopting proper conduct. Crossing the ocean in a dream means booty. If one sees strong waves bringing seawater to his street without causing damages in a dream, it means that a ruler or a great person will enter or visit that locality. Bathing in seawater in a dream means repentance from one's sins. Seeing the ocean from a distance in a dream means that calamities, temptations and trials are coming to one's community. If one sees the sea receding, whereby he can see the edges of the earth it covers in a dream, it means diminishing of his authority and control, or that the wrath of God Almighty has descended upon that locality. This calamity could be carried by one's own government, economic tribulations, drought, or one's enemies. Standing over seawater in a dream means attaining something one did not seek. Walking in the air above the seawater in a dream represents the person's good intentions, his clarity, faith and certitude. If a sick person sees himself taking ablution in seawater in a dream, it means that he will recover from his illness, or it could mean payment of one's debts and relief from worldly pressures. (Also see Water)

October: (See Earthquake; Thunder)

Oculist: (See Ophthalmologist)

Odor: Smelling a bad odor in a dream means hearing bad words, or it could mean distress. Smelling odor that emanates from under the armpit in a dream means headache, nasal congestions, cold, or hearing bad news, divulging secrets, dispelling rancor and jealousy, or it could mean relaxing after an exhausting workday, contracting an eye disease, or it could mean loathsomeness. If a child smells such an odor from under his armpit in his dream, it means that he has reached his puberty, or it could mean an illness or an accident that could take away his life. (Also see Cloud of smoke; Perspiration; Smell)

Offensive odor: (See Odor; Perspiration)

Offering: (Immolation; Sacrifice; Vow) In a dream, an offering represents the wife who is the delight of her husband, or the child who is the delight of his father. An offering in a dream also represents one's good deeds, although it also could mean trouble, adversities, enmity, dispute, fight, argument with one's family, an invasion, or profits from hunting. (Also see Immolation; Sacrifice)

Office: (Employment) In a dream, an office means attaining a leadership position, or it could mean degradation, contemptible position, parsimony, living under tight circumstances, poverty, worrying about one's children and fear for one's future.

Officer: *(See Exhibition)*

Officiant: (Wedding) An officiant in a dream means a wedding, a divorce, or he could represent a pimp, depending on the mental condition, or the type of work one who is seeing the dream performs. *(See Saddler)*

Offspring: *(See Backbone)*

Oil mill: *(See Oil press)*

Oil press: (Oil mill; Oil refinery; Refinery) In a dream, an oil press represents spiritual guidance, knowledge, a foster mother or a wet nurse. *(Also see Sugar mill)*

Oil refinery: *(See Oil press)*

Oil[1]**:** (Food) Anointing oneself with oil in a dream means receiving blessed and lawful earnings, or it could mean recovering from an illness. Drinking oil in a dream has a bad connotation and implies a bad omen, an evil spell or an illness. However, olive oil in a dream also represents knowledge, wisdom, spiritual guidance, inner light, blessings and lawful earnings. Drinking any other type of oil in a dream such as oil from rape seeds of the crucifer family tree (*Brasica napus*), or cashew oil from the terebinth tree (*Pistacia terebinthus*), then it represents earning money from a suspicious source, or receiving illegal money. Oil in a dream also represents the light of the heart, spiritual growth, a growing insight, or it may denote birth control, murders, assassinations, or braking someone's bones. Oil in a dream also denotes a broker. If good oil turns putrid or stale in a dream, it means revoking one's covenant, while if a putrid or a stale oil turns good in a dream, it means growing awareness, certitude and adopting a good standard in dealing with other. *(Also see Extracting oils from seeds; Olives)*

Oils[2]**:** *(See Amber; Musk; Perfume)*

Ointment: *(See Electuary)*

Old man: *(See Elderly person)*

Old woman: In a dream, an old woman represents the ending of one's life in this world, sorrows, the hereafter, wine, or bearing children after having lost hope in one's fertility. An old woman in a dream also could represent deceit, cunningness, duplicity, backbiting, or slander. Seeing an old and sick woman in a dream may mean impotence, weakness, or disability. Seeing a thirsty old woman in a dream means drought. If she turns a young girl in the dream, then she represents rain. If an unknown old woman visits a sick person in a dream, it means his death. Otherwise, if an unknown old woman visits a pregnant woman in a dream, it means giving her the glad tidings of a son. If one is engaged in an important project and sees himself sleeping with an old woman in a dream, it means that his project will not succeed. An old woman in a dream also represents non-arable land. If one sees her wearing a veil in the dream, it means that he will meet with hardships and regret. If one sees an ugly old woman, or a hag in a dream, it means adversities and war. If a young woman sees herself as an old woman in a dream, it means earning respect and dignity. An unknown old woman in a dream also represents a bad crop for that year. If one sees an old woman descending from the skies and people are wondering about her, she represents the passing year. Seeing an ugly old woman in a dream also could mean glad tidings of an ending war, or the end of drought. An emaciated old woman in a dream represents a year of drought. If she gains weight and turns beautiful in the dream, she represents changes in the weather conditions, bringing a prosperous and a happy end for the farmers in that year. An ostentatious old woman in a dream represents a prosperous life, or good news that will arrive shortly. If she looks frowning or unhappy in the dream, then she represents distress and loss of prestige. If she looks ugly in the dream, she represents facing adverse conditions. If she is naked in the dream, she represents a scandal. If an old woman enters a house in a dream, it means prosperity and business success and if she leaves a house in the dream, it means the opposite. An unknown old woman in a dream has a stronger connotation than a known old woman. If one sees himself frequenting an old woman in a dream, his dream denotes his attachment to worldly gains. If an old woman who passed her menopause sees herself in a dream experiencing her menstrual period again and regaining her sexual drive, and if she sees herself engaged in sexual intercourse in the dream, it means that she will become religious and have strong material and spiritual success in her life if her sexual intercourse in the dream is marital intercourse and of a lawful nature. Otherwise, if it is unlawful, then it represents her attachment to worldly gains and neglects for her spiritual values. If a young woman sees herself being an old woman in a dream, it means that she will prosper and have a successful marital life.

Olfaction: *(See Body¹; Smelling)*

Olive tree: *(See Oil; Olives)*

Olives: (Blessed tree) In a dream, olives represent money, pleasures, or one's prosperity. An olive tree in a dream represents a blessed man who benefits his family, a chaste woman, or it could mean a son who may become a governor. A yellow olive in a dream represents heavy concerns about one's religious life. If one presses olives for oil in a dream, it means that he will earn blessings and benefits. If one sees himself watering an olive tree with olive oil in a dream, it means that he sleeps with his mother. The same interpretation applies if one sees himself watering a garden with vinegar. If one buys an olive tree, or eats from one, or drinks from its oil in a dream, it means blessings, or that he will marry a noble and a chaste woman. Seeing the leaves of an olive tree in a dream means following the straight path, or fulfilling one's spiritual obligations, guidance, light, reading the Qur'ān, comforting someone's heart, making money for a poor person, except if one eats the olive raw in the dream, then it means the opposite, or it implies poverty, indebtedness, or it could denote the place, or the direction it comes from. The leaves of an olive tree represent righteous people or spiritual leaders. The fruit of an olive tree represents easy money, or living a rich and a happy life. Selecting olives or pressing them for oil in a dream means toiling, or hardships. As for a sick person, olives in a dream mean regaining strength and recovering from his illness. The fruit itself and the leaves also denote assiduousness and resoluteness, however, olives in a dream also denote slow growing. *(Also see Oil)*

Omar: (The commander of the believers, Omar bin Al-Khattāb, may God be pleased with him.) Seeing him in a dream means longevity, trustworthiness and praiseworthy deeds. One who sees him in a dream will speak the truth, be just and call people to the straight path. He also may be able to attend to the Sacred House in Mecca in an auxiliary pilgrimage (*'Umrah*). If one shakes hands with Omar bin Al-Khattāb in a dream, it means that he will prosper and live a pious life, and he will be a vigilant and a strong believer, the value of whose deeds will surpass his fame. If one sees him frowning in a dream, it means that Omar is calling for justice, commanding what is good and forbidding what is evil. If there is a drought in a town and one sees Omar in a dream, it means that rain will fall and be a blessing for that land. If there is tyranny in that land and one sees Omar in his dream, it means that justice will prevail. If Omar hits someone with a stick, or warns him, or threatens him in a dream, it means that one must renounce the course of his current actions or deviation from God's path, or perhaps that someone in authority or a scholar will persecute him. If one sees himself being Omar in a dream, or if he wears one of his garments in a dream, it means that he will be awarded honor, a dignified status, or die as a martyr. If one sees Omar smiling in a dream, it means that he follows the correct precepts of God's Messenger, upon whom be peace, and emulates his practices. Seeing him in a dream also means that justice and truth will prevail in his time, or that he is a trustworthy person, or that the propagation of truth is prominent in his time. Seeing him in a dream also could mean signing a peace treaty with one's enemy, annihilating hatred with love, good luck with one's in-laws, renouncing one's attachment to worldly things, though being capable of winning it, or presiding over people with justice, love and compassion.

Omayyād mosque: *(See Masjid)*

Ombrograh: *(See Water level)*

Ombrometer: *(See Water level)*

Omelet: (Eggs) An omelet in a dream means prosperity, joy, celebrations, profits, or marriage. *(Also see Eggs)*

Ominous: (Threatening. *See Scowling*)

Omit: (Forget) Omitting something in a dream means worries, trouble, misplacing things, or heedlessness.

One-eyed: (Blind in one eye.) If one loses one of his eyes in a dream, it means that he may lose half of his wealth, or divorce his wife, or fail to attend to his religious obligations, or commit a major sin, or it could mean that he has wasted half of his life in vain. To be blind in one eye in a dream also could mean expecting something and hoping for its arrival, or it could mean loss of a brother or a son. If a humble and a hard-working person sees that, it testifies to the trueness of his faith. If an impious person, or a corrupt person, or an impostor sees that dream, it means distress, a sickness that could bring him near his death, or to lose one hand in an accident, or to lose one's wife, or sister, or partner, or loss of blessings, or becoming sacrilegious and profane. *(Also see Antichrist)*

Onion: Eating a raw onion in a dream denotes an evil happening. If a sick person eats a small amount of onions in a dream, it means that he will die from his illness, but if one sees himself eating a large quantity in his dream, it means that he will be cured of his illness. However, eating a green onion, or a scallion in a dream means prosperity and good health, though they will be accompanied with stress, sadness or separation from one's wife. Eating a strong smelling or a fragrant herb in a dream means contempt, loathing on the part of some members of his family toward him, or it could mean that hidden matters will finally surface. If such herbs are the type of bulbs that require skinning before eating, then they denote curiosity and eavesdropping, representing what is usually discarded. In a dream, onions for a businessman represent the element of money, and for a traveller it represents health, success and a safe return. Onions in a dream also mean distress and difficulties. Gathering onions in the field in a dream means suffering from harm caused by one's own family.

Open: *(See Unlock)*

Opening: *(See Window)*

Ophthalmia: *(See Eye inflammation)*

Ophthalmologist: (Eye doctor; Oculist) In a dream, an ophthalmologist represents a spiritual guide who brings people out of darkness into light and who brings peace and unity between beloveds. An ophthalmologist in a dream also represents a teacher who entices people to seek knowledge, to reflect in advance about the consequences of their actions and to develop a sharp sight. An ophthalmologist in a dream also could represent a pearl diver, an ocean diver, one who digs wells or restores old springs, or an eye expert who can tell the difference between false eyes from the true ones. An ophthalmologist in a dream also represents a preacher, or a counsellor who can show the difference between the path of righteous people and the path of the heedless ones. An ophthalmologist in a dream

311

also may represent someone who has something to say, or news to report.

Opium: *(See Intoxicants)*

Opponent: (Adverse; Contrast; Opposite) If one's opponent is a dead person in the dream, then the good luck goes to the living in wakefulness. If the opponent is alive, then the better luck goes to the departed person. Opposition in a dream brings forth the better of the two in wakefulness. *(Also see Orbit)*

Opposite: *(See Opponent)*

Opposition: *(See Opponent)*

Oppression: If one sees people oppressing one another in a dream, it means that a tyrant or an unjust ruler will seize their land. Oppression in a dream is also interpreted as guidance, and guidance in a dream is interpreted as oppression. *(Also see Injustice; Terrorization)*

Orange-blossom water: *(See Distilled water)*

Orange: *(See Colors; Safflower; Yellow)*

Orbit: (Sun or moon orbits) In a dream, these two orbits may represent encircling one's opponents, surrounding the path of debtors, a sign of a major meeting of leaders, adversities, or despise. The circle itself represents the noble and just people. *(Also see Opponent)*

Organize: (Adjust; Arrange; Institute) Organizing things in a dream means knowledge, or earning and saving lawful money.

Orgasm: *(See Pleasure; Sexual intercourse)*

Oriole: *(zool.)* In a dream, an oriole represents doubt, wonderment, subsiding, concealment, trusting, confiding, associating with people in authority, or fear of one's enemy.

Orion: *(See Constellations)*

Ornaments: (Decoration) In a dream, ornaments are a sign of poverty. If one sees the world decorated for him and he is able to ask for whatever he wishes from it in a dream, it means that he will become poor, or that he may face destruction. As for unusual ornaments that are not recognizable, or decorated lands one does not recognize, then ornaments are a good sign, and the same goes for wearing customary or traditional ornaments one is used to adorn himself with. *(Also see Earrings; Gem; Gold; Necklace)*

Orphan: (Foundling; Waif) Picking-up an abandoned infant in a dream means picking-up one's enemy, in conjunction to the story of Moses and Pharaoh. Picking up an abandoned child in a dream also could mean returning things to the way they should be, or dispelling distress and sorrow. If one sees himself planting an apple tree in a dream, it means adopting an orphan, or caring for one. To find oneself as an orphan in a dream means depression which is caused by injustice. To be an orphan in a dream also means feeling depressed because of one's love for a woman, loss of property or money.

Orthopedist: (Bonesetter) An orthopedist who corrects skeletal deformities and sets broken bones in a dream represents a pious governor who governs with justice, teaches righteousness, balances substances and conforms to equanimity. Seeing an orthopedist in a dream also means presumptuousness, might and audacity. He also represents officiousness, adroitness and resoluteness, for he discards the deficient and brings together what is broken. Seeing an orthopedist in a dream also means distress and trouble. He also represents an architect, and an architect represents an orthopedist in a dream. Thus, seeing him in a dream also means construction and could represent a generous person who comforts, accommodates and helps a needy person, or a wise man who comforts the broken hearts, a just judge, a great scholar, a shoe repairman, or a tailor. If one sees himself standing before an orthopedist in a dream because of a broken bone or another fracture and then complains about an abscess in his neck, and if the orthopedist opens that abscess with pliers to drain the puss in the dream, then it represents a debt one has to repay, or a votive offering one has to fulfill, or it could mean giving a testimony in court, or accepting the ruling of a scholar. If an orthopedist sets one's broken right arm and ties it to his neck in a dream, it means that someone will oblige him to do him a personal favor and consequently deprive him from attending other duties, or restrain him from serving other charities. The same interpretation is given for a broken leg.

Oryx: (Antelope; Gemsbok; Wild cow; Wild gazelle; Wild goat) In a dream, all kinds of genus oryx of the wild large African and Asian antelopes with long and straight horns represent a great leader, a pious and a reclusive person though he does not follow the prophetic traditions, or he could be an ascetic, or an innovator. If one finds the eyeball of an oryx in a dream, it means that he will marry a chaste and a beautiful woman whose life will be short. If one's head becomes that of an oryx in a dream, it means prosperity, or that he will receive an appointment to a leadership position. *(Also see Buffalo; Mountain goat)*

Oscillator: *(See Fan)*

Osprey: (Angel of death; Bone-breaker; Eagle) In a dream, an osprey represents a powerful and a mighty warrior, and a merciless man whom no one trusts. If one sees an osprey over his roof, or inside his house, or standing over his head in a dream, it represents the angel of death. Catching an osprey in a dream means frequenting a ruler and remaining constantly wary of him whether one obeys him, or opposes him in opinion. If an osprey scratches someone with his claws in a dream, it means depression and financial losses. Eating the flesh of an osprey in a dream represents a demanding person. An osprey in a dream also represents a ruler about whom people speak very scarcely, but who is the direct cause of the falling of many neighboring rulers. Seeing an osprey in a tree means profits, favors and blessings. A flying osprey in a dream means victory in one's life. An osprey standing on top of a mountain or a rock, or on a cliff in a dream means success for the one who is starting a new job or a new business. However, it also could mean bad news if one is afraid of something, or if he is travelling. As for rich and noble people, riding an osprey in a dream means death, while for poor people it means profits and success that will benefit their families and neighbors. An osprey in a dream also means returning from a journey. It is also glad tidings of success and profits if an osprey comes near someone in a dream and talks to him. If a pregnant woman begets an osprey in her dream, it means that she will give birth to a son who will grow to be a courageous soldier or a leader in his community. A dead osprey in a dream means death. If thieves or robbers see an osprey in a dream, it means that they will suffer the consequences of their evildoing. If an osprey caries someone in the air in a dream, it means rising in station and honor. Fighting an osprey in a dream means fighting people in authority. Carrying the emblem of an osprey in a dream means winning victory over one's enemy. A female osprey in a dream represents homeless women who are driven into prostitution, while osprey chicks in a dream represent children born from adultery.

Ostrich: (Mail; Male ostrich) In a dream, a male ostrich represents a servant, a Gypsy, a deaf person, a castrate, an eunuch, or announcing someone's death. An ostrich in a dream also represents wealth and blessings. If one sees himself slaughtering a male ostrich in a dream, it means homosexuality. Receiving a male ostrich in a dream means that one will become a man of knowledge, a judge, or preside over a high ranking post in conjunction with one's qualifications. Riding an ostrich in a dream also means carrying a postal pouch, or becoming a courier. Riding an ostrich in a dream also means living on unlawful money. Seeing an ostrich living in one's house in a dream means longevity. Carrying an ostrich in a dream means carrying one's sins. Finding an ostrich egg in a dream means pursuing a woman to satisfy an erotic intention.

Outcry: *(See Shout)*

Outdoor bench: *(See Bench)*

Outer: (Manifest)

Oven: (Fire; Furnace; Grill; Head of household; Kiln; Range) If one sees himself lighting an oven for heating, or cooking on it in a dream, it means increase in earnings and benefits for one's own growth. An oven in a house in a dream means bringing a solution to a problem, or winning victory over one's enemies. An oven without accumulation of ashes in a dream means a bad marriage. Dream interpretation of ovens varies sometimes depending on the type of oven one sees in his dream. A grilling oven in a dream means imprisonment for a free man and freedom for a jailed one. A grilling oven in a dream also represents a respected man of knowledge who is sought to deliver legal opinions or views of wisdom that will satisfy both parties in a claim. The house range in a dream represents the head of the household, the housekeeper, the butler, a treasure chest, one's coffer or a safety box. The baker's oven in a dream represents the governor's house, a juvenile correction house, fulfillment of one's needs, earning one's livelihood, or recovering from illness. If one bakes dough in a dream, it means satisfying one's needs, recovering from illness, winning victory over one's enemies, or opponent, winning a court case, teaching one's son a craft, sending one's child to a school, enlisting one's son in the army, or it could mean becoming wealthy. A bakery oven in a dream also represents one's source of income, revenues, or shop, or it could denote one's carnal self, its good and evil nature, or it could mean changes in one's life, profits and losses. Seeing an unknown bakery oven in a dream also represents the governor's house, or the court house because of the fires that are kindled therein from time to time—as fire in a dream signifies power and sovereignty. An oven in a dream also represents a marketplace. *(Also see Furnace; Heater)*

Overcoat: (Cap; Coat; Capote) Wearing an overcoat in a dream means strength and support. Wearing a decorated ceremonial overcoat in a dream signifies power, dispelling depression, or satisfaction of one's needs. *(Also see Cap; Coat; Raincoat)*

Overlay: *(See Blanket)*

Overseas cap: (Headgear) Seeing a headgear in a dream means recovering from an illness, or it could mean purification from sin. If a garment salesman visits a sick person in a dream, it means death. *(Also see Headgear)*

Overseas: *(See Invasion)*

Oversight: *(See Slip of a tongue)*

Overspread: *(See Blanket)*

Owl: In a dream, an owl represents a tyrant ruler, or a haughty and a dangerous thief who works alone without helpers. An owl in a dream also means being unemployed, or aversion of fear and bewilderment. In a dream, an owl also represents a traitor. If one sees himself fighting with an owl in a dream, it means facing a fight with someone. An owl in a dream also represents a person without steadfastness or determination to do what is right. If an owl falls inside his house in a dream, it means news of someone's death. An owl also represents thieves hiding in the darkness and under the shade of ruins, and of being annoyed about having to make an effort to earn one's livelihood.

Ox: *(See Bull)*

Oxidize: *(See Rust)*

P

Paddles: *(See Oars)*

Padlock: A padlock in a dream represents an employee who is treated roughly and unfavorably. A padlock made from wood in a dream represents deceit and hypocrisy. Locking one's door securely in a dream means managing and controlling one's business in accordance with the divine laws. If one's door does not have a lock in a dream, it means that one has no control over which way his life goes, and that he cares little about its consequences. Attempting to lock one's door, but to no avail in a dream means one's failure to complete an important project. Breaking a lock and entering a house in a dream represents a conqueror or benefits that will come through such a person. A padlock in a dream also represents a bolt, a door latch, one's son, a handicapped wife, taking shelter away from one's enemy, a hidden treasure, or a burial ground. A padlock in a dream also may denotes sorcery, concealing secrets, or hindrances obstructing one's travel plans. Putting a padlock on one's door in a dream means prosperity after suffering from poverty, or receiving honors after being humiliated. A padlock in a dream also could represent a bastard son, or a foundling. *(Also see Close; Lock)*

Pain: (Ache; Discomfort; Hurt) In a dream, pain means regret and sorrow. Suffering from a tooth ache in a dream means hearing painful words from a relative the particular tooth implies. Neck pain in a dream represents being ill-treated by one's friends. Neck pain in a dream also may indicate that one has betrayed his covenant, or that he has denied a promise. Shoulder pain in a dream signifies bad earnings. Stomach pain in a dream means spending money in sin and feeling regret for doing so. Pain in one's navel in a dream signifies ill-treatment of one's wife. Heart pain in a dream means having hidden bad qualities, or questionable religious sincerity. Liver pain in a dream means ill-treatment of one's children. Spleen pain in a dream means spoiling one's money by adding unlawful earnings to it. Severe spleen pain that could lead to one's death in the dream means loss of one's religious commitment. Lung and chest pain in a dream mean the nearing of one's death. Back pain in a dream means the death of one's brother, supporter, superior, or a close friend. Pain in one's thighs in a dream means causing harm to one's community. Pain in one's foot in a dream means money, or it could mean straying from God's path. *(Also see Body¹; Chest pain; Lungs; Teeth; Tooth)*

Painter: (Artist; Illustrator) In a dream, a painter represents knowledge, architecture, wisdom, writing poems, writing love songs or telling lies. A painter in a dream also represents someone who conceals his acts, or hides his true face. He also could represent alcoholism, falling in love, marriage, or having children. Some of the painter's works are beneficial while others are harmful. All depending on the quality of his work, its objectives, balance, resemblance to the object painted and authenticity. The characteristics of such a person in the dream may be that of a hypocrite in wakefulness, or an ostentatious person, a toadying person, a hypocrite, a panegyrist, or a lauding person, though he mostly looks as a good, sincere and a hard working person. The value of his paintings varies depending on the subject treated. A painter in a dream also represents a person who loves flattery, self-adulation, an eloquently speaking person, a liar, one who fails his promises, or he could represent strength and authority. *(Also see Architect; Artist; Paintings; Weaver)*

Paintings: (Art; Picture; Portrait) In a dream, paintings represent memories, guidance, or advice. Paintings in a dream also denote the passing of time, advancing of years, or the days of one's life. As for an immigrant, paintings in his dream mean reunion with his family, beloved, or commanding good and forbidding evil. *(Also see Painter)*

Palace: A palace in a dream represents a prison, tightness, shortage of cash, or loss of respect for an abominable and sinful person. If a rich person sees a palace in his dream, then it means rising in station, or repayment of his debts. Seeing a palace from a distance in a dream also means prosperity. A palace in a dream represents an unknown person, or a private person who maintains a steady religious life. Entering a palace in a dream means gaining authority, rising in station, and a growing religious adherence. If one sees himself managing his own palace in a dream, it means exaltation, power and reverence. If the palace he is managing in the dream belongs to someone else, then it means earnings from such a person. A palace in a dream also denotes good deeds. Entering a palace in a dream also means getting married. Entering a palace made of glass means a marriage that will not last. It is thus said that a palace in a dream can be interpreted in eight different ways: that is blessings, money, leadership, rank, management, authority, attaining one's goals and happiness. Residing in one of the palaces of paradise in a dream means leadership, victory, or marriage.

Palanquin: (Camel litter; Gocart; Handbarrow; Horse litter; Kajawah; Mahmal; Sedan chair) A palanquin, a litter, or a camel litter in a dream represent a woman. A camel litter carrying pilgrims in a dream represents the pilgrimage season, celebrations, festivals, joy and glad tidings in the town one may recognize in his dream. *(Also see Litter; Sedan chair)*

Paleness: (Yellow) Paleness of one's face in a dream means a sickness. If one sees his face bright yellow in a dream, it means that he will be among the exalted and blessed people in the hereafter. However, paleness of the face in a dream also may be interpreted as humiliation, jealousy, or hypocrisy. Paleness of the face in a dream also could mean devotion, standing up in prayers at night, observing night vigils, being in love, piety, contemplation, or being afraid of something. If one sees his face white and his body yellow in a dream, it means that what he shows outwardly is better than what he hides. On the other hand, if one's face is yellow and pale and his body is white in the dream, then it means that his heart is better than what others can perceive from his outer look. If both his face and body look pale and emaciated in a dream, it means an illness. Paleness of the face alone in a dream also means sadness or sorrow. Wearing a yellow garment in a dream means an illness, unless if it is made from silk. If one sees himself in a dream wearing a yellowish silk-brocaded cloak, it means religious fakery, or committing improprieties under the name of one's religion. *(Also see Yellow)*

Palm branch: (Spadix) A palm branch in a dream represents peace, love, unity, ascetic detachment from worldly attractions, knowledge and piety. *(Also see Palm leaves)*

Palm core: (Edible tuber) In a dream, a palm core represents an inheritance, lawful capital, youth, energy, a newborn, separation, or a miscarried fetus.

Palm fiber: (Rubbing cloth) Palm fiber in a dream represents new clothing, or an accumulated wealth that is bearing heavy on its owner because of the methods he uses to gather it, or because of failing to pay its due alms tax, or required charities.

Palm leaves: (Palm branch; Spadix) In a dream, palm leaves represent an ointment, purification, cleanliness, a nurse, a bridegroom, or a physician who performs circumcision. *(Also see Palm branch)*

Palm tree: (Date palm) A palm tree in a dream represents a sire, a scholar, a noble man or a wise man who imparts his knowledge and wisdom to others. Cutting a palm tree in a dream means the death of such a man. Seeing a plantation of palm trees, or an oasis or palm trees in a dream mean leading people and guiding them on the straight path. If a merchant or a trader sees a palm tree in his dream, it means business success. If a shopkeeper sees a palm tree in his dream, it also means profits. A dead and dried out palm tree in a dream represents a hypocrite. To uproot a palm tree in a dream means that a plague will befall that place, or it could mean suffering from the persecution of an unjust ruler. Uprooting a palm tree in a dream also means a dead end to one's plans, or it could mean a dispute. A palm tree in a dream also represents one's paternal aunt. Palm trees in a dream also represent Arab women. If one sees a seedling become a big palm tree in a dream, it means that a child in that community will grow to be a great scholar. It also connotes that a weak person will grow strong. Seeing a palm tree in a dream also means longevity, a scholar, a teacher, children, a wife, a house, a property, a king, a year, new clothing, money, or bearing a child. To prune or trim a palm tree in a dream means that one's adversity at his work or related to his travels will be dispelled. *(Also see Palmyra; Tree)*

Palm: (Hand) In a dream, the palm of one's hand represents one's fitness in wakefulness. Clapping one's hands in a dream could either mean joy and happiness, or it could mean nothing in wakefulness. Carrying a glove in one's hand in a dream means ceasing the course of wrongdoing. Slapping one's own face with both hands means sorrow, sadness, or calamities. Hitting the top of one's hand into the palm of the other hand means separation. In a dream, the palm of one's hand also represents one's strength. To stretch open one's palm in a dream signifies wealth and prosperity. Holding a tight fist in a dream implies poverty, or tight living conditions. If one sees hair growing in the palm of his hand in a dream, it means depression, distress and debts. Growing hair on top of one's hand in a dream indicates one's strength or virility. Seeing one's hand hanging down from the skies in a dream denotes one's connections with the ruler or people in authority. A stretched hand from the skies in a dream also could mean profits and blessings for a hunter, a builder and a real estate professional. In a dream, the palm of one's hand also represents his world. It also may mean ceasing a certain course of action. If one finds himself afraid, then sees the palm of a hand holding out before him in a dream, it means that his fears will be dispelled. A large and a stretched palm in a dream means prosperity and generosity. A close fist in a dream means stinginess. A nice looking palm of one's hand also signifies abstaining from evil, or failing to pay charity. The palm of one's hand in a dream also represents one's prayers and supplications, comfort, seeking the comfort of others, or receiving benefits from others. The palm of one's hand in a dream also represents a year, ways of life, money, leadership, a son, courage and desisting from evildoing. *(See Desisting from evildoing)*

Palmyra tree: A palmyra tree in a dream represents a wise man, a poet, or an astronomer. *(Also see Palm tree)*

Palpitation: (Heart; Pulsate; Throbbing) In a dream, palpitation means neglecting something, or abandoning it. If one sees his heart pulsating rapidly in a dream, it means changing his travel plans, or denying a marriage promise, or putting off a fight.

Pander: *(See Driver¹; Panderer; Pimp)*

Panderer: (Bully; Cadet; Pimp; Procurer) Seeing oneself as a panderer, or a pimp, but failing to see an accompanying prostitute in the dream represents a door-to-door salesman. Pandering in a dream also means giving a false testimony. *(Also See Driver¹; Primp)*

Panther: *(See Lynx)*

Panties: (Underpants; Underwear) If one discovers some wetness in his underpants in a dream, it means that his wife is pregnant. If one defecates in his underpants in a dream, it means a fight with his wife after which he will pay her something he owes her, or it could mean a fight that will end in divorce. If one wears his underpants inside-out in his dream, it means that he indulges in the loathsome and forbidden act of anal intercourse with his wife. If one sees himself wearing his underpants without the underwear shirt in a dream, it means poverty. Wearing fancy underpants in a dream means travels, or financial growth. Wearing new underpants in a dream means protecting one's chastity. Giving away one's old underpants in a dream means relief from difficulties. *(Also see Underwear; Pants)*

Pants: (Panties; Trousers; Underpants) In a dream, they represent a firm person who manages his affairs carefully. Wearing a new pair of pants in a dream also means that one will find a new job. *(Also see Panties)*

Paper: (Notebook; Record; Parchment) A sheet of paper in a dream represents an oath, a vow, or a pledge. Writing a note on a piece of paper in a dream means being ungrateful and perfidious toward others. A writer in a dream also represents someone who is burdened, pressured, doubtful and uncertain, whereby, writing has become his escape goat and a way out of his depression. If one's boss gives him a paper to write something on it in a dream, it means that he will solicit something from his boss and eventually receive it. If one feels uncertain about some people then sees himself holding a pen and a piece of paper in a dream, it means that his obscurity will be replaced with clarity. Holding a piece of paper in a dream also means attaining one's goal, or completing a project, or finalizing a program. A paper salesman in a dream represents someone who helps cunning people do their tricks. *(Also see Notebook; Paper; Write; Writer)*

Papermaker: (Parchment; Tree) A papermaker in a dream represents a person of knowledge, wisdom, guidance and eloquence.

Papers: (Books; Credentials; Letter; Newspaper; Records; Revelations; Scrolls; Studies) Papers in a dream represent witnesses, guidance, spiritual leaders, knowledge, warnings, or glad tidings. Holding papers in a dream means glad tidings and celebration. If a woman hands someone a piece of paper in a dream, then one may expect good news to arrive from one moment to another. If the woman who hands him the paper covers herself with a veil in the dream, it means that he should be careful. Carrying a folded piece of paper in a dream means that one may have an accident that could be the cause of his death. If one sees himself carrying a paper in his left hand in a dream, it means that he regrets something he did. Writing a paper with the left hand in a dream means writing poem, or committing abominable actions, or that one will beget a son from adultery. If a God fearing person sees himself looking at a paper written in a language he cannot decipher in a dream, it means that he will face humiliation or suffer from distress. If one is offered a wrapping paper and he finds a newborn baby wrapped inside it in a dream, it means that he will hire a servant with some strings attached to his employment. If one is given a newspaper, or a document but does not care to read it in his dream, it means that he may receive an inheritance. If one reads the title page of a newspaper in a dream, it also means that he may receive an inheritance. If he quickly browses through it in his dream, then it means debts. To see one's records of the Day of Judgment open before his own eyes in a dream, it denotes his faith, certitude, lack of doubt and true belief in what God's Messenger, upon whom be peace, brought from his Lord. *(Also see Book; Letter; Paper; Reference book; Write; Writing)*

Paradise: (Green garments) Seeing paradise and not entering it in a dream means glad tidings of a blessed deed one will perform. Only an equitable person may see it, not an unjust person. Should he desire to enter it when someone is preventing him from doing so in the dream means that he must exercise patience toward being prevented from attending a pilgrimage to Mecca. It also means that he could be prevented from repenting from a sin he is adamant at disqualifying from being a sin, then when suddenly he feels an urge to repent for it, he may be prevented from doing so. If one sees that one of the gates of paradise is closed in the dream, it means that one of his parents will pass away. If two of its gates are closed in the dream, it means that he will lose his parents. If all of its doors are locked in the dream, it means that his parents are displeased with him. If he enters paradise from whichever gate he pleases in the dream, it means that both of his parents are pleased with him. If one is let into paradise in a dream, it represents his death. It is also interpreted to mean that he will repent for his sins at the hands of a spiritual guide or a wise shaikh who will lead him into paradise. Entering paradise in a dream also may mean attaining one's goals, though paradise itself is surrounded with schemes and maneuvers. Seeing paradise in one's dream also means joining the company of revered people of knowledge and observing good conduct with people in general. If one sees himself entering paradise smilingly in a dream, it means that he constantly invokes God's remembrance. If one sees himself entering paradise with his sword unsheathed in a dream, it means that he commands good, forbid evil, and that he will receive blessings and praises in this world and in the hereafter. This dream also can be interpreted as earning one's martyrdom. If one sees himself sitting under the central Tūbā tree in paradise in a dream, it means blessings and prosperity in this world and in the hereafter. If one sees himself sitting in the gardens of paradise in a dream, it means that he will be blessed with sincerity and perfect religious adherence. Eating from the fruits of paradise in a dream means acquiring knowledge. Drinking from its rivers of honey and milk in a dream means receiving wisdom, inner knowledge and prosperity. Leaning against a tree in paradise in a dream represents the chastity of one's wife. Picking the fruits of paradise and feeding them to others in a dream means sharing knowledge with others or teaching them. If one is forbidden from having the fruits of paradise in a dream, it denotes his failure to properly attend to his religious duties. Drinking water from the fountain of abundance *(kawthar)* in a dream means attaining leadership and conquering one's enemy. Dwelling in a heavenly palace in a dream means marriage to a beautiful woman. Seeing Ridhwān, the guardian angel of paradise in a dream brings happiness, prosperity and a healthy life. If one sees angels coming before him and paying their regards in a dream, it means that he will sustain a great patience during a worldly trial that will lead him to paradise. If a sick person sees himself entering paradise in a dream, it means that he will recover from his illness, and it could represent earnings, piety, prosperity, dispelling distress and getting an answer to one's prayers. If one sees himself entering paradise carrying money and leading a herd of sheep in a dream, it means that he will enter it through his charity and paying his due alms. Entering paradise together with one's wife means a good family relationship and giving respect to one's wife. Seeing paradise in a dream also represents one's devotion, piety, renunciation, and being of benefit to one's companions. The trees of paradise in a dream represent the gnostics, the true servants of God Almighty and the callers to God Almighty. If one is thrown out of paradise in a dream, it means that he needs to understand the story of Adam, upon whom be peace. Circumambulating paradise in a dream means dispelling fear, overcoming one's difficulties, or getting married. *(Also see Key)*

Paralysis: (Cripple; Impediment; Justice; Wither) If one sees his right hand paralyzed in a dream, it denotes a great sin he has committed that warrants such a severe punishment. If the right hand is paralyzed in the dream, it means that one earns his money from practicing usury, or it could mean that he is unjust toward a poor and a weak person. If one's left hand is paralyzed in a dream, it means that either his sister or his brother may die shortly. If his thumb is paralyzed in a dream, it means that he will suffer from hardships because of his children. If the index or the middle finger are paralyzed in a dream, it means that one may suffer because of his sister. If one sees his ring finger paralyzed in the dream, it means that he will suffer pain and difficulties because of an ailment that will befall his mother or a female relative. If one sees his little finger paralyzed in a dream, it means that he may suffer because of a daughter. Any infliction in one's hand in a dream represents one's brothers, while any infliction of the fingers in a dream represents his children. If one sees his right hand paralyzed in a dream, it means that he will lose his source of income. If one's fingers are paralyzed in a dream, it means that he has committed an awful sin. If one sees his right hand paralyzed in a dream, it means he has caused major losses to an innocent person. *(Also see Body¹; Physical paralysis)*

Parchment: *(See Notebook; Paper)*

Pardon: (Absolution; Amnesty; Acquittal) If one forgives someone a sin, or a mistake, or an error in a dream, it means that God Almighty will forgive him his sins. It also means that he will live a long life, earn fame for his piety, live in God's protection, have a good heart and a forgiving nature. If one pardons a criminal in a dream, it also means that he will receive God's forgiveness in this world and on the Day of Judgment. To forgive and pardon someone when one has the power to do so in a dream represents one's faith, piety and fear of wrongdoing. If God Almighty, or if His Prophet (uwbp) pardon of forgive one's sins in a dream, it means that one will repent for his sin, receive guidance and attain a praiseworthy conclusion to his life in this world and in the hereafter. *(Also see Amnesty)*

Parents: (Eye-brows)

Parrot: (Any bright-colored tropical bird.) In a dream, a parrot represents a prodding man, a white slave trader, a liar and an unjust person. A parrot in a dream also can be interpreted as a philosopher whose son may also grow to be a philosopher. A parrot in a dream also represents a lively and an eloquent beautiful woman, or a brilliant, well articulated and a handsome looking boy. A parrot in a dream also represents an attractive foreign woman, or it could represent a swaggering man who constantly brags and boasts about himself, though he is filled with conceit, covetousness, and has an oppressive nature.

Partnership: (Affiliation; Alliance; Business association) In a dream, business partnership means happiness, or it could mean exaggeration in one's devotion toward God Almighty, or it could mean going to extremes to attain business success and prosperity in the world. If a poor person sees himself involved in a business partnership with a rich person in a dream, it means that he will become wealthy. If he is hoping for an inheritance, then seeing this dream means that it will come through, and that he will find a business partner. If one sees himself in a business partnership with a known person in a dream, it means that they deal justly and equitably with one another. If one's partner in the dream is an unknown old person, then he represents his grandfather and such a year will be a prosperous business year for him. If one's partner in the dream is a young man, then he represents an enemy, or it could mean that his opponent will be fair in dealing with him, though the person in the dream will remain suspicious but cannot legally dissolve his partnership. Partnership in a dream also means sincerity, loyalty, truthfulness and fulfilling one's agreement.

Partridge: (Francolin; Genus; Mountain quail; Woman) In a dream, a partridge represents a beautiful but a non-amicable woman. Catching a partridge in a dream means marrying such a woman. Catching many partridges in a dream means prosperity. A flock of partridges in a dream represents women. A partridge in a dream also represents smiling people. Eating the flesh of a partridge in a dream means buying new clothing, or storing food for one's family. If a married person sees himself catching a male partridge in a dream, it means that he will beget a blessed son. If a pregnant woman catches a partridge in a dream, it means that she will give birth to a daughter. Slaughtering a partridge in a dream means committing adultery. Driving or pushing a partridge in a dream means rebuking a woman. Owning a partridge in a dream means marrying an Asiatic or a Persian woman, or meeting with a wealthy woman, or marrying a woman who will betray him and bring no benefits to him.

Passage: *(See Road)*

Passing gas: *(See Fart)*

Passion: (Desire) In a dream, to fulfill a desire with great passion denotes the actions of the dwellers of hell-fire. *(Also see Desire)*

Paste: *(See Glue)*

Pastry chef: *(See Sweets)*

Pastry shop: *(See Seasonal sweets; Sweets; Sweets maker)*

Pastry: (Baklava; Blintz; Pie; Strudel; Tart) In a dream, pastries represent enjoyable earnings. *(Also see Seasonal sweets; Sweets)*

Path: *(See Road)*

Patience: (Fettering; Forbearance; Self-control) Exercising patience in a dream means glad tidings, or a warning about an adversity, or perhaps it could mean success in one's endeavors. If one exercises patience toward harm or adversities he suffers in a dream, it means that he will rise in station, or receive a financial reward, or it could mean enjoying good living, safety, good health and victory in one's life.

Patrol: (Sentinel; Watchmen) A patrol in a dream represents a warning to the person seeing it. Fleeing from a patrol of soldiers, then getting caught and interrogated by them, and if one is released thereafter in the dream, it means that he will repent for his shortcomings.

Pavilion: (Army; Canopy; Large tent) In a dream, a pavilion represents someone in command. Seeing a pavilion in a dream also means conquering one's enemy. A canopy in a dream represents someone who has less authority than the commander, a dome represents someone of a lower rank, and a tent in a dream means less than a dome. If a commander is seen leaving his pavilion in a dream, it means that he will lose some of his authority, or that he may die shortly. Unknown pavilions of either green or white colors in a dream mean healing, endowments, gifts, martyrdom, visiting the graves of righteous people, or a pilgrimage to Jerusalem. *(Also see Canopy; Tent)*

Pawn: (Collateral; Deposit; Hostage; Mortgage; Security) In a dream, a pawn represents goods that are deposited to secure a loan, or it could mean changes in one's life for the better. To deposit something valuable as a security for something worthless in a dream means falling in love with an insolent man who will abuse the woman, take advantage of her, or use her for his own interests. Signing a collateral in a dream also represents the lack of trust between the lender and the borrower. Otherwise, a security deposit may denote a journey. *(Also see Deposit; Hostage)*

Pay: *(See Coughing)*

Paying a debt: *(See Debt; Return; Returning from a journey)*

Peace: *(See Conciliation; Reconciliation)*

Peach tree: *(See Tree)*

321

Peacock: In a dream, a peacock represents a vain and a strutting person. A peacock in a dream also could represent a beautiful and a wealthy woman, or cheerful looking people. If one sees himself owning apeacock and a pigeon in a dream, it means that he is a pimp. A female peacock in a dream represents a bride, children, or wealth. Owning a peacock in a dream also means wandering, heedlessness, pride, ostentatiousness, backbiting, deceit, lies, confiding into one's enemy, loss of blessings, experiencing poverty after being rich and tightness after plenitude. Seeing a peacock in a dream also means jewelry, clothing, presidency, a beautiful wife, marriage and good children. Eating the flesh of a peacock in a dream means the death of one's wife and inheriting her wealth. To hold the radiant rain-bow colored plumules of a peacock in a dream means profits earned earned through a woman. To catch the chick of a peacock in a dream means profits through a son from that woman, or it could mean that one may beget a son. *(Also see Chicken)*

Pear: (Fruit) A pear in a dream means money, blessings, or a sickness. Eating it in season in a dream means benefits, income, or it could denote the arrival of a long awaited person. Eating pears out of season in a dream means a sickness or swelling, though if a sick person eats a pear in a dream, it means a cure for his illness, or it could mean earning unlawful money. Receiving a basket, or a plate of pears in a dream means receiving an inheritance. As for a pregnant woman, pears in a dream represent a son, and for an unmarried woman, they means marriage. Pears in a dream also signify the death of an ailing person and his burial.

Pearl diver: A pearl diver in a dream represents a royalty, a great person, or a man of authority. Diving into the seawater to catch pearls in a dream means entering into a business with someone in authority, then marrying a daughter from his family and begetting a beautiful son from her. Seeing a pearl diver in a dream also means seeking to learn about something, or seeking to borrow money from a merchant, or asking someone in authority for an important appointment, or it could mean adventuring into the business of treasure hunting. A pearl diver in a dream also represents someone who knows the inside secrets of things, or he could be a scholar, a gnostic, a seeker on the path, or an interpreter of the true meanings of the early prophetic teachings. *(Also see Diving)*

Pearl fishery: *(See Diving; Pearl diver)*

Pearl necklace: (Covenant; Husband; Qur'ân; Wisdom) A pearl necklace in a dream represents woman's beauty and ornaments. A pearl necklace, or a necklace made of corals in a dream also means piety, fear of wrongdoing, or an expression of reverence before God Almighty. All of that is subject to the value, beauty and clarity of the necklace, or the number of gems it holds. As for a woman, a pearl necklace in a dream represents her husband, or her young son. If a man sees himself wearing a pearl necklace in a dream, it means that he is a seeker of knowledge, spiritual understanding and wisdom. It could also mean fulfilling a covenant, making a promise, or getting married. If one's wife is pregnant, it means that she will give birth to a son who will grow to be a wise person, a man of knowledge, or a judge. This interpretation is possible in most cases except if the necklace breaks in the dream. In this case, if the necklace is broken, it means that one will break his promise, or forget his learning, become heedless, suffer eviction, deportation, or be exiled from his home or country. If one sees himself wearing one or even two pearl necklaces in a dream, it means that he subscribes to God's revelations, memorizes God's Words, recites the holy Qur'ân, speaks words of wisdom, and that he is one of the carriers of the divine trust who demonstrates trustworthiness, piety, trueness, religious commitment and beauty of character. All depending on the beauty, radiance and clarity of one's necklace. If one sees himself in a dream carrying many necklaces and decorations, and if he finds them heavy and unbearable to carry, it represents his incompetence, or his inability to complete a job. *(Also see Necklace)*

Pearl: (Beads; Jewel; Money; Tears; Women) Drilling wholes in pearls to string them in a dream means fulfillment of one's goals, easing one's passage, or facilitating one's marriage. In a dream, a pearl also means a son. If one's wife is pregnant, and if she hands him a pearl in his dream, it means that she will deliver a beautiful son. If the pearl has no glitter, or if he takes it from his wife and locks it inside a box in a dream, then it represents a servant. A pearl in a woman's dream means good news. If she is unwed, it means that she will get married. If one sees himself bartering a pearl or a gem for fake jewelry, or for chips of glass in a dream, it means that he has sold the reward of the hereafter for the temporary pleasures of this world, or that he has exchanged something precious for something worthless, or it could mean that he may commit a sin, or become an apostate. Pearls in a dream also represent the Qur'ān, manner of proper talking, bezels of wisdom, children, servants, integrity, beauty, or money. If one sees himself piercing a pearl in a dream, it means that he will give valuable interpretations to Qur'ānic verses. Swallowing pearls in a dream means forgetting what one has learned from the Qur'ān. Swallowing pearls in a dream also could mean acquiring wisdom and knowledge. Selling pearls in a dream means acquiring knowledge and growing to be famous and respected. Throwing pearls at people in a dream and seeing people collecting them while one remains aloof, represents a judge who issues his verdict, or admonishes people who accept what he says and abide by it accordingly. Receiving a pearl in a dream means caring for the daughter of a relative. Finding a pearl in a dream also means finding a wife. Borrowing a pearl from someone in a dream means begetting a son and giving him for adoption, or that the boy will die shortly after his birth. Pearls in a dream also mean becoming wealthy from an inheritance. As for a scholar, a pearl in a dream represents knowledge, and for a governor, it means expansion of his power. As for a merchant, it means a growing business, and for a craftsman in a dream, it means advancement in his craft. Pearls in a dream also represent the final step in adorning something and the proper way to display beauty, or they could represent fantasies and attractions. Drilling a hole in a pearl in a dream also means having sexual intercourse with a blood relation. Swallowing a pearl in a dream means hiding a testimony. Chewing on pearls in a dream means backbiting people. Vomiting pearls in a dream means scheming against people and deceiving them. Throwing a pearl into a river in a dream means helping people. Extracting a pearl from its shell, then throwing the pearl and keeping the shell in a dream means that one is involved in body snatching and in desecrating the graves. Opening a closet with a key and pulling out stored pearls from inside it in a dream means asking a question from a scholar. Counting pearls in a dream means going through hardships. Seeing pearls in a dream means becoming joyful and happy. Receiving a gift of pearls in a dream denotes a political appointment. Pearls in a dream also denote good words, money, or servants. A pearl necklace in a dream means marriage, or a bundle of money, or it could mean memorizing the Qur'ān. Carrying loads of pearls in a dream means carrying burdens. Throwing pearls to a swine or over a trash pile in a dream means giving knowledge to people who are not worthy of it, or people who do not understand it and who will consequently mock him. Burning pearls to cook with them rather than wood in a dream means putting a heavy burden on someone who cannot carry it and consequently having him explode. Large pearls in a dream provide for better connotations than the small ones. Pierced pearls in a dream mean easy and fast coming money. Pearls in a dream also may represent tears. *(Also see Counting pearls; Mother of pearl; Tears)*

Pebbles: In a dream, pebbles represent men, women, little children, or counted money. They also mean memorizing a book of knowledge, understanding it, knowing it by heart, or writing poems. They also mean performing one's pilgrimage to Mecca and pelting stones in the valley of Mina at a placed called Jamarât. Pelting stones in a dream also means harshness, toughness, slander, or youth. Collecting pebbles for pelting from a marketplace, a street, under the trees, or in a farmland in a dream means receiving financial benefits. Collecting pebbles at the foot of a tree in a dream means receiving a gift from a person in authority, or profits from the sea, learning at the hand of a good teacher, a gift from a wealthy wife, or they could mean the birth of a son if one does not have a son. Throwing pebbles in the sea in a dream means wasting one's money. Throwing pebbles in a well in a dream means benefiting from a marriage or a business. *(Also see Gravel, Pelting stones)*

Pecan: *(See Walnut)*

Pederasty: (Homosexuality; Lover of boys; Sodomize; Sodomy) Molesting a child, or forcing a boy to sodomy in a dream means committing an evil act, loss of one's capital to one's enemy, engaging in loathsome actions, losing dignity, or confronting an enemy. *(Also see Anus; Inkwell; Satan; Scorpion; Sexual intercourse; Sodomy)*

Peel¹: *(See Shell)*

Peel²: *(See Skinning an animal)*

Peephole: *(See Attic window; Window)*

Peg: (Pin; Pole; Stake; Tent peg) In a dream, a peg represents a high ranking person, a master, or a scholar. If a young man hits someone over his back with a wooden stick in a dream, it means that he will beget a son who will grow to be a hypocrite and an enemy to his father. Unplugging a peg or the pole of a tent in a dream means death. Driving a peg into the wall in a dream means liking to associate oneself with a great person. Driving a peg into a house in a dream means being in love with a woman from that family. Driving a wooden peg or a pin into wood in a dream means liking to befriend a teenager who is also a hypocrite. A metal peg in a dream represents money, strength, pain, distress, sorrow, or rising to a high ranking position to become firmly established therein. It also means being drafted to accept a governmental position, or it could mean impeachment from office or travels. If a peg is interpreted to represent a son or a wife in a dream, then it denotes longevity. Standing on top of a pole in a dream means acquiring knowledge from a great scholar. A peg in a dream also implies money, love, marriage, distress, sorrow, or hypocrisy.

Pelting stones: (Twenty one pebbles collected at Muzdalifa near the Plain of 'Arafâ during the pilgrimage season and are used to stone the devil at a place called Jamarât.) In a dream, pelting stones represent fidelity, paying one's debts, victory over one's enemy, or doing good deeds. To eat one of the stones which are intended for pelting in a dream means to devour or steal the property of a young orphan. Pelting stones in a dream also means fulfilling one's obligatory prayers and fasting, having earlier missed their performance for a legitimate reason. *(Also see Pebbles; Pilgrimage; Jamarât)*

Pelvis: *(See Abdomen)*

Pen: (Pencil; Tongue) In a dream, a pen represents knowledge, learning, a child, a tradesman, or commanding what is good and forbidding what is evil. If a tradesman or a craftsman sees a pen in his dream, it means that he will be successful in his trade, or that he will preside over people of the same trade. If a tradesman earns something with a pen, or writes an invoice with it in a dream, it means that he will be protected from poverty through his trade. If a writer sees himself carrying a pen, or holding a paper, or an inkwell in a dream, it also means having a source of income, protection against poverty, earning one's livelihood from writing, or from working under someone in authority. A pen in a dream also represents one's manager, his controller, a cosigner, a witness in an agreement, entering into a marriage agreement, or it could represent an intelligent son who will become a famous writer. Owning a pen or receiving a one as a gift in a dream means acquiring knowledge. Then, if one proceeds to write with it in his dream, it means receiving an appointment, or occupying a position of authority. Looking at a pen one is holding in his hand and seeing another pen laying beside him in a dream denotes having a half brother, or if one's mother is pregnant, it means that she will deliver a new son. A pen in a dream also means a guarantee. If one's wife is pregnant, then if he sees a pen laying beside an inkwell in his dream, it means that she will beget a son. Holding a pen in a dream also means making an oath. If one's pen is broken or scratched in a dream, it will reflect on his business, trade and livelihood. Moistening a pen from an inkwell in a dream means committing a sin. A pen in a dream also represents virtues by which one is known, or it could mean complying with a court judgement, or signing a court order, or it could represent a scholar, a judge, one's tongue, a sword, one's penis, a railway, generosity, abundance, human-kind, one's confidant, or winning victory over one's enemy. If one's pen looks in good condition in the dream, it means that one's oath or covenant is true. Otherwise, a defective pen in a dream represents a false oath, or a biased agreement. A pen in a dream also means longevity and prosperity. *(Also see Tongue)*

Penance: *(See Atonement; Tithe collector)*

Pencil sharpener: (Blade) A pencil sharpener in a dream represents a good son who is envied by people. Seeing a pencil sharpener in a dream means that one will be gifted with such a beautiful son. In a dream, a pencil sharpener also represents a writer or an author. If one sees himself holding a pencil sharpener in a dream, it means reconciliation with a woman with whom he has been separated for sometime.

Pencil: *(See Pen)*

Pendant: (Decoration. *See Necklace*)

Penny: (Cent; Money) For a pregnant woman, pennies in a dream represent a son, or a sign of gratitude, prayers and remembrance of God, or they could mean assaulting someone, or beating him. If one receives pennies in a stack in a dream, it means that someone will place a trust with him. Pennies in a dream also mean talking. If they look new, the conversation will be meaningful. Pennies in a dream also mean solving someone's problem, or performing one's prayers. Counting pennies in a dream means valuing one's deeds. Nickels, dimes, quarters, halves, or other coins or tokens in a dream represent worldly gains and prosperity. If pennies are tied to one's wrist in a dream, they represent his livelihood. Owing money in a dream means that one will be summoned to testify in a court of justice. If his pennies are old, chipped, or broken in the dream, they denote a faltering faith. Losing a penny in a dream means wasting time and money, or wasting one's words, or advising an ignorant person who will not heed his advice. If one's pennies carry the picture of a person in a dream, it means that both the carrier and the one who mints these pennies are innovators. Broken pennies in half in a dream represent an enmity that cannot be healed. Receiving money in a dream is better than giving it. If one's actual liquid asset turns into pennies in a dream, it means insolvency or bankruptcy. If one's little money grow in a dream, it means prosperity. *(Also see Cent; Money)*

Pepper: (Black pepper; Hot pepper) Pepper in a dream represents security money that insures the capital investment. Eating pepper in a dream means drinking a lethal drink or a bitter tasting medicine, or falling victim to a bad spirit, or earning money with commendation though through hard work. Pepper in a dream also means money if it is not used as food. Otherwise, if one eats pepper in his dream, it means distress or dismay.

Percentage: *(See Measure²)*

Perception: (Clarity. *See Glass)*

Perennial plant: *(See Iris)*

Perennials: *(See Meadow)*

Perfume bottle: In a dream, a scent bottle or a perfume bottle represents a guardian who is entrusted with an estate to manage, or a guardian who is entrusted with an inheritance to distribute as charity on God's path, or it could denote a woman or a child.

Perfume salesman: In a dream, a perfume salesman represents a gnostic, an ascetic, a devout worshiper, or a man of letters. Anyone who sits with him will carry some fragrance of his perfumes, or learn about an etiquette, adopt good manners, learn something about his arts, enjoy a happy surrounding, or earn praises, except if the perfume salesman is burning incense, for the smoke that emanates from burning incense in a dream denotes guarded praises. A perfume salesman in a dream also represents a beautician. Seeing him in a dream also means knowledge, guidance, earning praises or receiving a commendation. *(Also see Amber; Musk; Perfume)*

Perfume: (Oils) In a dream, perfume means acknowledgment, commendation, or hearing pleasing words. If one sees his bottle of perfume evaporating in the dream, it means regards accompanied with apprehension and danger. If a sick person smells perfumed oils in his dream, it means his death. If a woman perfumes herself in a dream, it means engaging in good deeds. If she is unmarried, it means that she will get married and the same goes for men. If a thief or an impostor anoint himself with perfume in a dream, it means that he will repent for stealing. *(Also see Amber; Galia moschata; Musk)*

Perfumery: (Perfume shop) In a dream, a perfumery represents happy news, marriages and children. *(Also see Amber; Marketplace; Musk)*

Permanent residence: (Mole)

Perplexity: *(See Darkness)*

Persecution: *(See Daniel)*

Persian: *(See Language)*

Personal guard: A personal guard in a dream represents night vigil, prayers, constant remembrance of God Almighty and invoking His attributes. On the other hand, seeing one's personal guard in a dream may mean evil or blatancy. *(Also see Keeper of the gate)*

Perspicacity: (Acumen; Astute; Discrimination; Physiognomy; Prophesying) If one finds himself capable of perceiving matters with astute sense, or to discriminate things with a clear mental keenness, or to even explain the future, or to prophesy, or to know what is hidden in a dream, it means that he will acquire all what is good, and that God Almighty will protect him so that no harm, or evil will ever touch him. Perspicacity in a dream also represents goodness and salvation.

Perspiration: (Offensive odor; Sweat) In a dream, perspiration means recovering from an illness, or it could represent the stench of death. As for a healthy person, perspiration means work, or a service followed by a wretched life. Perspiration in a dream also represents the common adversities in one's life. If one sees himself sweating profusely in a dream, it means that he will fulfill his goals, or satisfy his needs. Perspiration under one's armpit that produces an offensive odor in a dream represents an ailment or a plague. As for a governor, a merchant, or a tradesman, such a stench in a dream means hoarding money in an ugly way. Perspiration in a dream also means losing money, paying taxes, or toiling. *(Also see Odor; Smell)*

Perturbation: *(See Worries)*

Perverseness: *(See Twist)*

Pestilence: *(See Plague)*

Pestle: *(See Mortar)*

Petroleum: (Crude oil) In a dream, petroleum represents an adulteress, or unlawful money. Eating crude oil in a dream means receiving money from someone in authority. If one is drenched in petroleum in a dream, it represents adversities that will be driven by someone in authority. Crude oil in a dream also means money, evil, adversities and wars.

Phantom: (Ghost) A phantom in a dream represents money one will earn from a friendly person. If a pregnant woman sees a phantom in her dream, it means that she will beget a son. *(Also see Mirage)*

Pharaoh: (Enemy) Pharaoh is the enemy of God Almighty. If one sees pharaoh looking good in a dream, it means that the Imãm, the leader, or the person who leads the congregational prayers in his community is a goofy person, or that the congregation itself does not follow the proper religious rules. However, if pharaoh looks ugly in the dream, it means that both the Imãm and his congregation are good people. The same interpretation applies for any common enemy one may have. If one sees himself becoming a pharaoh in a dream, it means that he may become a leader, though it will be at the expense of his religious covenant. If people are talking about a specific pharaoh in a dream, it means that one will earn fame in that locality. *(Also see Orphan)*

Pharmacist: (Druggist) In a dream, a pharmacist represents a man of knowledge, or a librarian, for drugs and knowledge represent a cure for many illness.

Pharmacy: (Drugstore) In a dream, a pharmacy represents healing from an illness.

Philander: *(See Courting)*

Philologist: *(See Grammarian; Linguist)*

Phlegm: (Mucus) In a dream, phlegm or mucus represents money that does not grow. If the person in question is a scholar, then seeing phlegm in a dream means that he does not like to share his knowledge. *(Also see Nasal mucus)*

Physical fitness: (Health) Physical fitness in a dream denotes the opposite in wakefulness. On the other hand, it could mean enjoying blessings. *(Also see Physical paralysis)*

Physical paralysis: Paralysis in a dream means corruption in one's religious life, or introducing innovations to one's religion and suffering the consequences of playing with God's words. *(Also see Paralysis; Physical fitness)*

Physician: (Mother) A physician in a dream represents a wise man, or a religious doctor. A physician in a dream also represents a scholar, and a scholar in a dream represents a physician. If one sees a physician examining him in a dream, it means an improvement in his health condition. If one sees a religious scholar advising him in a dream, it means that hypocrisy and doubt will be dispelled from his heart. A physician in a dream also represents one's mother, or he could be an opponent, or an adversary. The death of one's physician in a dream means the death of one's mother. If a sick person sees a physician visiting him in a dream, it means that he will recover from his illness. If a physician visits a healthy person in a dream and write a prescription for him, it means that he will fall sick. Seeing or visiting a physician in a dream means exposing one's secrets, for a physician works to extract the patient's illness just like a snake charmer who brings a snake out of its hiding. A physician in a dream also represents a garbage collector, a street cleaner, a spy, a backbiter, or a fighter who sometime wins and sometime loses. To see oneself as a physician in a dream means attaining a high ranking position, or becoming a policeman, or a commander who controls people's livelihood. A physician in a dream also represents someone who provides spiritual as well as practical guidance, a social reformer, a judge, a preacher, a teacher, a tanner, or a copper. If one sees a just and a well known judge as a physician in a dream, it means that his compassion and welfare will encompass everyone in that locality. If one sees a known physician as a judge or a wise man in a dream, it means that one will become renowned, his status will rise and he will become a celebrated pioneer in his field. If he is not known to be a righteous physician, then it means that one will be visited with adversities, or it could mean that someone will die from malpractice, or it could mean persevering with daring attempts do increase one's business at the expense of people's lives. If one sees a physician selling coffins or folded shrouds in a dream, one should be suspicious of him in wakefulness even if people are fascinated by his charm. If one sees a physician working as a tanner in a dream, it shows the physicians ingenuity, knowledge of his trade and the many people who recover from their illness at his hand. The exception to that is when the tan is spoiled, or if it has a stench, or if it is ineffective in the dream, then it means that such a physician is a crafty swagger.

Physiognomy: *(See Perspicacity)*

Pickax: (Digging) A pickax in a dream represents strength, resoluteness, or contemplating good deeds. A pickax in a dream also may represent an opportunistic person who draws people to himself for selfish interests, interferes in everything, or craves wealth. *(Also see Construction worker)*

Pickles: Pickles in a dream signify disputes, distress and rivalry. Eating pickles in a dream means distress. Seeing pickles and not touching them in a dream means financial losses. Making pickles in a dream represents someone who suffers from many diseases and serious ailments. *(Also see Fruit pickle; Gherkins; Preserves)*

Picnic Basket: *(See Food basket)*

Picnic: *(See Earrings)*

Picture: Seeing one's picture on a wall in a dream means one's death and that his name will be itched on a gravestone. *(Also see Paintings)*

Pie: *(See Money; Pastry)*

Piebald: If one sees himself blotched with white spots in a dream, it means that he will be struck with a painful illness.

Piercing a hole in a pearl: If one sees himself piercing a hole in a pearl in a dream, it means that he will give a valuable commentary on Qur'ānic interpretations. *(See Daniel; Nose ring)*

Piercing a hole: (Boring) Piercing a hole in a dream means deception. Piercing a hole in a stone in a dream means investigating someone in authority. Piercing a hole in the wall of a citadel in a dream means being obsessed with virgin girls and desiring to deflower them. Piercing in a dream also means spying, pursuing someone's tracks, desecrating one's earnings by bringing unlawful money into them, or it could mean deterioration in the conduct of one's children. Digging an underground tunnel in a city in a dream means searching for someone. Digging an underground tunnel to reach the inside of a house in a dream means trying to court a woman, exerting an irresistible influence on her, then luring her to deceive her. *(Also see Tunnel)*

Piety: *(See Prostration)*

Pig: (Swine) In a dream, a pig represents someone who is devoid of human dignity, or someone who lacks integrity. *(Also see Lizard; Transformation)*

Pigeon racing: *(See Racing)*

Pigeon: (Dove; Ringdove; Turtledove) Seeing a pigeon in a dream means glad tidings. It is also said that God Almighty will accept the prayers of one who sees pigeons in his dream. In a dream, a pigeon also represents a trustworthy messenger, a truthful friend, a comforting beloved, a chaste wife, striving to sustain one's family, or a fertile woman with a large family. The cooing of pigeons in a dream means lamentation. Pigeons eggs in a dream represent one's daughters or female neighbors. A domesticated pigeon in a dream represents a beautiful woman from Arabia. Pigeon's nest in a dream represents women's parties. Pigeon chicks in a dream represent the boys in a family. Pigeon's rumbling or roar in a dream means reproof or censure for a fault. A white pigeon in a dream means spirituality, a green pigeon represents piety, while a black pigeon denotes a mastery. A frightened pigeon in a dream means divorce or death. A landing pigeon in a dream represents the long awaited arrival of a beloved. Eating pigeon's meat in a dream means to steal money from one's own workers, to defraud them, or to cheat one's servants. Hunting pigeons in a dream means earning good money from wealthy people. As for an unwed person, seeing a pigeon inside his house in a dream means marriage. If a pigeon attacks someone then flies away with him in a dream, it means that happiness and joy will enter his life. However, doves in a dream may represent death. If one sees himself throwing something at a pigeon in a dream, it means that he slanders a woman, or writes secret correspondence with her. Reaching at a pigeon's nest to take its eggs in a dream means taking advantage of a woman, or swindling her money. Hunting pigeons in a dream means adultery. Seeing a pigeon standing over one's head, or tied to his neck or shoulders in a dream connotes one's relationship with his Lord. If in that sense the pigeon is an ugly one, it means that one's actions are of the same nature. Otherwise, it means the opposite. Plucking some feathers from a pigeon in a dream means money. Slaughtering a pigeon in a dream means marriage. (Also see Ringdove; Turtledove)

Pilgrimage rituals: (See 'Arafãt; Circumambulation; Cradle of Ismãïl; Ka'aba; Mina; Muzdalifa; Pelting stones; Responding; Sa'i; Station of Abraham; 'Umrah)

Pilgrimage season: (Mecca; Pilgrimage) Performing a pilgrimage during its season in a dream means dispelling one's worries, distress, apprehensions or trouble. Praying or delivering a sermon at the valley of Mina during the pilgrimage season in a dream, and if neither the person seeing the dream or anyone in his family or clan qualify for that, it means that someone with the same name among his acquaintances will do so. If this is not feasible, it means that he may face adversities, though become known for his good nature and deeds. If a learned person sees himself delivering a sermon at Mina, and if the people listen to him attentively in the dream, it means that he will rise in station and lead his people, or he could be appointed as a project manager or become an administrator. If one does not complete his sermon or prayers in the dream, it means that he will attain such a position, though he will be quickly removed from it. (Also see Pilgrimage)

Pilgrimage: (Hajj) Performing the pilgrimage to Mecca, fulfilling its obligatory pillars and celebrating its ceremonies in a dream represents one's spiritual and religious growth. It will bring him a great reward in this life and in the next, appease his fears, and imply that he is a trustworthy person. If this dream occurs during the pilgrimage season, it means profits for a merchant, recovery for the sick, finding guidance after heedlessness, or it could mean that one will perform his pilgrimage if he had not yet fulfilled this obligatory religious duty. If one's dream takes place outside the pilgrimage season, then it could mean the opposite. If one sees himself as a pilgrim in a dream, and if he disdains from actually perform his pilgrimage, though he possesses the means to do so, it means that he is a reprobate and an ungrateful person. Performing one's pilgrimage in a dream also indicates the necessity to serve one's parents and to be true to them, or the duty to serve one's teacher and be truthful with him. Performing one's pilgrimage in a dream also means visiting a gnostic, a saint, a shaikh, a scholar, or it it could mean getting married, acquiring knowledge, satisfying one's needs, recuperating from an illness, repenting from sin, or joining the company of pious people. If one travels to perform his pilgrimage using a vehicle in a dream, it means that he will receive help from God Almighty. If he travels on foot leading a camel in the dream, it means that he will do so with the help of a woman. If he rides an elephant in the dream, it means that he will perform his pilgrimage as a member of a governmental delegation. If one travels on foot in the dream, it means that he has made a vow which he must fulfil. Seeing oneself returning from a pilgrimage in a dream means profits and relief from stress. If one carries his provisions with him in the dream, it means that he stands before his Lord with piety and reverence. Carrying the pilgrims's provisions in a dream also means paying poor people their dues, or it could mean paying one's debts. If one sees himself going to perform his pilgrimage alone, and the people standing up to pay their farewell to him in a dream, it means that he will die shortly. *(Also see 'Arafāt; Circumambulation; Cradle of Ismāīl; Ka'aba; Mina; Muzdalifa; Pelting stones; Responding; Sa'i; Station of Abraham; 'Umrah)*

Pilgrims' camp: *(See Mina)*

Pillage: *(See Spoils)*

Pillars: (Corner stone; House) In a dream, a pillar represents one's wife and money. *(Also see Black stone; Ka'aba)*

Pillow: (Softness; Support; Throw pillow) In a dream, a pillow represents money, a husband, a wife, a confidant, or children. A pillow in a dream also represents a women who knows another woman's secret and who keeps it hidden from people's knowledge. A stolen pillow in a dream means the death of one's servant. The king's pillow in a dream represents his deputies, ministers and administrators. As for most people, a pillow in a dream represents one's intimate friends and brethren. The interpretation of a pillow in a dream is also similar to that of a mattress or a carpet. As for scholars, a pillow in a dream denotes their piety and righteousness. Carrying a pillow in a dream also represents earnings, a cushion, rest, or an illness.

Pimp: (Inverted; Queer) Seeing a pimp in a dream means moving from a clean place to a loathsome one, or from a vagina to the anus. A pimp in a dream also represents a pervert, or an inverted person who exhibits sexual desire for both sexes. *(Also see Panderer; Thread)*

Pimple: (Abscess; Boil; Postulate; Pus; Swelling; Tumor; Ulcer) When one sees that he has contracted pimples that open, and if pus starts running from them in the dream, it means benefits or a booty. In general, open wounds and pimples in a dream represent money and profits, unless if they appear in high concentration or cause sufferings in the dream. Thus, pimples could represent money that keeps coming as long as the pus has not dried in the dream. *(Also see Swelling)*

Pin: (Safety pin) In a dream, a pin represents miseries and wretchedness. If the pin does not have a head in the dream, then it represents someone who offers invaluable services for a small compensation, or it could mean starting a married life with little furnishings. A pin in a dream also represents a renowned brother, or a companion who defends his friend. *(Also see Peg; Skewer)*

Pinch: (Bite off; Nip; Tweak) Pinching someone in a dream means envying him, or plotting to get some of his money which he will eventually get. Pinching someone in the butts in a dream means betraying him with his wife. Pinching someone in the belly in a dream means wishing to get some of his savings. Pinching someone in a dream means hurting him with words. Pinching or biting someone's hand in a dream may represent a snake bite, or a bite of a scorpion. Pinching someone's hand in a dream also means receiving unlawful money then incurring heavy losses, or it could mean paying a hefty fine.

Pine tree: *(See Evergreen; Tree)*

Pine: (Seeds; Terebinth; Tree) Pine trees and their fruit in a dream mean loneliness and bewilderment during travels. Climbing a pine tree in a dream means triumph, success and hearing good news. Pine nuts in a dream represent the pine tree itself. A pine nut in a dream also represents a renowned person who has a noble character, a godly person who is respected, holy but poor, or it could represent someone who has little to offer, or a person who shelters thieves out of compassion. The same interpretation applies to owls and crows. Building a door for one's house from pine wood in a dream means hiring a servant or a doorman who has little politeness and who is filled with foolish ideas. If a merchant or a businessman builds such a door in a dream, it means that he will unknowingly employ a thief.

Ping-Pong ball: *(See Ball)*

Pipe dream: *(See Rainbow)*

Piper: (Jester; Music) In a dream, a piper represents someone who is longing for something, or who is anxious to say or do something, or he could denote vain talk. A wedding piper in a dream represents festivities. The court piper in a dream represents an army going to war. A piper in a dream also represents an obituarist, an announcer of a murder, someone who exposes an adulterer, or one who uncovers a secret prostitution ring and exposes it leaders. A piper in a dream also may denote one's anus. An unknown piper in a dream means suffering from a venereal disease. A piper in a dream also could represent a mourner, a good mother, or perhaps a bad mother who is bereaved of her child.

Pisces: *(astr. See Moon)*

Pistachio: Eating pistachio in a dream means earning blessed money. A pistachio tree in a dream represents a courageous and a generous man. Pistachio itself in a dream means money. Plucking and eating fresh green pistachios in a dream means hardships and toiling. Dried pistachios in a dream mean evil, an argument or fighting. Eating salted pistachios in a dream means profits from the sea and land, and for a pregnant woman, it could mean that she is close to delivering her baby.

Pit¹: (Snake pit. *See Tongue*)

Pit²: (Core. *See Date pit*)

Pitch: (Conifers; Resin) In a dream, it means travels. *(Also see Conifer tree)*

Pitcher: A pitcher, a jog or any similar container in a dream means repentance for a sinner. It also means a son for a pregnant woman. A pitcher in a dream also represents an extremely intelligent child who is recognized to fathom many hidden secrets. Collecting pitchers in a dream represents good deeds that can lead one to paradise. A pitcher in a dream also represents a sword. When a pitcher is highly priced in a dream, it denotes the high rank of the one who is interested in buying it. A pitcher in a dream also means playfulness, joy or laughter. A glass pitcher in a dream represents one's wife, marriage to a rich and a beautiful woman, a secret affair, or a friend one is proud to have. A glass pitcher in a dream also represents a spouse who cannot be trusted with a secret, or someone who is never content to be married or to have children. A pitcher in a dream also represents a prostitute, or a neighboring woman who is crafty and unflinching. *(Also see Urn)*

Pith: (Core; Kernel; Quintessence) The pith of any matter in a dream represents beneficial knowledge, sincerity in one's words and actions, and his innermost righteousness. *(Also see Martingale)*

Place of worship: *(See Masjid; Mosque)*

Placing things: To place things in the proper position, or to move them to a better place, or to give them a better environment in a dream means commanding what is good and forbidding what is evil. To downgrade things by placing them in an unfitting environment in a dream means the opposite, or it could mean bartering good for evil, or unjustly depreciating and devaluating an object.

Plague: (Pestilence) In a dream, a plague means itch, scabies, sycosis, or mange. To be inflicted with any type of such plagues in a dream means suffering from the same in wakefulness. If one sees a city struck with a plague in a dream, it means that he will witness the wrath of God Almighty befalling it. A plague in a dream also represents one's grave, religious innovation, a journey that will take a full year, or a penalty imposed by the ruler. If one sees himself in a city which is struck by a plague in a dream, it means war. *(Also see Epidemic disease)*

Plain of 'Arafāt: *(See 'Arafāt)*

Plait: *(See Braiding)*

Planning: Planning and organizing matters or events in a dream means rising in status. Planning in a dream also means justification of one's responsibilities or actions.

Plant lice: *(See Nit)*

Plant: If an inconsistent or a thoughtless person sees a plant in his dream, it means blessings, receiving praises, guidance, growing determination, or becoming decisive.

Plantations guard: *(See Rural warden)*

Planting a tree: (Seedling; Tree) Planting a tree in a dream means receiving honors or befriending a noble person, depending on the value, quality and substance of such a tree. Planting a seedling that does not grow in a dream means growing pains, depression and sufferings. A tree that grows in the dream represents one's dealing with others. In this sense, it could either grow or die. The branches of a tree represent one's brethren and children. *(Also see Tree)*

Planting: Seeing an arable land or planting it in a dream means finding work, or doing someone a favor with ulterior motives, or performing a duty from which one hopes to receive benefits at a later time. Planting in a dream also means that one's wife will become pregnant. If one sees himself planting in other than a fertile ground in a dream, it means that he engages in sodomy. *(Also see Crop; Seeds)*

Plaster: Seeing plaster in any form in one's dream means preserving one's dignity, holding to one's status and position, or it could mean persevering in one's goals. Plaster in a dream also could be interpreted as having a good marriage, good children, assiduity, concern for one's religious duties, applying knowledge to one's words, ability to appreciate and to express one's gratitude, recovering from an illness, buying new clothing, or drafting a just agreement. Gypsum in a dream has the same interpretation. If a renunciate or a pious person sees plaster or gypsum in his dream, it becomes a proof of an unlawful or sullied substances mixing with their earnings, or it could mean engaging in religious innovations, neglecting to follow the prophetic example, or becoming a hypocrite. *(Also see Plasterer)*

Plasterer: A plasterer in a dream represents a hypocrite and a trouble maker or an agitator. His presence in a dream also could mean the smoothing of one's affairs, or dispelling of one's trouble and quelling the fire of his surrounding evil. *(Also see Mortar carrier; Plaster)*

Plate: In a dream, a plate represents one's beloved, or it could mean going through hard times, or it could represent locusts or money. A plate in a woman's dream represents the best man in her circles. If a man sees a plate in his dream, it represents the most respected woman in his circles. If one sees a covered plate being taken out of the room of a sick person, the contents represent the cause of his illness.

Playing games: *(See Games)*

Playing: *(See Games)*

Plead: *(See Soliciting advice)*

Pleasure: (Enjoyment; Orgasm; Sexual climax; Sexual pleasure) In a dream, pleasure means something which is temporary, or a short lived benefit. Sexual enjoyment in a dream also means committing the forbidden act of adultery, or it could denote usury, or a deceptive sale. Sexual pleasure in a dream also may mean arrogance, pride about one's properties, business partnership, or a marriage where the wife will enjoy what she receives and the husband will benefit from satisfying his desire. *(Also see Sexual intercourse)*

Pleat: (Fold) In a dream, a pleat means forgiveness, pardon, concealing, or suppressing one's anger, or depletion of one's sustenance, or the end of one's life.

Pledge of allegiance: (Contract; Homage) Making a pledge of allegiance to the blessed family of God's Prophet, upon whom be peace, or to their descendents, or true gnostics and leaders among his followers in a dream means following true guidance, walking on the straight path and truly observing the divine laws and abiding by them. Making a pledge of allegiance to the governor of a seaport city in a dream means winning victory over one's enemy, glad tidings, honoring piety, being grateful to one's Lord and oft-praying for salvation and forgiveness. Making a pledge of allegiance to an impious person or to an evil companion in a dream means helping evil people. Making a pledge to someone under a tree in a dream means receiving blessings from God Almighty.

Pledge: *(See Paper; Pledge of allegiance; Promise)*

Plenitude: *(See Kawthar)*

Pleurisy: Inflammation of the chest membrane in a dream represents a sinner who is punished as a warning, and perhaps driven through his illness to induce him to repent for his sins.

Plinth: *(See Base)*

Plover: (Sea gull; Seabird; Shorebird) A plover or any type of seabirds in a dream represent travels, tardiness, delinquency in one's dealings, putting things in the wrong place, or praying at the wrong time.

Plow: *(See Rake; Shovel)*

Plowing: Plowing in a dream means marriage. If one sees himself plowing a field that belongs to someone else in a dream, it means that he will end by marrying that man's wife. *(Also see Earth)*

Ploy: *(See Chess)*

Pluck¹: *(See Fruit)*

Pluck²: (Animal's heart, liver, lung and windpipe.) In a dream, animal's pluck represent savings from solid gold bullions, or they could represent woman's jewelry.

Plucking out facial hair: If a rich person sees himself plucking out his facial hair in a dream, it means losing money, while if a poor person sees that, it means that he will repay his debts. *(Also see Shaving; Temples)*

Plucking roses: *(See Rose)*

Plug: Plugging one's ears in a dream means doubt, divisiveness, or uncertainty. It also means that someone will lie to him.

Plum tree: *(See Tree)*

Plum: In a dream, plums in season represent health and welfare. Otherwise, out of season, plums represent distress and difficulties. However, everybody draws benefits from seeing a plum tree in a dream. If one sees himself eating a sweet and ripened plum in a dream, it means that he will satisfy his pleasures, passions, and wantonness. If it tastes sour in the dream, then it represents his fear. A plum tree in a dream also represents a rich person, or a spendthrift who is also dangerous but courageous when facing adversities, and who may become wealthy early in his life though he may die young. Eating plum out of season in a dream means suffering from a severe illness. Plucking a plum from its tree in a dream means seizing money from a dying person. Plums in a dream also represent the glad tidings of recovering what is lost if they are good, and a warningrn about what is evil should it happen again. A plum in a dream also represents a good brother, or a good looking and a respectable companion. The same interpretation applies for all types of berries. *(Also see Tree)*

Plumber: (Tinsmithing) In a dream, a plumber represents a teacher, a trainer, a painter, a photographer, or one who lies in his words and actions.

Plunderer: *(See Spoils; Wrecker)*

Plural marriage: *(See Polygamy)*

Pluviometer: *(See Water level)*

Poached eggs: *(See Boiled vegetables)*

Poem: Memorizing a poem or a verse from a poem in a dream means engaging in a business from which one will acquire great knowledge, or it could mean profits or success in whatever trade one chooses to practice. If one sees himself in a court of justice reciting poems for money in the dream, it means that he will give a false testimony. If he recites a poem for a gathering in a dream, it means that he will relate a wise saying, though he himself inclines to hypocrisy. If one sees himself listening to a poem in a dream, it means that he will associate himself with a group of people who do not foster the truth. In a dream, poems also represent falsehood or vain talk. Reciting a poem or listening to one and memorizing its verses in a dream means that one should take heed to what it says. If the poem one is listening to in his dream contains wisdom or a divine revelation, then it does mean good. Composing a poem, or memorizing it in a dream also means losing one's status, dismissal from one's job, weakness in one's religious adherence, suffering from depression, adversities, suffering from slander by one's enemy, or it could represent a crafty ploy. If one composes a defamatory poem or a satirical poem in a dream, it means that he slanders others for fun or profit. If it is lauding someone, then it means that he will become poor. If he sings his poem with a melody in the dream, it represents a satirical attitude toward someone, doubt about someone, or failure to complete one's work. *(Also see Poet)*

Poet: (Charmer; Poet; Reciting) A poet reciting his verses in a dream represents a man who brings peace to people's hearts, entertains them and dispels anger from their hearts if God's name is mentioned in his poem. If he does not mention the name of God Almighty in the dream, then his words may be baseless and false. A poet in a dream also represents someone who pieces together a conversation, or who embellishes his words with lies, or who deceives people by giving them bad advice, encourages them to do wrong and to abstain from what is right, or misleads them with deceptive words. In general, seeing a poet in a dream means concoctions, lies, adultery, alcoholism, greed, or someone who writes poems for money and fame. If the person seeing the dream memorizes poetic verses containing words of wisdom, or verses glorifying God Almighty, or praising His Messenger upon whom be peace, or if one becomes a poet who recites such poems in the dream, it means that he will acquire knowledge, status, honor and receive guidance. In a dream, a poet also represents a seducer who says something and does something else. *(Also see Poem; Snake charmer)*

Poetry: (Poems) Selling poems in a dream denotes a person who barters his religion for the meager price of temporary worldly pleasures.

Poison: (Money) In a dream, poison means money. If one drinks poison and if his body swells and emits pus in the dream, it means profits. If his body does not show such effects in the dream, it means sorrow and distress. A lethal quantity of poisons in a dream means death. If a poor person sees himself drinking poison in a dream, it means that he will get married. Giving someone a poisonous drink in a dream means committing adultery. Drinking poison in a dream also could mean using a remedy, and it could represent an antidote or longevity. *(Also see Money; Mustard)*

Poker: (Fire iron; Fomenter) Using a poker for stirring fire in a dream means adversities, visitations and suffering.

Pole: *(See Peg)*

Police dog: *(See Dog)*

Policeman: (Crocodile; Guardian; Mercury; Thunder; Watchman) A policeman in a dream represents security and peace, prayers, a secret friendship, a hidden love, protection against Satan or his party, or perhaps he may represent one's guardian dog. A policeman in a dream also represents the angel of death, a fright, or distress. If a policeman brings his helpers with him in a dream, it means a scare, sorrows, sufferings, punishment, or a danger. He also may represent an evil person, a perfidious and a harmful beast or a lion. If someone in authority sees himself befriending a policeman in a dream, it means that he will make a new covenant, or introduce an amendment to the law, or draft a new constitution which he will sign. If one sees himself putting a policeman in prison in a dream, it means that he will engage in a political fight. *(Also see Crocodile; Lieutenant; Mercury¹)*

Polishing: (Burnishing; Shining) A wood finisher polishing a piece of furniture in a dream represents a minister, an administrator, or a statesman who deals with the high and the low. Seeing a polisher in a dream also means befriending a righteous man who points out one's pitfalls and helps him to remove his ills and to correct himself. *(Also see Sanding)*

Politician: *(See Counselor; Figure; Star)*

Pollen: (Inflorescence; Money; Spadix; Spathe; Spores) In a dream, pollen means money or a pregnancy. If a sick person sees pollen in his dream, it means that he will recover from his illness, or it could mean his death. Pollen in a dream also means hoarding merchandise or provisions. If one picks a spathe or two in his dream, it means that he may beget a child or two. If one eats pollen in his dream, it means that he will live from the revenues of such children. Observing the florescence of trees in a dream means the rising of one's star and anticipation of benefits. Seeing a yellow spathe and not eating from it in a dream represents the anger of a landlord toward his ranchers. Pollen in a dream also means money or illness. Picking up spores of pollen in a dream also means the illness of one's wife that could lead to her death, or receiving a sizeable inheritance.

Pollination: *(See Wind)*

Pollution: *(See Cloud of smoke)*

Pollux: *(See Constellations)*

Polygamy: (Multiple spouses; Plural marriage; Second wife) Having a second wife along with the first in one household in a dream means sickness, losses, harm, blindness, bad deeds, exposing one's private life, divulging one's secrets, distress, dismay and sorrow.

Pomegranate: Eating pomegranate seeds in a dream means earning easy money. A pomegranate in a dream also represents savings. If it is ripened and tastes sweet, it represents a beautiful woman, a town, a son, a one thousand dollars, a one hundred dollars, or ten dollars depending on the type of work one performs. If a pomegranate is eaten unripened in the dream, it represents suspicious money. As for a ruler or a governor, a pomegranate in a dream represents a city. If he brakes one in a dream, it means that he will conquer or rule that city. The skin of a pomegranate represents the city's walls, its seeds represent its people and its juices represent its resources, industries and wealth. If a sick person eats the skin of a pomegranate in a dream, it means that he will recover from his illness. A pomegranate in a dream also means a coffer, a beehive, or a honeycomb. If the seeds are white in the dream, they represent little money. If they are red, then they represent a sizeable profit. A pomegranate in a dream also denotes fear or a journey. A fresh looking pomegranate in a dream represents a young virgin. A broken pomegranate in half in a dream represents a deflowered girl, a divorcée or a widow. A rotten or a spoiled pomegranate in a dream represents an unchaste woman. A sour tasting pomegranate in a dream represents unlawful money, worries, or disturbances. If one sells pomegranates in a dream, it means that he will sell the everlasting reward of the hereafter for the temporary pleasure of this world. Drinking pomegranate juice in a dream means spending for one's livelihood. A pomegranate tree in a dream represents a pious, respected and a rich man. If he is a merchant, his business will always multiply. The thorns of a pomegranate tree in a dream represent the obstacles that restricts a believer from falling into or committing a wrongdoing. Cutting down a pomegranate tree in a dream means severing one's blood ties, or neglecting one's duty toward his family.

Pond: (Brook; Pool; Washing basin) In a dream, a pond represents a noble, generous, magnanimous, dominant and a beneficial person. If the pond is filled with water in the dream, it represents a generous and a well respected person. If one takes his ritual ablution from it in the dream, it means that he will escape from danger by God's leave, and if he drinks from its water, it means that he will receive a financial gift from a person in authority. Reaching a pond in a dream means walking into adversities, betrayal and perfidy.

Pool: *(See Pond)*

Poor: *(Also see Poverty; Serving)*

Poppy: (Herb) Eating it in a dream means receiving a comfortable income. Seeing the lights of its showy flowers in a dream means flags and banners. *(Also see Flag)*

Popular trend: *(See Tambourine)*

Porcupine: (Hedgehog) In a dream, a porcupine represents someone who is constantly depressed, easily annoyed, who quickly gets angry and who has little compassion. A porcupine in a dream also represents deceit, spying, betraying someone, hiding, or evil.

Porridge: (Gruel) In a dream, porridge means travel by land, abstinence, piety and fear of wrongdoing. Eating porridge in a dream means release from prison, attaining a high ranking position, finding a lost property, or having excellent religious standing. Porridge is mostly made from flour and milk. The flour comes out of grinding. The milk emanates from the udders of an animal and the porridge is cooked on fire, thus all three can be interpreted according to their individual meaning. Eating porridge in a dream during the summertime means stress, adversities, trouble and a fight. *(Also see Breakfast food)*

Porter: (Carrier; Carrying weight; Burdens; Forbearance; Serving others) In a dream, a porter or a carrier represents a school bus driver who is entrusted with bringing the children to school, then taking them back home. Whatever appearance he shows in the dream, it will indicate the mental state of the school bus driver. A porter in a dream also represents someone who is carrying his own sins and burdens. To see oneself as a porter in a dream means doing penance. If a porter enters before a sick person in a dream, it means recovering from an illness. *(Also see Tithe collector)*

Portrait: *(See Painting)*

Post: *(See Column)*

Postal package: *(See Envelope)*

Posterior: *(See Back)*

Postponement: *(See Deferment)*

Pot: (Cooking pot; Vessel) In a dream, a cooking pot represents one's wife, his livelihood and home, while the lid represents the husband. If the pot looks in a good condition and of value in one's dream, then it represents his nobility and honor. A pottery cookware salesman in a dream represents comfort and one does not need to travel to earn his livelihood, while a copper cookware or other types of cookware salesman in a dream represent a livelihood based on travelling from door to door. A cooking pot in a dream also represents a scholar or a man of knowledge who is sitting in the teacher's chair, while the meat, vegetables and spices inside the pot represent his knowledge, wisdom and their benefits for the seeker. A pot on fire with water boiling inside it in a dream represents a divorced woman. A pot in a dream also represents a handsome looking man who cares about his neighbors' opinions. A pot in a dream also could represent a housekeeper. Whatever happens to it in a dream could affect the housekeeper. If there is a sick person in a family, and if one sees a cooking pot he does not know what's inside it in a dream, the stove here represents his bed, the fire represents his depression and the boiling water represents his worries. If the boiling stops, and if the contents start to cool down, and if the fire is put off in one's dream, it means that he will recover from his illness. Putting a pot with meat and vegetables on the stove in a dream means imposing oneself on someone to receive a favor. If the meat is cooked in his dream, it means that one will greatly benefit from such a person, and his earnings will be lawful. If the meat does not cook, it means that whatever he earns through the other person will be unlawful. Stirring a pot in a dream means backbiting someone. If one eats directly from the pot in a dream, it represents money one could save otherwise beside other benefits. If the pot one is stirring in his dream does not contain any meat or food, it means that he will ask a poor person to do something beyond his means, and consequently he will not benefit from his doing. A cooking pot in a dream also represents one's relentlessness toward his enemy. A pot in a dream also denotes one's contentment and his acceptance of his destiny and of the divine providence. A pot in a dream also represents a woman or money. The sauce represents lawful earnings that are accompanied with some hassles. *(Also see Earthenware pot; Jar)*

Potter: In a dream, a potter represents someone who handles pots and pitchers, or he could represent a servant, a housekeeper, women, girls or daughters. Seeing a potter in a dream also means pride about one's lineage, wealth, or beauty.

Pouch: Entrusting someone with a pouch filled with money in a dream means confiding a secret to him. If the pouch looks good, then one's secret is important. If not, then the secret is useless. If the other person opens the pouch to see what is inside it in the dream, it means that he does not keep a secret. *(Also see Purse; Sack; Suitcase; Trunk)*

Poultry: Seeing a farmer who raises poultry for living in a dream will dispel one's distress and and replace sorrow with happiness. Seeing him also could mean recovering from an illness.

Pounding one's head: Pounding one's head, or smiting one's forehead, or shaking one's head in a dream means begetting a son at an advanced age.

337

Poverty: (Beggar; Enamored; Emaciated; Hobo; Homeless; Indigence; Love; Mendicant; Poor) Poverty in a dream means richness in wakefulness. Seeing oneself poor and hungry in a dream means that one will wake up to a great meal, or it could mean that he has stored sufficient provisions and satisfactory sustenance for sometime to come. If one sees himself as a poor beggar in a dream, it means that he prays incessantly and often asks God Almighty for extra favors and blessings. Seeing a group of needy people and beggars in a dream connotes the death of a rich person in that locality, and it is a sign for poor people to go and collect the charitable donations his heirs will distribute after his death. If someone sees himself asking for something, and if he is given what he is asking for in a dream, it means that he will receive money without trouble, or that he will earn easy money, for earning one's livelihood with mere asking in a dream means a business without capital investment, or receiving without having to give anything in return. It is also said that if one sees himself as a poor person in a dream, it means that he will earn benefits in wakefulness. *(Also see Beggar; Hobo)*

Power of attorney: *(See Proxy)*

Praises: Praising God Almighty and thanking Him in a dream means receiving benefits and a great reward. It also means finding guidance for one's religious life. Praising God Almighty in a dream is also interpreted as begetting one or two sons who will grow to become religious scholars. As for a poor man, praising God Almighty in a dream means wealth. If one sees people praising him in a dream, it means that he will live up to it and do good. If he sees them showering him with money in the dream, it means that they are speaking ill of him.

Praising God: *(See Praises)*

Prance: (Swagger) To move around in a conspicuous manner in a dream represents one's perception of his religion. It also means attaining a worldly rank that will end soon after. If one recognizes a subject relating to some earnings in his dream, then he should seriously and carefully examine the lawfulness of its source. *(Also see Walking)*

Pranks: *(See Prance; Write; Writer)*

Prayer beads: In a dream, prayer beads represent a righteous and a pious woman, a lawful and blessed livelihood, or loyal soldiers. *(Also see Beads)*

Prayer mat: A prayer mat in a dream represents a pious woman, or it could mean receiving a religious duty, or a spiritual appointment.

Prayer niche: *(See Miḥrāb)*

Prayers[1]: *(See Amulet; Invocation; Prostration; Supplications)*

Prayers[2]: *(arb. Ṣalāt)* Performing one's required daily prayers in a dream means fulfillment of one's promise, attainment of one's goals, or relief and comfort after distress. Praying at a door, or in front of a bed in a dream denotes a funeral. If one sees himself alone making the call to prayers *(Azān)* then establishing it *(Iqāmah)* in the dream, it means that he will strive to do good and to eliminate evil in his life. If one completes his prayers with the traditional greetings to the right and then to the left in a dream, it means that his worries and concerns will be eliminated, and that he will pursue the path of love and unity. If one pays the greeting only to the right in his dream, it means that he will seek to correct only some of his religious concerns. If he pays the greeting to the left side only in the dream, it means that he will be troubled for sometime to come. Paying the regards of peace *(Salām)* at the end of one's prayers in a dream means pursuing one's path, following the proper religious traditions, completing one's job, resignation from one's job, receiving an important appointment, dismissal from work, travels, or profits. If one ends his prayers beginning his greetings from the left, then proceeding to the right in a dream, it means innovation, or that he follows the path of evil. If one ends his prayers without the traditional greetings in the dream, it means that he is more interested in collecting his immediate profits than in protecting his capital investment. *(Also see Call to prayers; Five time prayers; Greetings; Imām; Impurities; Pharaoh; Prostration)*

Preach: *(See Preacher; Setting out)*

Preacher: (Khatïb; Sermon) A preacher delivering his sermon in a dream represents purity, submission, repentance, crying, rising in station, longevity, mixing with a fellowship of believers, commanding what is good and forbidding what is evil, celebrations, weddings, or anniversary meetings. If an unwed woman sees him in her dream, it means that she will get married through a third party involvement. The same goes for an unwed man, or it could indicate his search for a wife. If a suitable person sees himself being a preacher in a dream, it means that he will be appointed to manage a sensitive position of authority. If one sees himself delivering a sermon (*Khutba*) in accordance with the prescribed method and prophetic traditions in a dream, it means that he will be helped at doing his work. If he wears a white garment instead of a black one when delivering his sermon in the dream, it means that he will rise in station and that his earnings will increase. If one sees himself sitting down rather than standing up when delivering his sermon in a dream, it means that he will preside over his companions. If one sees himself sitting on the pulpit rather than standing up and delivering his sermon in a dream, this maybe interpreted as afflictions and disgrace. If an unqualified person sees himself delivering a sermon during the pilgrimage season in a dream, in this case his dream may refer to someone in his company who will do so, or it may mean that he will suffer from an illness or a mishap. If he delivers a sermon and people hearken to his words in the dream, it means that he will become a respected and obeyed guardian or leader. If he does not finish his sermon in the dream, it means that his guardianship will not last, or that he will resign or be fired from his job. If a woman sees herself delivering a sermon and admonishing people in a dream, it means that she will gain power, or marry a strong and a righteous man. If she sees herself giving a sermon on Friday's congregational prayers in a dream, it means that she will be divorced, or conceive a child from adultery. *(Also see Friday; Setting out)*

Precious stone: *(See Carnelian-red; Gem; Hyacinth; Jewel; Sapphire)*

Precision scale: *(See Balance)*

Predatory birds: *(See Bird; Eagle; Falcon; Hawk; Sakr; Vulture; etcetera)*

Preemption: (Gift; Intercession; Option; Redeem; Right) In a dream, preemption means reconciling with one's enemy, marriage of an unwed person, observance of one's prayers, conceiving a child, or receiving money.

Pregnancy: (Childbearing; Planting) In a dream, a pregnancy indicates woman's success, diligence and assiduity in pursuing her goals. In a dream, pregnancy also means receiving recognition, respect and prosperity. If a man sees himself pregnant in a dream, it means that he suffers from heaviness in his life, or it could represent one's fear of exposing his problems in public. In general, pregnancy in a dream represents material gains. If a woman sees herself pregnant in a dream, it means difficulties and adversities beside some troubling secrets she maybe hiding. However, for a learned man, pregnancy in a dream may represent increase in his knowledge, while for a craftsman, it means achieving unrivalled excellence in his trade. Pregnancy in a dream also means being madly in love, or having passionate attachment to someone, or planting seeds in the wrong place, or being bisexual or a deviate, or suffering from dropsy, or perhaps it could mean that a thief will enter his house to steal something, or to hide a stollen object, or that one may steal something and hide it from its true owner, or that he may get sick from eating spoiled food, or it could mean that he may bury a dear person, or that he is affected and a liar, or he may hide his real beliefs and show a better standing in public, or it may represent an accident or a fire. As for a woman, her pregnancy in a dream means losing her virginity before marriage, or that she will marry an unsuitable person. If a barren woman sees herself pregnant in a dream, it means a bad harvest for that year, or it could mean a robbery in her neighborhood. If an unmarried woman or a young virgin sees herself pregnant in a dream, it means that she will find a compatible husband. Pregnancy in a dream has many meanings. In a dream, woman's pregnancy means wealth, and man's pregnancy means pain and sorrow. However, generally speaking, pregnancy in a dream also could mean prosperity and material success. The extent of wealth is measured by the number of months of such pregnancy and the size of one's growth in the dream. This is true whether it is a man or a woman in the dream. If a young boy who is under the age of puberty sees himself pregnant in a dream, it represents his father, and if a young girl who is under the age of menstruation sees herself pregnant, then it represents her mother. If a man sees his wife pregnant in a dream, it reflects his desire for material success. If one sees his pregnant wife delivering a baby boy in a dream, it means that she will give birth to a girl and the opposite maybe true, except if it is common for the person in the dream to experience in wakefulness what he sees in his dream. If one sees himself delivering a baby from his mouth in a dream, it means his death, or it could mean that he will use poised and pleasant words in a conversation with someone he is careful not to offend. If a man gives birth to a baby boy in a dream, it means that he will carry a heavy burden then escape from it, or it could mean that he will vanquish his enemy, or it could mean that he may escape from a treacherous woman. If a pregnant woman sees herself delivering a child in a dream though having not had sexual intercourse with her husband, it means that she will discover a hidden treasure. A pregnant animal in a dream denotes benefits or profits. *(Also see Carrying someone; Delivering a baby; Transformation)*

Prejudice: *(See Jaundice; Jealousy)*

Prenuptial agreement: *(See Contract; Dower)*

Prepuce: (Apostate; Hard earned money; Sin; Uncircumcised; Weakness. *Also see Circumcision)*

Prescribe: *(See Setting out)*

Prescription: *(See Grammarian)*

Present: *(See Donation)*

Presentation: *(See Exhibition)*

Preserved Tablet: *(See Tablet)*

Preserves: A jar of preserves in a dream means adversities, distress, or it could represent repayment of one's debts. *(Also see Fruit pickle; Gherkins; Pickles)*

President: *(See Presiding)*

Presiding: If one sees himself in a dream presiding over a group of people, or becoming the head of a household, or a leader of a community, etcetera, it denotes distress, pressure, burdens, sorrows, loss of livelihood, or it could mean a sickness. If a woman sees that, it may mean her death. If the type of presidency is suited for women only, then the opposite interpretation may apply. *(Also see King)*

Press: (Mill) Building a press in a dream represents urban developments and prosperity for that place. The lack of a press or a mill in a town in a dream means poverty, the death of a foster mother or that of a wet nurse. In a dream, all types of juices and oils when freshly pressed in a dream represent freedom, relief, release from prison, dispelling distress, money, or sexual intercourse. *(Also see Mill; Sugar mill; Oil press; Thrust)*

Pressing olives: *(See Extracting oils from seeds)*

Prestidigitator: *(See Juggler)*

Pretending: Pretending to be in love in a dream means going astray. If a knowledgeable person pretends to be enamored in his dream, it means that he deceives people with his ornate presentations, and that his actions contradict their common standards. If a little person displays such pretension in his dream, it means that he will rise in station, strengthen his religious adherence, and have a better understanding of his spiritual goals and real purpose in life.

Pretzel: (Bagel; Bread; Twist) Pretzels in a dream mean travels, hoarding money, evil, or having an argument. Eating a pretzel in a dream also means prescribing to a healthy diet. If someone who has no teeth receives a hard pretzel in his dream, it means distress, burdens and trouble. Eating a pretzel in a dream also means recurrence of good and bad experiences.

Preventive medicine: *(See Grammarian)*

Prick: *(See Spur)*

Pride: (Conceit; Vainglory; Vanity) In a dream, pride or vainglory signifies oppression and injustice. Every conceited person in a dream is an unjust person in reality. If one sees a deceased person showing pride in a dream, it means that he is one at whom God Almighty does not look on the Day of Judgment, and particularly if he looks different in the dream. If one is proud of himself, his wealth, or power in a dream, it means that he oppresses others.

Priest: (Clergyman; Conjecture; Monk; Prognosticator) A priest in a dream connotes faith, renouncing the world, staying away from suspicion, or he could represent an Imām, a guide, an example to be followed, or a wise man whose instructions people respect and obey. A priest in a dream also could represent someone who follows conjecture, or someone who does not see his own faults. If a regular person sees himself as a priest in a dream, it means benefits for others, rising in station and fame. If a layman sees himself speaking like a preacher, a soothsayer, a fortuneteller, an astrologer or a priest in a dream, it means that he lies and engages in falsehood.

Primate: *(See Gibbon; Monkey)*

Prison guard: In a dream, a prison guard represents repercussions that could influence the veiling or unveiling of secrets.

Prison: (Cage) Imprisonment in a dream means benefits, money and comfort. It also could mean the reversal of one's condition for the worst. Becoming a prisoner in a dream also could mean making unnecessary and wasted efforts to unveil a secret. In general, prison in a dream means difficulties and humiliation. If one sees a known personality or a government administrator imprisoned or jailed, it could mean the same. If one sees himself incarcerated in a large prison in a dream, it means that he will stand before a strong person who will delegate an important responsibility to him, and from which he will gain spiritual advancement. If he is incarcerated in an unknown jail which is built from plaster in a dream, then it represents his grave. If one sees himself locked and tied-up inside a house in a dream, it means a positive advancement in his life. If in such a place one sees himself being tortured in a dream, it means that his benefits and profits will be greater. If a woman sees herself imprisoned in a dream, it means that she will marry an important person or an older person. If in one's dream the prison is administered by a religious authority, it means that one correctly prescribes to his religion. If it is a civil prison, then it means adversities, sufferings and distress caused by hypocrisy and by blaming others. An unknown prison in a dream means the world. A prison in a dream also represents an ill-natured wife, a difficult cause, silence, or controlling one's tongue, the perfidy of one's enemy, accusations, allegations, associating with rich people, one's grave, suspension of travels because of an illness, losing one's drive, poverty, or unhappiness. Entering a prison in a dream also means longevity, or reuniting with one's beloved. If one chooses to live in a sanctuary away from people in a dream, it means that he will be protected from sin. If a sick person leaves his prison cell in a dream, it means that he will recover from his illness. If a prisoner sees the gates of his jail open, or if there is a hole in the wall, or a ray of light, or if the ceiling of one's prison disappears and he can see the skies and stars above him, or if he can see them through the walls of his cell in a dream, it means that he will escape from jail. A prison in a dream also represents the safe return of a traveller, or the death of a sick person. If one sees himself imprisoned and tide-up by someone in authority in a dream, it represents adversities he wishes for them to be removed. Walking out of such an imprisonment in a dream means relief from such adversities If one is travelling, it means that he is a heedless, and if he is sick, it means that his sickness is a prolonged one. It is also said that imprisonment in a dream may mean that one's prayers are answered and that his difficulties and distress will be removed. If one sees himself incarcerated in an unknown jail of an unknown location and whose dwellers have uncommon appearance in a dream, such a prison then represents his grave. If a sick person sees himself walking out of an unknown prison, or out of a tiny house into a large open space in a dream, it means that he will recover from his illness and fully enjoy his life. If one sees himself incarcerated in a prison he does not recognize in a dream, it means that he will marry a woman through whom he will prosper and have children. If one sees himself tied-up inside his own house in a dream, it means that he will profit and witness blessings that will show in his household members. If one who is experiencing difficulties in his life sees himself tied-up to a chair or to a wall in a dream, it means that his problems and fears will be dispelled. If one sees himself building a prison in a dream, it means that he will meet a righteous man, or an Imām who will guide him on the straight path. A prison in a dream also represents paralysis, arrogance, self-deception, or incarcerating troublesome people. If one sees a deceased person in jail in a dream, it means that he is in hell. If one sees himself imprisoned in a dream, it also means that he may enter a forbidden place, a house of a prostitution, or a tavern. *(Also see Cage; Imām; Mental hospital)*

Probe: *(See Court; Digging up the past)*

Procrastination: *(See Deferment)*

Procurer: *(See Driver; Panderer; Pimp)*

Procyon: (Star. *See Dog*)

Product: (Aliment; Food) Any product which is touched by fire in the process of its manufacturing, preparation, or cooking in a dream means arguments and disputes.

Profane: *(See Irreligious)*

Profanity: *(See Curse)*

Professional singer: *(See Singing)*

Profile of a person: *(See Figure)*

Profits: *(See Milk)*

Profligacy: (Dissolute; Immoral; Shameless) In a dream, profligacy signifies ingratitude, disbelief, or denial of the truth. If a pregnant woman acts shamelessly in a dream, it means that she will soon deliver her baby, or it could represent a recalcitrant child, or a rebellious son.

Profligate: *(See Profligacy)*

Promise: (Debt; Pledge) Making a promise in a dream means indebtedness to the second party. If one also fulfills his promise in the dream, it denotes his true intention, faith and certitude. Making a good promise in a dream means blessings, profits and longevity. Receiving a good promise from one's enemy, or opponent in a dream means evil. Receiving a bad promise from one's enemy in a dream means good. A promise in a dream is a good deed. The recipient of the promise in wakefulness is the one who makes that pledge in the dream.

Prompting: (Incite; Induce; Lure; Urge) To urge someone to feed the hungry or to do good deeds in a dream means repentance of a sinner, or attracting one's good luck, or following the exemplary conduct of God's Prophet upon whom be peace.

Proof: To prove something in a dream is a testimony of one's right. To argue and prove one's case in a dream means a dispute with a colleague, whereby the one who wins the case in the dream is at fault in wakefulness.

Property taxes: *(Also see Cauterize; Tax collector; Taxes)*

Prophesying: *(See Perspicacity)*

Prophet's mosque (uwbp): *(See Masjid)*

Prophet: In a dream, each one of God's prophets, upon all of them be peace and blessings, is like a compassionate father toward his son, who is trying to save his child from the hell of this world and the hell-fire in the hereafter. In a dream, a prophet also represents a teacher, a tutor, a shaikh, a warning, or glad tidings. If one sees them standing in a stately form, or if one prays behind them, or follows them on the road, or eats something from their delicious food, or drinks from their drink, or if one is anointed with their perfume, or learns something from them, or acquires a particular knowledge from them in a dream, it demonstrates his trueness, faith in God's oneness, following His Messenger and being faithful to his traditions. Otherwise, if one walks before them, or leads them into a narrow lane, or stones them, or mocks them, or argues with them in a dream, it means that he is an innovator and a heedless person. This could also mean that he will be persecuted by his superiors, for a prophet in a dream also represents a ruler or a king, and God's prophets are in truth the guardians of the souls, and they are kings in this world and in the hereafter. A prophet in a dream also represents a religious scholar, because religious scholars are the heirs of the prophets, upon all of them be peace. Religious scholars also know God's prophets better than the common people. They understand their message and follow their traditions of glorifying God's Oneness, devotion, piety, prayers, charity, acting upon what they know and admonishing others to follow the path of truth and righteousness. A prophet in a dream also represents one's superior, a preacher, a righteous Imãm, a conscientious teacher and a caller to God Almighty. Seeing any of God's prophets looking gracious, stately and courtly in a dream also represents his people's devotion, or that a major and a positive change will take place among his followers. If such a prophet looks spurious, unhappy in a dream, or if he appears in a state that does not befit God's prophets, it means that his followers in the world have deviated from his path and created their own religion, opposing his commands, falsifying and interpreting his message to their own liking and abusing his admonition. If one claims to be a prophet in a dream, it means that he will become known in his field, or if he qualifies, he may become a ruler, a judge, a teacher or a caller to God Almighty, commanding what is good and forbidding what is evil. Otherwise, it means that he will be inflicted with a great calamity because of a falsehood he fosters, or innovations he practices. If one becomes a messenger in a dream or a caller to God Almighty, and if someone hearkens to him and accepts his message in the dream, it means that he will rise in rank. Otherwise, it means that he will become a broker, a liar, a defrauder, a swagger, depending on his level of knowledge, or it could mean that he will be struck with a major calamity in his life. Such a calamity will be of the same caliber, degree and nature that a messenger of God Almighty may have suffered from his own people. Seeing one of God's prophets in a dream also means living the experience of time, space and condition in which he saw him in the dream. Wearing the cloak of one of God's prophets in a dream means attaining one's goals, or presiding over people, or acquiring true knowledge. Consequently, one will become renowned, revered and his opinions will be respected by most people. If one becomes a prophet in a dream, it means that he will die as a martyr, or become poor and be gifted with patience and endurance. He will then be granted victory, and God willing, all his needs will be satisfied. Emulating the devotion of a prophet in a dream means trueness in one's faith, compliance with God's religion, certitude and determination. Becoming one of God's prophets, upon all of them be peace and blessings, in a dream means commanding good and forbidding evil, suffering from adversities and distress equal to those endured by such a prophet, then one will escape from destruction or humiliation by God's leave and through His subtle kindness. If one sees a prophet suffering from poverty and asking for help in a dream, it means that God Almighty will satisfy all the needs of the person seeing such a dream for the sake of the blessings reserved for that prophet. If one kills a prophet in a dream, it means that he will betray a trust, negate a promise, or deny a covenant. Living in the time of one of God's prophets on earth in a dream means honor, dignity, success, piety and wealth if one is suited for such gifts. Otherwise, it means that Satan is deceiving him. If a prophet of God Almighty beats a righteous and a sincere believer in a dream, it means that he will attain peace and salvation in his life in the hereafter. If a prophet talks to someone in a dream, it means that he will receive blessings, honor, status, knowledge, wisdom and fame in his life. *(Also see Muhammad, upon whom be peace.)*

Proportion: *(See Measure²)*

Prostate: *(Also see Circumcision)*

Prostration: (Faith; Prayers; Gratitude; Piety; Fear of wrongdoing; Repentance; Reward; Strength; Truthfulness) If one sees himself prostrating in submission to God Almighty in a dream, it means that he will be cured of arrogance, and he will establish the correct spiritual and religious life, quickly achieve what his heart desires in both spiritual and material gains, and he will triumph over his enemy. Prostrating oneself in a dream also means repenting from sin, feeling regret, salvation, escaping from danger, or receiving pardon. Prostrating during a war in a dream means humiliation before one's enemy, a fight, business losses, or it could mean standing helpless before closed doors. Prostrating oneself before God Almighty on top of a mountain in a dream means vanquishing a strong enemy, while prostrating on top of a hill means submission to a strong man. Prostration in a dream also means faith in God Almighty, joining the company of God's messenger upon whom be peace, in paradise, longevity and improving one's spiritual life. If one sees a piece of gold prostrating to a piece of silver in a dream, it means that a nobler person will submit to a lowly one. *(Also see Prayers²)*

Protection: *(See Closet; Hide-out; Veil; Wife)*

Protégée: *(See Sponsorship)*

Province: *(See City)*

Provisions: (Supplies) Carrying traveller's provision in a dream is a sign of piety, richness for a poor person, or repayment of a loan.

Proxy: (Authorization; Power of attorney) A signed document empowering someone to represent the principal in a dream represents accumulated sins. If one is commissioned to administer someone's will in a dream, it means prosperity, indisputable control, or a license to operate someone else's assets. If the person delegating that authority is sick, then signing a proxy means recovering from his illness. However, if he is healthy, then it means that he may fall sick, because a proxy means delegating an agency. If one is seeking an office in the government, and if he signs a proxy in a dream, it means that he will win it.

Prunes: (Cherries) In a dream, prunes or cherries represent easy money, recovering from illness, happiness, joy and celebrations.

Psalms of David: In a dream, the Psalms of God's prophet David (uwbp) represent wailing, lamentation, crying, repentance, fear of wrongdoing, devotion, harmony between people, unity, good luck, flute music and percussions, learning about strange news, or earning one's livelihood from reciting poems, or from delivering sermons.

Ptolemy: *(See New year's day)*

Pub: (Inn; Hostel)

Pubes: (Pubic region) Shaving the pubic region in a dream means overcoming stress, or repaying one's debts. The female pubes in a dream represent a garden or divorce, and the same interpretation may apply for her menstrual period. In a dream, if one looks at his pubic region and finds no hair therein, it means that he may indulge in a wrongdoing out of ignorance, and consequently suffers financial losses as a penalty. If one's pubic region is hairy or in need of shaving in the dream, it represents money earned through corruption. *(Also see Bath; Body¹; Hair)*

Pubescence: *(See Young man; Young woman)*

Pubic region: *(See Pubes)*

Public announcement: *(See Book)*

Public bath: *(See Bathhouse; Turkish bath)*

Publication: *(See Book)*

Pulmonary: *(See Lungs)*

Pulpit: *(See Minbar)*

Pulsate: *(Also see Nerves; Palpitation)*

Pumpkin: (Gourd; Squash; Zucchini) In a dream, a pumpkin represents a scholar, or a highly trained physician who cares about his patients and who is loved by the people, who asks for little and who rarely asks for anything for himself. A pumpkin in a dream could also denote medicine and particularly when cooked. Eating pumpkin in a dream also means guidance, following good example, or it could mean temptation. Eating a pumpkin in a dream also means recovering a lost object, or reuniting with one's beloved, or correcting one's spiritual thoughts. Eating raw pumpkin in a dream means becoming scared of roaming spirits *(See Jinn)*, or it could mean fighting with someone. Resting under the shade of a pumpkin in a dream means soliciting peace and safety. It is also said that a pumpkin plant in a dream represents a poor person. Finding a pumpkin in the middle of a plantation of melons in a dream means recovering from a dangerous illness. A pumpkin in a dream also could mean censure, reproof, or a scolding. Eating a cooked pumpkin in a dream also means acquiring knowledge, or memorizing some of it, or it could mean reestablishing broken ties. Pumpkin in a dream also means distress, trouble, tight financial standing, sickness, or imprisonment. A pumpkin in a dream also denotes vigilance and clarity of mind. Serving plates or kitchen utensils that are made from dried pumpkin skin in a dream represent beautiful, humorous and noble women. Eating a pumpkin curry dish in a dream means distress, sadness and sorrow. Eating a steamed pumpkin without spices in a dream may mean earnings. *(Also see Food)*

Punch: (Box; Fist fight; Strike) In a dream, punching someone means speaking to him with roughness. Holding a fist in a dream means abstaining from performing one's obligatory prayers. Punching someone in a dream also means using base and ignoble words in a fight between believers, or it could mean revenge, indebtedness, a court appeal, a summon or a lawsuit. *(Also see Spur)*

345

Punishment: *(See Cauterize; Seal)*

Pupil: *(See Assistant teacher)*

Puppy: *(See Dog)*

Purple: The color purple in a dream represents a brilliant and a skillful housemaid. If one sees himself lifting something of purple color in a dream, it means that he will hire or kiss a housemaid. Purple in a dream is also interpreted to mean a beautiful woman. In general, the sweet aroma of a purple plant among other fragrant plants represent a woman who has little care for stability, or it may represent a short lived child, or it could mean health problems. If the color purple is mixed in a bouquet of flowers in a dream, it means love, affection and harmony. *(Also see Colors)*

Purse: In a dream, a purse represents the chief minister, an assistant manager or a vice-chairman. He is the one who remains with his superior at all times, discusses with him confidentiality, and transmits his messages. A purse in a dream also represents a war thirsty person or an influential person. Seeing a purse in a dream also means a job for an unemployed person, temptation, or lamenting the dead. *(Also see Bag; Pouch; Sack; Wallet)*

Purslane: (*bot.* A low trailing succulent herb.) In a dream, purslane represents a person with exaggerated hopes. This is why this type of sprout is also called: 'Stupid sprout.' *(Also see Sprout)*

Pursuit: (Claim; Search; Wanted) In a dream, pursuit means one's destiny, or death. If one sees himself wanted by his enemy in a dream, it means that he may die shortly. On the other hand, pursuit in a dream also could represent things that foster one's pride, such as knowledge, schooling, degrees, money, or work. If one sees himself pursued by someone in a dream, it means sorrow and distress. Pursuit in a dream also represents one's goal in life. If one is not a fugitive, then to see himself wanted in a dream means appeasement of his fears. If one sees an ugly looking person searching for him in a dream, he then represents an unwanted catastrophe, or a mishap. If one is caught by his claimant, then it means increase of his fears. If one sees himself pursuing something, or seeking to get something in a dream, it means that he will attain his goal or at least a part of it.

Pus: In a dream, pus means a continuous source of money. Puss-filled sore in a dream represents the growing of one's savings, a show of prosperity, a monthly pay off to a band of criminals, or it could mean slander. Anything that runs from one's body such as puss, purulence, sperms, etcetera, in a dream means unlawful money. If one sees pus coming out of a sore or a boil in a dream, then it represents the male or the female sexual organs. *(Also see Pimple)*

Pushball: *(See Ball)*

Pushing someone: *(See Driving force)*

Put in irons: *(See Bond¹; Fetter)*

Pyramids: Seeing the pyramids of Egypt in a dream means receiving news from a distant place. As for an unmarried person, seeing the pyramids of Egypt in a dream means his marriage to a foreigner, or embracing his or her religion, ideals, or it could mean pursuing one's schooling in arts and science. Seeing the pyramids of Egypt in a dream also denotes a place of distraction, playfulness, music, dances, drinking alcohol, a tavern, imagery, idols, or forms.

Qaḍā': *(arb. See Five times prayers)*

Quail: (A mountain short-winged and a stout-bodied bird; Mountain quail; Partridge; Woman) In a dream, a mountain quail represents a thief, a confidant, or a pimp who secretly conducts his business of soliciting clients for his prostitutes. However, a quail in a dream also represents a blessed food, an answer to one's prayers, repelling a calamity, or overcoming an adversity. In dream interpretation, a quail also could represent a double-faced person. If a hobbyist finds himself seeking to hear the cry of a quail in a dream, it means profits from suspicious sources, or earnings made from reciting poems, singing, gambling, or it could mean squandering money. In this sense, seeing a quail in a dream could represent a crime which is punishable by death or life imprisonment.

Quake: *(See Tremor)*

Quantity surveyor: *(See Measurer)*

Quarrel: *(See Dispute; Gambling)*

Quartz: *(See Stone²)*

Qubba: *(See Dome²)*

Queen: *(See Chess queen)*

Queer: *(See Pimp)*

Question: (Vestige) In a dream, a question means pursuing someone's tracks, following a sign, or ascertaining the truth. If one sees himself asking questions in a dream, it means that he is seeking knowledge and that he will humble himself before God Almighty Who will raise him up in station.

Questioning: *(See Reckoning)*

Quick pace: *(See Hurry)*

Quicksilver: *(See Mercury)*

Quince: (Fruit) A quince in a dream denotes a sickness. However, if a sick person eats this fruit in his dream, it means that he will recover from his illness. If a governor eats quince in his dream, it means that he will achieve his goals. If a healthy person eats it in his dream, it means that he will receive spiritual guidance. If a merchant eats it in his dream, it means prosperity. Extracting juice from a quince in a dream means undertaking a business trip and reaping good benefits from one's venture. A quince tree in a dream represents a prudent, discrete and a firm man from whom no one can benefit, or it could represent a vile person. A green quince in a dream is better than a yellow one. A quince in a dream also represents a beautiful and a noble woman. Many interpreters disliked the quince fruit because of its yellowish color, and they mostly qualify it to mean sickness because of the constipation it causes if eaten raw. However, its yellowish color also can be interpreted as the color of gold. Seeing or eating a quince in a dream also means travelling with good companions, though some of them may be of no benefit. However, in general a quince or a quince tree in a dream can still be interpreted in a positive sense under all circumstances.

Quintessence: *(See Pith)*

Quiver: (Case; bag) In a dream, a quiver represents a good wife, a trustworthy companion, or one's confidant. If one draws arrows from his quiver in a dream, it means that he will beget a son. Buying a quiver in a dream means getting married. Receiving a quiver as a gift in a dream denotes a political appointment.

Qur'ān reader: (Holy Book; Qur'ānic recital) Reciting the Holy Qur'ān in a dream means admonition to do good and to forbid evil. *(Also see Qur'ānic recital)*

Qur'ān: (Garden; Holy Book; The Last Revelation) In a dream, the holy Qur'ān represents a garden because when one looks at it, it looks like a beautiful garden and its verses are the fruit of knowledge and wisdom the reader can pluck. Learning a Qur'ānic verse, a saying of God's Prophet (uwbp), a prophetic tradition, or a craft in a dream means richness after poverty, or guidance after heedlessness. If one sees himself in a dream reading from the pages the holy Qur'ān, it signifies honor, command, happiness and victory. Reciting the Qur'ān by heart and without reading the pages of the holy Book in a dream means proving to be true, or having a true claim, being pious, commanding what is good and forbidding what is evil. If one is told a verse from the holy Qur'ān in a dream, he should understand it, memorize it and comply with the same. If the verse reads about mercy or glad tidings or other admonitions in the dream, the interpretation of one's dream should be the same. If the Qur'ānic verses recited in the dream connote an advice, one should act upon it in order for him to reap its benefits. If one hears a Qur'ānic verse containing a warning, promising punishment for the disbelievers, or announcing a swift retribution for their sins, then one should immediately repent for his sins, even if the verses relate to previous nations or times. If one sees himself reciting the Qur'ān and under- standing what it says in a dream, it denotes his vigilance, intelligence, faith and spiritual awareness. If a Qur'ānic verse is recited to someone, and if he does not agree with the divine judgement in the dream, it means that he will suffer harm from someone in authority, or that a punishment from God Almighty will soon befall him. If an unlettered person sees himself reading the holy Qur'ān in a dream, it could also mean his death, or his reading of his own records. If one sees himself reading the holy Qur'ān without true interest in it in a dream, it means that he follows his own mind, personal interpretations and innovations. If one sees himself eating the pages of the holy Qur'ān in a dream, it means that he earns his livelihood from his knowledge of it. If one sees himself completing the reading of the entire Qur'ān in a dream, it means that a splendid reward from his Lord is awaiting him, and that he will get whatever he asks for. If a disbeliever sees himself reading the holy Qur'ān in a dream, the verses of admonition will help him in his life, the verses of punishment will be his warning from God Almighty and the parables will denote his need to contemplate the meaning. If one sees himself writing the verses of the holy Qur'ān on slabs of a mother of pearl, or on a piece of cloth in a dream, it means that he interprets it according to his own liking. If one sees himself inscribing a Qur'ānic verse on the ground in a dream, it means that he is an atheist. It is also said that reading the Qur'ān in a dream means fulfillment of one's needs, clearing of one's heart and establishment of one's success in his life. If one discovers that he has memorized the Qur'ān in a dream, though in wakefulness he has not memorized it, it means that he will own a large property. Hearing the verses of the holy Qur'ān in a dream means the strengthening of one's power, reaching a praiseworthy end to his life, and that one will be protected from the envy and jealousy of evildoing people. If a sick person sees himself reciting a verse from the holy Qur'ān, but could not remember to what chapter it belongs in the dream, it means that he will recover from his illness. Licking the holy Qur'ān in a dream means that one has committed a major sin. Reciting the holy Qur'ān in a dream means increase in one's good deeds and rising in his station. *(Also see Holy Book; Pearl necklace; Reading)*

Qur'ănic commentaries: *(arb. Tafsīr. See Reference book)*

Qur'ănic recital: Reading the holy Qur'ăn or part of it in a dream means rising in station, gaining power, repenting from sins, prosperity, paying one's debts, witnessing the truth, or delivering a trust to its rightful owner. Reciting the holy Qur'ăn with a beautiful voice in a dream means honor, dignity and good fame. Reading the holy Qur'ăn and adding one's own words to it in a dream means wavering from the truth, or betraying one's promise or covenant. If in the latter case one does not understand the meaning of what he is saying in the dream, it means that he will give a false testimony in a court of justice, or that he will be involved in something evil the consequences of which cannot be foreseen. If one sees people listening to his recital of the Qur'ăn in a dream, it means that he will command a job, and that people will follow his instructions. Hearing, or reading any Qur'ănic chapter which is customarily read for a deceased person in a dream, signifies the death of a sick person in that family. Professional Qur'ăn readers in a dream represent the leading people of the society. To hear a professional Qur'ănic recital in a dream means that people in authority will soon gather in the place where the recital is seen in one's dream. If one sees himself reading his book of records on the Day of Judgment in a dream, and if he is an unlettered person in wakefulness, it means that he will become rich after having suffered from poverty, and that he will answer all the questions he will be asked on the Day of Reckoning, or that he will be protected by God Almighty from what he fears most. This happens if one's reading of his own records is positive, but if it reads his sins and pitfalls in the dream, then it denotes distress, trouble, or sufferings. *(Also see Holy Book; Reading)*

Qur'ănic verses: Reading or listening to Qur'ănic verses in a dream may carry needed interpretations related to one's current studies of God's holy Book. If they indicate verses of mercy in the dream, it means that he will receive it, and if they carry admonition in the dream, and unless one immediately repents, they mean a punishment for one's sins. *(Also see Pearl necklace)*

R

Rabbit: In a dream, a rabbit represents a coward man, a wife, an evil woman, or someone who talks continuously about unimportant matters. Eating rabbit meat in a dream means getting little money, or profiting from a woman. A rabbit's foot in a dream represents superstition or a talisman.

Rabī'u Thānī: *(See Arabic months)*

Rabī'ul Awwal: *(See Arabic months)*

Racing: (Car racing; Competition; Contest; Horse race; Pigeon racing) Racing on foot in a dream means activities, actions, accomplishments, workout, amusement, playfulness, idling, a vacation, or travelling without a purpose. If a sick person sees himself racing in a dream, it means his death. If a poor person sees himself racing in a dream, it means financial gains. If a traveller sees himself racing in a dream, it means returning to his home. Horse racing in a dream means indulging in what is forbidden, arrogance, self-deceit, or guaranteeing the success of what has no prospect of succeeding. Horse racing in a dream also could mean engaging in a dangerous adventure that could lead to one's death, corruption and divisiveness. Pigeon racing in a dream means sodomy. Car racing in a dream means exceeding the boundaries of safety, or crossing into the boundaries of danger.

Radiance: *(See Light)*

Radish: In a dream, a radish represents a nomad, a pilgrim, lawful money, blessed earnings, or starting something with a good intention then regretting it.

Rage: *(See Anger)*

Ragman: *(See Junk dealer)*

Raiment: (Knighthood; Robe) To put on a new raiment in a dream means a knighthood for a person who has lost his rank or position. It also means rising in station for an appointed person, wearing a new garment, or having constant disputes with one's wife. Wearing a new raiment in a dream also could represent one's love to preside over others or to be perceived as a great person.

Rain: (Clouds; Drizzling; Life; Vapor; Water) If no harm or destruction is caused by a rainstorm in a dream, then it means blessings, profits and mercy. Rain in a dream also represents life, an earthly being, or fulfillment of a promise. If the rain falls exclusively on a particular location in a dream, it means sorrow and distress for its dwellers, or it could mean the loss of a beloved. If one sees rain falling exclusively over his house in a dream, it means personal blessings. Otherwise, it he sees it falling over the whole town in the dream, it means blessings for everyone. Rain falling exclusively over one's house in a dream also means that someone will fall sick in that house, or suffer from a debilitating and excruciating pain. If the skies rain stones or blood in a dream, it means calamities and punishment for people's sins. If it rains dust or sand in a dream, it represents an unjust ruler in that locality. If the skies rain dirt without dust, it also means prosperity and a good harvest. If a traveller sees rain in a dream, it means hindrances along his journey. A destructive rainstorm in a dream denotes dishonesty, cheating with measures, or the spread of sodomy in the community. Seeing a destructive rainstorm tearing down structures, destroying homes and pulling down tress in a dream represents a punishment for the corruption and sins of the dwellers of that place. A good rain in a dream could mean reconciliation with one's enemy, or it could mean helping a needy person. Rain in a dream also represents a caravan of camels, and a caravan of camels in a dream represents rain. A good rain in a dream also means prosperity, happiness, refilling wells with rainwater, the gushing forth of springs with sweet, fresh and pure waters. Rain in a dream also means reviving an old and a stagnant matter, or it could mean benefits, profits, blessings, relief from distress, payment of debts, or feeling relief. In a dream, a good rain means blessings, a good harvest and profits for a farmer. If the skies rain honey, butter, oil, or food people like in the dream, it means blessings for everyone. Rain in a dream also represent mercy from God Almighty, a helping hand, knowledge, wisdom, the Qur'ān, rejuvenation, revival, resurrection and life. If one sees himself standing under a cover, a roof, or behind a wall to take shelter from a rainfall in a dream, it means that he may suffer because of someone slandering him. If the rain falls in season in one's dream, it means roadblock barring travels, business losses, inability to get medicine for a sick person because of one's poverty, or it could mean imprisonment. If one washes himself in the rain, or takes a ritual ablution to perform his prayers, or washes his face with it, or washes away filth in a dream, it means repentance from sin, receiving spiritual guidance, or abolishing religious innovations and polytheism from one's heart. If he is poor, it means that God Almighty will enrich him and satisfy his needs, or if he needed something from a ruler or a governor, it means that his request will be answered favorably. Drinking from rainwater and if it is clear and pure in the dream, it means receiving blessings and benefits. If the water is dirty and polluted in the dream, it means a sickness. *(Also see Water)*

Rainbow: (Fantasy; Illusion; Pipe dream) In a dream, a rainbow means peace and tranquility. If the red color is dominant in the dream, then it means witnessing bloodshed during the same year. If the yellow color is more dominant in the dream, it means an illness. If the green color is more dominant in the dream, then it means safety, peace and tranquility. A rainbow in a dream also means marriage. Seeing a rainbow over one's right side in a dream means blessings. If it appears on one's left side in the dream, then it means prosperity and a good harvest. As for poor people, seeing a rainbow on one's right side also means richness, while for a rich person it means short lived difficulties. A rainbow in a dream also represents wonders, or a military coup. If thunder accompanies the rainbow in the dream, then it means war.

Rain gauge: *(See Water level)*

Raincoat: (Overcoat; Trench coat) In a dream, a raincoat means comfort, superiority, backing, cooperation and strength. As for a merchant, wearing a raincoat in a dream means prominence, distinction and fame in his field. Wearing a heavy raincoat in a dream means profits in one's material and spiritual life. Wearing a cotton overcoat in a dream means lesser benefits. Wearing silk brocaded overcoat in a dream signifies attachment to one's worldly gains and disregard for one's religious and spiritual benefits. Being the only person who is wearing an overcoat or a raincoat in a dream means becoming poor and mixing with good people by displaying praiseworthy qualities. *(See Overcoat)*

Rainworm: *(See Worms)*

Raise: (Allowance) In a dream, a raise means satisfying one's needs and it could indicate the house servant, or an employee.

Raisins: Eating raisins in a dream means profits no matter what kind or color they are.

Rajab: *(See Arabic months)*

Rake: (Shovel) A rake in a dream represents an employee or a servant. Its function is to sweep and gather dirt or manure and all of that means money in a dream. Only one who uses a rake in wakefulness will see one in his dream. As for an unmarried person, seeing a rake in a dream means getting married and protecting one's chastity, or uniting with one's beloved, or it could mean a crop, a good appetite, a ladle, a son, a comfortable financial standing, a hard working man, a helper, a hard working and a patient woman, or business activities. *(Also see Shovel)*

Ram: In a dream, a ram represents a noble person. Holding a ram by its wool in a dream means taking money from a noble person. Holding a ram from its horn in a dream means being restrained by a noble man from engaging in something. Holding a ram from its buttock in a dream means controlling or managing the interests of a noble man, or it could mean inheriting him, or marrying his daughter. Holding a ram from its belly in a dream means taking money from a noble person. Killing a ram for other than food in a dream means killing a noble person. If one kills a ram during a wartime in a dream, then it represents his enemy. A slaughtered ram in a dream represents a murder. Buying a ram from a butcher in a dream means that a noble and a great person will come to need the person seeing the dream who will save him from a foreseeable danger, or help him to recover from an illness. Slaughtering a ram in a dream means recovering from an illness. Carrying a ram over one's head in a dream means caring or managing the business or accounts of a noble and a rich person. Riding a ram and driving it at will in a dream means conquering a great person. If one sees a ram riding him in a dream, then it means that such a great and powerful person will rise above him and control his life. Breaking the horns of a ram in a dream means weakening a powerful person. Fighting with a ram in a dream also means fighting with a powerful person. Whoever wins the fight in the dream, will eventually win it in wakefulness. Seeing a dead ram in a dream means the death of such a great person. Dividing the meat of a ram in a dream means dividing the wealth of a great person after his death. Sacrificing a ram to eat and to distribute from its meat as a charity to poor and needy people in the dream means the release of a prisoner, his escape from capture, dispelling distress and worries, payment of one's debts, attending the annual pilgrimage to God's House in Mecca, or recovering from an illness. Slaughtering and skinning a ram then hanging it in a dream means stripping one's enemy from his money and wealth. Seeing a skinned ram inside one's house in a dream means the death of a relative. If it is the leg of a ram, then it means the death of the closest relative. Broiling a ram in a dream means governing for one year after which period one may be imprisoned. The number of rams in a dream represents the number of years. Thus, seeing them also represents the number of years one will serve in his job. The wool of a ram in a dream means money. A ram in a dream also represents the muezzin in a mosque, a general in the army, a deposed ruler, or a humiliated person. If a ram attacks someone in a dream, it signifies an attack by one's enemy. If a ewe becomes a ram in a dream, it means that one's wife will no longer bear children. If one is not married, then it means winning victory in his life. *(Also see Ewe; Sacrifice; Sheep)*

Ramadãn: *(See Arabic months; Fasting)*

Rancher: *(See Stableman)*

Rancor: (Grudge; Hatred; Spite) To have rancor or to suffer from others' rancor in a dream means attaining a high rank, or becoming a governor. Rancor in a dream also represents unlawful earnings. *(Also see Anger; Handcuff; Grudge)*

Range: *(See Oven)*

Rank: (Ceremony; Religious rank) Awarding a meek person a ceremonial rank or a station of honor in a dream represents a wedding, a job, or a good deed through which God Almighty will raise such a person in station. *(Also see Rising in station)*

Ransom: *(See Enemy; Enmity)*

Rape: *(See Adultery)*

Rapture: *(See Delight)*

Rare book: *(See Reference book)*

Rash: *(See Hives)*

Rasp: *(See File)*

Rat: A rat in one's house in a dream means that he will emigrate from one land to another. If the person seeing the dream owns a house, it means that he will sell it. Rats in one's house in a dream also represent thieves one must guard his house against, or that he must guard himself against the betrayal of a close acquaintance. Eating a rat in a dream means backbiting others, or earning unlawful money. In general, rats in a dream represent insolence, causing damage, fornication, adverse marital conditions, or problems in the upbringing of one's children. Catching a rat in a dream means suffering from humiliation and despise.

Ratio: *(See Measure²)*

Raven: (Carrion crow; Crow; Hooded crow; Rook) In a dream, a raven represents a high ranking man, a forbearing and a patient person, or a strong and a well feared person. *(Also see Crow; Rook)*

Razor strop: *(See Hone)*

Razor: (Straight razor) In a dream, a straight razor represents a son. If one causes wounds to a pigeon or an animal with a razor in a dream, the razor then represents his tongue and the base language he hurls at people. Seeing a straight razor in a dream also signifies perfidy, enmity and the use of harsh language.

Reading: Reading the front page of a letter, a paper, or a book in a dream means receiving an inheritance. Reading the last page, or the back cover of a book in a dream means indebtedness. Reading a book in a dream also means receiving an inheritance. If one finds himself as a lettered person and if he reads well in his dream, it means that he will attain a high ranking job. If one sees himself reading his book of records in a dream, it means that he will repent for his sins. Reading a book in another language in a dream means travelling to such a country, or going to places one is not familiar with and performing a job that will earn him fame. If one sees himself reading a book in a foreign language and is unable to properly decipher its words in a dream, it means that he will escape from a potential danger he could face in such a land, or it could mean falling sick in a foreign country, then recovering from one's illness before returning to one's homeland. *(Also see Language; Qur'ānic recital; Reckoning)*

Rear side: *(See Back; Buttock)*

Rebellious child: *(See Profligacy; Recalcitrant child)*

Rebellious son: *(See Profligacy; Recalcitrant child)*

Rebuke: (Calumniation; Fire; Harsh words; Slander. *See Blame; Censure)*

Recalcitrance: *(See Recalcitrant child)*

Recalcitrant child: (Accursed; Disobedient; Disrespectful; Rebellious; Undutiful) To see a recalcitrant child who stubbornly refuses to obey his parents in a dream means committing a major sin, such as associating partners to God Almighty, or committing a violent crime or a murder, etcetera. *(Also see Disobedience)*

Receiving: *(See Giving)*

Reciting: *(See Poem)*

Reckoning: (Day of Reckoning; Doomsday; Resurrection) Seeing the reckoning of a deceased person in a dream denotes his sufferings in the hereafter. If a traveller is asked to account for his travel expenses, and if he is treated with kindness during the reading of his report in the dream, it means profits from his journey and a safe return to his homeland. If one reckons himself in a dream, it means that he will repent for his sins. If one is brought for judgment on the day of reckoning, and if his questioning is made easy in the dream, it means that God has blessed him to marry a pious wife who has love and compassion for him, and who cares about his interests. If his questioning is strict and detailed in the dream, it means that he will incur losses. If a person sees himself questioned, probed and investigated in a court by people he does not recognize in the dream, it means that he has strayed into innovation, and that he will remain accountable for his actions. If he sees them well dressed and fragrant, congratulating him and greeting him with the salutation of peace: "'As-Salāmu Alaikum'", then it is an indication of his righteousness and good deeds. *(Also see Intercession; Reading; Resurrection)*

Recognition: *(See Fame)*

Recognize: *(See Uncertainty)*

Reconciliation: Reconciliation between a husband and a wife in a dream connotes the consequences of an illness, embracing one's former religion, or it could mean returning to one's old trade. *(Also see Conciliation)*

Record keeper: (Accountant; Calculator; Drawing board; Gambler; Inscription tablet; Speculator) A calculator in a dream represents a painter or a photographer. If one sees himself as a calculator, an accountant, or a record keeper in a dream, it means that he might become a secretary, a writer, a stockbroker, a jobber, a dealer, a speculator, an operator, a bookmaker, a bookie, or an operator of a gambling table. *(Also see Abacus)*

Record keepers: (Angels; Spiritual) Representing the heedful angels in charge of guarding the writings of the Preserved Tablets, and the heavenly beings or scribes in charge of recording peoples' deeds. In a dream, the blessed angels in charge of keeping peoples' records represent the gnostics, the renowned people of knowledge, religious scholars and the trustworthy ones. Seeing the scribes of the records in one's dream brings him glad tidings in this life and in the next. If the person lives a pious life, it means that the heavenly paradise is his final abode, but if he is impious, it could represent a clear warning. Meeting the blessed angels in charge of keeping peoples' records in a dream also means facing adversities, then becoming free from one's trials. *(Also see Scribes²)*

Records: *(See Book)*

Red anemones: *(bot.)* In a dream, anemones represent fire, red cheeks, blushing, a beauty mark, the sickness of one's brother or sister.

Red rose: *(See Rose)*

Red-brown beard: *(See Reddish beard)*

Red: (The color red; Dignity; Nobility; Happiness) Wearing a red silken garment in a dream means a sickness. If a warrior sees himself wearing a red silken garment in a dream, it means that he will be decorated for his chivalry. Red in a dream also represents the world, its glitters and material pleasure. *(Also see Blushing)*

Reddish beard: (Red-brown) Unless one has a reddish beard as the natural color of his hair, having a reddish beard in a dream means trials or temptations, and particularly if gray hair is mixed with it.

Reddish-brown: *(See Maroon)*

Reed: (Cane) A reed in a dream represents the worst of people, or it could connote engaging in a despicable and a loathsome conversation. Leaning on a stick of reed in a dream represents the short span of life which remains for such a person, and it could mean that he will become poor before he dies. Reed in a dream also represents a frugal person who has loyalty to nothing, and who has no respect for the common norms or ideals. If one sees strips of reed turn into strips of silver or gold in a dream, then they denote good and valued deeds. Reeds in a dream also signify prosperity and wealth which is made from lawful earnings, a pure and a chaste wife, or good children. However, reeds in a dream also represent hypocrites, and if one hears their sound in his dream, it means an argument, or a fight. *(Also see Caning; Sugar cane)*

Reference book: (Compilation; Encyclopedia; Qur'ānic commentaries; Manual; Journal; Papers; Rare book; Source book) Reading any reference book, Qur'ānic commentaries, or compilation of the prophetic sayings in a dream means correcting one's actions and thoughts and walking on the straight path. Reading the studies of religious scholars or science books in a dream means acquiring knowledge and benefiting from it. Reading history books or journals in a dream means becoming close to people in the government. Reading a book on logic, rhetorics or explicative apposition in a dream means working in an amazing field of science and discoveries.

Refinement: *(See Elegance)*

Refinery: *(See Oil press)*

Reflection: Seeing one's picture reflected in a wall means his death, and connotes that his name will be itched on his gravestone.

Refuge: (Cave; Den; Harbor; Retreat; Sanctuary)

Refund: *(See Tax refund)*

Refuse: *(See Garbage)*

Regent: *(See King)*

Regret: (Hastiness) In a dream, regret represents hastiness, and hastiness represents regret.

Reins of power: *(See Bridle; Reins)*

Reins: (Bridle; Harness) In a dream, reins represent mastery of one's craft, control of his trade, or it could signify power and a strong financial standing. Reins in a dream also represent a coachman, or the driver who never disobeys his master, and who goes wherever he is told to go. Riding on a workhorse who is fitted with a harness, or on a bridled nag in a dream means occupying an important office and letting everyone who works for the leader make an oath of allegiance before hiring them for work. If the bridle and the martingale are unadorned in the dream, then such a dream represents a humble person, and connotes that his heart is better than what his outer look may suggest. Reins in a dream also connote safety or a safety belt. Wearing a harness in a dream means safety, and that one does not interfere with others' business or talk about them. However, should one who has to appear in court see himself wearing a harness in a dream, it means that his proof will not be accepted by the judge, and subsequently he will lose his case. If the reins of one's horse are broken in a dream, it could mean the death of his driver. Reins in a dream also denote chastity, guardianship and protection. They also represent the obligatory payment of alms tax which cleanses and protects one's capital. If the reins or the harness fall from one's hand in the dream, it means corruption in one's religious life, a decline in his devotion, or that one's wife will become unlawful to him (i.e., living together after a divorce), or that she will remain in his house without a legal marriage. To see oneself bridled in a dream also means refraining from sin, or observing a voluntary religious fast. A broken bridle in a dream is good for one who service it and bad for its owner. *(Also see Bridle)*

Reject: In a dream, rejecting something means ingratitude or disbelief.

Relationships: (Bond; Connection; Liaison) To have important connections in a dream means compelling one's enemy to retreat or to accept one's conditions. To have strong relationships in a dream cools the divine wrath, as does giving charity in secret. This is true unless one's connections or circle gathers a group of evil companions, or if one is mingling with a band of conspirators.

Relaxation: (Ease; Leisure; Repose; Rest) To see oneself relaxing after toiling in a dream means wealth after poverty, or a happy marriage after a miserable one. If a sick person sees himself relaxed in a dream, it means the nearing of his death, and taking a rest from the adversities and toiling of this world. On the other hand, relaxing in a dream may mean misery, worries and unhappiness.

Relief: *(See Death; Freedom; Manumission; Slaughter)*

Religion of Islām: *(See Islām)*

Religion: *(See Rope; Spool; Uncertainty; Veil)*

Religious commitment: *(See Rope)*

Religious doctors: *(See Legist; Scholars)*

Religious endowment: *(See Endowment)*

Religious rank: *(See Rank)*

Religious rites relating to a newborn: *(See 'Aqīqah rites)*

Religious scholar: *(See Legist; Scholars)*

Relish: *(See Pickled fruit)*

Remembrance of God: *(See Zikr)*

Reminiscence: *(See Institute)*

Remorse: *(See Worries)*

Renegade: *(See Betrayal)*

Renowned: *(See Fame)*

Renter: *(See Carrier)*

Reorganization: *(See Bankruptcy; Fraudulent bankruptcy; Slave)*

Repairing: Repairing a broken jar or a utensil in a dream means correcting oneself, giving medicine to a sick person, or setting a broken bone.

Repel: Repelling someone in a dream means ingratitude, or disbelief.

Repentance: In a dream, repentance means release from prison. It also means reversing the course of one's life to attain success and to replace failure. If one sees himself refraining from evil and sins in a dream, it means that he will be tried with an adversity, then repents to regain honor after humiliation. If one repents for a sin he is not even aware of in a dream, it may be feared that he will fall into its trap, though the conclusion will turn positive. If a musician or an adulterer repents from sin in a dream, it means that he may experience poverty after richness. *(Also see Prostration; Tithe collector)*

Reprimand: *(See Blame; Censure)*

Reproof: *(See Blame; Censure)*

Repudiation: (Desertion; Denial; Divorce; Estrangement) Repudiating one's wife in a dream means unveiling or exposing disturbing secrets. Repudiation in a dream also denotes a vow one has forgotten about. Repudiation in a dream also denotes having loathsome sexual preferences, or desiring anal intercourse with one's wife, or it could mean running away from one's enemy.

Requital: (Retaliation; Retribution) In a dream, requital means longevity, departure from one's past, or it could mean instituting justice, or performing penance that will purify the person from his sins, such as prayers, voluntary fasting and alms giving. *(Also see Atonement)*

Rescind: *(See Marriage bond; Reconciliation)*

Research: Inciting someone to research, or to impel one's animal to drive faster in a dream means investigating the secrets of life after death, or explaining its meaning. *(Also see Impel)*

Reservoir: *(See Water level)*

Resignation: *(See Justice)*

Resigned: *(See Despair; Uptight)*

Resin: (Conifers; Pitch) In a dream, resins mean travels. *(Also see Conifer tree)*

Respite: Granting respite or a timetable to another person in a dream represents one's own sufferings. If this is done in anger in the dream, then the measure of sufferings will be awesome.

Responding: *(arb. Talbiyah)* Responding to a call, or uttering and repeating a formula *"Labbaika Allāhumma Labbaik,"* during the pilgrimage season in a dream means that one will capture his enemy and bring him to justice. Loud answering to a call in a dream means complaining before a judge, and winning the case thereafter. *(Also see Hajj; Feast of Immolation; Pilgrimage)*

Resurrection: (Day of Reckoning; Day of Resurrection; Last Day; Reckoning; Rising of the dead; Trumpet of Resurrection) Seeing the Day of Resurrection, or Doomsday in a dream is a serious warning for a sinner, or it could represent a warning for someone who is contemplating a sinful act. Seeing the Day of Resurrection in a dream also denotes justice. Being the only person resurrected on such a day means one's death. Standing up awaiting one's judgement on the Day of Resurrection in a dream means travels. If one sees himself and his wife being the only people who are brought for judgement of the grand Day of Gathering in a dream, it means that he is being unjust. If a warrior sees the Day of Resurrection in a dream, it means that by God's decree, the aggressor shall be defeated. The land of the grand gathering in a dream represents a chaste woman or a noble man. The blowing of the Trumpet of Resurrection in a dream represents the salvation of the righteous ones. Seeing any of the great extraordinary events or signs that shall precede the Day of resurrection in a dream means glad tidings for a believer who does good, and a warning for a disbeliever to correct himself and repent for his sins before its coming. Seeing the Day of Resurrection in a dream also denotes that some of the major signs are actually taking place, such as blood shedding, spread of evil, belligerence of atheism, pride about wealth, ruling of the working class, building high rises, the end of the era of kings on earth, or it could remind the person of the prophesied signs, such as the rising of the sun from the West, the emergence of a beast that will speak with a human tongue, the rising of the Imposter *(arb. Dajjāl. Antichrist)*, etcetera. Seeing the Day of Resurrection in a dream also represents the spread of evil, the presence of an extended police force, and the ruling of large armies and dictatorships around the world. Thus, seeing the Day of Resurrection in a dream is a reminder and a warning to the one who sees it. If one sees the graves splitting open, dead people resurrected back to life and are walking out of them accompanied with their angels in a dream, it means that justice will prevail in that land. If one experiences the resurrection in a dream, then discovers that the world went back to continue its prior course , it means that justice will dominate that land for a while, then it will be followed by a tyranny that will be carried by people who are not even suspected to be of such character. Such a dream also could be interpreted to suit a person who is seeking the impossible, or one who is adamant at pursuing the path of wrongdoing, falsehood and lies. Recognizing the eminent final signs of the Day of Reckoning in a dream means that one is unaware of his heedlessness and such dream constitutes a warning. If one's reckoning is easy in a dream, it denotes his wife's piety, compassion and love for him. If one's reckoning is detailed and painful in a dream, then it represents major losses. If one's good deeds weigh heavier than his bad deeds in the dream, it means that his devotion is true and that his reward will be greater. If one sees himself carrying the scale to weigh his own deeds in a dream, it denotes his righteousness and correctness. If one sees an angel handing him his records and telling him to read his own book in the dream, it also means that he is on the right path. Walking on the bridge of the Day of Judgment, carrying one's own records and crying in a dream means that one is praying for God's forgiveness and to ease his reckoning. If one sees the Doomsday in a dream, it means that he will escape from dangerous enemies, or that perhaps a major trial will befall the dwellers of that place. If one crosses the Bridge of Judgement in a dream, it means that he will escape a major trial, or perhaps it could represent a major hurdle one may have to cross in this life. If one sees himself carrying his book of records in his right hand in a dream, it means that he will win righteousness, wealth and honor. If one sees himself carrying his book of records in his left hand in a dream, it means that he will fall into sin and the consequent poverty and need of others, for wealth and adultery do not mix. If one witnesses the emergence of the Imposter (*Antichrist*) in a dream, it signifies new trends, innovations and masses straying from the straight path. *(Also see Intercession; Reckoning; Rising of the dead; Trumpet of Resurrection)*

Retaliation: *(See Driving force; Requital)*

Reticent: *(See Naked)*

Retreat: (Sanctuary; Spiritual retreat. *arb.* I'tikâf) The place where one may see himself observing a spiritual retreat in a dream represents what the person is inclined to do. If it is a mosque in the dream, it means blessings or a marriage to a righteous woman. If one's retreat takes place inside his own shop in the dream, it means that his business has become his primal concern. In a dream, a spiritual retreat represents devotion, prayers, hunger, votive fast, depression, humbling oneself, controlling one's passions and desires. If one secludes himself in a known location in a dream, it means that such a place is a source of comfort. If one takes refuge in his shop in a dream, it means clinging to one's livelihood. *(Also see Hermitage; Temple)*

Retribution: *(See Requital)*

Return of one's soul back to its Lord: (Death; Give up the ghost; To die) In a dream, the return of one's soul back to its Lord means remitting a trust to its rightful owner, the recovery of a sick person from his illness, the release of a prisoner from jail, or perhaps it could represent the reunion of beloveds.

Return: (Return from a journey) When one returns from a trip in a dream, it means paying one's dues, dispelling sorrow and sadness, escaping from ill consequences, receiving a reward, or repenting from sin. *(Also see Debt)*

Returning a merchandise: (Business) Returning a merchandise to the merchant in a dream represents a highway robber, a thief, obstructing the trade, delaying a traveller, failing to observe the laws, or being careless about violating the law.

Returning from a journey: *(See Debt; Return)*

Reunification: *(See Reunion)*

Reunion: (Reunification) To sit with one's beloved, enjoying love, affection and unity in a dream means marriage or prosperity. Sitting with one's beloveds and enjoying one's financial accomplishments in the dream means loss of rank and wealth. If a woman sees herself sitting with her beloved in a dream, it means that they will get married. A visit of one's beloved in a dream means valuing and cherishing one's happiness.

Reverence: *(See Majesty)*

Reverie: *(See Moon)*

Reversal of sentence: *(See Wrecker)*

Review officer: (Military. *See Exhibition*)

Reviewer: *(See Critic)*

Reward: *(See Compensation; Bribe)*

Rheum: *(See Mucous)*

Rhinoceros: In a dream, a rhinoceros represents a great king or a powerful ruler. If one sees himself milking a rhinoceros in a dream, it denotes money one may earn from such a great person. Riding a rhinoceros in a dream means rising above such a ruler, or it could mean betraying him.

Ribs: (Women) In a dream, ribs represent women. Whatever may affect one's ribs in a dream will manifest in his wife, for it is said that Eve was created from Adam's rib. Ribs in a dream represent a protective shield. Their parable is like that of a tent and its pillars, a house and its foundation, the roof of a house, or a boat and its boards. Ribs in a dream also represent relatives of different social environments, or they could represent their stations of love, unity, compassion toward one another, or help they render to one another. Ribs in a dream also denote secret deeds or concealed actions. Ribs in a dream also mean punishment. If one sees his ribs standing out, or exposed in a dream, he may face punishment for a crime or a sin he has committed. If one's ribs grow strong and the flesh surrounding them becomes healthier in a dream, then they represent prosperity, recovering from an illness, gaining weight, or growing fat. If one sees himself in a dream without ribs, it means that he will lose what the ribs represent of either a wife, a child, money or perhaps, he could have engaged in something wrong, thinking it to be right. One's ribs in a dream also mean a sickness, or bending of one's shoulders because of old age. Eating one's own ribs in a dream means becoming a burden to his family and relatives, or it could mean that he may sell wood for living, or work at a lumberyard. *(Also see Body¹)*

Rice drink: *(See Amazaki)*

Rice flour: In a dream, rice flour means a blessing or a favor. *(Also see Flour)*

Rice pudding: In a dream, rice pudding means celebrations, a reception, a wedding, a contract, knowledge, or prosperity.

Rice: In dream, rice means money which is earned with toiling, distress, or passion.

Richness: Richness in a dream means poverty or contentment. *(Also see Star)*

Ride: (Animal; Carrier; Mount; Vehicle) A vehicle in a dream represents care, concern, attaining one's purpose, or it could mean reaching one's destination through striving and hard work. To ride an animal in a dream means following one's desires and passions. However, to be carried by any animal, or by any type of vehicle in a dream is a sign of honor and authority. Riding a horse one cannot control in a dream means following one's passions and wantonness. If one is able to adequately tame his horse and control it in the dream, it means that he will be saved from adversities. Riding an elaborately dressed horse for a parade, being surrounded by servants and an entourage in the dream means receiving an inheritance, or it could mean becoming the guardian of an estate one will inherit in a short while. Riding over the shoulder of another man and forcing him to accept it in a dream represents one's funeral, and it means that the other person will have no choice but to carry the coffin. If the person carrying him in the dream is willingly doing so, then it means that he will care for his needs and bear his encumbrance. Riding over someone's shoulders in a dream also means facing an major adversity. Should he meanwhile fall down in the dream, it means that such a trial will not take place. If one sees himself riding over someone's shoulder backward in a dream, it means that he does not accept any advice or excuse, or it may mean that he turns to the other side if he is asked for help, or it may mean that he engages in the forbidden sexual intercourse during women's menstrual period, or that he engages in sodomy. To see a horseman leading a procession or a caravan of travellers in a dream means taking a distant journey, or it could represent business activities, or recovering from an illness.

Ridhwân: (The archangel Ridhwân, peace be upon him.) Seeing the guardian angel of paradise in a dream means blessings and comfort in one's life, glad tidings, an unalterable happiness, and protection from illness. In a dream, Ridhwân (uwbp) represents the treasurer of the king and his messenger, seeing him also could mean fulfilling a promise, or satisfying one's needs. If one has disagreements with his superiors then if he sees Ridhwân (uwbp) in a dream, it means that they will wind up in blessings and harmony, and particularly if Ridhwân (uwbp) hands the person a heavenly fruit or a heavenly garment, or meets him cheerfully with a comforting smile, showing a sign of God's pleasure with him. Seeing him (uwbp) in a dream also denotes a divine grace which is bestowed secretly and openly upon the one who sees him. Seeing Ridhwân (uwbp) in a dream also denotes a happy life, joy, peace, comfort and blessings in this world and in the next. If one sees the heavenly angels coming before him to congratulate him in a dream, it means that God Almighty has forgiven that person his sins and endowed him with the gift of patience and forbearance through which he will triumph in this life and be blessed in the next. *(Also see Paradise)*

Rift: *(See Rupture of relations)*

Right hand: *(See Food)*

Righteous men: *(See Scholars; Shepherd)*

Righteous people: (Companions of God's Prophet, upon whom be peace; Followers; Successors) Seeing God's blessed people and His righteous ones, or any of the early companions of God's Messenger (uwbp), whether such a companion is known or not in a dream represents blessings in one's life and denotes one's correct following of their example, and their advice or comments in one's dream must be heeded. To see oneself as one of such true ones, or to enter their circles in a dream means that one is following their example and enjoying or suffering similar trials to theirs, then he will triumph over his enemies. To see one of the companions living in a city in a dream also represents the joy, happiness, prosperity, and justice the inhabitants of such a city enjoy under the leadership of a righteous governor. *(Also see Companions of the Prophet; Scholars; Serving; Shepherd)*

Rigor: *(See Harshness)*

Rind: *(See Shell)*

Ring polishing: (Gem polishing) A ring stone polisher in a dream represents someone who offends or injures people with his words.

Ring: In a dream, a ring represents peace, tranquility, authority, a wife, a child, or a job, the reward of which will equal the value and size of the gemstone which is placed on it. If one's wife is pregnant, and if he sees himself wearing a golden ring in a dream, it means that she will give birth to a son. The king's ring in a dream represents his kingdom. Cutting off a tight ring with a pair of pliers in a dream means the end to one's authority. Any incrustations on one's ring in a dream represent his goals. If the gemstone of one's ring falls in a dream, it may mean the death of his child, or the loss of his business. A broken ring in a dream means divorce. Wearing a ring made of iron in a dream means that one will receive benefits though with great strain on him. Wearing a golden ring carrying a precious stone in a dream means that such benefits will come with ease. If it is a plain ring or a band with no stone, it means engaging in a strenuous project and getting nothing out of it. Rings made of ivory or from an animal's horn in a dream represent glad tidings for a woman. Seeing someone in authority stamping a document with his ring as a seal in a dream means that one will receive an important political appointment. If one who is accustomed to wearing a silver ring sees himself offering it as a gift to whoever he wishes in a dream, it means that he will preside over an honorable post. Wearing the governor's ring in a dream means an appointment as a dignitary, or inheriting such a rank from one's father. If one's father does not hold such a position, then it means the opposite of one's wishes. Finding a lost ring in a dream means earning money from a foreign land, or having a new born son, or it could mean a marriage to a righteous woman. If the stone of one's ring seems unstable in the dream, it means that one will be fired form his job. Removing one's ring in a dream means that one maybe removed from his job. If a woman sees herself removing her wedding ring in a dream, it means the death of either her husband or of a close relative. A ring in a dream also connotes a band, an encumbrance, or a shackle. If one's ring disappears and only the stone remains in the dream, it means that once the responsibilities are gone, good memories of the person will remain. A man wearing a golden ring in a dream represents innovation, and the results will bring about afflictions, betrayal, or a revolt. Wearing a tight ring in the dream means that one will be let off from a vicious woman, or that he will be spared from a wicked duty. A borrowed wedding ring in a dream represents an ownership that will not last. If one buys an engraved ring in a dream, it means that he will own something he never owned before, such as a house, a vehicle, or perhaps he may get married, or bear a child. If one sees rings being sold in the open market in a dream, it means that the estates of the high society are for sale or it could represent foreclosure. If one sees the skies raining rings in a dream, it means that he will conceive a child during that year. If he is unwed, it means that he will marry a rich and a virgin young woman during that same year. If they are gold rings in the dream, it means that such a woman has lost her wealth. If one places a ring in his little finger then removes it to place it on his ring finger, then removes it again to place it on his middle finger in the dream, it means that he solicits customers for a prostitute. If one notices his ring sometime in his little finger, then in his middle finger, then in his ring finger without his doing in the dream, it means that his wife will betray him with another man. If he sells his ring for pennies or a handful of sesame, or for little flour in a dream, it means that he will separate from his wife, though they will have respect for one another, or it could mean that he will offer her a good financial arrangement. Receiving a ring that is inlaid with a precious stone from one's son in a dream represents the good character and qualities of such a son. A stone which is made from worthless glass beads in the dream denotes a weak authority. A ring that is inlaid with a green sapphire in the dream means begetting an intelligent son who will become a great man of knowledge. A wooden ring in a dream represents a hypocritical woman. If a woman is offered a ring in a dream, it means that she will get married, and for a married woman, it means that she will give birth to a son. If the ring in one's dream is interpreted to mean money or clothing, then it represents one's status and high esteem his field. Receiving a ring as a gift in a dream also means happy news, or a marriage to a beautiful woman. Seeing an atheist who publicly brags about his actions and thoughts wearing a ring and turning its stone toward the palm of his hand in a dream, it means that he engages in sodomy. If a believer turns his ring inside during prayers in a dream, then it represents his modesty. Wearing a ring that carries two gemstones, one to the outside and the other to the inside in a dream means that one may chair two important appointments, material and a spiritual ones, or inner and outer ones. Wearing a ring with a carnelian-red stone in a dream means an end to one's poverty. If a pious person, a religious person or an ascetic receives a silver ring from God Almighty in a dream, it means his salvation on the Day of Judgment. If he receives a silver ring from God's Messenger (uwbp) in a dream, it represents a gift of a greater knowledge. If it is gold, iron, or copper, then it has negative consequences, because iron rings represent the chains of the dwellers of hell-fire. Somehow, to wear a simple band in one's dream is better than wearing a heavy ring. Heavy rings in a dream also may connote an assassination or deceit. On the other hand, large rings in a dream also can be interpreted to mean something great, or something which entails sizable benefits. Lead rings in a dream mean weak authority. If one sends his ring to some people who returns it to him in the dream, it means that he is asking to betroth someone from such a family, but his request will be declined. If one sees his ring being forcefully pulled out from his finger in a dream, it means that he will lose his rank or whatever the ring represents to him. If one loses his ring in a dream, it means that he will experience something he hates to see it happening to him. *(Also see Games; Solomon's ring)*

Ringdove: (Dove; Pigeon; Turtledove) A ringdove in a dream represents a rebellious son, or a son who lies excessively, or a wife who lacks devotion and tenderness, who is void of piety, who lies constantly, who possesses a difficult character, or who consents only to her own opinion and interpretations of things. A ringdove in a dream also represents a beautiful and an energetic woman who likes to show off. *(Also see Pigeon; Turtledove)*

Ringworm: *(See Herpes)*

Ripe: *(See Fresh)*

Ripping: To tear open one's garment in a dream means divorce, or marrying a virgin girl.

Rising in station: (Rank; Status) In a dream, rising in station means falling in people's esteem. Love to preside over others in a dream means the reversal of one's conditions for the worst. If one sees himself in a dream working hard at winning a leadership position, and if he wins an election in the dream, it means that he will grow in arrogance, then suffer from humiliation. Turning down an offer for a high ranking position or an elevated station in a dream means earning respect, honor, status and happiness. *(Also see Army's flag; Rank)*

Rising of the dead: (Resurrection) Seeing the rising of all the dead on the Day of Judgment in a dream represents people attending to their daily business and seeking profits where some will win while others will lose. *(Also see Resurrection)*

Rising prices: *(See Bread)*

Rising-up: *(See Awakening)*

Rising: *(See Ascending in the skies)*

Risk: *(See Gambling)*

Ritual ablution: *(See Ablution; Ritual bath)*

Ritual bath: (Ablution; Ghusul; Ritual ablution; Wash) A ritual bath *(arb. Ghusul. Islāmic Law)* is customarily performed on a festival day, or before the Friday congregational prayers, before starting a pilgrimage, after recovering from an illness, or is necessitated by the emission of sperms either during one's sleep or following a marital intercourse. A ritual ablution is also given to a deceased person before his funeral and burial, or otherwise is taken by the undertaker himself after washing the dead. To take a ritual ablution in a dream before the Friday congregational prayers means purifying oneself, washing oneself from sin, repenting from sin, serving one's parents, or being true to one's friends. Taking a ritual ablution for any of the above reason during the wintertime and using cold water in the dream means distress, trouble or a sickness. If hot water is used, then it means profits, benefits and recovering from sickness. Taking a ritual ablution in a dream before attending a festival means getting married. Taking a ritual ablution after seeing either a solar or a lunar eclipses in a dream means an adversity, and the same applies if one takes a ritual ablution in a dream before the prayers of asking for rain. To take a ritual ablution after washing a deceased person in a dream means abandoning one's association with heedless people. If the person who performs such an ablution is mentally deranged, it means that he will wake-up cured from his condition. Taking a ritual ablution prior to joining the sacred pilgrimage in a dream means happiness, success, victory over one's enemy, paying one's debts, or reuniting with one's beloveds. Taking a ritual ablution before circumambulating the sacred House in Mecca in a dream means working for one's livelihood, serving rich people, or caring for one's wife and parents. If a sick person sees himself taking a ritual ablution then putting on a new garment in a dream, it means that he will soon recover from his illness. Taking a ritual ablution in a dream also could mean the release of a prisoner, payment of one's debts, dispelling one's distress, or it could mean richness, prosperity, attending the sacred pilgrimage in Mecca, or having a successful business. If one does not put a new garment after taking his ritual ablution in the dream, it means that he will be able to lighten his burdens, or recover his good health. Walking into a pond, or descending a well, or stepping into a bathtub to take a bath in a dream means marriage. Washing oneself with soap during such an ablution means dispensing of one's debts, or dispelling one's stress. Washing one's garment after taking a _Ghusul_ in a dream means correcting one's conduct, pursuing the correct religious life, paying one's debts, or washing away one's filth. If one sees a deceased person washing himself before his burial in a dream, it means relief for one's dependents and increase of their wealth after him Giving a ritual ablution to a deceased person in a dream also means that someone will repent for his sins at the hand of the undertaker. If a deceased person asks someone to wash his clothes for him in a dream, it means that he needs someone to pray for him, or to intercede on his behalf before his Lord, or to pay charity for the benefit of his soul, or to pay his debts, or to fulfill his will, or to do him justice. If one does fulfills the deceased person's wish and washes his clothes for him in the dream, it means the redemption of such a person. _(Also see Ablution)_

Ritual impurity: _(See Excretion; Feces)_

Rituals of the pilgrimage: _(See 'Arafāt; Circumambulation; Cradle of Ismāīl; Ka'aba; Mina; Muzdalifa; Pelting stones; Responding; Sa'i; Station of Abraham; 'Umrah)_

River: In a dream, a river represents a noble and a great person. Walking into a river in a dream means befriending or encountering such a person. Drinking from a river in a dream means trials, but if the water is clear, it means enjoying prosperity and a happy life. Jumping from one bank of a river to the other in a dream means escaping from adversities, dispelling distress or anguish, and it means winning victory over one's enemy. In a dream, a river also denotes travels. Swimming in a river in a dream means working in the government. If the river runs through the streets and markets, and if one sees people bathing in it or taking their ritual ablution in it in one way or another it in a dream, such a river then represents the justice of a ruler. If the river floods the streets, or runs through people's homes and damages their properties and personal belongings in the dream, then the river represents an unjust ruler, or it could represent an invading army. If a river flows from one's house and causes no harm to anyone in a dream, it represents one's good intentions or deeds. If one becomes a river in a dream, it means his death. Murky waters in a dream signify worries and fearing a great man. Crossing from one side of a river into another in a dream means dispelling one's fears or worries. It also could mean severing one's association with such a man only to meet with another one. Jumping from the middle of a river to the riverbank in a dream means escaping from the wrath of a ruler. Losing something in a river means suffering harm and damages from a ruler. A river flowing inside one's house in a dream means prosperity. If one sees people drinking from it in the dream, it denotes his generosity and sharing of his wealth with needy people, or it could mean imparting knowledge to others.

If a poor person sees a river flowing inside his house in a dream, it means that he will drive a member of his household out of his house because of an abominable and a sinful act, or adultery. A river in a dream also means a good deed or a regular income. A river with murky and putrid waters in a dream represents hell-fire. Seeing one of the heavenly rivers of paradise in a dream means prosperity. The heavenly river of milk in a dream represents God's gift of the innate knowledge and criterion which is given to His creation, and it represents submission to His sovereignty and obedience to His commands. Seeing the heavenly river of non-intoxicating wine in a dream means elation and intoxication from one's love for God Almighty. Seeing the heavenly river of honey in a dream means knowledge or the Holy Qur'ān. Drinking from Egypt's Nile in a dream means receiving a great wealth, gold and power. *(Also see Euphrates; Kawthar; Walking on water; Water)*

Rivulet: *(See Fountainhead; Spring; Stream)*

Road: (Avenue; Direction; Path; Trail; Way) A road in a dream represents the divine law. Seeing many roads in a dream denotes deviation from God's path, or it could mean religious innovation. Walking on a side road, or yielding at a fork in a dream means going astray. If a highway robber attacks someone in a dream, it means that he will suffer from the loss of a friend. If one sees a ruler strolling through a rugged road in a dream, it means that he will establish justice and pave the way to righteousness and prosperity. A straight road in a dream represents God's path, or it could represent one's true faith in God's revelations, or in following the practice of God's Messenger, upon whom be peace, or following the guidance of one's teacher or shaikh. Walking on a straight path in a dream means repenting from one's sins and finding guidance. Seeing many roads in a dream means hesitancy, fluctuations in one's faith, doubt, heedlessness, or apostasy. A road in a dream also represents a craft, eternity, the past, aging, continuity, the good example, or the bad example. A boat following the correct sea lane in a dream means salvation. A road in a dream also represents a woman, one's livelihood, truth, or death. If a merchant sees himself walking on a road in a dream, it means that he will find new avenues to earn more money. A hidden road in a dream means pride, innovation and self-deception. *(Also see Lane; Roadless terrain; Wending one's way)*

Roadless terrain: (Rugged terrain) Walking a rugged terrain, then suddenly seeing oneself walking through plains in a dream means overcoming one's difficulties. Walking through roadless terrain in a dream also means stress, adversities, toiling, stagnation of one's business, or it could mean looking into the ample opportunities of one's life. A roadless terrain in a dream also means fear of wrongdoing, straying from the path of righteousness, or walking the avenues of innovation. A roadless terrain in a dream also means dullness or stupidity, while a plain in a dream signifies intelligence and keenness. *(Also see Road)*

Roaring: (Clamor) In a dream, roaring means witnessing social disorder, a public outcry, participating in a religious festival, or in an important event that involves the interest of all people. *(Also see Shout; Sound of animals)*

Roast: *(See Boiler; Deep frying; Kettle)*

Roasted meat: (Grilled meat; Restaurant) To buy roasted or grilled meat from a restaurant in a dream means enrolling one's children in a school and entrusting them to a good teacher to educate them and properly train them. The owner of such a restaurant represents an educator, a trainer or a shaikh. Buying from him in a dream also means hiring a worker who is trained at the hands of an experienced master. If one sees himself roasting or grilling meat in a dream, it means that he may become a tax collector, a physician, a jailer, a torturer, a thief, or a murderer. Seeing someone roasting meat on fire in a dream may denote a wedding, a picnic, or celebrating the birth of a new child. If the meat is well-cooked in a dream, it means good news. Otherwise, if the meat is still uncooked in the dream, it means a headache and stress caused by one's son. Roasting a whole sheep in a dream means money. Eating the meat of a roasted sheep in a dream means money earned through one's son. Roasting a calf in a dream means appeasement of one's fears, or news about one's wife giving birth to a son, or it could mean standing in court before a judge. Eating anything that is touched by fire in a dream means profits. If one sees a roasted leg of sheep talking to him in a dream, it means that he will escape from an accident, a danger, or gain a strong foothold, or become well established in this world. A broiled rib in a dream represents a woman, for Eve was created from Adam's rib. The chest represents plants and servants. The belly represents the children. A roasted leg in a dream represents woman's earnings that her husband regularly swindles from her. If it is uncooked, then it means slander or backbiting. Eating roasted or boiled meat in a dream also could mean hard earned money, fears, sorrows, pain and sufferings, an illness, or persecution. Broiling a female sheep, or a ewe in a dream represents an illness that may befall one's mother, wife or a relative. Broiling meat in a dream also means strength, marriage, health, wealth, the arrival of a traveller, love, unity, spying, telling on others, losing all benefits, squandering money, severing one's relationship with his family, cutting one's blood ties, or it cold denote a fever. (Also see Stakes)

Roasting: (See Boiler)

Robber: (Thief) In a dream, a thief represents a liar, or humiliation inflicted upon such a person. (Also see Crocodile; Robbery; Thief)

Robbery: (Burglary; Garding; Possessing) In a dream, a robbery means adultery or usury. If the thief is unknown in the dream, then he represents the Angel of Death. If the thief is known to the owner of the house, it means that he will benefit from his knowledge, his trade, a good word of wisdom, or from someone's advice. If an unknown thief enters one's house and steals his washing basin, or his blanket, or a feminine item, or a similar house item in a dream, it may mean the death of one's wife, or of a woman in his immediate family. If a known thief robs someone of his money in a dream, it means that he slanders him. If it is an unknown old man in the dream, it means that a close friend will backbite him. A robbery in a dream also has positive connotations, except for a swaggerer who lives on betraying others. If one sees himself sneaking up to steal something in a dream, it means that thieves will burglarize his house or business. If one sees himself stealing something in a dream, it means that he will commit adultery or lie. (Also see Thief)

Robe: (See Garment; Raiment)

Roc: (arb. *Rukhkh*; A legendary Arabian bird.) Seeing the legendary giant roc in a dream means fast travelling news coming from Western regions, or it could represent distant travels, playing with words, taunt with a serious subject, or just prattling.

Rocking chair: In a dream, a rocking chair means intelligence, clarity, or it could represent a hard working student.

Rocks: (Stone) Mountain rocks in a dream represent strong believers who hold fast to their religious duties. If one sees himself trying to lift a heavy rock, testing his strength in a dream, it means that he will face a strong opponent. If he succeeds at lifting it in the dream, it means that he will win his battle. Otherwise, it could mean that he will lose it. If one sees stones hitting him, or falling over his head in a dream, it means that his superior will delegate heavy responsibilities to him, compel him to do a personal favor, depend on him or impose a service on him. In this case, it means that one's advice will have effect and his opinion will be respected. Throwing stones in every direction from a high altitude in a dream means being unjust toward others, or it could mean being in a position of strength. If one sees women throwing stones at him using a slingshot in a dream, it means sorcery and a bad spell. If a poor person sees himself hitting a rock with a staff to split it, and suddenly water gushes forth from it in the dream, it means that he will become rich. A rock in a dream also represents hard working women who are patient and bearing their sufferings with determination. A rock in a dream also means longevity, construction, forgetfulness, cattle, impudence, shamelessness, fornication, a dissolute life, immorality, or heartlessness. Seeing a town scattered with rocks in a dream also could mean lower prices. If a rock is interpreted as a rank, then it means a lasting one. If it denotes one's wife, then it means that she is patient and content. A rock in a dream also represents a threshold, a house, or a statue. Seeing a mountain of rocks in a dream represents heartless, brutal and cruel men, or it could denote their dwellings. If one sees himself drilling a hole into a rock in a dream, it means that he is searching for something hard to get, though he will be able to reach as far as he reaches through drilling in his dream. Descending upon a rock in a dream is interpreted the same as descending upon a mountain in a dream. Rocks in a dream are also interpreted to mean dead people, heedlessness, ignorance, or immorality. *(Also see Stone)*

Rodent: *(See Mouse)*

Roll up: *(See Wrap up)*

Roller: (Any tropical bird of the Coraciidae family; Eurasian roller; Canary that rolls or trills its notes.) In a dream, a roller represents a beautiful and rich woman.

Rome: (Italy) Seeing the city of Rome in a dream means attainment of one's goal, or it could denote the defeat of his purpose.

Roof gutter: *(See Gutter; Roof)*

Roof: In a dream, a roof represents a noble and a well respected woman or man. If one sees himself running on top of a roof in a dream, it means that he will be struck with a calamity. Sitting on top of a roof in a dream during the summertime means comfort, dispelling aggravations, recovering from an illness, or divulging secrets.

Rook: (Carrion crow; Crow; Raven) Capturing a rook in a dream means receiving an inheritance, or it could mean presenting the truth before a jury in a court of justice that will be refuted, then presenting the judge with a false version that will be accepted. A rook in a dream also represents a highway robbery. *(Also see Crow)*

Room: *(See Chamber)*

Rooster: (Fighter) In a dream, a rooster represents the man of the house and a chicken represents the lady of the house. If one is offered a rooster in a dream, it means that he will beget a son who will spend his life serving others. A rooster in a dream also represents a man of bad character who also mixes serious talk with joking, and whose words carry no weight. A rooster in a dream also represents a servant who has compassion toward his master. Receiving a rooster as a gift in a dream means making peace with a friend. If one sees himself slaughtering a rooster in a dream, it means that he does not heed the call to prayers. A rooster hence represents the caller to prayers. Seeing a rooster in a dream also denotes increase in one's wisdom and knowledge, or frequenting the circles of knowledge. If one becomes a rooster in a dream, it means that he may die shortly, or it could mean that he will become knowledgeable about setting a timetable for the daily prayers. A rooster in a dream also represents a preacher, a reader of sermons, a singer, a man who commands good but does not practice it, a sexually obsessed person, a broker, a guard, a generous man, a man with good will and determination, or a man with a large family who gives preference to helping others, and contents himself with little.

Roots: (Edible roots. *See Taro*)

Rope: (Cable; Hawser) In a dream, a rope represents an agreement, a promise, or a covenant. A rope which is extended down from the heavens in a dream represents God's Book. However, a rope in a dream also represents rank, respect and prosperity, or it could mean deception, misleading others, or sorcery. Holding to a rope in one's dream represents one's strict adherence to God's path. If the rope is made from fibers in the dream, it means that the one holding it is a rough person. If it is made from leather in the dream, then it represents a bloody person. If the rope is made from wool in the dream, then it represents a religious person. Twisting a rope in a dream means going on a trip. Twisting it around one's own neck in the dream means getting married. Throwing it over one's shoulders in the dream means an important appointment resulting from a business trip. Twisting one's beard to make a rope out of it in a dream means perjury, receiving a bribe and giving a false testimony. Twisting a rope, making one, or measuring it in a dream means travels. Attaching a rope to a wooden stick or a staff in a dream means indulging in an evil act, or engaging in sorcery. *(Also see Cable)*

Rose oil: *(See Rose)*

Rose(s): (Blossoms; Kiss) In a dream, a rose represents a noble person, a woman, a newborn son, or it could represent the homecoming of a long awaited traveler. Plucking roses from a rosebush in a dream means harvesting honor, love, prosperity and blessings. Kissing a white rose in a dream means kissing a God-fearing woman. Plucking a red rose in a dream means kissing a fun loving woman. Smelling the fragrance of a yellow rose in a dream means kissing a sick woman. A bouquet of roses in a dream means kisses, one after the other. A rosebud in a dream means a miscarriage. A rose in a dream also represents an estranged wife, or it could mean a dying woman, a losing business, a short lived happiness, or a promise that does not last. Receiving a rose from a young man in a dream means receiving a promise that will not hold too. Seeing a crown of roses over one's head in a dream means getting married. Roses on a tray in a dream signify the pleasure of youth that does not last, or they could denote the temporary joy of this world. Roses in a dream also signify praiseworthiness, or enjoying a good reputation. Rose oil or attar which is made from the petals of damask roses in a dream means intelligence, clarity of mind, a friendly and a gentle person. If a sick person sees himself laying on a bed of flowers in a dream, it means that he might die within forty days, because forty days represent the life span of a rose blossom. Cutting off a rosebush in a dream means distress. Harvesting roses in a dream means joy.

Rose-water: *(See Distilled water)*

Rosebush: *(See Rose)*

Rough: *(See Rude)*

Row: (Line) To see people standing in a row in a dream means love and unity, performing one's duties, or it could mean attending a congregational prayer.

Rubber stamp: *(See Ring; Seal)*

Rubbing grease: *(See Grease)*

Rudders: *(See Ship)*

Rude: (Coarse; Rough) If someone in authority becomes rude, or if he is witnessed to be rude in a dream, it means loss of his job.

Rue: (*Peganum harmala; L., bot.* Herb of grace) A wild African rue plant the seeds of which resemble sesame seeds. Seeing it in a dream means investing lawful money to save a bad investment from an unlawful source. Seeing a rue plant in a dream, also known as herb of grace, means great profits, or multiplying one's earnings.

Ruffled hair: In a dream, seeing one's hair ruffled means stinginess and love to hoard money, or doing little for others.

Rug: (Mockado carpet; World) In a dream, a rug is interpreted to represent the world.

Rugged terrain: *(See Roadless terrain)*

Ruḥāniyyeen: *(See Angels)*

Rukū': *(See Bowing in prayers)*

Ruler: *(See Governor)*

Rumble: *(See Murmur)*

Rumbling of one's stomach: In a dream, rumbling of one's stomach means a family dispute, an argument, or an antagonistic competition between relatives. *(Also see Body¹)*

Rump: *(See Backside)*

Running away: (Escape; Fear; Take flight) Running away from something in a dream means turning to God Almighty and seeking refuge in Him for safety and protection. Running away in a dream also could mean receiving an appointment, or it could mean repentance from a sin, or it could mean one's death. If one sees himself running away to escape from an enemy he fears in a dream, it means that he will be safe. If a man of knowledge or a scholar sees himself running away from an enemy in fear in a dream, it means that he will be asked to sit as a judge, or to govern. If one sees himself running away but has no fear in the dream, it means his death. *(Also see Escape from danger; Take a flight)*

Rupture of relations: (Breach; Break; Enmity; Rift; Cutting off) Enmity among relatives and rupture of relations in a dream means straying away from God's path, heedlessness, paying a penalty, or it could mean suffering from being exiled as a punishment. *(Also see Enmity)*

Rural warden: (Keeper; Plantations guard; Warden) In a dream, a rural warden represents a rich person. If he looks at walnut trees in the dream, it means that he will control business interests for foreign people. If a warden looks at glass in a dream, it means that he will guard women's interests.

Rust: (Corrosion; Oxidize; Smut) In a dream, rust or corrosion represents an ostentatious and an affectatious person who displays piety and devotion during the day and contempt during the darkness of the night. It also could represent a thief, a highway robber, or a weak, tardy and negligent person, or a person who hoards money and likes to live alone.

S

Saber guard: *(See Knife handle)*

Sable: (Fur; Marten) In a dream, a sable represents an ungrateful person, a disbeliever, or an unjust person who lives in isolation, amasses wealth and no one can benefit from his riches until he dies. *(Also see Fur coat; Fur)*

Saboteur: *(See Tar)*

Sack: (Bag; Pouch; Suitcase; Trunk) A sack or any packing container in a dream represents travels, or activities in general. A sack in a dream also represents the body of a human being. An empty sack in a dream then means death. Seeing a sack within a sack in a dream represents the knowledge one benefited from during his life in this world. If the second sack contains money in the dream, it means that one's knowledge is true. If it contains change, it means that one is still studying and needs to further his knowledge. A sack in a dream also represents one's personal and secret life. In a dream, if one makes a cut through a sack and throws its contents asunder, it means that his private and intimate life will be exposed and becomes the subject of people's talk. If one's money falls through a hole in the bag or a purse he carries, the bag also represents his body and the money represents his soul, which is an indication of his death. If one finds termites or moths inside his sack in a dream, it also means death. Thus, a sack in a dream denotes what a person represents, or it could mean one's heart. *(Also see Bag; Pouch; Purse; Suitcase; Trunk)*

Sacking needle: (Needle; Upholsterer's needle) A sacking needle in a dream represents a woman, because of its threading hole. Holding a sacking needle in a dream means travels, or if one's wife is pregnant, it means that she will beget twin girls.

Sacrament: *(See 'Aqïqah rites)*

Sacred mosque: *(See Masjïd)*

Sacrification: *(See Cupping)*

Sacrifice: (Immolation) To offer a sacrifice in a dream means to fulfill one's promises, relief from difficulty, healing of the sick, or increase in one's earnings. If the one offering a sacrifice interprets dreams as a profession, then it means that he has misinterpreted someone's dream, that he gave him bad advice, or sacrificed the interest of the person in question. Sacrificing in a dream also means receiving an inheritance. If a pregnant woman sees such a dream, it means that she will bear a righteous son. *(Also see Abraham; Ismāïl; Immolation; Lamb; Offering; Ram; Sheep)*

Saddle cloth: In a dream, a saddle cloth represents marriage, a judicial or a political appointment, moving to a new house, moving to a new shop, or it could mean travels.

Saddle mount: In a dream, a saddle mount represents a boy, a dependable and a trustworthy servant, woman's vagina, or the foundation of a house. If one sees himself putting his right foot in it in a dream, it means that he will have sexual intercourse with his wife. A saddle mount in a dream also represents one's vehicle, comfort, job, travels, a carpet, a farm, wife, son, honest money, or a presidency. If one finds that his saddle mount has a cut, or if it disappears in the dream, it means that he will sell his saddle, or his vehicle, or that his dear servant may die shortly. *(Also see Saddle)*

Saddle: (Appearance; Burden; Control; Hamper; Impose; Money; Seat; Seat of authority; Woman) A saddle in a dream represents the end of one's sufferings, difficulty, or bad luck, or it could mean planning a journey. Mounting a saddle in a dream means getting married for comfort and companionship. Descending from a saddled animal in a dream means repentance from a wrongdoing after excessive indulgence in its sensations for a while. An unmounted saddle in a dream represents a woman. Seeing a saddle in a dream also represents sexual intercourse. If a dog, a pig, or a donkey sits in one's saddle in a dream, it means that an ignoble person will betray him with his wife. Riding with a saddled animal in a dream also means continuous success, or a growing victory. A broken saddle in a dream means death. To dismount a saddle in a dream also means divorcing one's wife. *(Also see Saddle mount)*

Saddlebags: In a dream, a saddlebag represents expensive merchandise, comforts, or travels.

Saddler: In a dream, a saddler represents someone who has determination, and who takes matters into his own hands. This element also may represent a religious person, or the officiant or a Muezzin who performs wedding ceremonies.

Saddling an animal: Improper saddling of an animal for a ride in a dream means imposition upon oneself or others, or it could mean unnecessary and inadequate going out of one's way.

Safā: *(arb.* Hill of Safā; Mecca. *See Rituals of the pilgrimage; Sa'i)*

Safar: *(See Arabic months)*

Safe: *(See Closet; Protection; Veil; Wife)*

Safety pin: *(See Pin)*

Safflower: (Dyestuff; Orange) Safflower in a dream represents a pleasant party that will be interrupted or followed by bad news. Safflower in a dream also represents one's working tools, a war proclamation, the defeat of those who call for a war, and women's role in provoking a fight. If safflower is planted around the thorny tragacanth plant *(bot. Astragalus)* in a dream, it means receiving overwhelming benefits one did not anticipate.

Saffron: (Aroma; Perfume; Stigma) In a dream, If dried saffron does not stain the skin or a gown, then it represents lauding someone, commending him, or speaking good of someone. If its color does stain the skin or one's gown in the dream, then it represents an illness. Grinding the dried purple saffron flowers in a dream to use it as powder, or as an additive for making perfumes in a dream represents a severe illness, though many people will pray for the recovery of the person who is struck by it, but to no avail. It is also said that saffron in a dream represents benefits, except if it touches one's skin or stains it. Grinding saffron in a dream means producing something one will view with pride and be amazed by its results, though again, one's efforts will be followed by a severe illness. Grinding saffron in a dream means illness, exposing secrets, divulging confidential information, or it could mean deeds that will bring happiness, or it could denote studying, or acquiring knowledge. If a woman sees herself grinding saffron in a dream, it means that she is a lesbian, or a female homosexual. *(Also see Miller)*

Sagittarius: *(astr.* See Moon)

Sa'i: *(arb.* Encompassing the two hills of Safā and Marwa; Mecca; Rituals of the pilgrimage) Encompassing the two hills of Safā and Marwa in a dream denotes one's righteousness and correctness. It also means reconciliation between two people, quelling a conflict, mediating between two people and bringing about a just and a peaceful agreement. If the one who is walking between the two hills in the dream is a judge, it means that he will be just and equitable. If he is a husband, it means that he will be just with his wife, or true to his parents. If one is ill, it means that he will recover from his illness and return to earning his livelihood. *(Also see Rituals of the pilgrimage)*

Sail maker: A sail maker in a dream represents travels, preparing oneself to start a business, to equip a major project, or to get married.

Sailboat: *(See Ship)*

Sails: (Captain; Manager; Ship) In a dream, the sails of a ship represent its captain, or they could represent a good manager, or they could mean gaining power. If one sees sails being raised to honor him in a dream, it means that he will attain power, leadership, honor and exaltation. If a ruler or a general of an army sees such a dream, it means that he will remain strong and secured from enemy attacks.

Saint tree: *(See Tree)*

Saker: (Falcon; Hawk) In a dream, a saker means a son, high rank, authority, or a respected, dignified and awe-inspiring person who comes from noble lineage though he is unjust. If one sees a saker pursuing him in a dream, it means that he has incurred the wrath of a strong and a courageous man who does what he says. Seeing a saker without a fight in a dream means profits, and the same interpretation applies to most hunting birds or animals. Owning a hunting saker who is well trained and obedient in a dream means gaining authority, or becoming unjust and ungodly. Owning a disobedient saker that does not hunt in a dream means begetting a son who will grow to manhood and be independent. A saker in a dream also signifies might, rank, victory, attaining one' goals, adversities, death, prison, shackles, adornment, or tightening one's grip on expenses. A trained saker in a dream also represents an articulate man of knowledge, verses an untamed saker in the dream.

Ṣalāt: *(arb. See Five times prayers)*

Sale: If one sees himself as a prisoner being sold in a slave market in a dream, it means honor if the buyer is a woman, and difficulties if the buyer is a man. The higher the price he is auctioned for, the better or worse is his luck. In a dream, the more loss the buyer incurs, the better it is for the traded subject and vice-versa. There is also a difference between seeing oneself being auctioned and being sold. Being auctioned in a dream means evil. To sell means to part with. In a dream, the buyer is the seller and the seller is a buyer. Selling means giving preference and value to the merchandise. If what is being sold is worldly, the preference is then given to one's benefits in the hereafter. Selling in a dream also means exchanging one condition with another. However, bartering in a dream means to exchange the benefit of things, or to share them. If for example one sees himself in a dream trading something of no value for something precious, and if he is a warrior, it means that he will die as a martyr. Selling a free man in a dream means rotation of power and reaching a praiseworthy end. As it happened in the story of Joseph son of Jacob, upon both of them be peace. *(See Introduction)*

Salesman: If one sees himself in a dream invoking false oath, or making false claims to market his merchandise, it means that he will turn into that state to live in falsehood and oppose his own conscious. This includes prejudice, belittling the value of things, underweighing the selling measures, or accumulating interest from usury. A wheat salesman in a dream denotes someone who loves the world and does not think about his life in the hereafter. If one sees himself receiving money for his merchandise, or if he discards his profits from the sale in his dream, such an act maybe rewarding. Selling yarn in a dream means travel. Selling salt in a dream means earning extra money. Selling expensive fashion clothing and declining from taking money in a dream represents a trustworthy person who will attain a high ranking position. A fruit salesman in a dream represents a hard-working man who gives priority to his religious life over that of the world. An aromatic herbs salesperson in a dream represents a soft hearted man who cries easily, or a Qur'ān reader who recites its verses in an emotional way that affects his listeners. Birds salesman in a dream represents a pimp, while a lead salesman in a dream represents someone with meagre goals.

Ṣaliḥ: (God's prophet Ṣāliḥ, upon whom be peace. He is the descendent of the people of Thamūd, the son of 'Abir, the brother or Arām, the son of Sām, the son of Noah, upon whom be peace. The prophet Ṣāliḥ delivered God's message to the tribe of Thamūd who lived in the North-Western corner of the Arabian peninsula, in Petraea between Medina and Syria, 700 B.C.) Seeing God's prophet Ṣāliḥ (uwbp) in a dream means that one may suffer from the persecution of arrogant and ungodly people then triumph over them, by God's leave, in a war between truth and falsehood. Seeing him (uwbp) in a dream also means that one may give up his struggle against such people, following a major clash and display of differences. It also shows that the one who sees him in a dream is a righteous and a true believer.

Salsola kali: *(See Mill)*

Salt shaker: *(See Salt)*

Salt: (Condiment; Veteran) In a dream, salt means easy money, common people and a good person. Seeing an argument between two adversaries and witnessing salt placed between them in a dream means that they will allay their differences and make peace. If common salt becomes spoiled in a dream, it means that a plague, injustice, or a drought will befall the people of that locality. Salt in a dream also signifies hard work, or an illness. Table salt in a dream also means asceticism, renunciation and detachment from the material world. It also means blessings, honesty and comfort. Eating bread with salt in a dream means contentment with little from this world. A salt shaker in a dream represents a good and a dutiful woman. Discovering salt in a dream means adversities and a severe illness. Salt in a dream also represents balance, usability of things and acceptability of everything. This includes knowledge, religion, wife, money, child and lawful earnings. Salt in a dream also means appeasement of one's fear, peacefulness, developing patience and forbearance. Salt in a dream also represents a medicine, a remedy, drugs, love, tenderness, unity, compassion, earning suspicious money, or a conspiracy. Receiving a fish preserved in salt in a dream means good news. Olives treated with salt in a dream means recanting one's promise.

Saltwort: *(See Mill)*

Salve: *(See Electuary)*

Sanctimonious: *(See Besmear)*

Sanctuary: In a dream, a sanctuary represents marriage to a righteous woman. *(Also see Hermitage; Retreat; Temple)*

Sand: In a dream, sand represents money. Carrying a handful of sand in a dream means pursuing a business. If one carries a heavy load of sand in a dream, it means that he will suffer for his sins. Swallowing sand or gathering it in a dream denotes savings. Walking on sand in a dream means pursuing either a spiritual or a mundane interest, or it could represent a sad event, a fight, or committing injustice toward one's own soul or against others. Depending on the quantity seen in one's dream, gathering sand may mean shackles, a siege, life or death, poverty or richness, and honor or humiliation. Sand in a dream also means toiling or difficulties. If a woman sees herself walking on sand in a dream, it means the death of her husband. If a man sees such a dream, it means the death of his wife. Red sand in a dream represents a high ranking position. White sand in a dream means profits for fortunetellers. Yellow sand in a dream means repentance, recovering from an illness, or tightening of one's livelihood. A pile of sand collected at the feet of a tree in a dream represents a construction project, or urban expansion. *(Also see Hourglass)*

Sandals: *(See Shoes)*

Sandglass: *(See Hourglass)*

Sanding: (Wood sanding) In a dream, sanding represents a person who extricates the truth and cleans it from slur through painstaking efforts, knowledge, wisdom and experience.

Sandpiper: (Bird) A sandpiper in a dream represents a virgin, a woman, or a wife.

Sanitation: (Garbage; Refuse; Sweeping) Sanitation in a dream means profits for its professionals, a street sweeper, or a garbage collector. If a poor person sees himself engaged in such a profession in his dream, it means easing of his difficulties, and making money from a new employment. If a rich person sees himself managing such a business in his dream, it means profits, leadership, honor and earning everyone's respect. *(Also see Garbage; Sweeping the floor; Trash collector)*

Sapphire: In a dream, sapphire represents an honorable, noble, dignified, wealthy and a prosperous woman. *(Also see Stone²)*

Sarcophagus: (Casket; Coffin; Mummy case) A dead person or a mummy inside a sarcophagus in a dream represents unlawful money. If the coffin is empty in the dream, then it represents a house of evil, or an evil person who is sought by people of the same trade. *(Also see Coffin)*

Sash: *(See Cummerbund)*

Sasin: *(See Mountain goat)*

Sasquatch: (Bigfoot; Fabulous being; Fictitious creature) In a dream, a Sasquatch represents a person of little intelligence and who leads himself to a breakdown. Such a person disrupts his life by his own actions and becomes despised in people's eyes.

Satan: Seeing the accursed one in a dream means evil, sin, lying, stealing, jealousy, sorcery, separation between husband and wife, disdain from performing one's prayers, or it could mean preaching falsehood. Seeing the accursed one in a dream also means propagation of an invented world or ideas. If in a dream one becomes Satan, it is interpreted as loosing one's sight. If one kills Satan in a dream, it means that he will deceive and conquer a deceiver and an evil person. In a dream, the accursed Satan also represents an enemy of the body and the soul. He deceives, cheats, disbelieves, as well as he is ungrateful, jealous, capricious, arrogant, heedless, impetuous, or he could represent a leader, a minister, a judge, a policeman, a man of knowledge, a preacher, a hypocrite, or one's own family and children. Seeing Satan in a dream also means villainy, dirt, passion and sexual devilry. If one sees Satan attacking him in a dream, it means that he earns his money from usury. If Satan touches him in a dream, it means that someone is slandering or trying to deceive his wife. If one is sick or under stress, and if he sees Satan touching him in a dream, it means that he will put his hand on material wealth. If one is suffering from the consequences of devilry while he recognizes his trials and remains steadfast in remembering God Almighty and calling upon Him for help in a dream, it means that he has many enemies trying to deceive him or to destroy him, though they will eventually fail, and in turn, they will be defeated by God's leave. If one sees Satan following him in a dream, it means that an enemy is pursuing him to deceive him, and consequently one will lose his status, rank and the benefits of his knowledge. If one sees himself inwardly talking with Satan in a dream, it means that he will join hands with his own enemy, and his strike will be against the righteous people, though he will ultimately fail. If one sees Satan teaching him something in a dream, it means that he will fabricate a story, speak falsehood, or recite poems filled with lies. If one sees that Satan has descended upon him in a dream, it means that he engages in falsehood and sin. If one sees himself presiding over a band of satans, controlling them, commanding them, and if they obey him in the dream, it means that he will receive a seat of honor and he will be feared by his friend and foes. If one ties Satan with chains in a dream, it means that he will win victory in his life together with might and fame. If one sees himself deceived by a group of satans in a dream, it means that he will suffer financial losses or lose his job. If Satan strips someone from his clothing in a dream, it means that the latter will lose a battle to an enemy. If one sees Satan whispering something in his ear in dream, it means that he will be dismissed from his job. If one sees himself defying and fighting Satan in a dream, it means that he is a true and a strong believer who obeys his Lord and who holds fast to his religious obligations. If Satan frightens him in a dream, it means that the latter is a sincere deputy and a protégé of God Almighty, and that God will safeguard him from any fear of the accursed Satan or his army. If one sees a meteor or a flame shooting at Satan in the skies in a dream, it means that there is an enemy of God Almighty in that locality. If that person is a ruler, then his secrets will be exposed, and if he is a judge, it means that a just punishment will befall him for his injustice. If one sees Satan happy in a dream, it means that he engages in sensuality, passion and loathsome actions. In general, Satan is a weak enemy, if one sees himself fighting him with resoluteness in a dream, it shows that he is a religious and a pious person. If Satan swallows someone or penetrates inside his body in dream, it means a fright, losses and sufferings. Satan in a dream also represents builders or ocean divers who work as spies. Seeing them in a dream also could mean backbiting or slandering. If one sees himself as a Satan in a dream, it means that he constantly frowns with people and that he is quick to harm them, or that he may work at cleaning sewers, or perhaps he may perish in a fire, or die as a heedless person.

Satisfaction: Satisfaction in a dream means relief from difficulties and repentance from sin.

Saturn: (Planet) In a dream, the planet Saturn represents subjugation, rulership, deputyship, power of attorney, or seeking any of the above. If one sees the planet Saturn close to the moon in dream, it means that he is thinking of business expansion, real estate, properties, or buildings. The planet Saturn in a dream also represents a person who lives in the wilderness and mixes with wildlife, buffalos, dears, peacock, francolin, parrots, or any beautiful looking animal, or it could represent a caterpillar, silk, or a stripped fabric denoting an architect, or a caller to prayers, or any courteous employee who willingly and wholeheartedly serves others. The planet Saturn in a dream also means punishment, poverty, business losses or adversities.

Sauce pan: If a traveller sees a sauce pan in his dream, it may mean drowning. A sauce pan in a dream also represents the house manager, the butler, the governor, the judge, the superintendent, the tax collector, or the internal revenues administrator.

Sausages: *(See Meat)*

Saw: In a dream, a saw represents a forgiving person, or a mediator who negotiates back and forth. A saw in a dream also may represent a judge, an arbitrator, or marriage. A saw in a dream also means division of assets, a scale, or a perfidious person who loves to create division between a husband and a wife, and to separates between them. A saw in a dream also represents a cunning person, unfair dealings between people, hypocrisy, evil, an informant, or sexual intercourse. A saw in a dream also represents a helper, strength, profits, a public ordinance, a proclamation, a learned person, or a judge. A lumberman's saw in a dream represents an astringent and an austere headman. A marble saw in a dream signifies running out of tricks, or presenting an unsatisfactory proof. A handsaw in a dream represents a layman, a miller, or sieve merchant, etcetera.

Scabies: *(See Plague)*

Scale beam: *(See Steelyard)*

Scale: (Balance; Measure) Seeing a scale in a dream means renewal of one's business. Depending one the truthfulness by which one weighs his business, or product, a scale in a dream also means profits or a fine. Receiving a scale as a gift in a dream means that one may become a judge. The same applies if one sees himself transformed into a scale in a dream. If one sees merchants short weighing their merchandise in a dream, then a scale will represent a judge who deviates from justice. *(Also see Balance; Measure²; Measurer; Weight)*

Scallion: *(See Onion)*

Scarab: (Dung beetle; Evil spell; Charm) In a dream, a scarab represents vileness, a despicable nature, or mixing with lowly people.

Scarce: *(See Little)*

Scarcity: *(See Famine)*

Scarf: *(See Head cover)*

Scepter: (Authority; Mace) A scepter in a dream means good conduct, emulating the leading example of the Prophet Muhammad, upon whom be peace, rising to a high ranking position, or becoming an authority. A scepter in a dream also could represent a wild son, a crooked man, or a hypocrite. Playing with a scepter in dream means using the help of such a person and assisting him to lay hands on his rivals. The crosier represents the human heart and the staff represents man's tongue. Thus, playing with a scepter in a dream means playing at will. Whatever may affect a scepter in a dream can be interpreted as affecting one's son or his tongue. If one sees himself hitting a small ball with a septer, or playing with a ball in his dream, it represents a dispute with his wife, or a fight with a hypocritical person. A scepter in a dream also indicates the presence of jinn spirits, wars, devastations, or it could represent past benefits. Hitting someone with a scepter in dream means getting what one desires from him, but through crooked ways. If one sees his governor or his boss carrying a scepter in dream, it means that he will be appointed to head an important project.

Scholars: (Early companions; Legist; Masjid; Men of knowledge; Mosque; Religious doctors; Righteous men) A scholar in a dream represents glad tidings, a promotion, or a commendation and it represents one who acts upon what he knows and says. Seeing one of the early scholars in a dream means increase in one's knowledge, for they were the wise representatives of God's message on earth. Seeing them also means increase in one's wisdom, happiness, joy, and one's dream could mean that one will stand to admonish people or counsel them. Seeing the early righteous people and the blessed companions of God's Prophet, upon whom be peace, in a dream means growth of one's righteousness. If one sees a scholar who is considered to be a reference in religious knowledge, and if one accepts his admonition in the dream, though in wakefulness he does not follow this school of thought, it means that he will be tried with an adversity that will be remembered by people for sometime to come, though his testimony will be accepted by the people. If a well-known early scholar appears in one's dream when the dwellers of that locality are experiencing adversities, economic distress or a drought, it means that their calamity will be lifted. Seeing an unknown scholar, or an unknown religious doctor in a dream means that a physician or a philosopher may visit one's house. *(Also see Legist; Companions of the Prophet; uwbp; Masjid; Mosque)*

School: (Institute; Learning; Tutoring) In a dream, a school represents its teachers, scholars, a gnostic, a school of thought, or its founder. Seeing a school in a dream also could mean divorcing one's wife then returning her to wedlock. It also means righteousness, establishing the divine laws, promoting a business, or inviting trouble. *(Also see Institute)*

Scission: *(See Cutting off)*

Scissors: (Clippers; Shears) In a dream, scissors mean slander and causing harm to someone's reputation without regard for the truth. Scissors in a dream also represent a legal guardian who discerns between true and false. Holding a pair of scissors in a dream means delivering a brother for one's first born son, or having two businesses feeding one another, unless if one is unmarried, then holding a pair of scissors, or a nail clipper in a dream means getting married. If one sees a pair of scissors falling from the skies in a dream, they represent the scissors of destiny and the end of his life in this world. Clipping people's beards in a dream means backbiting them. A pair of scissors in a dream also represents business partners. Sheep shearing with a pair of scissors in a dream means prosperity. Holding a pair of scissors in a dream also means a dispute that requires a judge or a mediator.

Scoop: *(See Shovel)*

Scorch: *(See Cauterize; Seal)*

Scorpio: *(astr. See Moon)*

Scorpion: (Calamity; Misfortune) A scorpion in a dream means distress, dismay and trouble caused by a chatterer or a backbiter. A scorpion in a dream also means that one may be deceived by someone with a scorpion quality, and particularly if he uses a short haircut around the ears in the dream. A scorpion in a dream also represents a backbiter and an enemy from within one's family. If one catches a scorpion inside his own house and throws it at his wife in the dream, it means that he engages with a loathsome and a forbidden sexual relationship with her from the anus. If a scorpion attacks people in a dream, the scorpion there represents a homosexual. A yellow scorpion in a dream represents a fierce enemy, though he would have more patience in getting at his prey. A yellow scorpion in a dream also means incoming money. Killing a yellow scorpion in a dream means making a good investment that will show profits. The sting of a scorpion in a dream represents the benefits one will receives and they will not remain long in one's possession. If scorpions pierce through the walls of one's house in a dream, it means the death of one's enemy. A scorpion in one's pants in a dream represents an enemy who blackmail or takes advantage of one's wife. Eating a cooked or a broiled scorpion in a dream means making money behind the back of one's enemy, or winning a just inheritance case against one's opponent. Eating an uncooked scorpion in a dream means backbiting a corrupt person. Eating a scorpion uncooked in a dream also means getting unlawful money. A scorpion coming out of one's anus in a dream means begetting children who will turn enemies of their father. Swallowing a scorpion in a dream means letting an enemy inside one's house. A scorpion inside one's shirt or shop in a dream represents trouble and distress regarding one's livelihood. A scorpion sitting on one's bed in dream represents an inside enemy. A scorpions inside one's stomach in a dream represents the enmity of one's employees or children who work for their father. A scorpion in a dream also represents someone who speaks his mind and does not know his friend from his enemy. A scorpion in a dream also represents an enemy who lacks determination or will. Killing a scorpion in a dream means that one will capture and destroy his enemy. If one sees something that resembles a scorpion but is not a scorpion in a dream, it means that he has suspicion about someone who is not an enemy. The stingers of a scorpion in a dream represent one's tongue. (Also see Sting)

Scourge: (Whip) In a dream, a scourge means fulfilling one's needs, attaining one's goal, or subjugating one's enemy to accept one's conditions. If one's scourge is cut in two pieces during a fight, or while lashing someone in a dream, it means loss of power. If the rope splits, it means weakening of one's authority. If one sees himself driving an animal with a whip in a dream, it means praying to Almighty God to ease his burdens and to facilitate his earnings. If one sees himself riding a horse and hitting him hard with a scourge in a dream, it means that he is in dire need and is praying for a way out of his difficulties. If one sees himself lashing a sitting person with a scourge in a dream, it means admonishing him, and if the other person is scared, or if he shields his face with his arm in the dream, it means repentance from sin. If he is not hurt by the scourge in the dream, it means that he is stubborn and does not accept the good advice. If he bleeds in the dream, it means that he is beaten unjustly. If the victim's blood splashes and stains one's clothes in the dream, it means that he will receive suspicious or unlawful money from his victim. If one's scourge is bent in the dream, it means a mental disorder, or that one's assistant is a reckless or an impatient person.

Scowling: (Frowning) Scowling in a dream connotes a misfortune.

Scraps: (See Trash)

Scratch: (Injury; Wounds) In a dream, a scratch represents financial harm. If one sees another person scratching him in a dream, it means that he will cause him partial financial loss, or pain with respect to a family member, or perhaps he will accuse him of something, then compensate him for injuring his reputation. If the scratch gets infected, bleeds, or produces pus or purulence in the dream, it means that the assailant will slander him and cause a major collapse to his business. If the scratch is over one's forehead in the dream, it means that he may die quickly. A scratch in a dream also represents a bad reputation, an acronym, or a nickname such as stingy, insolent, or apostate, etcetera. A scratch in a dream also means recanting one's statement. (Also see Scratching)

Scratching: (Itch) Scratching in a dream represents the element of caring for one's kin, though headache may follow. If the itch stops in the dream, it means reaping the benefits of one's deeds. (See Body[1])

Scream: (See Shout)

Screeching of a pen: The screeching sound of a pen in a dream represents a writer, or writing on paper, or writing on a chalkboard. Such screeching in a dream also could represent the chalkboard itself, or teachers of various grades. As for most people, hearing the screeching of a pen in a dream means divulging secrets, or attacking people's reputation in the process of attaining one's selfish goals.

Scribble: (See Write)

Scribe: (Secretary; Tailor. See Writer)

Scribes: (Angels; Record keepers) If a pious person sees the recording angels in a dream, it means glad tidings, prosperity, happiness and joy in this world and in the hereafter. If an ungodly person sees them in a dream, it means that he should correct his life and seek the company of pious and good people. (Also see Record keepers)

Scrolls: (See Book; Letter; Table of contents; Tablet; Write)

Sculpturing: (See Stonemasonry; Wood sculptor)

Scum: (See Foam; Sludge)

Scythe: (Death; Mowing; Sickle) In a dream, a scythe means profits, good harvest, good news, true news, or the harvest of one's life. *(Also see Scissors)*

Sea gull: *(See Plover)*

Sea onion: *(See Squill)*

Sea: *(See Ocean)*

Seabird: *(See Plover)*

Seafood restaurant: (Fish) In a dream, a seafood restaurant represents adversities, fights, evil, stress, depression, or relief from difficulties. *(Also see Fishery)*

Seal: (Brand; Lock; Stamp) If one sees a person in authority placing the seal of his ring on a document in a dream, it means that he will receive an important appointment. To see someone branding and sealing people's hearing, sights, mouth or hearts in a dream means that God Almighty abhors their actions and qualities. If a qualified person sees himself stamping cases of merchandise, or sealing coffers with his ring in a dream, it means that he may receive such a position or become a controller. If he is poor, it also means that his needs will be promptly satisfied. *(Also see Cauterize)*

Seaman: (Captain; Mariner; Sailor) In a dream, a seaman or the captain of a ship represents a jailor, a ghetto leader, a coach driver, a minister, an army general, a manager, a mediator, or a carrier.

Seaport: In a dream, a seaport represents a trustworthy person one can consign or store his belongings with him in trust.

Sear: (Scorch. *See Cauterize; Back; Seal)*

Search: *(See Piercing a hole; Pursuit; Tunnel)*

Searching for someone: *(See Piercing a hole; Tunnel)*

Seasonal sweets: In a dream, seasonal sweets represent witnessing an annual festival, or the reelection of a just ruler. *(Also see Pastry)*

Seat of authority: *(See Chair; Saddle)*

Seat: (Chair) One's seat in a dream represents his capital, wealth, work, profit, joy, happiness, a good son, or a wife who is content with what she has. Seeing a deceased person sitting relaxed in a comfortable chair in a dream means that he is in paradise. A chair in a dream also represents a contractual agreement, making an oath, peace, tranquility and comfort, or it could mean establishing a business partnership. *(Also see Chair; Saddle)*

Seclusion: *(See Hermitage)*

Second wife: *(See Polygamy)*

Secret service: *(See Bodyguard)*

Secret: (Confiding) A secret in a dream means marriage. If someone tells a secret that does not denote marriage, then it means becoming a shareholder in a business, or it could mean trusting someone, or inheriting him. *(Also see Confiding)*

Secretary: (Keeping a secret; Scribe; Secretary of state; Tailor; Vice-regent; Writer) In a dream, a secretary represents someone who is acquainted with the ins-and-outs of a business, or a woman who is aware of the private life of her employer, or she could be his wife or his mistress. *(Also see Keeping a secret)*

Security: *(See Guarantee; Pawn)*

Sedan chair: A sedan chair in a dream means moving from one place to another, activities, travels, business, or a noble and a well respected woman. *(Also see Palanquin; Litter)*

Sedatives: *(See Intoxicants)*

Seedling: *(See Planting a tree)*

Seeds: Planting seeds in a dream represent the element of progeny and procreation.

Scattered seeds on the ground in a dream mean bearing a child for each seed. As for the grains that are germinated for medicinal purpose, when seen in a dream, they mean acquiring knowledge that helps the person in question to increase his or her piety and ascetic detachment from worldly matters. Pumpkin, cucumber, eggplant, sweet basil, chard, onion, cabbage, Indian corn and melon seeds in a dream mean abating or ceasing of difficulties and disturbances, or they could mean recovering from a terminal illness. If one sees himself trying to plant something which is not a plant, or to place a seed in an unsuitable ground in a dream, it means that he is wasting his money and squandering his property. To plant seeds in a dream also could mean knowledge, wealth or recognizing a noble trade. Sprouted seeds in a dream represent honor and status. However planting seeds in a dream also represent mixing with evil people. *(Also see Earth; Extracting oils from seeds)*

Seeping: (Leaking) Seeping water from a crack in a wall in a dream means adversities and distress caused by a brother or an in-law.

Seer: (Dream interpreter) If a seer who predicts events or a dream interpreter sees himself falling into a deep well in a dream, it means that he will be involved with the life of governors, or high society who will seek his council to interpret their dreams. *(Also see Dream interpreter)*

Seizing: *(See Gripping)*

Self-control: *(See Patience)*

Selling: *(See Sale)*

Semen: (Sperm) In a dream, semen represents a growing and a lasting capital, whether there is little or much of it. If one sees a drop of semen coming out of his reproductive organs in a dream, it denotes money that will surface. If the man's semen spatters over his wife in the dream, it means that he will buy her a new garment. Owning an earthenware jar filled with semen in a dream means uncovering a hidden treasure, or becoming wealthy. If the husband is spattered with the semen of his wife in a dream, it means that he will satisfy his desire for her and attain his purpose. Drinking water from one's own reproductive organ in a dream means lustfulness. If the husband sees a thick yellowish fluid flowing from his wife's sexual organ in a dream, it means that she will give birth to an unhealthy child. If a reddish fluid flows instead in the dream, it represents a short lived child. If it comes out as a black fluid in the dream, it means that such a child will grow to dominate the family and to be an unjust master of the household. The ovum of a beautiful woman in a dream means happiness, wealth and children. Semen in a dream also means attaining one's goal, comfort, or wasting one's capital, divulging one's secrets, or the death of a child. If a farmer sees semen in his dream, it means that he will work on a barren land and make it fertile. *(Also see Impurity; Sexual intercourse; Vagina)*

Semolina: *(See Flour)*

Seniors: *(See Elders)*

Sentinel: *(See Patrol)*

Separate: *(See Sieve)*

Separation: *(See Pencil sharpener; Wall)*

September: *(See Earthquake; Thunder)*

Sequins: (Glitters; Pilgrimage; World) Wearing a garment which is adorned with brilliant silk and decorated with glittery sequins in a dream means money or prosperity. If the color of the sequins is red in the dream, it means renewal of his material success. If it is yellow in the dream, it means wealth which is accompanied with health problems. All types and colors of sequins in a dream represent money except the yellow ones.

Sergeant: (Military) To see oneself as a sergeant in the army, or as a lieutenant in the police in a dream means gaining power, respect, fame, commendation, or perhaps one may become a muezzin in a mosque.

Sermon: *(See Preacher; Pulpit)*

Servants: (Angels; Vinegar) If one sees servants carrying platters of food, sweets and fruits to serve in one's house in a dream means that someone in that house who had a long illness has just recovered from it, or that he may die as a martyr. Servants in a dream also represent glad tidings. If a king, a merchant, or a man of knowledge see himself eating from the hand of a servant or a nurse in dream, it represents his authority, knowledge, wisdom, falling sick, or it could mean business expansion. *(Also see Slave)*

Serviette: *(See Towel)*

Serving: To serve the poor in a dream, to humble oneself to them, to lower one's wings to the believers, to stand before the righteous people with respect and obey their instructions in a dream means being extremely lucky in God's sight, and that one can anticipate a good conclusion to his life in this world. It also could mean joining the company of gnostics and the circles of righteous people in this world, and God willing, one will rise in station in this world and in the hereafter.

Sesame oil: In a dream, sesame oil represents someone who enjoys a material and a spiritual life. If burned, then its light means guidance, and if heated to fry something, then it represents something valuable. Eating sesame oil or using it as an ointment in a dream means profits, comfort, honor, rank, good deeds, or having prior knowledge about something.

Sesame seeds: In a dream, sesame seeds represent blessed earnings, and the same goes for its butter or oil. Like that, in a dream, all kinds of seeds denote lawful money. If one sees himself planting sesame seeds in a dream, it means that he will preside over a growing business, or it could represent an expanding trade, or a flourishing craft, happiness in one's life, or becoming a renunciate. The meaning of dry sesame seeds in a dream denotes greater opportunities than the fresh ones. If the seeds are fried or sautéed, then they denote a greater evil and hardships. Sesame seeds and mustard seeds in a dream denote good only when seen by a physician. Otherwise, for the majority of people, seeing sesame seeds in a dream could mean a sickness, fever, or even poison.

Seth: (The prophet Seth, upon whom be peace.) Seeing God's prophet Seth, upon whom be peace, in a dream means prosperity, contentment, blessings, joy, children, honor and a happy life by God's leave. Seeing him (uwbp) in a dream also means becoming a guardian over a blessed and an important child, or it could denote an important appointment one will manage with decency, integrity and honor, for the prophet Seth, upon whom be peace, was the first appointed guardian on earth.

Setting out: (Preach; Prescribe) Setting out to command what is good and to forbid what is evil in a dream means benefiting others and comforting them. If a sick person sees himself standing up to defend proper moral values, to explain what is true and to refute what is false in a dream, it means that he will enjoy a quick recovery from his illness. If one sees someone's infant setting out to walk in a dream, it means that it will take him a longer time to walk.

Settlement: *(See Conciliation; Reconciliation)*

Severing: *(See Cutting off)*

Severity: *(See Harshness)*

Sexual climax: *(See Pleasure; Sexual intercourse)*

Sexual drive: *(See Sexual intercourse)*

Sexual intercourse: (Adultery; Coitus; Fornication; Hugging; Instinct; Lesbian; Molesting; Sexual drive; Sleeping together, Sodomy; Tribadism) If a man sees himself having sexual intercourse with another man in a dream, it means that both of them have lost their moral dedication, that have become aimless, turned stingy toward their own dependents and generous toward others. It also means loss of one's capital, or divorcing one's wife. If a poor person sees such a dream, it means that he will fall sick, or attract an incurable disease. To have sexual intercourse with a male in a dream also means falling into sin, committing the unlawful, or engaging in sexual intercourse with a female member of one's own family, a blood relation, or a consanguineous person whom one is forbidden to marry. Molesting a child in a dream means suffering from a great affliction. Fornication with a young servant in a dream means suffering from continuous stress and a lasting depression. Sleeping with a beautiful woman one recognizes in his dream means profits. Sleeping with an ugly looking old woman in a dream means the opposite. Having sexual intercourse with an unknown woman in a dream represents the type of interactions and dealings one fosters with people in general. Accordingly, and depending on the condition of the woman one is sleeping with in a dream, one's actions will substantiate. Sleeping with someone's wife in a dream means engaging in a profitable business with the husband. If a sick person sees himself having sexual intercourse with his mother in a dream, it means his death, for the mother here represent the earth. If a woman sees herself engaging in tribadism, or a lesbian relationship with another woman she knows in a dream, it means that she will confide her personal life to her, or divulge all her secrets, become her intimate friend or a fan, shares opinions with her and emulate her actions and look in public. If she does not know that woman in the dream, it means that she will indulge in sin. If a married woman sees herself engaging in tribadism with another woman in a dream, it means that she will separate from her husband or become a widow. Engaging in sexual intercourse with a deceased person, be it a man or a woman in a dream means one's own death, unless if one is travelling, then it could mean visiting that country where the deceased person is buried. Any sexual intercourse in a dream that culminates in ejecting semen and necessitates a complete ritual ablution in wakefulness represents disturbed dreams, or engaging in a forbidden sexual intercourse from the anus, or it could represent wet dreams. Having sexual intercourse in a dream also signifies paying one's debts, or it could mean relief from pressures. Having sexual intercourse with a prostitute in a dream means love for the world, or it could mean profits. Having sexual intercourse with one's wife in a dream means success in one's trade. Having sexual intercourse with a heavenly woman in a dream means religious and spiritual attainment. *(Also see Anus; Semen; Pleasure; Sodomy; Tears; Vagina)*

Sexual organ: *(See Looking at a sexual organ; Span)*

Sexual pleasure: *(See Pleasure)*

Sha'bān: *(See Arabic months)*

Shackles: *(See Bond¹; Fetter; Yoke)*

Shade: (Changes; Cover; Shelter) Witnessing a shade in the summertime in a dream means comfort, profits, honor, or becoming the protégé of a great person. If one sees a shade in the winter in a dream then it means trouble, distress, adversities, or soliciting the company of people who foster innovation. Shade in a dream also represents the governor of one's town, a man of knowledge, a pious person, an ascetic, or a religious student on the path. Seeking refuge in the shade away from the heat of the sun in a dream means comfort, profits, or escaping from harm. As for a woman, shade in her dream represents her husband. If an unmarried woman sees herself seeking the shade in a dream, it means her marriage and that she will marry a rich and a powerful person. If one finds it cold to sit in the shade in his dream, then if he seeks to sit under the sun to worm himself up, it means that his poverty will be dispelled, for cold in a dream also means poverty. *(Also see Shadow)*

Shadow: (Under the sun, in the dark, or otherwise.) In a dream, a shadow represents changes affecting one's life in the world and his elevation or abasement. A shadow in a dream also means guidance, repentance, true monotheism and contemplating the Maker and His creation. If one moves but does not see his shadow moving in a dream, it means abrogating the laws, discarding what is permissible, adopting what is unlawful, death, becoming motionless, or losing one's senses. The same interpretation applies if one's shadow disappears under the sunlight, or under the moonlight, or in the night lights, or if his reflection disappears from the water surface, or from any shiny surface. If one sees his shadow dancing in a dream, it means falsehood, lies, stealing people's money, shifting one's faith according to one's personal interests, or that he criticize the conduct of God's Prophet, upon whom be peace. Dancing one's shadow over a carpet in a dream means invoking evil spirits, speaking their words after being possessed by them, and it means trials, temptations and evil. *(Also see Shade)*

Shahāda: *(arb. Tashahhud)* A sitting posture during one's prayers which includes the proclamation of God's oneness *(i.e., I bear witness that God is one, no associate has He, and I bear witness that Muhammad is His servant and Messenger.)* To see oneself offering the testimony of faith in a dream means the lifting of his adversities and achievement of his goals.

Shaking one's head: Shacking one's head in a dream means begetting a son at an old age.

Shaking: *(See Shivering; Tremor)*

Sham: *(See Labor)*

Shameful act: (Abominable; Contemptible; Disgraceful; Loathsome) To engage in a shameful act in a dream represents one's objectionable character and reprehensible behavior in wakefulness.

Shameless: *(See Profligacy)*

Sharing a table: *(See Messmate)*

Shark[1]: (Deceiver. *See Con artist*)

Shark[2]: (Fish) A shark in a dream represents high spirit, or it could mean belonging to the upper class or to a noble lineage.

Shaved head: If a woman sees her head shaved in a dream, it means her divorce, or the death of her husband.

Shaving: Shaving one's hair in a dream relates to one's personal customs. If he is used to have short hair and sees himself shaving his head in a dream, it means that he will pay a fine as an atonement. If he sees his head shaved in the summertime, and if he is used to doing so, it means benefits, comfort, or recovering from a migraine headache. If one sees his hair shaved during the winter in a dream, it means difficulties, adversities, penalties, or a sickness. Shaving one's head in a dream also means paying one's dues, appeasement of one's fears, and success in one's life. Shortening one's hair in a dream also means appeasing his fears. If one is suffering from depression and he sees his head shaved in a dream, it means an end to his trouble, or payment of his debts. It also means abasement, disgrace, deception, or death. If a soldier sees his head shaved in a dream, it means that he will lose his strength and esteem. If one sees himself chipping his hair in bits in a dream, it means that he will lose people's respect. Shaving one's head in a dream for someone who does not usually shave it also may mean an affliction or an illness. If a woman sees her head shaved in a dream, it means divorce, or the death of her husband. If she sees her hair sheared in a dream, it means confinement to her house. If she sees her husband giving her a beautiful haircut and talking to her affectionately in a dream, it means spiritual growth, delivering a trust, or paying one's debts. Trimming women's hair in a dream means inability to conceive children. Cutting one's hair in a dream means losing one's strength. Shaving half of one's beard in a dream means losing one's source of income and dignity. Plucking out one's facial hair in a dream is worst than shaving it, and particularly when hair louses up one's face or attractiveness. Nevertheless, plucking out one's facial hair in a dream also could depict amelioration of one's condition or look. Shaving one's backside or abdomen in a dream means paying one's debts. Shaving, clipping, or adjusting one's moustache in a dream means lightening one's burdens, though it also could represent a mishap. If a rich person sees himself shaving his pubic hair or using a depilatory agent for that purpose in a dream, it means the loss of his wealth, or it could mean that he has overpaid for a property he has just purchased. If a poor person sees that, it means that he will become financially solvent. If one sees himself shaving it with a razor blade, it represents benefits from one's spouse. *(Also see Beard)*

Shawwāl: *(See Arabic months)*

Shearer: (Sheep shearing) In a dream, a sheep shearer represents a barber, an evil fight, or squandering money. *(Also see Scissors)*

Shearing: *(See Barber; Shaving)*

Shears: *(See Scissors; Shearer)*

Sheath: (Covering) For those who love wealth, a sheath in a dream means guarding one's money, but it could also mean being extravagant, or living lavishly. A sheath in a dream also means guarding one's secrets, getting married, or becoming pregnant.

Shedding one's skin: *(See Skin inflammation)*

Sheep shearing: *(See Scissors; Sheep)*

Sheep: A herd of sheep in a dream represents a good flock, obedient subjects, or good citizens. Sheep in a dream also signify joy, happiness, festivities, a wife, children, a farmland, properties, prosperity or wealth, and particularly when one pays the due alms tax on his money making ventures and liquid assets. Owning a herd of sheep in a dream represents a growing wealth. Passing by a herd of sheep in a dream means passing a gathering of men who have no brain. If a herd of sheep faces someone in a dream, they represent a group of people who will welcome him with a fight which one will eventually win. Receiving a herd of sheep as a gift in a dream means a political appointment, knighthood, knowledge, the seat of justice, or a blessing in one's life. Shearing off the wool of a sheep in a dream is a warning that one should remain aloof for three days. Both the white sheep and the black sheep in a dream mean profit, though the benefits one draws from a white sheep are greater. Seeing a herd of sheep in a dream means continuous happiness. Walking by a slaughter house or a tripe shop and witnessing the heads and trotters of sheep in a dream mean longevity. To find oneself transformed into a sheep in a dream means a booty or winning something. Seeing a sheep in one's dream also represents an obedient son. If one's wife is pregnant, and if he is presented with a sheep as a gift in a dream, it means that she will deliver a boy. Otherwise, the remaining little domesticated animals represent headache, because of the responsibility involved in caring for and in upbringing the boys, except for the girls, for they represent worldly success and profits. If one sees himself slaughtering a sheep in a dream, it means that one of his boys will shortly die, or perhaps it could be the son of someone he knows. A sheep trader in a dream represents a good man who is intuitive and who spends his money on the path of seeking knowledge, or to propagate the same. If one sees himself having a fat tail like that of a sheep in a dream, it means that his livelihood will depend on the revenues of his offspring. In a dream, a sheep also represents a righteous man. *(Also see*

Counting sheep; Ewe; Ram; Trader)

Sheepskin: *(See Wool)*

Shelf: (Secretary) In a dream, shelves represent one's confidant, the keeper of his secrets, one's secretary, one who veils noble women's personal pitfalls, or one who creates a facade for some charitable women. To see a shelf that carries some unique or precious collectibles in one's house or shop in a dream means that one may beget an intelligent son who is diversified and capable, and who will grow to become a renowned man of knowledge. A shelf supported with rods in a dream represents a chaste woman who protect her husband's secrets. A shelf in a dream also represents a trustworthy business partner who labors hard for the success of the business, and who respects and guards his partner's interests.

Shell: (Husk; Peel; Rind; Shuck; Skin) Almond, walnuts or the like nutshell in a dream signify clothing or sustenance. If a pregnant woman sees nutshells in her dream, they mean a miscarriage. A shell or a husk in a dream represents hypocrisy, affectation, ostentatiousness and a swelled head. *(Also see Skin)*

Shelling: (Bombing; Shooting) Shelling someone or a place in a dream represents an excuse or a stratagem. Shelling in a dream also means defaming the people of knowledge, slandering them, or exploiting a religious subject for fame and profits. Shelling someone or a place in a dream also may mean adversities and trials. Shelling the castle of one's enemy in a dream means speaking the truth, or invoking a strong prayer. *(Also see Shooting arrows)*

Shelter: (Gulf. *See Shade)*

Shepherd's dog: *(See Dog)*

Shepherd: (Bucket; Watering) In a dream, a shepherd represents a leader, a teacher or a governor. If one sees himself herding his sheep and not knowing how far they have spread in the fields in the dream, it means that he reads the Qur'ānic revelations but does not fathom their meaning. Herding camels in a dream means presiding over people from a different land. Herding one's flock in a dream means serving one's people with compassion, and caring for their interests. Sheep in a dream also represent righteous men. A shepherd in a dream also represents a high rank, a position of authority, or justice toward others. *(Also see Righteous people)*

Sherbert salesman: *(See Bartender)*

Shia'it: *(See Ali, God bless his countenance)*

Shield: (Armor; Coat of mail) A broad piece carried by warriors for their protection during their fight. In a dream, a shield means a faithful but an arguing friend. It also represents a well-mannered and a true person, or a sincere person who protects his friends and helps them. A valuable shield in a dream represents a beautiful and a wealthy wife, or any female acquaintance or relative. If the shield is worthless in the dream, then it means the opposite. *(Also see Armor)*

Shine: *(See Light)*

Ship: (Boat; Human being; Might; Mother; Prison; Star; Salvation; Stress) Seeing a ship in a dream means escape from danger, overcoming adversities, recovering from an illness, or it could represent rain after a severe drought. If one who is experiencing adversities sees a ship or a boat anchored in a harbor in his dream, it means that his adversities will be lifted shortly. If one sees himself pulling it, or driving it on dry land in a dream, it means that he is a hypocrite or a pimp. If he rides a ship along with righteous people in a dream, it means that he is guided on the straight path and that his sins will be forgiven. If one reaches the shore and leaves the boat in a dream, it means that he will live in safety and happiness, and he will escape from the danger of his enemies. If one who is dismissed from his work sees himself on a boat in a dream, it means that he will be rehired to occupy the same office and regain his authority, or that he may take

384

a dangerous trip during which he may either die or escape from death. If one thinks that the ship does not befit his class or rank in the dream, it means that he will face danger. If one's ship is drowning, and if another ship comes to its rescue in the dream, it means that one will escape from a great danger to fall into the hands of a strong person, or that he will escape from a danger, though should he disobey its captain and abandon the second ship in his dream, it means that he may disobey his leader and go astray. Recovering one's ship from the deep in a dream means regaining power. If the ship in one's dream is interpreted as power, it means that he will lose his power or authority. If the ship is interpreted as burdens and difficulties, it means that he will overcome them through prayers or giving charity, or taking a medicine if he is ill. If one's ship drown, and if he sees himself floating in the water holding to a panel or debris from the ship in the dream, it means that he will face the wrath of someone in authority. If he is holding a leadership position, it means that he may lose it. If he is a merchant, it means that he may go bankrupt. If he still dies from his trial in the dream, it means that he may be killed, and his death will still be an escape from something he feared most. An empty ship in a dream means business profits. Seeing a passenger ship transporting people in a dream means safety. If the ship is floating still in the dream, it means imprisonment. To hold to the rope of a ship in a dream represents a religious person who joins the company a pious teacher. Even if one sees himself dropping the ropes, or lowering the anchor in his dream, it means that he will remain in the company of such a person. Riding a ship along with one's family, relatives and friends in a dream means honor, prosperity and escape from one's enemies. If one sees himself crossing the sea with a small boat in the dream, it represents a danger he will face. Seeing a ship floating nicely in a dream means happiness. Standing on the shore and watching a ship in the sea in a dream means receiving glad tidings. If one sees the ship ascending in the skies in a dream, it represents slow coming benefits, and if the ship is descending from the sky, it denotes fast coming benefits. The beams of a ship represent religious men, faith, holding fast to one's religion, or they could mean complications. The sails of a ship in a dream represent its captain. The crew represents servants. The rowing oars, the rudders, or the propellers in a dream represent the movement of the ship, or the children of its owner. The condition of a ship represents the state of the person seeing the dream or his living condition. If one rescues a drowned ship in a dream, it means that he will discover a treasure, or it could mean marriage if one is unwed, or a financial gift for one who works for a governor. If one sees himself as a ship ebbing and stretching as the tide fall in the sea, then if the sea calms in the dream, it means that he will receive a high ranking appointment, leadership, authority and honor. If one sees a ship floating over a sea of blood in a dream, it means adultery. If the ship sinks, and if some of its debris and boards remain afloat in the dream, it may mean the death of one's mother, for one's mother was once his ship. Buying a ship in a dream means getting married. Carrying oars in a dream means knowledge. A flying ship in a dream means the death of its rider. A flying ship in a dream also may represent another type of vehicle, or it could mean a coffin or a funeral. If one dies inside a ship that has sunk in a dream, it means that he will be saved from suffering in the hereafter, and he will also escape from what he fears most in this world. If he finds a hole in the ship in his dream, it means that he may escape from drowning. A ship in a dream also represents a heavy built woman. In a dream, a ship also represents the Bridge of Judgement (Ṣirāṭ) that will be stretched on the Day of Resurrection for the creation to cross into the land of the Grand Gathering. A ship in a dream also represents salvation, avoiding ignorance, or overcoming temptation. If a sick person sees himself riding in the morgue of a ship with dead people in a dream, it means that he will escape from the trials of this world. If a healthy person who is seeking knowledge does so in a dream, it means that he may meet with a spiritual teacher to benefit from his knowledge and wisdom, and to escape from ignorance. If an indebted person does so in his dream, it means that he will repay his debts, while for a deprived person, he too will find plenitude and acquire wealth from unexpected sources. If one sees his ship sailing to the shore, then if it becomes amphibious, driving him on dry land in the dream, it means that he will waiver in his faith and deviate from the path of truth to follow innovations, hypocrisy and insolence. If he is not seeking knowledge, it means that he will divorce his wife, then proceed to live with her in sin. If he is a merchant, it means that his business will stagnate and he will seek unlawful methods to market his merchandise. In a dream, a ship also represents good deeds, righteous companions, associating with a wise man, a good fellowship, praiseworthy deeds, a handcraft, stagnation of one's business, fear, hope, salvation, a mosque, a marketplace, one's father, one's mother, master, teacher, educator, wealth, a house, an adulteress, a vehicle, one's wife, or his servant. A ship in a dream also represents a tavern in the sense that one enters it sober and leaves it light headed. A ship in a dream also represents the human form and its body represents his body. Its oars represent his hands. Its front represents his head. Its contents represent his brain. Its boards represent his ribs, and its ropes represent his veins, etcetera. If one sees a ship sitting on top of a mountain in a dream, it means safety, or escape from a danger, or protection from one's enemy. If it sinks in the sea in the dream, it also means that he is one of the dwellers of hell-fire. If the ship turns into iron in the dream, it means longevity. Eating the wood of a ship in a dream means receiving a sizeable inheritance, or it could mean eating forbidden meat. If one sees a ship talking to him and soothing his understanding in a dream, it means that he will listen to the admonition of a wise man. Seeing Noah's arc in a dream means happiness, joy, festivities, salvation, relief from stress and worries, protection from drowning, marriage and a presiding position, or victory over one's enemy. (*Also see Boat; Helm*)

Shipment: *(See Cargo)*

Shirt: (Blouse) One's shirt in a dream represents his piety, godliness, livelihood, knowledge, or it could mean glad tidings. Putting on a new shirt in a dream means marriage to a woman who has no relatives or kin. If a woman puts on a shirt or a blouse in a dream, it also means her marriage. A torn shirt in a dream means divorce. If one's shirt is torn in a dream, it means breaking up a business partnership. A shirt in a dream also represents one's religious and worldly concerns. Wearing a shirt without sleeves in a dream means having piety but no money, for sleeves in a dream represent money. If the pocket of one's shirt is torn in the dream, it means poverty. Having a wardrobe filled with shirts in a dream represent one's reward in the hereafter. Wearing a white shirt in a dream means piety and religious assiduousness. Receiving a shirt as a gift in a dream means blessings and profits. Wearing a dirty and a torn shirt in a dream means poverty, distress and afflictions. If a woman sees herself wearing a new, large and comfortable blouse in a dream, it denotes her piety, religiousness, happiness and the enjoyment of a rich life in this world. The same could reflect the state of her husband. Wearing a green or a white shirt in a dream denotes piety. Wearing a blue shirt in a dream may not be praiseworthy. Wearing a red shirt in a dream means fame, while a yellow shirt in a dream means an illness. A wet shirt in a dream means obstacles in one's travels. If one's wet shirt dries in the dream, it means that his hurdles have been removed. Wearing a shirt without a collar, a pocket, buttons, or button holes in a dream means wearing one's shroud at the time of his preparation for burial. Wearing a shirt with stripes in a dream means travels, or it could mean performing a pilgrimage.

Wearing a shirt that does not properly cover one's body in the dream means falling short in performing one's religious duties. Wearing a black shirt in a dream means sorrow, distress and worries. Wearing one's shirt inside-out in a dream means reversal of one's condition, or having a loathsome and a forbidden type of sexual relationship with one's wife from the anus. A shirt in a dream also represents one's house or shelter. If one's shirt is torn in half vertically in a dream, it means relief from anxiety or depression. If one's shirt is torn from the back in a dream, it means that one will suffer from defamation, or be falsely accused of sexually harassing or abusing a woman. If one's shirt is torn from the front in the dream, then it becomes a proof of his guilt. Seeing the shirt of the Prophet Joseph (uwbp) in a dream means that an emissary of good intent will bring glad tidings, and for someone who is suffering from eye problems, it means that he will recover his sight.

Shivering: (Shake; Shudder) Shivering in a dream means fear of God Almighty.

Shock: (Blow) A shock that leads to pain, suffering and crying in a dream means loss of a child or money. *(Also see Tremor)*

Shoemaker: (Beautician; Broker; Woman) A shoemaker in a dream represents someone who brings peace and unity between adversaries, a lawyer, a peace-maker, a scholar or a shaikh who specializes in jurisprudence relating to inheritance laws. A shoemaker in a dream has many meanings. Some shoemakers specialize in repairing women's shoes. In that case, in a dream, he represents a pimp or a brothel owner. As for those specializing in men's shoes, seeing him in a dream means travel, or employing people to work in one's business. *(Also see Tailor)*

Shoes: (Sandals) In a dream, a pair of shoes represent one's son, a vehicle, a friend, a brother, a business partner, or travels. Wearing a pair of shoes without heels in a dream means having a barren wife. Walking with one shoe in a dream means separation between husband and wife, or the breakup of a business partnership. Taking off one's shoes in a dream means victory and rising in station.

Shooting arrows: In a dream, shooting arrows is interpreted like shelling someone or a place. Otherwise, they means backbiting people or slandering them. Shooting arrows in a dream also could mean taking medicine, or giving an injection to a patient. If the arrows do not have arrowheads in the dream, then they mean disappointment. If one shoots arrows and finds himself also at the receiving end in a dream, it means that he will attain his goal of meeting his Lord. However, if he remains in this world, it means that he will rise in station and receive honor. If one sees two rows of people shooting arrows at each other in his dream, it means that the successful ones would be right and the losers would be at fault. Shooting arrows at people in a dream then means backbiting people, slandering them, or it could mean vain talking. If one constantly fails his aim in his dream, it means that he has an evil speaking tongue. Hitting one's target in a dream means attaining one's goals, or speaking the truth regarding someone he knows. Wearing a white garment and standing on top of a mountain and shooting arrows toward the East and the West in a dream means attaining a vast control over people and lands, if one qualifies. One's arrows in a dream also represent his message or writings. *(Also see Arrows; Hunting; Shelling)*

Shooting: (Hunter; Hunting) Shooting in a dream means heedlessness, or pursuing the avenue of women, lust and the company of its people. *(Also see Hunter)*

Shop: In a dream, a shop represents one's wife, child, life, death, property, pride, servant, vehicle, or personal secrets.

Shopping bag: Seeing or carrying a shopping bag in a dream represents someone who strives to serve his family, or one who brings his household what they desire. A shopping bag in a dream also may represent one's wife, son, or a charitable endowment.

Shorebird: *(See Plover)*

Short hair: Shortening one's hair in a dream means appeasing one's fears. *(Also see Hair; Shaving)*

Shoulders: (Friend; Responsibility; Support) Riding over the shoulders of one's enemy in a dream means committing a wrongdoing or a shameful act against someone. If there is no enmity between the two, and if one sees himself riding over the shoulders of his friend in a dream, it means that he will earn something from him. Carrying someone over one's shoulders in a dream means being indebted to him. Carrying a hypocrite over one's shoulders in a dream could mean that one may work at a lumberyard, or deliver wood for living. One's shoulders in a dream also represent his parents, brothers, partners, one's station, or beauty. Anything that affects them in a dream will show in any of the above. Shoulders in a dream also represent one's partner, his employee, assistant, or a close friend. As for a prisoner, having large shoulders in a dream means serving a long term imprisonment. Aching shoulders in a dream may represent the sickness of one's brothers. Shoulders in a dream also represent one's child, or the weight and amount of responsibilities one can assume. *(Also see Body¹; Ride)*

Shout: (Call; Cry; Human call; Outcry; Shout; Scream) Shouting at a gathering of people in a dream means winning the title of a statesman, authority and power in an election, or presiding over people. If one sees himself shouting alone in a dream, it means that he will lose his power and his words will have impact. Shouting in a dream also denotes social turmoil, agitation caused by war, an earthquake, the drowning of a ship, or the spread of a new disease that will force people to turn to God Almighty for help. *(Also see Calling someone)*

Shouting: *(See Calling someone)*

Shove: *(See Thrust)*

Shovel plow: *(See Rake; Shovel)*

Shovel: (Harrow; Mattock; Plow; Scoop; Trowel) In a dream, a shovel represents a wife for an unmarried person. She will keep no secret, though she will spare no expense to save her husband from poverty. A shovel in a dream also means dispelling distress, overcoming trouble, or satisfying one's debts. A shovel in a dream also may represent a trustworthy person one can depend on during hard times, or in times of adversities. Holding a shovel in a dream means receiving benefits and blessings, for a shovel collects dirt as well as valuables. A shovel in a dream also may represent a woman, profits, or business activities. *(Also see Rake; Spade)*

Shrill sound: *(See Wind)*

Shrine: (Grave; Tomb) The graves of martyrs, holy men, saints or their shrines in a dream represent innovation, heedlessness, intoxication, adultery, corruption, or fear. Seeing the shrine of a saint or a shaikh, or the grave site of a martyr who is venerated by people in a dream means witnessing either good or evil happenings. It also could represent the pilgrimage season, religious gatherings, precious metals, a treasure, or offerings. *(Also see Dome²; Cemetery)*

Shroud: (Wrap) A shroud in a dream means covering one's private parts, or it could mean having a secret affair, concealing one's action while displaying a deceptive appearance, or it could mean marriage with an incompatible spouse. Wearing a shroud in a dream also may mean earning money from adultery. If one sees a shroud and does not wear it in his dream, it means that he will be lured to engage in adultery, though he will abstain. Being wrapped in a shroud like a dead person in a dream means one's death. If one's head and feet are still uncovered in the dream, it represents his religious failure and corruption. The smaller is the wrap shrouding the deceased in a dream, the closer he is to repentance and the larger is the wrap and more complete is his preparation for burial in the dream, the further he is from repentance. *(Also see Shrouding; Undertaker)*

Shrouding: Shrouding the body of a deceased person in a dream is a cause of happiness for a sad person and repentance for a sinner. If someone sees himself brokering on behalf of a friend or a relative to purchase a shroud for him in a dream, it means that he will pay and intercede on behalf of someone who strayed from God's path, whom one regularly admonishes and advises to correct his actions and thoughts. It also means helping him against poverty or adversities, because death is the culminating phase of practicing one's religion in this world. A shroud in a dream also connotes a prison, or committing a major sin. Shrouding the dead after washing the body in a dream means washing it from impurities. *(Also see Burial; Camphor; Disrobe; Mummification; Shroud)*

Shrubs: *(See Buckthorn)*

Shu'aib: (God's prophet Shu'aib, upon whom be peace, a great-grandson of Madyan and one of the children of God's prophet Abraham, upon whom be peace.) Seeing him a dream means that one lives among people who fake their measures, cheat in their weight, withhold things that are due and do mischief. Such people will cause him harm, though at the end one will triumph over them, beget daughters and live happily with them. If the prophet Shu'aib (uwbp) looks ghastly in the dream, it means that one may lose his sight.

Shuck: *(See Shell)*

Shudder: *(See Shivering)*

Shut: *(See Close)*

Shyness: Shying from God Almighty, or refraining from indulgence in evil and forbidden acts in a dream represents a strong faith, profits, or that one will receive spiritual guidance.

Siamese cat: *(See Tomcat)*

Sickle: *(See Scythe)*

Siddiqün: He is the arc angel Saddiqün, upon whom be peace, who is in charge of interpreting the meaning of dreams and visions, or giving explanatory parables drawn from the heavenly Preserved Tablet. Seeing him (uwbp) in a dream represents glad tidings, festivities, fulfilling promises, recognizing the inevitability of death, enjoying life, travels, coming home, marriage, children, a high ranking appointment, gaining power, victory, or perhaps defeat and humiliation. Whatever this blessed angel of dreams gives or tells will take effect as it is, for he is in charge of such a duty. The arc angel Saddiqün in a dream also represents the speaker of the house, the translator of the palace, the one who delivers the royal decree and knows the inner secrets. Seeing him in a dream also represents piety, medicine, clarity, perspicacity, transparency of one's vision, the school teacher who keeps looking at the blackboard, the librarian, an official speaker, logs, or books.

Sideswipe: *(See Digging up the past)*

Siege: (Besiege) In a dream, a siege represents an ambush or constipation. It also means having patience, determination and steadfastness. A siege in a dream also means victory over one's enemy.

Sieve: (Bolter; Colander; Filter; Separate; Sift; Sort; Strainer) In a dream, a sieve represents knowledge, discerning, honor, rank and discriminating between truth and false. A sieve in a dream is like a detector of true banknotes from counterfeit, a person who chooses his words, a choosy person of the type of work he does, or a discriminating buyer, a pious person, or it could represent a comb. If a sieve is given as a collateral, or as a promissory note in a dream, it means that the depositor will flunk his promise, for a sieve does not retain water. *(Also see Bolter; Strainer)*

Sift: *(See Sieve)*

Sifter: *(See Bolter; Sieve)*

Sigh: A deep sigh in a dream means initiating a project which demands are cumbersome and which progress is slow and painful. In general, deep sighs in a dream indicate an involvement that will cause sufferings.

Signing a loan: Signing a loan in a dream means being put under a court restraint. *(Also see Borrowing; Lending money; Write)*

Signs of the last hour: *(See Resurrection)*

Silence: (Abstaining from reply; Desistance; Dumbness; Muteness)

Silk brocade: *(See Brocade)*

Silk merchant: Seeing him in a dream means celebrations and joy because of the beautiful colors he displays in his shop. Seeing him in a dream also may represent a social worker, a spiritual guide, or a psychologist who is expert at solving problems and promoting peace. *(Also see Brocade; Silk)*

Silk: Seeing loose silk in a dream means being enamored, or falling in love. If a person in authority wears silk in a dream, it represents his arrogance. Wearing yellow or red silk in a dream means a sickness. If a warrior wears one of these two colors in his dream, it means that he will be decorated for his chivalry. If a man of knowledge is adorned with silk in a dream, it means that he is desirous of worldly status, or that he will lead people astray through innovation. As for the rest of people, wearing silken garments in a dream means that one's deeds are worthy of paradise, though such a person may attain leading ranks and success in the world as well. Wearing a silken garment in a dream also means marriage to a woman from a noble lineage. Wearing a silken shawl without patterns in a dream is better than a cotton or a woolen shawl and particularly a patterned one. *(Also see Silk merchant)*

Silkworm: *(See Butterfly; Caterpillar; Worms)*

Silly: *(See Fool; Stupidity)*

Silver cage: *(See Marriage)*

Silver: (Woman) Silver in a dream represents hard earned money or savings. In dream interpretation, the substance of silver and that of a woman are the same. A silver coin in a dream represents a beautiful woman. Extracting silver in a dream means taking advantage of a woman. If one finds abundance of silver in his dream, it means that he will uncover a treasure. Melting silver in a dream means having an argument with one's wife that will become the talk of the town. Receiving silverware or silver cups as a gift in a dream means being entrusted with money or personal items for safe keeping. The same interpretation goes for receiving a silver mirror in a dream as long as one does not look into it. Once he looks into the mirror in his dream, it means adversities, defamation, and loss of respect, for only harm could come from looking into a silver mirror in a dream. Silverware, silver cups or silver pitchers, as well as the golden ones in a dream also may represent good deeds that lead to paradise, or they could mean good business and prosperity. To see expensive silver items mixed with trivial imitations in a dream means innovation and suspicious behavior. Silver ornaments in a dream mean forcing one's way, or obliging a jealous person to revert the course of his actions. Buying something with silver coins of unknown origin, or placing them inside a silver bowl in a dream means hiding something suspicious, or receiving something as a trust that one should keep with honesty, then return it to its rightful owner when asked to do so.

Singer: A singer in a dream represents celebrations, parties, festivals, travelling around the country, or a preacher. *(Also see Singing)*

Singing: (Chanting; Song) Singing in a dream means falsehood and trouble. Having a beautiful voice in a dream may represent a profitable business. Otherwise, if one sings off key in his dream, it means that he is venturing into a losing business. A singer in a dream also represents a wise person, a preacher, or a physician. The location where the singing has taken place in the dream will experience lies, falsehood and separation between beloveds because of jealousy, envy and perfidy. Singing in a dream also connotes evil, disputes and fights. If a professional singer, a musician, or a music writer sees himself singing his repertoire in a dream, it means benefits and profits. If the singing is bad, or off key in the dream, then it could mean lack of work, meekness, or it could mean having little opinion about oneself. If one sees himself singing while walking in a dream, it means earning a comfortable livelihood, being content and having a good opinion about oneself. Singing in the bathroom or under a shower in a dream means speaking unclear words, or having a dispute. If a rich person sees himself singing in the streets or in a marketplace in a dream, it means a scandal, or it could carry bad connotation. If a poor person or an evil person sees such a dream, it means that he has lost his mind. If a pious person sees himself singing in the streets or in a marketplace in a dream, it means that he will witness deceit and trials. *(Also see Hornet; Singer)*

Sin: (Inequity; Wrongdoing) To see one's movements hampered by sin in a dream means debts. To confess one's sins in a dream means dignity and honor. To commit a sin in a dream means borrowing money.

Sinus congestion: Sinus congestion in a dream means a sickness that will be followed by fast recovery, comfort and rejoicing.

Ṣirāṭ: *(arb. See Bridge of the Day of Judgement)*

Sirius: (Constellation; Star. *See Dog*)

Sisters: (Bread) Holding two loaves of bread in a dream means the marriage of two sisters to one man, one after the other.

Sitting: In a dream, sitting means inactivity, idling, failure, disappointment, paralysis and for an old woman, it may mean ceasing to bear children.

Siwāk: *(arb. See Toothbrush)*

Size: *(See Tallness)*

Skewer: (Brochette; Fastener; Leaning; Piercing; Pin) Skewers in a dream mean fulfilling one's needs, satisfying one's goals, reconciling two friends, or interceding to give advantage to someone for his comfort, or they cold mean money. A skewer in a dream also represents the butler of the house, or the household servant who manages its business, teaches many workers their duties, arts, and commands the various interests of his employer.

Skies: (Castle; Child; Firmament; Heavens; House; Mother; Oath; Ocean; Prison; Teacher; Town; Wife; Wonders) In a dream, the sky represents itself. Whatever descends from it or comes from that direction in a dream will materialize. If fire falls from the sky over people's homes in a dream, it means plagues, illness, pleurisy, smallpox, or death and destruction. If fire falls over the marketplace in the dream, it means higher prices. If it falls over the fields and farmlands in the dream, it means that the crops could either burn, freeze, or be struck by a swarm of locusts or by other harmful insects. If what falls from the sky indicates prosperity, such as honey, oil, figs, barley, or money, etcetera, in the dream, it means a good rain and a good harvest for that year. Whatever falls from the sky of good or bad may represent the government and the hardships it inflicts upon the people, or the benefits it may bring them. Climbing to the sky with a rope, a ladder, or using a staircase in a dream means exaltation, rising in station, good luck and support. If one climbs without a common medium in a dream, it means fear and arrogance. If his intention in climbing is to spy on others in the dream, it means that he may work as a spy. If one descends safely from the sky in the dream, it means that he will escape and be spared the consequences of his sin. If he falls and breaks or fractures a bone or so in the dream, it means that he may suffer such accident in wakefulness. If a sick person sees himself climbing to the sky, and if he does not return to earth in the dream, it means that he may die from his illness. If he comes back in the dream, it means that his illness will increase and his difficulties will reach their peak, though God willing, he will recover from his illness, unless he falls into a hole in a dream. In that case the hole represents his grave. If one sees the sky shooting arrows causing people wounds, injuries and bleeding in a dream, it means taxes and confiscation of properties by the government. If the arrows hit people's ears and eyes only in the dream, it means that major trials and temptations will strike at everyone. If the arrows fall without causing harm to anyone, and if people rush to collect them in the dream, they represent a booty that people will come to win, or a divine gifts people will enjoy. To rise close to the sky in a dream means nearness to one's Lord. This is particularly true for pious people and for true believers. Nearing the sky in a dream also represents a supplication needing an immediate answer, and God willing such prayers will be answered. Nearing the sky in a dream also could mean going before the governor of one's town, or any person from whom one may need something, i.e., a teacher, a man of knowledge, a father, or a wife. If one sees the sky falling over his head in a dream, it means that the roof of his house may cave in, or that he will die from an illness he already suffers. If one sees himself climbing and entering the sky in a dream, it means that he will die as a martyr. If one sees himself standing in the sky in a dream, it means that he will command or admonish others. If one sees himself in the sky looking down at something on earth in a dream, it means that he will rise in station, then he will regret something he missed. If one sees the sky green in a dream, it means prosperity and a good harvest. If one sees the sky turned into iron in a dream, it means drought or scarcity of rain. If one falls from the sky in a dream, it means that he may abandon his faith, become a reprobate, or that he may be struck with a major calamity that will be driven by an unjust person. If the iron sky splits open, and if an old man appears from behind it in the dream, such an old person represents the grandfather of the people of that town or tribe. Consequently, people will enjoy a good harvest, prosperity and happiness. If it is a young man that appears in the dream, then he represents an enemy and an evil that may befall the people following such dream. If a sheep appears from the sky in a dream, then it means profits. If camels appear, then they represent rain. If a lion appears in the dream, it represents an unjust ruler. If the sky becomes one solid piece in the dream, it means drought. If it rips apart and its doors become wide open in the dream, then it means rain or an answer to people's prayers. If one sees himself reaching out and touching the sky in a dream, it means that he is seeking an important goal, and that he will fail to attain it. If one sees himself rising near the lower heavens in a dream, it means worldly gains, or profits and status in either material or spiritual realms. If one looks toward the sky, whether to the East or to the West in a dream, it means travels. If one sees himself stealing the sky and hiding it in a jar in a dream, it means that he may steal a copy of the holy Qur'ān and hides it with his wife. If one sees the sky wide open in a dream, it means blessings and benefits. If one sees himself rising toward the sky in a flat posture in a dream, it means that he will become emaciated, or suffer losses in his business. On the other hand, if one sees himself rising without difficulty and without being laid on his back in a dream, it means exaltation, success and safety from any harm that could be driven by one's enemies. If one bites the sky in a dream, it means that a calamity will strike at him, or it could mean business losses, failure to attain one's goals, or an argument with one's superior at work. If one sees himself touring the sky then returning to earth in a dream, it means that he may become an astronomer, or an astrologer and gain fame in his field. If one sees himself leaning his back to the sky in a dream, it means that he may win a leadership position, or win victory over his opponents. If one sees himself in the sky having a form different than that of human beings in a dream, it means that he may leave this world unblessed. If one sees himself hanging down with a rope from the sky in a dream, it means that he will govern after someone else's, or inherit his post. However, if the rope breaks in the dream, it means that he may lose such an opportunity. If one sees a lighted candle in the sky which luster and brightness dims the light of the sun in a dream, it represents a solar eclipse. If one sees the sky being build in his presence in a dream, it means that he lies in his testimonies. Falling from the sky in a dream also could be a warning against falling into sin. Falling from the sky in a dream with one's head down means longevity. If one sees himself in the sky but could not remember when did he enter it in a dream, it means that God willing he is already in paradise. If one sees radiance, or scintillating rays of light coming through the sky in a dream, it means guidance. If he sees dark clouds coming through the sky in a dream, it means that he could stray from God's path. If he sees a scourge descending from the sky in a dream, it means that plagues and adversities will befall the people as a chastisement for their sins, or for crimes they have committed. As for gnostics and people of knowledge, seeing the sky in a dream means clarity, vision, placing one's interests in heavenly matters, or travelling to distant lands, or engaging in importing and exporting goods. Climbing into the sky in a dream also means falsehood, false beliefs, lies, or talking about God Almighty without the proper knowledge or guidance. Climbing into the sky in a dream also could mean seeking one's livelihood, satisfying one's needs, or fulfilling a promise. Skies in a dream also represent the ocean because of their vastness and the countless number of creation living therein, or they could represent the ripening of fruits, or the conclusion of one's work, or they could represent one's helmet, armor, wife, money, religion, death, or they could indicate slander and falsehood against someone who descends from them after being raised, and they could mean making peace with one's enemies, or they could represent the shares allotted for each one of God's creation, the good and the bad, people's sustenance and that of beasts, gains, losses, blessings or afflictions. *(Also see Ascending in the skies; Celestial spheres; Heavens; Star)*

Skin inflammation: (Thinning; Shedding one's skin) If one sees his skin thinned or inflamed between his legs in a dream, it means that he will marry a rich woman who will give him her wealth. If one sees himself shedding his skin or skinning himself in a dream, it means money he will part with, and if he is sick, it means his death. *(Also see Dry skin; Skin)*

Skin: One's skin in a dream represents the element that cloaks the human being, veils his wealth and what he wills for his heirs. Skin in a dream also represents the elements of father, might, wealth, garment, farm, state of worship, faith, polytheism, or it could mean one's enemy, friend, wife, house, beloved, son, or what protects the human being from harm. A healthy skin in a dream represents a healthy life, and a diseased skin means weakness. A discolored skin in a dream means sickness. If a deceased person is seen wearing a healthy and a beautiful skin in a dream, it represents his good state or condition in the life after death. If a sick person sees himself being skinned like a goat in a dream, it means his death. Being skinned in a dream also represents a robbery in one's house, or it may represent a tyrant, or an unjust ruler. If he is healthy, it means that he will become poor and his ill qualities will be exposed. Fat which is collected under the skin represents the strength of one's faith and religious adherence. If one sees himself wearing the skin of a snake in a dream, it means that he will unmask his animosity toward others. In general, wearing animals skin in a dream means receiving an inheritance. If one sees himself having a fat tail like that of a sheep in a dream, it means that his livelihood will depend on the revenues of his offspring. If he sees his body grown, it means that he will prosper accordingly. Being fat in a dream means prosperity and knowledge, and being emaciated means poverty and ignorance. (Also see Body¹; Body²; Shell)

Skinning an animal: (Peel) In a dream, skinning an animal represents an unjust ruler, a tyrant, an oppressor, a policeman who takes people's money and disappears, or a policeman who can be bribed.

Slander: (Calumniation; Fire; Harsh words; Rebuke)

Slapping on the cheek: (Blow; Criticize; Smack) To lightly slap someone in a dream means to reprimand him, or to oblige him to recognize a favor, boasting about one's generosity, or constantly reminding the other person of some shabby assistance. If one playfully slaps someone lightly on his cheek in a dream, it also means that the latter owes him something or a favor and the opposite is interpreted accordingly. Slapping someone's face with anger in a dream means that the victim will triumph over the assailant. To slap someone in a dream also means recognition of his seniority or superiority. Threatening someone in a dream also maybe a recognition of his superiority. (Also see Digging up the past; Slapping; Threat)

Slapping: (Striking) Slapping someone on his cheek in a dream means cautioning him or warning him about his heedlessness. If a woman gently slaps her own cheeks in a dream, it means glad tiding of a son she will conceive at an advanced age, or after having lost hope in conceiving children. However, slapping someone's face in a dream also could mean injustice, an illness, or cold. (Also see Slapping on the cheek)

Slaughter: (Astray; Injustice; Kill; Murder; Relief) In a dream, slaughter means displeasing one's parents, or it could mean injustice. If one sees himself in a dream slaughtered, he should pray hard and seek refuge in God Almighty to help him. If one sees corpses of slaughtered people scattered around him in a dream, it means profits and achievement of his goals. Seeing slaughtered people in a dream also may mean that they have gone astray. If one sees a man or a butcher slaughtering him in a dream, it means that he will triumph over his assailant. If he is imprisoned, it means that he will be set free. If he is seized by fear, it means that he will reach safety and regain his equanimity and peacefulness. If he is a war captured prisoner, it means that he will be set free. If he is a leader, it means that his sovereignty will widen. Slaughtering someone in a dream means being unjust toward him. Slaughtering a pigeon in a dream means getting married. Cutting a piece of flesh from one's backside in a dream means that he engages in sodomy. If one finds himself slaughtered but does not know who killed him in the dream, it means that he is an innovator, or it could mean that he will forge a testimony. Murdering one's own father or mother in a dream means disobeying them or assaulting them and becoming damned. To slaughter a woman in a dream means adultery, or eliciting sexual intercourse with her. To slaughter a fowl or the female of any bird or animal in dream means deflowering a young girl. To slaughter a son in a dream means that such a son is ruthless and unjust toward his parents. If one kills himself in a dream, it means that he married a woman who is unlawful to him. (Also see Slaughter house)

Slaughterhouse: (Abattoir) A slaughterhouse in a dream represents loss of lives, the return of souls to their Lord, bloodshed, skinning animals, or it could mean fetidness. A slaughterhouse in a dream also means weddings, festivities, celebrations and banquets, or it could represent tyranny, adultery, or a brothel. If a sick person sees himself entering a slaughterhouse in a dream, it means the end of his life and the dividing of his assets after his death. If a healthy person enters a slaughterhouse and if his garment become stained with blood in a dream, it means a sickness, adversities, or debts. If one sees hogs or pigs being slaughtered therein, his dream means that he will witness the end of innovators, the contemptible, the evil ones, and the abominable people. Meanwhile, if people are afraid of someone, the dream then signals the end of such a person. A slaughterhouse in a dream also represents a dungeon, a torture room, or a primitive prison. Entering a slaughterhouse in a dream may also mean that the police is investigating allegations related to such a person. A slaughterhouse in a dream also represents a procuress or a white slaver. (Also see Slaughter)

Slave: (Bondman; Servant; Submission) If a free man sees himself as a slave, and if he recognizes the person who enslaved him in the dream, it means that he will serve such a person, or perhaps he may blackmail him. Becoming a slave in a dream also means excessive borrowing of money until one becomes a slave to his lenders, or that the compounded interest of his loans weigh heavy on his family, or it could mean reorganization of one's business, or that he may work for his lender to repay his debts, or it could mean that he may develop heart problems, or any debilitating illness. If one is sold as a slave in a dream, it means that he will regain honor and dignity, or perhaps fall in a trap, for selling a free person in a dream means humiliating him. Selling a human being in a dream also connotes a good end, such as that in the story of God's prophet Joseph, upon whom be peace. If a bondman sees himself free in a dream, it means that he will experience ease after he was subjugated to difficulties and hardships, or it could mean paying his debts, recovering from an illness, attaining one's goals, or perhaps he may become a true servant of God Almighty, who commands good and forbids evil, establishes regular prayers, pays his charities and fears wrongdoing. Being a slave in a dream also means distress. Being sold in a dream also means worries, unless if the buyer is a woman, then it means that he will be honored and well treated. His value and comfort then will depend on the price he is sold for in the dream. If an unmarried woman is sold as a slave in a dream, it means that she will marry the one who bought her. If a man sells his wife in a dream, it means that he will divorce her. If one is captured and turned into a slave by his enemy in a dream, it means that he will learn something about humiliation and submissiveness.

Sledge: (See Hammer)

Sleep: Sleeping in a dream means heedlessness or joblessness. In general, sleeping or feeling sleepy in a dream has negative connotations except for someone who is scared, or who expects an adversities or sufferings he may experience otherwise. This is because sleep abates all fears, annihilates them and clams one's distress. Sleeping in a graveyard in a dream means a sickness. Sleeping over a grave in a dream means death for a sick person and joblessness for a healthy person. Sleeping in a dream also means stagnation, heedlessness, or infringing upon God's commands, or discrediting or denying the consequences of negating them. Sleeping in a dream also could represent a blessed journey, such as seeking knowledge or doing good deeds. It also means disregard for worldly attractions, or despite for its glitters. Sleeping people in a dream also represent mass annihilation, death, murders, rising prices, or it could denote things which people are unaware of. If in fact the people are unaware or uncertain about something, and if one sees them in such a state of slumber in a dream, it means that God Almighty will remove that blind, and they will see things clearly. If one sees himself sleeping or laying on his back in a dream, it means that he will gain power and financial success in the world. Sleeping with the face down in a dream means losing one's job, or it could mean poverty. Sleeping on the floor in a dream means owning a land, being a rich person, or having children. Sleeping for an unmarried woman in a dream means that she will get married shortly. The sleeping of an unjust ruler in a dream means a temporary relief for the people. Sleeping in a dream also means intoxication of the mind, ecstasy, a sickness, neglecting one's duties, disunity, humiliation, or death. Sleeping under a tree in a dream means having a large progeny. *(Also see Doze; Sleeping on the stomach: Slumber; Turning in one's sleep)*

Sleeping on the stomach: *(See Sleep; Turning in one's sleep)*

Sleeping pad: *(See Mattress)*

Sleeping together: *(See Sexual intercourse)*

Sleeplessness: (Insomnia) In a dream, sleeplessness means loss of a beloved, the death of a child, separation between lovers, or leaving one's family and travelling to a foreign country.

Sleeves: Sleeves in a dream represent money. Thus, large sleeves denote a greater amount of money than tight ones, and long sleeves in a dream mean more money than short ones. Torn sleeve in a dream signify poverty, exposure, or desistance of divine favors.

Sleigh bell: *(See Bell)*

Slime: *(See Sludge)*

Sling: *(See Slingshot)*

Slingshot: (Sling; Catapult) Bringing a slingshot before a sick person in a dream means transporting him to a new place, or it could mean his death and burial. A slingshot in a dream also means removal of a guardian from his office, or recovering from drug addiction, or it may represent a messenger. Using a slingshot to cast stones at others in a dream also means rightly invoking a strong curse on them. If one sees a woman using a slingshot to throw stones at him in a dream, it means sorcery or witchcraft. A slingshot in a dream also denotes just and harsh words. Holding a slingshot and preparing to shoot in a dream represents one's strength and determination to say something just and true. If one carries a slingshot but adoes not use it to cast stones in the dream, it means that he will repent for his sin.

Slip of a tongue: (Cutting remark; Oversight) A slip of one's tongue, or to slip in a cutting remark in a dream may mean walking on a slippery surface, or vice-versa. *(Also see Slippery surface)*

Slip: (Under garment; Underpants) In a dream, a slip represents a free woman. A woman wearing an underwear slip in a dream denotes marriage. If she is wearing a flashy red slip in the dream, it means that she will be accused of wrongdoing. If a respectable woman adventures with her slip into the streets in a dream, it means that her misfortune will become the talk of the town.

Slippers: (Glass slippers; Hoof; Protection; Wooden clogs; Wooden slippers.) Slippers in a dream represent property, protection, a ring, or preventing evil happening. Wearing a pair of slippers in a dream also means a journey, or travelling by sea, or it could mean buying a new vehicle. Tight slippers in a dream means tightness in one's livelihood, entanglements, or being pursued by debt collectors. Removing one's slippers in a dream means putting an end to one's strains. Wearing embroidered slippers coupled with a shawl over one's shoulders in a dream means increase in one's wealth and respect. Wearing them in the winter is more beneficial then wearing them in the summer where they mean distress. Seeing one's slippers on fire or if they fall into a well in a dream may mean the death of one's wife. In a dream, a pair of new slippers that are elongated like a boat means tight circumstances and debts. Slippers in a dream also represent money which is earned from a foreign country or from an import and export business. If slippers in a dream are interpreted to mean protection, then losing them in a dream could mean loss of one's job. If they are interpreted to mean religion, then losing them in a dream means relief from difficulties, or an end to one's trials. Wearing a pair of simple slippers in a dream means taking a trip to a distant place, or a marriage to a young virgin. If one's slippers are worn-out in a dream, it means that one may marry an unwed woman or a widow. Losing a slipper in a dream means losing half of one's assets. Finding a pair of lost slippers in a dream means occupying oneself with worldly business rather than serving one's benefits in the hereafter, or it could mean delinquency in attending one's religious duties. Wearing wooden slippers in a dream means repentance from sin, engaging in an argument, acquiring knowledge, or exposing a secret one would rather conceal from others. Walking with glass slippers in a dream means being a hypocrite and a bad companion whose friendship does not last, and whoever befriends someone wearing glass slippers in a dream will suffer from adversities and hardships because of him. *(Also see Wooden clogs)*

Slippery surface: Walking on a slippery surface, or tripping over a slippery surface may mean abolition of a wrongdoing one has committed in the past. It also means forgetfulness, distraction, slowing of mental keenness, or diversion from one's pursuit of knowledge. *(Also see Slip of a tongue)*

Slipping: *(See Slip of a tongue; Tripping)*

Sludge: (Black mud; Scum; Slum; Profits; Capital for business; Glad tidings; Dominance) In a dream, a sludge means good news and particularly if one cannot find clean water near it. If a poor person trips into sludge in a dream, it means that his will satisfy his needs. If an unmarried person sees sludge in his dream, it means that he will get married, and he will have a family, a father-in-law and a mother-in-law. Though this gain of his will be accompanied with trials and difficulties. Nevertheless, it will also remain under control.

Slum: *(See Sludge)*

Slumber: In a dream, slumber means appeasing one's fears and getting some peace. Slumber in a dream also means repentance from sins, guidance, victory over one's enemy, prosperity, or stabilization of market prices.

Slumberous: *(See Yawning)*

Smack: *(See Slapping on the cheek)*

Smallpox: In a dream, smallpox represents debts, or being pursued by debt collectors. It also can be interpreted as increase in one's earnings. If one sees his son struck by smallpox in a dream, it denotes blessings for the son.

Smashing: (Bang; Collide; Hit; Impact; Knocking) To bang one's head against a rock or a wall in a dream means suffering from failing to perform one's night prayers. *(arb. 'Ishā)*

Smell: Smelling a sweet fragrance in a dream means uneasiness or a light illness. Smelling a bad odor in a dream means hearing or speaking bad words, or it could mean distress or depression.

Smelling an apple: Smelling an apple inside a mosque in a dream means getting married. If a woman sees herself smelling an apple during a reception in a dream, it denotes her misconduct, and that she could commit an abominable sin during that same evening. *(Also see Nose)*

Smile: Smiling in a dream means happiness and true adherence to one's religion.

Smiting one's forehead: (Blow; Pound; Shake; slap) In a dream, pounding one's head, or smiting one's face means begetting a son at an old age.

Smoke: (Fumes) In a dream, smoke means a partnership, an investment, or it could represent outside money which someone has placed with one's own capital for business. Smoke in a dream also may mean meekness, or loss of property or capital. However, seeing smoke in a dream may mean profits only for one whose livelihood stems from dealing with fire. In a dream, smoke also represents an appalling or a horrifying calamity wherever it may appear. *(Also see Clouds of* *smoke; Sparks)*

Smothering: *(See Extinguishing a fire)*

Smut: *(See Besmear; Rust)*

Snail: A snail in a dream means that one will move away from his place or town.

Snake bite: *(See Snake; Sting)*

Snake charmer: (Diphtheria; Quinsy; Tracer; Tracker) A snake charmer in a dream represents mixing with evil people, participating in a competition, or racing against one's enemy. If a sick person sees himself sitting with his snakes in a dream, it means that he will recover from his illness and live a long and a happy life. If the basket carries silkworms instead of a snake in his dream, it means repentance of a sinner, or prosperity of a poor person, or it could mean changing a bad profession for a good one. The presence of a snake charmer in a dream also represents the presence of a deceiver, any taunting profession, or it could mean an illness or suffocation. *(Also see Tracker)*

Snake-cucumber: (Cucumber; Large cucumber; Squirting cucumber) Seeing or eating the large variety of cucumber known as snake-cucumber in a dream means blessed money, a good business, or buying a new property. On the other hand, a snake-cucumber in a dream may represent money that does not remain long in one's hand. If a woman sees a snake-cucumber in a dream, it means that she is pregnant. *(Also see Cucumber)*

Snake: (Boy; Contemptible person; Enemy; Hidden treasure; Idolatry; Innovators; Power; Unjust ruler; Woman) A snake in dream represents a person who lives in a valley. A snake in a dream also means enmity from one's in-laws or children, or it could represent the evil and jealousy of one's neighbor. A sleeping snake in a dream means a sleeping enemy. As for an unjust person, a water snake in a dream means receiving help, or it could represent a verdict. Owning a snake in a dream means gaining power and authority. Its flesh represents enemy money, or it could mean joy. If one sees himself wearing the skin of a snake in a dream, it means that he will unmask his enmity toward others. Killing a snake in a dream and staining one's hands with its blood means destroying one's enemy. A snake in one's dream also represents a rich enemy, for its poison means money. If one sees snakes being killed in the streets in a dream, it means a war. A small snake in a dream represents a little child. Hunting snakes in a dream means tricking or deceiving one's enemies. A black snake in a dream represents a strong enemy. A white snake in a dream represents a weak enemy. If one sees a snake talking to him and saying nice words to him in a dream, it means enjoying pleasant moments with one's adversary, or benefiting at the hands of one's enemy. If the snake talks harshly to him in a dream, it means suffering from tyranny and oppression caused by one's enemy. Becoming a snake in a dream means being contemptible against one's own religion. Seeing oneself as a half-snake half-human in a dream means being able to neutralize half of the enemy's power. Discovering a snake skin which is made from gold in a dream means that one will discover a hidden treasure. If a snake swallows someone in a dream, it means that he will reach a powerful position. If one sees a snake sitting over his head in a dream, it means that he will earn the respect of people in authority. A field which is covered with snakes in a dream represents a destructive rain. A snake with a horn in a dream represents a profitable business. Black snakes and pythons in a dream represent army generals. Water snakes in a dream represent money. If one sees his garden covered with snakes in a dream, it means that its trees will bear fruits and exceed the normal crop. A snake coming out of its hole in a dream represents a son. A snake leaving one's house in a dream means its destruction or demolition. Killing a snake in a dream means marriage. Tapeworms or other intestinal worms in a dream represent one's relatives and their children. Seeing snakes eating on one's table in a dream means separation between friends. Desert snakes in a dream represent highway robbers. In general a snake or a serpent in a dream represent jealousy, envy, perfidy, swindling people's properties, deceit and an avowed enmity. (*Also see Belt; Sting*)

Snare: (Catch; Hunt; Lure) In a dream, a snare means deception, duplicity and fraud. If one is captured or held with a snare in a dream, it means that he will be victimized. If one places a snare to catch an animal or a bird with it in a dream, it means that he earns his money through deception and fraud. (*Also see Trap*)

Sneezing: (Anger; Ascertain; Cold; Disdain; Disregard; Exhale; Fury) Sneezing in a dream means reassessing something about which one had doubt. Thus, sneezing in a dream could mean acknowledging the truth, and that is why people's common reply is "God bless you." Sneezing in a dream also could mean the death of a sick person, or experiencing agony, distress, adversities, or facing a disturbing problem. If one who is experiencing such trials sees himself sneezing in a dream, it means that the time has come to dispel them. If a poor person sneezes in a dream, it means that he may wake up to find that help is coming his way. Sneezing in a dream also could mean paying one's debts, or recovering from a cold or a nasal congestion, or it could mean exasperation, fury, rage, anger, or frowning. If one sneezes with force in his dream, it means that he should beware of a strong enemy and the possibility of suffering losses at his hands.

Snoring: Snoring in his dream means getting hold of one's enemy or exposing him, or it could mean enjoying peace and comfort, or dispelling one's fear. Seeing someone else snoring in a dream means that he is a heedless person.

Snot: (*See Nasal mucus; Phlegm*)

Snow: Snow in a dream means profits, or it could mean a cure for an illness. If snow and fire coexist beside one another in a dream, they represent love, passion and companionship. If one sees snow in its season, then it means washing away one's difficulties and exposing one's enemies or jealous companions. Seeing snow in other than wintertime in a dream means an illness, paralysis, or obstacles hindering one's travel plans, or it could mean sufferings, swearing, or deceit. A heavy snow storm in a dream means oppression, while a light snowfall or flurries mean benefits to one's town. Melting snow in a dream means dispersal of agony, or it could mean the end of depression. Like rain, snow in a dream is a sign of divine mercy and a good harvest. When heavy, it represents a calamity, and when light, it is a blessing. Standing under a snowfall in a dream signifies enemy blows. (*Also see Snowball*)

Snowball: (*See Ball; Snow*)

Snuff: (Inhaling pulverized tobacco or powdered medicine.) Inhaling snuff in a dream is a sign of devastation, lacking a sense of continuity, needing to conceive a child, needing one's mother, seeking the help of one's superior, or it could denote a mental illness. If one sees himself snuffing tobacco or other herbs, or powdered medicine in a dream, it means that his anger has reached a stage he could no longer bear.

Soaking: (*See Infusion*)

Soap: In a dream, soap represents the washing away of one's sins, dispelling distress and adversities, or paying one's debts. Seeing a soap boiler inside one's house in a dream represents a visit by the undertaker. A bar of soap in a dream also represents a funny person. Washing a shirt with soap in a dream means recovering from an illness, or repenting from sin. A bar of soap in a dream also means hearing a story, writing a story, bringing a deposition before a judge, or it could simply mean washing one's dirt.

Soar: (*See Kite*)

Sociability: *(See Adulation; Flattery)*

Social acquaintances: *(See Connections)*

Social connections: *(See Connections)*

Sock: *(See Stocking)*

Sodom and Gomorrah: *(See City; Lot¹)*

Sodom: *(See Lot¹)*

Sodomize: *(See Pederasty; Sexual intercourse; Sodomy)*

Sodomy: (Homosexuality; Pederasty; Sodomize) Sodomy in a dream means a meeting between two men to engage in an evil act. To see an unknown person forcibly subjecting the one seeing the dream to engage in sodomy means letting oneself be overcome by an enemy. *(Also see Pederasty; Vagina)*

Softness: *(See Pillow)*

Solar eclipse: *(See Eclipse; Skies)*

Solar system: *(See Stars)*

Soldiers: (Angels; Travel) Soldiers in a dream represent God's arc angels and the soldiers of mercy, while mercenaries in a dream represent the soldiers of punishment. If one sees himself as a soldier eating his meal inside the chambers of a king in a dream, it means that he will control a land without much efforts on his part. If one's name is listed as a soldier in a dream, it represents his welfare, satisfaction, or that he will continue his education. If a bedridden person sees himself as a soldier in a camp, or that he is discharged from the army in a dream, it means that his illness will end in his death, or it may mean difficulties, distress and losses. A gathering of soldiers in a dream means destruction of the wrongdoers and victory of the righteous ones. A soldier carrying a scourge or arrows in a dream also represents good conduct. A count of one hundred soldiers in a dream represents the chastisement and calamity which God Almighty inflicts upon the people of the earth because of their sins at the conclusion of each century, or at the beginning of a new one. Seeing one thousand soldiers in a dream represents the blessed Night of Power which occurs near the end of the fasting month of Ramadān. If soldiers are led by a prophet, a king, a wise man, or a man of knowledge in one's dream, it means victory for the believers. If one sees an army entering a town in a dream, they could represent rain. *(Also see Night of Power)*

Solemn promise: *(See Offering)*

Soliciting advice: (Appeal; Begging; Bequeath; Plead) To solicit the advice of a religious scholar, a learned person, a lawyer, or a judge in a dream means to need them in a conflict. If a rich person asks a poor person for something or for a favor in a dream, it means that he could suffer in hell-fire unless he repents from his sins and bigotry. *(Also see Advice; Beggar)*

Solomon's ring: (A gift from God Almighty; Authority) If a ruler or a rich person sees himself wearing Solomon's ring in a dream, it means that his authority, wealth, lands, travels and all his goals will be successful and grow further. If someone invokes spirits for a living, then wearing Solomon's ring in a dream will make him rich. Seeing or finding Solomon's ring in a dream also means renewing one's term of leadership, or a manifestation of a great confounding wonder that will bewilder everyone. *(Also see Ring; Solomon)*

Solomon: (God's prophet Solomon, upon whom be peace.) God Almighty subjugated the wind to serve the prophet Solomon. Seeing him (uwbp) in a dream denotes leadership, the seat of a judge, acquiring wisdom, or giving religious interpretations if the person who sees him in a dream qualifies. This vision becomes stronger if the Prophet Solomon crowns the person, or places a ring on his right hand, or sits him beside himself on his throne. Seeing him (uwbp) in a dream also means overcoming adversities and hardships, and receiving a divine endowment of an exalted station in this world, and greater blessings in the hereafter. Seeing him (uwbp) in a dream also means trials with women and ingratitude on their part. If the person who sees God's prophet Solomon in a dream is a governor, it means that he will be dismissed from his functions, though his authority will be restored later on, or he could through cheating, marry a rich woman. If the one who sees God's prophet Solomon in a dream practices sorcery, witchcraft, black magic, or invoking jinn or evil spirits, it means that he will profit from his trade and become wealthy after having lost hope in attaining such benefits, or he could triumph over his enemy. Whoever sees God's prophet Solomon (uwbp) in his dream will receive God's favors, including clear visions, clarity of religious interpretations, the ability to learn many languages, or he could become a translator, or perhaps could master the Arabic language. Seeing Solomon in a dream also means that one will recover from an illness. If one gets hold of Solomon's staff in a dream, it means that he will engage in slander or calumny, and if he is sick, it means his death. Seeing or finding Solomon's ring in a dream means renewing one's term of leadership, or a manifestation of a great and a confounding wonder that will bewilder people. If a woman sees God's prophet Solomon (uwbp) in a dream, it means that she will deceive her husband. Seeing him (uwbp) in a dream also means that one may acquire knowledge about herbal medicine. If one sees him laying dead on his bed in a dream, it means that the calif, an army commander, a leader, or a man of knowledge will die in that locality and whose death will remain undetected, or undisclosed for sometime. Seeing him (uwbp) in a dream also means increase in one's travels, supremacy over one's enemy and subjugation of one's friends and foes to his orders should he qualify. Seeing him (uwbp) in a dream also denotes riches, sovereignty, distant but fast travels and receiving blessings, peace and protection. *(Also see Solomon's ring)*

Solution: *(See Complications; Solving a complicated problem)*

Solving a complicated problem: Solving a complicated problem, or dissolving a solid element into liquid in a dream represents profits and easing of one's problems, abating one's concerns, neutralizing a sorcerer's act, or nullifying the intent of an evil spell.

Son: In a dream, a son may mean a daughter or a servant.

Song: *(See Singing)*

Songs of God's love: *(See Zikr)*

Sophistication: *(See Elegance)*

Sorcerer: *(See Worshipping fire)*

Sorcery: (Black magic; Magic arts; Witchcraft) If one sees women throwing stones at him using a slingshot in a dream, it means sorcery and a bad spell. Sorcery in a dream also means deception and arrogance. If one sees himself practicing sorcery, or if he is bewitched by a sorcerer in a dream, it means separation between husband and wife through falsehood. Sorcery in a dream also connotes disbelief, a ruse, shrewdness, or ingratitude. If the sorcery is done by jinn in the dream, their effects will be stronger. *(Also see Magic arts; Spit out)*

Sorrel: (Heartburn)

Sort: *(See Sieve)*

Sound of animals: In a dream, the sound of a crowd means money beside other benefits. The bleating of sheep in a dream means distress and fear. The neigh of horses in a dream means might and honor. The barking of a dog in a dream means vain talk and meddling in others' business. The sound of a lynx in a dream means pampering oneself and wantonness. The cooing of pigeons in a dream means crying, sorrows or marriage. The chirp of swallows in a dream means beneficial words. The croaking of frogs in a dream means beatings or death. The sound of bells and the hissing of snakes in a dream represents a fight, an argument, a warning, or a war. The braying of donkeys in a dream means cursing in the darkness. The braying of mules in a dream means vain talk, or it could mean indulging in suspicious acts. The mooing of a cow in a dream means temptation. The gurgling or braying of camels in a dream signifies travels and difficulties. The roaring of a lion in a dream means threats. The yowling of a tomcat in a dream means uproar, backbiting, defamation and insinuation. The yapping of foxes in a dream means a warning for one to escape from danger, or to move from one field into another. The howling of a wolf in a dream means robbery. The squeak of a mouse in a dream means profits, reunion, love and peace. The crying of a female gazelle in a dream means longing for one's homeland. The barking of a jackal in a dream means a mission of good intent, or a forthcoming evil. *(Also see Dog; Listening; Roaring; Speaking; Voice)*

Sound of birds: *(See Sound of animals)*

Sound of walking: *(See Tap)*

Sound: (Human sound. *See Voice*)

Soup: Sopped bread with meat and broth or soup in a dream represent man's livelihood. The amount of food one eats from a bowl of soup represents the portion of life one has spent, and the balance in the bowl represents what is left. Looking at a bowl of soup and being afraid to eat from it in the dream means longevity which is accompanied with comfort and ease. Eating fat-free soup in a dream means wishing for death because of one's poverty or illness. Soup with bread but without meat in a dream represents a high ranking position without benefits. Eating a lion's soup in a dream means presiding over heartless and inhumane people, along with mistrust and fears. Eating a dog's soup in a dream means presiding over a loathsome and a despicable business, working with evil people and earning black profits. If the soup has no fat in the dream, it means deprivation, poverty and humiliation. Eating the sopped bread of such soup means death. Eating a falcon's or eagle's soup in a dream means taking a business trip, or making profits out of ignorant people who unwillingly submit to their losses.

Source book: *(See Reference book)*

Spade: (Shovel) In a dream, a spade means profits. *(Also see Shovel)*

Spadix: *(See Palm branch; Palm leaves; Pollen)*

Span: (Hand; Measure) In a dream, a span denotes architecture, renewing one's wardrobe, or travel. A span in a dream also could represent a compass, or the male sexual organ. If one sees himself fighting with a spear that measures about a span in the dream, it means that he will seduce a virgin.

Spaniel: *(See Dog)*

Spanish fly: (Blister beetle) A Spanish fly is a bad omen if seen in a dream by someone who indulged in abominable and loathsome actions. As for the majority of people, seeing a Spanish fly in a dream is more ominous. However, if a druggist, or a pharmacist sees a Spanish fly or a blister beetle in his dream, then they connote medicinal benefits.

Sparks: In a dream, sparks represent ugly words. If one sees sparks hitting him in a dream, it means that he will hear harsh words pronounced against him by someone in authority. If one's clothing ignites and burns from sparks in the dream, it means aggravation of his condition. If smoke engulfs the sparks in one's dream, then they represent an awesome adversity. Whenever smoke appears in one's dream, it represents an appalling and a horrifying calamity. If the sparks cause secondary burns in the dream, then they represent a weak enemy who slanders him and one may bear the consequences of such slander with patience, and its evil and fire will eventually diminish. If one sees a major eruption of sparks in his dream, they represent a major calamity. If a spark falls in the midst of a gathering in the dream, it means a fight and harm. Sparks in a dream also represent one's children. If sparks burn one's face in a dream, they mean continuous suffering and disturbances. Sparks in a dream also mean evil deeds, sins and crimes that call for punishment in hell-fire. *(Also see Flint Stone)*

Sparrow: A sparrow or a hawk in a dream represents an ignorant and unjust ruler. Both command lesser controlling domains than the eagle. Holding a sparrow or a hawk in a dream means that one will capture a thief. If one sees himself producing a sparrow or a hawk out of his urethral canal, it means that he will bore a son who will possess courageous and frivolous character. Holding a sparrow in a dream also means choosing a community of elders and volunteering one's services. *(Also see Hawk)*

Spasmodic inhalation: *(See Hiccup)*

Spathe: *(See Pollen)*

Speaking in other languages: *(See Language)*

Speaking: (Hearing; Language; Listening; Talking; Words) Speaking different languages in a dream means richness. The words of a deceased person in a dream are always true. The same goes for birds speaking in a dream and their speech denotes glad tidings, prosperity, knowledge and understanding. If an animal talks with someone in his dream or tells him: "I saw a dream..." then if the animal refrains from relating such a dream, it means a fight, a battle, losses, or an argument. If a dog, a panther, or a falcon speaks to someone and tells him a dream in a dream, it means glad tidings, great earnings, benefits and joy. In general, birds talking to humans in a dream mean benefits and rising in rank. If a snake speaks gently with someone in a dream, it means that he will receive benefits from an enemy. If a beast talks to someone in a dream, it means his death. If one's head or nose talk to him in a dream, it means that whoever these two members represent in one's life *(See Body¹)* will suffer from an adversity. If a tree speaks to someone in his dream, it means benefiting from that line of thinking. A talking tree in a dream means a fight, or the end of one's exile. The speech of a tree in a dream also could mean exaltation. Whatever a baby says in a dream is true. It also could mean falling into sin. If a godly and a spiritual person sees a baby talking to him in a dream, it means that he will witness wonders or a miracle, or become a witness to an unbelievable agreement. The speech of inanimate objects in a dream always means good, provides a lesson or gives advice. Animal talk in a dream also represents punishment and suffering. The talk of one's limbs in a dream means trouble from one's relatives, or it could mean committing a sin. The speech of moving shadows in a dream means evoking jinn or evil spirits. Being possessed by such spirits and speaking on their behalf in a dream signifies temptation, trouble, corruption and evil. Any words that agree with God's revelations in a dream must be hearkened to and complied with. The opposite is also true. If a limb talks to someone in his dream, it denotes advice one will receive from a relative. Animal talk in a dream denotes leaning toward friendships and finding peace in the company of pious people, or it could mean working to earn one's livelihood. If a wall speaks to someone in a dream, it means a warning of separation, or it could mean renouncing the city and seeking to live in the wilderness, near uninhabited ruins, or near a graveyard. Hearing a voice commanding one to do something in a dream means glad tidings. Hearing God Almighty on the Day of Judgement in a dream means rising in station, performing good deeds and nearness to one's Lord. Listening to the Holy Words of God Almighty in a dream also denotes the spread of justice and righteousness, and such a dream could represent a ruler who cares for his subjects. If a godly and a pious person sees that in a dream, it means that he will renounce the world and seek the comfort and the blessings of the hereafter. *(Also see Exhaustion from speaking; Listening; Sounds of animals)*

Spearhead: In a dream, a spearhead means patience, determination, bearing difficulties, facing evil people, or it could mean a bridge or tools.

Spearman: A battle between spearmen in a dream represents a blow of fate, a mishap, or a calamity. The way to avoid such a mishap is by spending money and efforts on God's path. Such a battle also could mean an attack against one's religion, a calumny, or speaking ill of another person's faith, or speaking ill of righteous people, or being sarcastic about religion, or it could mean slander, defamation, confuting someone, defaming him, vilification, or making libelous statements against someone. If one sees himself stabbing someone with a spear, a sword, a lance, or a wooden post in a dream, it means making or publishing libelous statements about someone, and in that case, he is the assailant and he is liable for his actions, also he will be subjected to the same destiny. If one stabs, wounds, or threatens someone with any of the above weapons, or if he points them toward the other person but does not attack him in the dream, it means that he will be tempted to slander or defame him, then he will withhold himself from doing so. If one sees people fighting with spears in a dream, it means that a plague will strike that place, or it could mean rising prices. If one sees them rebelling against the government in the dream, it means that prices will fall.

Speckles: *(See Freckles)*

Specks of dust: Counting specks of dust or gathering them in a dream means trials, injustice, aggression, or temptations. Specks of dust in a dream also represent one's progeny, money, longevity, or they could represent soldiers, weak people, or God's soldiers. Seeing a room full of dust in an unusual place, or a closed place where they usually do not gather means knowledge, or they could mean immeasurable wealth.

Speech writer: *(See Tongue)*

Speech: *(See Language)*

Spell out: (Divulging) If one speaks or spells out something that is supposed to remain a secret in a dream, it may mean reaching an elevated position, gaining respect for one's words and opinions, or it could mean speaking publicly about one's charities.

Sperm: *(See Semen)*

Spermaceti: *(See Amber)*

Spica: *(See Constellations)*

Spider: In a dream, a spider represents a malicious woman, or a weak, perfidious and a distant man. A spider in a dream also represents a weaver, an ascetic or a monk. If one sees a spider in his dream, it may mean that he will meet a pious and a religious man. Weaving a web in a dream means becoming weak. A spider in a dream also could represent a pleasing wife. If one sees a spider hanging down from the ceiling in a dream, it indicates a severe winter in that area. *(Also see Tarantula)*

Spikes of grain: Seeing spikes of grain in a dream means money and profits that will multiply. Green spikes of grain in a dream represent prosperity and a good harvest, while dry spikes of grain mean drought. Spikes in a dream also represent the days, months and years of one's life, or the wealth contained in this world, its natural resources, or its coffers. Carrying a bunch of green spikes in one's hand in a dream means knowledge or profits. Collecting spikes of grain from different spots in a farm one recognizes in a dream means that he will receive regular payments or a wage from the owner of that farm.

Spikes: (Fishbones)

Spinal column: *(See Backbone; Body¹)*

Spindle whorl: (Spinning; Yarn) Owning a spindle whorl in a dream means marriage, while losing it in a dream means divorce. To place the spindle on the spinning wheel in a dream means reconciliation between husband and wife. A spindle whorl in a dream also means steadfastness, profits from a business, or it could mean marriage for a single person. *(Also see Spinning)*

Spindle: If a woman sees a spindle in her dream, it means that she will beget a daughter or have a new sister. If a thread line of a spindle breaks in a dream, it means that a traveller will be delayed. Spinning a wire with a spindle in a dream means using the help of a stranger. In a dream, a spindle also represents a messenger, a collector, or a vehicle. *(Also see Spindle wheel; Spinning)*

Spinning wheel: A girl operating a spinning wheel in a dream represents contentment, giving things their true worth, or devoting one's life to a good cause. If the girl keeps on weaving, then when she finishes her work she unravels the fabric in the dream, it means God's wrath, afflictions, or destruction. *(Also see Spindle; Spinning; Wheel)*

Spinning: (Yarn) If a woman sees herself working on a spinning wheel and quickly trying to finish her work in a dream, it means that a traveller will soon come home, or that an expected visitor will arrive. If she sees herself taking her time in spinning her wool in a dream, it means that either she or her husband will undertake a journey. If the thread breaks inside the bobbin in her dream, it means cancellation of her plans to travel. If she sees herself in a dream spinning cotton threads, it means separation from her husband. During such a separation, she will cease asking her husband for her bridal dower, and later on she will return to him. If she sees herself spinning linen in a dream, it means that she will seek the company of righteous people to acquire wisdom and knowledge. If a man sees himself spinning cotton, or linen in a dream, it means that he will suffer humiliation, or he may engage in a job which he cannot do properly. If the threads he is spinning turn thin in the dream, it means that he toils hard through his work but fails to do it properly. If the threads turn too thick in the dream, it means that he will undertake a business trip and reap success from it. If a man sees a woman spinning cotton in her house in a dream, it means that she will betray her husband with someone else. If one sees himself spinning wool, fur, or hair in his dream, it means that he will undertake a profitable business trip. To undo a spun thread in a dream means renouncing one's allegiance, or breaking one's promise, or denying one's commitment. *(Also see Ball of thread; Pledge of allegiance; Spindle)*

Spireas: *(See Meadow)*

Spirits: *(See Intoxicants)*

Spiritual gathering: (Admonition; Fellowship; Gathering; Meeting; Religious meeting) If one who does not qualify to be a spiritual leader or a scholar sees himself holding a religious gathering and admonishing people to do good and to forbid evil in a dream, it means distress and an illness which he is praying hard for it to be lifted by God's leave. However, if he does speak wisdom during such a spiritual gathering in his dream, it means praying hard to have one's distress and illness lifted by God's leave. Consequently, and God willing, he will recover from his illness and be able to dispel his adversities. His condition will change from tightness to abundance. He will repay his debts and overcome his oppressors. If one sees a spiritual gathering where God's Name is glorified, the holy Qur'ān is read and wisdom is spoken in his dream, it means that such a place will be established as a spiritual center or as a mosque. Such a place will also become a center where spiritual leaders and governors will gather and speak. If love songs of light nature are played during such a gathering in a dream, it means that falsehood will overtake such a place. If one sees himself sitting in the center stage, in the middle of learned people and religious scholars in a dream, it means that he will receive a greater knowledge and honor in his life. A gathering that involves a court case, or a marriage in a dream represents an unknown adversity that will safely pass. Admonishing people in a public gathering in a dream means that one's command will be obeyed. Sitting in the center stage in a spiritual gathering in a dream represents one's station or rank, or it could represent one's wife, child, property, or personal secretary. Anything that happens to such a gathering in the dream may reflect on any of them. *(Also see Fellowship; Gathering; Mosque)*

Spiritual guide: *(See Army's flag; Minaret; Spiritual gathering)*

Spiritual leader: *(See Army's flag; Minaret; Spiritual gathering)*

Spit out: (Imprecation; Witchcraft) Spitting over something in a dream, or blowing over a knot and spitting on it with an imprecation in a dream means witchcraft. *(Also see Spittle)*

Spitefulness: *(See Enmity)*

Spittle: Saliva or spittle in a dream represents the element of one's strength. If in a dream one seems to have a dry mouth, it represent his inability to do what his competition can do. Spitting against a wall in a dream means spending one's money in a good cause, or engaging in a profitable business. Spitting on the floor in a dream means purchasing land. Spitting against a tree in a dream means to recant one's promise. Spitting at another person in a dream means despising him. Warm saliva in a dream means long life, while cold saliva represents a short life. Thè color of one's saliva in a dream shows the state of one's spirit. Spiting blood or phlegm in a dream means speaking ill of others.

Spleen pain: *(Also see Body¹; Pain; Spleen)*

Spleen: *(ant.)* A healthy spleen in a dream means that one's coffers are well protected and that he will enjoy success in his life. If one's spleen is inflamed or larger than usual in the dream, it means that one will fail to achieve his goals, or to change his general condition, or that he will become physically weakened by a debilitating illness. Suffering from one's spleen in a dream means that one will spoil or waste a great wealth which he is supposed to use to support his family. *(Also see Body¹)*

Splice: *(See Twist)*

Split: A split in a branch of a tree in a dream means that a member of one's family will brace against him.

Spoils: If one sees himself pillaging or plundering something in a dream, it means that he will recant a covenant, or ruin something useful, stray from God's path, or it could mean that he will marry a young girl whom he will abuse sexually. If what he ruins is a cast of precious metal in the dream, then it denotes bad words he speaks, or jealousy and envy he carries. *(Also see Booty)*

Sponger: *(See Leech)*

Sponsoring a child: *(See Sponsorship)*

Sponsorship: (Guarantee; Legal guardianship; Support; Tutelage) To take the responsibility of caring for someone, or to sponsor someone, or to become a legal guardian of someone, or to guarantee someone in a dream means blessings, profits, or victory over one's enemy. A sponsorship in a dream also signifies steadfastness and resoluteness of both the guarantor and his protégée. It is also said that sponsoring someone in a dream means to cause him harm. Guaranteeing someone or something in a dream means profits. Sponsoring a child in a dream means advising an enemy. *(Also see Guarantee; Legal guardian)*

Spook: *(See Ghost; Mirage)*

Spool: In a dream, a spool means keeping one's secrets, or it could represent a gracious man, or a trustworthy person who lends his help to others and benefits them in their worldly affairs. If one sees himself carrying a spool while taking his ritual ablution in a dream, it means that he will seek the help of a righteous believer who holds fast to the rope of God Almighty. In that sense, a spool represents the element of religious life and the rope in a dream signifies religion, which is one's connection to his Lord. Carrying a spool when performing one's ablution in a dream means that one will be permanently cured from ills and become free from debts. A spool in a dream also means an active servant, or a talkative son. *(Also see Ball of thread; Rope)*

Spoor: *(See Tracker)*

Spores: *(See Pollen)*

Spread¹: *(See Date Spread)*

Spread²: *(See Measure)*

Spread³: *(See Hanging clothes)*

Spring: (Ascent; Creation; Fountainhead; Season) In a dream, a spring represents money, a child who may die young, a short lived marriage, acquiring an important job that does not last, or a fast disappearing happiness. *(Also see Fountainhead)*

Sprinkler: (Water sprinkler) In a dream, a sprinkler means rejuvenation, renewal of life, revival of old practices, or extinguishing a fire.

Sprout: (Garden greens; Leguminosae) A fresh sprout in a dream means distress, but if it is dry, then it means a good harvest, or clean money which is earned with joy. If one sees himself gathering a bunch of green sprouts in a dream, it denotes a warning. If one recognizes its substance in his dream, interpreting the element then goes back to its innate quality. Entering into a field of sprouts in a dream means a marriage into the family who owns that farmland, or it could mean a business partnership. If one sees himself bartering green sprouts for bread in a dream, it means aversion to poverty. Eating cooked sprouts in a dream means benefits in every respect. If one sees himself in a dream exchanging quails and manna *(See Manna)* for green sprouts and garlic, it means that he will be subjugated to poverty and humiliation. Purslane in a dream represents someone who has exaggerated hopes. This is why this type of sprout is also called: 'Stupid sprout.' *(Also see Garden herbs; Lentil)*

Spur: (Prick; Punch; Strike) In a dream, to spur someone means to pursue a satanic act, then be struck with fear, or run away, although one will survive and ultimately triumph over his act.

Spy glass: *(See Binoculars)*

Spy: (Diver) In a dream, a spy represents jinn *(See Jinn)* or an evil influence. *(Also see Diver)*

Squandering money: *(See Shearer)*

Squash: *(See Pumpkin)*

Squeak of a mouse: *(See Sound of animals)*

Squeaking of the door: In a dream, squeaking of the door means an evil caused by a guard, or a fight between husband and wife, or it could mean divulging a secret. *(Also see Screeching of a pen)*

Squill: (Onion) In a dream, a squill represents an obscene and corrupt person who is notorious for his pranks. Holding a squill in one's hand in a dream means seeking something that will earn him the worst reputation.

Squinting of the eyes: Squinting of the eyes in a dream means evil talk, or perhaps it could mean good news.

Squirrel: *(See Fur)*

Squirting cucumber: *(See Snake-cucumber)*

Stabilizer: (Balancer; Evenness; Weight stabilizer) A weight stabilizer in a dream represents equilibrium, justice, truthfulness and beneficial knowledge.

Stableman: (Barn; Cattle-ranching; Fodder; Forage) In a dream, a stableman represents a rich and a generous person who is known for his good deeds. Seeing a stableman in a dream also means managing one's business, showing kindness to others, distributing charity, helping foreigners, assisting travellers, turning one's attention to slothful people, or feeding the homeless. *(Also see Driver)*

Staff¹: *(See Scepter; Solomon; Staff²; Transformation)*

Staff²: (Rod; Wand; Scepter; Stick) In a dream, a staff represents a distinctive, strong, generous and a helpful person. Holding a staff in a dream means depending on a person who also carries some imprints of hypocrisy. Through such a person, one will attain his goals, gain strength and overcome his enemy. Leaning on a hollow staff in a dream means losing one's wealth and keeping it a secret. If the staff of a governor, or a leader, or a manager is broken in a dream, it means that he will lose his post. If he is a merchant, it means that he will lose his business. If one sees himself hitting the ground with his staff in a dream, it means that he will have control over that land, preside over its people, or triumph over the landlord. If one turns into a staff in his dream, it means a quick death. A broken staff in a dream represents a sickness that will lead to debilitation and complete loss of power. A staff in a dream also means giving orders, victory over one's enemies, or attainment of one's goals. If the staff is made from a branch of a palm tree in a dream, it means isolation. If it is made from a branch of an almond tree in the dream, it means banishment. If it is made from a branch of a plum tree in a dream, it means religious hypocrisy. A staff in a dream also could represent a snake or sorcery. Hitting someone with a staff in a dream means using harsh language with him. If a poor person hits a rock with his staff, and if water gushes forth from the rock in the dream, it means prosperity. If a rich person sees such a dream, it means increase in his wealth. The water that comes out of a rock in a dream also could represent sweet earnings. A wooden staff in a dream represents a vile person, or irreligious man, because wood in a dream means hypocrisy. *(Also see Scepter; Solomon; Transformation)*

Staircase: *(See Stairway)*

Stairway: (Conveyor; Steps; Travels) In a dream, stairways represent the vehicle of rising in station, advancement in worldly gains, seeking the blessings of the hereafter, and the rising of one's station in the hereafter. A stairway in a dream also could represent the days of one's life and their term. If one sees a staircase which he recognizes in the dream, it could represent the servant of a house, its owner, or its accountant. If a sick person sees himself climbing an unknown staircase which is leading him to the upper room from where he can see paradise in the dream, it means that he may die from his illness and reach what he saw. If obstacles hinder his way or impede his climb in the dream, it means that he is detained, and the immediate blessings of such a gift will be veiled to him. Descending a staircase in a dream means arriving from a journey, resigning from one's job, impeachment, or it could represent a pedestrian. If one's descent leads him to his family, house, or farmland in the dream, it means money. If what he reaches at the end of the staircase is unknown, and if one meets people, or souls he does not recognize in the dream, it also denotes what we have earlier explained. If during one's climb or descent he falls into a well, or if a giant bird grabs him and flies away with him, or if a beast devours him, or if he steps into a boat that sails away as he steps into it, or if he takes a step to find himself riding an animal, or a vehicle of some type, the staircase then represents the stages of one's life and what he encountered during the journey of his life, all replayed or screened before his eyes at the point of descending into his grave, or as a book one reads after his death. If he does wake up and finds himself healthy and fit, it means that he will become a tyrant, an unjust person, an atheist and a reprobate. If one sees himself descending a staircase that leads him into a mosque, lush foliage, green fields, a fresh breeze of spring, or into a pond to take a ritual ablution to perform his prayers in the dream, it means that he will become a true believer, repent for his his sins and abandon his blameworthy conduct. Otherwise, if he descends upon adverse elements such as snakes, lions, steep hills, corpses, or a field of scattered remains in a dream, then it represents major trials and adversities. If the steps are made of clay in one's dream, they indicate positive signs. However, a stairway could be regarded as unfavorable if its steps are made of backed bricks. If they are made of stones in the dream, they mean business success, along with a heart like a stone. If the staircase is made of wooden steps in the dream, it means reaching a high rank which is compounded with hypocrisy. If they are made of gold in the dream, then they mean achieving success and gaining authority. If they are made of silver in the dream, they represent one's entourage and attendants. Climbing a staircase in a dream also means sharpening one's intellect and awareness. In a dream, a stairway is also interpreted to mean leading a life of ascetic detachment and devotion. Coming near a staircase in a dream also means attaining success and a growing piety. Each step represents a different station. Climbing a staircase in a dream also represents the dangers one may have to cross. Seeing a staircase with five steps in a dream represents the five time prayers, or the pulpit where the Imām stands to deliver his Friday sermon. That is why some interpreters qualify the staircase in one's dream as glad tidings, good news, prayers, charity, alms giving, fasting, or a pilgrimage. God knows best.

Stake: *(See Peg)*

Stale bread: (Cheap; Inexpensive; Shoddy prices)

Stall: *(See Carriage house)*

Stammer: Stammering in a dream means acquiring knowledge and a better religious understanding, or it may mean eloquence in speech. Stammering in a dream also means attaining a high ranking position, or winning victory over one's enemies.

Stamp: *(See Seal; Cauterize)*

Standing up for the truth: *(See Setting out)*

Star: (Astral; Celestial spheres; Constellation; Dog star; Moon; Procyon; Sirius; Stars) In a dream, a star represents the best and the most noble of people. Seeing the stars scintillating with lights and gathered inside one's house in a dream means that great people, or some of the leaders of the country will meet at that house. If the stars are gathered in one's house, and if their light is dimmed in the dream, it means that such people will secretly meet in that house under constraint, or because of a calamity. Holding a star in one's hand in a dream means begetting a noble son who will grow to be a great leader. Stealing a star in a dream means stealing a valuable thing. Seeing a star falling from the skies in a dream means that a calamity will befall that place and it will particularly affect the life of a great and noble person, or it could mean the death of the governor of that town. In general, stars in a dream represent political leaders, the most knowledgeable of scholars, the most noble of people in the society and the richest of the rich. Seeing many stars inside one's house in a dream also may signify having a large family. Seeing the seven major stars, or the fixed stars of the solar system in a dream represents the trades, businesses, knowledge and the leadership in the land. Each of such stars brings a different luck. Seeing a brilliant star in a dream means happiness and leadership. If a rich person sees the skies without stars in a dream, it means loss of his wealth. If a poor person sees the skies without stars in a dream, it means his death. Holding little stars in one's hand in a dream means acquiring fame and presiding over people. Seeing a star over one's head in a dream means becoming renowned and surpassing one's associates, or it could mean serving in a high ranking position. If one sees brilliant stars gathering in one place in his dream, it means that he will reap benefits from a business trip, or safely return home from such a successful business trip. Riding a star in a dream means leadership, strength and wealth. If one sees the stars fixed under his roof in a dream, it means a calamity, or destruction of one's house, or it could mean the death of the head of the household. Eating stars in a dream means swindling people of their money. Swallowing a star in a dream means mixing with noble people and sharing one's personal life with them, or it could mean insulting or slandering the companions of God's Prophet upon whom be peace. Sucking on a star in a dream means learning at the hands of great scholars or a wise shaikh. If a fortuneteller or an astrologer sees himself eating stars in a dream, it means that he will be selected to fill an important job from which he will prosper. As for the majority of people, eating stars in a dream means death. Seeing the stars scattered in a dream means the death of great leaders or scholars, or it could mean a war. Seeing the stars falling down on earth then disappearing, or the lights of meteors entering the earth atmosphere in a dream, represents a great destruction and death. The falling of small stars in a dream signifies the death of unknown people and the meek ones, while the falling of large stars represent the death of renowned people. Seeing the stars falling from the skies also could mean becoming bald or losing one's hair. Whereby, the stars represent one's hair and the skies represent one's head. Seeing the stars during the daylight time in a dream means scandals, notoriety, or major events and calamities. Seeing the morning stars in a dream means a wedding. Becoming a star in a dream means acquiring wealth and fame. Seeing stars that denote the coming of winter in a dream means distress and sorrow, while seeing the stars that denote the coming of summer in a dream mean happiness and good living. *(Also see Celestial spheres; Ship)*

Starling: *(zool.)* In a dream, a starling represents an ascetic, one who surrenders to God's will, a true believer, a patient man, a traveller or a companion on the road. If one sees himself holding a starling in a dream, it means that he will meet someone of such caliber. If he eats its flesh, or pulls out its feathers in the dream, it means that he will receive benefits. A starling in a dream also may represent the element of mixing good deeds with bad ones, or a person who is neither rich or poor, neither honest or vile. Seeing a starling in a dream also means humiliation, being content with little, or it may represent a writer. *(Also see Swallow)*

Stars: *(astr.* Horoscope) Watching the stars in a dream means presiding over people. *(Also see Celestial spheres; Moon)*

State¹: (Abode; Changing condition vs. station; Dwellings; Transient)

State²: (Government)

Station of Abraham: *(Maqām Ibrāhïm, arb.)* One who stands at the Station of Abraham at the Sacred Mosque in Mecca and offers his prayers in a dream is a pious person who observes the divine laws and who may be invited to perform a pilgrimage. If a terrified person sees himself entering inside the Station of Abraham in a dream, it means that all his fears will be dispelled and that he will reach the abode of safety. Entering the station of God's prophet Abraham, upon whom be peace, in a dream also means receiving honors, seeking knowledge, or receiving an inheritance from one's father or mother. Standing up or sitting at the Station of Abraham in a dream also may signify living by the divine laws until one's soul returns to its Lord. *(Also see Abraham)*

Station: In a dream, attaining a station means receiving an irrevocable award, as compared to reaching a state which denotes a transitory passage and a condition which is subject to constant changes.

Statue: (Idol) A statue in a dream represents falsehood, inventions, make-shift, fiction, illusion, heedlessness, or a nice looking person who is full of deception. Worshipping a statue in a dream means lying to God Almighty, or that one worships what his mind tells him to worship, whether it is a physical object or a child of one's imagination. If it is a carved wooden statue in the dream, it means that he ingratiates himself to rich people, or to an unjust person in authority through his religion. If the statue is built from wood in the dream, it means that one seeks religious arguments or disputes. If the statue is made of silver in the dream, it means that one elicits sexual relationship with his servant, or with a foreign woman, or perhaps just a friendship. If the statue is made of gold in the dream, it means that one may commit an abominable action, or a religious inequity, or seeks profits from someone at the expense of displeasing God Almighty and consequently, one will suffer financial losses or health problems. If the statue combines mixed material of bronze, copper, steel, iron, or lead in the dream, it means that such a person uses his religious garb to make profits, and that he often forgets about his Lord. A statue in a dream also means travels. Seeing a golden or a silver statue in a dream also could mean prosperity. Seeing a bronze statue of a young woman moving around in a dream means a good harvest, prosperity, or travels. If the statue is bigger than life-size, then it means a fright. Statues in a dream also represent one's children, his sexual drive, or his determination. If one sees himself worshiping a statue in a dream, it means that he is engaged in falsehood, giving preference to his personal desires and passions over obeying his Lord's commands. If one sees himself worshiping a golden statue in a dream, it means that he will solicit business from someone who worships God Almighty, though he will also suffer losses from such an association. It also means that he will lose his investment and it will show the weakness of his faith. If one sees himself worshiping a statue made of silver in the dream, it means that he uses his religion to make business out of it, or to betray others through it, or that he will solicit the help of someone to do evil, or that he may sexually abuse a young girl who trusts his religious appearance. If one sees a statue and does not associate it with worship, or if he does not see anyone worshiping it in his dream, his dream then represents financial gains. A statue in a dream also means to be enamored with a woman or a boy. Statues in a dream also could mean deafness, idiotic behavior, dumbness, attachment to anything in this world, making an idol out of it, such as one's love and attachment to his position, status, business, wife, beloved, house, or child, etcetera. If one owns a statue in a dream, it means that he may marry a deaf, or a dumb, or a non-intelligent woman, or that he may beget a child who will grow up having one or more of these defects. In whatever condition one sees the statue in his dream, it will reflect on any of the above. A statue in a dream also represents a generation. If the statue is missing something in the dream, such defect will definitely manifest in one's society. Seeing a statue in a dream also could reflect one's strength and determination. If one breaks a statue, or lames it, or damages it in a dream, it means that he will vanquish his enemy and earn rank and fame. If the statue in the dream portrays a particular woman, or if it is interpreted to represent a specific woman, then she will be quiet, intelligent and serene, or it could mean that she is stupid and has pride.

Status: *(See Rising in station)*

Steak: (Meat) In a dream, a steak represents an unavoidable evil happening, or it could represent a passing danger. Sliced meat in a dream also could mean happiness, quick earnings, fertility, or exposure of what man should keep personal and private. Seeing a butcher slicing meat in a dream could mean fights, evil, war, divisions in the society, or mixing the lawful with the unlawful, or usury, or fulfilling one's needs.

Steam: *(See Vapor)*

Steamroller: (Mortar) In a dream, a steamroller represents a hard-working man, or a person who tries to make good of an investment but fails to succeed. A steamroller in a dream also represents force, adversities, aberration, despotism, or it could mean bringing things down to proper level and correcting the course of one's life.

Steelyard: (Scale beam) A steel yard in a dream represents a difficult son, or a husband with a temper that is difficult to balance. Seeing a steelyard in a dream also denotes knowledge, guidance, following the path of truth, or it could represent a judge, or a great king and his land, his subjects, secrets, hearing, sight, justice and responsibilities.

Steep incline: *(See Ascent)*

Steeping: *(See Infusion)*

Steer: *(See Bull; Cow)*

Steering wheel: Holding onto a steering wheel in a dream means pursuing one's own destiny and whatever good or bad it brings. Controlling a steering wheel in a dream means that adverse conditions will turn easy through one's determination and perseverance.

Stench: *(See Odor; Perspiration)*

Steps: (Conveyor; Stairway)

Sterile: *(See Impotence)*

Stern: *(See Scowling)*

Stew: (Indian meal; Indian stew) Cooking a dish of boiled meat and vegetables in a dream means profits and prosperity for a poor person. Cooking Indian stew which is a meal consisting of corn and other vegetables in a dream means poverty, worship, or devotion. Cooking unripened vegetables in a dream means an illness. If one cooks a nice meal for himself in a dream, it means that he will be honored, or it could mean a political appointment, or money. If someone else cooks one's meal in a dream, it may denote double-crossing, deception, or perhaps it may mean receiving help from someone according to one's own intention or state. *(Also see Boiled vegetables; Kitchen; Ladle)*

Steward: *(See Wick)*

Stigmatize: *(See Besmear)*

Sting: The sting of a scorpion, or the bite of a snake in a dream means falling into sin, or committing a wrong action. *(Also see Scorpion)*

Stinger: (Tongue. *See Scorpion; Sting*)

Stink: *(See Odor; Perspiration)*

Stir up: *(See Digging up the past)*

Stockbroker: *(See Termite)*

Stocking: (Sock) In a dream, stockings represent wealth and prevention, as long as they are not worn. Once seen worn in a dream, they mean business losses. If one's mother is alive, it means that he will migrate with her to another country, or it could mean that she will be deprived of her son. If the socks are new and have a clean smell in the dream, it means that one regularly pays his due alms, that he is praised for his character and that his money will grow in a lawful way. If his socks are old or emit bad odors in the dream, it means that he withholds paying the obligatory alms tax, that he is uncharitable, worthy of blame and that his wealth will quickly disappear.

Stomach pain: *(See Body¹; Pain)*

Stomach: In a dream, the stomach represents the elements of property, family, secrets, one's mate, prison, grave, health, sickness, friend, wayfarer, one's religious life and nature of one's devotion. If in a dream one sees his stomach open, it means that his business may be temporarily put out of commission, or that he may lose any benefits he used to derive from it up to then. The other aforementioned elements also may apply. If the person in question is a pregnant woman, and if she sees her baby or any part of it comes out of her open stomach, this may mean that a jailed person in her family will be set free, or that the family graves will be desecrated, or that the body of someone in her family will be exhumed, thus uncovering its diseases and infestations, or it could mean that one's personal life will become public knowledge. If one is actually complaining of such an illness, his dream means that he will find a cure for it. If one sees that he has no stomach in a dream, it means that he may lose a friend, or that his guardian may die shortly, or that he may become a religious, ascetic and devoted worshiper. If one sees fire coming out of his stomach in a dream, it means that he will repent for stealing the properties of orphans. If one sees himself crawling on his stomach in a dream, it shows him being needy and striving to barely feed himself, or it may denote his materialistic character. The stomach in a dream also represents the plains of a valley. It also can be interpreted as one's tribal belonging or a branch of his lineage. Entering a stomach in a dream means travels, imprisonment, or returning home from one of the two. If one sees himself inside the womb of his mother while he is traveling in a foreign land in a dream, it means that he will return to his motherland to die and be buried there. *(Also see Body¹; Rumbling of one's stomach)*

Stone coffin: *(See Sarcophagus)*

Stone hammer: *(See Hammer; Stone¹)*

Stone tomb: *(See Grave; Sarcophagus)*

Stone¹: (Rock) A discarded stone in a dream represents a dead person. It could also represent people with hardened hearts, heedless, or jobless people. It is common among the people of knowledge to describe an ignorant person as a stone. Owning a precious stone in a dream could mean buying one in wakefulness, or it may mean gaining a strong foothold over someone of the same caliber, or it could mean a marriage to a compatible person. If one sees himself petrified in a dream, it means that he disobeys his Lord, in that sense, if he is sick, it means that he may die from his illness, or he may be inflicted with a stroke that will leave him paralyzed. A falling stone over the world in a dream means the wrath of God Almighty, a calamity, or that an unjust person will rule the land. If the stone splits asunder or explodes after falling in the dream, it means that the harm will touch every house. Carrying bags full of stones or moving mountains in a dream means attempting to do something difficult. Hanging a stone around one's neck as a charm in a dream means that an affliction or an evil will take place. If a poor person sees himself hitting a rock with a staff to split it, then if water gushes forth in the dream, it means that he will strike it rich. Stones in a dream also may represent devotion, asceticism, or godly people. If a godly person or an ascetic sees himself possessing a stone in a dream, it means that the blessings he receives will show in his community, and people will seek him to pray for their needs. Owning a wheat grinding stone, a juicer, porphyry, or any therapeutic or medicinal stones in a dream represent a respected or a revered person such as one's father, one's master, teacher, shaikh, friend, relative, physician, gnostic, a learned person, honorable people, a property, comfort, profits, benefits, or a rewarding trade. Such stones also may be interpreted as extensive travels. *(Also see Pebbles; Rocks)*

Stone²: *(See Carnelian-red; Gem; Jewel; Ring)*

Stonecutter: Seeing a stonecutter in a dream means that one is close to committing a major sin. A stonecutter in a dream also means enmity or divisiveness. A stone cutter in a dream also represents an experienced person at dealing with, treating and healing the pains of the hardened hearts. *(Also see Stonemasonry)*

Stonemason: *(See Stonemasonry)*

Stonemasonry: (Cutting stones; Stone carving; Sculpturing) Building a structure in a dream from masonry rather than baked brick represents elevation of one's status, success, or stretching one's hopes. It also could denote concerns about protecting one's wife, adopting what is beneficial, conducting scientific research, or preserving one's heritage. Building the base, the foundation, or the pillars from uncut stones rather than marble in a dream connotes humiliation and poverty. If one sees that the gravestones were changed from marble into unfinished stones in a dream, it means alteration of a will left by the deceased. *(Also see Building)*

Stoning to death: *(See Stoning)*

Stoning: (Capital punishment; Cleansing; Curse; Damn; Death; Lapidate) Stoning someone in a dream means insulting him, backbiting him, or it could mean slandering a woman. Stoning someone to death in a dream means purification from sin only when it relates to fulfilling the divine laws.

Storage: (Ferro concrete; Chaste wife)

Stork: In a dream, a stork represents sociable and sharing people. However seeing a flock of storks gathering in the wintertime in a dream means a meeting of thieves and highway robbers, or it could represent the enemy's army, cold weather, air pollution, or strong winds. Seeing a dispersed flock of storks in a dream is then a good sign for a traveller, or it could mean returning home from a business trip.

Storm: *(See Wind)*

Storyteller: In a dream, a storyteller may represent the Imām of a mosque, or the Khaṭīb who delivers the Friday sermon. A storyteller in a dream also may represent one's livelihood, or intestinal and bowel problems, or he could represent travels. If the stories are new, then they mean disturbances in one's life. If they are stories of chivalry, then they represent a war. A pleasant story one tells to a king, or to man of authority in a dream represents wealth, or great profits which are distributed equitably. As for a merchant, hearing a pleasant story in a dream represents easy and quick profits from his business, and for a craftsman, it represents a sizeable contract, or an important new account. *(Also see Comedian; Humorist)*

Story: *(See Storyteller)*

Stove: *(See Fireplace)*

Straight razor: *(See Razor)*

Strain: Exerting efforts to one's utmost, or to the point of straining oneself in a dream means the death of a sick person, or it could represent laboring hard to sustain one's dependents.

Strainer: A strainer in a dream represents a noble servant. *(Also see Sieve)*

Strand of hair: (Bun; Tuft; Wisp) If a pregnant woman sees a strand of hair in her dream, it means that she will beget a blessed son. A strand of hair hanging over one's head in a dream means money. Carrying several tufts in a dream represents one's neighbors. If a woman sees herself having a long strand of hair in a dream, it means that her son will become a leader. If she sees her hair thick in the dream, it means that she will do something that will make her famous. If people see her thick strand of hair, it means that she will be exposed for something wrong she has committed. Black hair represents a respected and a handsome looking husband. If the woman sees herself without a head cover in a dream, it means that her husband has left her and he will not return back to her. If she is not married, it means that she will never marry. If she sees herself having charcoal colored hair in a dream, it means that she will live from her husband's wealth or inheritance. *(Also see Black hair)*

Strangulation: (Hanging) If one strangles himself with his own hands, or if he hangs himself with a rope which he attaches to the ceiling in a dream, it means that he is sufferings from depression, distress, or sorrow. It also could mean that he will not reside in his present house, or in the place where he saw himself strangled. The same interpretation goes for seeing oneself suffering from asphyxia. *(Also see Suffocation)*

Strap: *(See Bond¹)*

Stratagem: *(See Advice)*

Straw mat: *(See Carpet; Mat)*

Straw: In a dream, straw represents richness, prosperity and a good harvest, for one who gathers straw ends and brings them home. Eating straw in a dream means poverty and hunger. Locking or placing straw in an unsuitable container such as safe or a dresser in a dream means depression and destruction of cattle feed. Straw in a dream represents charities. Abundance of straw in a dream also represent a community where the female count exceeds the number of men. Wheat straw in a dream means goodness and trustworthiness. *(Also see Wheat straw)*

Strawberry mark: *(See Birthmark)*

Strawberry: *(See Mulberry)*

Stream: (Brook; Creek; Irrigation; Rivulet; Watering) In a dream, a stream represents the course of one's livelihood, his source of income, his shop, his trade, travels and the like interests. A stream in a dream also could mean festering wounds, waterskin, watering irrigation, the resting area on the highway, one's throat which is the watering access of his body, or it could represent life if it is public property. If it is a private property, then it represents the life of the person who digs out such a stream. A stream in a dream also represents a good life, or the comfort of its owner. If its water flows over its banks in the dream, then it represents sorrows, crying, or sadness. If one sees a stream flowing through people's homes in a dream, then such a stream represents a happy life and particularly when its water is colorless and sweet tasting. If one sees himself as the owner of a stream, a spring, or a watercourse which he establishes as a charity in a dream, it means that he will become a leader, a president, or happily serve his community. If one cleans a rivulet then finds it filthy again, or finds it filled with trash in his dream, it represents diarrhea. If he sees water flowing under his feet in a dream, then it means dropsy. If one sees a stream of water running through a town where people are filling their jars, drinking its water and thanking God for His blessings in a dream, it means that a calamity is removed and is replaced with peace, safety and tranquility. If the people are inflicted with adversities or a drought, then it means prosperity and rains, food, or money and their merchandise will not stagnate. If the water in the stream is murky, or salty, or running outside its canal, then it represents a coming calamity that will cause mass sufferings, or a sickness such as cold in the winter and fever in the summer, or it could mean that they will hear bad news about some travellers, or it could represent a richness which is acquired from an unlawful source, or it could mean that he will receive tainted money. If one sees a watercourse flowing only in the direction of his house, then such adversities will be his lot. If one sees a stream flowing in the direction of his house, or garden in a dream, it means a marriage or conceiving a child. A stream of flowing blood rather than water in a dream represents the deviation of one's wife. If one sees a stream running off its course, or damaging people's crops in a dream, it means bad news. Blocking the path of a stream in a dream means separation between a husband and a wife, or avoiding a sinful action between unmarried relatives. If one sees himself standing behind a rivulet in a dream, it means that his wife will inherit him. If one sees the water of a stream flowing toward his own home or garden, and if he finds that its water has turned into blood in the dream, it means that someone will marry his wife after him. Drinking fresh water from a rivulet, a stream, or a river in a dream represents the joy of living or longevity. A murky water of a rivulet or a stream in a dream means a fright, difficulties, or a sickness. Streams in a dream also represent the veins and the blood that flows through the human body. *(Also see Fountainhead; Meadow; Spring)*

Street vendor: In a dream, if a street vendor is selling woolen garments or golden jewelry, then one's dream denotes benefits. If he is selling silk merchandise in the dream, then it denotes harm.

Strength: In a dream, strength signifies wealth that is accompanied with an illness.

Stress: In a dream, stress means tightness of income, or it could represent the consequences of one's wrongdoing, or the punishment for his sins.

Stretcher: (Dolly; Litter) In a dream, a stretcher or a dolly represents a hard-working man who earns his livelihood through toiling and sufferings. There are no advantages in seeing a stretcher in a dream and particularly if one is brought before a sick person, then it means his death and departure from this world. A stretcher in a dream also represents an abode or a hostel.

Strike: *(See Spur)*

Striking: *(See Punch; Slapping; Spur)*

String instruments: Seeing string instruments in a dream means recovering from an illness, or they can represent man's spinal cord, or his spinal column, strength, sternness, relentlessness, health condition, or physical fitness. Seeing string instruments in a dream also means gaining some understanding about human nature, or the physiology of the human being, or they could represent medicine or astronomy. If a bachelor sees string instruments in his dream, it may mean that he will get married. If a wife sees herself playing a string instrument in her dream, it means that she will put a child in her lap. If one sees himself playing a string instrument in front of the governor's house in a dream, it means that he will preside over people should he qualify. Otherwise, it could mean that he will piece together or fabricate a story. Seeing a lute or a guitar in a dream denotes no harm if one sees them or intends to hold them, except if one hears their music. Playing or hearing a string instrument in a dream represents lies. Playing them in one's house in a dream represent a calamity that will befall that family. It is also said that playing such an instrument in a dream also means winning fame and presiding over others, though it could also denote distress for the player. If a string of such an instrument breaks in a dream, it means relaxation and relief from stress. A broken string of a lute or a guitar or similar instrument in a dream represents a precious property that causes its owner a headache. Every time he remembers it, he suffers from heartburn or stomach pain. Seeing such an instrument by a layman or a hard-working person in a dream means consolation and a lesson to learn from life. Seeing it by an insolent person in a dream means further corruption, while if a a tyrant or an unjust person sees it in a dream, it means oppressing others, terrorizing them and cutting them off from their families. *(Also see Banjo; Musician)*

String: *(See String instruments)*

Stripped: *(See Naked)*

Strive: *(See Efforts; Struggle)*

Stronghold: *(See Castle; Citadel; Fortress)*

Strudel: *(See Pastry)*

Struggle: *(See Inner-struggle; Jihād; Wrestling)*

Strutting: *(See Walking)*

Stubbornness: *(See Obstinacy)*

Students' leader: *(See Assistant teacher)*

Stuffed fish: *(See Stuffed turkey)*

Stuffed fowl: *(See Stuffed turkey)*

Stuffed lam: *(See Stuffed turkey)*

Stuffed Turkey: (Stuffed fish; Stuffed lam; Stuffing) In a dream, a stuffed turkey means holdings, reserves, profits from an investment, marriage, a festive dinner, or it could mean recovering from an illness. The grease collected in the bottom of a pan in the dream represents money earned from a woman.

Stuffing: *(See Stuffed turkey)*

Stumble: *(See Tripping; Walking)*

Stump: *(See Firewood)*

Stun: (Stupefy) If one is stunned by someone in a dream, it represents suffering and trouble driven by perfidy and jealousy of the other person.

Stupefy: *(See Stun)*

Stupid sprout: *(See Sprouts)*

Stupidity: Acting stupidly in a dream means money or profits. If a farmer acts silly in a dream, it may mean a good harvest for that year. Otherwise, the farmer's dream could be meaningless.

Submerse: *(See Diver; Spy)*

Submission: *(See Islām; Slave)*

Submissiveness: *(See Meekness; Humiliation)*

Substitute: *(See Commutative contract)*

Subterranean storehouse: *(See Underground granary)*

Suburban area: *(See City; Village)*

Subversive people: *(See Tar)*

Successors: *(See Companions of the Prophet; Companions; Followers; Righteous people)*

Suck: (Bleed; Drain; Tap) To suck someone in a dream means to take money from him. Sucking someone's breast in a dream means swindling money from his wife. Sucking someone's nose in a dream means taking money from his pocket. Sucking someone's thigh in a dream means taking money from his clan.

Suckling: *(See Breast; Breast-feeding; Milk)*

Suds: *(See Foam)*

Suffocation: (Strangulation) Suffocating in a dream means that one has taken upon himself a responsibility greater than what he can handle, or that he is intimidated into accepting a heavy responsibility, or that he abused a trust or a leadership position. If his suffocation is caused by an illness in the dream, then it represents a chastisement for a sin or an injustice he has committed. If his suffering increases to near strangulation and death in the dream, it means that he is required to repay all the benefits he drew from holding such trust. If he dies in his dream as a consequence of his suffocation, it means that he will lose his battle with the owner and become poor. If he comes back to life after dying in the dream, it means that in a while, God Almighty will reinstate him in his position after his trying experience. He also may regain power and bring his opponents to justice. *(Also see Strangulation)*

Sugar cane: (Cane; Juice; Reeds) In a dream, sugar cane means toiling and suffering, rabbling, or clamor in the area in which it is seen in a dream. Sugar cane in a dream also could represent a noble lineage, acquiring an honorable knowledge, or earning a spiritual advancement. Sugar cane in a dream also represents chaste and noble women or pious men. If one sees a field of sugar cane planted in inadequate terrain, then means destruction, ruin, or archaeological excavations that will lead to exposing the past and exhuming the dead, or it could mean a wailing party of women showing their grief and sorrow. A field of sugar cane in a dream also represents the ability to hide something, or to redo something, or to declare a war, or it could mean signing a business agreement, a marriage contract, celebrating old times and events, freedom from imprisonment, releasing prisoners, recovering from an illness, or exhuming the dead. Chewing or sucking on a stick of sugar cane in a dream means becoming talkative or repetitive. If one sees himself making juice out of sugar cane in a dream, it means prosperity and wealth. Sugar cane in a dream also represents money that one earns from a stingy person. *(Also see Juice; Reed)*

Sugar mill: (Mill) A sugar mill in a dream represents success in the world, sufferings, burial, money, usury, the release of prisoners, a bathhouse, a lavatory, discarding what is shameful, waters, spinning, breathing, a college, or a fellowship house. In general, all types of mills represent good news and guidance. *(Also see Oil Press)*

Sugar: (Kiss; Sweet) Sugar in a dream represents joy, festivities, recovering from an illness, dispelling anxiety, putting worries aside, fulfilling one's aspirations, reaching one's goals, completing one's duty, a noble wife, a blessed son, an intelligent child, or a son who is a genius in all crafts. If sugar is interpreted as money in the dream, then it means lawful money, and if it is interpreted as a man of knowledge, his knowledge is then free from innovation. A piece of sugar candy means a kiss, money, a child, truthfulness, sincerity in words and actions, recovering from an illness, financial comfort after difficulties, or it could represent profits from a farming business, or from collecting the sap from maple trees in season. A large quantity of sugar in a dream means hearsay or vain talk. Selling sugar in a dream may stimulate hypertension or discomfort. *(Also see Sugar cane)*

Suḥūr: *(arb.)* To take the last meal before daybreak during the month of Ramadān in a dream means wearing down one's enemy, repentance of a sinner, guidance to a disbeliever, or it could mean earning little money. If one thinks that he took such a meal in his dream, it means that he may commit a wrongdoing then repent and ask for forgiveness.

Suicide: *(See Disbelief; Killing)*

Suit of mail: *(See Leather shield)*

Suitcase: In a dream, a suitcase represents two brothers, two sons, partners, or perhaps it could mean travels. Having a suitcase, buying or receiving one as a gift in a dream means relief from difficulties. A suitcase in a dream also could represent an ambassador. *(Also see Sack)*

Suite: *(See Chamber)*

Sulfur: In a dream, sulfur represents a liar or tainted money. If used as a fuel for cooking in a dream, sulfur then means guidance, benefits and dispelling worries, or distress, because it burns quickly and its smoke dissipates fast.

Sultān: *(See King; Sun)*

Sun-dried bricks: *(See Adobe)*

Sun: (King; The Fourth heaven; Planet) In a dream, the sun represents a great king, the vice-regent, a father, a prince, a commander, gold, or a beautiful woman. If one sees himself turned into a sun in a dream, it means that he may receive a dominion that will stretch as far as the radiance one sees in his dream. If one sees himself holding the sun in a dream, it means that he will gain strength and wealth that will come about through someone in the government. If one receives the sun hanging as a necklace in a dream, it means that he will win a seat in the senate. If he goes near the sun or sits inside it in a dream, it means that he will acquire power, wealth and support. Should he qualify, the stretch of his power will extend between the two horizons he sees in his dream, or it may mean that he will acquire a knowledge coupled with fame. If one sees that he owns the sun in a dream, it means that his words will be respected and listened to by someone in authority. If someone in authority sees the sun looking clear and brilliant in the dream, it means that his authority will grow, or that he will assist someone in leadership. Otherwise, it means that he will live happily and acquire lawful wealth. If a woman sees such a dream, it means that she will enjoy her marriage and receive what pleases her from her husband. If the sun rises inside one's house in a dream, it means that he will receive an important political appointment, or that he should be careful about his association with someone in authority, or it may mean marriage. If the sun rises inside one's house and lights the entire house in the dream, it means that he will receive honor, dignity, rank and fame. If a woman sees the sun rising inside her house in a dream, it means that she will marry a wealthy person, and that her horizon will expand. The radiance of the sun in a dream means reverence, might and justice of the ruler of that land. If one sees the sun talking to him in a dream, it means that he will be honored and commended by the governor. If one sees the sun or the moon talking to him, and if he then strolls away with them in the dream, it represents his death. If one sees the sun rising from an unusual direction in a dream, it represents a beneficial knowledge he will acquire. If the sun shines over one's head and not the rest of his body in a dream, it means that he will receive a prominent responsibility. If its rays rise to shine over his feet and not the rest of his body in the dream, it means a farming project that brings him prosperity and lawful earnings. If the sun discretely shines over one's belly and without people's noticing it in the dream, it means that he will be struck with leprosy. If it shines over his chest and not the balance of his body in the dream, it means a sickness. If a woman sees that the sun has embraced her from her neck down in a dream, it means that she will marry a person in authority and for one night only. Should such a person divorce her the next morning, it means that she may become a prostitute. If the sun rises from one's open belly in a dream, it means his death. If one sees the sun setting and himself walking behind it, it also means death. If one sees himself walking behind the sun in a dream, it means that he will be captured and imprisoned. If one sees the sun turned into an old man in a dream, it means that the governor will become a pious and God-fearing person. Otherwise, if the sun turns into a young man in the dream, it represents his weakness. If one sees blazes of fire straying away from the sun in a dream, it means the impeachment of some members of the governor's cabinet or someone from his counsel. If one sees the sun turned red in a dream, it means corruption. If it turns yellow in the dream, it means an illness. If it turns black in the dream, it means losses. If one seeks the sun after it sets in a dream, it means that whatever is destined for him whether it be good or bad has passed. If one sees the sun rising at times different than its usual sun rising time in a dream, it means that an uprising against the government will take place in different parts of the country. If one sees himself with the sun in a dream and should he be working in the government, or the army, it means that he will betray his superior, or the ruler of that land. Otherwise, it means that his condition will deteriorate and life will turn against him. If the sun has no rays in the dream, it means that the governor or the general of the army will

419

lose respect. If he is an administrator, it means that he will be dismissed from his function. If he is a subject or an employee it means that he will lose his source of income. If a woman sees a sun that has no rays in a dream, it means that her husband will deprive her of her needs. If one sees the sun split in two in a dream, it means losing one's dominion. If one sees the sun falling down in a dream, it means that a major calamity will befall the inhabitants of the earth. If it falls over the earth in the dream, it means the death of one's father. Gazing at the sun in a dream means gaining authority and dominion, or presiding over the people of one's locality. If a traveller sees the sun too bright in a dream, it means that he will return home safely. If one sees the sun rising from the East and setting in the West with a clear brightness in a dream, it means blessings for that land. If one swallows the sun in a dream, it means distress, sorrow or death. If the sun rises from the West, then it means defamation, exposing the ills of the person seeing it, or divulging a secret. The rising of the sun from the West also means recovering from an illness, and for a businessman, it means profits from that direction, but in general, it may mean revealing a secret, or it could mean a scandal or death. The same interpretation is given if one sees the sun rising from the South to set in the North. If the sun changes its nature in a dream, it means trouble in that land. If one sits under the sun in a dream, it means that he will receive honor and blessed profits. Grabbing some rays of the sun in a dream means receiving undiminishing wealth. The sunrise in a dream also means waking people up to go to work, seeking one's livelihood, begetting a son, or releasing a prisoner. If one is hiding something, then seeing the sun in his dream means that his secret will be exposed. If one sees the rays of the sun falling over his bed or threatening him in a dream, it means a painful sickness, or inflammation of the skin. If the sun rays which are falling over his bed provide him with good energy in the dream, it means a good harvest, or good health. If travellers see many suns in the sky in a dream, it means profits and prosperity. Running away from the sun in a dream means that one may leave his wife, or he may run away from the governor of that land, or escape from an evil. If the sun and the moon meet in one's dream, it means a royal marriage, or a marriage between a beautiful woman and a wealthy man. Clouds covering the rays of the sun in a dream means an illness. If one carries the sun in a bag in a dream, it means money. The sun in a dream also could represent a wise man, or a teacher one whose company is sought. Otherwise, the sun in a dream could represent, the governor, one's husband, wife, child, mother, daughter, aunt, father, or grandfather and the above interpretations will relate to such a person. Whatever happens to the sun in the dream, will then affect such people. If one sees the sun rising, then immediately setting in the same direction in a dream, it means a newborn who may die shortly after his birth, returning an ex-prisoner to jail shortly after his release, earning amazing amounts of money, or repenting from sin, reverting to wrongdoing, the return of a bride to her parent's house immediately after her wedding night, or it could mean reconciliation between husband and wife. If one sees the sun and the moon shinning on him in a dream, it means that his parents are pleased with him. If one sees himself prostrating to the sun or the moon in a dream, it means that he will commit an awful sin, or a heinous crime. In a dream, the sun also represents one's livelihood, earnings, spiritual guidance, following the truth, new garments, or recovering from a serious illness. Seeing many suns in the sky in a dream means the spread of religious innovations. If the brightness of the sun grows beyond normal to become unbearable in the dream, it means adversities. Eating up the sun in a dream means benefiting from its services and prospering from its rays, or that one may become a man of knowledge, a scholar, an astrologer, or a fortuneteller. If the rays of the sun cause burns to someone in a dream, it means that he will fall in love with a beautiful face, or perhaps he will be hurt by someone he adores, or it could mean loss of spiritual direction, or it could be a severe warning about a woman he loves. If a woman sees herself carrying the sun in a dream, it means that she will find a husband, or bear a son. If one sees the sun talking to him in a dream, it means that he will discover a mystery or acquire knowledge about spirits, or he could become a translator, an analyst, or a consultant. Seeing the sun, the moon and the stars together in a dream denotes adversities, jealousy on the part of one's own family, or they could denote fear. If the rays of the sun burns the crop in a dream, it means a devastation and a plague or rising prices. *(Also see Eclipse; Heavens)*

Sunshine: *(See Light; Sun)*

Superciliousness: (Disdain; Haughtiness) For one who desires to earn respect from others, superciliousness in a dream means grovelling, servility, toadying, or loosing rank.

Supermarket: *(See Marketplace)*

Supervisor: In a dream, a supervisor represents a seeker of knowledge, remembrance of God Almighty, prayers, family reunion, or marriage of an unwed person.

Supplication: (Imploring; Invocations) In a dream, supplications represent worship, a special prayer, or asking for a specific need. Invocations in a dream mean that one's needs are satisfied. If one's supplications are done under dire need, or if they involve strong emotions, sobbing or grief in the dream, then they represent trying moments in one's life, or they could mean temptations. Loud or solemn supplications in a dream may indicate a special prayer for rain. If the supplications do not call for God's favors, or if they are not directed toward Him in the dream, then they represent falsehood. If the supplications are silent in the dream, they could mean that one will beget a blessed son. If one sees a group of people gathering in a circle of prayers, or doing Zikr and invoking the divine attributes in a dream, then they represent a gathering of children, growth, blessings, or waiving away sufferings. If one sees himself praying to God Almighty, or that prayers are invoked on his behalf in a dream, it means happiness and money. Supplications in God's house or in a mosque in a dream are more beneficial than prayers which are offered anywhere else. If one prays in the dark in a dream, it means that he will be saved from trials. If one sees himself imploring another person in a dream, it means that he fears him. *(Also see Prayers; Zikr)*

Support: *(See Brace; Family support; Pillow; Sponsorship)*

Suppository: *(See Medicine)*

Suppressing one's anger: (Anger) Suppressing one's anger in a dream means having good qualities, receiving a commendation, blessings, doing good for those who appreciate and those who do not appreciate good favors. *(Also see Anger; Suppressing one's feelings)*

Suppressing one's feelings: If a sick person sees himself suppressing his feelings, or down-playing his pain and sufferings in a dream, it means that he will shortly recover from his ailment. *(Also see Suppressing one's anger)*

Suppression: *(See Terrorization)*

Surety: *(See Guarantee)*

Surgery: Surgery in a dream represents the real limb which is operated on in one's dream. If a young man or a young woman see themselves having an operation where their chest is opened, or having an open heart surgery for example in a dream, it means that they are in love. As for elderly people, it means distress. Having a minor surgery on the thumb in a dream means signing a loan. *(Also see Body[1]; Chest)*

Surrender: *(See Islām)*

Susan: (Lily of the valley. *See Hyacinth*)

Suspicion: Being suspicious in a dream means committing a sin.

Swaddle: (Diaper) A swaddle in a dream represents a pregnant woman, a broken bone, or defeating one's enemy. If one sees his wife swaddled in a piece of cloth and if he unwraps her in a dream, it means that he will divorce her. Seeing a fugitive, a sick person, a traveller, or a prisoner swaddled in a dream may not purport advantages or a favorable end.

Swagger: *(See Ghee; Prance; Write; Writer)*

Swallow: (*zool.* Starling) A swallow in a dream represents money, a blessed man, a blessed woman, or an intelligent and a learned boy. Catching a swallow in a dream means seizing what is unlawful for one to take. A house filled with swallows in the dream represents lawful earnings. A swallow in a dream is also interpreted to represent a man of good character, and who is pious and amicable. Helping a swallow in a dream means that one may assist a kind person in his life. Catching a swallow in a dream also means being unjust toward one's wife. Eating a swallow in a dream represents a fight. If one sees swallows flying away from his house in a dream, it means that his wife or a relative will abandon him, or separate from him and travel away from that town. In general, swallows and starlings in a dream represent people who are financially comfortable, or they could represent death, grief, or good deeds, movement, chanting, benevolence, or weddings. Seeing a swallow in a dream also may mean marriage to a trustworthy woman, or it could represent a good household manager. If one is transformed into a swallow in a dream, it means that thieves will rob his house. Seeing a dead swallow in a dream is a warning to revert one's actions and to engage in doing good.

Swallowing: To swallow something one is chewing in a dream means debts, or collectors demanding their money. To swallow dust or sand in a dream means poverty, giving someone a warning look, greed, or it could mean bribing someone in authority. *(Also see Chewing; Food)*

Swan's meat: Eating swan's meat in a dream means benefits drawn from pious and religious people. *(Also see Dusk; Meat)*

Swathe: *(See Wrap up)*

Sweat: *(See Perspiration)*

Sweeping the floor: (Cleaning; Sanitation) Sweeping the floor, or caring for the floor matt or carpet in a dream means to care for one's community or family. Sweeping dirt or cleaning a floor in a dream means financial benefits for people who do that professionally. Sweeping someone else's house in a dream means receiving money from him. If a rich person sees himself sweeping a floor in a dream, it means poverty, or loss of a business. *(Also see Cleaner; Garbage; Sanitation; Trash collector)*

Sweet almond: *(See Almond)*

Sweet fragrance: *(See Smell)*

Sweet marjoram: *(See Marjoram)*

Sweet water: *(See Euphrates)*

Sweets maker: (Baker; Pastry chef) A pastry chef in a dream represents a man of knowledge, catering a wedding, vesting ranks of authority, or children. A sweets maker in a dream also represents a good and a gentle person, a compiler of literary works, a scientist, a slanderer, or an agitator. *(Also see Sweets)*

Sweets shop: In a dream, a sweets shop represents faith in God Almighty and submission to His will.

Sweets: Seeing or eating sweets in a dream indicates one's sincerity in his religious attendance, release of a prisoner, arrival of a traveller, recovery of a sick person, marriage of an unwed person, guidance, repentance, learning the

Qur'ān, buying new clothing for one's children, having a loyal servant, or earning blessed monies. Seasonal sweets in a dream represent witnessing an annual festival, or the reinstatement of a just ruler. To feel saturated with sweets in a dream means self-conceit, lies, or it could mean extollment, or speaking nice words. Eating sweets in a dream also means suffering from cold symptoms. Though, eating fermented sweets or preserves in a dream may represent a cure. If a sweet is made from the basic four ingredients (i.e., honey, sugar, flour and manna or dates, or other fillings) in a dream, it means happiness, longevity, or escaping from the consequences of a dangerous business one ventures in with greed. As for a believer, eating sweets in a dream means tasting the blessings of one's faith, though for a disbeliever, it means indulging in the pleasures of this world. *(Also see Pastry; Seasonal sweets; Sweets maker)*

Swelling: Swelling in a dream means increase in one's earnings, or earnings that will be quickly spent, or it could mean increase in one's knowledge. Swelling in a dream also signifies pride, self-adulation, or a hidden claim. If a swelling from inflammation subsides in a dream, it means the return of a traveller, calming the fury of an angry person, controlling the exasperation of an outraged person, things returning to normal, appeasement of a repulsive person, or loss of one's job. *(Also see Pimple)*

Swells: *(See Waves)*

Swerving: *(See Cave)*

Swimmer: A swimmer in a dream represents someone who strives to serve his superiors or people in the government, though little is what he can offer. *(Also see Swimming)*

Swimming: (Employment; Knowledge; Prison) If a man of knowledge sees himself swimming in the ocean in a dream, it means that he will attain his goals. If he enters the water of the ocean then comes back to the shore in a dream, it means that he will commence his path of seeking knowledge then abandons it. Swimming in a dream also means going to jail. Swimming on sand in a dream means that one may be incarcerated; that his living conditions in his jail will be constricted, and that he will suffer in his prison from hardships equal to the difficulties he encounters during his swim in the dream. If one sees himself swimming inside his own house in a dream, it means that he will work for a ruthless, wicked and an unjust employer who will entrap him in his service through a business deal. Consequently, God Almighty will help him out of his entanglements. If one is afraid of swimming in the dream, it means that he is scared of someone in authority. If he runs away from swimming in a dream, it means that he will escape from him. If one sees himself entering waters where he can swim successfully in a dream, it means that he will engage in a major project, lead an important job, or acquire authority and power. If one swims on his back in a dream, it means that he will repent for a sin. If he swims in the sea and finds its water stagnant in the dream, it means that he will serve someone in authority, though his job will bring him nothing but trouble and the wrath of his employer. If he still manages to cross the sea in his dream, it means that he will escape from dangers his employment could inflict upon him. If he swims with fear in a dream, it means trouble, imprisonment, or a sickness he will endure depending on the type of needed efforts or distance he has to cross. Should he think in the dream that he will not be able to make it, then it means his death. If he shows courage during his swim in the dream, it means that he will be able to escape from such a dangerous job. Troubled waters in a dream mean adversities. Swimming successfully across troubled waters in a dream means overcoming one's adversities. Any sea or agitated waters in a dream represent the authorities or the state, whether it be a swamp, a lake, a pond, a sea, or an ocean. If one sees himself drowning in a river, or a lake, then if he is carried by others and laid on dry land motionless like a fish in a dream, this also means trials and adversities. If one is saved from drowning before he wakes-up from his sleep in the dream, it means that he will triumph over his trials. Otherwise, if he dies from it in the dream, it means that he may die from such adversities. If during his swim one meets a ship that pulls him out of the waters, or to which he holds or grabs, it also means escape from adversities. If one drowns in the dream, it means that he may die as a martyr, though having previously indulged in many sins. To walk on water, whether it is the sea or a river in a dream means good spiritual standing, religious assiduousness and a strong faith and determination. Walking on water in a dream also could be interpreted as ascertaining something about which one may have doubt, or placing one's trust in God Almighty before embarking on a dangerous trip. *(Also see Air)*

Swindle: *(See Chisel; Crow)*

Swine: (Pig) In a dream, a swine represents an avowed and a fierce enemy who is perfidious, worrisome, anxious, who does not act upon what he says and who lies and tricks people. Riding a swine in a dream means that he will earn a large some of money. If one eats it raw, cooked, or broiled in the dream, it means that he swallows unlawful money, or knowingly eats impermissible food. Walking like a swine in a dream means turning quick profits from an investment or a business, or it could mean that one will acquire what his heart desires. A wild pig in dream is a sign of a severe cold weather. Eating ham in a dream carries benefits for all people, though it is unlawful for Muslims. If one sees a pig in his bed in a dream, it means that he will commit adultery. Little pigs in a dream represent adversities and distress for their owner, or for the person seeing the dream. A domesticated swine in a dream means good harvest, prosperity, or satisfying one's needs and desires. Seeing a swine in a dream also may mean presiding over people of opposing or diverse opinions, or it could mean divorce, evil happenings, spendthrift, acquiring demonic nature, earning illegal money, or having a large progeny. If a pig causes harm to someone in a dream, it represents the perfidy of one's rival. Swine's milk in a dream represents a heartbreaking loss of money, or it could mean committing a major sin. If one sees little pigs entering his house in a dream, it represents an official inspection of one's private life. If one sees himself kicking little pigs out of his house in a dream, it means that he will resign from working for the government.

Swing: (Toy) To see oneself in a dream swinging on a rope means faltering in one's faith. Swinging on a suspended seat in a dream also means heedlessness, or looking at random in search for a true religion.

Swiss chard: *(See Chard)*

Swoon: *(See Faint)*

Sword hilt: *(See Knife handle)*

Sword: (Blade; Power; Scabbard) In a dream, a sword represents a son, a king, a clan, a tribe, a farm, a property, or a woman. If a sword is interpreted as power, then it means diligence, and if it is interpreted as words, it means clarity of speech. If it is interpreted as one's father, then it represents the father's pride of his son. If one's sword is weighing heavy and is being dragged with difficulty in the dream, it means an appointment that is difficult to bear, though one will draw benefits from it. If one hands his wife the blade in the dream, it means that she will bear a son. If he hands her the sword sheathed in the dream, it means that she will bear a daughter. An iron sword in a dream represents a son. A brass sword in a dream means a rich son. A lead sword in a dream means an effeminate son. A wooden sword in a dream means a son who is a hypocrite, and a tarnished sword in a dream represents an unattractive son. To draw out one's sword from its sheath in a dream could represent some words one is prepared to say. If the sword is sharpened, bright and scintillating in the dream, it means that his words will be sweet and true. If it looks rusted or tarnished in the dream, it means that his words will be harsh and false. If the sword is heavy in the dream, it means that he will say words which are even heavy on him to bear. If the sword has a crack in the dream, it means that his words will be rejected, and his intention will vex. If one's sword falls to the floor in the dream, it means that one may divorce his wife. If one's sword is seen laying beside him in the dream, it means that he is a man of authority. If the loop or the belt breaks and the sword falls in the dream, it means loss of one's power. If the hilt breaks in the dream, it may mean the death one's wife. If one is given a sheath without a sword in a dream, it means that he will keep something in trust. If the handle of one's sword breaks in the dream, it means that either one's father, uncle, aunt, or mother may die shortly. If the blade breaks in the dream, it means that one's servant, or assistant-worker may die shortly. If one sees swords flying in the air in a dream, they represent a plague. A sword in a dream also could represent one's anger, or his tight financial circumstances. Swallowing a sword in a dream means gathering the spoils of war. If a sword swallows someone in a dream, it means a snakebite. In a dream, the sheath of a sword represents a woman. Hitting someone with a sword in a dream means insulting him with harsh words. Sheathing one's sword in a dream means marriage. If the blade ceases to cut in a dream, it means that one's words will bear no weight. If one is hit with a sword, and if he loses his hand, his leg, or receives wounds in the dream, it means having an argument that involves one's father, son, or brother, etcetera, depending which limb and what member of one's family it represents. If one's head is cut off with a sword in a dream, it means that the one who received the blow will triumph over the one who beheaded him, or receive benefits through him. If one's body is dismembered with a sword in a dream, it means that he may travel far, or that his progeny will disperse across the land. A sword in a dream also represents wealth, power or knowledge. Waving a sword during a duel in a dream means becoming known in one's field or profession. (Also see Duel; Knife)

Sycamore tree: (bibl. Fig tree; Mulberries tree; Maple tree) In a dream, this large shade tree represents beneficial and lawful earnings which keep multiplying. A sycamore tree in a dream also represents a rich and a strong person who benefits others. A sycamore tree in a dream also could be interpreted as a beautiful and a rich woman, or it may represent suffering from heart disease or sight problems. (Also see Mulberry tree; Tree)

Sycophancy: (See Adulation; Flattery)

Sycosis: (See Plague)

Sympathy: (See Condolences)

Synagogue: (See Church; Temple)

Syphilis: (Piper; Venereal disease)

Syrup vendor: (See Bartender)

T

Table companion: *(See Messmate)*

Table of contents: (Chapters; Drawers; Scrolls) In a dream, the table of contents represents the subject of a hardcover book containing the bezels of wisdom, or a book of knowledge. It also means a rich woman, a rich man, a report card, forthcoming benefits, a register, an astrological sign, a scroll, or a drawer.

Table: (Dining table) A dining table with its food ready to serve in a dream means blessings, accepting an invitation to dinner or lunch, financial comfort, status and winning victory over one's enemy. In this case, one's enemy is hunger. The food placed on the table represents a booty. Clearing the dinner table in a dream means cessation of comfort and blessings. The dinning table of one's house in a dream represents his livelihood and sustenance, an important project that requires the help of many people, or a great person who is gracious, true and generous. Sitting on such a table in a dream means joining the company of such great man. If the dining table is topped with clean food and fresh bread in the dream, it means love between friends and brethren. To have little food and some bread on the table in a dream means lack of such love between brethren. Accepting the invitation to share a loaf of bread with someone in a dream means love, unity and prescribing to the prophetic traditions. If one sees one or two dishes on his table in a dream, it means profits for oneself and sustenance for his dependents. Having good appetite in a dream means longevity. If the dining table is cleared after one's meal in the dream, it denotes the conclusion of one's life. If a crowd of people sits on a table to partake their meal in a dream, they represent one's dependent. If two opponents sit on the same table in a dream, it means war, and particularly if their is broiled meat and herbs on the table. The dining table in the dream then represents the battlefield, and eating their meal means fighting. A dining table in a dream also represents piety. If one shares his meal in a dream, it means that he will meet new friends and enjoy their company, then a conflict will rise concerning his livelihood and earnings. *(Also see Food; Guest; Invitation; Hospitality; Table)*

Tablet: (Blackboard; Preserved Tablet; Records; Scrolls) Seeing the heavenly Preserved Tablet in a dream means unveiling one's actions and thoughts, glad tidings for someone suffering from adversities, recovering from an illness for an ailing person, or falling into sin for people whose indulgence in abominable action is a common way of life. As for godly and righteous people, seeing the Preserved Tablet in a dream means guidance relating to what God Almighty has written of commands and prohibitions. As for niggardly people, seeing the Preserved Tablet in a dream means acquaintance with one's written shares and certainty about one's limitations and his life in this world. Seeing it also means preserving knowledge, cataloging references, or saving money for one's family and heirs. It also represents a guardian for one's properties, treasurer, the keeper of one's secrets, or a controller. Seeing the Preserved Tablet in a dream also could denote enjoying peace after experiencing fear. If a ruler sees the Preserved Tablet in a dream, it means that his sovereignty will expand, or it could mean that he will discover a great treasure. As for the tablets that were revealed to God's prophet Moses, upon whom be peace, seeing them in a dream represents witnesses, spiritual guides, guidance or admonition. A wooden blackboard in a dream represents one's wife, child, farmland, or finding peace after suffering from fear, or it could mean knowledge if one is a seeker of such avenues. In general, all boards in a dream represent admonition or prohibition of sin. Receiving a writing tablet from an Imām in a dream means an appointment to leadership, knowledge, understanding, or becoming an Imām, except if what is written on the blackboard in the dream implies admonition to do good, then the tablet means guidance and mercy. If the blackboard is made of iron in the dream, it means that one will beget a son who will become a great scholar and a strongman. A polished board in a dream means that one's son will become a man of courage who accomplishes what he intends, acquires what he wants, and who will rarely be defeated. If the blackboard is corroded in the dream, it means that one's son will have no dynasty. If the blackboard is made of stone in the dream, it means that his heart will be like a rock. If the blackboard is made of copper in the dream, it means that one's son will grow to be a hypocrite. If it is made of lead in the dream, it means that one's son will be an effeminate person. A tablet in a dream also denotes a woman and the writing on it represent her children, or it could represent an intelligent and a good natured boy who accepts what he learns from his teacher. Receiving a blackboard from someone in authority in a dream means gaining power. If a pregnant woman sees a blackboard in a dream, it means that she will beget a son.

Taḥayyāt: (*arb.* Testimonial greetings) The last segment of the regular Islāmic prayers which is recited in a sitting posture. Once completed, one may ask for his personal needs or pray for others. If one reaches this segment of his prayer in a dream, it represents a condition or an agreement that must be fulfilled between two partners, or it could mean finding a guardian for one's intended wife (i.e., her father, uncle, brother, etcetera), without whom the marriage is not legitimate. Reciting the Taḥayyāt in a dream also means bartering material property for spiritual gains.

Tail: Having a tail in a dream means having a following of people or students.

Tailor: (Couturier; Marriage) A tailor in a dream represents unity, a peacemaker, a scribe, a secretary, or an officiant who conducts the marriage ceremony and witnesses the signing agreement. A tailor in a dream also represents someone who regrets his wrongdoing, or amends his conduct for the better. To become a tailor and sew one's own garments in a dream means struggling to build one's livelihood. If one sees himself unable to do a good sewing job in a dream, it means that he is trying to bring opposites together but to no avail. Sewing a robe for a woman in a dream means that he will be afflicted with a major trial. If one sees himself as a tailor or altering garments in a dream, it means prosperity, setting up a business venture, getting married, having a progeny, or putting things where they belong. A tailor in a dream also represents piety and a good character. (*Also see Shoemaker; Alterations*)

Tailoring: (*See Alterations*)

Take flight: (Flee; Run away) If one sees himself turning and running away in the face of a battle in a dream, it means that he may contract a venereal disease, or suffer from syphilis. Taking flight in a dream also may mean reverting to what is proper. On the other hand, it may mean falling into sin to earn God's wrath and the despise of the common people. If one sees himself taking refuge in a group of people, enticing them to fight in a dream, it means that he is adventuring with his head by walking the path of evil, or by backbiting others. (*Also see Escape from danger; Running away; Turning*)

Taking the middle course: (*See Middle course*)

Taking the road: (*See Wending one's way*)

427

Talbiyyah: *(See Responding)*

Talisman: *(See Amulet)*

Talkative: *(See Exhaustion from speaking; Spool)*

Talking: *(See Exhaustion from speaking; Speaking)*

Tall person: *(See Figure; Tallness)*

Tallness: (Height; Size) To see oneself taller than usual in a dream means increase in knowledge and wealth. If a man of authority sees that, it means expansion of his power. If he is a merchant, it means business prosperity. If one sees himself extremely tall and beyond the tallest human being in a dream, it means the nearing of his death, or it could mean his downfall. It is ominous for a tall person to see himself short in a dream, for it also denotes falling in rank, losing respect, or nearing one's death. Even seeing oneself shorter in a dream means death. If one sees his figure taller in a dream, it means that his authority will expand and he will win victory over his enemies. Tallness of one's figure in a dream also denotes longevity. If a short person sees himself tall in a dream, it denotes self-deception and boastfulness, or it could represent his stinginess. *(Also see Figure)*

Tallow-chandler: (Wax-chandler) In a dream, a chandler represents festivities, joy, happiness, death, illness, guidance, knowledge, desire, or crying.

Tallow: *(See Fat)*

Tamarisk tree: *(See Tamarisk; Tree)*

Tamarisk: (bot.) In a dream, tamarisk represents someone who hurts the rich and benefits the poor. *(Also see Tree)*

Tambourine: (Drum; Musical instruments) In a dream, a tambourine means adversities, pain and sufferings. It also means fame for the one carrying it. If a girl dancer carries it in the dream, it means that she may win a lottery, or acquire a publicly known fortune. The sound of a tambourine in a dream represents a recognized and a baseless fallacy. Seeing a man carrying a tambourine means fame for him and for whoever accompanies him in the dream. A woman carrying the tambourine in a dream also means that she will become famous, or it could indicates a new social trend. In general, when musical instruments are used in one's dream, playing them in a festival, a wedding, or in any type of celebration means trials. *(Also see Musical instruments)*

Tan: (Brown skin) In a dream, tan skin represents mixed ancestry.

Tangle: *(See Fog)*

Tank: *(See Cistern; Vat)*

Tankard: (Dull-witted; Dummy; Idiot; Mug) In a dream, a tankard represents a housekeeper or a servant. A tankard or a mug in a dream represent the household servants who consent to sexual abuse or sexual relationship with their employer. Drinking from a tankard in a dream also means earning money through one's servants or employees. A broken tankard in a dream signifies the death of one's servant or employee. *(Also see Mug)*

Tanner: (Changing hide into leather or curing it; Dye) Seeing a tanner in a dream is interpreted the same as seeing a cupper. *(See Cupping)*. Both specialties cure something. If one sees a physician becoming a tanner in a dream, it denotes his expertise and the large number of people who benefit from his treatments. Unless one finds the tanning to be faulty, then it indicates a non-professional person. If seeing a tanner in a dream is understood to denote material benefits, then in reality, he represents an escape from death. If he is understood in relationship with religious matters, then seeing him means feeding the poor and hungry during a drought or a famine. A tanner in a dream also represents a peacemaker, a physician, or a guardian. However, it is possible to interpret a tanner in a dream to mean distress, adversities, or an unjust person. *(Also see Dye; Vat)*

Tannery: (Leather dying factory) A tannery in a dream has the same interpretation as that of a slaughterhouse. It also represents a school, a fellowship house, or similar places where the mind and spirit are taught and reared to correct oneself, to hold to what is true and to discard what is false. A tannery in a dream also represents a patient, forbearing and a hard-working woman, a housekeeper, or a child. Perhaps a tannery in a dream also could denote a harsh, wretched and a contemptible woman, though she likes cleanliness and guards herself from others' impurities. *(Also see Dye; Vat)*

Tanning drum: *(See Vat)*

Tap dancer: *(See Dancer; Tap)*

Tap¹: (African steps; Footsteps; Loud steps; Tap dancing; Sound of walking) In a dream, loud steps represent distinguished wealthy merchants who are envied for their richness by everyone, and who are despised for their stinginess.

Tap²: *(See Suck)*

Tapeworm: Intestinal worms in a dream represent one's relatives and their children. *(Also see snake)*

Tar: Hot tar in a dream represents a guard who prevents saboteurs or subversive people from causing damage to one's property. Wearing a garment drenched with tar in a dream means indulging in sin and mixing with its people.

Tarantism: *(See Tarantula)*

Tarantula: (Hairy spider; Spider) A tarantula in a dream represents a loathsome and an evil woman who interferes with people's business and damages their interests, or who destroys what they repair and denies having anything to do with their sufferings. In a dream, this interpretation is based on the legendary nervous disease, formerly believed to be caused by a poisonous bite of a tarantula. Thus, when this harmless hairy spider is seen in a dream, it also could represent a lethal enemy of a fierce sting, scowling, or a despising look. *(Also see Spider)*

Tarâwïẖ: *(arb. See Five times prayers)*

Taro: (Edible roots of a tropical plant; *Colocasia antiquorum; bot.;* Large Egyptian potato) Eating taro in a dream means sufferings, adversities and trouble.

Tarragon: *(bot.)* In a dream, tarragon represents a vile person. Tarragon is originally grown from African rue and is sprouted in vinegar for a full year before it is planted to grow a new herb. Tarragon in a dream also represents someone who has learned about pious conduct by associating with pious people before he developed his own. Tarragon in a dream also signifies treachery or betrayal.

Tart: *(See Pastry)*

Tasbïẖ: *(arb. See Five times prayers)*

Tassels: (Fringes) In a dream, tassels represent money, power, evil, falsehood, or a following. A tassel maker in a dream represents evil and doubt, or he could represent a school teacher, or perhaps having a large progeny.

Tatter: *(See Lice)*

Tattoo: If a person sees his hands tattooed with henna in a dream, it means that he cheats to earn his livelihood, or that he tricks others to get what he needs. Consequently, he will be exposed and his enemy will rejoice at his misfortune. If a woman sees her hands tattooed in a dream, it means that she will trick someone to repossess her rightfully owned jewelry. If the tattoo is made with gold in the dream, it means performing an old but a polite trick. If the tattoo is done with mud in the dream, it means praising God Almighty. If a woman sees the lines of her tattoo mixing together, or as though the dye has started to run in the dream, it means difficulties with her children. If a man sees his feet dyed and tattooed in a dream, it means that he will be tried with family problems. If a woman sees her feet dyed and tattooed in a dream, it means that she will suffer from an abusive husband. *(Also see Dye; Henna)*

Taurus: *(astr. See Moon)*

Tavern: A tavern in a dream means getting high after feeling low and depressed. It also means dispelling one's strains and distress, or it could represents a prostitute, an abused woman, or adversities because of the damages and liabilities a tavern may bring. If one promises to do something, then if he sees a tavern in his dream, the tavern then represents the terms of his agreement, or that he is engaged in a shabby or a covert action against his boss. If a sick person sees himself in a tavern in a dream, it means that his time is up. If a pious person sees himself entering a tavern in a dream, it means that he may be lured into temptation.

Tax collector: Collecting taxes in a dream means compelling someone or forcing him to pay due alms, or it could mean coercing someone to live with him. If one sees himself as a tax collector in a dream, it means that he will earn respect, or that he will be forced to ask everyone for permission regarding everything he does. A tax collector in a dream also means paying one's debts, or he could represent a policeman, an emissary, a treasurer, or a safe.

Tax refund: If a ruler or a governor sees himself vomiting in a dream, it means that he will refund people taxes he unjustly collected from them. *(See Vomiting)*

Taxes: (Due alms; Property taxes)

Tayammum: *(arb.)* Performing one's ritual ablution but without water in a dream means the nearing solutions of one's problems. Tayammum is usually performed instead of the regular ablution in the absence of water, or because of a preventing illness, etcetera. However, observing the religious rites and substance of the act remains solemn. Tayammum in a dream also may mean a journey, or an illness. If the act is performed with a dry surface such as wood, stone, dry sand, earth, or a substance that does not stick to the skin in a dream, it means that one's travel plans may be infeasible, or it could mean that he will become cheep, or pursue his evil desires. To perform tayammum while water is accessible in a dream means falsehood and hypocrisy. It also means hoping for forgiveness while adamantly pursuing the avenues of wrongdoing, giving preference to one's interests in the world over his lasting benefits in the hereafter, preferring masturbation over lawful sexual intercourse, or being a hypocrite, and it could mean recovering from a terminal illness, or release from prison. *(Also see Enacting; Ablution)*

Teacher: (Bucket; Grammar teacher; Language teacher) In a dream, a teacher represents a strong person who does people favors and particularly those who learn at his hand unless if he takes monetary compensation for his work in the dream. An elementary school teacher in a dream represents a commander, a judge, a scholar, or a trainer. A grammar teacher and a language teacher in a dream represents honor, dignity, exalted rank, helping others, having impor- tant connections with people in authority, scholars, or he could represent understanding, clarity of speech, easy life, profits, marriage, children, or parents. A teacher in a dream also represents a bird hunter who presides over the affairs of ignorant people. *(Also see Educator; Engraver; Grammarian; Language; Writer)*

Teak: (Indian oak; Timber) In a dream, teak represents a feverish illness.

Tearing down one's shirt: To tear open one's garment in a dream means divorce.

Tears: (Pearls) In a dream, cold tears mean happiness while warm tears mean sadness. Running tears over one's cheeks without crying in a dream mean slander that carries weight. Guarded tears in someone's eyes that do not flow over his cheeks in a dream mean storing illegal money, or disguising the unlawful source of one's income which one's adversaries will eventually unveil or expose. If such tears are finally shed in the dream, they mean that one will willingly spend such money, or get rid of it to conceal his act. If one sees tears running from his right eye and entering his left eye in the dream, it means that his son and daughter may engage in sexual intercourse, and he must immediately separate between their rooms, and teach them about the lawful and the unlawful. Tears which come during yawning in a dream signify payment of an unjust fine. Seeing tears during the daylight time, or under the sun, or in front of a fire in a dream means business losses caused by one of these three elements. Tears in a dream also signify loneliness, leaving one's homeland, or yearning to see one's beloved, or they may represent pearls. (Also see Pearl)

Teasing bow: (See Carder; Cotton)

Teenage boy: (See Young man)

Teenage girl: (See Young woman)

Teeth[1]: (Acrimony; Dice; Grasping; Longevity; Migration) Falling teeth in a dream means longevity, or living past one's contemporaries. Collecting one's lost teeth in a dream means longevity, or it could mean having a large progeny. If one cannot find his teeth in the dream, it means that his family will die before him, or that a member of his clan will emigrate to a new land. If one finds a lost tooth in a dream, it means the return of an immigrant to his homeland. If the upper teeth fall into one's hand in the dream, they represent profits. If they fall in his lap in the dream, they mean a son, and if they fall on the floor in the dream, they means death. If the lower teeth fall in the dream, they mean pain, sufferings, sorrows and distress. Falling teeth in a dream also mean paying one's debts. If a tooth falls in a dream, it means payment of a loan, while the number of fallen teeth represent the number of debts to be satisfied. If one's teeth fall without pain or a cause in the dream, then they represent worthless deeds. If they fall because of a gum disease or cause pain in the dream, then they mean being forced to part with something from one's house. If the front teeth fall and cause pain and bleeding in the dream, they represent one's incompetence or inability to complete a project. If the front teeth fall without pain or bleeding in the dream, then they mean losing one's property. Falling teeth in a dream also denote a long illness that may not necessarily culminate in death. If one collects his fallen teeth in a dream, it also means that he can no longer conceive children. If one's teeth fall into his lap in the dream, it means having a large progeny. If one's wife is pregnant, and if he pulls out a tooth without difficulty or pain in the dream, it means that his wife will give birth to a son. If his gums bleed, it means that he will forsake his family, except if he owed someone money, then it means that he will be asked to pay, or that he will be forced to comply. Collecting fallen teeth in a dream also means saying something one will regret. If a religious person loses his teeth in a dream, it means that he should be more assiduous in his devotion, and votive fasting will surely help him as a start. If one loses his teeth and finds himself unable to eat properly in the dream, it also means poverty. Falling teeth in a dream also denote spending one's money to acquire spiritual knowledge, then recuperating one's investment through a new and a blessed business. (Also see Body[1]; Pain; Tooth)

Teeth[2]: (Setting the tooth on its edge.) To set one's tooth on its edge in a dream means a betrayal carried by a member of one's family the tooth represents. This includes one's children, wife, partners, or employees. To set one's teeth on their edge in a dream also could mean changes in one's behavior that may lead to a changing attitude on the part of such family members. (Also see Body[1]; Tooth)

Telescope: *(See Binoculars)*

Tell a lie: *(See Lying)*

Telling the future: *(See Perspicacity)*

Temple: (Altar; Retreat; Sanctuary) Temples, sanctuaries or retreats in a dream represent security, peace, finding a shelter away from fear, and victory over one's enemy. A temple in a dream also represents children, weddings, benefits, profits, prudence, or having reservations about one's dealings with others. A Christian temple in a dream represents the clergyman who officiates the masses, or it could represent the recital of Psalms or Gospels therein, and it may denote offerings. *(Also see Church; Hermitage; Retreat)*

Temples: *(anat.)* In a dream, one's temples represent two noble and blessed sons. Anything that affects them in the dream will affect one's sons. Temples in a dream also could mean recovering from an illness. If one is suffering from a migraine headache sees his temples turn into iron in a dream, it means that he will find a cure for his illness. One's temples in a dream also may be interpreted as money. Plucking out the facial hair from someone's temples in a dream means borrowing money from him, and the lender will take pride in lending him money. If a rich person sees himself plucking out his facial hair in a dream, it means that he may lose his wealth. If a poor person sees that dream, it means that he will repay his debts. *(Also see Body¹)*

Temptation: *(See Trouble; Wine)*

Tender: *(See Fresh)*

Tennis ball: *(See Ball)*

Tent peg: *(See Peg)*

Tent: (Canopy; Pavilion) In a dream, a tent means travels, a grave, a wife or a house. A camp of tents in a dream represents clouds. If a tent is raised over someone, and if he is a merchant, it means that his business will grow. If he is a soldier, it means that he will rise in rank. If he is unwed, it means that he will get married. If one sees a white tent raised beside his tent in a dream, it represents a righteous person who commands what is good and forbids what is evil. It also means that he will repent for a hideous sin. If one sees the moon inside his tent in a dream, it means that he will illicit sexual intercourse with a boy or with a young girl from a noble family. Seeing unknown white or green tents in a valley represent the graves of martyrs. *(Also see Canopy; Pavilion)*

Termite: (Broker; Stockbroker; Wood warm) In a dream, termites represent jealousy, envy, perfidy, competition in knowledge, or search for arguments. If one sees termites in his carry-on bag, or eating from his staff in a dream, they mean his death. Termites in a dream also represent a slanderer who tricks wealthy people to make his commission by advising them to place their money into bad investments. If a sick person sees termites inside his house or clinging to his skin in a dream, it also means his death. If one sees termites eating his wooden door, table or bed in a dream, they mean an illness. Termites in a dream also means having a large family with little income.

Terra firma: *(See Dry land)*

Terror: *(See Fear; Fright)*

Terrorization: (Oppression; Suppression; Tyranny) Terrorizing others or oppressing them in a dream denotes a mental sickness, depression, psychological weakness, or actions that will bring their author closer to hell-fire. Terrorizing others in a dream represents one's own losses and humiliation. Terrorizing people in a dream also means poverty, loss of business, a severe illness, or it could represent profits that will turn into losses. *(Also see Oppression)*

Testator: *(See Legal guardian)*

Testicles: (Male reproductive glands) In a dream, testicles represent the elements of husband and wife, one's two children, trade, business, doors, doormen, money pouch, or the female members of one's family, including sisters, daughters, mother or aunts. Whatever affects one's testis in a dream may manifest in events affecting any of the above.

Testifying to God's Oneness: *(See Carnelian-red; Taḥayyāt)*

Testimonial greetings: *(See Carnelian-red; Taḥayyāt)*

Testis: *(See Testicles)*

Tetter: *(med. See Herpes)*

Theft: *(See Robbery)*

Theologian: *(See Legist; Scholars)*

Thief: (Assassin; Illness; Robber) In a dream, a thief represents an illness, deficiency in one's character, or a physical ailment. If the thief is a black man, it means that the illness relates to one's black bile. If the color of his skin is red, then it relates to one's blood. If the color of his skin is yellow, then it relates to his galls. If the color of his skin is white, then it relates to his chest and phlegm. Whatever a thief takes in the dream should be interpreted in relation to the substance of what he took. If he takes nothing from one's house, then it denotes a passing ailment. If one catches the thief, or holds to his shirt in the dream, it means that he knows the cure. A thief in a dream also represents an assassin, the angel of death, a visitor, or someone asking for marriage. If there is a sick person in the house and a thief enters that house in a dream, it means the death of the ailing person. If a thief comes to one's house and takes nothing from it in a dream, it means the recovery of sick person from his illness. A thief in a dream also can be interpreted to represent a cunning person, a deceiver, an adulterer, a hunter, a backbiter, someone who asks for things that do not belong to him, a lion, a snake, a Satan, eavesdropping, or one's mind, desire and passions. If a scholar sees a thief in his dream, it means that he will learn wisdom from an anecdote. A thief in a dream also represents a liar, or the humiliation inflicted upon such a person. *(Also see Crocodile; Illness; Robbery)*

Thigh pain: *(See Body¹; Pain)*

Thigh: (Limb) One's thighs in a dream represent his family or clan. Anything that affects them in the dream will manifest in his family or clan. If one sees his thighs missing something in a dream, it means that he is a foreigner, or that he does not know his lineage or ancestry. Experiencing pain in one's thigh in a dream means doing harm to one's own family or clan. If one sees that a piece of skin is crafted to his thigh in a dream, it means that someone will attribute a son to him, and it will turn to be a false allegation. Thighs in a dream also represent the pillars of one's house, the head of a household, one's wife, one's husband, son, master, earnings, business, vehicle, or wealth. One's thighs in their beautiful condition in a dream also represent the correctness of one's prayers, or they may represent his garment, tools, or chair. Imputation of one's thigh in a dream means taking a long journey and dying in a foreign country. *(Also see Body¹; Foot; Leg)*

Thimble: A thimble in a dream means money, a child, a wife, a young intelligent worker, a vehicle, travels, or a needed competitor for the better promotion of one's business. A thimble in a dream also means dire need, tight circumstances, difficulties, or perhaps it could represent one who is crafty and who deceives children. Placing a thimble in the wrong finger in a dream means committing adultery, neglecting one's prayers, or the falling sick of the person such finger represents in the dream. *(Also see Fingers; Five fingers)*

Thinning: (Skin inflammation) If one sees his skin thinned or inflamed between his legs in a dream, it means that he may marry a rich woman who will give him her wealth. If one sees himself shedding his skin or skinning himself in a dream, it represents money he will part with, and if he is sick, it means his death.

Thirst: (Desire; Dryness) In a dream, thirst represents stagnation of businesses, dullness of the real estate market and unsalability of farm products. Thirst in a dream also means poverty, slump, recession, or yearning for a beloved, desiring to be with him and missing him. Thirst in a dream also could represent religious corruption. If a thirsty person sees himself searching for water but could not find it in a dream, it means that he will escape from a misfortune. If one sees himself standing thirsty before a source of water or a well but cannot drink from it or reach it in a dream, it means that he will fail to reach his goal. Thirst in a dream also means being corrupt, or it could represent one's need to get married to preserve his chastity.

Thorns: (Affliction; Bristling with perplexity) In a dream, thorns represent a harsh, difficult, repulsive and a distressful person. Thorns in a dream also represent indebtedness, signing a loan, temptation, degeneration of moral standards, or social unrest. If a thorn pierces someone in a dream, it means that he will be tried with temptations, or that he will be hurt from something he hates. Walking on thorns in a dream means delaying or postponing payment of one's debts upon maturity. Thorns in a dream also represent ignorant and evildoing people who uphold respect for nothing, and who have won neither material nor spiritual success in their lives. Thorns in a dream also represent pain and sufferings, complexity of matters, sorrows, distress, difficulties, love, injustice, or harm caused by women.

Thread: Holding a thread in one's hand in a dream means looking for an alibi or a proof to support one's argument and win a case. Twisting a thread, or tying it around someone neck, then dragging him or her in a dream represents a pimp soliciting clients for a prostitute. Knots in a thread mean sorcery or evil spells. A white thread in a dream represents the dawn, and a black thread represents the night. *(Also see Ball of thread; Pimp; Rope; Spool)*

Threat: Receiving a threat in a dream means victory over one's assailant, opponent, or adversary, or it could mean developing a defence mechanism against any danger from that side. If the threat comes from an unknown person, such a person is a Satan, particularly if the threat is directed against one's prayers, charitable actions, or devotion. A threat in a dream also represents the trials of a love story. *(Also see Slapping on the cheek)*

Threshing: To beat grains out of husks in a dream represents savings one accumulates from a long and a hard-working job. Threshing in a dream could represent money which is earned through someone else's labor, or it could mean acquiring knowledge.

Threshold: In a dream, a threshold represents one's gown, garment, one's adornment, makeup, money, or it may denote closing a subject, spreading it, or it could represent a beautiful woman who embodies all the attributes man desires, including beauty, good character, intelligence, wealth and fertility. Buying a new threshold or sitting on one in a dream means that either the husband or the wife may suffer a bodily injury. If one sees himself sitting under the threshold of his door in a dream, it represents an adversity or an illness. If one sees himself being carried over the threshold of his door in a dream, it represents his funeral. *(Also see Doorstep; Door lintel; Doorplate)*

Thrift shop: *(Also see Used clothing)*

Throat: (Life; chastity. See Body[1])

Throbbing: *(Also see Palpitation)*

Throne: *(See Carriers of the Divine Throne; Chair; Divine Throne)*

Throng: *(See Crowd)*

Throw in the towel: *(See Towel)*

Throw pillow: *(See Pillow)*

Throw: *(See Cast²; Thrust)*

Throwing apples : If one sees the ruler or the governor throwing apples at him in a dream, it means that he is sending him his emissaries, and usually such a dream carries glad tidings. *(Also see Cast²)*

Throwing stones: Throwing stones from a high altitude down in every direction in a dream means being unjust toward others though from a position of strength. *(Also see Cast²; Stoning; Hazelnut; Rocks)*

Thrust: (Hurl; Press; Shove; Squeeze; Throw) In a dream, thrust means engaging in a narrow sighted project, entering a close race, entertaining a project of little importance, participating in a project with a narrow or a difficult way out, or perhaps it could mean death.

Thrusting: *(See Bullfight; Thrust)*

Thumb: If one measures a house or a shop with his thumb in a dream, it means that he will own that place. *(Also see Measure)*

Thunder: (Curse; Omen; Policeman; Warning sign) In a dream, thunder without rain means a scare, a warning or an ultimatum. It also represents good promises, gracious orders, or the sound of drums. Seeing thunder in a dream means repayment of one's debts, and for a sick person, it means recovering from his illness. Thunder, lightening and rain in a dream represent fear for a traveller, or the greed of a merchant. Hearing about an awesome blast in a distant land in a dream means that the dwellers of that place will be struck with a major calamity or sudden mass casualties. The sound of thunder in a dream represents a murder, a fight, a dispute, an argument, lack of religious attendance, loss of money, or the release of a prisoner. A thunderstorm with rain when needed in a dream represents a good harvest for that year. Hearing a thunderous sky without seeing the lightening in a dream means an assassination, deception, falsehood or slander. Hearing the sound of thunder in a dream also means being reprimanded by a higher authority. There are no benefits in hearing the sound of thunder in the darkness without seeing lightening in the dream, this would be interpreted as apostasy or disloyalty. This can be particularly true when it is accompanied with an earthquake. If one hears thunder in its season in a dream, it means good news and blessings. Otherwise, out of its usual season, thunder in a dream represents an army on the move, or a foreign occupation of a country. Hearing the sound of thunder in a dream also represents hymns, praising God Almighty, glorifying Him, or it could mean a sickness, fear, deafness, or the sound of drums in a wedding. If the one seeing the dream is an atheist, it means that he will be guided and have faith in God Almighty. If he is a sinner, it means that he will repent for his sins. Hearing the roaring of thunder in a dream on the first day of **October** means death. If it is heard during the first six days of that month, it means benefits, or lower prices, but if it is heard near the end of the month, then it means a plague or a disaster. Hearing the sound of thunder at any other time during the month of October in a dream means evil. If it is heard during the month of **November** in a dream, it means blessings for the land, prosperity, the spreading of God's words in a new land, the falling of a comet in a populated area, the death of a leader, a pollution that will devastate bird life, or a heavy rainstorm with limited damages. If the sound of thunder is heard during the first ten days of **December** in a dream, it means the death of famous people within the Western hemisphere, inflation, rising prices, degradation of social behavior, decrease in harvest, inflation, or playing dirty politics. Hearing the sound of thunder during the last seven days of December in a dream means that the winter will be cold and dry, though the forthcoming spring will be cool and wet. Hearing the sound of thunder in the first six days of the month of **January** in a dream means that a major event will take place, such as an earthquake, death, destruction, or a war in Iraq. If this dream is witnessed during the last week of the month of January, then it represents a solar eclipse, or the death of a Western leader, a plague, or the birth of a planet that signifies the destruction of a great city on earth. Hearing the sound of thunder on the first day of **February** in a dream means a good harvest, lowering or stabilization of prices, discovering a new disease in the East, death in the seas, heavy rains in Mecca, fear, devastation and famines in Ethiopia, or that a Western leader will move his armies to the East and control the land for a short period of time. Hearing the sound of thunder during the first six days of **March** in a dream means good harvest, lowering of prices, stabilization of the market and prosperity. Hearing the sound of thunder at the end of March in a dream means famines, destruction, or that a swarm of locusts may devastate the lands, or it could mean a drought that will kill African cattle. Also in this type of dreams, if the sound of thunder is heard on the twenty first day of **April**, it means that Western armies will drive East and establish military bases there. If the first of April happens to be a Sunday, then March will be a month of great fear and disturbances in the East, meanwhile, a conflict between the Western armies will end by the death of a Western leader and the defeat of his army. If the dream is seen on the eleventh day of April, it may mean that earthquakes or cyclones will devastate many countries. If the dream takes place on the thirteenth day of April, then it means that inflation will strike and price hiking will burden the common people. If the dream is seen on the seventeenth day of April, it purports a major political dispute between the leaders of the world, and if it is seen on the twenty second day of April, it means that a disastrous evil will contaminate many societies. If the dream takes place on the twenty third day of the month of April, it means abundance, falling prices, fertility in the lands, while if it is seen on the twenty fifth day of April, it will mean price hiking. If it is seen on the twenty ninth day of April, it means that blessings, fertility, relief and joy will spread in the land. If the sound of thunder is heard during the first nine days of the month of **May** in a dream, it means the death of noble and leading people in Turkey. During that period, rain will be in abundance, the land will be fertile and the farms most productive. If the dream takes place between the tenth and the twentieth day of the month of May, it means plagues. If the sound of thunder is heard in a dream during the first ten days of **June**, it means the death of renowned scholars, people of knowledge, religious leaders, or noble people in Egypt. Meanwhile, prices will fall, and abundance will ease the economy into a major economic turnaround. If the dream is seen during the first six days of **July**, it means that good rain will fall during the following December and that the land will be fertile. During that year, several Western leaders will die, and a war may take place in Persia. Meanwhile, evil will spread throughout Egypt, and it will be brought about by its own leaders. If the dream takes place during the last seven days of July, it means that peace will spread throughout the earth, prices will fall in Iraq and in East Africa, and a new disease will affect fruit trees, banana trees, date trees, though wheat will be available in abundance, even if the farmers were concerned about it in the early part of the year. If the sound of thunder is heard during the month of **August** in a dream, it means blessings for the people in Syria and the people of Azerbaijan on the Caspian Sea. At that time, sea passages will be blockaded, the highways will be forsaken and a war may take place in China. If the sound of thunder is heard at the end of the month of August in a dream, it means the end of a drought in Egypt, rising prices, death, earthquakes, or major political changes. If the sound of thunder is heard during the first eight days of **September** in a dream, it announces a drought during the early part of the year that will be followed by heavy rains and results in a good harvest. It also means that a long and destructive war will take place. If the thunder takes place on the tenth day of September in one's dream, then it means a drought in Morocco. God knows best what He has reserved for His creation and He is the best of judges.

Thunderbolt: Thunderbolts in a dream are signs of punishment, illness or death. If a thunderbolt hits and burns something in the dream, it means false rumors, damages, financial losses, recession, or dumping of merchandise. A thunderbolt in a dream also means a warning for a sinner, the punishment for his crime, devastation, calamities, diseases, tornados, plagues, a blast, a major political shift, tyranny, decapitation, a bad death, inceneration, burining people alive, or a robbery. If one is under surveillance, then seeing a thunderbolt in a dream means a crackdown on his house or business. If thunderbolts strike people's homes in a dream, they mean the arrival of covetous and despicable criminals in the company of decent and innocent people who are not aware of the true identity of their companions. If thunderbolts strike the fields and damage the crop in a dream, they represent taxes or an investigation. If one sees a town hit and burnt with a thunderbolt in a dream, it means that an unjust governor will rise in that town, and his government will bring fear, rising prices, economic chaos, injustice or war. If a thunderbolt does not carry fire in the dream, then it represents a new leader. *(Also see Earthquake)*

Thyme: *(See Wild thyme)*

Tiara: *(See Headgear)*

Tickling: Tickling someone in a dream means interfering in his business, or denying him access to it.

Tides: (Ocean) In a dream, swimming in troubled waters or high tides means adversities, or having to face a strong opponent.

Tie: (Bond; Knot) A tie in a dream represents longevity, old age and the possible bending of one's back. *(Also see Band; Bond¹; Captivated; Contract; Fond; Knot; Untying something)*

Tied-up: *(See Handcuff)*

Tiger: (Leopard) In a dream, a tiger represents a tyrant, an unjust ruler, or an avowed enemy. Killing a tiger in a dream means vanquishing such an enemy. Eating the flesh of a tiger in a dream means money, profits and honor. Riding on a tiger in a dream means power and sovereignty. A tiger inside one's house in a dream represents an insolent person who attacks one's family. Seeing a tiger or a leopard in one's dream means receiving money from an insolent or an artful person. A struggle with a tiger in a dream means fighting with an insolent person. Tiger's bite in a dream represents damage caused by such a person. A tiger in a dream also represents either a man or a woman. It also represents deceit, trickery, an illness, or eye irritation. Tigress milk in a dream represents enmity. Seeing a tiger in a dream also could mean repenting from sin. *(Also see Fur; Milking a tiger)*

Tight shirt: Wearing a buttoned and a tight shirt, a blouse, or other apparel in a dream means experiencing tight circumstances, or reuniting with a traveller returning home, or it could mean marriage for an unwed person. *(Also see Clothing)*

Tile maker: A tile maker in a dream represents distress, adversities, trouble, hoarding money for the benefit of others, or he could represent anyone who has no descendents or posterity. In a dream, a tile maker also represents wealth, a palace, the high society, beauty, unity and love. Laying tiles in a dream means preparing oneself for something important, or building a corridor or a pathway.

Tiller: *(See Helm)*

Timber: *(See Firewood; Teak)*

Timepiece: *(See Clock)*

Tinner: *(See Fuller)*

Tinsmith: In a dream, a tinsmith represents a cadet, a procurer or a pimp.

Tinsmithing: *(See Plumber; Tinsmith)*

Tippler: In a dream, a tippler represents an alcoholic, a drunkard or an inebriate. *(Also see Wine)*

Tithe collector: (Atonement; Penance) In a dream, a tithe collector represents someone who interferes in people's business. Seeing the tithe collector in a dream also denotes adversities, calamities, heavy losses, disasters, or trials that befall a believer to direct him to repent, to wash his heart from impurities, and to free him from the burdens of his sins. *(Also see Atonement)*

Tithe: (Alms giving; Charity. *See Alms Tax; Tithe collector)*

Title: *(See Fame)*

Toaster oven: *(See Oven)*

Tobacco: *(See Snuff)*

Toes: Toes in a dream represent good deeds. *(Also see Body¹; Foot)*

Toga: (Persian toga; Roman toga. *See Cap)*

Toil: *(See Labor)*

Toilet: (Lavatory) In a dream, a toilet means relief from distress, satisfying one's innate needs, a bathhouse, taking a ritual ablution, a place where one's secrets are exposed, a place where one hides his money, a treasury, a coffer, a rest room, or a place to reflect. Washing the toilet's floor in a dream means becoming poor. A flooded toilet in a dream means distress, pregnancy, or prosperity. To fall into a toilet in a dream means imprisonment. Pouring honey or milk into the toilet bowl, or urinating blood in a dream means sodomizing. Looking into the toilet bowl and finding blood in it in a dream implies that one engages in the forbidden sexual intercourse with his wife during her menstrual period. A toilet in a dream also represents a guard. *(Also see Bathroom)*

Tomb: *(See Shrine)*

Tomcat: (Book of records; Cat; Reckoning; Siamese cat; Thief) In a dream, a tomcat means a thief or a servant. A cat in a dream also represents an evil and a treacherous woman. The same interpretation is given for anyone who compasses people, or guards them, or someone who harms the interests of his employer more than he benefits him. If a tomcat scratches someone or bites him in a dream, it means that he will fall sick for a full year. The bite of a wildcat in a dream is more dangerous and has greater implications. If one sees a tomcat sitting peacefully and quietly in his house in a dream, it means that he will have a comfortable, peaceful and a profitable year. Otherwise, a large wildcat in the dream represents a troublesome year. Selling a tomcat in a dream means spending one's money in various charities. Eating a cat in a dream means learning about sorcery. If one sees himself transformed into a tomcat in a dream, it means that he lives from stealing and seeks what is harmful. A tomcat entering one's house in a dream represents a robber. Whatever a tomcat takes from one's house in the dream will be looted by such a thief. Killing or beating a tomcat in a dream means catching a thief or killing him. If one extracts fat from a cat in a dream, it means that he will receive stolen money or a share thereof. Fighting with a tomcat in a dream means an affliction with a long and a debilitating illness that will be followed by a complete recovery. If the tomcat loses the fight, and if the man is already sick, it means that he will recover from his illness shortly thereafter. Otherwise, if he loses in the dream, it means that his illness has reached its peak. A cat or a tomcat in a dream also represent reckoning, estrangement of one's wife, her roughness with her husband, or they

438

could represent ill behaved children with their parents, fights, theft, adultery, lack of loyalty, eavesdropping, taunting, roaring, clamor, a bastard son, a foundling or an orphan. On the other hand, a cat in a dream could represent a toadying person, dancing, being playful and kind, though awaiting to jump at the first opportunity to spoil others' peace. If the cat, the tomcat and the mouse, or the lamb and the wolf become friends in the dream, it means hypocrisy, affectation and loss of moral standards. A civet cat in a dream represents a man who may have a suspicious look, though his character and conduct are exemplary. *(Also see Cat)*

Tongue: (Interpreter; Pen; Speech writer; Stinger; Translator) In a dream, one's tongue represents his translator or his business manager. One's tongue in a dream also represents the chief cause of sin. Moving one's tongue without speaking in a dream means committing a sin. Seeing an increase in size, width, or length of one's tongue in a dream means strength and overcoming one's enemy. If one's tongue becomes elongated with no cause for dispute or argument in a dream, it means having a bad tongue, or backbiting others, speaking ill about others, or using base and despicable language. Having a long tongue in a dream also could mean clarity in one's speech and eloquence in one's expressions. Having two tongues in a dream means acquiring a second language or a second trade, using a proof other than one's own in a court of justice, or winning victory over one's enemy. If one finds his tongue tied in a dream, it means stagnation of his business, or it could mean poverty. If black hair grows over one's tongue in a dream, it means a fast coming evil. If gray hair grows over one's tongue in a dream, then it means a slow coming adversity. Hair growing over one's tongue in a dream also means writing or reciting a poem. One's tongue in a dream also represents the perfect alibi, the beauty and eloquence of one's presentation, a professional presentation, good fame and good conduct. If a governor's tongue is cut off in a dream, it means the death of his interpreter or his speech writer. The human tongue in a dream also represents his pen and his signing authority. If one's tongue becomes long and reaches the skies in a dream, it means that he will be impeached or deposed from his leadership position following his tyranny and injustices. If the tongue of a leader or a ruler becomes long in a dream, it also signifies the expansion of his power and the infallibility and effectiveness of his commands. One's tongue in a dream also symbolizes a milk suckling baby, a lion in his den, or an intelligent warrior. Thus, if one lets a lion out of a lair in a dream, it denotes his tongue, or hurting people's feeling or reputation with one's tongue. If one sees himself without a tongue in a dream, it may mean the death of an infant. If one has to appear in court and sees his tongue cut off in a dream, it means that his proof will be rejected by the judge. If only the side of one's tongue is cut off in a dream, it means that he has doubts about the testimony of his witness. If he is a merchant, it means that he will lose an important business deal. If he is a student, it means that he will not complete his schooling. It is also said that when one's tongue is cut off in a dream, it means that he is a forbearing person. If the wife's tongue is cut off in a dream it means that she is a chaste and a pious woman. If a wife cuts off the tongue of her husband in a dream, it means that she will flirt with him and show him tenderness and love. Cutting off the tongue of a poor person in a dream means giving something to an impudent person to shun off his evil. If a poor person cuts off the tongue of another poor person in a dream, it means a fight between them. If one's tongue sticks to his palate in a dream, it means that he will deny or reject someone's right, refute the truth, or lie about a trust he received to keep for a time. Eating one's tongue or biting on it in a dream represents an act one will regret. If a governor sees that in a dream, it means that he swindles people's money and receives bribes. Biting on one's tongue in a dream also means remaining mostly silent, withholding one's advice, or controlling one's fury and anger. Biting one's tongue in a dream also could denote gluttony. Cutting off one's tongue in a dream means invalidating one's argument or proof, or preventing him from asking for anything. The cutting off of a poet's tongue in a dream means giving him money for his recitation. Seeing one's tongue black in a dream means that one may preside over his own people. If he is a wretched person, it means that he is a liar. If someone who is scared of something sees his tongue in a dream, it means that he will lose his battle and become subject to defamation and humiliation. If a wretched person sees himself having many tongues in a dream, it means that he will have a large family. Having many tongues in a dream also means speaking many foreign languages. If one's tongue is split in half in a dream, it means that he is a liar. Having many tongues and of many colors in a dream means telling different and contradictory stories, or it could represent a music writer. If people touch one's tongue or suck it in a dream, it means that they are acquiring his knowledge. It also represents people toadying or lobbying in official business. One's tongue in a dream also represents a hidden treasure, a hidden knowledge, a toadying servant, an employee, one's house, a vehicle, a skilled enemy, a seedling of a fruit bearing tree, a bad wife, a barren woman, one's spoken and irretrievable words, earnings, collecting garbage, following someone's traces, a policeman, or a prisoner. An animal's tongue in a dream represents one's life or death, because for an animal, his tongue is like a hand through which he takes things. If a scholar's tongue is cut off in a dream, it means that he will lose his argument, or it could mean the death of his assistant, student or son. Losing one's tongue in a dream represents the malicious joy of one's enemy, family, or neighbors for one's losses, or it could mean the death of a beloved, severing a relationship, or a plant disease that will affect one's fruit bearing trees. Perhaps losing one's tongue in a dream could mean separation between husband and wife, divorce, losing one's job, or moving to a new town. Having two tongues in a dream also means backbiting others, or having two faces with people, for people say that so-and so has two tongues or two faces. If the second tongue does not impede the person from speaking in the dream, then it denotes his truthfulness, love and affection toward others. One's tongue in a dream also may represent something one fears, such as the collapsing of a roof over his head, or it could represent an enemy. It also means isolating oneself from people of knowledge and wisdom, or it could mean remaining mostly silent, minding one's own business, or offering devotion and being grateful to God Almighty for His gifts and blessings. One's tongue in a dream also represents a captured prisoner of war, or a snake hiding in its pit. Looking at one's tongue in a dream means controlling what comes out of it. (Also see Body[1]; Exhaustion from speaking; Language; Spell out)

Tongues: (See Tweezers)

Tooth: [1] Teeth in a dream represent one's identity, age , clan, a boy, a girl, his family, money, servants, domestic animals, employees, weapons, life, death, unity, separation, trusts, or savings. In a dream, male's or female's upper teeth represent the male members of one's family from the father's side, and the teeth of the lower jaw represent the female members of one's family from the mother's side. The closer the teeth are to the incisor, the closer is the relative. Divided in two sections, the upper right incisor represents the father, and the upper left incisor represents the paternal uncle, or it could represent one's sisters, sons, or a close friend. The upper canines represent one's cousin, or two friends who are as close as cousins. The bicuspids represent one's uncles from the mother's side and their children, while the molars represent the grandparents and the grand children. The lower right incisor represents the mother, and the lower left incisor represents one's aunt from his father's side, or they could represent two sisters, two daughters, or two close friends who have the same compassion, concern and love. The lower canines represent one's female cousin from either the father or the mother's side. The lower canine tooth, or the eyetooth represents the sire of the house, or the landlord. The upper and the lower molars also represent the furthest members of one's family, including the grandmother and her grand daughters. If a tooth moves in its place in the dream, it means an illness. If it falls, or if it is lost, then it means death of the person to whom it is attributed, or it could possibly mean that he will be separated from him and can no longer see him. If one saves his lost tooth and does not bury it in the dream, it means that someone will come forth and be to him as good as that relative. Otherwise, if he does bury it, then it means the death of his relative. [2]In a dream, the human limbs also represent the members of his family, and whatever condition they portray in one's dream may become visible in the members of his family. Similarly, whatever may affect one's teeth in a dream can be interpreted as affecting such family members. If one's incisors look beautiful and bright in the dream, they denote the power, honor and prosperity his father or uncle will gain. If extra incisors grow in one's mouth in a dream, it means that one's family will grow by either a new born brother or a new son. If one finds his teeth slightly deteriorating in a dream, it means a trial, or that his family will engage in a disgraceful act that will bring him shame. If one attempts to pull out his teeth in a dream, it means that he may spend his money unwillingly, pay a fine, or separate from his parents, thus cutting off his blood ties, or he may become untrue to his relatives. If one's teeth turn yellow or black in a dream, such a dream also represents a disgraceful act that will bring shame upon one's family. Yellow teeth in a dream mean spending money to restore one's reputation, or it could mean being knowledgeable in one's own esteem. Developing bad mouth odor in a dream represents bad connotations resulting from praises one's family may receive. Deteriorating teeth in a dream represent weakness in one's family. If one sees people biting him in a dream, it means that he could have pretended something in public, though he fortunately restrained himself. [3]If one's mouth in a dream is interpreted to represent his household, then the teeth of the right side represent the boys, and those on the left side represent the girls. On the other hand, the teeth on the right side could represent the older generation, and the teeth on the left side could represent the younger generation. The incisors represent the young men in the family, and the canines represent the young girls. As to the molars, they represent elderly people. If one loses a molar tooth in a dream, it means the death of an elderly person in his household. [4]Human teeth in a dream also represent one's business and management of his life. In that case, the molars represent one's private life, the eyetooth represents what is semi-public, while the front incisors represent what is openly practiced, one's public character, words and deeds. If one sees his teeth broken in a dream, it means that he pays his debts slowly. Long teeth in a dream mean enmity or a fight between members of one's household. If one sees his teeth curved and deteriorating, and if one decides that it is better to pull them out in a dream, it means that he will escape from great adversities and dangers. If one's teeth turn gold in a dream, they represent benefits for a teacher or a preacher. Otherwise, golden teeth for everyone else in a dream mean fire, illness, Candida, or an illness that is caused by one's bile. If one's teeth become glass or wood in a dream, it means his death. If they turn silver in the dream, it means harm or losses. If one's front teeth fall and new ones grow instead in the dream, they represent major changes in one's life. If one sees himself forcefully pushing his tongue against his teeth in a dream, it means that he speaks ill of his own family, or it could mean problems in one's house. If the crown or the enamel of one's eyetooth is damaged, or if it falls in a dream, it means the death of one's son. [5] Teeth in a dream represent one's clan, close relatives, or distant cousins. The molar teeth represent the male members and the incisors represent the female members. Unnecessarily pulling out one's teeth in a dream means paying a fine, losing one's capital, or severing relationship with members of one's family. Discovering one or two cavities in one's teeth in a dream means that one may beget one or two sons. Developing bad mouth odor in a dream means belittling someone's ideas, or it could mean a family dispute. Fallen teeth in a dream may denote that the husband and the wife sleep in separate beds, or it may mean poverty, or that one may die in a foreign land, or that the term of one's life span in this world may be extended. If one pulls out his teeth and buries them in the dream, it means that his entire clan or family will die before him. Pulling out one's teeth in a dream also means exposing one's secrets. Losing a tooth in a dream may imply a punishment for a wrongdoing. If one finds the teeth of his upper jaw and those of the lower jaw intermixed in the dream, it means that the women control the men in his or family. Flossing one's teeth in a dream means dispersal of one's family, or loss of money and property. If after flossing one's teeth some meat fiber remains stuck between the teeth in the dream, it means that he backbites his family members. [6] Teeth in a dream also represent a pearl necklace, a grinder, or an army formation. The right wing, the left wing and the front assault formation, or they could mean severing blood ties. The incisors may represent the heart of a human being. Teeth in one's pocket or in the palm of one's hand in a dream represent one's brothers. If one has an incarcerated relative, and if he sees his teeth pulled out in a dream, it means the release of his relative from prison. Pulling out one's teeth in a dream could mean the return of a traveller to his homeland. Tartar in a dream represents weaknesses in the family. Black or broken teeth in a dream mean sorrow caused by one's relatives. Wisdom teeth in a dream represent one's followers, while the incisors and the canines represent his wealth, adornment, pride, or child. The changing of their color into yellow or black in a dream mean changes in one's life. If one's teeth turn into iron in a dream, they mean strength. Losing one's teeth in a dream also could mean losing one's job. Pulling out one's teeth in a dream so that no one can see them means infertility, or loss of one's business, loss of one's savings, a bad relationship with one's family, an evil act toward one's family, or it could mean that he will try to sustain his business through a loan, then suffer from bankruptcy. Having a bad tooth in wakefulness and pulling it out in a dream means trying to comfort or appease a difficult person whose hurtfulness will eventually cease. Replacing a tooth with a bridge in a dream means recovering losses, or balancing one's business. Having an extra tooth in a dream means losing one in wakefulness. *(Also see Body¹; Pain; Teeth)*

Toothbrush: (Boy; Broom; Employee) A toothbrush in a dream is a sign of hygienic conditions, prosperity, purity, cleanliness, repentance, or asking someone for forgiveness. Brushing and cleaning one's teeth in a dream is also a sign of being religious, a family person, a concerned relative and a generous kin. If one sees himself brushing his teeth, and if his gums bleed in the dream, it means that he will become free from his sins and curtail his evildoing, or it could mean the opposite, that is to proceed with abhorrent actions, cause harm to one's own family, steal their money, or defame them. Brushing one's teeth in a dream also could mean reservation and prudence with one's words, purifying oneself from sin, faith after disbelief, paying one's debts, doing what pleases God Almighty, fulfilling one's promises, a pregnancy, or a marriage. *(Also see Broom)*

Tooth ache: *(See Pain; Teeth; Tooth)*

Topaz: (Chrysolite; Gem) In a dream, topaz represents a good man who is courageous, well behaved, a true friend, a pious person, or a religious person. If topaz is understood to denote money in the dream, then it represents lawful earnings. Topaz in a dream also represents the substance of speech, the essence of knowledge, and the good quality of a true human being.

Torah: Reciting the Torah but not recognizing what it is in a dream means that one may become a fatalist. To own a copy of the Torah for a king or ruler in a dream means that he will conquer a land or make peace with its people on his terms. If he is learned in real life, it means that either his knowledge will increase or that he will invent what is not ordained, or he may tend to lean toward jovial company. Seeing the Torah in a dream also means finding what is lost, welcoming a long awaited traveller, or it could represent someone who follows the Jewish faith. As for an unmarried person, owning a Torah in a dream means getting married to a woman from a different religion, or it could mean marrying a woman without her parents' consent. Seeing the Torah in a dream also may mean extensive travels. If one's wife is pregnant, it means that she will bear a child who resembles his father. If one's wife is pregnant, and if he sees himself holding the Torah in a dream, it means that she will beget a daughter, for the gender of the word Torah is feminine. It also means that he will mix with evil companions. Similar interpretations are given to carrying other scriptures. To see the Torah, or the Evangel, or the Gospel in a dream is as though one has seen God's Prophet Muhammad, upon whom be peace, because his name (uwbp) is mentioned in all three of them. It could also mean betrayal, negating a covenant, or desiring what is shoddy.

Torch: (Beacon) Carrying a torch in a dream means knowledge, wisdom, guiding and leading the people on the straight path, or it could represent someone people depend on to learn about the truth. However, such a person will enjoy no luck, and he will receive little appreciation for his work.

Torn garments: (Goodwill; Secondhand. *Also see Used clothing*)

Tornado: (Changing course; Storm; Wind) A tornado in a dream means death and destruction. *(Also see Cloud of destruction; Wind)*

Torpor: (Apple tree)

Torrent: (Inundation; Tumultuous outburst. *See Flood*)

Torturer: *(See Executioner)*

Toss: *(See Cast²)*

Tourist: A tourist in a dream represents a student seeking knowledge, a buyer, a customer, or a merchant.

Towel: (Apron; Serviette) A towel in a dream represents one's servant, employee, housekeeper, or it could represent a pilgrimage to Mecca. In a dream, a towel also represents one's wife, and for a woman it represents her husband. If a towel is used as a mat during sexual intercourse in a dream, then it represents a discrete servant who protects his mistress's secrets, or it could represent money that serves woman's needs and those of her children. To throw a towel at someone in a dream means to slam the door in his face, or it could mean separation between two people. To throw in the towel in a dream also means to give up one's fight.

Tower: Standing inside a tower in a dream means that one should not feel safe from the blows of his enemy, or expect to be secured and safe in his own environment when someone calls upon him for something. If he is sick, it means that he may die from his illness. Standing on top of a tower or a wall in a dream means that one will conquer or capture a dangerous person. If one stands over or inside a tower that is no longer in use in a dream, then it represents his grave. *(Also see Grave)*

Town: *(See Village)*

Toy: (Swing)

Tracer: *(See Snake charmer; Tracker)*

Trachoma: *(See Water)*

Tracing footsteps: *(See Tracker)*

Tracker: (Spoor; Tracing footsteps) A tracker in a dream connotes divulging secrets, exposing people's private life, or he could represent knowledge, or a student who is investigating the works of masters from the past. *(Also see Snake charmer)*

Trade: Any product that is touched by fire in the process of its manufacturing means arguments and disputes.

Trader: A garment trader in a dream represents a person who loves the world and who is proud about his personal success in it. A milk merchant represents a knowledge seeker. A cattle trader represents an affectatious person who loves to show off. A sheep merchant in a dream may represent a good man who is intuitive and who spends his money on the path of seeking knowledge or to propagate the same.

Tragacanth: *(See Safflower)*

Trail: *(See Road)*

Trait: (Caprice; Distinguishing quality; Temper) In a dream, a trait represents someone who is impulsive, or who has an arbitrary change of mind, or someone who does not know rest in his work, or someone who does not know an end to his pursuit of success, or it could represent an argumentative person. The good or bad of such a character may show depending of the place, circumstance, or temper of the moment in the dream.

Tramp: *(See Destitute; Hobo)*

Transfixed: *(See Eyes)*

Transformation: (Changing form) Transformation by substitution in a dream where one thing is converted into something else. If a withered tree is transformed into a blossoming one in a dream, it means political changes, changes in worldly conditions, or reversal of conditions from good to bad, or from bad to good. This element includes the transformation of inner substances or physical ones. For example, if sees himself as an old person in a dream, when in real life he is young, it means progress in his spiritual life and gaining honor. If he is an old person and sees himself as a young boy in a dream, it means indulging in wrongdoing. If one sees a known old person regaining his youth, it means that the material conditions of the person seeing the dream will turn around to one's advantage or otherwise. i.e., richness into poverty and vice-versa, or if he is sick, he will recover from his illness. If one is transformed into a beautiful shoot of green or a blossoming branch of a tree in a dream, it means that he may die within a short time. Becoming taller in a dream means longevity, prosperity, or begetting a son. If one finds himself missing partial mental keenness or physical abilities or a limb in a dream, it means that he may suffer losses relating to his worldly interests. If a man sees himself transformed into a woman, and wears her apparels, ornaments and make-up in a dream, it means that he may suffer humiliation, adversities and abuse. If a woman sees herself transformed into a man, or if she grows a beard in a dream, it means that she will reestablish her connection with a missing child. As a man in the dream, and if she is pregnant, it means that she will beget a son who may die in his early youth, but if she is not pregnant, it means that she is no longer fertile. If one sees himself flying with wings in a dream, it means travels. If one sees himself transformed into a wooden staff in a dream, it represents his insolence. If one sees himself transformed into an iron rod in a dream, it means longevity. If one sees himself transformed into a bridge in a dream, it means that he may become a ruler, a wise man, or a man of knowledge whom people will seek to benefit from his wisdom. If a person sees his sick child turn into a bird in a dream, it means the death of the child. If one sees himself turned into a beast in a dream, it means that he will be segregated from the believers to live alone because of his evil qualities. If one sees himself turned into a deer, a gazelle or an antelope in a dream, it means that he will become obsessed with his sexual life, or that he will become mentally deranged to the degree of indulging in bisexual practices. If he turns into a pig in a dream, it means prosperity surrounded with absence of human dignity. If one sees a steer transformed into a wolf in a dream, it represents a government employee who will turn unjust. However, according to Islāmic interpretations of the human transformation into a lower category of creatures phenomena, if such transformation takes place in real life, it connotes a curse and a punishment, and it does not last for more than three days, and it will culminate in death. *(Also see Changing form)*

Transgression: *(See Infringement; Injustice)*

Transient: (Dwellings; House; Interim; Loan; Temporary)

Translator: (Tongue)

Transparent hood: *(See Canopy)*

Transportation: *(See Car; Driver)*

Transvestite: *(See Vagina)*

Trap: (Hunter's snare; Hunting trap; Net; Snare) In a dream, a trap means deception, duplicity and fraud. If one falls victim to a hunting trap in a dream, it means that he will be victimized. If one sets a trap and catches an animal or a bird with it in the dream, it means that he earns his money through deception and fraud. In a dream, a trap also represents a man who fosters little moral standards, or one who does not prescribe to any religious code of conduct, and who is smart but deceitful. Setting a trap or a net to catch a bird in a dream means setting a trap to bring a powerful person to his knees. If a woman sees herself setting a trap in a dream, it means that she desires to bear a child from her husband, though if she does get pregnant, she may have a miscarriage.

Trash collector: (Garbage) A trash collector in a dream represents a deprived person, someone who toils hard to serve others, or someone who struggles hard to comfort others. A trash collector in a dream also represents a short lived richness, a short lived poverty, or a stingy person who keeps hoarding money. *(Also see Garbage; Sanitation; Sweeping the floor; Trash)*

Trash: (Debris; Scraps) In a dream, trash represents the unavoidable a traveller hates to see, or fears of what he may reap from his journey. *(Also see Trash collector)*

Traveller's pouch: *(See Food basket)*

Travels: (Hotel; Inn; Millstone; World) In a dream, travels mean discovering people's substance or character. If a poor person sees himself travelling in a dream, it means that he will become rich. If one hosts travellers in a dream, it means that he may receive news from that direction. Travelling in a dream also means changing condition, state, environment, or that one may have to wash the floor of a house, or change his employer, repent for his sin, or satisfy what his heart desires. Travelling on foot in a dream means owing a debt that is weighing heavy in one's heart. Moving out of an unknown house in a dream means travelling. If a sick person sees himself travelling from one land into another that he could not recognize in his dream, it means his death. If a traveller sees himself carrying a food basket in a dream, it means that he will take a positive look at things, or that he will make a practical move that will benefit him and his family. *(Also see Reckoning; Saddle-mount; Stairway; Tent)*

Treasure box: (Jar; Preserves) If one finds a treasure box that is filled with jewelry in a dream, it means that he may acquire a large property, or it could mean joy or marriage. A treasure box in a dream also means being proud of one's child, or it could represent a wife who is concerned about the welfare of her family. It could also represent a book. Seeing a jar of preserves which is used in fermenting liquids in a dream connotes adversities and distress, or it may mean satisfying one's debts.

Treasure hunting: *(See Diving; Pearl diver)*

Treasure-trove: *(See Hidden treasure)*

Treasure: (Hidden treasure; Knowledge; Wheel) Discovering a treasure in a dream means acquiring knowledge. If one is a merchant, then it means profits from his business, or spending money generously on God's path. If one is a ruler, it means expansion of his powers and it denotes his justice. Seeing a treasure in a dream is interpreted in relation to one's type of trade. A treasure in a dream also represents a business. Discovering a hidden trunk with little money inside it in a dream means a short lived difficulty, but if the trunk is stashed with money, then it means distress, sadness and sorrow. In many instances, discovering a treasure in a dream may mean death, or it could mean becoming rich, or complying with a court order. Discovering a great treasure in a dream means martyrdom. Discovering a treasure and rejoicing in the dream means loss of one's money or business. Discovering a treasure in a dream also could mean ease in one's life, receiving an inheritance, distress, trouble, wearing a new garment, a wife, cheating on one's taxes, or it could mean avoiding to pay alms tax, or hindering the distributions of charitable endowments. A treasure in a dream also represents a profitable business, or it could represent a money changer, a jeweler, or remembering something. Discovering a treasure that is difficult to reach in a dream represents a stingy person who hinders the distribution of charities, or if he is a scholar, it means that he does not like to share his knowledge with others, and if one is a judge, it means that he is unjust. If a woman discovers a treasure in her dream, it means that she is careful about spending money and managing her household. If the trunk has no cover or lid in the dream, then it means the opposite.

Tree leaves: (Leaf) In a dream, tree leaves represent clothing, except for the leaves of a fig tree for they represent sorrow.

Tree: An apple tree in a dream represents a good man who serves and cares about his community. A crack in a tree in a dream represents members of one's family who will brace against him. A palmyra tree in a dream represents a wise man, a poet, or an astronomer. Seeing one, or sitting under it in a dream means meeting such a person. An oak tree in a dream means profits, prosperity, honor, associating with heedless people who live in the mountains, or perhaps it could mean visiting righteous people or a renunciate who lives in the wilderness or in uninhabited ruins. A mimosa tree in a dream represents stinginess, evil, or pursuing the actions of the dwellers of hell-fire. A buckthorn tree that grows datelike fruit in a dream represents a noble and a generous woman, or it could represent a noble and a generous man. The greener is its color, the greater is the person. Seeing this tree in a dream means that one will rise in station, acquire knowledge, and grow in piety. Eating its fruit in a dream means an illness. Climbing this tree in a dream means stress and difficulties. If one acknowledges the condition of a specific tree in wakefulness then sees the same in his dream, it means that such condition will last. In general, trees in a dream represent women or men of different tempers or personalities. Trees in a dream also represent fights. Unknown trees mean distress, worries, adversities and fears, particularly if one sees them in the dark in his dream. Sitting under the shade of a tree in a dream means profits and money, or it could mean dependence on people in authority, or befriending rich people for their money. As for one who is pursuing the path of innovation, it means that he will repent and follow the path of righteousness if it is a fruit-bearing tree. Taking shelter under a tree that bears no fruit in the dream means pursuing something that will bear no comfort or benefits. Fragrant trees, flowering trees, a Moringa tree, or a henna plant in a dream represent people of knowledge, religious scholars, teachers or preachers who teach what they do not practice. As for citrus trees in a dream, they represent righteous people, wise men and people of inner and outer awareness who practice what they preach. Palm trees, walnut trees, or the like trees in a dream represent people of the upper social class from whom no one can get anything, or no one will even attempts to ask them for anything. As for the poplar trees, the evergreen cypress trees, or the saint trees in a dream, they represent stinginess and avariciousness. In a dream, any kind of maple or other trees that renew their leaves annually represent poverty, richness, memorizing things, forgetfulness, celebrations, or sadness. In a dream, any kind of large trees that do not shed their leaves in the winter represent longevity, richness, jealousy, or steadfastness in one's religion. Climbing a tree in a dream means escaping from danger, or carefully avoiding something worrisome. Seeing an unknown tree inside one's house in a dream means that fire may consume such a house, or that a fight may break the family apart. Common types of trees and city trees in a dream represent enemies, or men seeking lawful earnings. Planting a seedling in a dream means getting married to a girl from a renowned family and gaining rank. A plane tree, a sycamore, or the like trees in a dream represent great, strong and famous men who have no wealth, nor do they benefit anyone. A thorny tree in a dream represents a perplexed man. If one cuts a tree in a dream, it may mean the death of his wife, or that he will infringe upon a contract, or break a covenant. If a tree dries out in a dream, it means that a traveller may die in an accident, or that a sick person may die from his illness. If one sees a king or a man in authority carving some emblems on the trunk of a tree in a dream, it means that he is designing a plan to destroy someone. If he cuts it down with a scythe or a sickle in the dream, it means that he is demanding something, the other party cannot deliver. If one takes money from a tree in his dream, it means that he will earn lawful and blessed money from people who deal with the same type of trees, or that he will live in their vicinity. Planting trees in one's garden in a dream means bearing children. A plane tree represents longevity. Peach or plum trees in a dream represent a short life. Seeing a group of trees surrounded with aromatic plants in a dream means that a group of men will gather to mourn someone, or to lament a loss. Tree leaves in a dream represent money. A tree outside one's house in a dream represents one's clan or servants. A female tree inside a house represents a woman, and a male tree represents a man. It is a bad omen to see the forbidden tree in a dream. In a dream, to see the tree near which God Almighty spoke to Moses, upon whom be peace, means nearness to God Almighty. A dead tree in a dream represents guidance and wealth, for it is a source of fuel. Sitting under the shade of a tree along with a group of people, praising and glorifying God's attributes in a dream means receiving God's blessings in this world and in the hereafter. Seeing the heavenly Tūbā tree in a dream means a good end, or living an ascetic life, or it could mean helping others. Seeing mountain trees in a dream means performing supererogatory devotion, work, or receiving unexpected profits. A palm tree in a dream represents a good word and a true one. It also represents Muslims' testimony of faith: 'There is no God except Allāh, Muhammad is the Messenger of Allāh.' Seeing a garlic tree, or an onion plant, or a perennial vine of the gourd family, or the colocynth tree (*Citrullus colocynthis; bot.*) in a dream means hearing harsh words or evil talk. Plucking fruits other than what the mother tree bears in a dream means carrying someone else's money or property. A tree bearing a fruit other than its own in a dream represents an adulterous wife who bears a child from someone other than her husband. Cutting a tree in a dream means killing someone, or it could mean an illness. Climbing a tree in a dream means meeting a strong man. Coming down from a tree in a dream means parting with someone. Falling down from a tree in a dream means death resulting from fight. If one's right hand breaks from such fall in the dream, it means the death of his brother or his sister in a fight. If the leg breaks in the dream, it means losing one's money. If one sees blessed trees such as an olive tree with thorns in a dream, it means that such thorns will prevent him from wrongdoing or from falling into sin. A walnut tree in a dream represents hard earned money. Trees in a dream also represent shops, businesses, tables, festivities, servants, cattle, restaurants, money, hidden treasures, storage houses, religions or sects. If a storm damages a tree, burns it, or causes it to falls in a dream, it means the death or murder of a man or a woman. A date or a palm tree in a dream also represents a famous person, a man of knowledge, the wife of a king, or the mother of a president. If it is an olive tree, then it represents a man of knowledge, a preacher, a passenger, a judge or a physician. Like that, trees are interpreted according to their substance, value, or the harm or benefit they bring, their roots, origin or age. Seeing a vineyard bearing grapes in the winter in a dream means that one will be deceived by a woman or a man during a business transaction, thinking that they are rich. A quince tree in a dream represents an intelligent person who does not use his intelligence to benefit himself or others. An almond tree in a dream represents a foreigner or a passenger. Cane or reed plants in a dream represent opposition, punishment or help. A pomegranate tree in a dream represents a pious and a religious person, and its thorns represent the obstacles that could prevent him from falling into sin. A lotus tree in a dream represents a noble and a gracious person. A colocynth tree in a dream represents a good but cowardly and easily scared man who has no real devotion and fails to practice his religious duties. An oak tree in a dream represents a king, a gnostic, a poet or a fortuneteller. An indigo plant in a dream represents a knowledgeable Arab. A dried out palm tree in a dream represents a hypocrite. If a storm uproots a tree in a dream, it means a calamity or a plague. A banana tree in a dream represents a rich person who correctly manages his religious and his material life. A jujube tree in a dream represents a joyful and a happy person, or it could represent power and leadership. A fig tree in a dream represents someone who benefits his family, and who treats his enemy with justice. A berry tree in a dream represents a generous person. A pistachio tree in a dream represents a wealthy person who also possess a good humor, and who is generous with his family and friends. A peach tree in a dream represents a correct person, though few can benefit from him, or it could represent a hypocrite or a handsome looking person, or perhaps a rich woman. If one pluck its fruits in a dream, it means that he will marry her. An apple tree in a dream represents a person with steadfastness and determination. A plum tree in a dream represents a rich and a courageous man. A pear tree in a dream represents a Persian who practices herbal medicine. A tamarisk tree in a dream represents a hypocrite, or it could mean a thief who benefits poor people and harms the rich. A bullace, a wild small plum tree, or a damson tree in a dream represent someone who benefits everyone. A sycamore tree in a dream represents a good person who is steadfast in his servitude to others, though who is also firm, equitable, powerful and rich. A carob tree in a dream represents a man of little benefit to others. A lemon tree in a dream represents a beneficial person, or a rich woman who is known for her charities. *(Also see Sycamore tree; Evergreen; Oak tree; Palm tree; etcetera)*

Trellis: *(See Vineyard)*

Tremble: (Shake; Shiver; Tremor) Seeing one's head trembling in a dream means gaining honor and rising in station. If one's right hand trembles or shakes in a dream, it means difficulties in earning his livelihood. If one's right leg trembles in a dream, it means profits from one's family or clan. If one's left leg trembles in a dream, it means business losses. The same applies to the trembling or the shocking of any part of one's body. *(See Body¹; Tremor)*

Tremor: (Labor pangs; Labor throes; Quake; Shaking; Shock) A tremor in a dream represents plants blooming, grass growing, vegetations sprouting, the blossoming of garden flowers, and the ripening of fruits. If a pregnant woman sees an earth tremor in her dream, it represents labor throes. *(Also see Earthquake; Shock; Tremble)*

Trench coat: *(See Raincoat)*

Trench: (Defenses) If it relates to the king or the ruler and his army in the dream, a trench then means one's men and wealth. If the trench relates to a scholar in the dream, then it represents his advisors, or his circle of intimates who support his theories. If it relates to one's wife, the trench then represents her guardian or her father. If it relates to one's son, the trench then represents his parents. Noticing a city without a trench or a castle to defend it in a dream means failure to pay alms or charities, wasting money, losing knowledge, the spread of evil, or an enemy attack against that city.

Trespassing: (Allurement) In a dream, trespassing means corruption, straying from God's path, denying the truth, or refusing to follow common sense.

Trials: *(See Trouble)*

Triangulum: *(See Constellations)*

Tribadism: *(See Hone; Sexual intercourse)*

Trickery: In a dream, trickery means betrayal, deception, misleading others, or it could mean war. *(Also see Advice; Tricks)*

Trickling sand: *(See Hourglass)*

Tricks: (Conjuring; Jugglery; Magic arts) In a dream, tricks represent deceit, chicanery, pride, artificiality, or temptation. *(Also see Magician)*

Trickster: *(See Juggler; Tricks)*

Tricktrack: *(See Backgammon)*

Tripe shop: *(See Sheep; Trotter)*

Tripping: (Debts; Slipping; Step lightly; Stumble) To stumble by catching one's foot or hurting one's toe in a dream means accumulating debts. If one's toe bleeds from tripping out in the dream, it means acquiring unlawful or tainted money to pay other debts, or it could mean suffering a great financial loss. *(Also see Walking)*

Trotter: (Tripes) In a dream, trotters represent an orphan's property or money. Eating trotters or licking up their marrow in a dream signifies swindling the trusted inheritance of an orphan by his guardian. Eating tripes in a dream means defrauding rich and honorable people from their monies, for a sheep is the most noble animal, comparatively speaking, after the human being. *(Also see Sheep)*

Trouble: (Money; Temptation; Trial) In a dream, trouble mean money and money means trouble. Seeing oneself in a dream wealthy and having many children means trouble, trials and temptations.

Troubled waters: Swimming in troubled waters or in high tides in a dream means adversities, or having to face a strong opponent.

Trough: *(See Manger)*

Trousers: *(See Paints)*

Trout: *(See Fish)*

Trowel: *(See Shovel)*

Truce: (Armistice; Cease fire; Cessation) Negotiating a truce, or witnessing one between two armies in a dream means cessation of fear, relaxing, recovering of a sick person from his illness, caring for the wounded, extending the chances of one's survival, profits, business, marriage, rebuilding, doing good, or performing one's prayers.

Truffle: In a dream, a truffle represents an honest and a likeable man whose company is sought by noble people. A truffle in a dream also represents money earned through a woman. Eating truffle in a dream means earning money from a relative through legitimate means.

Trumpet of Resurrection: Hearing the sound of the trumpet of the Day of Resurrection in a dream means hearing the truth. Blowing in the trumpet of the arc angel Isrāfīl (uwbp) in a dream means salvation of the righteous ones. In a dream, the sound of this trumpet invokes fear incurring news that cause shivers and trembling in people's hearts. If one hears it alone, then the news are exclusive for him. If everyone hears its sound in the dream, then it is a public affair. If one hears the sound of the trumpet and anticipates that everyone has heard it too in a dream, it means plagues and adversities, for the first blow indicates the end of the world and the death of everyone in it. The second blow indicates their resurrection back to life, which will be followed by the Grand Gathering for the Day of Judgment. If a sick person hears the first blow in a dream, it means that he will shortly recover from his illness. If the town is inflicted with a calamity, then hearing it in a dream means that people's adversities will be lifted. If there is a drought, it will end and food prices will go back to normal. If one hears the second blow of the trumpet of resurrection in a dream, it means prosperity, revealing what is hidden, exposing long kept secrets, recovering from an illness, release from prison, reunion of beloveds, or meeting with people who have just arrived from a long journey. *(Also see Blowing; Rising of the dead; Resurrection)*

Trumpet: Hearing the sound of a trumpet or a horn in a dream means going to war. If one blows into a horn in the dream, it means that he will face adversities, and if one sees himself playing the trumpet, it means that he will receive glad tidings. *(Also see Trumpet of Resurrection)*

Trunk: In a dream, a trunk represents a wife, a beautiful woman, one's house, or one's shop. In a dream, a trunk also represents marriage for an unwed person, prosperity for a poor person, travels, or an ambassador. *(Also see Sack; Suitcase; Treasure box)*

Trust in God: To express one's trust in God Almighty in a dream signifies the end of adversities and the achievement of one's goals. To proclaim one's trust is God in a dream is an indication of true faith, recognition of God's supremacy, cessation of adversities and victory over one's enemy. Putting one's trust in God Almighty in a dream also means repenting from sin. Otherwise, perhaps it may indicate the infallibility of one's destiny, though the end result of one's encounter with his adversities will prove him triumphant.

Trust: *(See Deposit)*

Trustee: *(See Legal guardian)*

Trusting someone: *(See Deposit)*

Truth: Recognizing the truth through seeing a light or hearing the admonition of the holy Qur'ān in a dream means walking on the straight path and abstaining from falsehood or from mixing with its people. In the case of a sick person, it means his death. *(Also see Almond; Sanding)*

Truthfulness: In a dream, truthfulness represents one's faith and certitude. Being truthful in a dream means avoiding adversities.

Tuberculosis: In a dream, it represents an illness, debts, a journey that necessitates living a simple life, being filthy, or it could represent a rare form of art.

Tuft[1]: (Crest) A tuft in a dream represents a little boy.

Tuft[2]: *(See Strand of hair)*

Tumor: (Abscess; Boil; Ulcer. *See Pimple*)

Tunnel: (Burrow; Hole; Underground passage) In a dream, a tunnel represents trickery and deception. If one sees himself digging a tunnel or a hole for someone else in a dream, it means tricking and deceiving him. If one enters the tunnel that he dug in the dream, it means that he will fall in his own trap. If one enters a tunnel or a burrow and cannot see light at the end of it, or if a traveller digs a hole, enters it and can longer see the skies or the stars above him in the dream, it means that thieves will rob him from his luggage, or that he will be high-jacked, or stopped by a band of highway robbers. If one sees himself taking an ablution or a bath inside the tunnel or in the hole in a dream, it means that he will arrest the robbers and recover his property. If one enters a tunnel and takes a bath inside it in a dream, it means that he will pay his debts, or repent for his sins, or if he is incarcerated, it means that he will be released. If one digs a tunnel and draws water from it or discovers a hole filled with still water inside it in a dream, it means that he earns his livelihood from trickery and deception. *(Also see Piercing a hole)*

Turban: (Crown; Headgear; Tiara) In a dream, one's turban represents his family tree, his paternal uncle, or his paternal aunt. In a dream, one's turban also represents his crown, strength, integrity, state, or wife. If one's turban is taken away from him in a dream, it means that he may lose his job, divorce his wife, or lose his wealth. The same interpretation is given for one who sees himself wearing a golden turban in a dream. If a prophet of God Almighty, or a ruler crowns someone with a turban in a dream, it means that he will receive an important appointment, or that he may marry a pious woman. Putting on a turban in a dream means increase in one's strength, expansion of one's control, growth in one's business, or it could mean becoming wealthy. If the turban is made of wool in the dream, it means a spiritual appointment, and if it is made of silk in the dream, then it means living a corrupt state of mind, or earning unlawful money. Wearing a second turban on top of the first one in a dream means increase in one's power. Fixing a turban for oneself in a dream means taking a journey. A yellow turban means sickness. A black turban means happiness and unity. Wearing a turban in a dream also could mean that one may lose his sight. If a bewildered person sees himself wearing a turban in a dream, it means that his fears will dissipate. *(Also see Crown; Headgear)*

Turkish bath: (Bathhouse; Rest room; Sauna; Steam room; Sweat room) Seeing the attendant of a public bath facility in a dream means paying one's debts, dispelling one's problems, ending one's difficulties and washing oneself from sin. On the other hand, seeing him in a dream also could mean depression or a sickness. If one sees himself as the attendant of a Turkish bath facility or a bathhouse, and if he stood by and did not serve the customers in the dream, it means that he is a pimp and a bastard who brings benefits to no one but rather wrath. If one sees himself wearing a white uniform and serving people in a dream, it means that he washes people's hearts and dispels their trouble. Public bath in itself denotes many meanings. *(Also see Toilet)*

Turkish: *(See Language)*

Turning in one's sleep: If one sees himself turning in his sleep and putting his face down, or resting on his stomach in a dream, it means that he will turn away from his faith and lose both his earnings in this world and in the hereafter. If one sees the reverse, which is turning from resting on one's stomach to lying on his back in a dream, it means that he will repent for his sins. It also represents his willingness to face the people and to correct his wrongdoing. If the subject is a woman, then sleeping on her stomach in a dream means that she is refusing to sleep with her husband. *(Also see Running away; Take a flight; Sleep)*

Turnip: In a dream, turnip represents a strong woman from a village, a curious villager, or it could mean distress and worries. If one sees turnip growing in the field in a dream, it means having unhappy children.

Turquoise: (Precious stone) Turquoise in a dream signifies victory and success in one's life, or it could mean longevity. If a pregnant woman sees herself holding to a dagger or a knife with a turquoise haft in a dream, it means that she will give birth to a son who will live to advanced age.

Turtle: In a dream, a turtle represents a woman who likes to adorn herself and to make herself noticeable to please men. A turtle in a dream is also interpreted as a man of knowledge, or a chief justice, because she is most knowledgeable and God fearing amongst the sea creatures. In a dream, a turtle therefor could represent a devout worshipper who reads the scrolls of God's prophet Abraham, upon whom be peace, or any of the holy scriptures. Seeing a pet turtle in a house or a town in a dream means that the people of knowledge in that locality are well respected. Seeing a turtle living in a dump, then it represents a knowledgeable person living in the midst of ignorant people who care little about learning anything from him. Eating a turtle in a dream means profits, benefits, or money. If one sees a turtle inside his house, or if he owns one in a dream, it means that he will benefit from the company of a learned person who is acquainted with ancient manuscripts, or in interpreting ancient scrolls. If one sees a turtle lying on its back in a dream, it means that there is a man of knowledge in that town people do not recognize. If one sees a well kept and fed turtle sitting on a brocade in the dream, it means that the people of that town honor their scholars. However, a turtle in a dream also can be interpreted as deception, trickery, spying, hiding, evil and acquisition of weapons.

Turtledove: (Dove; Pigeon; Ringdove) A turtledove in a dream represents a poet or a singer. Seeing a turtledove in a dream during the springtime means benefits and goodness, or it could mean the return of a long awaited traveller, satisfaction of one's need, fulfillment of one's intent, or overcoming distress. Seeing a turtledove during other seasons in a dream means delays. As for a pregnant woman, seeing a turtledove in a dream means that she will beget a son. A turtledove in a dream also represents a pious woman or a blessed son. (*Also see Pigeon; Ringdove*)

Tutelage: (*See Sponsorship*)

Tutoring: (*See School*)

Tūbā tree: (*See Tree*)

Twanging: (Nasal speech) If one sees himself speaking with a twang in a dream, it means difficulties, or it could mean that he will be mocked for his opinions.

Tweak: (*See Pinch*)

Tweezers: (Tongues) In a dream, a pair of tweezers represents a hard-working and a patient boy. It also means blabber, or employment for a jobless person.

Twilight: (Dusk) Twilight in a dream means taking an oath, or it could represent the political or military move of a ruler and his deputies.

Twine: (*See Twist*)

Twist: (Bend; Curve; Perverseness) In a dream, twisting something means hypocrisy, absurdity, or twisting and changing God's words, or attributing a personal saying to God Almighty, and making it sound like an authentic revelation. Twisting one's turban a cap or a rope in a dream also means travels. (*Also see Twisting a rope*)

Twisting a rope: (Splice; Entwine; Twine) To splice a rope or a thread, or to twist a rope around oneself, or to whorl it around a spindle, or to make a bobbin in a dream means undertaking a journey. If it comes out thin in the dream, then the outcome of one's journey is meager. If the rope comes out thick and strong in the dream, it means that the outcome of one's journey is beneficial. If the twisting of the rope or the thread is easy in the dream, it means that one's endeavor is free from constraint. If one sees himself plucking the hair of his beard and twisting it like a rope in a dream, it means that he will receive a bribe to make a false testimony in court. Twisting a rope or a thread in a dream also could mean signing a contract, establishing a partnership in a business, or signing a marriage contract. *(Also see Beard; Twist)*

Tying a knot: *(See Contract)*

Tyke: *(See Dog)*

Tyranny: If one suspects himself to be a tyrant in a dream, it means that his desires and passions are uncontrollable, that he has strayed from the straight path, and that his wantonness has incriminated him. In this case, he can be justly considered as one of the dwellers of hell-fire. *(Also see Terrorization)*

U

'Ūd: (*arb*. Aloe perfume; Civet; Incense burning 'Ūd) Aloe or 'Ūd wood chips or incense sticks in a dream represent a vocative and an articulate person who has a praiseworthy reputation. Carrying a chip of 'Ūd or aloe incense in a dream means finding a lost object, or hearing comforting words. Smelling the fragrance of 'Ūd or seeing the smoke of 'Ūd burning in a dream means receiving a commendation and experiencing a fright along with it. Seeing 'Ūd or an Aloe tree growing inside one's house in a dream means begetting a son who will grow to be a sire or a leader in his community. (*Also see Aloe perfume; Civet*)

Ulcer: (Abscess; Boil; Tumor. *See Pimple*)

Umbilicus: *(See Body¹)*

'Umrah: (*arb*. Minor Hajj; Pilgrimage; Visiting God's House in Mecca) Performing the minor pilgrimage to God's House in Mecca during the great pilgrimage season signifies the end of one's life, or it could mean reaching the peak of one's illness. Performing the minor pilgrimage also known in Arabic as 'Umrah in a dream also could mean increase in one's wealth, longevity, success in one's life, or acceptance of one's prayers. (*Also see Pilgrimage; Rituals of the pilgrimage; Sa'i*)

Unbalance: *(See Delirium; Distraction)*

Unbeliever: *(See Irreligious)*

Uncertainty: (Doubt) In a dream, uncertainty means heedlessness or being allured by Satan. Uncertainty and doubt about all religions in a dream represents adjuration and ingratitude. If a person who is concerned about religious explanations sees himself unable to recognize what faith he belongs to, or what direction to turn to in a dream, it represents doubt and lack of knowledge or certitude. If a seeker or a student on the path sees himself searching at no avail for a place to pray in a dream, it represents a blocking on his path, or obstruction of his learning. As for a merchant, uncertainty in a dream represents obstacles hindering his efforts from receiving any significant benefits from his business.

Uncle's beard: Holding one's uncle's beard in a dream means inheriting him through unlawful means.

Unclothed: *(See Naked)*

Under garment: *(See Slip)*

Underground granary: (Granary; Pantry; Storrage room; Subterranean storehouse) An underground grain storage house in a dream represents a caring mother, a single parent or a foster mother. This interpretation comes from the example of a fetus in his mother's womb and its dependence on her to supply the necessary nourishment. Once the stored food is consumed, then it is necessary to depend on a new source. If one sees an underground granary demolished or filled with dirt in the dream, and if his mother is sick, it means that she may die from her illness. If one's wife is pregnant, it means that she will soon deliver her infant. A demolished underground granary in a dream means finding a buyer for one's grains, and the dirt that fills the storehouse in the dream represents money. If the stored grain turns into dirt in a dream, it means that market prices will come down, or it could mean the loss of one's investment. Seeing a granary filled with food in a dream means that one's wife is pregnant. If a fire consumes the stored grain in a dream, it means rising prices. If one sees a granary filled with sugar or dates in a dream, it means that prices will stabilize and become attainable, while the type of food stored therein will be in limited supplies and consequently, its price will rise. If a sick person falls into an underground granary in a dream, it means his death, or drowning in the sea, or facing a highway robbery. As for one who is engaged in a fight, an underground granary in his dream represents a prison or a visit to a brothel.

Underground passage: *(See Tunnel)*

Undertaker: If a sick person sees an undertaker washing and shrouding him in a dream, it means his death or relief from his agony. An undertaker in a dream also means payment of one's debts, or repentance. If one sees himself washing a deceased person with boiling water in a dream, it means that the latter is suffering in hell-fire. *(Also see Grave digger; Hot water; Mortician; Ritual bath; Shrouding)*

Underwear: *(Panties; Underpants)* One's underwear in a dream represents his chastity. If one discovers wetness in his underpants in a dream, it means that his wife is pregnant. Seeing one's underpants soiled with feces in a dream means divorce. Wearing one's underpants inside-out in the dream means indulging in a loathsome and a forbidden act of anal intercourse with one's wife. Wearing one's underpants without the underwear shirt in a dream means poverty. Wearing fancy underpants in a dream means travels or financial growth. Wearing a new set of underpants in a dream means modesty and protection of one's chastity. Giving away one's old underpants in a dream means relief from pressure.

Undressed: *(See Disrobe; Naked)*

Undutiful child: *(See Recalcitrant child)*

Uneasiness: *(See Worries)*

Unfinished business: *(See Incomplete job)*

Unfold: *(See Hanging clothes)*

Ungodly: *(See Irreligious)*

Uniform: Wearing a soldier's uniform in a dream means a war. Wearing any uniform in a dream represent the type of work involved in using such a uniform. *(Also see Bodyguard)*

Unit of weight: (Measure; Weight) In a dream, a unit of weight may signify distress or it could mean relief. A unit of weight in a dream also represents the elements that are measured or weighed with it. In a dream, a unit of weight also could represent one's confidant or personal secretary. *(Also see Half a bushel; Measure²; Weight)*

Unjust ruler: When injustice is practiced by a ruler in a dream, it means the opposite. In fact, seeing an unjust ruler in a dream could signify comfort, peace, safety, tranquility, protection of the society, or urban developments. *(Also see Injustice; Justice)*

Unlawful: (Unlawful earnings; Impermissible; Illegal) Earning illegal money in a dream means falling into sin, or that a religious person will go astray. The opposite represents the lawful.

Unloading: Unloading one's burdens, or unloading one's cargo in a dream means paying charity and doing good for the benefit of those who appreciate and those who do not appreciate.

Unlock: (Open) To unlock a closed or a sealed door, or to open a sealed container, or a location in a dream means easing of one's difficulties, and it could represent the way to prosperity.

Unmarried: *(See Virgin)*

Unseen: *(See Perspicacity)*

Untying something: Untying something in a dream means bewilderment, loneliness, being reprimanded, or stinginess. *(Also see Knot)*

Upholsterer's needle: *(See Sacking needle)*

Upholsterer: In a dream, an upholsterer represents someone who is proud of himself or his work, or he could represent a singer, a helper, a teacher, resting after a long-working day, or someone who curbs the intentions of hypocrites, obliges them, and defrauds them of their assets.

Upper room: *(See Stairway)*

Uptight: (Anxious; Disheartened; Dispirited) Feeling uptight in a dream may mean an illness or death. *(Also see Despair)*

Urge: (Entice; Incite; Induce; Lure. *See Prompting)*

Urinating: Urinating in a dream means wasting money in an unnecessary or an unlawful way. It also means a marriage to an unsuitable or a non-compatible person. Frequency of urination in a dream means receiving regular income. On the other hand, suppression of urine in a dream means the opposite, or it may mean hastiness, or making an incorrect decision. If one sees himself urinating in an unknown place, in someone else's house, a lodge, a town, etcetera in a dream, it may mean kinship with its people. Wetting one's underpants in a dream means a newborn in the family. Urinating in the sea in a dream mean paying taxes or giving charity. Urinating in a valley in a dream means expansion of one's progeny. Emitting bad odor after urination while others are looking with despise in a dream means defamation, or exposing one's ills in public. Drinking urine in a dream means earning unlawful income. If one sees his servant or employee urinating inside a well or a stream in a dream, it means that someone from his family will betray its interests. Urinating in a dream also means dispelling distress.

Urine: *(Also see Excretion; Glass bottle; Impurity; Urinating)*

Urn: (Cistern; Container; Storing; Waterskin) In a dream, each type of urn is interpreted differently. A large urn represents a prostitute. In a dream, a cistern or any large conical jar made of porous clay and used in storing water represents a caretaker, a custodian or a curator, the head of the household, his safe, or his shop. If the urn is seen inside a house in a dream, it represents a rich woman who is always in grief. If it is connected to a water wheel in the dream, it represents a rich man who carries heavy responsibilities and who spends his money on God's path. A waterskin in a dream represents a chaste woman. Drinking from a waterskin in a dream means receiving money or benefits from such a woman. If one sees himself drawing water from a storage tank then pouring it into an urn in the dream, it means that he will take advantage of such a woman. A wine pitcher in a dream means discovering a treasure. If one sees an urn containing vinegar in a dream, it represents a pious and a God-fearing person. If it stores butter or ghee for cooking in the dream, it represents a rich man who hides his wealth. If it stores pickles in the dream, it denotes a sick person. If an urn falls from one's hands and breaks in the dream, it means a divorce. *(Also see Pitcher)*

Ursa Major: *(See Constellations)*

Ursa Minor: *(See Constellations)*

Urticaria: *(See Hives)*

Used clothing: (Attire; Goodwill; Secondhand) Buying used clothing in a dream means poverty, but selling worn garments in a dream means good deeds, for in that case, one repels his aggravation or unwarranted adversities. A thrift shop salesperson in a dream represents a layman. Selling used clothing in a dream also means putting an end to one's problems.

'Uthmān: ('Uthmān bin 'Affān, God be pleased with him. The third of the four righteous califs) Seeing him in a dream means celebrating knowledge, being a godly person, friendship and love for others, lowering one's wings before God Almighty and to the believers among His creation, and he represents a trustworthy leadership. Seeing 'Uthmān bin 'Affān in a dream also could mean facing the aggression of one's enemy and losing to them by winning martyrdom. It also means having a great luck, prosperity, kinship with noble people, or being a pious and a religious person. One who sees 'Uthmān, God be pleased with him, in a dream will become a scholar. If one sees him doing business in a dream, it means that one is seeking worldly profits, though he likes to adorn himself with a religious garb and titles but lacks true piety. If one sees him besieged inside his own house in a dream, it means that he will persecute and oppress a great scholar or a man of God. Seeing him alive and dealing with people in a dream means being chaste, pious, reverent and earning the jealousy of one's own circles.

Uvula: If one's uvula is swollen to the extent of blocking his mouth, or impeding his breathing in a dream, it means covetousness, love to hoard money, frugality, miserliness, or the nearing of one's death.

'Uzair: (See Ezra)

V

Vagabond: *(See Destitute)*

Vagina: A vagina in a dream signifies relief for someone who is experiencing hardship, pressure, or sorrow. It also could mean satisfaction of one's needs, fulfillment of one's desire, marriage, partnership, exposing a secret, working with minerals, protecting women's chastity, imprisonment, the house entrance, the front door, travels, the prayer niche inside a mosque, one's innermost secret, running water, heat, an oven, a garment, a canyon, discovering a cure for an illness and feeling happy about it, finding an elixir, feeling relief after having sexual relationship with one's spouse, a grave, distress, one's wife, fire, a burning desires, family reunion, having children, dispelling doubt about what is right and what is wrong, clearly identifying true from false, finding guidance, or heeding admonition. If a man looks at a woman's vagina in a dream, it represents his wicked state of mind, needs, desires, humiliation, or it could represent the high standard a woman has achieved in his eyes. If a woman looks at a man's sexual organ in a dream, it represents her strength and manlike drive. If a prisoner finds himself having a vagina in a dream, it means his release from prison, and for someone who is depressed, it means relief from his depression. If one has to appear in court, it means that he will win his case. If one is facing an opponent, it means that he will conquer him. Seeing the vagina of an elderly woman in a dream means loss of business. If one reenters the womb of a woman through her vagina in a dream, it means his death. A vagina in a dream also could represent a blood sucker, a murderer, or a deceitful person who portrays piety during the day, then shows his teeth at night. A vagina in a dream also represents a shameless and an insolent worker, or it could represent a bird's nest. In this sense, capturing a bird, or looking inside a bird's nest in a dream means getting married. If a woman sees water entering her vagina in a dream, it means that she will conceive a child. If a woman's vagina turns into iron or into any metal in the dream, it means that she has lost all hope in accomplishing her aspirations, satisfying her desires or needs. *(Also see Blowing into the vagina; Looking at a sexual organ; Semen; Effeminate; Sexual intercourse; Sodomy)*

Vain talk: *(See Naked)*

Vainglory: *(See Pride)*

Valley: *(See Wadi)*

Vanity: *(See Pride)*

Vapor: In a dream, vapor represents a symptom of cataract that makes one's eye cloudy and obscures his sight. If during the summer one sees vapor exhaling from his mouth in a dream, which is a common phenomena in cold weather, it means an internal disease, or exposing one's secrets. If the person in question in such a dream is a believer on the path, he may become heedless. If he is a man of knowledge, he may invent a provoking trend. On the other hand, vapor in a dream may imply falsehood, lies and idle talk. *(Also see Clouds)*

Varanidae: *(See Monitor[2])*

Vascular blockage: (Clot; Coagulation) When one is suffering from blood thickening or clotting, then retaining or flushing any part thereof in a dream means liquidation of stagnant merchandise, or recovering from an illness. When such an illness is not common, then seeing it in a dream means cognizance of a bad action, discovering a robbery in one's house, desecration of the grave of a relative, body snatching, or exhuming a body and moving it to another grave. Vascular blockage in a dream also represents abrogating one's promise, failing to fulfill a vow, denying a promise, or other related matters. *(Also see Blood)*

Vast control: *(See Finished business)*

Vat: (Tank; Tanning drum; Tannery; Woman) A vat in a dream holds the same interpretation as a tannery, except if a tannery represents an independent woman in a dream, then a vat will represent an inhibited woman. A vat in a dream also represents a bathhouse, death by drowning, or dying under a collapsing structure.

Vegetables: *(See Boiled vegetables)*

Vehicle: *(See Car)*

Veil: (Attire) In a dream, a woman's veil represents her religion. For a woman, wearing a veil in a dream means marriage, prosperity, beauty. Wearing a black veil in a dream means marrying a poor man. If a man sees himself wearing a veil in a dream, it means that he will commit adultery with his female servant. *(Also see Apparel; Climbing a mountain; Closet; Khimār; Protection; Uncertainty; Wife; Yashmak)*

Veins: (Blood ties; Family; Relative; Vessel) The veins of the children of Adam represent their tribal belonging or clan. The parable of one's veins is like that of a tree and its branches. One's veins in a dream represent his family members, depending which part of the body they belong to. The condition and beauty of one's veins in a dream denote their counterpart in one's family. If one sees his vein split open in a dream, it means the death of a relative. The same dream also could denote deceit, evil, an accident or a calamity. Otherwise, it could represent a divided family. Exposed veins in a dream mean difficulties. The point of pulsation in one's veins or the arteries, or the veins of the carpal tunnel in a dream represent one's livelihood, job, income, or the elderly people of his family. If a rich person sees a specific quantity of blood running through his veins in a dream, it means that he will lose an equal portion or percentage of his money. Otherwise, if a poor person sees that dream, it means that he will earn an equal amount of money. *(Also see Aorta; Blood; Body¹; Jugular vein)*

Vela: *(See Constellations)*

Venereal disease: (Piper)

Venter: *(See Abdomen)*

Venus: (Planet; Woman) In a dream, the planet Venus represents a beautiful woman. Seeing the planet Venus in a dream means getting married to an attractive and a beautiful woman of no kinship to him, though her beauty will lead many people into temptation. The planet Venus in a dream also could mean allegations, playfulness, complaisance, jokes, images, idolatry, jewelry, nudity, pictures of beautiful women, or it could mean beautiful clothing. Seeing the planet Venus in a dream also means allegations, accusations, or that one may pursue any of the aforementioned elements, or he may establish a friendship with someone who follows such avenues, or perhaps he may marry an attractive and a beautiful woman, a foreign woman, or a famous singer. If one sees the planet Venus mixing with the moon, or if its position is lower than the moon, or if it is burning in the dream, then Venus represents one's daughter, or it could mean mixing with crazy or stupid people, or listening to vain talk. *(Also see*

Constellation; Heavens)

Verbal abuse: *(See Fire)*

Vermin: *(zool.* Game; Graveyard) A vermin or any bird that kills game or dwells near the graveyards in a dream represents a procurer or a prostitute.

Vertical wound: In a dream, a vertical wound represents a friendship, commendation, or unity.

Vestige: *(See Question)*

Veteran: *(See Salt)*

Veterinarian: In a dream, a veterinarian is a person who adorns and beautifies distinguished and honored people, and who supports and assists them in developing strength. Seeing a veterinarian in a dream also means performing a marriage ceremony, travels, a pharmacist or a merchant. In a dream, a veterinarian also means nursing the wounded soldiers in the battlefield. A veterinarian in a dream also may be interpreted as one's physician, one who practices righteousness, a wise man, a specialist in setting broken bones, cupping, or practicing bloodletting medicine.

Viaduct: *(See Arched bridge; Bridge)*

Vice-regent: (Calif; Caliphate; Deputy; Human being; Minister; Ruler; Secretary of state; Vizier) In a dream, a vice-regent represents someone whom people seek for his knowledge, or to learn the mastery of his craft, or he could represent an appointed justice of the peace. He also represents someone who inherits good and bad qualities, or whose character is different privately from the way he portrays himself in public. If one sees the vice-regent of the land in a stately appearance, or if he sees himself in such a form in a dream, it denotes his good state in this world and his success in the hereafter. Seeing him wearing an unsuitable garment in a dream reflects one's own state, or it may mean that his current religious state is weak, though it may become better at a latter stage of his life. A vice-regent or a calif in a dream also represents someone who establishes the laws of his religion and follows the example of God's Prophet, upon whom be peace. Whatever he is wearing in the dream connotes one's own state, or the growing or diminishing of his devotion. If one who is promised something sees the vice-regent or the calif in his dream, it means that his promise will be fulfilled, and his wishes will come true. Seeing him in a dream also means that someone from a different circle is backbiting him, or speaking of him without his consent, or that people are reporting him to the authorities, or that scholars are discussing him, or mentioning his work. A vice-regent or a calif in a dream also represents aloofness, seclusion, truthfulness, volunteering one's services, commanding what is good and forbidding what is evil, developing one's own certitude and faith, repentance, abstaining from sinful actions, imprisonment, sickness, or travels. If one sees himself being awarded the seat of the vice-regent or calif in a dream, though he does not suit the position, it means that adversities and temptations will befall the land, though the people of knowledge and the righteous ones will escape such danger. It could also mean that he will suffer humiliation, and that the people whom he manages may rise to preside over him.

Viergo: *(See Constellations)*

Vigilance: *(See Wakefulness)*

Vilify: *(See Insult)*

Village: (City; Suburban area; Town) A village in a dream represents injustice that will be followed by destruction as a consequence of people's sins. Entering a well fortified village in a dream means fighting with someone. Crossing a village into a city in a dream means changing a menial job into a more respectable one, or perhaps it could mean downgrading a good deed one has performed, thinking of it as unimportant, or regretting it, or it could mean doing something good and thinking of it as evil, or perhaps it could mean showing indecisiveness and doubt. Entering a village in a dream also means governing it, or presiding over its people, or it could mean commencing a new job. Walking out of a village in a dream means escaping from evil. Seeing a destroyed village in a dream means heedlessness or a calamity caused by the sins of its dwellers. Seeing a well-built village in a dream shows the piety and righteousness of its people. Seeing ancient edifices or ruins inhabited again in a dream represents people's repentance from sin. A village in a dream also could signify injustice, innovations, corruption, disregarding the divine laws, or discarding the moral standards set by the community. A village in a dream also could represent ants' underground nest or colony, while an anthill in a dream represents a village. If a village is completely destroyed by fire, or floods, or freezing temperature, or by locusts, or plagues in one's dream, it means suffering under the oppression of an unjust ruler or a tyrant, or it could mean destroying an anthill. Moving from a village into a city in a dream means leaving one's toiling and hardships behind him. Moving from a city into a village means the opposite, and signifies leaving comfort and safety to meet with discomfort and fear. *(Also see City)*

Vinegar: (Servant) In a dream, vinegar means money that is earned and spent in piety with blessings contained therein, or it could mean longevity, or wasting the least time possible in doing one's work. Vinegar sediments in a dream represent ignoble or evil money that carries meager benefits, or which is deemed shoddy. In a dream, vinegar and its container represent a servant and her dwellings. Drinking vinegar in a dream means enmity with one's household, or it could mean a family quarrel. As for a prisoner, drinking vinegar in a dream means his release from prison. Good vinegar in a dream means income and blessings, though when rarefied or stale, it means struggling to earn one's livelihood. It also means toiling to make ends meet, or it could mean hardships. Vinegar in a dream also may mean marital problems, difficulties with one's children, or a conflict at work. Vinegar in a dream also represents one's bosom friend. To water one's garden with vinegar in a dream means sleeping with one's mother.

Vineyard: (Espalier; Grapevine; Trellis; Woman) A vineyard in a dream represents honor and strength, and the same goes for all fruit trees. A vineyard in a dream is also interpreted to represent a wealthy woman. Cutting branches from a grapevine in a dream means receiving money from a noble woman. Thus, an espalier in a dream represents a generous woman. A grapevine in the wintertime in a dream represents a woman who has lost her wealth, though one still thinks that she is rich. Plucking a bunch of grapes from an espalier in a dream means spending one's money on a woman. If one sees it but does not pluck any grapes from it in the dream, it means that he will be spared unnecessary expenses. A grapevine in a dream also represents marriage. A trellis for grapevines in a dream represents a beautiful, a noble and a rich woman. The same interpretation is given for the garden surrounding it. To see a close-up view of a vineyard with its clusters of grapes and leaves in a dream means gaining financial benefits from associating with a community of believers. *(Also see Wine press)*

Vintage: *(See Wine press)*

Vintager: *(See Wine press)*

Violation: (Rights. *See Destruction*)

Virgin: (Chaste; Girl; Unmarried) Seeing a virgin woman in a dream means distress, adversities, or business difficulties, while seeing a woman in a dream means comfort and success. *(Also see Bride)*

Virgo: *(astr. See Constellations; Moon)*

461

Visibility: *(See Appearance)*

Visiting God's House in Mecca: *(See Pilgrimage; 'Umrah)*

Visiting holy sites: Visiting the Prophet's Mosque in Medina in a dream means seeking God's nearness and his pleasure through good deeds. It also means feeling safe, mixing with people of knowledge, associating with people of religious ranks, joining the company of knowledge seekers, and developing sincere love for the family of God's Prophet, upon whom be peace, serving and loving those who love his progeny. Visiting the Prophet's Mosque in a dream also means love, knowledge and guidance. Visiting Al-Aqṣā Sacred Mosque in Jerusalem in a dream means blessings, understanding the inner meaning of important spiritual subjects and miraculous events, or reflecting upon the Nocturnal Journey of God's Messenger (uwbp), the night in which the eight heavens were decorated to receive and honor him when he was called upon to come before God Almighty. Visiting the grave of God's Prophet Abraham, upon whom be peace, in a dream means obedience to one's parents, being true to them, seeking their love, blessings and pleasure with sincerity and trueness with one's words and actions. Visiting holy sites in a dream also means seeking knowledge and wisdom, having love for charitable people, associating with good people, seeking to learn one's religion at the hand of a pious teacher, to receive blessings and benefits in this life and in the next. *(Also see Muhammad, upon whom be peace; Mecca; Medina)*

Vizier: (Calif; Caliphate; Minister; Ruler; Secretary of state; Vice-regent)

Voice: In a dream, the human voice represents one's reputation or fame, and its strength or weakness reflects one's state of mind or the condition of his health. Raising one's voice in a dream means unjustly presiding over a crowd of people. Hearing a human voice in a dream means chairing an important responsibility. If the human voice emanates from an animal in the dream, it denotes great benefits and particularly if the animal speaks pleasing and soothing words or words of truth. If one raises his voice above the voice of a man of knowledge, a shaikh or a teacher in a dream, it means that he will commit a sin. A weak voice in a dream represents a man. Intentionally lowering one's voice in a dream means being indebted to someone, or it could mean humility. If a man of authority or a policeman lower his voice in a dream, it means that he maybe dismissed from his job, or he maybe reprimanded or disciplined for his misconduct. The sound produced by the ringing of coins in a dream represents temptation, allurement, or a fight between stockbrokers or money exchangers. The clank of money in a dream also means either good or bad news, or it could mean hearing good words, a wise speech, or words one likes to hear more about, if they are given as a sign of friendship or as a dower. If the clanking of money is made in jest in the dream, then it represents a fight one does not wish to end. The sound of a hornet represents a person who defames or discredits others, or whose evil cannot be removed without acquiring the help of a like person. The bleating of a ewe in a dream means kindness shown by one's mistress, his wife, or by a gracious man. The bleating of a billy goat or a ram in a dream means happiness and prosperity. The neighing of horses in a dream means receiving guidance from a noble person, or it could represent a courageous soldier. The braying of a donkey in a dream means hideousness, or the ugly character of a despicable enemy. The braying of a mule in a dream means a hardship which is combined with a difficult person, or it could mean vain talk, or indulging in suspicious acts. The mooing of a calf, a cow, or a steer in a dream means a riot. The gurgling of a camel in a dream represents a blessed journey, a pilgrimage, a successful business trip, or toiling and hardships. The roaring of a lion in a dream represents alarm, esteem, fear, or being threatened by someone in authority. In general, the sound of animals in a dream connotes adversities or fear. The neighing of horses in a dream means an invasion or might. The barking of dogs in a dream means vain talk, interference in others' business, regret, intending to harm others, hostility toward others, or dissonance. The blaring of a leopard in a dream means coquetry, vanity and wantonness. The blaring of a lynx in a dream means a false promise from an unsteady, oft-hesitant, or a greedy person and taking advantage of him. The cooing of pigeons in a dream means lamenting, or having marital intercourse. The chirp of swifts in a dream means good words or an admonition from a wise person. The croaking of frogs in a dream represents the ringing of bells, feeling overjoyed, employment for a teacher, rising to leadership, or it could mean hearing harsh words. The hissing of a snake in a dream means a warning or a fight with someone who hides his enmity. The braying of a donkey in a dream means cursing one's adversaries. The roaring of a lion in a dream means threats or boasts. The yowling of a tomcat in a dream means uproar, backbiting, defamation and insinuations. The squeak of a mouse in a dream means profits, reunion, love and peace, or it could mean harm one could suffer because of an interfering person or a robber. The crying of a female gazelle in a dream means longing for one's homeland. The yapping of foxes in a dream means a warning to escape, to move from one field into another, or it could mean suffering from jealousy, perfidy or lies. The howling of a wolf in a dream means a robbery, or fear of a brutal thief. The barking of a jackal in a dream means a mission of good intent, a forthcoming evil, women's cries for help, or the cry of people who abandoned all hope. The sound of a pig in a dream means taking advantage of a stupid enemy and stripping him of his money. The sound of an ostrich in a dream means hiring a trustworthy and a courageous servant, or bringing a new employee into one's business. Most dream interpreters dislike to interpret the meaning of the sound of peacocks or chicken and note that they mostly mean sorrow and distress, while others interpret the cawing of crows to mean separation or announcing someone's death. However, in dream, any ugly or coarse sound represents sorrow and distress while any pleasant sound in a dream represents happiness and joy. (Also see Invisible caller)

Volleyball: (See Ball)

Vomit: (Repentance; Throw up) Vomiting in a dream means returning things to their rightful owner, divulging secrets, or of regaining one's health through control of his stomach. Throwing up clean food in a dream means ease in one's life. If a poor person vomits blood in his dream, it means receiving money, begetting a son, or the return of a relative from a journey. If the blood is collected in a bowl in the dream, it means that one's son will survive a major illness, or it could mean that one's relative may come to stay with him. However, if the blood is spilled on the floor, then it may mean the death of either the son or the relative. If one's intestines or bowels come out during vomiting in the dream, it means the death of a child. As for a sick person, vomiting in a dream means his death. Vomiting a snake in a dream also means death, or distancing oneself from one's enemies. Vomiting in a dream also means wasting money on food, or unnecessary dieting for a poor person. Vomiting in a dream also has positive connotations for a poor person, but has negative ones for a rich person. If a ruler or a governor sees himself vomiting in a dream, it means that he will refund people taxes he unjustly collected from them. If one licks back what he vomits in the dream, it means that he is indifferent about repaying a debt that he can easily afford. If one vomits inside a basin in a dream, it means repentance from his wrongdoing, or it could mean giving a woman a share from unlawful money. If one suffers during vomiting and finds the taste disgusting in his dream, it means that he is forced to confess and apologize for his wrongdoing, though he does not like being caught. It could also mean paying damages, health problems, or it could mean a financial misfortune. Vomiting blood in one's dream means repentance from sin, restraining oneself from indulging in what is forbidden, or it could mean satisfying one's debts, or fulfillment of a vow. If one drinks wine, then vomits the same in his dream, it means that he has received some tainted or unlawful money that he will remit to its rightful owner and repent for his sin. If one gets drunk then throws up in his dream, it means that he is a stingy person who does not take good care of his own family. If one swallows a pearl then throws up honey in his dream, it means that he will render a correct interpretation of some Qur'ânic verses. Drinking milk then vomiting it in a dream means turning away from the truth. Drinking milk and vomiting honey in a dream means repentance from sin. Drinking blood in a dream then vomiting it as milk also means repentance from sin. If one's vomit is yellow and bitter in taste in the dream, it means repentance after having paid the price of one's crime. If one vomits mucus in his dream, it means that he will voluntarily repent from wrongdoing. Throwing up food in a dream means giving away something to someone who needs it. Swallowing what one is throwing up before it leaves his mouth in a dream means to go back on one's word. Eating what one has just vomited in a dream means prosperity and fame. Vomiting excessively in a dream means that one will reach near his death or die from a severe illness.

Vow: *(See Offering)*

Vulpicula: *(See Constellations)*

Vulture: (Candor; Eagle; Enemy; Evil; Imbecile; Thieves) A vulture in a dream represents a stupid, abominable and a lewd person. When seen during a daylight dream, it means a grievous illness. If one sees a vulture inside his house in a dream, it means sending help to assist someone in difficulty. Capturing a vulture in a dream means a fight or war. A flock of vultures descending upon a town in a dream represent an occupying army with merciless soldiers who will plunder such town. If a sick person sees a vulture inside his house in a dream, it means the approach of his death. As for a tanner and a potter, or the like craftsmen, seeing a vulture in a dream means profits or benefits. As for physicians or sick people, a vulture in their dream purports evil. In general, vultures in a dream represent highway robbers, a band of thieves who are not residents of that town, people who refuse to earn their livelihood through honest work, or it could represent an undertaker, a body snatcher, a grave digger, or a lewd and an insulting person. *(Also see Eagle)*

Wadi: (Valley) Seeing a ravine or a valley with a dry watercourse in a dream means going on a tiering trip, taking a long journey, or it could represent an intractable person. Seeing a wadi in a dream denotes good deeds, or making offerings to please God Almighty. A wadi in a dream also represents its dwellers, a tribe from that region, or its plantations. If one sees the wadi blossoming with fruit trees, fragrant flowers, a running water course, or if one hears nice words during such a dream, it means that he will rise in station, or mingle with people in power, or receive an appointment in the government, and for a righteous person, it means that miraculous events and blessings will be shown at his hands by God's leave. Seeing a wadi in a dream also means rain, and that the ravine will be filled with rainwater. A wadi in a dream also could represent a prison because of the steep mountains surrounding it and the difficulty in crossing it. Seeing oneself in a wadi floating in the air until one reaches a desired altitude in a dream means working for a powerful person. A wadi in a dream also represents a warrior, a bandit, a highway robber or a lion. If a wadi obstructs one's journey in a dream, it may represent a robbery, heavy rain, or having to face a dangerous person. If one is not travelling, then it means distress, adversity, harm, imprisonment, fear, or illness. Crossing a wadi in the wintertime in a dream means escaping from danger. Digging a wadi in a dream means the death of a family member. Falling into a steep wadi in a dream and feeling no pain or incurring no harm from it in a dream means that one will receive a gift from someone in authority or from his superior. Inhabiting a valley with no vegetation in a dream means performing one's pilgrimage to Mecca. To wander aimlessly in a wadi in a dream means writing a poem. *(Also see Flying)*

Wages: (Compensation. *See Bribe*)

Wagtail: *(See Crow)*

Waif: *(See Orphan)*

Wailing: *(See Lamenting)*

Waist belt: (Belt; Cincture; Waistband) A waist belt in a dream represents a wife who owns a house or a property. A waist belt in a dream also could represent happy children, and for rich people it represents their housekeeper or their servants. As for everyone else, a waist belt in a dream means adornment, or money depending of its quality and value in the dream. *(Also see Belt; Cincture; Waistband)*

Waistband: (Belt; Cincture; Waist belt) If a depressed person sees a waistband in his dream, it means relief from stress. A dirty waistband in a dream means depression and problems for a usually happy person. *(Also see Belt; Cincture)*

Wakefulness: (Alertness; Keenness of mind; Vigilance) Wakefulness in a dream signifies keenness of mind, perseverance in one's objective, completion of one's work, retracting one's steps to reverse an act of wrongdoing, or it could mean longevity. Waking up someone from his sleep in a dream means guiding him or showing him the road.

Walk around: *(See Circumambulation)*

Walking in the air: *(See Air)*

Walking on the moon: *(See Moon)*

Walking on water: Walking on water in a dream represents one's strong faith, certitude and trust in God Almighty. This is particularly true if while waking one also speaks words of wisdom. Otherwise, walking on water in a dream also could mean clarifying a complex issue. Walking on water in a dream also could mean undertaking a dangerous venture and trusting one's affairs to God's protection. If one walks back from the water to the dry land in a dream, it means that he will satisfy his needs or fulfill his intentions. In a dream, waking on water represents one's good intention, clarity and certitude. Walking on water in a dream also means unveiling a mystery, the need to trust one's affairs into God's hand, or it may mean approaching a danger, or it could mean that the accumulated pressures one is enduring are bearing heavy on him. It also means placing one's trust in God Almighty before embarking on a trip that could entail some danger. To walk on water, whether it is an ocean or a river in a dream also denotes good spiritual standing, religious assiduousness and strong faith, certitude and determination. *(Also see River; Water)*

Walking the streets: A man compassing the streets in a dream represents a guide, a shaikh, a spiritual guide, a preacher, a teacher, a peacemaker and one who accepts what is good and discards what is evil.

Walking: (Jogging; Prancing; Strutting; Tripping) Walking straight in a dream means profits, seeking the path of righteousness and unwavering in one's religious commitment. Walking through the markets in a dream means carrying a will, or should one qualify for leadership, it means that he may be appointed to fill such a position. Walking barefooted in a dream means dispelling distress and portraying a good religious character. The meaning of walking in a dream implies an expression of meekness and submissiveness before one's Lord, and it could mean seeking to earn one's livelihood. Jogging in a dream means victory over one's enemy. Walking backward in a dream means reversing one's decision, cancelling a commitment, or it could represent corruption in one's religious practices. Strutting or prancing in a dream represents an ugly state of mind that is coupled with evil actions. Falling down over one's face during walking in a dream means loss of benefits in this world and in the next. Tripping while walking in a dream means exposure of one's ills, and suffering the consequences of wrongdoing. To cause someone to trip while walking in a dream means ridiculing him, or delivering him a humiliating blow. To walk earnestly and steadily in a dream represents one's good intention. Travelling on foot in a dream means facing danger. Walking while bowing one's head in a dream means longevity, or it could mean recovering from a long illness. Walking over the clouds in a dream means rain. Walking with a cane in a dream means old age, or an illness which will require the help of a cane. Hopping on one foot in a dream means losing half of one's wealth. Having several feet in a dream means losing one's sight. If the governor sees himself having many feet in a dream, it means that he will be impeached from his office. If one sees inanimate objects such as a tree, a rock or a mountain walking in a dream, it represents major adversities and plagues. The movement of inanimate objects in a dream also means being dogmatic about one's spiritual stand. Walking like animals in a dream means emulating ignorant people, seeking the unattainable, or being a hypocrite, unless if the animal is permissible for food, then such style of walking means offering good deeds. *(Also see Jogging; Prancing; Sound of walking; Strutting; Tripping)*

Wall Gecko: (Lizard) A wall gecko in a dream represents an evil person who is proud of himself, who encourages mischief, and dampens people's spirit to do good. A gecko in a dream also represents a backbiter and a slanderer. Getting hold of a gecko in a dream means encountering such a person. Eating a gecko in a dream means backbiting people. If a gecko takes a bite from someone's flesh in a dream, it means that someone will speak ill of him in public. A gecko in a dream also represents an avowed enemy who incessantly belittles his opponent and who drives from one place to another. *(Also see Lizard)*

Wall: A wall in a dream represents knowledge, guidance, cognizance, knowing secrets, judgment, or separation between friend. Standing by a wall or sitting on it, and depending on its conditions in a dream represents one's own state. A wall in a dream also represents a strong, wealthy, powerful and religious person. If the wall needed urgent repairs, and if a group of people come to rescue it in the dream, it represents a man of knowledge, or the Imãm of a mosque who has lost his control or respect, then some friends will come to his rescue and to help him restore his rank. If a successful businessman sees the walls of his house collapsing in a dream, it means that he will recuperate a lost treasure. If one sees a wall caving over his head, or falling over other people in a dream, it means that he has committed many sins and unless his repents, his punishment will be swift. The caving-in of a wall toward the inside of a house in a dream means an illness, but if it falls toward the outside in the dream, it means death. Seeing a crack in the wall in a dream means that someone in the family will brace against him. Grabbing to a wall in a dream means the nearing of one's death, pending how firmly one is grabbing to it in the dream. Grabbing to a wall in a dream is also interpreted as holding firmly to one's interest in a strong person. If one builds a wall then tears it down in a dream, it means that he will attempt at destroying someone's livelihood, or perhaps kill him. If one sees and recognizes a wall in his dream, it represents a close friend who may die from depression. A wall in a dream is also interpreted as a mighty person who cannot be managed except through kindness. Jumping over a wall in a dream means reverting from being a believer to a disbeliever, or accepting and following the advice of a disbeliever. Seeing one's picture reflected in a wall in a dream means one's death, and that his name will be itched on his gravestone. If a traveller sees himself returning to his house, whereby its walls are renewed, it means that he will get married. Seeping water from a crack in a wall in one's dream means adversities and stress. *(Also see Walls of the city)*

Wallet: (Money bag; Money belt; Money pouch; Purse) A wallet in a dream means getting married or begetting a son. A wallet in a dream also represents money placed in a wallet, or it could represent a key. If one's wallet falls in a sea or in a river, it means loss of one's capital at the hand of people in authority. If it falls into a fire, it means losing one's money to a greedy, envious and an unjust person. It is also said that one's wallet in a dream could represent his body. If one's wallet is taken away from him in a dream, it means his death. Carrying a money belt in a dream means having knowledge one has earned in the first half of his life. If it contains some change only in the dream, it means that one has to pursue the path of knowledge and further his studies.

Wallflower: *(Bot. See Gillyflower)*

Walls of the city: In a dream, the walls of a city represent strong men, a strong ruler, or a treasurer who is concerned about guarding the interests of his people. The walls of a city in a dream also represent the most pious and devout worshiper in that city, its most renowned men of knowledge, its supreme justice, or its just ruler. Seeing the walls of a city in a dream also means joy, festivities and celebrations. *(Also see Balcony; Castle; Citadel; Wall)*

Walnut tree: *(See Tree)*

Walnut: A walnut tree in a dream represents a stingy foreigner, a backbiter, a slanderer, a difficult person who cares only for his selfish interests. A walnut in a dream also represents a healthy body, or it could mean extensive travelling.

Playing with walnut in a dream means playing with unlawful earnings. If a woman sees a walnut tree in her dream, it means longevity. A walnut in a dream also means a husband. Crushed walnuts in a dream mean easy money. Eating pecans from a hickory tree in a dream means speaking the truth.

Wandering: (Astray; Error; Lost) Walking on a straight highway and still losing one's way in a dream means deviating from the path of truth. If the road in the dream is twisted or curved, then it means allurement, trespassing, misguidance, or erring from God's path, or it could mean seeking a way out of error. If one is lost in the dream, it means that he will become heedless, and if he finds his way thereafter, it means that he will receive someone's guidance and accept it.

Waning of one's wealth: *(See Coal)*

Wanted: *(See Pursuit)*

Wantonness: *(See Desire)*

War correspondent: (Correspondent; Exchanging letters; Spy) Exchanging letters between two army camps in a dream means nearing the end of one's life, quelling a riot, accepting the truth, following what is lawful, death of a sick person, or the victory of an oppressed person. If one becomes a war correspondent in a dream, it means that he may become a spy, or be promoted in his field. *(Also see War)*

War: (Fight) In a dream, war means deception, betrayal, misleading, or trickery. War in a dream also means inflation, rising prices, a plague, food lines, adversities and stress. If a soldier sees himself fighting an enemy in a dream, it means that he will gain benefits and success in his life. *(Also see War correspondent)*

Warble fly: (Enemy; Spy)

Warden: *(See Rural warden)*

Wardrobe: A wardrobe in a dream means glad tidings and good news that maybe announced in few days. *(Also see Dressing room)*

Warrior's helmet: *(See Helmet)*

Washbowl: *(See Basin)*

Washer: (Cleaner) A washer in a dream represents an educator or a teacher who attends to ignorant people though they care little about his advice. Seeing a washer in a dream also means relief from stress, avoiding trouble, or preparing for a journey. *(Also see Washing)*

Washing a garment: *(See Filth)*

Washing the dead: (Undertaker) If one sees a deceased person washing himself before burial in a dream, it means relief for one's dependents and increase of their wealth after him. Washing a deceased person in a dream means that someone will repent at the hand of the undertaker. If a deceased person asks someone to wash his clothing in a dream, it means that he needs someone to pray for him, or to intercede on his behalf before his Lord, or pay charity for the benefit of his soul, or to satisfy his debts, or to fulfill his will, or to seek justice for his death. If one does wash the garment of the deceased person in the dream, it means the redemption of that person. Washing a deceased person with boiling water in a dream means that the latter is suffering in hell-fire. *(Also see Grave digger; Hot water; Ritual bath; Undertaker)*

Washing : (Brass polisher; Dishwasher; Washer) A dishwasher or a brass polisher in a dream represent an interior decorator, or someone who beautifies and embellishes people's properties, or one who attracts people to himself. A washer in a dream is also interpreted as a righteous man, a gnostic, a preacher, a teacher, or one who polishes people's hearts with his admonitions. *(Also see Washer)*

Wasting money: *(See Penny)*

Wastrel: *(See Hobo)*

Watch: (Timepiece; Wristwatch. *See Clock*)

Watchful: *(See Conscious; Carefulness; Concern)*

Watching the stars: *(astr.)* Watching the stars in a dream means presiding over people.

Watchman: (Policeman; Security)

Watchtower: (Cupola; Minaret; Observatory) In a dream, a watchtower represents a notable person. Seeing a watchtower from a distance in a dream means victory over one's adversary, attainment of one's goals, rising in rank, or it could mean happiness. If a merchant sees a watchtower in a dream, it means prosperity, presiding over his fellow merchants and gaining power. Building a watchtower in a dream has the same interpretation as building an edifice or a house.

Water carrier: (Delivering water) In a dream, a water carrier represents a man of piety and trueness, because he practices the best of deeds and particularly if he does not receive a wage for his delivery in the dream. If one sees himself filling a bottle of water and delivering it to a house, it represents his earnings. A water carrier in a dream also represents a gnostic who heals the illness of people's hearts with his knowledge, love and wisdom. A water carrier in a dream also represents one who can go near high ranking people. He also represents one who delivers people's belongings to their hands. A water carrier in a dream also may denote evil, burdens, fights, dancing, or whirling. If a water carrier delivers someone a glass of water in a dream and receives money for it, it represents a responsibility or a burden he will carry, or perhaps that the other person may receive accumulated profits from his business.

Water jug: In a dream, a water jug means travels, or it could represent a woman who becomes pregnant then have a miscarriage or abortion. The water represents the fetus and the jug represents the mother's womb.

Water level: (Artificial lake; Farm pond; Ombrometer; Ombrograh; Pluviometer; Rain gauge; Reservoir) The water level of an artificial lake or a reservoir in a dream represents God's mercy, blessings, rain, celebrations, festivals, a wedding, the pilgrimage season, a good harvest, or the governor's mansion. Seeing the city's reservoir full to capacity means glad tidings and prosperity. If one finds the water level low, and if the waterside is covered with crusts, mildew, decay and produces a fetid odor in the dream, it means drought and adversities. The city's reservoir in a dream also represents its governor. Whatever condition it portrays in the dream, be it good or bad, will be exhibited in his work. In a dream, all gauges that are used in measuring the water level have the same interpretation. *(Also see Water)*

Water lily: (Lily; Hyacinth; Nenuphar; Nubile; Nymph) In a dream, a water lily means life, hiding, concealment, travels by sea. If a traveller by sea sees a water lily in his dream, it means that his ship may drown. A water lily in a dream also represents a lawfully earned money from which one spends for his charities to please his Lord. A water lily in a dream also means sorrow, sadness, illness, a man with different faces, someone whose actions are tainted, or whose temper is changing constantly. Having a bouquet of water lily in a dream means changes, illness, sorrow or endurance.

Water mill: (Manager; Rich man; Treasurer) A water mill in a dream represents a person who handles large amounts of cash, or who is an extremely wealthy person. If one seeks him, his needs will be satisfied and he will not return empty handed. If one sees a water mill in operation in a dream, it means coming profits, or benefits for one's life and his family through the person operating it. A water mill in a dream also represents one's helpers, clan, easing of one's difficulties, or it could mean rain. *(Also see Hand mill)*

Water passage: *(See Canal)*

Water wheel: (Noria) In a dream, this type of water wheel which is used to raise and discharge water from a low level stream into a higher ground means help, assistance, keeping one's promise, or complying with preset conditions. *(Also see Noria)*

Water: (Life; Rain; River; Vapor) Water in a dream represents a happy life, money, prosperity, expansion of one's business, increase in one's income, or it could mean marriage. If one sees the water pure and abundant in his dream, it means lowering of prices, peace and social justice. If one sees himself chewing on water in a dream, it means toiling and hardships related to earning his livelihood. Drinking a glass of water in a dream means protection against any danger from one's enemy and it denotes a prosperous year for the one who drinks it in a dream. Drinking more water in a dream than what one usually drinks in wakefulness means longevity. If one glass of water does not quench one's thirst in the dream, it means discord between husband and wife. If one immerses his hand in water in a dream, it means that he will play with money and confuse himself. Fresh potable water or a well in a dream also could be the immediate cause of a trial, fight or calamity. Giving someone a glass of water in a dream is glad tidings of a child. Drinking a glass of spring water in a dream means conceiving a child, or that he will receive benefits from his wife. In this sense, glass in a dream represent the substance of a woman and water represents a fetus. Drinking hot water in a dream means distress and adversities. If one is pushed into a pond or a river of clear water in a dream, it means receiving a pleasant surprise. Seeing oneself submerged in a body of water in a dream means facing a trial, distress, bewilderment and adversities. Carrying a jar of clear water in a dream means receiving an inheritance. Asking people for water to drink in a dream means lying to them by claiming to be needy. Stagnant water in a dream means imprisonment, distress, or depression. It is said that stagnant water in a dream has weaker meaning than running water. Bad smelling or putrid water in a dream represents a wretched life. Bitter water in a dream means a bitter life. Boiling water in a dream means suffering from heat. If boiling water is used during the daylight in a dream, it means suffering from chastisement, afflictions and punishment for one's sins. If used during the nighttime in a dream, then it means fear of evil spirits. Salty water in a dream means hardships and difficulties in earning one's livelihood. Murky waters in a dream represent unlawful earnings. Black colored water in a dream means destruction or family problems. Drinking black colored water in a dream also may mean blindness. Yellow water in a dream means an illness. Boiling water, blazing water, or oozing water in a dream means change of one's status, or being deprived of God's favors for lack of gratitude and for being a hindrance against those who do good. Drinking polluted seawater in a dream means turbulences, distress and sufferings that will be brought about by someone in authority. If seawater runs inside one's dwelling place or business, and if one drinks from it in a dream, it means an illness. If everyone drinks from it in the dream, then it means a plague. Murky water in a dream denotes a tyrant. If a sick person bathes in murky water then walks out of it in a dream, it means that he will recover from his illness. If he is facing adversities, it means that he will be able to overcome them. If he is incarcerated, it means that he will be released. Pure potable water in a dream means salvation. Saltwater in a dream means distress. If one sees murky water gushing froth from a water well in a dream, it means a bad marriage. Walking on water in a dream represents the strength of one's faith, certitude and trust in God Almighty. This is particularly true if while walking one also speaks words of wisdom and piety. Otherwise, walking on water in a dream could mean ascertaining something that is not too clear. Walking on water in a dream also means undertaking a dangerous trip and trusting in God Almighty for protection and guidance. Walking on water in a dream also means undertaking a dangerous venture. If one walks back from the water to dry land in a dream, it means that he will satisfy his needs or desire. Falling into a deep sea or a deep river but not reaching the bottom of it in the dream means wealth and prosperity, for the world in a dream represents a deep ocean. If one falls into a river and if he is overcome by water in a dream, it means that he will fall sick. If he drowns in a river in a dream, it means his death. Falling into water in a dream also could mean happiness, joy, or blessings. Observing the reflection of one's face in the waters looking beautiful in a dream shows kindness toward one's household and neighbors. Reaching a pond of clear water in a dream means speaking good words. Pouring water inside a bag in a dream means spending money to please a woman. Pouring water over a place where it is of no benefit in the dream means wasting one's money. Floods in a dream means distress, suffering and corruption, depending on their strength. If the water level of a dam or a river rises and inundates people's homes and businesses and becomes a threat to people's lives in a dream, it means discord and trials after which evil people will be eliminated from that place. If one sees water flowing over his own roof in a dream, it means a quick distress, or a permanent stress that will be brought by someone in authority. Sweet potable water in a dream represents lawful earnings, a good heart, knowledge, revival, recovering from a dangerous illness, a wife, a husband, or marriage. If one drinks a sweet and a refreshing glass of water from a permissible cup in a dream, it means that his marriage is proper. Otherwise, if the container from which one drinks in his dream is unlawful, it means that his marriage is illegal from a religious point of view. Water in a dream also denotes the drink of poor people, or what gallant people exchange and share among themselves. If a thirsty person quenches his thirst with water in a dream, it means comfort, appeasement of one's bewilderments, prosperity verses poverty, or reuniting one's family. Bathing in fresh spring water in a dream means payment of one's debts. If sweet and potable water becomes salty in a dream, it means apostasy, or straying from the path of God Almighty and meeting with insurmountable difficulties. Carrying water in a container in a dream means conceiving a child and increase in one's income. Abundance of water at a time when it is supposed to be low, or drought at a time when it is supposed to be raining in a dream means injustice, abuse, high prices, divided opinions, weaknesses, or payment of financial damages. Clear water in a dream also means recovering from trachoma. The explosion of a water tank or a pipe in a dream means distress, trouble and adversities. Green colored water in a dream means a long illness or a wretched life. Drinking black colored water in a dream means becoming blind. Sucking water in a dream means tight circumstances. If unexpectedly one is showered with hot water in a dream, it means a fever, an illness or a scare from evil spirits, the intensity of which is relevant to how hot is the water. If one's garment gets wet in a dream, it means changes in one's travel plans, or it could mean delaying a project, or failure of one's plans. If a poor person sees himself carrying a container of water in a dream, it means money. If a rich person sees that dream, it means marriage, or conceiving a child. Carrying water in a purse, socks, a cloth, or in any porous material in a dream means pride about one's wealth, status, attainments, fame and living conditions. Pouring water into a container in a dream means getting married. Bathing in cold water in a dream means repenting from sin, recovering from an illness, release from prison, payment of one's debts, or dispelling one's fears. Drawing water from a well in a dream means earning money through deception and fraud. Channeling irrigations to water a garden or a farm in a dream means earning money from a woman. If the trees of one's garden or farm do blossom in the dream, it means conceiving a child from such a woman. Watering a garden or a farm in a dream also means having sexual intercourse with one's wife. If pure water gushes forth from one's mouth in a dream, it means that he is a gnostic and people will benefit from his knowledge, wisdom and admonition. If one is a young merchant, it means that he is a truthful person. Sweet water in a dream also represents the element of faith in God Almighty, while saltwater represents the element of atheism. In a dream, water also means wealth. Seeping water from a crack in a wall means adversities and distress caused by a brother or an in-law. (*Also see Distilled water; Earth; Ophthalmologist; River; Walking on water*)

Watercourse: *(See Canal)*

Watercress: (*bot. Nasturtium officinale*) Watercress is the legume of the dwellers of hell-fire. If one sees it in a dream, it means that he follows the conduct of the dwellers of hell-fire.

Waterfall: *(See Cataract)*

Watering a herd: Watering a herd in a dream means profits from travels.

Watering hose: (Water) A watering hose in a dream means rain, or watering the grass or the garden plants. A watering hose in a dream also represents positive developments in one's life, or it could mean correcting oneself, becoming more vigilant, having less need for excessive sleep, or it could mean overcoming one's adversities.

Watering: (Drink one's fill; Quench one's thirst; Irrigation) To drink one's fill after being thirsty in a dream means satisfaction and ease in one's business, end of one's difficulties, richness after poverty, repentance from sin, recovering from sickness, continuing one's education after a long interruption of one's studies, attending to one's spiritual interests, or it could mean inclining toward a religious life. Quenching one's thirst in a dream also means being healthy, religious and rightful.

Waterless plain: *(See Desert)*

Waterskin: *(See Bottle; Urn)*

Waterthrush: *(See Crow)*

Waves: (Swells) In a dream, waves means coming adversities, sufferings and punishment for one's sins.

Waving a sword: *(See Duel; Sword)*

Wax-chandler: (Tallow-chandler) In a dream, a chandler represents festivities, joy, happiness, death, illness, guidance, knowledge, desire, wantonness, or crying.

Way: *(See Road)*

Weakness: Weakness in a dream means strength. However, of one sees himself debilitated or emaciated, then it means weakness of his faith, failure to perform one's religious obligations, sterility, impotence, or sorrow and depression.

Wealth: Wealth for a poor person in a dream means trouble, because wealth can divert a poor person from the straight path. Wealth in a dream also denotes a righteous wife, a successful business, imposing one's conditions upon his enemy, or subduing the evil of a jealous friend.

Weapon: (Arm) In a dream, a weapon means power and victory, or it could mean overcoming a disease. If one sees himself carrying a weapon while others around him are not armed in the dream, it means that he may become a leader in his community or field. If one notices people admiring his weapon in a dream, it represents their jealousy and envy toward him. If one sees himself carrying a weapon which he uses with mastery, it represents his maturity and fulfillment of his goals. However if a sick person sees himself carrying a weapon, it may mean his death, satisfying one's religious duties, or correcting himself. If he feels fear while carrying that weapon in the dream, it means that God Almighty will cure him from his illness. If he is travelling, it means that he will return home safely. If one is stripped from his weapon in a dream, it represents his weakness. If one adorns himself with a weapon in a dream, it means that he will acquire knowledge to help him overcome ignorant people, or wealth to shelter him from poverty, or it could mean victory over his enemy. A weapon in a dream also represents medicine, or a wife who protects her husband's chastity and shelters him against evil, or from desiring other women. (Also see Sword)

Weariness: (See Breathing difficulty)

Wearing a mask: (See Mask)

Weasel: (Marten; Mongoose) In a dream, a weasel represents an insolent person, a fool and a stupid man who is unjust and ruthless. If a weasel enters a house in a dream, it means that evil or adversities may take place inside one's dwellings. A weasel is the only mammal that can kiss a snake. Thus, seeing a weasel in a dream may represent a prostitute or adultery. Fighting with a weasel in a dream means fighting with a prostitute or an adulteress.

Weaver: (Knitting) In a dream, a weaver represents a problem solver, garments, travels, or hesitation. Seeing a weaver in a dream also may indicate the death of sick person, or lowering his corps into his grave. (Also see Architect; Artist; Painter)

Weaving: (Cloth) Weaving a cloth or hanging it in the air in a dream means going on a journey.

Wedding band: (See Ring)

Wedding officiant: (See Officiant)

Wedding: If one sees himself as a bridegroom on his wedding night, accompanied with musicians and dancers in the dream, it means that he may die in that place. If one sees himself having marital intercourse with his bride, but could not see her or recognize her, nor is she named to him in the dream, it also means his death. If one sees and recognizes his bride, or if she is named as his bride in the dream, then it means acquiring wealth. (Also see Bride; Locksmith; Star)

Weeds: In a dream, weeds represent someone who is loved by his family, though they do not benefit from him. He differs with those close to him and draws himself closer to those who envy him. He lives distant from his true friends, but close to his enemies. (Also see Grass; Unwanted)

Weight stabilizer: (See Stabilizer)

Weight: (Unit of weight) In a dream, a unit of weight represents a criterion, or commanding what is good and forbidding what is evil. It also means admonition, reprimand, power, authority, guidance, truthfulness, writing or signing an agreement, or it could represent the burdens of one's sins. (Also see Measure²; Unit of weight)

Well: In a dream, a well inside one's house means prosperity, riches, a wife, business, a teacher, poverty, deception, fulfillment of one's needs, travels, goals, stinginess, generosity, or it could mean a servant. The structural condition of each well in a dream has its own interpretation. A well in a dream also represent a woman who has a loud laughter, or it could represent a pleasant and an inspiring woman. If a woman sees a well in a dream, it means meeting a man of good character. If one sees himself looking into a well in a dream, it means that he is thinking about a particular woman for marriage. A well in a dream is also interpreted to represent knowledge, marriage, a big man, prison, ties, or deception. If one digs a well and finds water in it in his dream, it means that he will marry a wealthy woman whom he will deceive. If the water gushes forth, rises and runs outside of an old well in the dream, it represents crying and grief in that place. Digging a well and finding water to channel for one's garden in a dream means taking an herbal remedy to cure one's impotence, or to save his marriage. Falling into a well of muddy waters in a dream means that one may become subject to the tyranny of an unjust ruler. If the water he falls into is clear in the dream, it means that he will willingly work to serve a righteous man and for a nominal wage. Falling into a well in a dream also means demotion, or it could mean travels. Sitting at the edge of a well in a dream means dealing with a deceiving person. A collapsed well in a dream represents a dying woman. Reaching a well which is dug for the general public to draw from its water means getting relief after suffering from difficulties. Finding a well adjacent to a barmaid in a dream means finding a spiritual teacher, or joining a fellowship and a school for the seekers. If one sees the well of Zamzam quenching the thirst of people in a particular neighborhood other than Mecca in a dream, it means that a gnostic will come to that town, and whose knowledge and wisdom will greatly benefit its people. It also may denote the bounty and blessings which are imparted to that town, or it could denote the victory of its people over their real enemy. Drinking from such a well in a dream means fulfillment of one's intentions and satisfaction of his needs. In a dream, a well also means a prison or depression. If one is in such a state, it means that his adversities will dissipate, and that he will reestablish himself in the circles of people in authority. If the person in the dream is a seer who predicts events, then he may be involved in the circles of governors, particularly to interpret their dreams. It is possible that he also might receive emissaries of notable people who will bring him what pleases him. It also could mean a fight in one's family involving jealousy, envy, betrayal, though at the end one will triumph over them. Falling into a well in a dream also means being indicted in an alleged crime from which one is clearly innocent. A well in a dream is also interpreted as levying taxes, or it could mean circumcision. Digging a well in a dream also represents a crafty and an artful deceiver.

Wending one's way: (Direction) To wend one's way, or to take the road, or to go in the direction of the door in a dream means establishing the course of one's life on the basis of righteousness, or finding the real cause of things, or it could mean success, depending on how close one gets to his goal in the dream. *(Also see Road)*

Whale: (Fish; Jonah; Sea life) In a dream, a whale represents an oath, the temple of righteous people and the prayer mat of the devotees. Seeing a whale in a dream also means strains, depression, loss of rank, or a growing anger. Seeing the whale which swallowed God's prophet Jonah (uwbp) in a dream means dispelling one's fears, prosperity for a poor person and the coming relief for someone in distress. In a dream, a whale also represents the chief minister of sea life, while the ocean represents the king or the ruler. *(Also see Fish)*

Wheat straw: Wheat straw in a dream means goodness and trustworthiness.

Wheat: (Grains) In a dream, wheat means money well earned. Buying wheat in a dream means increase in one's earnings, or in the number of his children. If one sees a ruler placing a stick and steering inside a bushel of grains in a dream, it means rising prices. Planting wheat in a dream means doing a good deed for God's pleasure. Walking in wheat fields in a dream means offering a service to God Almighty. If one plants wheat but it sprouts barley instead in a dream, it means ostentatiousness. If it grows blood in the dream, it means that he profits from usury. Eating green wheat in the fields from its spikes in a dream means gaining spiritual progress through ascetic detachment. Eating cooked wheat in a dream means afflictions. Holding a bundle of ears of wheat, or placing them inside a pot in a dream means profits equal to the number of spikes one has gathered. Harvesting wheat outside the season in a dream means death, destruction, deception and trials for the people of that locality. Harvesting green spikes of wheat in the dream means the death of a young person, but if they are yellow and dry, then they mean the death of an elderly person. Bartering wheat for barley in a dream means replacing the Qur'ānic recital with interest in poetry. Seeing wheat over one's bed in a dream represents one's wife. Planting its seeds in a dream means conceiving a child. In a dream, wheat also represents a cautious person who manages his affairs with wisdom and who spends his money to help people without being a spendthrift.

Wheel[1]: In a dream, a wheel represents a treasurer or travels. A rolling wheel in a dream means the ongoing process of living and earning one's livelihood. If the wheel suddenly stops or brakes in the dream, it means that one may lose his job, or it may mean the cancellation of a journey. Wheels in a dream also represent the changing phases of businesses, or the changing hands of their owners. If the rolling wheel produces a sweet sensation or an enchanting sound in the dream, it means good news. Otherwise, a roaring sound of a wheel means a cry of jealousy or selfish love. A spinning wheel which is used for either wool or silk in a dream means blessed profits, comfort, or a marriage.

Wheel[2]: *(See Helm)*

Wheels: *(See Car; Wheel)*

Whip: *(See Scourge)*

Whistling: In a dream, whistling represents pagan customs. If one hears a whistle or produces one in a dream, it may indicate an illness, or it could represent a vacant house or a ghost town.

White rose: *(See Rose)*

White: The color white. If one sees his face white in the dream, it means sickness. If he sees his cheeks radiant white in the dream, it means honor, bounty and a high rank in his community. White in a dream also represents elderly people. *(Also see Colors)*

Whitewasher: *(See Fuller)*

Whorl: *(See Spindle whorl)*

Wick: (Housekeeper; Lamp; Steward) A candle wick in a dream represents a steward, a housekeeper or a butler. If the wick burns-up completely in one's dream, it means the death of any of the above. If a sparkle falls on a piece of cotton fabric and burns it in the dream, it means that he or she may fall victim to into evildoing. If the wick is extinguished in the dream, it means that a sick person in that family may soon die from his illness, or that the family will receive news of the death of a close relative. *(Also see Lamp stand)*

Wickedness: If one recognizes a wicked act in a dream, it represents his evil end, or that he may become an apostate. If one speaks of something evil in his dream, it denotes a wicked act he will commit toward someone in wakefulness.

Widow: If a widow sees herself wearing a crown studded with gems in a dream, it means that she may marry a wealthy person from another country. If the crown is of gold in the dream, it means that she may marry an old man whom she will inherit.

Wife: A wife in a dream represents a partner, an enemy, an unjust ruler, one's opponent, prosperity, a vehicle, earthly wealth, worldly pleasures, the combination of comfort and toiling, or she could mean honor, class, or whatever indication of personality or character the wife may stand for in the dream. *(Also see Climbing a mountain; Closet; Hide-out; Khimār; Marriage; Protection; Veil)*

Wild beast: *(See Beast)*

Wild cow: *(See Oryx)*

Wild gazelle: *(See Oryx)*

Wild goat: *(See Mountain goat; Oryx)*

Wild ox: *(See Buffalo; Oryx)*

Wild plants: (Forest; Hidden; Manifest; Woods) Eating wild plants in the wilderness in a dream represents hard earned money. Wild plants are also interpreted as a person whose goodness is hidden and whose heart is better than what his appearance may suggest. *(Also see Wild thyme)*

Wild thyme: In a dream, wild thyme means hoarding money, or it could mean virility and rejuvenation of one's sexual appetite. In a dream, wild thyme also means continuous blessings, power, a good business, a woman or a child. Seeing wild thyme in the field is better than seeing it cut in a dream, for once any fragrant plant is cut in a dream, then it means distress and worries. *(Also see Wild plants)*

Wildcat: *(See Tomcat)*

Will: (Bequest; Grandfather) In a dream, a will represents the relationship between two people. A will in a dream also means making peace between adversaries, or it could mean a meeting between two people from different towns.

Willow: *(See Moringa)*

Wimble: *(See Drill)*

Wind Instruments: *(See Flute; Oboe)*

Wind[1]: *(See Fart)*

Wind[2]: (Blow; Changing course; Hurricane; Storm; Trap; Tornado; Wonder) In a dream, winds represent the person in authority or the leader. In that sense, winds in a dream represent the sphere of one's control and his power to change things, or to maneuver people's interests. Winds in a dream also may represent a leader, his army, commands and helpers. Wind was once one of the servants of God's Prophet Solomon, upon whom be peace, as it moved under his command by God's leave. A stormy wind in a dream may represent calamities, destruction, or plagues. A tornado in a dream means destruction or a calamity. On the other hand, wind in a dream may also mean pollination, good harvest, prosperity, victory, or success. However, winds in a dream also represent illness, rheumatism, sneezing, aching, or headaches, etcetera. If one sees the wind carrying him and transporting him from one place to another with no fear on his part, and if there are no clouds or darkness in the skies in the dream, it means that he may preside over people, should he qualify for that, or if he wished to do so, or it could represent his business success, or that he will liquidate his merchandise, should it be stagnant or unsalable. If the winds lift someone who is seized by fear or tyranny, and if the winds carry with them dark clouds, or a cloud of dust in the dream, and if the person is travelling when he sees the dream, it means that he will face great difficulties. If he is ill, then his illness will intensify, or it could mean that some higher order will persecute him, or perhaps a judge will rule against him. If one sees a huge tornado or a tropical storm carrying people, trees, homes, or cattle in the air to scatter them over its path of destruction, then it represents a major plague, or a calamity affecting that region. Poisonous winds or polluted air in a dream represent a feverish illness. A stormy wind accompanied with thunder in a dream represents a tyrant. If the wind carries someone from one place to another in the dream, it means that he may travel there, but he may never return to his homeland. A gentle wind or a breeze in a dream represents grace and blessings for the people and the land. A storm of dust in a dream represents destruction in the land. However, winds in a dream always represent tidings from God Almighty. If the wind is not accompanied with a good witness or a cheering element in the dream, then it means cessation of blessings for that land. If the wind is accompanied with a stridulous or a shrill sound in the dream, it means a severe punishment for that place. If a general of an army sees himself leading his soldiers and is preceded by a stormy wind in a dream, it means that he will be victorious and that he will triumph over his enemy. However, if a storm faces him at his arrival to the battlefield in the dream, it means that he will lose his battle. If one sees a storm uprooting the trees in his dream, it means that the government of that land will mass murder its own people. A southern wind in a dream means illness, diseases, or death. A southern wind is sometimes interpreted as rain and prosperity. If one witnesses a slow moving wind in his dream, it means that he will consent to the actions of a group of evildoing people. If the wind blows from a known direction in the dream, it means mercy and blessings, or that one may receive good news from that direction. Winds in a dream also mean asking for one's needs, or fulfilling them. A gentle breeze in a dream, represents travel and joy. If one sees the wind colored red in the dream, it represents a recalcitrant child. (Also see Fan)

Windmill: In a dream, a windmill represents a harsh fight between two people, or and end of a major dispute between two people. A windmill in a dream also could represent one's helpers, or representatives, or it could mean rain. (Also see Fan; Mill)

Window: (Attic window; Aperture; Opening; Peephole) In a dream, a large window represents a woman of good character and conduct, while a tight window means the opposite. If a man sees himself sitting inside a window in a dream, it means that he will divorce his wife in public. If one sees himself sitting at a distance from the window in a dream, it means that he will secretly divorce his wife. In a dream, the windows of a house also represent an outsider who is aware of the inner secrets of such a house. A window in a dream also means relief from difficulties, overcoming distress, renewing festivities and celebrating anniversaries. Depending on their direction in the dream, windows also mean news, women, or children. Seeing the glass of one's window tainted or colored means planting seedlings, inflorescence, conceiving children, continuing one's education, buying new clothes, or crowning someone. Sitting tied-up inside a window box in a dream means getting married. (Also see Attic window)

Wine pitcher: (See Urn)

Wine press: (Grapes; Juice; Vineyard; Vintage; Vintager) Pressing grapes to make wine in a dream means corruption and evil. (Also see Extracting oils from seeds; Juice; Vineyard)

Wine: (Alcoholic; Beer; Drunkard; Enmity; Evil; Hatred; Inebriate; Temptation; Tippler) Wine in a dream represents unlawful earnings, illegal tender, or easy money. Drinking wine in a dream means committing a major sin, or it could mean becoming wealthy. It also could imply verbal abuse, temptation, or enmity. A river of wine in a dream means adversities. Wine in a dream also represents marriage consent, or dismissal from one's job. Mixing wine with water in a dream means mixing legal and illegal money, or it could represent earnings from a business partnership with a woman. Pressing grapes to make wine in a dream means serving someone in authority whose employment allows one to achieve noticeable successes in life. If one is invited to a drinking party where he finds platters of fruit and pitchers of wine in the dream, it represents his martyrdom. If a sick person sees himself drinking wine in a dream, it means that he will receive the right medicine and recover from his illness. Drinking wine in a dream also means losing one's senses, or it could denote an evil happening. Drinking wine in the company of mentally disturbed people along with sedatives, drugs, music, dancing, farce, or ridiculous actions in a dream means that one will brake his pledge of allegiance to his guardian or ruler, deny his covenant to his Lord, or that he may start a war against his ruler. If a scholar sees himself drinking wine in a dream, it means that his knowledge will grow. If it is grape wine in the dream, it means that he will eat grapes outside of their season, or that he may require a drug preparation as a cure for an ailment, or it could mean earning lawful money, or falling into a shameful act. If he buys wine or presses it in the dream, it means that he will foster religious distortion, an act that will cause him to suffer from a curse. Wine in a dream also represents lies, prattle, divulging secrets, adultery or crimes. Drinking wine in a competition or for fun in a dream means loss of one's money or child. If the person is a hard-working laborer, it means that he may experience some temporary comfort, or that he may marry an older woman. Drinking wine in a dream also means suffering from a state of stupor. Seeing a departed person drinking non-intoxicating wine with joy in a dream means that he is dwelling in paradise. This is only true if he was not in the habit of drinking alcohol in this world. However, wine in a dream could be a good sign for one who is intending to get married, because of its water content. *(Also see Beer; Grapes; Intoxicants; Juice; Non-alcoholic wine; Urn; Vineyard)*

Wing: *(See Air; Arm[1])*

Wings: (Guild) If one sees himself flying with wings in a dream, it means travel. Wings in a dream also represent one's children. If one sees his wings feathered, this could represent his prosperity or authority. If someone sees himself flying with someone else's wings in the dream, it means that he will receive his help and support. In that sense, traditional people say: "So and so flew with so and so's wings." Having wings and not using them to fly with in a dream means acquiring worldly wealth. A broken wing in a dream represents a severe illness one's son may attract. If one experiences the excruciating pain from his wings being pulled off his shoulders in a dream, it may mean the death of his son. A wing that does not allow one to fly in a dream means a wound or a permanent scar in one's life that will slow his progress. It also could represent a punishment for one's sins. *(Also see Arm[1]; Transformation)*

Winking: (Regret; Sign; Spite) Winking in a dream means rancor and spite. To see oneself winking at someone in a dream means triggering an act one will regret.

Winning the presidency: *(See Bees)*

Winning the election: *(See Bees; Figure)*

Wisdom tooth: *(See Teeth; Tooth)*

Wise men: *(See Elders)*

Wish: *(See Zamzam)*

Wisp: *(See Strand of hair)*

Witch: (Bat. *See Hyena*)

Witchcraft: *(See Magic arts; Sorcery; Spit out)*

Witness: (Eyewitness; Legitimacy; Testify; Truth) An eyewitness in a dream means triumphing over one's enemy, testifying to the truth and refuting falsehood. If one sees himself as a true signing witness to an agreement in a dream, it means that he will triumph over his enemies. If one sees himself witnessing a contract or putting his seal on a testimony in a dream, it means that he will loan money to the second party in the contract. If one sees himself bearing a true testimony before someone and against the other in a dream, it means that he will attend the pilgrimage in Mecca.

Witter: *(arb. See Five times prayers)*

Wolf: (Thief; Trifler; Womanizer; Year) In a dream, a wolf represents a fierce enemy, an unrelenting thief, or a liar. If one sees a wolf entering his house in a dream, it means that a thief will burglarize his house and that he will chase and capture him. If one sees himself raising a wolf's cub in a dream, it means that he will raise an abandoned child of a thief who upon growing up will bring that family much pain, suffering, divisiveness and loss of property. Seeing a wolf in a dream also could represent false allegations one may fabricate to assault an innocent person. If one sees a wolf turning into a steer in the dream, it means that a boy who is used to stealing will repent for his sin, turn to honesty, trustworthiness and grow to become a good and a generous person. Seeing a wolf in a dream also means receiving praises from one's superior at work, or it could represent profits from one's job. If a wolf chases someone in a dream, it means that the person will see happiness, or it could mean his martyrdom. A wolf in a dream also represents the days of the year, or it could mean the four seasons. If one turns into a gentle lamblike wolf in a dream, it means that he is a thief who will repent for his sin. If one turns into a wolf in a dream, it means that he will earn personal joy and happiness. Wolf's milk in a dream represents fear, stress, or forfeiture of a project. A wolf in a dream also represents a tyrant, a weak thief, or a liar. A clash with a wolf in a dream means a clash with a rival. If a wolf and a dog make a pact of friendship in a dream, it means that one will witness hypocrisy and deceit.

Woman: (Beads; Garden; Glass; Pearls; Ribs; Silver; World) A beautiful looking woman in a dream represents a year of comfort, peace and prosperity. A woman in a dream also represents a coffer, one's store, or his hiding place. A woman in a dream also represents the earth, the world or a graveyard, for one returns to it after that he cames out of it. A woman in a dream also represents a prison, a confidant, a tree, a well, an inkwell, a house, or a partner who shares wealth and pleasure with the husband. Seeing a beautiful woman entering one's house in a dream means joy and happiness, money that will not last, or the reversal of one's condition from harsh to amiable. A fat woman in a dream represents a prosperous year. Seeing an unknown woman in a dream has better connotations than seeing a woman one knows. A young woman in a dream represents an enemy. An old woman in a dream represents the world. If one sees his wife looking like a man in a dream, she then represents his grandfather, or she could represent prosperity for that family. If one sees his wife carrying him in a dream, it means that he may fall sick, or perhaps that he may become rich. Seeing a female of unknown species in a dream means loss of money. If one sees his wife getting married to someone else in a dream, it means that he may deviate from God's path, then repent for his sin. A woman in a dream also represents wealth, the world, a farm, pleasures or authority, for a wife governs the needs of her husband and controls his life in one way or another. If a woman sees her crown stolen in a dream, it means the death of her husband. If a woman sees her head shaved in a dream, it means divorce, or it could mean the death of her husband. *(Also see Belt; Crown; Glass bottle; Glass; Gray hair; Ribs; Silver; Vat; Women)*

Womanizing: *(See Courting; Yarn salesman)*

Women: In a dream, women represent the world, its glitters and pleasures. If one sees women coming toward him in a dream, it means his success in the world. If they walk away from him in the dream, it means his poverty in the world. Sitting content in the company of women in a dream means lack of work. *(Also see Woman)*

Wood sculptor: In a dream, a wood sculptor represents someone who caters to a group of hypocrites and defrauds them of their money.

Woodcutter: (Disposer of estates; Guardian) In a dream, a woodcutter represents the person in charge of distributing one's inheritance, since it is he who disposes of the dead branches of a tree. In a dream, a woodcutter also represents an agitator, winter profits, eavesdropping, gossip, burdens, or sins.

Wooden bowl: (Bowl) In a dream, a wooden bowl represents the world, or earning money from a business during a trip, while a porcelain or a ceramic bowl in a dream signifies earnings from a local business. A bowl in a dream also represents one's condition, state, or the management of his affairs. Licking a bowl, or licking one's fingers after cleaning the bowl with one's hand in a dream means consuming one's share in this world and the nearing of one's death. A wooden bowl in a dream also represents a woman, a housekeeper, the workplace, or one's shop. If one sees a gathering of people or scholars partaking in a sweet meal from a large wooden bowl in a dream, it represents a community project that unites people's hearts and allows them to share their knowledge. If one sees a group of people gathering to eat a fish or a piece of rotten meat in a dream, it means that a group of evil people are gathered to take advantage of a prostitute. *(Also see Bowl)*

Wooden clogs: (Sandals; Shoes; Slippers) A wooden clog maker in a dream represents piety, asceticism, repentance from sin, purity, cleanliness, a hygienic person, or a marriage into a family of outcasts. *(Also see Slippers)*

Wooden slippers: *(See Slippers; Wooden clogs)*

Woods: (Forest; Wild plants)

Woodworker: *(See Carpenter; Construction worker)*

Wool: Wearing a woolen garment in the winter in a dream means profits and benefits. Wearing it during the summertime represents strain, distress and adversities. Wearing a woolen garment in a dream also means lawful money and prosperity. Sleeping over a sheepskin in a dream means becoming rich from associating with a rich woman, or from a marriage to a rich woman. Burning wool in a dream means religious contempt, or loss of capital. If a man of knowledge sees himself wearing a woolen garb in a dream, it means that he is leaning toward an ascetic life, or that he will become a caller to God's path, teach people to love the eternal comfort of the hereafter and to despise the temporary pleasures of this world. Wearing a woolen cloak with nothing under it in a dream means receiving money from a noble and a well respected person. A dog wearing sheepskin in a dream represents a lowly person who subsidizes his business through a well known and a respected person. If one sees a lion wearing a sheepskin in a dream, the lion here represents a tyrant who confiscates people's money and property. Wool in a dream also represents purity, clarity and asceticism, except if the wool is coarse or unsuitable to wear, then it means poverty or humiliation. *(Also see Spinning)*

Words: (Speaking; Speech) In a dream, using good, wise and beneficial words means benefits, improvement and amelioration of one's life. If one speaks incomprehensible words in his dream, it means the opposite. If one sees one of his limbs speaking against him in a dream, it means that someone will report him to the authorities, or become a witness against him in a court of justice. *(Also see Ring; Speaking; Stone polisher)*

Workhorse: (Nag) A workhorse in a dream represents man's endeavor and serious striving. The more fit a workhorse in a dream, the better is one's determination and drive. If a workhorse speaks to a man in a dream, it means income and fame. Riding on the back of a workhorse in a dream means taking a long journey, or it could mean taking money from one's wife. If a dog attacks a workhorse in a dream, it represents an enemy who will follow his wife. A blond workhorse in a dream means sad news. A workhorse in a dream also means a conflict, a foreigner, a wife, a husband or a servant. A gray workhorse in a dream represents a high rank, and a black workhorse means prosperity. *(Also see Horse)*

Workman: *(See Construction worker)*

World[1]: (Creation; Lower world; Material; Woman) In a dream, the world represents a woman, and a woman represents the world. If one sees himself departing from this world in a dream, it means that he may divorce his wife. If one sees the world as totally destroyed and that he is the only remaining soul in it in a dream, it means that he may lose his sight. If one sees as though the entire world is placed before him to take whatever he desires from it in a dream, it means that he may become poor, or that he may die shortly after that dream. Seeing the world in a dream also means distractions, jokes, deception, arrogance, negating promises, failing one's promises, theft, cheating, trickery, sufferings, a prostitute, adversities, sickness, paying fines, mental depression, limitations, appointments, dismissals, or disappointments. It also may be interpreted as one's wife, child, material growth, business success, good harvest, awakening, victory, love, or a beloved with two faces. Whether the world appears beautiful or ugly in one's dream, it could mean any of the above interpretations. Seeing the world in one's dream also could be a divine guidance, showing the person what he or she must see and understand in this world. If one sees himself walking away from the world in the dream, it means that he may become a renunciate. If one embraces the world in the dream, it means that he will amply satisfy his desire for it. If one sees himself running after it and the world running away from him in the dream, it means that the world will ultimately deceive him and lead him into temptation. In a dream, the world also represents the holy Qur'ân, which is the radiant full moon of this world. (Also see Travels)

World[2]: (Dwellings; Hotel; House; Inn; Rug; Temporary abode; Traveller's resting place)

Worms: (An organism living on another; Children; Insects; Parasites; Silkworm) In a dream, worms represent daughters or children living under their father. The same goes for all worms, annelids, intestinal worms, or parasites that live on cadavers. Seeing tapeworms coming out of one's backside in a dream represents one's grandchildren. If one sees worms coming out of his mouth in a dream, it means that some members of his family are plotting against him, though he knows about it, and he will finally escape from their danger, but at his own expense. If one sees worms coming out of his stomach in a dream, it means that he will distance himself from evil companions. Consequently, he will regain honor and purity. Worms leaving one's body in a dream mean overcoming distress, or paying alms tax. Worms in a dream also represent one's enemies. A silkworm in a dream means a customer in one's shop, or it could represent one's profession. Silkworms in a dream usually mean financial benefits, though in some circles they represent illegal money, or guesswork. (Also see Earthworm)

Worries: (Anxiety; Perturbation; Uneasiness) Worries in a dream mean regret, repentance, blaming oneself, attrition and remorse.

Worshipping fire: (Fire worshipper; Magi; Magus; Mazdaism; Sorcerer) Seeing an old man worshipping fire in a dream means facing a person who cares little about obliterating his enemy. Seeing oneself worshiping fire in a dream means apostasy, committing adultery, theft, murder, making a false oath, polytheism, or being an unjust person. Turning away from worshipping fire to embrace Judaism or Christianity in a dream means experiencing major changes in one's life. Worshipping fire in a dream means desiring worldly pleasures. Worshipping the fire in a dream also means desiring to work for the ruler or a king, or it could mean going astray. If the fire one is worshipping is not lit in the dream, it means that he is seeking unlawful earnings.

Wound: (Bleeding; Cut; Injury) A wound in a dream means compensation money that will come out of an injury one may suffer, and it will show. A cut in the right hand in a dream means money which is earned from a family business. If the left hand receives the cut, such profits will come through a female relative. If one sees his left foot bleeding from a cut, it means that he will earn money from a farming business. If his injury is in his back, then such profits will come from his children. If his wound starts bleeding in the dream, it means a debt which he must repay, even if it is difficult for him to do so at present. Every bleeding wound in a dream represents a financial obligation. In a dream, a head wound which does not bleed is a sign that one should guard his money. A wound which does not bleed in a dream also represents recognition by others. If a man of authority is wounded in an accident, whereby his flesh splits open, and his bones are dissected in a dream, it means that he will live a long life to see the burial of most of his relatives. If an army general sees his left hand wounded in a dream, it means that his army will double in size. If his right hand is wounded in the dream, it means that the area of his control will expand. If one suffers from a wound in his stomach in the dream, it means growth in his financial standing. If one is wounded in his thigh in the dream, it means that his clan will grow stronger. If one sees himself wounded in his legs in a dream, it means longevity. If one's foot is wounded in the dream, it means that his authority and control will become firmer. If one receives a cut and no blood runs out of his wound in a dream, it means that the assailant will say something true about his victim, representing the answer the person in the dream needs to realize. A bleeding wound in a dream also means being subject to backbiting, though what will be said is true. If one sees an angel piercing his stomach with a sword, whereby he thinks that he is dead in the dream, it means that he may suffer from an ulcer which will ultimately heal. If the sword inflicts a wound in his neck in a dream, it means prosperity which will mostly benefit his progeny. *(Also see Horizontal wound; Surgery; Vertical wound)*

Wrap up: (Roll up; Swathe) In a dream, a wrap represents one's limbs. To wrap up something in a dream means turning the page on something, closing a book, retracing one's steps, winding up a conversation, or controlling the spread of a rumor. *(Also see Wrap; Wrapping)*

Wrap: To see oneself wrapped in a blanket or a cloth in a dream means being serious about one's work and earning an honest livelihood. It also means receiving a medal of honor, recognition, or an endowment for his noble virtues. *(Also see Shroud; Wrap up)*

Wrapping: (Cloth; Cover) Wearing a wrapping around one's waist in a dream represents a husband and a wife who live together without sexual relationship. A wrapping in a dream also may represent a dullish or a simple-minded child. *(Also see Wrap up; Wrap)*

Wrecker: (Demolishing; Desperado; Destroying; Plunderer; Reversal of sentence) A wrecker in a dream has negative connotations. He represents a person with many contradictions, a violator of others' rights, someone who breaks things apart, who ruins things, someone who negates his promises or covenants, or one who breaks his own rules. On the other hand, if a wrecker demolishes something to replace it with something better, or to reverse an unjust sentence in the dream, he then represents a true human being, and one's dream carries a positive meaning. *(Also see Spoils)*

Wrecking ball: (Crane) A wrecking ball in a dream represents a message carrier. If one sees a wrecking ball hitting him in a dream, it means that he will receive a strong message which will be carried by a strong and a merciless emissary.

Wrestling match: In a dream, a wrestling match means a dispute between two people, even if it were between a man and a lion. The winner's stand in a dream is always better than that of the loser. If the match is between two men, then the one who challenges in the dream will be the loser in wakefulness. *(Also see Wrestling)*

Wrestling: (Fight; Struggle) If one sees himself wrestled to the ground in a dream, it means that he may lose his wealth. However, the one who is wrestled to the ground in the dream will ultimately be victorious. The winner in the dream is the loser in wakefulness. If there is a witness during the fight, then it could mean that the winner in the dream may become the winner in wakefulness. This could also happen if the winner in the dream has better preparedness, or if he is fighting for his food, such as in a struggle between a beast and a human being. If one sees two friends fighting a wrestling match in a dream, the loser in the dream has better standing in wakefulness. Wrestling in a dream also could mean a sickness that may befall the loser, or it could denote the consequences of an illness. If one sees himself battling with a beast, and if he kills the beast in the dream, it means relief from difficulties and dispelling of his sorrows and sufferings. If one reaches the throes of death in his fight in the dream, it means that he will triumph over his enemies. *(Also see Wrestling match)*

Wretched life: *(See Perspiration; Poverty)*

Wretched: *(See Deserted; Emptiness)*

Write: (Jot down; Scribble; Writing) Writing in a dream signifies a trick, a gimmick or a conspiracy. A writer in a dream represents a cunning and a fraudulent person. If one's handwriting looks illegible, or inelegant in the dream, it means that he will repent for dishonesty and from defrauding people. Writing on a scroll or on a legal pad in a dream means that one may receive an inheritance. Writing in a notebook in a dream means dodging, or repudiation. Writing a novel or a book in a dream means receiving unlawful money, or it could mean falling sick. If one sees himself writing a book or a letter and finishes it in his dream, it means that he will complete a project and fulfill his goals. If he fails to complete his book or his letter in the dream, it means that something will hamper, or stand in the way of completing his project. Writing with the left hand in a dream means indulging in loathsome actions, going astray, or perhaps having a son who is born from adultery, or it could mean that one may become a poet. Signing a deed, a check or a legal contract in a dream means failing to fulfill an agreement. If one sees someone he knows drafting a contract between them in a dream, it means that the other person will defraud him, mislead him in a business deal and drive him astray. If one finds himself illiterate and incapable of writing in a dream, it means that he is depressed, though God Almighty will show him a way out of his difficulties. If an illiterate person sees himself trying to learn how to write and read in a dream, it means that he will benefit from something he feared for a long time, or it could mean that he will go through hard times. If a learned person finds himself incapable of writing anything in a dream, it means depression, fear, toiling and obstruction of his business. *(Also see Book; Letter; Paper; Sign)*

Writer: (Author; Book; Letter; Scribe; Secretary; Starling; Write) A writer in a dream represents a dishonest, cunning, deceitful and a fraudulent person. If a writer sees himself unlettered in a dream, it means that he will forget his pranks, or lose his mind, or waste his religion, or develop a weak spiritual standing, or become poor. If one sees himself as an unlettered person, then if he suddenly becomes a writer in a dream, it means that he will develop pranks and deceive his opponent or enemy. Discovering oneself as a writer in a dream means that one will attend to the comfort of others rather than to his own comfort. Consequently he will get exhausted from such exercise and find that he gained nothing from it. If a sick person sees such a dream, it means his death. If a worker sees that dream, then it connotes his honesty and loyalty, or it could mean that he will be promoted, or get a raise from his employer. A writer in a dream also represents a tailor, a farmer, or a locomotive engineer. Seeing a scribe, or the secretary of managerial people, or someone in authority in a dream means that one may become one of them, or it could mean that he will rise in station, or improve his life. *(Also see Paper; Write)*

Writing: *(See Book; Letter; Write)*

Y

Yaḥyā: (God's prophet Yaḥyā, upon whom be peace; John) Seeing him (uwbp) in a dream means being endowed with piety, love for God Almighty, fear of wrongdoing and being distinct and unequalled in one's time. Seeing God's prophet Yaḥyā in a dream also means that one will acquire power and receive glad tidings.

Yapping: *(See Sound of animals)*

Yarn salesman: (Mill; Spinning; Yarn) A yarn salesman in a dream represents a contract, an agreement, planning, spinning, or womanizing.

Yarn: *(See Ball of thread; Spinning)*

Yashmak: (*Turk.* Double veil worn by Muslim women; Apparel; Attire; *arb.* Khimār; Niqāb) A yashmak or a veil covering the lower part of the face up to the eyes in a dream represents a young girl who will live a long life, or it could represent one who devotes her life to religious and spiritual studies. *(Also see Khimār; Veil)*

Yawning: (Slumberous) In a dream, yawning means an illness or an affliction. It also represents an insolent act that pleases Satan. Yawning in a dream also means a surprise charge at one's enemy. It also means a reward, because it prevents the person from speaking. Yawning in a dream also means a terminal illness.

Year: (Age; Period; Time) In a dream, a year represents drought, doubt, difficulties, threats, scientific advancement, trials, temptations. If one identifies a year in a dream, during a drought season, it means a good harvest. As for a pregnant woman, identifying a year in a dream means delivering her child. Seeing a year in a dream means experiencing an adversity, or witnessing someone else's trials and learning a lesson from it, or to repent of one's own sins.

Yearning for one's homeland: *(See Yearning)*

Yearning: To feel a yearning or a desire to see one's homeland in a dream means divorce between a husband and a wife, or separation between friends, or it could mean becoming rich after being poor. Yearning in a dream also connotes evil if accompanied with crying or lamenting.

Yelling: *(See Call)*

Yellow rose: *(See Rose)*

Yellow scorpion: *(See Scorpion)*

Yellow: (Color) Wearing a yellow silken garment in a dream means a sickness. If a warrior sees himself wearing a yellow silken garment in a dream, it means that he will be decorated for his chivalry. Yellow in a dream also represents strains. *(Also see Colors; Paleness)*

Yielding: *(See Driving force)*

Yogurt: *(See Cheese)*

Yoke of matrimony: *(See Marriage; Yoke)*

Yoke: (Bond; Bondage; Harness; Shackles; Yoke of matrimony) In a dream, a yoke means benefits for most people except for people in bondage. In their case, seeing a yoke in a dream means harsher subjugation to their masters. If someone is suffering from bondage, or if a prisonor of war, or a political prisoner sees a broken yoke in a dream, it means that he will be set free. The wooden frame which is attached to the plough-iron or the colter in a dream means marriage, bearing children, or work. A yoke in a dream also represents the turning of circumstances against one's liking, or meeting with obliging conditions.

Young boy: *(See Boy)*

Young man: (Teenage boy) An unknown young man in a dream represents an enemy. If the young man is known in the dream, then whatever strength, harshness, weaknesses, deceit, perfidy, or character he displays, they denote the same character in wakefulness. Walking behind an unknown young man in a dream means pursuing one's enemy and conquering him. If one meets an unknown young man whom he dislikes in a dream, it means that such an enemy will surface and people will abhor him. If one happens to like him in the dream, then it means that he will face an enemy whom most people like and sympathize with. If a young man sees himself turned into an old person in a dream, it means that he will suffer major losses in his life. A young man or a teenager in a dream mostly represents an enemy, for a teenager rarely respects or heeds the advice of his peers. A young man in a dream also represents deceit, betrayal, energy, or stubbornness, though he also could represent blessings and gratitude.

Young woman: (Teenage girl) A young girl in a dream represents an enemy however she may look. Seeing a well dressed and pleasingly adorned young woman in a dream means hearing pleasing news coming from an unexpected person. Seeing a young and a beautiful looking female servant in a dream means blessings, a favor, joy and festivities. In a dream, seeing an unknown young girl is more advantageous than seeing a known one. The strongest in meaning are those teenage girls who are presentable, well mannered and beautifully dressed. If she is seen dressed with modesty in the dream, then she represents goodness, chastity, discreteness, and following the correct religious conduct. If she adorns herself and plays up her charms in the dream, then such goodness will be public. If a young girl sees herself as an old woman in a dream, it means that she will live with modesty and preserve her chastity. If an old woman sees herself turned young again in the dream, it means regaining her strength, sexual desire and fertility. If she engages in lawful sexual intercourse in marriage, it denotes strong religious adherence. If she engages in sexual intercourse with someone without marriage in the dream, then her dream represents her love for the world and attachment to its glitters. If one sees an old woman turned young in a dream, then the above explanation becomes stronger. However, if one is poor, it means that her basic needs will be secured. If one has lost her chances in this world, it means that she will have a new opportunity, or if she is sick, it means that she will recover from her illness. Seeing a young girl frowning in a dream means that one may hear disturbing news. If she looks emaciated, then one's dream denotes poverty. If she is naked in the dream, it means business losses and defamation. Marrying a virgin teenage girl in a dream means wealth. *(Also see Little girl)*

Yowling: *(See Lamenting; Sound of animals)*

Yūnus: *(See Jonah)*

Yūsuf: *(See Joseph)*

Z

Zachariah: (*Zachar;* to remember + *ya;* God; The prophet Zachariah, upon whom be peace.) If one sees the prophet Zachariah in a dream, it means that God Almighty will restore fertility to him and to his wife at an advanced age. Seeing God's prophet Zachariah (uwbp) in a dream also means begetting a righteous son who will grow to be a sire. *(Also see Zikr)*

Zacharias: *(See Zachariah)*

Zamzam: (Well of Zamzam; Ka'aba; Mecca) If one sees the well of Zamzam quenching the thirst of people and if it is situated in a particular neighborhood, or in a town other than Mecca, it signifies that a gnostic will come to reside in that place and whose knowledge and wisdom will benefit its people. Drinking water from the blessed well of Zamzam in a dream also means recovering from an illness. If one drinks Zamzam water after having placed an intention in his dream, for example: to acquire knowledge, grow in wisdom, become wealthy, to recover from an illness, to conceive a child, to receive forgiveness for one's sins or any lawful desire in a dream, it means that God willing, one's wish will come true. *(Also see Gutter; Well)*

Zebra: (Donkey; Ingratitude; Sin) If one sees a domesticated zebra in a dream, it means benefits and profits. Transformation of a donkey into a zebra in a dream means evil. If a zebra enters one's house in a dream, it means that an evil person will enter that house, or that one will bring an evil person to his house. *(Also see Donkey)*

Zendik: *(arb.* Atheist. *See Cent)*

Zikr: (Hymn; Remembrance of God; Songs of God's love; Supplications) If one sees himself in a dream participating in a circle of people remembering God Almighty, or calling upon His most beautiful name, or invoking His divine attributes, or reading the Qur'ān, or reciting devotional songs, it means that such location will be built as a holy place to celebrate God's praises. The goodness of that place depends on the quality of reading, or the degree of devotion seen in the dream. When it is an ascetic song in the dream, it means that one's deputyship is established correctly, but if one sees himself singing a sensual love song, then it means temptations. If one sees himself repeatedly calling God's name in a dream, it means that he will win victory over his enemy. Calling people to God and reminding them of His attributes in a dream represents the work of a preacher who admonishes people, helps them to the shore of safety, and distances them from their sins and their consequences. If a merchant sees himself calling upon God's beautiful names in a dream, it means that his business will be saved from bankruptcy. If a disbeliever, a profane or a secular person sees himself in a state of remembering God Almighty and calling upon His most holy attributes in a dream, it means that he may fall sick, or face great adversities, while in his heart, he will remain pleading with God Almighty for mercy and relief, though he may remain silent in public regarding his inner faith, and in fear of being ridiculed by his own circles. If during his dream one speaks words of truth and wisdom, it means that he will recover from his adversity and be cured from his illness. Furthermore, he will move into a more comfortable life and begin a life of sharing and doing good deeds in this world, or he may receive guidance and light, and faith will permeate his heart. If one says his prayers with a twang in a dream, it means that he will linger in difficulties, and that people will mock him too. *(Also see Supplications)*

Zircon: (Gem; Mineral; Ring; Stone) In a dream, zircon represents unity and affection between husband and wife, or it could mean a contract between two partners, or reconciliation between two enemies, or it could represent the correctness of one's faith. *(Also see Stone²)*

Zodiac signs: *(See Celestial spheres; Constellations; Dog; Star)*

Zollikoferia spinosa: *(See Citrus medica)*

Zucchini: *(See Pumpkin)*

Zuhur: *(arb. See Five time prayers)*

Zul-Hijjah: *(See Arabic months; 'Arafāt)*

Zul-Qarnain: (Zul-Qarnain, peace be upon him.) Seeing him in dream means that one will intercede before a great person on behalf of someone else and satisfy his needs.

Zul-Qi'dah: *(See Arabic months)*

INDEX TO ENTRIES

E

GENERAL INDEX

510

511

BIBLIOGRAPHY

Al-Aṣfahāni, *Abu Naʻīm, Ḥilyat-ul Awliyā*, Beirut, 1988

Al-Bukhāri, *Saḥīḥ Al-Bukhārī*, Dār Al-Arabiya, Beirut 1985.

Al-Fairuzabādi, *Al-Qāmūs Al-Muḥīt*, Beirut , 1968.

Al-Ghazālī, *Abu Ḥāmid, Iḥyā ʻUlūm Al-Deen*, Cairo 1957.

Al-Jabarti, Abdu-Raḥmān, *ʻAjāʼib ul-Āthār Fi Al-Tarājim Wal-Āthār*, Cairo 1877.

Al-Suyūṭi, *Tafsīr Al-Jalālain Wa Asbāb Al-Nuzūl.*

Al-Zayyāt, Ḥabīb, *Khazāʻin Al-Kutub Fi Dimashq*, Cairo 1903.

Al-Ẕāhiri, Ibn Shāhīn, *Al-Isharāt Fi ʻIlm Al-ʻIbārāt.* Cairo National Library.

Ibn Kathīr, *Tafsīr Al-Qurʻān Al-ʻAzeem.*

Ibn Seerīn, Muḥammad, *Muntakhab Al-Kalām Fi Tafsīr-ul Aḥlām*, Dar Al-Fikr, Cairo 1964.

Nābulsi, Abdul-Ghani, *Taʻatīr ul Anām Fi Taʻabīr-ul Manām*, Cairo 1964.

Zirkli, Khayruddeen, *Al-Aʻalām*, Beirut 1984.